COMPILATION OF SELECTED UNITED STATES COAST GUARD AND MARITIME TRANSPORTATION RELATED LAWS

VOLUME 5

Updated through the 118th Congress.

Prepared By M. TWINCHEK

2025

Forward

This Compilation of Selected United States Coast Guard and Maritime Transportation Laws is a resource for those interested in U.S. laws governing the Coast Guard. This compilation includes laws governing United States Coast Guard and its establishment; the Coast Guard Academy; water pollution; lifesaving; ports and waterways; merchant marines; and other aspects of the United States Coast Guard.

The materials included comes from publicly available, open source information, prepared for the public by the Office of the Legislative Counsel of the U.S. House of Representatives and the Office of the Law Revision Counsel.

Items listed as a Statute Compilation do not appear in the U.S. Code or that have been classified to a title of the U.S. Code that has not been enacted into positive law. Each Statute Compilation incorporates the amendments made to the underlying statute since it was originally enacted and are current as of the date noted.

This compilation is not an official document and should not be cited as evidence of any law. The official version of Federal law is found in the United States Statutes at Large and in the U.S. Code, the legal effect of which is established in sections 112 and 204, respectively, of title 1, United States Code.

A special thanks is extended to the Office of Law Revision Counsel and the House Office of the Legislative Counsel for providing the U.S. Code and statute compilations; and to the Government Publications Office for hosting and making these available for use to the public. An additional thank you is offered to the staff of the House and Senate Committees who were gracious in responding to inquiries and providing background information on the legislation included.

Questions and comments may be directed to:

M. Twinchek
Email: mtwinchek@outlook.com

Contents

ELIJAH E. CUMMINGS COAST GUARD AUTHORIZATION ACT OF 2020 DIVISON G OF THE WILLIAM M. (MAC) THORNBERRY NATIONAL DEFENSE AUTHORIZATION ACT FOR FISCAL YEAR 2021

PUBLIC LAW 116-283

AS AMENDED THROUGH P.L. 118-159

William M. (Mac) Thornberry National Defense Authorization Act for Fiscal Year 2021

[(Public Law 116–283)]

[As Amended Through P.L. 118–159, Enacted December 23, 2024]

AN ACT William M. (Mac) Thornberry National Defense Authorization Act for Fiscal Year 2021

Be it enacted by the Senate and House of Representatives of the United States of America in Congress assembled,

SECTION 1. SHORT TITLE.

(a) IN GENERAL.—This Act may be cited as the "William M. (Mac) Thornberry National Defense Authorization Act for Fiscal Year 2021".

(b) REFERENCES.—Any reference in this or any other Act to the "National Defense Authorization Act for Fiscal Year 2021" shall be deemed to be a reference to the "William M. (Mac) Thornberry National Defense Authorization Act for Fiscal Year 2021".

SEC. 2. ORGANIZATION OF ACT INTO DIVISIONS; TABLE OF CONTENTS.

(a) DIVISIONS.—This Act is organized into eight divisions as follows:

* * * * * * *

(7) Division G—Elijah E. Cummings Coast Guard Authorization Act of 2020

* * * * * * *

(b) TABLE OF CONTENTS.—The table of contents for this Act is as follows:

* * * * * * *

DIVISION G—ELIJAH E. CUMMINGS COAST GUARD AUTHORIZATION ACT OF 2020

SEC. 8001. SHORT TITLE.

This division may be cited as the "Elijah E. Cummings Coast Guard Authorization Act of 2020".

SEC. 8002. [14 U.S.C. 106 note] DEFINITION OF COMMANDANT.

In this division, the term "Commandant" means the Commandant of the Coast Guard.

TITLE LVXXXI—AUTHORIZATIONS

SEC. 8101. AUTHORIZATIONS OF APPROPRIATIONS.

Section 4902 of title 14, United States Code, is amended—

(1) in the matter preceding paragraph (1), by striking "year 2019" and inserting "years 2020 and 2021";

(2) in paragraph (1)(A), by striking "provided for, $7,914,195,000 for fiscal year 2019." and inserting"provided for—

"(i) $8,151,620,850 for fiscal year 2020; and

"(ii) $8,396,169,475 for fiscal year 2021."

(3) in paragraph (1)(B), by striking "subparagraph (A)—" and inserting "subparagraph (A)(i), $17,035,000 shall be for environmental compliance and restoration.";

(4) by striking clauses (i) and (ii) of paragraph (1)(B);

(5) in paragraph (1), by adding at the end the following:

"(C) Of the amount authorized under subparagraph, (A)(ii) $17,376,000 shall be for environmental compliance and restoration."

(6) in paragraph (2)—

(A) by striking "For the procurement" and inserting "(A) For the procurement";

(B) by striking "and equipment, $2,694,745,000 for fiscal year 2019." and inserting"and equipment—

"(i) $2,794,745,000 for fiscal year 2020; and

"(ii) $3,312,114,000 for fiscal year 2021."

; and

(C) by adding at the end the following:

"(B) Of the amounts authorized under subparagraph (A), the following amounts shall be for the alteration of bridges:

"(i) $10,000,000 for fiscal year 2020; and

"(ii) $20,000,000 for fiscal year 2021."

(7) in paragraph (3), by striking "and equipment, $29,141,000 for fiscal year 2019." and inserting"and equipment—

"(A) $13,834,000 for fiscal year 2020; and

"(B) $14,111,000 for fiscal year 2021."

; and

(8) by adding at the end the following:

"(4) For the Coast Guard's Medicare-eligible retiree health care fund contribution to the Department of Defense—

"(A) $205,107,000 for fiscal year 2020; and

"(B) $209,209,000 for fiscal year 2021."

SEC. 8102. AUTHORIZED LEVELS OF MILITARY STRENGTH AND TRAINING.

Section 4904 of title 14, United States Code, is amended—

(1) in subsection (a), by striking "43,000 for fiscal year 2018 and 44,500 for fiscal year 2019" and inserting "44,500 for each of fiscal years 2020 and 2021"; and

(2) in subsection (b), by striking "fiscal years 2018 and 2019" and inserting "fiscal years 2020 and 2021".

SEC. 8103. DETERMINATION OF BUDGETARY EFFECTS.

The budgetary effects of this division, for the purpose of complying with the Statutory Pay-As-You-Go Act of 2010, shall be determined by reference to the latest statement titled "Budgetary Effects of PAYGO Legislation" for this division, submitted for printing in the Congressional Record by the Chairman of the House Budget Committee, provided that such statement has been submitted prior to the vote on passage.

SEC. 8104. AVAILABILITY OF AMOUNTS FOR ACQUISITION OF ADDITIONAL NATIONAL SECURITY CUTTER.

(a) IN GENERAL.—Of the amounts authorized to be appropriated by—

(1) section 4902(2)(A)(i) of title 14, United States Code, as amended by section 8101 of this division, $100,000,000 for fiscal year 2020; and

(2) section 4902(2)(A)(ii) of title 14, United States Code, as amended by section 8101 of this division, $550,000,000 for fiscal year 2021,

is authorized for the acquisition of a National Security Cutter.

(b) TREATMENT OF ACQUIRED CUTTER.—Any cutter acquired using amounts available pursuant to subsection (a) shall be in addition to the National Security Cutters approved under the existing acquisition baseline in the program of record for the National Security Cutter.

SEC. 8105. PROCUREMENT AUTHORITY FOR POLAR SECURITY CUTTERS.

(a) FUNDING.—Of the amounts authorized to be appropriated by—

(1) section 4902(2)(A)(i) of title 14, United States Code, as amended by section 8101 of this division, $135,000,000 for fiscal year 2020; and

(2) section 4902(2)(A)(ii) of title 14, United States Code, as amended by section 8101 of this division, $610,000,000 for fiscal year 2021,

is authorized for construction of a Polar Security Cutter.

(b) PROHIBITION ON CONTRACTS OR USE OF FUNDS FOR DEVELOPMENT OF COMMON HULL DESIGN.—Notwithstanding any other provision of law, the Secretary of the department in which the

Coast Guard is operating may not enter into any contract for, and no funds shall be obligated or expended on, the development of a common hull design for medium Polar Security Cutters and Great Lakes icebreakers.

SEC. 8106. SENSE OF THE CONGRESS ON NEED FOR NEW GREAT LAKES ICEBREAKER.

(a) FINDINGS.—The Congress finds the following:

(1) The Great Lakes shipping industry is crucial to the American economy, including the United States manufacturing base, providing important economic and national security benefits.

(2) A recent study found that the Great Lakes shipping industry supports 237,000 jobs and tens of billions of dollars in economic activity.

(3) United States Coast Guard icebreaking capacity is crucial to full utilization of the Great Lakes shipping system, as during the winter icebreaking season up to 15 percent of annual cargo loads are delivered, and many industries would have to reduce their production if Coast Guard icebreaking services were not provided.

(4) 6 of the Coast Guard's 9 icebreaking cutters in the Great Lakes are more than 30 years old and are frequently inoperable during the winter icebreaking season, including those that have completed a recent service life extension program.

(5) During the previous 10 winters, Coast Guard Great Lakes icebreaking cutters have been inoperable for an average of 65 cutter-days during the winter icebreaking season, with this annual lost capability exceeding 100 cutter days, with a high of 246 cutter days during the winter of 2017-2018.

(6) The 2019 ice season provides further proof that current Coast Guard icebreaking capacity is inadequate for the needs of the Great Lakes shipping industry, as only 6 of the 9 icebreaking cutters are operational, and millions of tons of cargo was not loaded or was delayed due to inadequate Coast Guard icebreaking assets during a historically average winter for Great Lakes ice coverage.

(7) The Congress has authorized the Coast Guard to acquire a new Great Lakes icebreaker as capable as Coast

Guard Cutter *Mackinaw* (WLBB-30), the most capable Great Lakes icebreaker, and $10 million has been appropriated to fund the design and initial acquisition work for this icebreaker.

(8) The Coast Guard has not initiated a new acquisition program for this Great Lakes icebreaker.

(b) SENSE OF THE CONGRESS.—It is the sense of the Congress of the United States that a new Coast Guard icebreaker as capable as Coast Guard Cutter *Mackinaw* (WLBB-30) is needed on the Great Lakes, and the Coast Guard should acquire this icebreaker as soon as possible.

SEC. 8107. PROCUREMENT AUTHORITY FOR GREAT LAKES ICEBREAKER.

(a) IN GENERAL.—Of the amounts authorized to be appropriated by section 4902(2)(A)(ii) of title 14, United States Code, as amended by section 8101 of this division, $160,000,000 for fiscal year 2021 is authorized for the acquisition of a Great Lakes icebreaker at least as capable as Coast Guard Cutter *Mackinaw* (WLBB-30).

(b) REPORT.—Not later than 30 days after the date of the enactment of this Act, the Commandant shall submit to the Committee on Commerce, Science, and Transportation of the Senate and the Committee on Transportation and Infrastructure of the House of Representatives a plan for acquiring an icebreaker as required by section 820(b) of the Frank LoBiondo Coast Guard Authorization Act of 2018 (Public Law 115-282).

SEC. 8108. POLAR SECURITY CUTTER ACQUISITION REPORT.

Not later than 1 year after the date of the enactment of this Act, the Commandant shall submit to the Committees on Transportation and Infrastructure and Armed Services of the House of Representatives, and the Committees on Commerce, Science, and Transportation and Armed Services of the Senate a report on—

(1) the extent to which specifications, key drawings, and detail design for the Polar Security Cutter are complete before the start of construction;

(2) the extent to which Polar Security Cutter hulls numbers one, two, and three are science ready; and

(3) what actions will be taken to ensure that Polar Security Cutter hull number four is science capable, as described in the

National Academies of Sciences, Engineering, and Medicine's Committee on Polar Icebreaker Cost Assessment letter report entitled "Acquisition and Operation of Polar Icebreakers: Fulfilling the Nation's Needs" and dated July 11, 2017.

SEC. 8109. SHORESIDE INFRASTRUCTURE.

Of the amounts authorized to be appropriated by section 4902(2)(A) of title 14, United States Code, as amended by section 8101 of this division, for each of fiscal years 2020 and 2021, $167,500,000 is authorized for the Secretary of the department in which the Coast Guard is operating to fund the acquisition, construction, rebuilding, or improvement of the Coast Guard shoreside infrastructure and facilities necessary to support Coast Guard operations and readiness.

SEC. 8110. MAJOR ACQUISITION SYSTEMS INFRASTRUCTURE.

Of the amounts authorized to be appropriated by section 4902(2)(A)(ii) of title 14, United States Code, as amended by section 8101 of this division, $105,000,000 is authorized for the hangar replacement listed in the fiscal year 2020 Unfunded Priority List.

SEC. 8111. POLAR ICEBREAKERS.

(a) IN GENERAL.—Section 561 of title 14, United States Code, is amended to read as follows:

"SEC. 561. Icebreaking in polar regions

"(a) PROCUREMENT AUTHORITY.—

"(1) IN GENERAL.—The Secretary may enter into one or more contracts for the procurement of—

"(A) the Polar Security Cutters approved as part of a major acquisition program as of November 1, 2019; and

"(B) 3 additional Polar Security Cutters.

"(2) CONDITION FOR OUT-YEAR CONTRACT PAYMENTS.—A contract entered into under paragraph (1) shall provide that any obligation of the United States to make a payment under the contract during a fiscal year after fiscal year 2019 is subject to the availability of appropriations or funds for that purpose for such later fiscal year.

"(b) PLANNING.—The Secretary shall facilitate planning for the design, procurement, maintenance, deployment, and operation of icebreakers as needed to support the statutory missions of the Coast

Guard in the polar regions by allocating all funds to support icebreaking operations in such regions, except for recurring incremental costs associated with specific projects, to the Coast Guard.

"(c) REIMBURSEMENT.—Nothing in this section shall preclude the Secretary from seeking reimbursement for operation and maintenance costs of the *Polar Star*, *Healy*, or any other Polar Security Cutter from other Federal agencies and entities, including foreign countries, that benefit from the use of those vessels.

"(d) RESTRICTION.—

"(1) IN GENERAL.—The Commandant may not—

"(A) transfer, relinquish ownership of, dismantle, or recycle the *Polar Sea* or *Polar Star*

"(B) change the current homeport of the *Polar Sea* or *Polar Star*; or

"(C) expend any funds—

"(i) for any expenses directly or indirectly associated with the decommissioning of the *Polar Sea* or *Polar Star*, including expenses for dock use or other goods and services;

"(ii) for any personnel expenses directly or indirectly associated with the decommissioning of the *Polar Sea* or *Polar Star*, including expenses for a decommissioning officer;

"(iii) for any expenses associated with a decommissioning ceremony for the *Polar Sea* or *Polar Star*

"(iv) to appoint a decommissioning officer to be affiliated with the *Polar Sea* or *Polar Star*; or

"(v) to place the *Polar Sea* or *Polar Star* in inactive status.

"(2) SUNSET.—This subsection shall cease to have effect on September 30, 2022.

"(e) LIMITATION.—

"(1) IN GENERAL.—The Secretary may not expend amounts appropriated for the Coast Guard for any of fiscal years 2015 through 2024, for—

"(A) design activities related to a capability of a Polar Security Cutter that is based solely on an operational requirement of a Federal department or agency other than the Coast Guard, except for amounts appropriated for design activities for a fiscal year before fiscal year 2016; or

"(B) long-lead-time materials, production, or postdelivery activities related to such a capability.

"(2) OTHER AMOUNTS.—Amounts made available to the Secretary under an agreement with a Federal department or agency other than the Coast Guard and expended on a capability of a Polar Security Cutter that is based solely on an operational requirement of such Federal department or agency shall not be treated as amounts expended by the Secretary for purposes of the limitation under paragraph (1).

"(f) ENHANCED MAINTENANCE PROGRAM FOR THE POLAR STAR.—

"(1) IN GENERAL.—Subject to the availability of appropriations, the Commandant shall conduct an enhanced maintenance program on the Polar Star to extend the service life of such vessel until at least December 31, 2025.

"(2) AUTHORIZATION OF APPROPRIATIONS.—The Commandant may use funds made available pursuant to section 4902(1)(A), to carry out this subsection.

"(g) DEFINITIONS.—In this section:

"(1) POLAR SEA.—The term '*Polar Sea*' means Coast Guard Cutter *Polar Sea* (WAGB 11).

"(2) POLAR STAR.—The term '*Polar Star*' means Coast Guard Cutter *Polar Star* (WAGB 10).

"(3) HEALY.—The term '*Healy*' means Coast Guard Cutter *Healy* (WAGB 20)."

(b) CONTRACTING FOR MAJOR ACQUISITIONS PROGRAMS.—Section 1137(a) of title 14, United States Code, is amended by inserting "and 3 Polar Security Cutters in addition to those approved as part of a major acquisition program on November 1, 2019" before the period at the end.

(c) REPEALS.—

(1) COAST GUARD AND MARITIME TRANSPORTATION ACT OF 2006.—Section 210 of the Coast Guard and Maritime Transportation Act of 2006 (14 U.S.C. 504 note) is repealed.

(2) COAST GUARD AND MARITIME TRANSPORTATION ACT OF 2012.—Section 222 of the Coast Guard and Maritime Transportation Act of 2012 (Public Law 112-213) is repealed.

(3) HOWARD COBLE COAST GUARD AND MARITIME TRANSPORTATION ACT OF 2014.—Section 505 of the Howard Coble Coast Guard and Maritime Transportation Act of 2014 (Public Law 113-281) is repealed.

(4) FRANK LOBIONDO COAST GUARD AUTHORIZATION ACT OF 2018.—Section 821 of the Frank LoBiondo Coast Guard Authorization Act of 2018 (Public Law 115-282) is repealed.

SEC. 8112. ACQUISITION OF FAST RESPONSE CUTTER.

(a) IN GENERAL.—Of the amounts authorized to be appropriated under section 4902(2)(A)(ii) of title 14, United States Code, as amended by section 8101 of this division, $265,000,000 for fiscal year 2021 shall be made available for the acquisition of four Fast Responses Cutters.

(b) TREATMENT OF ACQUIRED CUTTERS.—Any cutter acquired pursuant to subsection (a) shall be in addition to the 58 cutters approved under the existing acquisition baseline.

TITLE LVXXXII—COAST GUARD

Subtitle A—Military Personnel Matters

Subtitle B—Organization and Management Matters

Subtitle A—Military Personnel Matters

SEC. 8201. GRADE ON RETIREMENT.

(a) Retirement of Commandant or Vice Commandant.—Section 303 of title 14, United States Code, is amended by adding at the end the following:

"(d) Retirement under this section is subject to section 2501(a) of this title."

(b) RETIREMENT.—Section 306 of title 14, United States Code, is amended—

(1) in subsection (a), by inserting "satisfactorily, as determined under section 2501 of this title" before the period;

(2) in subsection (b), by inserting "satisfactorily, as determined under section 2501 of this title" before the period; and

(3) in subsection (c), by inserting "if performance of duties in such grade is determined to have been satisfactory pursuant to section 2501 of this title" before the period.

(c) GRADE ON RETIREMENT.—Section 2501 of title 14, United States Code, is amended—

(1) in subsection (a)—

(A) by striking "Any commissioned officer, other than a commissioned warrant officer," and inserting" Commissioned Officers.—

"(1) IN GENERAL.—A commissioned officer"

(B) by striking "him" and inserting "the commissioned officer";

(C) by striking "his" and inserting "the commissioned officer's"; and

(D) by adding at the end the following:

"(2) CONDITIONAL DETERMINATION.—When a commissioned officer is under investigation for alleged misconduct at the time of retirement—

"(A) the Secretary may conditionally determine the highest grade of satisfactory service of the commissioned officer pending completion of the investigation; and

"(B) the grade under subparagraph (A) is subject to resolution under subsection (c)(2)."

(2) in subsection (b)—

(A) by inserting "Warrant Officers.—" after "(b)";

(B) by striking "him" and inserting "the warrant officer"; and

(C) by striking "his" and inserting "the warrant

officer's"; and

(3) by adding at the end the following:

"(c) RETIREMENT IN LOWER GRADE.—

"(1) MISCONDUCT IN LOWER GRADE.—In the case of a commissioned officer whom the Secretary determines committed misconduct in a lower grade, the Secretary may determine the commissioned officer has not served satisfactorily in any grade equal to or higher than that lower grade.

"(2) ADVERSE FINDINGS.—A determination of the retired grade of a commissioned officer shall be resolved following a conditional determination under subsection (a)(2) if the investigation of or personnel action against the commissioned officer results in adverse findings.

"(3) RECALCULATION OF RETIRED PAY.—If the retired grade of a commissioned officer is reduced pursuant to this subsection, the retired pay of the commissioned officer shall be recalculated under chapter 71 of title 10, and any modification of the retired pay of the commissioned officer shall go into effect on the effective date of the reduction in retired grade.

"(d) FINALITY OF RETIRED GRADE DETERMINATIONS.—

"(1) IN GENERAL.—Except as provided in paragraph (2), a determination of the retired grade of a commissioned officer under this section is administratively final on the day the commissioned officer is retired, and may not be reopened.

"(2) REOPENING DETERMINATIONS.—A determination of the retired grade of a commissioned officer may be reopened if—

"(A) the retirement or retired grade of the commissioned officer was procured by fraud;

"(B) substantial evidence comes to light after the retirement that could have led to a lower retired grade under this section and such evidence was not known by competent authority at the time of retirement;

"(C) a mistake of law or calculation was made in the determination of the retired grade;

"(D) in the case of a retired grade following a conditional determination under subsection (a)(2), the investigation of or personnel action against the commissioned officer results in adverse findings; or

"(E) the Secretary determines, under regulations prescribed by the Secretary, that good cause exists to reopen the determination.

"(3) REQUIREMENTS.—If a determination of the retired grade of a commissioned officer is reopened under paragraph (2), the Secretary—

"(A) shall notify the commissioned officer of the reopening; and

"(B) may not make an adverse determination on the retired grade of the commissioned officer until the commissioned officer has had a reasonable opportunity to respond regarding the basis of the reopening.

"(4) RECALCULATION OF RETIRED PAY.—If the retired grade of a commissioned officer is reduced through the reopening of the commissioned officer's retired grade under paragraph (2), the retired pay of the commissioned officer shall be recalculated under chapter 71 of title 10, and any modification of the retired pay of the commissioned officer shall go into effect on the effective date of the reduction in retired grade.

"(e) INAPPLICABILITY TO COMMISSIONED WARRANT OFFICERS.—This section, including subsection (b), shall not apply to commissioned warrant officers."

SEC. 8202. AUTHORITY FOR OFFICERS TO OPT OUT OF PROMOTION BOARD CONSIDERATION.

(a) ELIGIBILITY OF OFFICERS FOR CONSIDERATION FOR PROMOTION.—Section 2113 of title 14, United States Code, is amended by adding at the end the following:

"(g)(1) Notwithstanding subsection (a), the Commandant may provide that an officer may, upon the officer's request and with the approval of the Commandant, be excluded from consideration by a selection board convened under section 2106.

"(2) The Commandant shall approve a request under paragraph (1) only if—

"(A) the basis for the request is to allow the officer to complete a broadening assignment, advanced education, another assignment of significant value to the Coast Guard, a career progression requirement delayed by the assignment or education, or a qualifying personal or professional circumstance, as determined by the Commandant;

"(B) the Commandant determines the exclusion from consideration is in the best interest of the Coast Guard; and

"(C) the officer has not previously failed of selection for promotion to the grade for which the officer requests the exclusion from consideration."

(b) ELIGIBILITY OF RESERVE OFFICER FOR PROMOTION.—Section 3743 of title 14, United States Code, is amended to read as follows:

"SEC. 3743. Eligibility for promotion

"(a) IN GENERAL.—Except as provided in subsection (b), a Reserve officer is eligible for consideration for promotion and for promotion under this subchapter if that officer is in an active status.

"(b) EXCEPTION.—A Reserve officer who has been considered but not recommended for retention in an active status by a board convened under subsection 3752(a) of this title is not eligible for consideration for promotion.

"(c) REQUEST FOR EXCLUSION.—

"(1) IN GENERAL.—The Commandant may provide that an officer may, upon the officer's request and with the approval of the Commandant, be excluded from consideration by a selection board convened under section 3740(b) of this title to consider officers for promotion to the next higher grade.

"(2) APPROVAL OF REQUEST.—The Commandant shall approve a request under paragraph (1) only if—

"(A) the basis for the request is to allow an officer to complete a broadening assignment, advanced education, another assignment of significant value to the Coast Guard, a career progression requirement delayed by the assignment or education, or a qualifying personal or professional circumstance, as determined by the Commandant;

"(B) the Commandant determines the exclusion from

consideration is in the best interest of the Coast Guard; and

"(C) the officer has not previously failed of selection for promotion to the grade for which the officer requests the exclusion from consideration."

SEC. 8203. TEMPORARY PROMOTION AUTHORITY FOR OFFICERS IN CERTAIN GRADES WITH CRITICAL SKILLS.

(a) IN GENERAL.—Subchapter I of chapter 21 of title 14, United States Code, is amended by adding at the end the following:

"SEC. 2130. [14 U.S.C. 2130] Promotion to certain grades for officers with critical skills: captain, commander, lieutenant commander, lieutenant

"(a) IN GENERAL.—An officer in the grade of lieutenant (junior grade), lieutenant, lieutenant commander, or commander who is described in subsection (b) may be temporarily promoted to the grade of lieutenant, lieutenant commander, commander, or captain under regulations prescribed by the Secretary. Appointments under this section shall be made by the President, by and with the advice and consent of the Senate.

"(b) COVERED OFFICERS.—An officer described in this subsection is any officer in a grade specified in subsection (a) who—

"(1) has a skill in which the Coast Guard has a critical shortage of personnel (as determined by the Secretary); and

"(2) is serving in a position (as determined by the Secretary) that—

"(A) is designated to be held by a lieutenant, lieutenant commander, commander, or captain; and

"(B) requires that an officer serving in such position have the skill possessed by such officer.

"(c) PRESERVATION OF POSITION AND STATUS OF OFFICERS APPOINTED.—

"(1) The temporary positions authorized under this section shall not be counted among or included in the list of positions on the active duty promotion list.

"(2) An appointment under this section does not change the position on the active duty list or the permanent, probationary, or acting status of the officer so appointed, prejudice the officer in regard to other promotions or appointments, or abridge the rights or benefits of the officer.

“(d) BOARD RECOMMENDATION REQUIRED.—A temporary promotion under this section may be made only upon the recommendation of a board of officers convened by the Secretary for the purpose of recommending officers for such promotions.

“(e) ACCEPTANCE AND EFFECTIVE DATE OF APPOINTMENT.—Each appointment under this section, unless expressly declined, is, without formal acceptance, regarded as accepted on the date such appointment is made, and a member so appointed is entitled to the pay and allowances of the grade of the temporary promotion under this section beginning on the date the appointment is made.

“(f) TERMINATION OF APPOINTMENT.—Unless sooner terminated, an appointment under this section terminates—

“(1) on the date the officer who received the appointment is promoted to the permanent grade of lieutenant, lieutenant commander, commander, or captain;

“(2) on the date the officer is detached from a position described in subsection (b)(2), unless the officer is on a promotion list to the permanent grade of lieutenant, lieutenant commander, commander, or captain, in which case the appointment terminates on the date the officer is promoted to that grade;

“(3) when the appointment officer determines that the officer who received the appointment has engaged in misconduct or has displayed substandard performance; or

“(4) when otherwise determined by the Commandant to be in the best interests of the Coast Guard.

“(g) LIMITATION ON NUMBER OF ELIGIBLE POSITIONS.—An appointment under this section may only be made for service in a position designated by the Secretary for the purposes of this section. The number of positions so designated may not exceed the following percentages of the respective grades:

“(1) As lieutenant, 0.5 percent.

“(2) As lieutenant commander, 3.0 percent.

“(3) As commander, 2.6 percent.

“(4) As captain, 2.6 percent.”

(b) [14 U.S.C. 2101] CLERICAL AMENDMENT.—The analysis for subchapter I of chapter 21 of title 14, United States Code, is amended by adding at the end the following:

"2130.	Promotion to certain grades for officers with critical skills: captain, commander, lieutenant commander, lieutenant."

SEC. 8204. CAREER INTERMISSION PROGRAM.

(a) IN GENERAL.—Subchapter I of chapter 25 of title 14, United States Code, is amended by adding at the end the following:

"SEC. 2514. [14 U.S.C. 2514] Career flexibility to enhance retention of members

"(a) PROGRAMS AUTHORIZED.—The Commandant may carry out a program under which members of the Coast Guard may be inactivated from active duty in order to meet personal or professional needs and returned to active duty at the end of such period of inactivation from active duty.

"(b) PERIOD OF INACTIVATION FROM ACTIVE DUTY; EFFECT OF INACTIVATION.—

"(1) IN GENERAL.—The period of inactivation from active duty under a program under this section of a member participating in the program shall be such period as the Commandant shall specify in the agreement of the member under subsection (c), except that such period may not exceed 3 years.

"(2) EXCLUSION FROM YEARS OF SERVICE.—Any service by a Reserve officer while participating in a program under this section shall be excluded from computation of the total years of service of that officer pursuant to section 14706(a) of title 10.

"(3) EXCLUSION FROM RETIREMENT.—Any period of participation of a member in a program under this section shall not count toward—

"(A) eligibility for retirement or transfer to the Ready Reserve under either chapter 841 or 1223 of title 10; or

"(B) computation of retired or retainer pay under chapter 71 or 1223 of title 10.

"(c) AGREEMENT.—Each member of the Coast Guard who participates in a program under this section shall enter into a written agreement with the Commandant under which that member shall agree as follows:

"(1) To accept an appointment or enlist, as applicable, and

serve in the Coast Guard Ready Reserve during the period of the inactivation of the member from active duty under the program.

"(2) To undergo during the period of the inactivation of the member from active duty under the program such inactive service training as the Commandant shall require in order to ensure that the member retains proficiency, at a level determined by the Commandant to be sufficient, in the military skills, professional qualifications, and physical readiness of the member during the inactivation of the member from active duty.

"(3) Following completion of the period of the inactivation of the member from active duty under the program, to serve 2 months as a member of the Coast Guard on active duty for each month of the period of the inactivation of the member from active duty under the program.

"(d) CONDITIONS OF RELEASE.—The Commandant shall prescribe regulations specifying the guidelines regarding the conditions of release that must be considered and addressed in the agreement required by subsection (c). At a minimum, the Commandant shall prescribe the procedures and standards to be used to instruct a member on the obligations to be assumed by the member under paragraph (2) of such subsection while the member is released from active duty.

"(e) ORDER TO ACTIVE DUTY.—Under regulations prescribed by the Commandant, a member of the Coast Guard participating in a program under this section may, in the discretion of the Commandant, be required to terminate participation in the program and be ordered to active duty.

"(f) PAY AND ALLOWANCES.—

"(1) BASIC PAY.—During each month of participation in a program under this section, a member who participates in the program shall be paid basic pay in an amount equal to two-thirtieths of the amount of monthly basic pay to which the member would otherwise be entitled under section 204 of title 37 as a member of the uniformed services on active duty in the grade and years of service of the member when the member commences participation in the program.

"(2) SPECIAL OR INCENTIVE PAY OR BONUS.—

"(A) PROHIBITION.—A member who participates in such a program shall not, while participating in the program, be paid any special or incentive pay or bonus to which the member is otherwise entitled under an agreement under chapter 5 of title 37 that is in force when the member commences participation in the program.

"(B) NOT TREATED AS FAILURE TO PERFORM SERVICES.—The inactivation from active duty of a member participating in a program shall not be treated as a failure of the member to perform any period of service required of the member in connection with an agreement for a special or incentive pay or bonus under chapter 5 of title 37 that is in force when the member commences participation in the program.

"(3) RETURN TO ACTIVE DUTY.—

"(A) SPECIAL OR INCENTIVE PAY OR BONUS.—Subject to subparagraph (B), upon the return of a member to active duty after completion by the member of participation in a program—

"(i) any agreement entered into by the member under chapter 5 of title 37 for the payment of a special or incentive pay or bonus that was in force when the member commenced participation in the program shall be revived, with the term of such agreement after revival being the period of the agreement remaining to run when the member commenced participation in the program; and

"(ii) any special or incentive pay or bonus shall be payable to the member in accordance with the terms of the agreement concerned for the term specified in clause (i).

"(B) LIMITATION.—

"(i) IN GENERAL.—Subparagraph (A) shall not apply to any special or incentive pay or bonus otherwise covered by such subparagraph with respect to a member if, at the time of the return of the member to active duty as described in that subparagraph—

"(I) such pay or bonus is no longer authorized by law; or

"(II) the member does not satisfy eligibility criteria for such pay or bonus as in effect at the time of the return of the member to active duty.

"(ii) PAY OR BONUS CEASES BEING AUTHORIZED.—Subparagraph (A) shall cease to apply to any special or incentive pay or bonus otherwise covered by such subparagraph with respect to a member if, during the term of the revived agreement of the member under subparagraph (A)(i), such pay or bonus ceases being authorized by law.

"(C) REPAYMENT.—A member who is ineligible for payment of a special or incentive pay or bonus otherwise covered by this paragraph by reason of subparagraph (B)(i)(II) shall be subject to the requirements for repayment of such pay or bonus in accordance with the terms of the applicable agreement of the member under chapter 5 of title 37.

"(D) REQUIRED SERVICE IS ADDITIONAL.—Any service required of a member under an agreement covered by this paragraph after the member returns to active duty as described in subparagraph (A) shall be in addition to any service required of the member under an agreement under subsection (c).

"(4) TRAVEL AND TRANSPORTATION ALLOWANCE.—

"(A) IN GENERAL.—Subject to subparagraph (B), a member who participates in a program is entitled, while participating in the program, to the travel and transportation allowances authorized by section 474 of title 37 for—

"(i) travel performed from the residence of the member, at the time of release from active duty to participate in the program, to the location in the United States designated by the member as the member's residence during the period of participation in the program; and

"(ii) travel performed to the residence of the member upon return to active duty at the end of the participation of the member in the program.

"(B) SINGLE RESIDENCE.—An allowance is payable

under this paragraph only with respect to travel of a member to and from a single residence.

"(5) LEAVE BALANCE.—A member who participates in a program is entitled to carry forward the leave balance existing as of the day on which the member begins participation and accumulated in accordance with section 701 of title 10, but not to exceed 60 days.

"(g) PROMOTION.—

"(1) OFFICERS.—

"(A) IN GENERAL.—An officer participating in a program under this section shall not, while participating in the program, be eligible for consideration for promotion under chapter 21 or 37 of this title.

"(B) RETURN TO DUTY.—Upon the return of an officer to active duty after completion by the officer of participation in a program—

"(i) the Commandant may adjust the date of rank of the officer in such manner as the Commandant may prescribe in regulations for purposes of this section; and

"(ii) the officer shall be eligible for consideration for promotion when officers of the same grade and seniority are eligible for consideration for promotion.

"(2) ENLISTED MEMBERS.—An enlisted member participating in a program under this section shall not be eligible for consideration for advancement during the period that—

"(A) begins on the date of the inactivation of the member from active duty under the program; and

"(B) ends at such time after the return of the member to active duty under the program that the member is treatable as eligible for promotion by reason of time in grade and such other requirements as the Commandant shall prescribe in regulations for purposes of the program.

"(h) CONTINUED ENTITLEMENTS.—A member participating in a program under this section shall, while participating in the program, be treated as a member of the Armed Forces on active duty for a period of more than 30 days for purposes of—

"(1) the entitlement of the member and of the dependents of the member to medical and dental care under the provisions of chapter 55 of title 10; and

"(2) retirement or separation for physical disability under the provisions of chapter 61 of title 10 and chapters 21 and 23 of this title."

(b) **[14 U.S.C. 2501]** CLERICAL AMENDMENT.—The analysis for subchapter I of chapter 25 of title 14, United States Code, is amended by adding at the end the following:

"2514.	Career flexibility to enhance retention of members."

SEC. 8205. DIRECT COMMISSIONING AUTHORITY FOR INDIVIDUALS WITH CRITICAL SKILLS.

(a) IN GENERAL.—Subchapter II of chapter 37 of title 14, United States Code, is amended by inserting after section 3738 the following:

"SEC. 3738a. [14 U.S.C. 3738a] Direct commissioning authority for individuals with critical skills

An individual with critical skills that the Commandant considers necessary for the Coast Guard to complete its missions who is not currently serving as an officer in the Coast Guard may be commissioned into the Coast Guard at a grade up to and including commander."

(b) **[14 U.S.C. 3701]** CLERICAL AMENDMENT.—The analysis for subchapter II of chapter 37 of title 14, United States Code, is amended by inserting after the item relating to section 3738 the following:

"3738a.	Direct commissioning authority for individuals with critical skills."

(c) **[14 U.S.C. 3701]** TECHNICAL AMENDMENT.—The heading for the first chapter of subtitle III of title 14, United States Code, is amended by striking "CHAPTER 1" and inserting "CHAPTER 37".

SEC. 8206. EMPLOYMENT ASSISTANCE.

(a) IN GENERAL.—Subchapter I of chapter 27 of title 14, United States Code, is amended by adding at the end the following:

"SEC. 2713. [14 U.S.C. 2713] Employment assistance

"(a) IN GENERAL.—In order to improve the accuracy and

completeness of a certification or verification of job skills and experience required by section 1143(a)(1) of title 10, the Secretary shall—

"(1) establish a database to record all training performed by members of the Coast Guard that may have application to employment in the civilian sector; and

"(2) make unclassified information regarding such information available to States and other potential employers referred to in section 1143(c) of title 10 so that States and other potential employers may allow military training to satisfy licensing or certification requirements to engage in a civilian profession.

"(b) FORM OF CERTIFICATION OR VERIFICATION.—The Secretary shall ensure that a certification or verification of job skills and experience required by section 1143(a)(1) of title 10 is rendered in such a way that States and other potential employers can confirm the accuracy and authenticity of the certification or verification.

"(c) REQUESTS BY STATES.—A State may request that the Secretary confirm the accuracy and authenticity of a certification or verification of job skills and experience provided under section 1143(c) of title 10."

(b) [14 U.S.C. 2701] CLERICAL AMENDMENT.—The analysis for such subchapter is amended by adding at the end the following:

"2713. Employment assistance."

Subtitle B—Organization and Management Matters

SEC. 8211. CONGRESSIONAL AFFAIRS; DIRECTOR.

(a) IN GENERAL.—Chapter 3 of title 14, United States Code, is amended by adding at the end the following:

"SEC. 321. [14 U.S.C. 321] Congressional affairs; Director

"The Commandant shall appoint a Director of Congressional Affairs from among officers of the Coast Guard who are in a grade above captain. The Director of Congressional Affairs is separate and distinct from the Director of Governmental and Public Affairs for the Coast Guard and is the principal advisor to the Commandant on all congressional and legislative matters for the Coast Guard and may have such additional functions as the Commandant may direct."

(b) [14 U.S.C. 301] CLERICAL AMENDMENT.—The analysis for chapter 3 of title 14, United States Code, is amended by adding at the end the following:

"321. Congressional affairs; Director."

SEC. 8212. LIMITATIONS ON CLAIMS.

(a) ADMIRALTY CLAIMS.—Section 937(a) of title 14, United States Code, is amended by striking "$100,000" and inserting "$425,000".

(b) CLAIMS FOR DAMAGE TO PROPERTY OF THE UNITED STATES.—Section 938 of title 14, United States Code, is amended by striking "$100,000" and inserting "$425,000".

SEC. 8213. RENEWAL OF TEMPORARY EARLY RETIREMENT AUTHORITY.

Section 219 of the Coast Guard and Maritime Transportation Act of 2012 (Public Law 112-213; 10 U.S.C. 1293 note) is amended—

(1) in the matter preceding paragraph (1), by striking "For fiscal years 2013 through 2018" and inserting "For fiscal years 2019 through 2025"; and

(2) in paragraph (1), by striking "subsection (c)(2)(A)" and inserting "subsection (c)(1)".

SEC. 8214. MAJOR ACQUISITIONS; OPERATION AND SUSTAINMENT COSTS.

Section 5103(e)(3) of title 14, United States Code, is amended—

(1) by redesignating subparagraphs (B) and (C) as subparagraphs (C) and (D), respectively; and

(2) by inserting after subparagraph (A) the following:

"(B) operate and sustain the cutters and aircraft described in paragraph (2);"

SEC. 8215. [14 U.S.C. 504 note] SUPPORT OF WOMEN SERVING IN THE COAST GUARD.

(a) ACTION PLAN.—

(1) IN GENERAL.—Not later than 180 days after the date of the enactment of this Act, the Commandant shall—

(A) determine which recommendations in the RAND gender diversity report can practicably be implemented to promote gender diversity in the Coast Guard; and

(B) submit to the Committee on Transportation and Infrastructure of the House of Representatives and the Committee on Commerce, Science, and Transportation of the Senate a report on the actions the Coast Guard has taken, or plans to take, to implement such recommendations.

(2) CURRICULUM AND TRAINING.—The Commandant shall update curriculum and training materials used at—

(A) officer accession points, including the Coast Guard Academy and the Leadership Development Center;

(B) enlisted member accession at the United States Coast Guard Training Center Cape May in Cape May, New Jersey; and

(C) the officer, enlisted member, and civilian leadership courses managed by the Leadership Development Center.

Such updates shall reflect actions the Coast Guard has taken, or plans to take, to carry out the recommendations of the RAND gender diversity report.

(3) DEFINITION.—In this subsection, the term "RAND gender diversity report" means the RAND Corporation's Homeland Security Operational Analysis Center 2019 report entitled "Improving Gender Diversity in the U.S. Coast Guard: Identifying Barriers to Female Retention".

(b) ADVISORY BOARD ON WOMEN AT THE COAST GUARD ACADEMY.—Chapter 19 of title 14, United States Code, is amended—

(1) by redesignating section 1904 as section 1906;

(2) by inserting after section 1903 the following:

"SEC. 1904. [14 U.S.C. 1904] Advisory Board on Women at the Coast Guard Academy

"(a) IN GENERAL.—The Superintendent of the Academy shall establish at the Coast Guard Academy an advisory board to be known as the Advisory Board on Women at the Coast Guard Academy (referred to in this section as the 'Advisory

Board').

"(b) MEMBERSHIP.—The Advisory Board shall be composed of not fewer than 12 current cadets of the Coast Guard Academy, including not fewer than 3 cadets from each current class.

"(c) APPOINTMENT; TERM.—Cadets shall serve on the Advisory Board pursuant to appointment by the Superintendent of the Academy. Appointments shall be made not later than 60 days after the date of the swearing in of a new class of cadets at the Academy. The term of membership of a cadet on the Advisory Board shall be 1 academic year.

"(d) REAPPOINTMENT.—The Superintendent of the Academy may reappoint not more than 6 cadets from the previous term to serve on the Advisory Board for an additional academic year if the Superintendent of the Academy determines such reappointment to be in the best interests of the Coast Guard Academy.

"(e) MEETINGS.—The Advisory Board shall meet with the Commandant at least once each academic year on the activities of the Advisory Board. The Advisory Board shall meet in person with the Superintendent of the Academy not less than twice each academic year on the duties of the Advisory Board.

"(f) DUTIES.—The Advisory Board shall identify opportunities and challenges facing cadets at the Academy who are women, including an assessment of culture, leadership development, and access to health care of cadets at the Academy who are women.

"(g) WORKING GROUPS.—The Advisory Board may establish one or more working groups to assist the Advisory Board in carrying out its duties, including working groups composed in part of cadets at the Academy who are not current members of the Advisory Board.

"(h) REPORTS AND BRIEFINGS.—The Advisory Board shall regularly provide the Commandant and the Superintendent reports and briefings on the results of its duties, including recommendations for actions to be taken in light of such results. Such reports and briefings may be provided in writing, in person, or both."

; and

(3) [14 U.S.C. 1901] by amending the analysis for such chapter—

(A) by amending the item relating to section 1904 to read as follows:

"1904. Advisory Board on Women at the Coast Guard Academy."

; and

(B) by adding at the end the following:

"1906. Participation in Federal, State, or other educational research grants."

(c) ADVISORY BOARD ON WOMEN IN THE COAST GUARD.—Chapter 25 of title 14, United States Code, is amended—

(1) [14 U.S.C. 2531] by redesignating subchapter II as subchapter III;

(2) by inserting after subchapter I the following:

SUBCHAPTER "Subchapter II—[14 U.S.C. 2521] ADVISORY BOARD ON WOMEN IN THE COAST GUARD

"SEC. 2521. [14 U.S.C. 2521] Advisory Board on Women in the Coast Guard

"(a) IN GENERAL.—The Commandant shall establish within the Coast Guard an Advisory Board on Women in the Coast Guard.

"(b) MEMBERSHIP.—The Advisory Board established under subsection (a) shall be composed of such number of members as the Commandant considers appropriate, selected by the Commandant through a public selection process from among applicants for membership on the Board. The members of the Board shall, to the extent practicable, represent the diversity of the Coast Guard. The members of the Committee shall include an equal number of each of the following:

"(1) Active duty officers of the Coast Guard.

"(2) Active duty enlisted members of the Coast Guard.

"(3) Members of the Coast Guard Reserve.

"(4) Retired members of the Coast Guard.

"(c) DUTIES.—The Advisory Board established under subsection (a)—

"(1) shall advise the Commandant on improvements to the recruitment, retention, wellbeing, and success of women serving in the Coast Guard and attending the Coast Guard Academy, including recommendations for the report on gender diversity in the Coast Guard required by section 5109 of chapter 51 of title 14;

"(2) may submit to the Commandant recommendations in connection with its duties under this subsection, including recommendations to implement the advice described in paragraph (1); and

"(3) may brief Congress on its duties under this subsection, including the advice described in paragraph (1) and any recommendations described in paragraph (2)."

; and

(3) **[14 U.S.C. 2501]** by amending the analysis for such chapter by striking the items relating to subchapter II and inserting the following:

"subchapter ii— advisory board on women in the coast guard

"2521. Advisory Board on Women in the Coast Guard.

"subchapter iii— lighthouse service

"2531. Personnel of former Lighthouse Service."

(d) RECURRING REPORT.—

(1) IN GENERAL.—Chapter 51 of title 14, United States Code, is amended by adding at the end the following:

"SEC. 5109. [14 U.S.C. 5109] Report on gender diversity in the Coast Guard

"(a) IN GENERAL.—Not later than January 15, 2022, and biennially thereafter, the Commandant shall submit to the Committee on Transportation and Infrastructure of the House of Representatives and the Committee on Commerce, Science, and Transportation of the Senate a report on gender diversity in the Coast Guard.

"(b) CONTENTS.—The report required under subsection (a)

shall contain the following:

"(1) GENDER DIVERSITY OVERVIEW.—An overview of Coast Guard active duty and reserve members, including the number of officers and enlisted members and the percentages of men and women in each.

"(2) RECRUITMENT AND RETENTION.—

"(A) An analysis of the changes in the recruitment and retention of women over the previous 2 years.

"(B) A discussion of any changes to Coast Guard recruitment and retention over the previous 2 years that were aimed at increasing the recruitment and retention of female members.

"(3) PARENTAL LEAVE.—

"(A) The number of men and women who took parental leave during each year covered by the report, including the average length of such leave periods.

"(B) A discussion of the ways in which the Coast Guard worked to mitigate the impacts of parental leave on Coast Guard operations and on the careers of the members taking such leave.

"(4) LIMITATIONS.—An analysis of current gender-based limitations on Coast Guard career opportunities, including discussion of—

"(A) shipboard opportunities;

"(B) opportunities to serve at remote units; and

"(C) any other limitations on the opportunities of female members.

"(5) PROGRESS UPDATE.—An update on the Coast Guard's progress on the implementation of the action plan required under subsection (a) of section 8215 of the Elijah E. Cummings Coast Guard Authorization Act of 2020."

(2) **[14 U.S.C. 5101]** CLERICAL AMENDMENT.—The analysis for chapter 51 of title 14, United States Code, is amended by adding at the end the following:

"5109. Report on gender diversity in the Coast Guard."

SEC. 8216. DISPOSITION OF INFRASTRUCTURE RELATED TO E-

LORAN.

Section 914 of title 14, United States Code, is amended—

(1) in subsection (a)—

(A) by striking "date" and inserting "later of the date of the conveyance of the properties directed under section 533(a) of the Coast Guard Authorization Act of 2016 (Public Law 114-120) or the date"; and

(B) by striking "determination by the Secretary" and inserting "determination by the Secretary of Transportation under section 312(d) of title 49"; and

(2) in subsection (c), by striking paragraph (2) and inserting the following:

"(2) AVAILABILITY OF PROCEEDS.—The proceeds of such sales, less the costs of sale incurred by the General Services Administration, shall be deposited into the Coast Guard Housing Fund for uses authorized under section 2946 of this title."

SEC. 8217. POSITIONS OF IMPORTANCE AND RESPONSIBILITY.

Section 2103(c)(3) of title 14, United States Code, is amended by striking "rear admiral (lower half)" and inserting "vice admiral".

SEC. 8218. [14 U.S.C. 719] RESEARCH PROJECTS; TRANSACTIONS OTHER THAN CONTRACTS AND GRANTS.

(a) IN GENERAL.—Chapter 7 of title 14, United States Code, is amended by adding at the end the following:

"SEC. 719. Research projects; transactions other than contracts and grants

"(a) ADDITIONAL FORMS OF TRANSACTIONS AUTHORIZED.—

"(1) IN GENERAL.—The Commandant may enter into—

"(A) transactions (other than contracts, cooperative agreements, and grants) in carrying out basic, applied, and advanced research projects; and

"(B) agreements with the Director of the Defense Advanced Research Projects Agency, the Secretary of a military department, or any other official designated by the Secretary of Defense under section 2371b of title 10 to participate in prototype projects and follow-on production contracts or transactions that are being carried out by such official and are directly relevant to the Coast Guard's cyber capability and Command, Control, Communications, Computers, and intelligence initiatives.

"(2) ADDITIONAL AUTHORITY.—The authority under this subsection is in addition to the authority provided in section 717 to use contracts, cooperative agreements, and grants in carrying out such projects.

"(3) FUNDING.—In carrying out paragraph (1)(B), the Commandant may use funds made available to the extent provided in advance in appropriations Acts for—

"(A) operations and support;

"(B) research, development, test, and evaluation; and

"(C) procurement, construction, and improvement.

"(b) RECOVERY OF FUNDS.—

"(1) IN GENERAL.—Subject to subsection (d), a cooperative agreement for performance of basic, applied, or advanced research authorized by section 717, and a transaction authorized by subsection (a), may include a clause that requires a person or other entity to make payments to the Coast Guard or any other department or agency of the Federal Government as a condition for receiving support under the agreement or transaction, respectively.

"(2) AVAILABILITY OF FUNDS.—The amount of any payment received by the Federal Government pursuant to a requirement imposed under paragraph (1) shall be deposited in the general fund of the Treasury. Amounts so deposited shall be available for the purposes of carrying out this section, to the extent provided in advance in appropriations Acts.

"(c) CONDITIONS.—

"(1) IN GENERAL.—The Commandant shall ensure that to the extent that the Commandant determines practicable, no cooperative agreement containing a clause described in subsection (c)(1), and no transaction entered into under subsection (a), provides for research that duplicates research being conducted under existing programs carried out by the Coast Guard.

"(2) OTHER AGREEMENTS NOT FEASIBLE.—A cooperative agreement containing a clause described in subsection (c)(1), or under a transaction authorized by subsection (a), may be used for a research project only if the use of a standard contract, grant, or cooperative agreement for such project is not feasible or appropriate.

"(d) EDUCATION AND TRAINING.—The Commandant shall—

"(1) ensure that management, technical, and contracting personnel of the Coast Guard involved in the award or administration of transactions under this section or other innovative forms of contracting are afforded opportunities for adequate education and training; and

"(2) establish minimum levels and requirements for continuous and experiential learning for such personnel, including levels and requirements for acquisition certification programs.

"(e) PROTECTION OF CERTAIN INFORMATION FROM DISCLOSURE.—

"(1) IN GENERAL.—Disclosure of information described in paragraph (2) is not required, and may not be compelled, under section 552 of title 5 for 5 years after the date on which the information is received by the Coast Guard.

"(2) LIMITATION.—

"(A) IN GENERAL.—Paragraph (1) applies to information described in subparagraph (B) that is in the records of the Coast Guard only if the information was submitted to the Coast Guard in a competitive or noncompetitive process having the potential for resulting in an award, to the party submitting the information, of a cooperative agreement for performance of basic, applied, or advanced research authorized by section 717 or another transaction authorized by subsection (a).

"(B) INFORMATION DESCRIBED.—The information referred to in subparagraph (A) is the following:

"(i) A proposal, proposal abstract, and supporting documents.

"(ii) A business plan submitted on a confidential basis.

"(iii) Technical information submitted on a confidential basis.

"(f) REGULATIONS.—The Commandant shall prescribe regulations, as necessary, to carry out this section.

"(g) ANNUAL REPORT.—On the date on which the President submits to Congress a budget pursuant to section 1105 of title 31, the Commandant shall submit to the Committees on Appropriations and Transportation and Infrastructure of the House of Representatives and the Committees on Appropriations and Commerce, Science, and Transportation of the Senate a report describing each use of the authority provided under this section during the most recently completed fiscal year, including details of each use consisting of—

"(1) the amount of each transaction;

"(2) the entities or organizations involved;

"(3) the product or service received;

"(4) the research project for which the product or service was required; and

"(5) the extent of the cost sharing among Federal Government and non-Federal sources."

(b) **[14 U.S.C. 701]** CLERICAL AMENDMENT.—The analysis for chapter 7 of title 14, United States Code, is amended by adding at the end the following:

"719. Research projects; transactions other than contracts and grants."

SEC. 8219. ACQUISITION WORKFORCE AUTHORITIES.

(a) IN GENERAL.—Subchapter I of chapter 11 of title 14, United States Code, is amended by adding at the end the following:

"SEC. 1111. [14 U.S.C. 1111] Acquisition workforce authorities

"(a) EXPEDITED HIRING AUTHORITY.—

"(1) IN GENERAL.—For the purposes of section 3304 of title 5, the Commandant may—

"(A) designate any category of acquisition positions within the Coast Guard as shortage category positions; and

"(B) use the authorities in such section to recruit and appoint highly qualified persons directly to positions so designated.

"(2) REPORTS.—The Commandant shall include in reports

under section 1102 information described in such section regarding positions designated under this subsection.

"(b) REEMPLOYMENT AUTHORITY.—

"(1) IN GENERAL.—Except as provided in paragraph (2), if an annuitant receiving an annuity from the Civil Service Retirement and Disability Fund becomes employed in any category of acquisition positions designated by the Commandant under subsection (a), the annuity of the annuitant so employed shall continue. The annuitant so reemployed shall not be considered an employee for purposes of subchapter III of chapter 83 or chapter 84 of title 5.

"(2)(A) ELECTION.—An annuitant retired under section 8336(d)(1) or 8414(b)(1)(A) of title 5, receiving an annuity from the Civil Service Retirement and Disability Fund, who becomes employed in any category of acquisition positions designated by the Commandant under subsection (a) after the date of the enactment of the Elijah E. Cummings Coast Guard Authorization Act of 2020, may elect to be subject to section 8344 or 8468 of such title (as the case may be).

"(i) DEADLINE.—An election for coverage under this subsection shall be filed not later than 90 days after the Commandant takes reasonable actions to notify an employee who may file an election.

"(ii) COVERAGE.—If an employee files an election under this subsection, coverage shall be effective beginning on the first day of the first applicable pay period beginning on or after the date of the filing of the election.

"(B) APPLICATION.—Paragraph (1) shall apply to an individual who is eligible to file an election under subparagraph (A) and does not file a timely election under clause (i) of such subparagraph."

(b) [14 U.S.C. 1101] CLERICAL AMENDMENT.—The analysis for subchapter I of chapter 11 of title 14, United States Code, is amended by adding at the end the following:

"1111. Acquisition workforce authorities."

(c) [14 U.S.C. 1102 note] REPEAL OF SUPERSEDED AUTHORITY.—Section 404 of the Coast Guard Authorization Act of 2010 (Public Law 111-281) is repealed.

SEC. 8220. VESSEL CONVERSION, ALTERATION, AND REPAIR PROJECTS.

(a) IN GENERAL.—Notwithstanding any provision of the Small Business Act (15 U.S.C. 631 et seq.) and any regulation or policy implementing such Act, the Commandant may use full and open competitive procedures, as prescribed in section 2304 of title 10, United States Code, to acquire maintenance and repair services for vessels with a homeport in Coast Guard District 17.

(b) APPLICABILITY.—Subsection (a) shall apply only if there are not at least 2 qualified small businesses located in Coast Guard District 17 that are able and available to provide the services described in such subsection.

(c) LIMITATION.—The full and open competitive procedures described in subsection (a) may only be used to acquire such services from a business located in Coast Guard District 17 that is able and available to provide such services.

SEC. 8221. MODIFICATION OF ACQUISITION PROCESS AND PROCEDURES.

(a) EXTRAORDINARY RELIEF.—

(1) IN GENERAL.—Subchapter III of chapter 11 of title 14, United States Code, is amended by adding at the end the following:

"SEC. 1157. [14 U.S.C. 1157] Extraordinary relief

"(a) IN GENERAL.—With respect to any prime contracting entity receiving extraordinary relief pursuant to the Act entitled 'An Act to authorize the making, amendment, and modification of contracts to facilitate the national defense', approved August 28, 1958 (Public Law 85-804; 50 U.S.C. 1432 et seq.) for a major acquisition, the Secretary shall not consider any further request by the prime contracting entity for extraordinary relief under such Act for such major acquisition.

"(b) INAPPLICABILITY TO SUBCONTRACTORS.—The limitation under subsection (a) shall not apply to subcontractors of a prime contracting entity.

"(c) QUARTERLY REPORT.—Not less frequently than quarterly during each fiscal year in which extraordinary relief is approved or provided to an entity under the Act referred to in subsection (a) for the acquisition of Offshore Patrol Cutters, the Commandant shall provide to the Committee on Commerce, Science, and Transportation of the Senate and the Committee on Transportation and Infrastructure of the House of Representatives a report that describes in detail such relief and the compliance of the entity with the oversight measures required as a condition of receiving such relief."

(3) [14 U.S.C. 1101] ANALYSIS FOR CHAPTER 11.—The analysis for chapter 11 of title 14, United States Code, is amended by inserting after the item relating to section 1156 the following:

"1157. Extraordinary relief."

(b) NOTICE TO CONGRESS WITH RESPECT TO BREACH OF CONTRACT.—Section 1135 of title 14, United States Code, is amended by adding at the end the following:

"(d) NOTICE TO CONGRESS WITH RESPECT TO BREACH OF CONTRACT.—Not later than 48 hours after the Commandant becomes aware that a major acquisition contract cannot be carried out under the terms specified in the contract, the Commandant shall provide a written notification to the Committee on Commerce, Science, and Transportation of the Senate and the Committee on Transportation and Infrastructure of the House of Representatives that includes—

"(1) a description of the terms of the contract that cannot be met; and

"(2) an assessment of whether the applicable contract officer has issued a cease and desist order to the contractor based on the breach of such terms of the contract."

SEC. 8222. ESTABLISHMENT AND PURPOSE OF FUND; DEFINITION.

Section 1461(a) of title 10, United States Code, is amended by inserting "and the Coast Guard" after "liabilities of the Department of Defense".

SEC. 8223. PAYMENTS FROM FUND.

Section 1463(a) of title 10, United States Code, is amended—

(1) in paragraph (1) by striking "and Marine Corps" and inserting "Marine Corps, and Coast Guard";

(2) in paragraph (2) by striking "(other than retired pay

payable by the Secretary of Homeland Security)"; and

(3) in paragraph (4) by inserting "and the Department of Homeland Security that" after "Department of Defense".

SEC. 8224. DETERMINATION OF CONTRIBUTIONS TO FUND.

Section 1465 of title 10, United States Code, is amended—

(1) in subsection (a)—

(A) by striking "(a) Not" and inserting the following:

"(a)(1) Not"

; and

(B) by adding at the end the following:

"(2) Not later than October 1, 2022, the Board of Actuaries shall determine the amount that is the present value (as of September 30, 2022) of future benefits payable from the Fund that are attributable to service in the Coast Guard performed before October 1, 2022. That amount is the original Coast Guard unfunded liability of the Fund. The Board shall determine the period of time over which the original Coast Guard unfunded liability should be liquidated and shall determine an amortization schedule for the liquidation of such liability over that period. Contributions to the Fund for the liquidation of the original Coast Guard unfunded liability in accordance with such schedule shall be made as provided in section 1466(b) of this title."

(2) in subsection (b)—

(A) in paragraph (1)—

(i) in the matter preceding subparagraph (A)—

(I) by inserting ", in consultation with the Secretary of the department in which the Coast Guard is operating," after "Secretary of Defense" ; and

(II) by inserting "and Coast Guard" after "Department of Defense";

(ii) in subparagraph (A)(ii) by striking "(other than the Coast Guard)" and inserting "members of the Armed Forces"; and

(iii) in subparagraph (B)(ii) by striking "(other than the Coast Guard)";

(B) in paragraph (2) by inserting "the Coast Guard Retired Pay account and the" after "appropriated to"; and

(C) in paragraph (3) by inserting "and Coast Guard" after "Department of Defense";

(3) in subsection (c)—

(A) in paragraph (1)—

(i) in the matter preceding subparagraph (A) by inserting ", in consultation with the Secretary of the department in which the Coast Guard is operating," after "Secretary of Defense";

(ii) in subparagraph (A) by striking "(other than the Coast Guard)" and inserting "members of the Armed Forces";

(iii) in subparagraph (B) by striking "(other than the Coast Guard)";

(B) in paragraph (2) by inserting ", in consultation with the Secretary of the department in which the Coast Guard is operating," after "Secretary of Defense";

(C) in paragraph (3) by inserting ", in consultation with the Secretary of the department in which the Coast Guard is operating," after "Secretary of Defense";

(4) in subsection (e) by striking "Secretary of Defense shall" and inserting "Secretary of Defense and, with regard to the Coast Guard, the Secretary of the department in which the Coast Guard is operating".

SEC. 8225. PAYMENTS INTO FUND.

Section 1466 of title 10, United States Code, is amended—

(1) in subsection (a)—

(A) in the matter preceding paragraph (1)—

(i) by striking "Secretary of Defense shall" and inserting "Secretary of Defense and the Secretary of the department in which the Coast Guard is operating, with respect to the Coast guard, shall"; and

(ii) by striking "each month as the Department of Defense contribution" and inserting "each month the respective pro rata share contribution of the Secretary of Defense and the Secretary of the department in which the Coast Guard is operating"; and

(B) in paragraph (2)(B) by striking "(other than the Coast Guard)"; and

(C) by striking the flush language following paragraph (2)(B) and inserting the following new subsection:

"(b) Amounts paid into the Fund under this subsection shall be paid from funds available for as appropriate—

"(1) the pay of members of the armed forces under the jurisdiction of the Secretary of a military department; or

"(2) the Retired Pay appropriation for the Coast Guard."

(2) by redesignating subsections (b) and (c) as subsections (c) and (d), respectively; and

(3) in subsection (c) (as so redesignated)—

(A) in paragraph (2)(A) by striking "liability of the Fund." and inserting "liabilities of the Fund for the Department of Defense and the Coast Guard."; and

(B) in paragraph (3) by inserting "and the Secretary of the Department in which the Coast Guard is operating" before "shall promptly".

Subtitle C—Access to Child Care for Coast Guard Families

SEC. 8231. REPORT ON CHILD CARE AND SCHOOL-AGE CARE ASSISTANCE FOR QUALIFIED FAMILIES.

(a) IN GENERAL.—Not later than 18 months after the date of the enactment of this Act, the Comptroller General of the United States shall submit to the Committee on Commerce, Science, and Transportation of the Senate and the Committee on Transportation and Infrastructure of the House of Representatives a report on child care and school-age care options available to qualified families.

(b) ELEMENTS.—The report required by subsection (a) shall include the following:

(1) FINANCIAL ASSISTANCE.—

(A) An assessment of—

(i) the subsidies and financial assistance for child care and school-age care made available by the Coast Guard to qualified families; and

(ii) the extent to which qualified families have taken advantage of such subsidies and assistance.

(B) The average number of days between—

(i) the date on which an application for a subsidy or other financial assistance for child care or school-age care is submitted by a qualified family; and

(ii) upon approval of an application, the date on which such subsidy or assistance is received by the qualified family.

(C) Recommendations for streamlining the payment of such subsidies and financial assistance.

(D) The amount of funding allocated to such subsidies and financial assistance.

(E) The remaining costs for child care or school-age care to qualified families that are not covered by the Coast Guard.

(F) A description of barriers to access to such subsidies and financial assistance.

(G) The number of qualified families that do not receive any such subsidies or financial assistance.

(2) REGULATION OF CHILD CARE SERVICES.—

(A) An assessment of—

(i) the regulations of States with respect to child care services (such as staffing, space and furnishings, safety, curriculum requirements, and allowable care hours); and

(ii) the effect that differences in such regulations may have on access to child care for qualified families.

(B) An assessment of—

(i) the regulations of the Coast Guard and the Department of Defense with respect to child development centers and other child care providers (including school-age care providers), and a comparison of such regulations with similar State regulations; and

(ii) the effect that such regulations may have on access to child care and school-age care for qualified families.

(C) The number of qualified families, and children, that do not have access to a Coast Guard child development center for child care.

(3) PARITY WITH DEPARTMENT OF DEFENSE.—The differences between child care and school-age care services offered by the Coast Guard and child care and school-age care authorities of the Coast Guard and the Department of Defense relating to the following:

(A) Authorized uses of appropriated funds for child care and school-age care services.

(B) Access to, and total capacity of, Coast Guard child development centers and Department of Defense child development centers.

(C) Child care and school-age care programs or policy.

(D) Coast Guard and Department of Defense programs to provide additional assistance to members and civilian employees with respect to child care and school-age care options.

(E) Respite care programs.

(F) Nonappropriated funds.

(G) Coast Guard family child care centers.

(H) Coast Guard and Department of Defense publicly available online resources for families seeking military child care and school-age care.

(4) FEASIBILITY.—An analysis of the feasibility of the Commandant entering into agreements with private child care and school-age care service providers to provide child care and school-age care for qualified families.

(5) AVAILABILITY.—An analysis of the availability of child care and school-age care for qualified families, including accessibility after normal work hours, proximity, and total capacity.

(6) RECOMMENDATIONS.—Recommendations—

(A) to improve access to child care and school-age care for qualified families;

(B) to ensure parity between the Coast Guard and the Department of Defense with respect to child care and school-age care;

(C) to expand access to child care and school-age care for all qualified families, including qualified families that have a child with special needs; and

(D) to ensure that regional child care and child development center needs at the unit, sector, or district level are identified, assessed, and reasonably evaluated by the Commandant for future infrastructure needs.

(7) OTHER MATTERS.—A description or analysis of any other matter the Comptroller General considers relevant to the improvement of expanded access to child care and school-age care for qualified families.

SEC. 8232. [14 U.S.C. 2922 note] REVIEW OF FAMILY SUPPORT SERVICES WEBSITE AND ONLINE TRACKING SYSTEM.

(a) MEMORANDUM OF UNDERSTANDING.—

(1) IN GENERAL.—The Commandant shall enter into a memorandum of understanding with the Secretary of Defense to enable qualified families to access the website at https://militarychildcare.com (or a successor website) for purposes of Coast Guard family access to information with respect to State-accredited child development centers and other child care support services as such services become available from the Department of Defense through such website. The memorandum shall provide for the expansion of the geographical areas covered by such website, including regions in which qualified families live that are not yet covered by the program.

(2) INCLUSION OF CHILD DEVELOPMENT CENTERS ACCESSIBLE UNDER PILOT PROGRAM.—The information accessible pursuant to the memorandum of understanding required by paragraph (1) shall include information with respect to any child development center accessible pursuant to the pilot program under section 8234.

(3) ELECTRONIC REGISTRATION, PAYMENT, AND TRACKING SYSTEM.—Not later than 1 year after the date of the enactment of this Act, the Commandant shall develop and maintain an internet website of the Coast Guard accessible to qualified families to carry out the following activities:

(A) Register children for a Coast Guard child development center.

(B) Make online child care payments to a Coast Guard child development center.

(C) Track the status of a child on the wait list of a Coast Guard child development center, including the placement and position of the child on the wait list.

(b) WAIT LIST.—

(1) IN GENERAL.—The Commandant shall maintain a record of the wait list for each Coast Guard child development center.

(2) MATTERS TO BE INCLUDED.—Each record under paragraph (1) shall include the following:

(A) The total number of children of qualified families on the wait list.

(B) With respect to each child on the wait list—

(i) the age of the child;

(ii) the number of days the child has been on the wait list;

(iii) the position of the child on the wait list;

(iv) any special needs consideration; and

(v) information on whether a sibling of the child is on the wait list of, or currently enrolled in, the Coast Guard child development center concerned.

(3) REQUIREMENT TO ARCHIVE.—Information placed in the record of a Coast Guard child development center under paragraph (1) shall be archived for a period of not less than 10 years after the date of its placement in the record.

SEC. 8233. [14 U.S.C. 2922 note] STUDY AND SURVEY ON COAST GUARD CHILD CARE NEEDS.

(a) STUDY.—

(1) IN GENERAL.—Not later than 1 year after the date of the enactment of this Act, and for each of the 2 fiscal years thereafter, the Commandant shall conduct a study on the child care needs of qualified families that incorporates—

(A) the results of the survey under subsection (b); and

(B) any other information the Commandant considers appropriate to ensure adequate tracking and future needs-based assessments with respect to adequate access to Coast Guard child development centers.

(2) CONSULTATION.—In conducting a study under paragraph (1), the Commandant may consult a federally funded research and development center.

(3) SCOPE OF DATA.—The data obtained through each study under paragraph (1) shall be obtained on a regional basis, including by Coast Guard unit, sector, and district.

(b) SURVEY.—

(1) IN GENERAL.—Together with each study under subsection (a), and annually as the Commandant considers appropriate, the Commandant shall carry out a survey of individuals described in paragraph (2) on access to Coast Guard child development centers.

(2) PARTICIPANTS.—

(A) IN GENERAL.—The Commandant shall seek the participation in the survey of the following Coast Guard individuals:

(i) Commanding officers, regardless of whether the commanding officers have children.

(ii) Regular and reserve personnel.

(iii) Spouses of individuals described in clauses (i) and (ii).

(B) SCOPE OF PARTICIPATION.—Individuals described in clauses (i) through (iii) of subparagraph (A) shall be surveyed regardless of whether such individuals use or have access to Coast Guard child development centers or other Federal child care facilities.

(C) VOLUNTARY PARTICIPATION.—Participation of any individual described in subparagraph (A) in a survey shall be on a voluntary basis.

(c) AVAILABILITY.—On request, the Commandant shall submit to the Committee on Commerce, Science, and Transportation of the Senate and the Committee on Transportation and Infrastructure of the House of Representatives the results of any study or survey under this section.

SEC. 8234. [14 U.S.C. 2992 note] PILOT PROGRAM TO EXPAND ACCESS TO CHILD CARE.

(a) IN GENERAL.—Commencing not later than 60 days after the date on which the report under section 8231 is submitted, the Commandant shall carry out a pilot program, based on the recommendations provided in such report, to expand access to public or private child development centers for qualified families.

(b) DURATION.—The duration of the pilot program under subsection (a) shall be not more than 3 years beginning on the date on which the pilot program is established.

(c) DISCHARGE ON DISTRICT BASIS.—The Commandant—

(1) may carry out the pilot program on a district basis; and

(2) shall include in the pilot program remote and urban locations.

(d) RESERVATION OF CHILD CARE SLOTS.—As part of the pilot program, the Commandant shall seek to enter into one or more memoranda of understanding with one or more child development centers to reserve slots for qualified families in locations in which—

(1) the Coast Guard lacks a Coast Guard child development center; or

(2) the wait lists for the nearest Coast Guard child development center or Department of Defense child development center, where applicable, indicate that qualified families may not be accommodated.

(e) ANNUAL ASSESSMENT OF RESULTS.—As part of any study conducted pursuant to section 8233(a) after the end of the 1-year period beginning with the commencement of the pilot program, the Commandant shall also undertake a current assessment of the impact of the pilot program on access to child development centers for qualified families. The Commandant shall include the results of any such assessment in the results of the most current study or survey submitted pursuant to section 8233(a).

SEC. 8235. IMPROVEMENTS TO COAST GUARD-OWNED FAMILY HOUSING.

Section 2922(b) of title 14, United States Code, is amended by adding at the end the following:

"(4) To the maximum extent practicable, the Commandant shall ensure that, in a location in which Coast Guard family child care centers (as such term is defined in section 8239 of the Elijah E. Cummings Coast Guard Authorization Act of 2020) are necessary to meet the demand for child care for qualified families (as such term is defined in such section), not fewer than two housing units are maintained in accordance with safety inspection standards so as to accommodate family child care providers."

SEC. 8236. BRIEFING ON TRANSFER OF FAMILY CHILD CARE PROVIDER QUALIFICATIONS AND CERTIFICATIONS.

(a) IN GENERAL.—Not later than 180 days after the date of the enactment of this Act, the Commandant shall brief the Committee on Commerce, Science, and Transportation of the Senate and the Committee on Transportation and Infrastructure of the House of Representatives on the feasibility of developing a policy to allow the transfer of a Coast Guard-mandated family child care provider qualification or certification between Coast Guard-owned housing units if, as determined by the Commandant—

(1) the qualification or certification is not expired;

(2) the transfer of the qualification or certification would not pose a danger to any child in the care of the family child care provider; and

(3) the transfer would expedite the ability of the family child care provider to establish, administer, and provide family home daycare in a Coast Guard-owned housing unit.

(b) BRIEFING ELEMENT.—The briefing required by subsection (a) shall include analysis of options for transferring a Coast Guard-mandated family child care provider qualification or certification as described in that subsection, and of any legal challenges associated with such transfer.

(c) RULE OF CONSTRUCTION.—The policy under subsection (a) shall not be construed to supersede any other applicable Federal, State, or local law (including regulations) relating to the provision of child care services.

SEC. 8237. INSPECTIONS OF COAST GUARD CHILD DEVELOPMENT CENTERS AND FAMILY CHILD CARE PROVIDERS.

(a) INSPECTIONS.—Section 2923 of title 14, United States Code, is amended by striking subsection (b) and inserting the following:

"(b) INSPECTIONS.—

"(1) IN GENERAL.—Not less than twice annually, the Commandant shall ensure that each Coast Guard child development center is subject to an unannounced inspection.

"(2) RESPONSIBILITY FOR INSPECTIONS.—Of the biannual inspections under paragraph (1)—

"(A) 1 shall be carried out by a representative of the Coast Guard installation served by the Coast Guard child development center concerned; and

"(B) 1 shall be carried out by a representative of the Coast Guard child development services work-life programs."

(b) FAMILY CHILD CARE PROVIDERS.—

(1) IN GENERAL.—Chapter 29 of title 14, United States Code, is amended by adding at the end the following:

"SEC. 2926. [14 U.S.C. 2926] Family child care providers

"(a) IN GENERAL.—Not less frequently than quarterly, the Commandant shall ensure that each family child care provider is subject to inspection.

"(b) RESPONSIBILITY FOR INSPECTIONS.—Of the quarterly inspections under subsection (a) each year—

"(1) 3 inspections shall be carried out by a representative of the Coast Guard installation served by the family child care provider concerned; and

"(2) 1 inspection shall be carried out by a representative of the Coast Guard child development services work-life programs."

(2) [14 U.S.C. 2901] CLERICAL AMENDMENT.—The analysis for chapter 29 of title 14, United States Code, is amended by adding at the end the following:

"2926. Family child care providers."

SEC. 8238. [14 U.S.C. 2922 note] EXPANDING OPPORTUNITIES FOR FAMILY CHILD CARE.

Not later than 1 year after the date of the enactment of this Act, the Commandant shall—

(1) establish a procedure to allow Coast Guard family child care centers to occur at off-base housing, including off-base housing owned or subsidized by the Coast Guard; and

(2) establish a procedure to ensure that all requirements with respect to such family child care programs are met, including home inspections.

SEC. 8239. [14 U.S.C. 2922 note] DEFINITIONS.

In this subtitle:

(1) COAST GUARD CHILD DEVELOPMENT CENTER.—The term "Coast Guard child development center" has the meaning given that term in section 2921(3) of title 14, United States Code.

(2) COAST GUARD FAMILY CHILD CARE CENTER.—The term "Coast Guard family child care center" means a location at which family home daycare is provided.

(3) FAMILY CHILD CARE PROVIDER.—The term "family child care provider" means an individual who provides family home daycare.

(4) FAMILY HOME DAYCARE.—The term "family home daycare" has the meaning given that term in section 2921(5) of title 14, United States Code.

(5) QUALIFIED FAMILY.—The term "qualified family" means any regular, reserve, or retired member of the Coast Guard, and any civilian employee of the Coast Guard, with one or more dependents.

Subtitle D—Reports

SEC. 8240. MODIFICATIONS OF CERTAIN REPORTING REQUIREMENTS.

(a) ESPECIALLY HAZARDOUS CARGO.—Subsection (e) of section 70103 of title 46, United States Code, is amended to read as follows:

"(e) ESPECIALLY HAZARDOUS CARGO.—

"(1) ENFORCEMENT OF SECURITY ZONES.—Consistent with other provisions of Federal law, the Coast Guard shall coordinate and be responsible for the enforcement of any Federal security zone established by the Coast Guard around a vessel containing especially hazardous cargo. The Coast Guard shall allocate available resources so as to deter and respond to a transportation security incident, to the maximum extent practicable, and to protect lives or protect property in danger.

"(2) ESPECIALLY HAZARDOUS CARGO DEFINED.—In this subsection, the term 'especially hazardous cargo' means anhydrous ammonia, ammonium nitrate, chlorine, liquefied natural gas, liquefied petroleum gas, and any other substance, material, or group or class of material, in a particular amount and form that the Secretary determines by regulation poses a significant risk of creating a transportation security incident while being transported in maritime commerce."

(b) COMPLIANCE WITH SECURITY STANDARDS.—Section 809 of the Coast Guard and Maritime Transportation Act of 2004 (Public Law 108-293; 46 U.S.C. 70101 note) is amended by striking subsections (g) and (i).

(c) MARINE SAFETY LONG-TERM STRATEGY.—Section 2116 of title 46, United States Code, is amended—

(1) in subsection (a), by striking "The strategy shall include the issuance of a triennial plan" and inserting "The 5-year strategy shall include the issuance of a plan";

(2) in subsection (b)—

(A) in the subsection heading, by striking "Contents of Strategy and Triennial Plans" and inserting "5-Year Strategy and Plan";

(B) in paragraph (1), in the matter preceding subparagraph (A), by striking "strategy and triennial plans" and inserting "5-year strategy and plan"; and

(C) in paragraph (2)—

(i) in the matter preceding subparagraph (A), by striking "strategy and triennial plans" and inserting "5-year strategy and plan"; and

(ii) in subparagraph (A), by striking "plans" and inserting "plan";

(3) in subsection (c)—

(A) by striking "Beginning with fiscal year 2020 and triennially thereafter, the Secretary" and inserting "Not later than 5 years after the date of the enactment of the Elijah E. Cummings Coast Guard Authorization Act of 2020, and every 5 years thereafter, the Secretary"; and

(B) by striking "triennial"; and

(4) in subsection (d)—

(A) in paragraph (1), by striking "No less frequently than semiannually" and inserting "In conjunction with the submission of the 5-year strategy and plan"; and

(B) in paragraph (2)—

(i) in the heading, by striking "Report to congress" and inserting "Periodic briefings";

(ii) in the matter preceding subparagraph (A), by striking "report triennially" and all that follows through "the Senate" and inserting "periodically brief the Committee on Commerce, Science, and Transportation of the Senate and the Committee on Transportation and Infrastructure of the House of Representatives";

(iii) in subparagraph (A)—

(I) by striking "annual"; and

(II) by striking "for the year covered by the report" and inserting "for the period covered by the briefing"; and

(iv) in subparagraph (B)(ii), by striking "plans" and inserting "plan".

(d) ABANDONED SEAFARERS FUND.—Section 11113(a) of title 46, United States Code, is amended—

(1) in paragraph (4), by striking "On the date" and inserting "Except as provided in paragraph (5), on the date"; and

(2) by adding at the end the following:

"(5) NO REPORT REQUIRED.—A report under paragraph (4) shall not be required if there were no expenditures from the Fund in the preceding fiscal year. The Commandant shall notify Congress in the event a report is not required under paragraph (4) by reason of this paragraph."

(e) MAJOR ACQUISITION PROGRAM RISK ASSESSMENT.—Section 5107 of title 14, United States Code, is amended—

(1) in subsection (a), by striking "April 15 and October 15" and inserting "October 15"; and

(2) in subsection (b)—

(A) in paragraph (2), by striking "the 2 fiscal-year quarters preceding such assessment" and inserting "the previous fiscal year";

(B) in paragraph (3), by striking "such 2 fiscal-year quarters" and inserting "such fiscal year";

(C) in paragraph (4), by striking "such 2 fiscal-year quarters" and inserting "such fiscal year"; and

(D) in paragraph (5), by striking "such 2 fiscal-year quarters" and inserting "such fiscal year".

SEC. 8241. REPORT ON CYBERSECURITY WORKFORCE.

(a) IN GENERAL.—Not later than 1 year after the date of the enactment of this Act, the Commandant shall submit to the Committee on Commerce, Science, and Transportation of the Senate and the Committee on Transportation and Infrastructure of the House of Representatives a report on how the Coast Guard plans to establish a workforce with the cybersecurity expertise to provide prevention assessments and response capacity to Operational Technology and Industrial Control Systems in national port and maritime environments.

(b) CONTENTS.—The report under subsection (a) shall include the following:

(1) A description of the number and skills of active duty and reserve Coast Guard members expected for initial operating capacity and full operating capacity of the workforce described in subsection (a).

(2) A description of the career development path for officers and enlisted members participating in the workforce.

(3) A determination of how the workforce will fulfill the cybersecurity needs of the Area Maritime Security Council and United States port environments.

(4) A determination of how the workforce will integrate

with the Hunt and Incident Response and Assessment Teams of the Cyber and Infrastructure Security Agency of the Department of Homeland Security.

(5) An assessment of successful models used by other Armed Forces, including the National Guard, to recruit, maintain, and utilize a cyber workforce, including the use of Reserve personnel for that purpose.

SEC. 8242. REPORT ON NAVIGATION AND BRIDGE RESOURCE MANAGEMENT.

(a) IN GENERAL.—Not later than 180 days after the date of the enactment of this Act, the Commandant shall submit to the Committee on Commerce, Science, and Transportation of the Senate and the Committee on Transportation and Infrastructure of the House of Representatives a report on the training and qualification processes of the Coast Guard for deck watch officers, with a specific focus on basic navigation, bridge resource management, crew rest, and qualification processes.

(b) CONTENTS.—The report under subsection (a) shall include the following:

(1) Recommendations for improving prearrival training, if necessary, and an assessment of how commercial industry best practices on prearrival training can be incorporated into military at sea watchkeeping.

(2) A detailed description of the deck watch officer assessment process of the Coast Guard.

(3) A list of programs that have been approved for credit toward merchant mariner credentials.

(4) A complete analysis of the gap between the existing curriculum for deck watch officer training and the Standards of Training, Certification, and Watchkeeping for officer in charge of a navigational watch at the operational level, Chief level, and Master level.

(5) A complete analysis of the gap between the existing training curriculum for deck watch officers and the licensing requirement for 3rd mate unlimited, Chief, and Master.

(6) An assessment of deck watch officer options to complete the 3rd mate unlimited license and the qualification under the Standards of Training, Certification, and Watchkeeping for

officer in charge of a navigational watch.

(7) An assessment of senior deck watch officer options to complete the Chief Mate and Master unlimited license and the qualification under the Standards of Training, Certification, and Watchkeeping for Chief Mate and Master.

SEC. 8243. REPORT ON HELICOPTER LIFE-CYCLE SUPPORT AND RECAPITALIZATION.

Not later than 180 days after the date of the enactment of this Act, the Commandant shall submit to the Committee on Commerce, Science, and Transportation of the Senate and the Committee on Transportation and Infrastructure of the House of Representatives a report that—

(1) includes an updated fleet life-cycle analysis and service life extension plan that includes dynamic components, and which clearly demonstrates the mission viability of the MH-65 through anticipated fleet recapitalization;

(2) includes a realistic sustainment budget necessary to achieve the operational availability rates necessary to meet MH-65 mission requirements through fleet recapitalization;

(3) includes an update on the status of the Coast Guard MH-65 helicopter recapitalization; and

(4) includes a description of any alternative, available, and cost-effective Government and civil systems, or updates, that the Coast Guard is considering for MH-65 operational missions, including Coast Guard cutter deployability requirements, in the event of delays to the future vertical lift program of the Coast Guard.

SEC. 8244. REPORT ON COAST GUARD RESPONSE CAPABILITIES FOR CYBER INCIDENTS ON VESSELS ENTERING PORTS OR WATERS OF THE UNITED STATES.

(a) IN GENERAL.—Not later than 1 year after the date of the enactment of this Act, the Commandant shall submit to the Committee on Commerce, Science, and Transportation of the Senate and the Committee on Transportation and Infrastructure of the House of Representatives a report on the response capabilities of the Coast Guard with respect to cyber incidents on vessels entering ports or waters of the United States.

(b) REVIEW.—The report under subsection (a) shall include a

review of each of the following:

(1) The number and type of commercial vessels of the United States subject to regulations under part 104 of title 33, Code of Federal Regulations (or any corresponding similar regulation or ruling).

(2) Policies and guidance issued by the Commandant, in accordance with guidelines on cyber risk management of the International Maritime Organization, to vessels of the United States.

(3) Measures to be taken by owners or operators of commercial vessels of the United States to increase cybersecurity posture on such vessels.

(4) Responses of the Commandant to cyber incidents on vessels described in paragraph (1) prior to the date of the enactment of this Act.

(5) Response protocols followed by personnel of the Coast Guard to a cyber incident on any vessel described in paragraph (1) experienced while that vessel is traveling to ports or waters of the United States.

(6) Oversight by the Commandant of—

(A) vessel-to-facility interface, as defined in section 101.105 of title 33, Code of Federal Regulations (or any corresponding similar regulation or ruling); and

(B) actions taken by the Coast Guard in coordination with vessel and facility owners and operators to protect commercial vessels and port facility infrastructure from cyber attacks and proliferation.

(7) Requirements of the Commandant for the reporting of cyber incidents that occur on the vessels described in paragraph (1).

(c) RECOMMENDATIONS AND APPROPRIATIONS.—The Commandant shall include in the report under subsection (a)—

(1) recommendations—

(A) to improve cyber incident response; and

(B) for policies to address gaps identified by the review under subsection (b); and

(2) a description of authorities and appropriations necessary to improve the preparedness of the Coast Guard

for cyber incidents on vessels entering ports or waters of the United States and the ability of the Coast Guard to prevent and respond to such incidents.

(d) FORM.—The report required under subsection (a) shall be submitted in unclassified form, but may contain a classified annex.

(e) VESSEL OF THE UNITED STATES DEFINED.—In this section, the term "vessel of the United States" has the meaning given such term in section 116 of title 46, United States Code.

SEC. 8245. STUDY AND REPORT ON COAST GUARD INTERDICTION OF ILLICIT DRUGS IN TRANSIT ZONES.

(a) FINDINGS.—Congress makes the following findings:

(1) The Coast Guard seizes an average of 1,221 pounds of cocaine and 85 pounds of marijuana each day in the transit zones of the Eastern Pacific Ocean, Caribbean Sea, and Southern maritime border approaches.

(2) The Joint Interagency Task Force-South (JIATF-South) estimates that it has a spectrum of actionable intelligence on more than 80 percent of drug movements into the United States from Central America and South America.

(3) The Coast Guard must balance asset allocation across 11 statutory missions. As such, the Coast Guard interdicts less than 10 percent of maritime noncommercial smuggling of illicit drugs into the United States from Central America and South America.

(4) In 2017, the Government Accountability Office recommended that the Commandant of the Coast Guard—

(A) develop new performance goals relating to the interdiction of illicit drugs smuggled into the United States, or describe the manner in which existing goals are sufficient;

(B) report such goals to the public;

(C) assess the extent to which limitations in performance data with respect to such goals are documented;

(D) document measurable corrective actions and implementation timeframes with respect to such goals; and

(E) document efforts to monitor implementation of

such corrective actions.

(b) STUDY.—The Secretary of the Department in which the Coast Guard is operating, in coordination with the Secretary of Defense and the heads of other relevant Federal agencies, shall conduct a study in order to identify gaps in resources that contribute to low interdiction rates for maritime noncommercial smuggling of illicit drugs into the United States from Central America and South America despite having actionable intelligence on more than 80 percent of drug movements in the transit zones of the Eastern Pacific Ocean, Caribbean Sea, and Southern maritime border approaches.

(c) REPORT.—Not later than 1 year after the date of the enactment of this Act, the Secretary of the Department in which the Coast Guard is operating shall submit to the Committee on Commerce, Science, and Transportation of the Senate and the Committee on Transportation and Infrastructure of the House of Representatives a report on the results of the study under subsection (b). Such report shall include—

(1) a statement of the Coast Guard mission requirements for drug interdiction in the Caribbean basin;

(2) the number of maritime surveillance hours and Coast Guard assets used in each of fiscal years 2017 through 2019 to counter the illicit trafficking of drugs and other related threats throughout the Caribbean basin; and

(3) a determination of whether such hours and assets satisfied the Coast Guard mission requirements for drug interdiction in the Caribbean basin.

(d) FORM.—The report required under subsection (a) shall be submitted in unclassified form, but may contain a classified annex.

SEC. 8246. REPORT ON LIABILITY LIMITS SET IN SECTION 1004 OF THE OIL POLLUTION ACT OF 1990.

Not later than 180 days after the date of the enactment of this Act, the Commandant shall submit to the Committee on Commerce, Science, and Transportation of the Senate and the Committee on Transportation and Infrastructure of the House of Representatives a report setting forth the following:

(1) Each liability limit set under section 1004 of the Oil Pollution Act of 1990 (33 U.S.C. 2704), including the statutory

or regulatory authority establishing such limit.

(2) If the Commandant determines that any liability limit listed in such section should be modified—

(A) a description of the modification;

(B) a justification for such modification; and

(C) a recommendation for legislative or regulatory action to achieve such modification.

SEC. 8247. REPORT ON COAST GUARD DEFENSE READINESS RESOURCES ALLOCATION.

(a) REPORT REQUIRED.—Not later than 180 days after the date of the enactment of this Act, the Comptroller General of the United States shall submit to the Committee on Transportation and Infrastructure of the House of Representatives and the Committee on Commerce, Science, and Transportation of the Senate a report on the allocation of resources by the Coast Guard to support its defense readiness mission.

(b) CONTENTS.—The report required by subsection (a) shall include the following elements:

(1) Funding levels allocated by the Coast Guard to support defense readiness missions for each of the past 10 fiscal years.

(2) Funding levels transferred or otherwise provided by the Department of Defense to the Coast Guard in support of the Coast Guard's defense readiness missions for each of the past 10 fiscal years.

(3) The number of Coast Guard detachments assigned in support of the Coast Guard's defense readiness mission for each of the past 10 fiscal years.

(c) ASSESSMENT.—In addition to the elements detailed in subsection (b), the report shall include an assessment of the impacts on the Coast Guard's non-defense mission readiness and operational capabilities due to the annual levels of reimbursement provided by the Department of Defense to compensate the Coast Guard for its expenses to fulfill its defense readiness mission.

SEC. 8248. REPORT ON THE FEASIBILITY OF LIQUEFIED NATURAL GAS FUELED VESSELS.

Not later than 1 year after the date of the enactment of this Act, the Commandant shall submit to the Committee on Transportation and Infrastructure of the House of Representatives and the Committee on Commerce, Science, and Transportation of the Senate a report on the following:

(1) The feasibility, safety, and cost effectiveness of using liquefied natural gas to fuel new Coast Guard vessels.

(2) The feasibility, safety, and cost effectiveness of converting existing vessels to run on liquefied natural gas fuels.

(3) The operational feasibility of using liquefied natural gas to fuel Coast Guard vessels.

SEC. 8249. COAST GUARD AUTHORITIES STUDY.

(a) IN GENERAL.—The Secretary of the department in which the Coast Guard is operating shall seek to enter into an arrangement with the National Academy of Sciences not later than 60 days after the date of the enactment of this Act under which the Academy shall prepare an assessment of Coast Guard authorities.

(b) ASSESSMENT.—The assessment under subsection (a) shall provide—

(1) an examination of emerging issues that may require Coast Guard oversight, regulation, or action;

(2) a description of potential limitations and shortcomings of relying on current Coast Guard authorities to address emerging issues; and

(3) an overview of adjustments and additions that could be made to existing Coast Guard authorities to fully address emerging issues.

(c) REPORT TO THE CONGRESS.—Not later than 1 year after entering into an arrangement with the Secretary under subsection (a), the National Academy of Sciences shall submit to the Committee on Transportation and Infrastructure of the House of Representatives and the Committee on Commerce, Science, and Transportation of the Senate the assessment under this section.

(d) EMERGING ISSUES.—In this section, the term "emerging issues" means changes in the maritime industry and environment that in the determination of the National Academy of Sciences are reasonably likely to occur within 10 years after the date of the enactment of this Act, including—

(1) the introduction of new technologies in the maritime

domain;

(2) the advent of new processes or operational activities in the maritime domain; and

(3) changes in the use of navigable waterways.

(e) FORM.—The assessment required under subsection (a) shall be submitted in unclassified form, but may contain a classified annex.

SEC. 8250. REPORT ON EFFECTS OF CLIMATE CHANGE ON COAST GUARD.

(a) IN GENERAL.—Not later than 1 year after the date of the enactment of this Act, the Commandant shall submit to the Committee on Transportation and Infrastructure of the House of Representatives and the Committee on Commerce, Science, and Transportation of the Senate a report on vulnerabilities of Coast Guard installations and requirements resulting from climate change over the next 20 years.

(b) ELEMENTS.—The report under subsection (a) shall include the following:

(1) A list of the 10 most vulnerable Coast Guard installations based on the effects of climate change, including rising sea tides, increased flooding, drought, desertification, wildfires, thawing permafrost, or any other categories the Commandant determines necessary.

(2) An overview of—

(A) mitigations that may be necessary to ensure the continued operational viability and to increase the resiliency of the identified vulnerable installations; and

(B) the cost of such mitigations.

(3) A discussion of the climate-change-related effects on the Coast Guard, including—

(A) the increase in the frequency of humanitarian assistance and disaster relief missions; and

(B) campaign plans, contingency plans, and operational posture of the Coast Guard.

(4) An overview of mitigations that may be necessary to ensure mission resiliency and the cost of such mitigations.

(c) FORM.—The report required under subsection (a) shall be

submitted in unclassified form, but may contain a classified annex.

SEC. 8251. [14 U.S.C. 504 note] SHORE INFRASTRUCTURE.

(a) IN GENERAL.—Not later than 1 year after the date of the enactment of this Act, the Commandant shall—

(1) develop a plan to standardize Coast Guard facility condition assessments;

(2) establish shore infrastructure performance goals, measures, and baselines to track the effectiveness of maintenance and repair investments and provide feedback on progress made;

(3) develop a process to routinely align the Coast Guard shore infrastructure portfolio with mission needs, including disposing of unneeded assets;

(4) establish guidance for planning boards to document inputs, deliberations, and project prioritization decisions for infrastructure maintenance projects;

(5) employ models for Coast Guard infrastructure asset lines for—

(A) predicting the outcome of investments in shore infrastructure;

(B) analyzing tradeoffs; and

(C) optimizing decisions among competing investments;

(6) include supporting details about competing project alternatives and report tradeoffs in congressional budget requests and related reports; and

(7) explore the development of real property management expertise within the Coast Guard workforce, including members of the Senior Executive Service.

(b) BRIEFING.—Not later than December 31, 2020, the Commandant shall brief the Committee on Transportation and Infrastructure of the House of Representatives and the Committee on Commerce, Science, and Transportation of the Senate on the status of the actions required under subsection (a).

SEC. 8252. COAST GUARD HOUSING; STATUS AND AUTHORITIES BRIEFING.

Not later than 180 days after the date of the enactment of this Act, the Commandant shall provide to the Committee on Transportation and Infrastructure of the House of Representatives and the Committee on Commerce, Science, and Transportation of the Senate a briefing on Coast Guard housing, including—

(1) a description of the material condition of Coast Guard housing facilities;

(2) the amount of current Coast Guard housing construction and deferred maintenance backlogs;

(3) an overview of the manner in which the Coast Guard manages and maintains housing facilities;

(4) a discussion of whether reauthorizing housing authorities for the Coast Guard similar to those provided in section 208 of the Coast Guard Authorization Act of 1996 (Public Law 104-324); and

(5) recommendations regarding how the Congress could adjust those authorities to prevent mismanagement of Coast Guard housing facilities.

SEC. 8253. PHYSICAL ACCESS CONTROL SYSTEM REPORT.

Not later 180 days after the date of the enactment of this Act, and annually for each of the 4 years thereafter, the Commandant shall submit to the Committee on Transportation and Infrastructure of the House of Representatives and the Committee on Commerce, Science, and Transportation of the Senate a report regarding the status of the Coast Guard's compliance with Homeland Security Presidential Directive 12 (HSPD-12) and Federal Information Processing Standard 201 (FIPS-201), including—

(1) the status of Coast Guard efforts to field a comprehensive Physical Access Control System at Coast Guard installations and locations necessary to bring the Service into compliance with HSPD-12 and FIPS-201B;

(2) the status of the selection of a technological solution;

(3) the estimated phases and timeframe to complete the implementation of such a system; and

(4) the estimated cost for each phase of the project.

SEC. 8254. STUDY ON CERTIFICATE OF COMPLIANCE

INSPECTION PROGRAM WITH RESPECT TO VESSELS THAT CARRY BULK LIQUEFIED GASES AS CARGO AND LIQUEFIED NATURAL GAS TANK VESSELS.

(a) GAO REPORT.—

(1) IN GENERAL.—Not later than 1 year after the date of the enactment of this Act, the Comptroller General of the United States shall submit to the Committee on Commerce, Science, and Transportation of the Senate and the Committee on Transportation and Infrastructure of the House of Representatives a report on the resources, regulations, policies, protocols, and other actions designed to carry out the Coast Guard Certificate of Compliance program with respect to liquefied natural gas tank vessels (including examinations under section 153.808 of title 46, Code of Federal Regulations) and vessels that carry bulk liquefied gases as cargo (including examinations under part 154 of title 46, Code of Federal Regulations) for purposes of maintaining the efficiency of examinations under that program.

(2) CONTENTS.—The report under paragraph (1) shall include an assessment of the adequacy of current Coast Guard resources, regulations, policies, and protocols to maintain vessel examination efficiency while carrying out the program referred to in paragraph (1) as United States bulk liquefied gases cargo, liquefied natural gas exports, and associated vessel traffic at United States ports increase.

(b) NATIONAL ACADEMIES STUDY.—

(1) IN GENERAL.—Not later than 6 months after the date on which the report required under subsection (a) is submitted, the Commandant shall enter into an agreement with the National Academies under which the National Academies shall—

(A) conduct an evaluation of the constraints and challenges to maintaining examination efficiency under the program as United States bulk liquefied gases cargo, liquefied natural gas exports, and associated vessel traffic at United States ports increase; and

(B) issue recommendations for changes to resources, regulations, policies, and protocols to maintain the efficiency of the program, including analysis of the following alternatives:

(i) Establishment of a Coast Guard marine examination unit near the Panama Canal to conduct inspections under the program on liquefied natural gas tank vessels bound for the United States, similar to Coast Guard operations carried out by Coast Guard Activities Europe and Coast Guard Activities Far East, including the effects of the establishment of such a unit on the domestic aspects of the program.

(ii) Management of all marine examiners with gas carrier qualification within each Coast Guard District by a single Officer in Charge, Marine Inspection (as defined in section 50.10-10 of title 46, Code of Federal Regulations) to improve the efficiency of their vessel examination assignments.

(iii) Extension of the duration of assignment of marine examiners with a gas carrier qualification at Coast Guard units that most frequently inspect vessels that carry bulk liquefied gases as cargo and liquefied natural gas tank vessels.

(iv) Increase in the use of civilians to conduct and support examinations under the program.

(v) Extension of the duration of certificates of compliance under the program for vessels that carry bulk liquefied gases as cargo and liquefied natural gas tank vessels that are less than 10 years of age and participate in a Coast Guard vessel quality program.

SEC. 8255. COMPTROLLER GENERAL OF THE UNITED STATES REVIEW AND REPORT ON COAST GUARD'S INTERNATIONAL PORT SECURITY PROGRAM.

(a) GAO REPORT.—Not later than 1 year after the date of the enactment of this Act, the Comptroller General of the United States shall submit to the Committee on Commerce, Science, and Transportation of the Senate and the Committee on Transportation and Infrastructure of the House of Representatives a report setting forth the results of a comprehensive review, conducted by the Comptroller General for purposes of the report, on the Coast Guard's International Port Security Program, including the findings, and any recommendations for improvement of the program, of the Comptroller General.

(b) REQUIRED ELEMENTS OF REVIEW.—The review required under subsection (a) shall include—

(1) review of the actions of the Coast Guard under the Coast Guard's International Port Security Program, since 2014, to enhance foreign port inspections;

(2) review of the actions of the Coast Guard to recognize and monitor port inspection programs of foreign governments;

(3) identification and review of the actions the Coast Guard takes to address any deficiencies it observes during visits at foreign ports;

(4) identify and review the benchmarks of the Coast Guard for measuring the effectiveness of the program; and

(5) review of the extent to which the Coast Guard and United States Customs and Border Protection coordinate efforts to screen and inspect cargo at foreign ports.

SEC. 8256. COMPTROLLER GENERAL OF THE UNITED STATES REVIEW AND REPORT ON SURGE CAPACITY OF THE COAST GUARD.

(a) GAO REPORT.—Not later than 60 days after the date of the enactment of this Act, the Comptroller General of the United States shall submit to the Committee on Commerce, Science, and Transportation of the Senate and the Committee on Transportation and Infrastructure of the House of Representatives a report setting for the results of a comprehensive review, conducted by the Comptroller General for purposes of the report, on the surge capacity of the Coast Guard to respond to a catastrophic incident (such as a hurricane), including the findings, and any recommendations for improvement, of the Comptroller General.

(b) REQUIRED ELEMENTS OF REVIEW.—The review required under subsection (a) shall include—

(1) a description and review of each Coast Guard deployment in response to a catastrophic incident after 2005;

(2) identification of best practices informed by the deployments described in paragraph (1);

(3) a review of the ability of the surge force of the Coast Guard to meet the demands of the response roles in which it was serving during each deployment described in paragraph (1);

(4) identification of any statutory or regulatory impediments, such as adaptability, planning, training, mobilization, or information and resource integration, to the surge capacity of the Coast Guard in response to a catastrophic incident;

(5) review of the impacts of a surge of the Coast Guard in response to a catastrophic incident on the capacity of the Coast Guard to perform its statutory missions;

(6) review of the capability of the Coast Guard to surge in response to concurrent or subsequent catastrophic incidents; and

(7) review and description of existing voluntary and involuntary deployments of Coast Guard personnel and assets in support of a United States Customs and Border Protection response to a national emergency (as defined in Presidential Proclamation 9844) on the surge capacity of the Coast Guard in the event of a catastrophic incident.

(c) DEFINITIONS.—In this section, the terms "catastrophic incident" and "surge capacity" have the meaning given such terms in section 602 of the Post-Katrina Emergency Management Reform Act of 2006 (6 U.S.C. 701).

SEC. 8257. COMPTROLLER GENERAL OF THE UNITED STATES REVIEW AND REPORT ON MARINE INSPECTIONS PROGRAM OF COAST GUARD.

(a) GAO REPORT.—Not later than 1 year after the date of the enactment of this Act, the Comptroller General of the United States shall submit to the Committee on Commerce, Science, and Transportation of the Senate and the Committee on Transportation and Infrastructure of the House of Representatives a report setting forth the results of a comprehensive review, conducted by the Comptroller General for purposes of the report, on the marine inspections program of the Coast Guard, including the findings, and any recommendations for improvement of the program, of the Comptroller General.

(b) REQUIRED ELEMENTS OF REVIEW.—The review required under subsection (a) shall include—

(1) an analysis of the demand for marine inspectors;

(2) an identification of the number of fully qualified marine

inspectors;

(3) a determination of whether the number of marine inspectors identified in paragraph (2) is sufficient to meet the demand described in paragraph (1);

(4) a review of the enlisted marine inspector workforce compared to the civilian marine inspector workforce and whether there is any discernable distinction or impact between such workforces in the performance of the marine safety mission;

(5) an evaluation of the training continuum of marine inspectors;

(6) a description and review of what actions, if any, the Coast Guard is taking to adapt to the current rise in United States export of crude oil and other fuels, such as implementing a safety inspection regime for barges; and

(7) an analysis of extending tours of duty for marine inspectors and increasing the number of civilian marine inspectors.

SEC. 8258. COMPTROLLER GENERAL OF THE UNITED STATES REVIEW AND REPORT ON INFORMATION TECHNOLOGY PROGRAM OF COAST GUARD.

(a) GAO REPORT.—

(1) IN GENERAL.—Not later than 1 year after the date of the enactment of this Act, the Comptroller General of the United States shall submit to the Committee on Commerce, Science, and Transportation of the Senate and the Committee on Transportation and Infrastructure of the House of Representatives a report setting forth the results of a comprehensive review, conducted by the Comptroller General for purposes of the report, on the Coast Guard Command, Control, Communications, Computers, Cyber, and Intelligence Service Center, including the findings, and any recommendations for improvement of the program, of the Comptroller General.

(2) REQUIRED ELEMENTS OF REVIEW.—The review required under paragraph (1) shall include—

(A) analysis of how the Coast Guard manages its information technology program, including information technology acquisitions, to meet its various mission needs and reporting requirements;

(B) analysis of the adequacy of the physical information technology infrastructure within Coast Guard districts, including network infrastructure, for meeting mission needs and reporting requirements;

(C) analysis of whether and, if so, how the Coast Guard—

(i) identifies and satisfies any knowledge and skill requirements; and

(ii) recruits, trains, and develops its information technology personnel;

(D) analysis of whether and, if so, how the Coast Guard separates information technology from operational technology for cybersecurity purposes;

(E) analysis of how the Coast Guard intends to update its Marine Information for Safety and Law Enforcement system, personnel, accounting and other databases, and implement an electronic health records system; and

(F) analysis of the goals and acquisition strategies for all proposed Coast Guard enterprise-wide cloud computing service procurements.

(b) REVIEW ON CLOUD COMPUTING.—Not later than 180 days after the date of the enactment of this Act, the Commandant shall submit to the Committee on Transportation and Infrastructure of the House of Representatives and the Committee on Commerce, Science, and Transportation of the Senate a detailed description of the Coast Guard's strategy to implement cloud computing for the entire Coast Guard, including—

(1) the goals and acquisition strategies for all proposed enterprise-wide cloud computing service procurements;

(2) a strategy to sustain competition and innovation throughout the period of performance of each contract for procurement of cloud-computing goods and services for the Coast Guard, including defining opportunities for multiple cloud-service providers and insertion of new technologies;

(3) an assessment of potential threats and security vulnerabilities of the strategy, and plans to mitigate such risks;

and

(4) an estimate of the cost and timeline to implement cloud computing service for all Coast Guard computing.

SEC. 8259. COMPTROLLER GENERAL OF THE UNITED STATES STUDY AND REPORT ON ACCESS TO HEALTH CARE BY MEMBERS OF COAST GUARD AND DEPENDENTS.

(a) STUDY.—

(1) IN GENERAL.—The Comptroller General of the United States shall conduct a study that examines access to, experience with, and needs under the TRICARE program of members of the Coast Guard and their dependents.

(2) ELEMENTS.—The study conducted under paragraph (1) shall analyze the following:

(A) The record of the TRICARE program in meeting the standards for care for primary and specialty care for members of the Coast Guard and dependents of those members, including members stationed in remote units.

(B) The accuracy and update periodicity of lists of providers under the TRICARE program in areas serving Coast Guard families.

(C) The wait times under the TRICARE program for appointments, specialty care, and referrals for members of the Coast Guard and dependents of those members.

(D) The availability of providers under the TRICARE program in remote locations, including providers for mental health, care for children with special needs, child and adolescent psychiatry, dental, and female health.

(E) The access of members of the Coast Guard and dependents of those members to services under the TRICARE program in comparison to the access to such services by personnel of the Department of Defense and dependents of such personnel.

(F) The liaison assistance between members of the Coast Guard and dependents of those members and the TRICARE program provided by the Coast Guard in comparison to such assistance provided by the Department of Defense.

(G) How delayed access to care, timeliness of care, and distance traveled to care may impact personnel readiness of members of the Coast Guard.

(H) The regions particularly impacted by lack of access to care and recommendations to address those access issues.

(b) REPORT.—Not later than 1 year after the date of the enactment of this Act, the Comptroller General shall submit to the Committee on Commerce, Science, and Transportation of the Senate and the Committee on Transportation and Infrastructure of the House of Representatives a report containing the findings, conclusions, and recommendations to improve access to quality, timely, and effective health care for members of the Coast Guard and dependents of those members from the study required under subsection (a).

(c) DEFINITIONS.—In this section, the terms "dependent" and "TRICARE program" have the meanings given such terms in section 1072 of title 10, United States Code.

SEC. 8260. COMPTROLLER GENERAL OF THE UNITED STATES STUDY AND REPORT ON MEDICAL STAFFING STANDARDS AND NEEDS FOR COAST GUARD.

(a) STUDY.—

(1) IN GENERAL.—The Comptroller General of the United States shall conduct a study that examines the health care system of the Coast Guard.

(2) ELEMENTS.—The study conducted under paragraph (1) shall analyze the following:

(A) The billets in clinics of the Coast Guard, whether for personnel of the Coast Guard or otherwise, including the number of billets, vacancies, and length of vacancies.

(B) The wait times for patients to attain an appointment for urgent care, routine physician care, and dental care.

(C) The impact of billet vacancies on such wait times.

(D) The barriers, if any, to improving coordination and access to physicians within the health care system of the Department of Defense.

(E) The accessibility and availability of behavioral health medical personnel at clinics of the Coast Guard, including personnel available for family counseling, therapy, and other needs.

(F) The staffing models of clinics of the Coast Guard, including recommendations to modernize such models.

(G) The locations and needs of Coast Guard units with or without clinics.

(H) How access to care models for members of the Coast Guard are managed, including models with respect to the time and distance traveled to receive care, the cost of that travel, and alternate options to secure care quickly and efficiently for members serving in units without a clinic.

(b) REPORT.—

(1) IN GENERAL.—Not later than 1 year after the date of the enactment of this Act, the Comptroller General shall submit to the Committee on Commerce, Science, and Transportation of the Senate and the Committee on Transportation and Infrastructure of the House of Representatives a report containing the findings, conclusions, and recommendations from the study required under subsection (a).

(2) ELEMENTS.—The report submitted under paragraph (1) shall include the following:

(A) An identification of the number of members of the Coast Guard and types of units of the Coast Guard serviced by the health care system of the Coast Guard.

(B) An assessment of the ability of the Coast Guard to conduct medical support at outlying units, including remote units.

(C) An assessment of the capacity of the Coast Guard to support surge operations using historical data from the 10-year period preceding the date of the report.

(D) An assessment of the impact to operations of the Coast Guard by extended wait times or travel times to receive care or other issues identified by the report.

(c) RECOMMENDATIONS.—Not later than 90 days after the date on which the report is submitted under subsection (b), the

Commandant shall submit to the Committee on Commerce, Science, and Transportation of the Senate and the Committee on Transportation and Infrastructure of the House of Representatives written recommendations for medical staffing standards for the Coast Guard based on each finding and conclusion contained in the report, including recommendations for health service technicians, flight surgeons, physician assistants, dentists, dental hygienists, family advocate services, pharmacists, and administrators, and other recommendations, as appropriate.

SEC. 8261. REPORT ON FAST RESPONSE CUTTERS, OFFSHORE PATROL CUTTERS, AND NATIONAL SECURITY CUTTERS.

(a) IN GENERAL.—Not later than 90 days after the date of the enactment of this Act, the Commandant shall submit to the Committee on Commerce, Science, and Transportation of the Senate and the Committee on Transportation and Infrastructure of the House of Representatives a report on the combination of Fast Response Cutters, Offshore Patrol Cutters, and National Security Cutters necessary to carry out Coast Guard missions.

(b) ELEMENTS.—The report required by subsection (a) shall include—

(1) an updated cost estimate for each type of cutter described in such subsection; and

(2) a cost estimate for a Sensitive Compartmented Information Facility outfitted to manage data in a manner equivalent to the National Security Cutter Sensitive Compartmented Information Facilities.

Subtitle E—Coast Guard Academy Improvement Act

SEC. 8271. [14 U.S.C. 101 note] SHORT TITLE.

This subtitle may be cited as the "Coast Guard Academy Improvement Act".

SEC. 8272. [14 U.S.C. 1901 note] COAST GUARD ACADEMY STUDY.

(a) IN GENERAL.—The Secretary of the department in which the Coast Guard is operating shall seek to enter into an arrangement with the National Academy of Public Administration not later than

60 days after the date of the enactment of the this Act under which the National Academy of Public Administration shall—

(1) conduct an assessment of the cultural competence of the Coast Guard Academy as an organization and of individuals at the Coast Guard Academy to carry out effectively the primary duties of the United States Coast Guard listed in section 102 of title 14, United States Code, when interacting with individuals of different races, ethnicities, genders, religions, sexual orientations, socioeconomic backgrounds, or from different geographic origins; and

(2) issue recommendations based upon the findings in such assessment.

(b) ASSESSMENT OF CULTURAL COMPETENCE.—

(1) CULTURAL COMPETENCE OF THE COAST GUARD ACADEMY.—The arrangement described in subsection (a) shall require the National Academy of Public Administration to, not later than 1 year after entering into an arrangement with the Secretary under subsection (a), submit to the Committee on Transportation and Infrastructure of the House of Representatives and the Committee on Commerce, Science, and Transportation of the Senate the assessment described under subsection (a)(1).

(2) ASSESSMENT SCOPE.—The assessment described under subsection (a)(1) shall—

(A) describe the level of cultural competence described in subsection (a)(1) based on the National Academy of Public Administration's assessment of the Coast Guard Academy's relevant practices, policies, and structures, including an overview of discussions with faculty, staff, students, and relevant Coast Guard Academy affiliated organizations;

(B) examine potential changes which could be used to further enhance such cultural competence by—

(i) modifying institutional practices, policies, and structures; and

(ii) any other changes deemed appropriate by the National Academy of Public Administration; and

(C) make recommendations to enhance the cultural competence of the Coast Guard Academy described in subparagraph (A), including any specific plans, policies, milestones, performance measures, or other information necessary to implement such recommendations.

(c) FINAL ACTION MEMORANDUM.—Not later than 6 months after submission of the assessment under subsection (b)(1), the Commandant of the Coast Guard shall submit to the Committee on Transportation and Infrastructure of the House of Representatives and the Committee on Commerce, Science, and Transportation of the Senate, a final action memorandum in response to all recommendations contained in the assessment. The final action memorandum shall include the rationale for accepting, accepting in part, or rejecting each recommendation, and shall specify, where applicable, actions to be taken to implement such recommendations, including an explanation of how each action enhances the ability of the Coast Guard to carry out the primary duties of the United States Coast Guard listed in section 102 of title 14, United States Code.

(d) PLAN.—

(1) IN GENERAL.—Not later than 6 months after the date of the submission of the final action memorandum required under subsection (c), the Commandant, in coordination with the Chief Human Capital Officer of the Department of Homeland Security, shall submit a plan to carry out the recommendations or the parts of the recommendations accepted in the final action memorandum to the Committee on Transportation and Infrastructure of the House of Representatives and the Committee on Commerce, Science, and Transportation of the Senate.

(2) STRATEGY WITH MILESTONES.—If any recommendation or parts of recommendations accepted in the final action memorandum address any of the following actions, then the plan required in paragraph (1) shall include a strategy with appropriate milestones to carry out such recommendations or parts of recommendations:

(A) Improve outreach and recruitment of a more diverse Coast Guard Academy cadet candidate pool based on race, ethnicity, gender, religion, sexual orientation, socioeconomic background, and geographic origin.

(B) Modify institutional structures, practices, and policies to foster a more diverse cadet corps body, faculty, and staff workforce based on race, ethnicity, gender, religion, sexual orientation, socioeconomic background, and geographic origin.

(C) Modify existing or establish new policies and safeguards to foster the retention of cadets, faculty, and staff of different races, ethnicities, genders, religions, sexual orientations, socioeconomic backgrounds, and geographic origins at the Coast Guard Academy.

(D) Restructure the admissions office of the Coast Guard Academy to be headed by a civilian with significant relevant higher education recruitment experience.

(3) IMPLEMENTATION.—Unless otherwise directed by an Act of Congress, the Commandant shall begin implementation of the plan developed under this subsection not later than 180 days after the submission of such plan to Congress.

(4) UPDATE.—The Commandant shall include in the first annual report required under chapter 51 of title 14, United States Code, as amended by this division, submitted after the date of enactment of this section, the strategy with milestones required in paragraph (2) and shall report annually thereafter on actions taken and progress made in the implementation of such plan.

SEC. 8273. ANNUAL REPORT.

Chapter 51 of title 14, United States Code, is further amended by adding at the end the following:

"SEC. 5111. [14 U.S.C. 5111] Report on diversity at Coast Guard Academy

"(a) IN GENERAL.—Not later than January 15, 2021, and annually thereafter, the Commandant shall submit a report on diversity at the Coast Guard Academy to the Committee on Transportation and Infrastructure of the House of Representatives and the Committee on Commerce, Science, and Transportation of the Senate.

"(b) CONTENTS.—The report required under subsection (a) shall include—

"(1) the status of the implementation of the plan required under section 8272 of the Elijah E. Cummings Coast Guard Authorization Act of 2020;

"(2) specific information on outreach and recruitment activities for the preceding year, including the effectiveness of the Coast Guard Academy minority outreach team program described under section 1905 and of outreach and recruitment activities in the territories and other possessions of the United States;

"(3) enrollment information about the incoming class, including the gender, race, ethnicity, religion, socioeconomic background, and State of residence of Coast Guard Academy cadets;

"(4) information on class retention, outcomes, and graduation rates, including the race, gender, ethnicity, religion, socioeconomic background, and State of residence of Coast Guard Academy cadets;

"(5) information on efforts to retain diverse cadets, including through professional development and professional advancement programs for staff and faculty; and

"(6) a summary of reported allegations of discrimination on the basis of race, color, national origin, sex, gender, or religion for the preceding 5 years."

SEC. 8274. ASSESSMENT OF COAST GUARD ACADEMY ADMISSION PROCESSES.

(a) IN GENERAL.—The Secretary of the department in which the Coast Guard is operating shall seek to enter into an arrangement with the National Academy of Public Administration under which the National Academy of Public Administration shall, not later than 1 year after submitting an assessment under section 8272(a), submit to the Committee on Transportation and Infrastructure of the House of Representatives and the Committee on Commerce, Science, and Transportation of the Senate an assessment of the Coast Guard Academy admissions process.

(b) ASSESSMENT SCOPE.—The assessment required to be sought under subsection (a) shall, at a minimum, include—

(1) a study, or an audit if appropriate, of the process the Coast Guard Academy uses to—

(A) identify candidates for recruitment;

(B) recruit applicants;

(C) assist applicants in the application process;

(D) evaluate applications; and

(E) make admissions decisions;

(2) discussion of the consideration during the admissions process of diversity, including—

(A) race;

(B) ethnicity;

(C) gender;

(D) religion;

(E) sexual orientation;

(F) socioeconomic background; and

(G) geographic origin;

(3) an overview of the admissions processes at other Federal service academies, including—

(A) discussion of consideration of diversity, including any efforts to attract a diverse pool of applicants, in those processes; and

(B) an analysis of how the congressional nominations requirement in current law related to military service academies and the Merchant Marine Academy impacts those processes and the overall demographics of the student bodies at those academies;

(4) a determination regarding how a congressional nominations requirement for Coast Guard Academy admissions could impact diversity among the student body and the ability of the Coast Guard to carry out effectively the Service's primary duties described in section 102 of title 14, United States Code; and

(5) recommendations for improving Coast Guard Academy admissions processes, including whether a congressional nominations process should be integrated into such processes.

SEC. 8275. COAST GUARD ACADEMY MINORITY OUTREACH TEAM PROGRAM.

(a) IN GENERAL.—Chapter 19 of title 14, United States Code, is further amended by inserting after section 1904 (as amended by this division) the following:

"SEC. 1905. [14 U.S.C. 1905] Coast Guard Academy minority outreach

team program

"(a) IN GENERAL.—There is established within the Coast Guard Academy a minority outreach team program (in this section referred to as the 'Program') under which officers, including minority officers and officers from territories and other possessions of the United States, who are Academy graduates may volunteer their time to recruit minority students and strengthen cadet retention through mentorship of cadets.

"(b) ADMINISTRATION.—Not later than January 1, 2021, the Commandant, in consultation with Program volunteers and Academy alumni that participated in prior programs at the Academy similar to the Program, shall appoint a permanent civilian position at the Academy to administer the Program by, among other things—

"(1) overseeing administration of the Program;

"(2) serving as a resource to volunteers and outside stakeholders;

"(3) advising Academy leadership on recruitment and retention efforts based on recommendations from volunteers and outside stakeholders;

"(4) establishing strategic goals and performance metrics for the Program with input from active volunteers and Academy leadership; and

"(5) reporting annually to the Commandant on academic year and performance outcomes of the goals for the Program before the end of each academic year."

(b) [14 U.S.C. 1901] CLERICAL AMENDMENT.—The analysis for chapter 19 of title 14, United States Code, is further amended by inserting after the item relating to section 1904 (as amended by this division) the following:

"1905. Coast Guard Academy minority outreach team program."

SEC. 8276. COAST GUARD COLLEGE STUDENT PRE-COMMISSIONING INITIATIVE.

(a) IN GENERAL.—Subchapter I of chapter 21 of title 14, United States Code, is further amended by adding at the end the following:

"SEC. 2131. [14 U.S.C. 2131] College student pre-commissioning

initiative

"(a) IN GENERAL.—There is authorized within the Coast Guard a college student pre-commissioning initiative program (in this section referred to as the 'Program') for eligible undergraduate students to enlist and receive a guaranteed commission as an officer in the Coast Guard.

"(b) CRITERIA FOR SELECTION.—To be eligible for the Program a student must meet the following requirements upon submitting an application:

"(1) AGE.—A student must be not less than 19 years old and not more than 27 years old as of September 30 of the fiscal year in which the Program selection panel selecting such student convenes.

"(2) CHARACTER.—

"(A) ALL APPLICANTS.—All applicants must be of outstanding moral character and meet other character requirements as set forth by the Commandant.

"(B) COAST GUARD APPLICANTS.—An applicant serving in the Coast Guard may not be commissioned if in the 36 months prior to the first Officer Candidate School class convening date in the selection cycle, such applicant was convicted by a court-martial or awarded nonjudicial punishment, or did not meet performance or character requirements set forth by the Commandant.

"(3) CITIZENSHIP.—A student must be a United States citizen.

"(4) CLEARANCE.—A student must be eligible for a secret clearance.

"(5) DEPENDENCY.—

"(A) IN GENERAL.—A student may not have more than 2 dependents.

"(B) SOLE CUSTODY.—A student who is single may not have sole or primary custody of dependents.

"(6) EDUCATION.—

"(A) INSTITUTION.—A student must be an undergraduate sophomore or junior—

"(i) at a historically Black college or university described in section 322(2) of the Higher Education Act of 1965 (20 U.S.C. 1061(2)) or an institution of higher education described in section 371(a) of the Higher Education Act of 1965 (20 U.S.C. 1067q(a)); or

"(ii) an undergraduate sophomore or junior enrolled at an institution of higher education (as defined in section 101 of the Higher Education Act of 1965 (20 U.S.C. 1001)) that, at the time of application of the sophomore or junior, has had for 3 consecutive years an enrollment of undergraduate full-time equivalent students (as defined in section 312(e) of such Act (20 U.S.C. 1058(e))) that is a total of at least 50 percent Black American, Hispanic, Asian American (as defined in section 371(c) of such Act (20 U.S.C. 1067q(c))), Native American Pacific Islander (as defined in such section), or Native American (as defined in such section), among other criteria, as determined by the Commandant.

"(B) LOCATION.—The institution at which such student is an undergraduate must be within 100 miles of a Coast guard unit or Coast Guard Recruiting Office unless otherwise approved by the Commandant.

"(C) RECORDS.—A student must meet credit and grade point average requirements set forth by the Commandant.

"(7) MEDICAL AND ADMINISTRATIVE.—A student must meet other medical and administrative requirements as set forth by the Commandant.

"(c) ENLISTMENT AND OBLIGATION.—Individuals selected and accept to participate in the Program shall enlist in the Coast Guard in pay grade E-3 with a 4-year duty obligation and 4-year inactive Reserve obligation.

"(d) MILITARY ACTIVITIES PRIOR TO OFFICER CANDIDATE SCHOOL.—Individuals enrolled in the Program shall participate in military activities each month, as required by the Commandant, prior to attending Officer Candidate School.

"(e) PARTICIPATION IN OFFICER CANDIDATE SCHOOL.—Each graduate of the Program shall attend the first enrollment of Officer Candidate School that commences after the date of such graduate's graduation.

"(f) COMMISSIONING.—Upon graduation from Officer Candidate

School, Program graduates shall be discharged from enlisted status and commissioned as an O-1 with an initial 3-year duty obligation.

"(g) BRIEFING.—

"(1) IN GENERAL.—Not later than August 15 of each year, the Commandant shall provide a briefing to the Committee on Transportation and Infrastructure of the House of Representatives and the Committee on Commerce, Science, and Transportation of the Senate on the Program.

"(2) CONTENTS.—The briefing required under paragraph (1) shall describe—

"(A) outreach and recruitment efforts over the previous year; and

"(B) demographic information of enrollees including—

"(i) race;

"(ii) ethnicity;

"(iii) gender;

"(iv) geographic origin; and

"(v) educational institution."

(b) [14 U.S.C. 2101] CLERICAL AMENDMENT.—The analysis chapter 21 of title 14, United States Code, is amended by inserting after the item relating to section 2130 (as added by this division) the following:

"2131. College student pre-commissioning initiative."

SEC. 8277. ANNUAL BOARD OF VISITORS.

Section 1903(d) of title 14, United States Code, is amended—

(1) by redesignating paragraphs (2) through (6) as paragraphs (3) through (7), respectively; and

(2) by inserting after paragraph (1) the following:

"(2) recruitment and retention, including diversity, inclusion, and issues regarding women specifically;"

SEC. 8278. HOMELAND SECURITY ROTATIONAL CYBERSECURITY RESEARCH PROGRAM AT COAST GUARD ACADEMY.

(a) IN GENERAL.—Subtitle E of title VIII of the Homeland Security Act of 2002 (6 U.S.C. 411 et seq.) is amended by adding at the end the following:

"SEC. 846. [6 U.S.C. 417] ROTATIONAL CYBERSECURITY RESEARCH PROGRAM

"To enhance the Department's cybersecurity capacity, the Secretary may establish a rotational research, development, and training program for—

"(1) detail to the Cybersecurity and Infrastructure Security Agency (including the national cybersecurity and communications integration center authorized by section 2209) of Coast Guard Academy graduates and faculty; and

"(2) detail to the Coast Guard Academy, as faculty, of individuals with expertise and experience in cybersecurity who are employed by—

"(A) the Agency (including the center);

"(B) the Directorate of Science and Technology; or

"(C) institutions that have been designated by the Department as a Center of Excellence for Cyber Defense, or the equivalent."

(b) CLERICAL AMENDMENT.—The table of contents in section 1(b) of the Homeland Security Act of 2002 (6 U.S.C. 411 et seq.) is amended by adding at the end of the items relating to subtitle E of such Act the following:

"Sec. 846. Rotational cybersecurity research program."

Subtitle F—Other Matters

SEC. 8281. STRATEGY ON LEADERSHIP OF COAST GUARD.

(a) IN GENERAL.—Not later than 180 days after the date of the enactment of this Act, the Secretary of the department in which the Coast Guard is operating shall develop and make available to the public a strategy to improve leadership development in the Coast Guard, including mechanisms to address counterproductive leadership in the Coast Guard.

(b) ELEMENTS.—The strategy shall include the following:

(1) Mechanisms to foster positive and productive leadership qualities in emerging Coast Guard leaders, beginning, at minimum, members at grade O-2 for officers, members at grade E-6 for enlisted members, and members training to become an officer in charge.

(2) Mechanisms for the ongoing evaluation of unit commanders, including identification of counterproductive leadership qualities in commanders.

(3) Formal training on the recognition of counterproductive leadership qualities (in self and others), including at leadership seminars and school houses in the Coast Guard, including means to correct such qualities.

(4) Clear and transparent policies on standards for command climate, leadership qualities, and inclusion.

(5) Policy to ensure established and emerging leaders have access to hands-on training and tools to improve diversity and inclusion.

(6) Policy and procedures for commanders to identify and hold accountable counterproductive leaders.

(c) COUNTERPRODUCTIVE LEADERSHIP DEFINED.—In this section, the term "counterproductive leadership" has the meaning given that term for purposes of Army Doctrine Publication 6-22.

SEC. 8282. [14 U.S.C. 1902 note] EXPEDITED TRANSFER IN CASES OF SEXUAL ASSAULT; DEPENDENTS OF MEMBERS OF THE COAST GUARD.

Not later than 180 days after the date of the enactment of this Act, the Commandant shall establish a policy to allow the transfer of a member of the Coast Guard whose dependent is the victim of sexual assault perpetrated by a member of the Armed Forces who is not related to the victim.

SEC. 8283. ACCESS TO RESOURCES DURING CREOSOTE-RELATED BUILDING CLOSURES AT COAST GUARD BASE SEATTLE, WASHINGTON.

(a) IN GENERAL.—With respect to the creosote-related building closures at Coast Guard Base Seattle, Washington, the Commandant shall, to the maximum extent practicable, enter into 1 or more agreements or otherwise take actions to secure access to resources, including a gym, that are not otherwise available to members of the Coast Guard during such closures.

(b) BRIEFING.—Not later than 60 days after the date of the enactment of this Act, the Commandant shall brief Congress with respect to actions taken by the Commandant to comply with subsection (a).

SEC. 8284. SOUTHERN RESIDENT ORCA CONSERVATION AND ENFORCEMENT.

(a) REPORT AND ACTION PLAN ON ORCA ENFORCEMENT OPPORTUNITIES. Not later than 180 days after the date of the enactment of this Act, the Commandant, in consultation with the Under Secretary of Commerce for Oceans and Atmosphere, shall submit to Congress a report on Coast Guard efforts to enforce southern resident orca vessel buffer zones and other vessel-related regulations in Puget Sound in coordination with existing Coast Guard fisheries enforcement, maritime domain awareness, the Be Whale Wise campaign, and other related missions. Such report shall include recommendations on what resources, appropriations, and assets are needed to meet orca conservation and related fisheries enforcement targets in the 13th Coast Guard District within 1 year of the date of enactment of this Act.

(b) SOUTHERN RESIDENT ORCAS.—The Commandant, in coordination with the Under Secretary of Commerce for Oceans and Atmosphere, shall undertake efforts to reduce vessel noise impacts on Southern resident orcas in Puget Sound, the Salish Sea, and the Strait of Juan de Fuca.

(c) PROGRAM.—

(1) IN GENERAL.—The Commandant shall—

(A) support the development, implementation, and enforcement of commercial vessel noise reduction measures that are technically feasible and economically achievable;

(B) establish procedures for timely communication of information to commercial vessel operators regarding orca sightings in Puget Sound and make navigational safety recommendations in accordance with the Cooperative Vessel Traffic Service Agreement; and

(C) collaborate on studies or trials analyzing vessel noise impacts on Southern resident orcas.

(2) VESSEL NOISE IMPACTS.—The Undersecretary of Commerce for Oceans and Atmosphere shall assess vessel noise impacts on Southern resident orcas in the program area and make recommendations to reduce that noise and noise related impacts to Southern resident orcas to the Commandant.

(3) COORDINATION.—In carrying out this section, the Commandant shall coordinate with Canadian agencies

affiliated with the Enhancing Cetacean Habitat and Observation (ECHO) program and other international organizations as appropriate.

(4) CONSULTATION.—In carrying out this section, the Commandant and the Undersecretary of Commerce for Oceans and Atmosphere shall consult with State, local, and Tribal governments and maritime industry and conservation stakeholders including ports, higher education institutions, and nongovernmental organizations.

SEC. 8285. SENSE OF CONGRESS AND REPORT ON IMPLEMENTATION OF POLICY ON ISSUANCE OF WARRANTS AND SUBPOENAS AND WHISTLEBLOWER PROTECTIONS BY AGENTS OF THE COAST GUARD INVESTIGATIVE SERVICE.

(a) SENSE OF CONGRESS.—It is the sense of Congress that—

(1) Coast Guard components with investigative authority should exercise such authority with due respect for the rights of whistleblowers; and

(2) the Commandant should—

(A) ensure compliance with the legal requirements intended to protect whistleblowers;

(B) seek to shield the disclosure of the identities of whistleblowers; and

(C) create an environment in which whistleblowers do not fear reprisal for reporting misconduct.

(b) REPORT REQUIRED.—Not later than 120 days after the date of the enactment of this Act, the Commandant shall submit to the Committee on Commerce, Science, and Transportation of the Senate and the Committee on Transportation and Infrastructure of the House of Representatives a report on the policy of the Coast Guard on the issuance of warrants and subpoenas and whistleblower protections by agents of the Coast Guard Investigative Service.

(c) ELEMENTS.—The report required by subsection (b) shall include the following:

(1) A discussion of current and any new policy of the Coast Guard on the issuance of warrants and subpoenas and whistleblower protections by agents of the Coast Guard Investigative Service, including Coast Guard Investigative Service Criminal Investigation Operating Procedure CIOP

2019-02, and the differences between such current policies and new policies.

(2) A plan (including milestones) for the implementation of the following:

(A) Incorporation of Coast Guard Investigative Service Criminal Investigation Operating Procedure CIOP 2019-02 into the next revision of the relevant Coast Guard investigative manual.

(B) Training on the policy described in paragraph (1) for the following:

(i) Agents and legal counsel of the Coast Guard Investigative Service.

(ii) Personnel of the Office of General Law.

(iii) Relevant Coast Guard headquarters personnel.

(iv) Such other Coast Guard personnel as the Commandant considers appropriate.

SEC. 8286. INSPECTOR GENERAL REPORT ON ACCESS TO EQUAL OPPORTUNITY ADVISORS AND EQUAL EMPLOYMENT OPPORTUNITY SPECIALISTS.

(a) IN GENERAL.—Not later than 90 days after the date of the enactment of this Act, the inspector general of the department in which the Coast Guard is operating shall conduct a study and develop recommendations on the need to separate Equal Opportunity Advisors and Equal Employment Opportunity Specialists, as practicable, through the pre-complaint and formal discrimination complaint processes, for the complainant, the opposing party, and the commanding officers and officers in charge.

(b) BRIEFING.—Not later than 30 days after the completion of the study required by subsection (a), the Commandant shall brief the Committee on Commerce, Science, and Transportation of the Senate and the Committee on Transportation and Infrastructure of the House of Representatives on the manner in which the Coast Guard plans to implement the recommendations developed as a result of the study.

SEC. 8287. INSIDER THREAT PROGRAM.

Not later than 180 days after the date of the enactment of this

Act, the Commandant shall brief the Committee on Transportation and Infrastructure of the House of Representatives and the Committee on Commerce, Science, and Transportation of the Senate on a plan to expand the Coast Guard Insider Threat Program to include the monitoring of all Coast Guard devices, including mobile devices.

TITLE LVXXXIII—MARITIME

Subtitle A—Navigation

SEC. 8301. ELECTRONIC CHARTS; EQUIVALENCY.

(a) REQUIREMENTS.—Section 3105(a)(1) of title 46, United States Code, is amended to read as follows:

"(1) ELECTRONIC CHARTS IN LIEU OF MARINE CHARTS, CHARTS, AND MAPS.—Subject to paragraph (2), the following vessels, while operating on the navigable waters of the United States, equipped with and operating electronic navigational charts that are produced by a government hydrographic office or conform to a standard acceptable to the Secretary, shall be deemed in compliance with any requirement under title 33 or title 46, Code of Federal Regulations, to have a chart, marine chart, or map on board such vessel:

"(A) A self-propelled commercial vessel of at least 65 feet in overall length.

"(B) A vessel carrying more than a number of passengers for hire determined by the Secretary.

"(C) A towing vessel of more than 26 feet in overall length and 600 horsepower.

"(D) Any other vessel for which the Secretary decides that electronic charts are necessary for the safe navigation of the vessel."

(b) EXEMPTIONS AND WAIVERS.—Section 3105(a)(2) of title 46, United States Code, is amended—

(1) in subparagraph (A), by striking "operates; and" and inserting "operates;";

(2) in subparagraph (B), by striking "those waters." and inserting "those waters; and"; and

(3) by adding at the end the following:

"(C) permit vessels described in subparagraphs (A) through (D) of paragraph (1) that operate solely landward of the baseline from which the territorial sea of the United States is measured to utilize software-based, platform-independent electronic chart systems that the Secretary determines are capable of displaying electronic navigational charts with necessary scale and detail to ensure safe navigation for the intended voyage."

SEC. 8302. SUBROGATED CLAIMS.

(a) IN GENERAL.—Section 1012(b) of the Oil Pollution Act of 1990 (33 U.S.C. 2712(b)) is amended—

(1) by striking "The" and inserting the following:

"(1) IN GENERAL.—The"

; and

(2) by adding at the end the following:

"(2) SUBROGATED RIGHTS.—Except for a guarantor claim pursuant to a defense under section 1016(f)(1), Fund compensation of any claim by an insurer or other indemnifier of a responsible party or injured third party is subject to the subrogated rights of that responsible party or injured third party to such compensation."

(b) [33 U.S.C. 2712 note] EFFECTIVE DATE.—This section and the amendments made by this section shall take effect 180 days after the date of enactment of this Act.

SEC. 8303. LOAN PROVISIONS UNDER OIL POLLUTION ACT OF 1990.

(a) IN GENERAL.—Section 1013 of the Oil Pollution Act of 1990 (33 U.S.C. 2713) is amended by striking subsection (f).

(b) CONFORMING AMENDMENTS.—Section 1012(a) of the Oil Pollution Act of 1990 (33 U.S.C. 2712(a)) is amended—

(1) in paragraph (4), by adding "and" after the semicolon at the end;

(2) in paragraph (5)(D), by striking "; and" and inserting a period; and

(3) by striking paragraph (6).

SEC. 8304. OIL POLLUTION RESEARCH AND DEVELOPMENT PROGRAM.

Section 7001 of the Oil Pollution Act of 1990 (33 U.S.C. 2761) is amended—

(1) in subsection (c)—

(A) in paragraph (1), by inserting ", technology," after "research";

(B) in paragraph (2)—

(i) by striking "this subsection" and inserting "paragraph (1)"; and

(ii) by striking "which are effective in preventing or mitigating oil discharges and which" and inserting "and methods that are effective in preventing, mitigating, or restoring damage from oil discharges and that";

(C) in paragraph (3) by striking "this subsection" and inserting "paragraph (1)" each place it appears;

(D) in subparagraph (A) of paragraph (4)—

(i) by striking "oil discharges. Such program shall" and inserting "acute and chronic oil discharges on coastal and marine resources (including impacts on protected areas such as sanctuaries) and protected species, and such program shall";

(ii) by redesignating clauses (iii) and (iv) as clauses (iv) and (v), respectively;

(iii) by inserting after clause (ii) the following:

"(iii) Research to understand and quantify the effects of sublethal impacts of oil discharge on living natural marine resources, including impacts on pelagic fish species, marine mammals, and commercially and recreationally targeted fish and shellfish species."

; and

(iv) by adding at the end the following:

"(vi) Research to understand the long-term effects of major oil discharges and the long-term effects of smaller endemic oil discharges.

"(vii) The identification of potential impacts on ecosystems, habitat, and wildlife from the additional toxicity, heavy metal concentrations, and increased corrosiveness of mixed crude, such as diluted bitumen crude.

"(viii) The development of methods to restore and rehabilitate natural resources and ecosystem functions damaged by oil discharges."

(E) in paragraph (5) by striking "this subsection" and inserting "paragraph (1)";

(F) by striking paragraph (7) and inserting the following:

"(7) SIMULATED ENVIRONMENTAL TESTING.—

"(A) IN GENERAL.—Agencies represented on the Interagency Committee shall ensure the long-term use and operation of the Oil and Hazardous Materials Simulated Environmental Test Tank (OHMSETT) Research Center in New Jersey for oil pollution technology testing and evaluations.

"(B) OTHER TESTING FACILITIES.—Nothing in subparagraph (A) shall be construed as limiting the ability of the Interagency Committee to contract or partner with a facility or facilities other than the Center described in subparagraph (A) for the purpose of oil pollution technology testing and evaluations, provided such a facility or facilities have testing and evaluation capabilities equal to or greater than those of such Center.

"(C) IN-KIND CONTRIBUTIONS.—

"(i) IN GENERAL.—The Secretary of the department in which the Coast Guard is operating and the Administrator of the Environmental Protection Agency may accept donations of crude oil and crude oil product samples in the form of in-kind contributions for use by the Federal Government for product testing, research and development, and for other purposes as the Secretary and the Administrator determine appropriate.

"(ii) USE OF DONATED OIL.—Oil accepted under clause (i) may be used directly by the Secretary and shall be provided to other Federal agencies or departments through interagency agreements to carry out the purposes of this Act."

(G) in paragraph (8)—

(i) in subparagraph (A), by striking "subsection (b)" and inserting "subsection (d)"; and

(ii) in subparagraph (D)(iii), by striking "subsection (b)(1)(F)" and inserting "subsection (d)"; and

(H) in paragraph (10)—

(i) by striking "this subsection" and inserting "paragraph (1)";

(ii) by striking "agencies represented on the Interagency Committee" and inserting "Under Secretary";

(iii) by inserting ", and States and Indian tribes" after "other persons"; and

(iv) by striking "subsection (b)" and inserting "subsection (d)";

(2) in subsection (d), by striking "subsection (b)" and inserting "subsection (d)";

(3) in subsection (e), by striking "Chairman of the Interagency Committee" and inserting "Chair";

(4) in subsection (f), by striking "subsection (c)(8)" each place it appears and inserting "subsection (e)(8)";

(5) by redesignating subsections (c) through (f) as subsections (e) through (h), respectively; and

(6) by striking subsections (a) and (b) and inserting the following:

"(a) DEFINITIONS.—In this section—

"(1) the term 'Chair' means the Chairperson of the Interagency Committee designated under subsection (c)(2);

"(2) the term 'Commandant' means the Commandant of the Coast Guard;

"(3) the term 'institution of higher education' means an institution of higher education, as defined in section 101(a) of the Higher Education Act of 1965 (20 U.S.C. 1001(a));

"(4) the term 'Interagency Committee' means the Interagency Coordinating Committee on Oil Pollution

Research established under subsection (b);

"(5) the term 'Under Secretary' means the Under Secretary of Commerce for Oceans and Atmosphere; and

"(6) the term 'Vice Chair' means the Vice Chairperson of the Interagency Committee designated under subsection (c)(3).

"(b) ESTABLISHMENT OF INTERAGENCY COORDINATING COMMITTEE ON OIL POLLUTION RESEARCH.—

"(1) ESTABLISHMENT.—There is established an Interagency Coordinating Committee on Oil Pollution Research.

"(2) PURPOSE.—The Interagency Committee shall coordinate a comprehensive program of oil pollution research, technology development, and demonstration among the Federal agencies, in cooperation and coordination with industry, 4-year institutions of higher education and research institutions, State governments, and other nations, as appropriate, and shall foster cost-effective research mechanisms, including the joint funding of research.

"(c) MEMBERSHIP.—

"(1) COMPOSITION.—The Interagency Committee shall be composed of—

"(A) at least 1 representative of the Coast Guard;

"(B) at least 1 representative of the National Oceanic and Atmospheric Administration;

"(C) at least 1 representative of the Environmental Protection Agency;

"(D) at least 1 representative of the Department of the Interior;

"(E) at least 1 representative of the Bureau of Safety and Environmental Enforcement;

"(F) at least 1 representative of the Bureau of Ocean Energy Management;

"(G) at least 1 representative of the United States Fish and Wildlife Service;

"(H) at least 1 representative of the Department of

Energy;

"(I) at least 1 representative of the Pipeline and Hazardous Materials Safety Administration;

"(J) at least 1 representative of the Federal Emergency Management Agency;

"(K) at least 1 representative of the Navy;

"(L) at least 1 representative of the Corps of Engineers;

"(M) at least 1 representative of the United States Arctic Research Commission; and

"(N) at least 1 representative of each of such other Federal agencies as the President considers to be appropriate.

"(2) CHAIRPERSON.—The Commandant shall designate a Chairperson from among the members of the Interagency Committee selected under paragraph (1)(A).

"(3) VICE CHAIRPERSON.—The Under Secretary shall designate a Vice Chairperson from among the members of the Interagency Committee selected under paragraph (1)(B).

"(4) MEETINGS.—

"(A) QUARTERLY MEETINGS.—At a minimum, the members of the Interagency Committee shall meet once each quarter.

"(B) PUBLIC SUMMARIES.—After each meeting, a summary shall be made available by the Chair or Vice Chair, as appropriate.

"(d) DUTIES OF THE INTERAGENCY COMMITTEE.—

"(1) RESEARCH.—The Interagency Committee shall—

"(A) coordinate a comprehensive program of oil pollution research, technology development, and demonstration among the Federal agencies, in cooperation and coordination with industry, 4-year institutions of higher education and research institutions, States, Indian tribes, and other countries, as appropriate; and

"(B) foster cost-effective research mechanisms,

including the joint funding of research and the development of public-private partnerships for the purpose of expanding research.

"(2) OIL POLLUTION RESEARCH AND TECHNOLOGY PLAN.—

"(A) IMPLEMENTATION PLAN.—Not later than 180 days after the date of enactment of the Elijah E. Cummings Coast Guard Authorization Act of 2020, the Interagency Committee shall submit to Congress a research plan to report on the state of oil discharge prevention and response capabilities that—

"(i) identifies current research programs conducted by Federal agencies, States, Indian tribes, 4-year institutions of higher education, and corporate entities;

"(ii) assesses the current status of knowledge on oil pollution prevention, response, and mitigation technologies and effects of oil pollution on the environment;

"(iii) identifies significant oil pollution research gaps, including an assessment of major technological deficiencies in responses to past oil discharges;

"(iv) establishes national research priorities and goals for oil pollution technology development related to prevention, response, mitigation, and environmental effects;

"(v) assesses the research on the applicability and effectiveness of the prevention, response, and mitigation technologies to each class of oil;

"(vi) estimates the resources needed to conduct the oil pollution research and development program established pursuant to subsection (e), and timetables for completing research tasks;

"(vii) summarizes research on response equipment in varying environmental conditions, such as in currents, ice cover, and ice floes; and

"(viii) includes such other information or

recommendations as the Interagency Committee determines to be appropriate.

"(B) ADVICE AND GUIDANCE.—

"(i) NATIONAL ACADEMY OF SCIENCES CONTRACT.—The Chair, through the department in which the Coast Guard is operating, shall contract with the National Academy of Sciences to—

"(I) provide advice and guidance in the preparation and development of the research plan;

"(II) assess the adequacy of the plan as submitted, and submit a report to Congress on the conclusions of such assessment; and

"(III) provide organization guidance regarding the implementation of the research plan, including delegation of topics and research among Federal agencies represented on the Interagency Committee.

"(ii) NIST ADVICE AND GUIDANCE.—The National Institute of Standards and Technology shall provide the Interagency Committee with advice and guidance on issues relating to quality assurance and standards measurements relating to its activities under this section.

"(C) 10-YEAR UPDATES.—Not later than 10 years after the date of enactment of the Elijah E. Cummings Coast Guard Authorization Act of 2020, and every 10 years thereafter, the Interagency Committee shall submit to Congress a research plan that updates the information contained in the previous research plan submitted under this subsection."

Subtitle B—Shipping

SEC. 8311. PASSENGER VESSEL SECURITY AND SAFETY REQUIREMENTS; APPLICATION.

Section 3507(k)(1) of title 46, United States Code, is amended—

(1) in subparagraph (B), by adding "and" after the semicolon at the end;

(2) in subparagraph (C), by striking "; and" and inserting a period; and

(3) by striking subparagraph (D).

SEC. 8312. SMALL PASSENGER VESSELS AND UNINSPECTED PASSENGER VESSELS.

Section 12121 of title 46, United States Code, is amended—

(1) in subsection (a)(1), by striking subparagraphs (A) and (B) and inserting the following:

"(A) was built in the United States;

"(B) was not built in the United States and is at least 3 years old; or

"(C) if rebuilt, was rebuilt—

"(i) in the United States; or

"(ii) outside the United States at least 3 years before the certificate requested under subsection (b) would take effect."

; and

(2) in subsection (b), by inserting "12132," after "12113,".

SEC. 8313. NON-OPERATING INDIVIDUAL.

(a) [46 U.S.C. 8701 note] IN GENERAL.—The Secretary of the department in which the Coast Guard is operating shall not enforce section 8701 of title 46, United States Code, with respect to the following:

(1) A vessel with respect to individuals, other than crew members required by the Certificate of Inspection or to ensure the safe navigation of the vessel and not a member of the steward's department, engaged on board for the sole purpose of carrying out spill response activities, salvage, marine firefighting, or commercial diving business or functions from or on any vessel, including marine firefighters, spill response personnel, salvage personnel, and commercial divers and diving support personnel.

(2) An offshore supply vessel, an industrial vessel (as such term is defined in section 90.10-16 of title 46, Code of Federal

Regulations), or other similarly engaged vessel with respect to persons engaged in the business of the ship on board the vessel—

(A) for—

(i) supporting or executing the industrial business or function of the vessel;

(ii) brief periods to conduct surveys or investigations, assess crew competence, conduct vessel trials, provide extraordinary security resources, or similar tasks not traditionally performed by the vessel crew; or

(iii) performing maintenance tasks on equipment under warranty, or on equipment not owned by the vessel owner, or maintenance beyond the capability of the vessel crew to perform; and

(B) not the master or crew members required by the certificate of inspection and not a member of the steward's department.

(b) SUNSET.—The prohibition in subsection (a) shall terminate on January 1, 2025.

(c) REPORT.—

(1) IN GENERAL.—Not later than 180 days after the date of the enactment of this Act, the Commandant shall submit to the Committee on Commerce, Science, and Transportation of the Senate and the Committee on Transportation and Infrastructure of the House of Representatives a report detailing recommendations to ensure that personnel working on a vessel who perform work or operate equipment on such vessel not related to the operation of the vessel itself undergo a background check and the appropriate training necessary to ensure personnel safety and the safety of the vessel's crew.

(2) CONTENTS.—The report required under paragraph (1) shall include, at a minimum, a discussion of—

(A) options and recommendations for ensuring that the individuals covered by subsection (a) are appropriately screened to mitigate security and safety risks, including to detect substance abuse;

(B) communication and collaboration between the

Coast Guard, the department in which the Coast Guard is operating, and relevant stakeholders regarding the development of processes and requirements for conducting background checks and ensuring such individuals receive basic safety familiarization and basic safety training approved by the Coast Guard;

(C) any identified legislative changes necessary to implement effective training and screening requirements for individuals covered by subsection (a); and

(D) the timeline and milestones for implementing such requirements.

SEC. 8314. CONFORMING AMENDMENTS: TRAINING; PUBLIC SAFETY PERSONNEL.

Chapter 701 of title 46, United States Code, is amended—

(1) in section 70107—

(A) in subsection (a), by striking "law enforcement personnel" and inserting "public safety personnel";

(B) in subsection (b)(8), by striking "law enforcement personnel—" and inserting "public safety personnel—"; and

(C) in subsection (c)(2)(C), by striking "law enforcement agency personnel" and inserting "public safety personnel"; and

(2) in section 70132—

(A) in subsection (a), by striking "law enforcement personnel—" and inserting "public safety personnel—";

(B) in subsection (b), by striking "law enforcement personnel" each place it appears and inserting "public safety personnel"; and

(C) by adding at the end the following:

"(d) PUBLIC SAFETY PERSONNEL DEFINED.—For the purposes of this section, the term 'public safety personnel' includes any Federal, State (or political subdivision thereof), territorial, or Tribal law enforcement officer, firefighter, or emergency response provider."

SEC. 8315. MARITIME TRANSPORTATION ASSESSMENT.

Section 55501(e) of title 46, United States Code, is amended—

(1) in paragraph (2), by striking "an assessment of the condition" and inserting "a conditions and performance analysis";

(2) in paragraph (4), by striking "; and" and inserting a semicolon;

(3) in paragraph (5), by striking the period and inserting "; and"; and

(4) by adding at the end the following:

"(6) a compendium of the Federal programs engaged in the maritime transportation system."

SEC. 8316. ENGINE CUT-OFF SWITCHES; USE REQUIREMENT.

(a) IN GENERAL.—Section 4312 of title 46, United States Code, is amended—

(1) by redesignating subsections (b), (c), and (d) as subsections (c), (d), and (e), respectively; and

(2) by inserting after subsection (a) the following:

"(b) USE REQUIREMENT.—

"(1) IN GENERAL.—An individual operating a covered recreational vessel shall use an engine cut-off switch link while operating on plane or above displacement speed.

"(2) EXCEPTIONS.—The requirement under paragraph (1) shall not apply if—

"(A) the main helm of the covered vessel is installed within an enclosed cabin; or

"(B) the vessel does not have an engine cut-off switch and is not required to have one under subsection (a)."

(b) CIVIL PENALTY.—Section 4311 of title 46, United States Code, is amended by—

(1) redesignating subsections (c), (d), (e), (f), and (g) as subsections (d), (e), (f), (g), and (h), respectively; and

(2) inserting after subsection (b) the following:

"(c) A person violating section 4312(b) of this title is liable to the United States Government for a civil penalty of not more than—

"(1) $100 for the first offense;

"(2) $250 for the second offense; and

"(3) $500 for any subsequent offense."

(c) [46 U.S.C. 4311 note] EFFECTIVE DATE.—The amendments made in subsections (a) and (b) shall take effect 90 days after the date of the enactment of this section, unless the Commandant, prior to the date that is 90 days after the date of the enactment of this section, determines that the use requirement enacted in subsection (a) would not promote recreational boating safety.

SEC. 8317. AUTHORITY TO WAIVE OPERATOR OF SELF-PROPELLED UNINSPECTED PASSENGER VESSEL REQUIREMENTS.

Section 8905 of title 46, United States Code, is amended by adding at the end the following:

"(c) After consultation with the Governor of Alaska and the State boating law administrator of Alaska, the Secretary may exempt an individual operating a self-propelled uninspected passenger vessel from the requirements of section 8903 of this title, if—

"(1) the individual only operates such vessel wholly within waters located in Alaska; and

"(2) such vessel is—

"(A) 26 feet or less in length; and

"(B) carrying not more than 6 passengers."

SEC. 8318. EXEMPTIONS AND EQUIVALENTS.

(a) IN GENERAL.—Section 4305 of title 46, United States Code, is amended—

(1) by striking the heading and inserting the following:

"SEC. 4305. Exemptions and equivalents"

(2) by striking "If the Secretary" and inserting the following:

"(a) EXEMPTIONS.—If the Secretary"

; and

(3) by adding at the end the following:

"(b) EQUIVALENTS.—The Secretary may accept a substitution for associated equipment performance or other safety standards for a recreational vessel if the substitution provides an equivalent level of safety."

(b) [46 U.S.C. 4301] CLERICAL AMENDMENT.—The analysis for chapter 43 of title 46, United States Code, is amended by striking the item relating to section 4305 and inserting the following:

"4305. Exemptions and equivalents."

SEC. 8319. RENEWAL OF MERCHANT MARINER LICENSES AND DOCUMENTS.

Not later than 60 days after the date of the enactment of this Act, the Commandant shall provide to the Committee on Transportation and Infrastructure of the House of Representatives and the Committee on Commerce, Science, and Transportation of the Senate a briefing on the Coast Guard's implementation of section 7106 of title 46, United States Code—

(1) an overview of the manner in which the Coast Guard manages and processes renewal applications under such section, including communication with the applicant regarding application status;

(2) the number of applications received and approved over the previous 2 years, or in the event applications were denied, a summary detailing the reasons for such denial;

(3) an accounting of renewal applications filed up to 8 months in advance of the expiration of a pre-existing license, including the processing of such applications and communication with the applicant regarding application status or any other extenuating circumstances; and

(4) any other regulatory or statutory changes that would be necessary to further improve the Coast Guard's issuance of credentials to fully qualified mariners in the most effective and efficient manner possible in order to ensure a safe, secure, economically and environmentally sound marine transportation system.

SEC. 8320. CERTIFICATE EXTENSIONS.

(a) IN GENERAL.—Subchapter I of chapter 121 of title 46, United States Code, is amended by adding at the end the following:

"SEC. 12108. [46 U.S.C. 12108] Authority to extend duration of vessel certificates

"(a) CERTIFICATES.—Provided a vessel is in compliance with inspection requirements in section 3313, the Secretary of the department in which in the Coast Guard is operating may, if the Secretary makes the determination described in subsection (b), extend, for a period of not more than 1 year, an expiring certificate of documentation issued for a vessel under chapter 121.

"(b) DETERMINATION.—The determination referred to in subsection (a) is a determination that such extension is required to enable the Coast Guard to—

"(1) eliminate a backlog in processing applications for such certificates; or

"(2) act in response to a national emergency or natural disaster.

"(c) MANNER OF EXTENSION.—Any extension granted under this section may be granted to individual vessels or to a specifically identified group of vessels."

(b) [46 U.S.C. 1201] CLERICAL AMENDMENT.—The analysis for subchapter I of chapter 121 of title 46, United States Code, is amended by adding at the end the following:

"12108. Authority to extend duration of vessel certificates."

SEC. 8321. VESSEL SAFETY STANDARDS.

(a) FISHING SAFETY TRAINING GRANTS PROGRAM.—Subsection (i) of section 4502 of title 46, United States Code, is amended—

(1) in paragraph (3), by striking "50 percent" and inserting "75 percent"; and

(2) in paragraph (4), by striking "2019" and inserting "2021".

(b) FISHING SAFETY RESEARCH GRANT PROGRAM.—Subsection (j) of such section is amended—

(1) in paragraph (3), by striking "50 percent" and inserting "75 percent"; and

(2) in paragraph (4), by striking "2019" and inserting "2021".

(c) [46 U.S.C. 4502 note] FISHING SAFETY GRANTS.—The cap on the Federal share of the cost of any activity carried out with a grant under subsections (i) and (j) of section 4502 of title 46, United States Code, as in effect prior to the date of enactment of the Frank LoBiondo Coast Guard Authorization Act of 2018, shall apply to any funds appropriated under the Consolidated Appropriations Act,

2017 (Public Law 115-31) for the purpose of making such grants.

SEC. 8322. MEDICAL STANDARDS.

(a) IN GENERAL.—Chapter 35 of title 46, United States Code, is amended by adding at the end the following:

"SEC. 3509. [46 U.S.C. 3509] Medical standards

"The owner of a vessel to which section 3507 applies shall ensure that—

"(1) a physician is always present and available to treat any passengers who may be on board the vessel in the event of an emergency situation;

"(2) the vessel is in compliance with the Health Care Guidelines for Cruise Ship Medical Facilities established by the American College of Emergency Physicians; and

"(3) the initial safety briefing given to the passengers on board the vessel includes—

"(A) the location of the vessel's medical facilities; and

"(B) the appropriate steps passengers should follow during a medical emergency."

(b) **[46 U.S.C. 3501]** CLERICAL AMENDMENT.—The analysis for chapter 35 of title 46, United States Code, is amended by adding at the end the following:

"3509. Medical standards."

Subtitle C—Advisory Committees

SEC. 8331. ADVISORY COMMITTEES.

(a) NATIONAL OFFSHORE SAFETY ADVISORY COMMITTEE; REPRESENTATION.—Section 15106(c)(3) of title 46, United States Code, is amended—

(1) in subparagraph (C), by striking "mineral and oil operations, including geophysical services" and inserting "operations";

(2) in subparagraph (D), by striking "exploration and recovery";

(3) in subparagraph (E), by striking "engaged in diving services related to offshore construction, inspection, and

maintenance" and inserting "providing diving services to the offshore industry";

(4) in subparagraph (F), by striking "engaged in safety and training services related to offshore exploration and construction" and inserting "providing safety and training services to the offshore industry";

(5) in subparagraph (G), by striking "engaged in pipelaying services related to offshore construction" and inserting "providing subsea engineering, construction, or remotely operated vehicle support to the offshore industry";

(6) in subparagraph (H), by striking "mineral and energy";

(7) in subparagraph (I), by inserting "and entities providing environmental protection, compliance, or response services to the offshore industry" after "national environmental entities"; and

(8) in subparagraph (J), by striking "deepwater ports" and inserting "entities engaged in offshore oil exploration and production on the Outer Continental Shelf adjacent to Alaska".

(b) TECHNICAL CORRECTIONS.—Section 15109 of title 46, United States Code, is amended by inserting "or to which this chapter applies" after "committee established under this chapter" each place it appears.

SEC. 8332. MARITIME TRANSPORTATION SYSTEM NATIONAL ADVISORY COMMITTEE.

(a) MARITIME TRANSPORTATION SYSTEM NATIONAL ADVISORY COMMITTEE.—Chapter 555 of title 46, United States Code, is amended by adding at the end the following:

"SEC. 55502. [46 U.S.C. 55502] Maritime Transportation System National Advisory Committee

"(a) ESTABLISHMENT.—There is established a Maritime Transportation System National Advisory Committee (in this section referred to as the 'Committee').

"(b) FUNCTION.—The Committee shall advise the Secretary of Transportation on matters relating to the United States maritime transportation system and its seamless integration with other segments of the transportation system, including the viability of the United States Merchant Marine.

"(c) MEMBERSHIP.—

"(1) IN GENERAL.—The Committee shall consist of 27 members appointed by the Secretary of Transportation in accordance with this section and section 15109.

"(2) EXPERTISE.—Each member of the Committee shall have particular expertise, knowledge, and experience in matters relating to the function of the Committee.

"(3) REPRESENTATION.—Members of the Committee shall be appointed as follows:

"(A) At least one member shall represent the Environmental Protection Agency.

"(B) At least one member shall represent the Department of Commerce.

"(C) At least one member shall represent the Corps of Engineers.

"(D) At least one member shall represent the Coast Guard.

"(E) At least one member shall represent Customs and Border Protection.

"(F) At least one member shall represent State and local governmental entities.

"(G) Additional members shall represent private sector entities that reflect a cross-section of maritime industries, including port and water stakeholders, academia, and labor.

"(H) The Secretary may appoint additional representatives from other Federal agencies as the Secretary considers appropriate.

"(4) RESTRICTIONS ON MEMBERS REPRESENTING FEDERAL AGENCIES.—Members of the Committee that represent Federal agencies shall not—

"(A) comprise more than one-third of the total membership of the Committee or of any subcommittee therein; or

"(B) serve as the chair or co-chair of the Committee or of any subcommittee therein.

"(5) ADMINISTRATION.—For purposes of section 15109—

"(A) the Committee shall be treated as a committee established under chapter 151; and

"(B) the Secretary of Transportation shall fulfill all duties and responsibilities and have all authorities of the Secretary of Homeland Security with regard to the Committee."

(b) [46 U.S.C. 55502 note] TREATMENT OF EXISTING COMMITTEE.—Notwithstanding any other provision of law—

(1) an advisory committee substantially similar to the Committee established by section 50402 of title 46, United States Code, and that was in force or in effect on the day before the date of the enactment of this Act, including the charter, membership, and other aspects of such advisory committee, may remain in force or in effect for the 2-year period beginning on the date of the enactment of this section; and

(2) during such 2-year period—

(A) requirements relating the Maritime Transportation System National Advisory Committee established by such section shall be treated as satisfied by such substantially similar advisory committee; and

(B) the enactment of this section shall not be the basis—

(i) to deem, find, or declare such committee, including the charter, membership, and other aspects thereof, void, not in force, or not in effect;

(ii) to suspend the activities of such committee; or

(iii) to bar the members of such committee from a meeting.

(c) [46 U.S.C. 55501] CLERICAL AMENDMENT.—The analysis for chapter 555 of title 46, United States Code, is amended by adding at the end the following:

"55502. Maritime Transportation System National Advisory Committee."

(d) MARINE HIGHWAYS.—

(1) [46 U.S.C. 55601] REPEAL.—Section 55603 of title 46, United States Code, and the item relating to that section in the analysis for chapter 556 of that title, are repealed.

(2) [46 U.S.C. 55601] MARINE HIGHWAYS PROGRAM.—The chapter heading of chapter 556 of title 46, United States Code, is amended to read “MARINE HIGHWAYS”.

(3) MARINE HIGHWAYS.—Section 55601 of title 46, United States Code, is amended—

(A) in the section heading by striking “Short sea” and inserting “Marine highways”;

(B) by striking “short sea” and inserting “marine highway” each place such term appears;

(C) in subsection (a)—

(i) by striking “transportation program” and inserting “transportation program to be known as the ‘America’s Marine highway program’ ”; and

(ii) by striking “mitigate landside congestion or to promote short sea transportation” and insert “provide a coordinated and capable alternative to landside transportation or to promote marine highway transportation”; and

(D) in subsection (b)—

(i) in the subsection heading by striking “Short Sea Transportation” and inserting “Marine Highway Transportation”; and

(ii) by striking paragraph (1) and inserting the following:

“(1) vessels documented under chapter 121 of this title;”

(4) CARGO AND SHIPPERS; INTERAGENCY COORDINATION AND RESEARCH.—Sections 55602 and 55604 of title 46, United States Code, are amended by striking “short sea” and inserting “marine highway” each place such term appears.

(5) RESEARCH ON MARINE HIGHWAYS TRANSPORTATION.—Section 55604 of title 46, United States Code, is amended in the section heading by striking**“short sea** and inserting “marine highway

(6) DEFINITION.—Section 55605 of title 46, United States Code, is amended—

(A) in the section heading by striking “Short sea” and inserting “Marine highway”; and

(B) by striking "short sea transportation" and inserting "marine highway transportation".

(7) [46 U.S.C. 55601] CLERICAL AMENDMENTS.—The analysis for chapter 556 of title 46, United States Code, is amended—

(A) by striking the item related to chapter 556 and inserting the following:

"Chapter 556— Marine Highways"

(B) by striking the item related to section 55601 and inserting the following:

"55601. Marine highways transportation program."

(C) by striking the item related to section 55604 and inserting the following:

"55604. Research on marine highway transportation."

; and

(D) by striking the item related to section 55605 and inserting the following:

"55605. Marine highway transportation defined."

SEC. 8333. EXPIRED MARITIME LIENS.

Section 31343(e) of title 46, United States Code, is amended—

(1) by inserting "(1)" before "A notice"; and

(2) by inserting after paragraph (1), as so designated by this section, the following:

"(2) On expiration of a notice of claim of lien under paragraph (1), and after a request by the vessel owner, the Secretary shall annotate the abstract of title to reflect the expiration of the lien."

SEC. 8334. GREAT LAKES PILOTAGE ADVISORY COMMITTEE.

(a) IN GENERAL.—Section 9307 of title 46, United States Code, is amended—

(1) in subsection (b)—

(A) in paragraph (1), by striking "seven" and inserting "8"; and

(B) in paragraph (2)—

(i) in subparagraph (B), by striking "representing the interests of" and inserting "chosen from among nominations made by";

(ii) in subparagraph (C), by striking "representing the interests of Great Lakes ports" and inserting "chosen from among nominations made by Great Lakes port authorities and marine terminals";

(iii) in subparagraph (D)—

(I) by striking "representing the interests of" and inserting "chosen from among nominations made by"; and

(II) by striking "; and" and inserting a semicolon;

(iv) by redesignating subparagraph (E) as subparagraph (F);

(v) by inserting after subparagraph (D) the following:

"(E) one member chosen from among nominations made by Great Lakes maritime labor organizations; and"

; and

(vi) in subparagraph (F), as so redesignated, by striking "with a background in finance or accounting,"; and

(2) in subsection (f)(1), by striking "2020" and inserting "2030".

(b) **[46 U.S.C. 9307 note]** COMMITTEE DEEMED NOT EXPIRED.—Notwithstanding section 9307(f)(1) of title 46, United States Code, in any case in which the date of enactment of this Act occurs after September 30, 2020, the Great Lakes Pilotage Advisory Committee in existence as of September 30, 2020, shall be deemed not expired during the period beginning on September 30, 2020 through the date of enactment of this Act. Accordingly, the committee membership, charter, and the activities of such Committee shall continue as though such Committee had not expired.

SEC. 8335. NATIONAL COMMERCIAL FISHING SAFETY ADVISORY COMMITTEE.

(a) NATIONAL COMMERCIAL FISHING SAFETY ADVISORY COMMITTEE.—

(1) AMENDMENTS TO SECTION 15102.—Section 15102 of title 46, United States Code, is amended—

(A) in subsection (b)—

(i) in paragraph (1)—

(I) by inserting "and provide recommendations in writing to" after "advise"; and

(II) in subparagraph (E), by striking "and" after the semicolon; and

(ii) in paragraph (2)—

(I) by striking the period and inserting "; and"; and

(II) by adding at the end the following:

"(3) review marine casualties and investigations of vessels covered by chapter 45 of this title and make recommendations to the Secretary to improve safety and reduce vessel casualties."

; and

(B) by adding at the end the following:

"(d) QUORUM.—A quorum of 10 members is required to send any written recommendations from the Committee to the Secretary.

"(e) SAVINGS CLAUSE.—Nothing in this section shall preclude the Secretary from taking emergency action to ensure safety and preservation of life at sea."

(2) AMENDMENTS TO SECTION 15109.—Section 15109 of title 46, United States Code, is amended—

(A) in subsection (a)—

(i) by striking "Each" and inserting the following:

"(1) IN GENERAL.—Except as provided in paragraph (2), each"

; and

(ii) by adding at the end the following:

"(2) MINIMUM REQUIREMENTS.—The committee established under section 15102, shall—

"(A) meet in-person, not less frequently than twice each year, at the call of the Secretary of a majority of the members of the committee;

"(B) hold additional meetings as necessary;

"(C) post the minutes of each meeting of the committee on a publicly available website not later than 2 weeks after the date on which a meeting concludes; and

"(D) provide reasonable public notice of any meeting of the committee, and publish such notice in the Federal Register and on a publicly available website."

(B) in subsection (f)(8)—

(i) by striking "Notwithstanding" and inserting the following:

"(A) REAPPOINTMENT.—Notwithstanding"

; and

(ii) by adding at the end the following:

"(B) LIMITATION.—With respect to the committee established under section 15102, members may serve not more than 3 terms."

(C) in subsection (j)(3)—

(i) in subparagraph (B), by striking "and";

(ii) in subparagraph (C), by striking the period and inserting "; and"; and

(iii) by adding at the end the following:

"(D) make all responses required by subparagraph (C) which are related to recommendations made by the committee established under section 15102 available to the public not later than 30 days after the date of response."

(D) by amending subsection (k) to read as follows:

"(k) OBSERVERS.—

"(1) IN GENERAL.—Any Federal agency with matters under such agency's administrative jurisdiction related to the function of a committee established under this chapter may designate a representative to—

"(A) attend any meeting of such committee; and

"(B) participate as an observer at meetings of such committee that relate to such a matter.

"(2) NATIONAL COMMERCIAL FISHING SAFETY ADVISORY COMMITTEE.—With respect to the committee established under section 15102, the Commandant of the Coast Guard shall designate a representative under paragraph (1)."

(E) in subsection (l), by striking "2027" and inserting "2029";

(F) by redesignating subsection (l) as subsection (m);

(G) by inserting after subsection (k) the following:

"(l) TECHNICAL ASSISTANCE.—

"(1) IN GENERAL.—The Secretary shall provide technical assistance to the Committee if requested by the Chairman.

"(2) COMMITTEE CONSULTATION.—With respect to the committee established under section 15102, the Chairman of the committee shall seek expertise from the fishing industry, marine safety experts, the shipbuilding industry, and others as the committee determines appropriate."

; and

(H) by adding at the end the following:

"(n) SAVINGS CLAUSE.—Nothing in this section shall preclude the Secretary from taking emergency action to ensure safety and preservation of life at sea."

SEC. 8336. [47 U.S.C. 352 note] EXEMPTION OF COMMERCIAL FISHING VESSELS OPERATING IN ALASKAN REGION FROM GLOBAL MARITIME DISTRESS AND SAFETY SYSTEM REQUIREMENTS OF FEDERAL COMMUNICATIONS COMMISSION.

(a) DEFINITION OF SECRETARY.—In this section, the term "Secretary" means the Secretary of the department in which the Coast Guard is operating.

(b) EXEMPTION.—Subject to subsection (c), the Federal Communications Commission shall exempt fishing vessels that primarily operate in the Alaskan Region, including fishing vessels that transit from States in the Pacific Northwest to conduct fishing operations in the Alaskan Region, from the requirements relating to carriage of VHF-DSC and MF-DSC equipment under subpart W of part 80 of title 47, Code of Federal Regulations, or any successor regulation.

(c) FUNCTIONAL REQUIREMENTS.—A fishing vessel exempted under subsection (b) shall—

(1) be capable of transmitting ship-to-shore distress alerts using not fewer than 2 separate and independent systems, each using a different radio communication service;

(2) be equipped with—

(A) a VHF radiotelephone installation;

(B) an MF or HF radiotelephone installation;

(C) a Category 1, 406.0-406.1 MHz EPIRB meeting the requirements of section 80.1061 of title 47, Code of Federal Regulations, or any successor regulation;

(D) a NAVTEX receiver meeting the requirements of section 80.1101(c)(1) of title 47, Code of Federal Regulations, or any successor regulation;

(E) survival craft equipment meeting the requirements of section 80.1095 of title 47, Code of Federal Regulations, or any successor regulation; and

(F) a Search and Rescue Transponder meeting the requirements of section 80.1101(c)(6) of title 47, Code of Federal Regulations, or any successor regulation;

(3) maintain a continuous watch on VHF Channel 16; and

(4) as an alternative to the equipment listed in subparagraphs (A) through (F) of paragraph (2), carry

equipment found by the Federal Communications Commission, in consultation with the Secretary, to be equivalent or superior with respect to ensuring the safety of the vessel.

(d) DEFINITION OF ALASKAN REGION.—Not later than 30 days after the date of enactment of this Act, the Secretary shall define the term "Alaskan Region" for purposes of this section. The Secretary shall include in the definition of such term the area of responsibility of Coast Guard District 17.

Subtitle D—Ports

SEC. 8341. PORT, HARBOR, AND COASTAL FACILITY SECURITY.

Section 70116 of title 46, United States Code, is amended—

(1) in subsection (a), by inserting ", cyber incidents, transnational organized crime, and foreign state threats" after "an act of terrorism";

(2) in subsection (b)—

(A) in paragraphs (1) and (2), by inserting "cyber incidents, transnational organized crime, and foreign state threats" after "terrorism" each place it appears; and

(B) in paragraph (3)—

(i) by striking "armed" and inserting ", armed (as needed),"; and

(ii) by striking "terrorism or transportation security incidents," and inserting "terrorism, cyber incidents, transnational organized crime, foreign state threats, or transportation security incidents,"; and

(3) in subsection (c)—

(A) by striking "70034," and inserting "70033,"; and

(B) by adding at the end the following new sentence: "When preventing or responding to acts of terrorism, cyber incidents, transnational organized crime, or foreign state threats, the Secretary may carry out this section without regard to chapters 5 and 6 of title 5 or Executive Order Nos. 12866 and 13563.".

SEC. 8342. AIMING LASER POINTER AT VESSEL.

(a) IN GENERAL.—Subchapter II of chapter 700 of title 46,

United States Code, is amended by adding at the end the following:

"SEC. 70014. [46 U.S.C. 70014] Aiming laser pointer at vessel

"(a) PROHIBITION.—It shall be unlawful to cause the beam of a laser pointer to strike a vessel operating on the navigable waters of the United States.

"(b) EXCEPTIONS.—This section shall not apply to a member or element of the Department of Defense or Department of Homeland Security acting in an official capacity for the purpose of research, development, operations, testing, or training.

"(c) LASER POINTER DEFINED.—In this section the term 'laser pointer' means any device designed or used to amplify electromagnetic radiation by stimulated emission that emits a beam designed to be used by the operator as a pointer or highlighter to indicate, mark, or identify a specific position, place, item, or object."

(b) **[46 U.S.C. 70001]** CLERICAL AMENDMENT.—The analysis for subchapter II of chapter 700 of title 46, United States Code, is amended by adding at the end the following:

"70014. Aiming laser pointer at vessel."

SEC. 8343. [46 U.S.C. 70034 note] SAFETY OF SPECIAL ACTIVITIES.

(a) IN GENERAL.—The Secretary of the department in which the Coast Guard is operating shall conduct a 2-year pilot program to establish and implement a process to—

(1) establish safety zones to address special activities in the exclusive economic zone;

(2) account for the number of safety zones established for special activities;

(3) differentiate whether an applicant who requests a safety zone for such activities is—

(A) an individual;

(B) an organization; or

(C) a government entity; and

(4) account for Coast Guard resources utilized to enforce safety zones established for special activities, including—

(A) the number of Coast Guard or Coast Guard Auxiliary vessels used; and

(B) the number of Coast Guard or Coast Guard

Auxiliary patrol hours required.

(b) BRIEFING.—Not later than 180 days after the expiration of the 2-year pilot program, the Commandant shall brief the Committee on Transportation and Infrastructure of the House of Representatives and the Committee on Commerce, Science, and Transportation of the Senate regarding—

(1) the process required under subsection (a); and

(2) whether the authority to establish safety zones to address special activities in the exclusive economic zone should be extended or made permanent in the interest of safety.

(c) DEFINITIONS.—In this section:

(1) SAFETY ZONE.—The term "safety zone" has the meaning given such term in section 165.20 of title 33, Code of Federal Regulations.

(2) SPECIAL ACTIVITIES.—The term "special activities" includes—

(A) space activities, including launch and reentry, as such terms are defined in section 50902 of title 51, United States Code, carried out by United States citizens; and

(B) offshore energy development activities, as described in section 8(p)(1)(C) of the Outer Continental Shelf Lands Act (43 U.S.C. 1337(p)(1)(C)), on or near a fixed platform.

(3) UNITED STATES CITIZEN.—The term "United States citizen" has the meaning given the term "eligible owners" in section 12103 of title 46, United States Code.

(4) FIXED PLATFORM.—The term "fixed platform" means an artificial island, installation, or structure permanently attached to the sea-bed for the purpose of exploration or exploitation of resources or for other economic purposes.

SEC. 8344. SECURITY PLANS; REVIEWS.

Section 70103 of title 46, United States Code, is amended—

(1) by amending subsection (b)(3) to read as follows:

"(3) The Secretary shall review and approve Area Maritime Transportation Security Plans and updates under this subsection."

; and

(2) in subsection (c)(4), by inserting “or update” after “plan” each place it appears.

SEC. 8345. VESSEL TRAFFIC SERVICE.

Section 70001 of title 46, United States Code, is amended to read as follows:

“SEC. 70001. Vessel traffic services

“(a) IN GENERAL.—Subject to the requirements of section 70004, the Secretary—

“(1) in any port or place under the jurisdiction of the United States, in the navigable waters of the United States, or in any area covered by an international agreement negotiated pursuant to section 70005, may construct, operate, maintain, improve, or expand vessel traffic services, that consist of measures for controlling or supervising vessel traffic or for protecting navigation and the marine environment and that may include one or more of reporting and operating requirements, surveillance and communications systems, routing systems, and fairways;

“(2) shall require appropriate vessels that operate in an area of a vessel traffic service to utilize or comply with that service;

“(3) may require vessels to install and use specified navigation equipment, communications equipment, electronic relative motion analyzer equipment, or any electronic or other device necessary to comply with a vessel traffic service or that is necessary in the interests of vessel safety, except that the Secretary shall not require fishing vessels under 300 gross tons as measured under section 14502, or an alternate tonnage measured under section 14302 as prescribed by the Secretary under section 14104, or recreational vessels 65 feet or less to possess or use the equipment or devices required by this subsection solely under the authority of this chapter;

“(4) may control vessel traffic in areas subject to the jurisdiction of the United States that the Secretary determines to be hazardous, or under conditions of reduced visibility, adverse weather, vessel congestion, or other hazardous circumstances, by—

“(A) specifying times of entry, movement, or departure;

"(B) establishing vessel traffic routing schemes;

"(C) establishing vessel size, speed, or draft limitations and vessel operating conditions; and

"(D) restricting operation, in any hazardous area or under hazardous conditions, to vessels that have particular operating characteristics or capabilities that the Secretary considers necessary for safe operation under the circumstances;

"(5) may require the receipt of prearrival messages from any vessel, destined for a port or place subject to the jurisdiction of the United States, in sufficient time to permit advance vessel traffic planning before port entry, which shall include any information that is not already a matter of record and that the Secretary determines necessary for the control of the vessel and the safety of the port or the marine environment; and

"(6) may prohibit the use on vessels of electronic or other devices that interfere with communication and navigation equipment, except that such authority shall not apply to electronic or other devices certified to transmit in the maritime services by the Federal Communications Commission and used within the frequency bands 157.1875-157.4375 MHz and 161.7875-162.0375 MHz.

"(b) NATIONAL POLICY.—

"(1) ESTABLISHMENT AND UPDATE OF NATIONAL POLICY.—

"(A) ESTABLISHMENT OF POLICY.—Not later than one year after the date of enactment of this section, the Secretary shall establish a national policy which is inclusive of local variances permitted under subsection (c), to be applied to all vessel traffic service centers and publish such policy in the Federal Register.

"(B) UPDATE.—The Secretary shall periodically update the national policy established under subparagraph (A) and shall publish such update in the Federal Register or on a publicly available website.

"(2) ELEMENTS.—The national policy established and updated under paragraph (1) shall include, at a minimum, the following:

"(A) Standardization of titles, roles, and responsibilities for all personnel assigned, working, or employed in a vessel traffic service center.

"(B) Standardization of organizational structure within vessel traffic service centers, to include supervisory and reporting chain and processes.

"(C) Establishment of directives for the application of authority provided to each vessel traffic service center, specifically with respect to directing or controlling vessel movement when such action is justified in the interest of safety.

"(D) Establishment of thresholds and measures for monitoring, informing, recommending, and directing vessel traffic.

"(E) Establishment of national procedures and protocols for vessel traffic management.

"(F) Standardization of training for all vessel traffic service directors, operators, and watchstanders.

"(G) Establishment of certification and competency evaluation for all vessel traffic service directors, operators, and watchstanders.

"(H) Establishment of standard operating language when communicating with vessel traffic users.

"(I) Establishment of data collection, storage, management, archiving, and dissemination policies and procedures for vessel incidents and near-miss incidents.

"(c) LOCAL VARIANCES.—

"(1) DEVELOPMENT.—In this section, the Secretary may provide for such local variances as the Secretary considers appropriate to account for the unique vessel traffic, waterway characteristics, and any additional factors that are appropriate to enhance navigational safety in any area where vessel traffic services are provided.

"(2) REVIEW AND APPROVAL BY SECRETARY.—The Captain of the Port covered by a vessel traffic service center may develop and submit to the Secretary regional policies in addition to the national policy established and updated under subsection (b) to account for variances from that national policy with respect to local vessel traffic conditions and volume, geography, water body characteristics, waterway usage, and any additional factors that the Captain considers appropriate.

"(3) REVIEW AND IMPLEMENTATION.—Not later than 180 days after receiving regional policies under paragraph (2)—

"(A) the Secretary shall review such regional policies; and

"(B) the Captain of the port concerned shall implement the policies that the Secretary approves.

"(4) MAINTENANCE.—The Secretary shall maintain a central depository for all local variances approved under this section.

"(d) COOPERATIVE AGREEMENTS.—

"(1) IN GENERAL.—The Secretary may enter into cooperative agreements with public or private agencies, authorities, associations, institutions, corporations, organizations, or other persons to carry out the functions under subsection (a)(1).

"(2) INTERNATIONAL COORDINATION.—With respect to vessel traffic service areas that cross international boundaries, the Secretary may enter into bilateral or cooperative agreements with international partners to jointly carry out the functions under subsection (a)(1) and to jointly manage such areas to collect, share, assess, and analyze information in the possession or control of the international partner.

"(3) LIMITATION.—

"(A) INHERENTLY GOVERNMENTAL FUNCTION.—A nongovernmental entity may not under this subsection carry out an inherently governmental function.

"(B) DEFINITION OF INHERENTLY GOVERNMENTAL FUNCTION.—In this paragraph, the term 'inherently governmental function' means any activity that is so intimately related to the public interest as to mandate performance by an officer or employee of the Federal Government, including an activity that requires either the exercise of discretion in applying the authority of the Government or the use of judgment in making a decision for the Government.

"(4) DISCLOSURE.—The Commandant of the Coast Guard shall de-identify information prior to release to the public, including near miss incidents.

"(e) PERFORMANCE EVALUATION.—

"(1) IN GENERAL.—The Secretary shall develop and implement a standard method for evaluating the performance of vessel traffic service centers.

"(2) ELEMENTS.—The standard method developed and implemented under paragraph (1) shall include, at a minimum, analysis and collection of data with respect to the following within a vessel traffic service area covered by each vessel traffic service center:

"(A) Volume of vessel traffic, categorized by type of vessel.

"(B) Total volume of flammable, combustible, or hazardous liquid cargo transported, categorized by vessel type as provided in the Notice of Arrival, if applicable, or as determined by other means.

"(C) Data on near-miss incidents.

"(D) Data on marine casualties.

"(E) Application by vessel traffic operators of traffic management authority during near-miss incidents and marine casualties.

"(F) Other additional methods as the Secretary considers appropriate.

"(3) REPORT.—Not later than 1 year after the date of the enactment of this paragraph, and biennially thereafter, the Secretary shall submit to the Committee on Commerce, Science, and Transportation of the Senate and the Committee on Transportation and Infrastructure of the House of Representatives a report on the evaluation conducted under paragraph (1) of the performance of vessel traffic service centers, including—

"(A) recommendations to improve safety and performance; and

"(B) data regarding marine casualties and near-miss incidents that have occurred during the period covered by the report.

"(f) RISK ASSESSMENT PROGRAM.—

"(1) IN GENERAL.—The Secretary shall develop a

continuous risk assessment program to evaluate and mitigate safety risks for each vessel traffic service area to improve safety and reduce the risks of oil and hazardous material discharge in navigable waters.

"(2) METHOD FOR ASSESSMENT.—The Secretary, in coordination with stakeholders and the public, shall develop a standard method for conducting risk assessments under paragraph (1) that includes the collection and management of all information necessary to identify and analyze potential hazardous navigational trends within a vessel traffic service area.

"(3) INFORMATION TO BE ASSESSED.—

"(A) IN GENERAL.—The Secretary shall ensure that a risk assessment conducted under paragraph (1) includes an assessment of the following:

"(i) Volume of vessel traffic, categorized by type of vessel.

"(ii) Total volume of flammable, combustible, or hazardous liquid cargo transported, categorized by vessel type as provided in the Notice of Arrival, if applicable, or as determined by other means.

"(iii) Data on near-miss events incidents.

"(iv) Data on marine casualties.

"(v) Geographic locations for near-miss events incidents and marine casualties, including latitude and longitude.

"(vi) Cyclical risk factors such as weather, seasonal water body currents, tides, bathymetry, and topography.

"(vii) Weather data, in coordination with the National Oceanic and Atmospheric Administration.

"(B) INFORMATION STORAGE AND MANAGEMENT POLICIES. The Secretary shall retain all information collected under subparagraph (A) and ensure policies and procedures are in place to standardize the format in which that information is retained to facilitate statistical analysis of that information to calculate within a vessel traffic service area, at a minimum, the incident rate, intervention rate, and casualty prevention rate.

"(4) PUBLIC AVAILABILITY.—

"(A) ASSESSMENTS AND INFORMATION.—In accordance with section 552 of title 5, the Secretary shall make any risk assessments conducted under paragraph (1) and any information collected under paragraph (3)(A) available to the public.

"(B) INFORMATION IN POSSESSION OR CONTROL OF INTERNATIONAL PARTNERS. The Secretary shall endeavor to coordinate with international partners as described in subsection (d)(2) to enter into agreements to make information collected, shared, and analyzed under that paragraph available to the public.

"(C) DISCLOSURE.—The Commandant of the Coast Guard shall de-identify information prior to release to the public, including near-miss incidents.

"(g) VESSEL TRAFFIC SERVICE TRAINING.—

"(1) TRAINING PROGRAM.—

"(A) IN GENERAL.—The Secretary shall develop a comprehensive nationwide training program for all vessel traffic service directors, operators, and watchstanders.

"(B) ELEMENTS.—The comprehensive nationwide training program under subparagraph (A) and any variances to that program under subsection (c) shall include, at a minimum, the following:

"(i) Realistic vessel traffic scenarios to the maximum extent practicable that integrate—

"(I) the national policy developed under subsection (b);

"(II) international rules under the International Navigational Rules Act of 1977 (33 U.S.C. 1601 et seq.);

"(III) inland navigation rules under part 83 of title 33, Code of Federal Regulations;

"(IV) the application of vessel traffic authority; and

"(V) communication with vessel traffic service users.

"(ii) Proficiency training with respect to use, interpretation, and integration of available data on vessel traffic service display systems such as radar, and vessel automatic identification system feeds.

"(iii) Practical application of—

"(I) the international rules under the International Navigational Rules Act of 1977 (33 U.S.C. 1601 et seq.); and

"(II) the inland navigation rules under part 83 of title 33, Code of Federal Regulations.

"(iv) Proficiency training with respect to the operation of radio communications equipment and any other applicable systems necessary to execute vessel traffic service authorities.

"(v) Incorporation of the Standard Marine Communication Phrases adopted by the International Maritime Organization by resolution on April 4, 2000, as amended and consolidated, or any successor resolution.

"(vi) Incorporation to the maximum extent possible of guidance and recommendations contained in vessel traffic services operator training, vessel traffic services supervisor training, or other relevant training set forth by the International Association of Marine Aids to Navigation and Lighthouse Authorities.

"(vii) A minimum number of hours of training for an individual to complete before the individual is qualified to fill a vessel traffic services position without supervision.

"(viii) Local area geographic and operational familiarization.

"(ix) Such additional components as the Secretary considers appropriate.

"(2) STANDARD COMPETENCY QUALIFICATION PROCESS.—

"(A) IN GENERAL.—The Secretary shall develop a standard competency qualification process to be applied to all personnel assigned, employed, or working in a vessel traffic service center.

"(B) APPLICATION OF PROCESS.—The competency qualification process developed under subparagraph (A) shall include measurable thresholds for determining proficiency.

"(3) INTERNATIONAL AND INLAND NAVIGATION RULES TEST.—

"(A) IN GENERAL.—All personnel assigned, employed, or working in a vessel traffic service center with responsibilities that include communicating, interacting, or directing vessels within a vessel traffic service area, as determined under the national policy developed under subsection (b), shall be required to pass a United States international and inland navigation rules test developed by the Secretary.

"(B) ELEMENTS OF TEST.—The Secretary shall determine the content and passing standard for the rules test developed under subparagraph (A).

"(C) TESTING FREQUENCY.—The Secretary shall establish a frequency, not to exceed once every 5 years, for personnel described in subparagraph (A) to be required to pass the rules test developed under such subparagraph.

"(h) RESEARCH ON VESSEL TRAFFIC.—

"(1) VESSEL COMMUNICATION.—The Secretary shall conduct research, in consultation with subject matter experts identified by the Secretary, to develop more effective procedures for monitoring vessel communications on radio frequencies to identify and address unsafe situations in a vessel traffic service area. The Secretary shall consider data collected under subparagraph (A) of subsection (f)(3).

"(2) PROFESSIONAL MARINER REPRESENTATION.—

"(A) IN GENERAL.—The Secretary shall conduct research, in consultation with local stakeholders and subject matter experts identified by the Secretary, to evaluate and determine the feasibility, costs and benefits of representation by professional mariners on the vessel traffic service watchfloor at each vessel traffic service center.

"(B) IMPLEMENTATION.—The Secretary shall implement representation by professional mariners on the vessel traffic service watchfloor at those vessel traffic service centers for which it is determined feasible and beneficial pursuant to research conducted under subparagraph (A).

"(i) INCLUSION OF IDENTIFICATION SYSTEM ON CERTAIN VESSELS.—

"(1) IN GENERAL.—The National Navigation Safety Advisory Committee shall advise and provide recommendations to the Secretary on matters relating to the practicability, economic costs, regulatory burden, and navigational impact of outfitting vessels lacking independent means of propulsion that carry flammable, combustible, or hazardous liquid cargo with vessel automatic identification systems.

"(2) REGULATIONS.—Based on the evaluation under paragraph (1), the Secretary shall prescribe such regulations as the Secretary considers appropriate to establish requirements relating to the outfitting of vessels described in such subparagraph with vessel automatic identification systems.

"(j) PERIODIC REVIEW OF VESSEL TRAFFIC SERVICE NEEDS.—

"(1) IN GENERAL.—Based on the performance evaluation conducted under subsection (e) and the risk assessment conducted under subsection (f), the Secretary shall periodically review vessel traffic service areas to determine—

"(A) if there are any additional vessel traffic service needs in those areas; and

"(B) if a vessel traffic service area should be moved or modified.

"(2) INFORMATION TO BE ASSESSED.—

"(A) IN GENERAL.—The Secretary shall ensure that a review conducted under paragraph (1) includes an assessment of the following:

"(i) Volume of vessel traffic, categorized by type of vessel.

"(ii) Total volume of flammable, combustible, or hazardous liquid cargo transported, categorized by vessel type as provided in the Notice of Arrival, if applicable, or as determined by other means.

"(iii) Data on near miss incidents.

"(iv) Data on marine casualties.

"(v) Geographic locations for near-miss incidents and marine casualties, including latitude and longitude.

"(vi) Cyclical risk factors such as weather, seasonal water body currents, tides, bathymetry, and topography.

"(vii) Weather data, in coordination with the National Oceanic and Atmospheric Administration.

"(3) STAKEHOLDER INPUT.—In conducting the periodic reviews under paragraph (1), the Secretary shall seek input from port and waterway stakeholders to identify areas of increased vessel conflicts or marine casualties that could benefit from the use of routing measures or vessel traffic service special areas to improve safety, port security, and environmental protection.

"(4) DISCLOSURE.—The Commandant of the Coast Guard shall de-identify information prior to release to the public, including near miss incidents.

"(k) LIMITATION OF LIABILITY FOR COAST GUARD VESSEL TRAFFIC SERVICE PILOTS AND NON-FEDERAL VESSEL TRAFFIC SERVICE OPERATORS.—

"(1) COAST GUARD VESSEL TRAFFIC SERVICE PILOTS.—Any pilot, acting in the course and scope of his or her duties while at a Coast Guard Vessel Traffic Service Center, who provides information, advice, or communication assistance while under the supervision of a Coast Guard officer, member, or employee shall not be liable for damages caused by or related to such assistance unless the acts or omissions of such pilot constitute gross negligence or willful misconduct.

"(2) NON-FEDERAL VESSEL TRAFFIC SERVICE OPERATORS.—An entity operating a non-Federal vessel traffic information service or advisory service pursuant to a duly executed written agreement with the Coast Guard, and any pilot acting on behalf of such entity, is not liable for damages caused by or related to information, advice, or communication assistance provided by such entity or pilot while so operating or acting unless the acts or omissions of such entity or pilot constitute gross negligence or willful misconduct.

"(l) EXISTING AUTHORITY.—Nothing in this section shall be construed to alter the existing authorities of the Secretary to enhance navigation, vessel safety, marine environmental protection, and to ensure safety and preservation of life and property at sea.

"(m) DEFINITIONS.—In this section:

"(1) HAZARDOUS LIQUID CARGO.—The term 'hazardous liquid cargo' has the meaning given that term in regulations prescribed under section 5103 of title 49.

"(2) MARINE CASUALTY.—The term 'marine casualty' has the meaning given that term in regulations prescribed under section 6101(a).

"(3) VESSEL TRAFFIC SERVICE AREA.—The term 'vessel traffic service area' means an area specified in subpart C of part 161 of title 33, Code of Federal Regulations, or any successor regulation.

"(4) VESSEL TRAFFIC SERVICE CENTER.—The term 'vessel traffic service center' means a center for the provision of vessel traffic services in a vessel traffic service area.

"(5) NEAR MISS INCIDENT.—The term 'near miss incident' means any occurrence or series of occurrences having the same origin, involving one or more vessels, facilities, or any combination thereof, resulting in the substantial threat of a marine casualty.

"(6) DE-IDENTIFIED.—The term 'de-identified' means the process by which all information that is likely to establish the identity of the specific persons or entities noted in the reports, data, or other information is removed from the reports, data, or other information."

SEC. 8346. TRANSPORTATION WORK IDENTIFICATION CARD PILOT PROGRAM.

Section 70105(g) of title 46, United States Code, is amended by striking "shall concurrently" and all that follows and inserting the following:"shall—

"(1) develop and, no later than 2 years after the date of enactment of the Elijah E. Cummings Coast Guard Authorization Act of 2020, implement a joint application for merchant mariner's documents under chapter 73 and for a transportation security card issued under this section; and

"(2) upon receipt of a joint application developed under paragraph (1) concurrently process an application from an individual for merchant mariner's documents under chapter 73 and an application from such individual for a transportation security card under this section."

TITLE LVXXXIV—MISCELLANEOUS

Subtitle A—Navigation and Shipping

Sec. 8401.	Coastwise trade.
Sec. 8402.	Towing vessels operating outside boundary line.
Sec. 8403.	Sense of Congress regarding the maritime industry of the United States.
Sec. 8404.	Cargo preference study.
Sec. 8405.	Towing vessel inspection fees review.

Subtitle B—Maritime Domain Awareness

Sec. 8411.	Unmanned maritime systems and satellite vessel tracking technologies.
Sec. 8412.	Unmanned aircraft systems testing.
Sec. 8413.	Land-based unmanned aircraft system program of Coast Guard.
Sec. 8414.	Prohibition on operation or procurement of foreign-made unmanned aircraft systems.
Sec. 8415.	United States commercial space-based radio frequency maritime domain awareness testing and evaluation program.
Sec. 8416.	Authorization of use of automatic identification systems devices to mark fishing equipment.

Subtitle C—Arctic

Sec. 8421.	Coast Guard Arctic prioritization.
Sec. 8422.	Arctic PARS Native engagement.
Sec. 8423.	Voting requirement.
Sec. 8424.	Report on the Arctic capabilities of the Armed Forces.
Sec. 8425.	Report on Arctic search and rescue.
Sec. 8426.	Arctic Shipping Federal Advisory Committee.

Subtitle D—Other Matters

Sec. 8431.	Plan for wing-in-ground demonstration plan.
Sec. 8432.	Northern Michigan oil spill response planning.
Sec. 8433.	Documentation of LNG tankers.
Sec. 8434.	Replacement vessel.
Sec. 8435.	Educational vessel.
Sec. 8436.	Waters deemed not navigable waters of the United States

Subtitle A—Navigation and Shipping

SEC. 8401. COASTWISE TRADE.

(a) IN GENERAL.—The Commandant shall review the adequacy of and continuing need for provisions in title 46, Code of Federal Regulations, that require a United States vessel documented under chapter 121 of title 46, United States Code, possessing a coastwise endorsement under that chapter, and engaged in coastwise trade, to comply with regulations for vessels engaged in an international voyage.

(b) BRIEFING.—Not later than 180 days after the date of the enactment of this Act, the Commandant shall provide to the Committee on Transportation and Infrastructure of the House of Representatives and the Committee on Commerce, Science, and Transportation of the Senate a briefing on the findings of the review required under subsection (a) and a discussion of how existing laws and regulations could be amended to ensure the safety of vessels described in subsection (a) while infringing as little as possible on commerce.

SEC. 8402. [46 U.S.C. 2101 note] TOWING VESSELS OPERATING OUTSIDE BOUNDARY LINE.

(a) DEFINITIONS.—In this section—

(1) the term "Boundary Line" has the meaning given the term in section 103 of title 46, United States Code;

(2) the term "Officer in Charge, Marine Inspection" has the meaning given the term in section 3305(d)(4) of title 46, United States Code; and

(3) the term "Secretary" means the Secretary of the Department in which the Coast Guard is operating.

(b) INTERIM EXEMPTION.—A towing vessel described in

subsection (c) and a response vessel included on a vessel response plan are exempt from any additional requirements of subtitle II of title 46, United States Code, and chapter I of title 33 and chapter I of title 46, Code of Federal Regulations (as in effect on the date of the enactment of this Act), that would result solely from such vessel operating outside the Boundary Line, if—

(1) the vessel is—

(A) operating outside the Boundary Line solely to perform regular harbor assist operations; or

(B) listed as a response vessel on a vessel response plan and is operating outside the Boundary Line solely to perform duties of a response vessel;

(2) the vessel is approved for operations outside the Boundary Line by the Officer in Charge, Marine Inspection and the Coast Guard Marine Safety Center; and

(3) the vessel has sufficient manning and lifesaving equipment for all persons on board, in accordance with part 15 and section 141.225 of title 46, Code of Federal Regulations (or any successor regulation).

(c) APPLICABILITY.—This section applies to a towing vessel—

(1) that is subject to inspection under chapter 33 of title 46, United States Code, and subchapter M of chapter I of title 46, Code of Federal Regulations (or any successor regulation);

(2) with only "Lakes, Bays, and Sounds" or "Rivers" routes recorded on such vessel's certificate of inspection pursuant to section 136.230 of title 46, Code of Federal Regulations (or any successor regulation);

(3) that, with respect to a vessel described in subsection (b)(1)(A), is operating as a harbor assist vessel and regularly engaged in harbor assist operations, including the docking, undocking, mooring, unmooring, and escorting of vessels with limited maneuverability; and

(4) that, with respect to a vessel that is described in subsection (b)(1)(B), is listed—

(A) on a vessel response plan under part 155 of title 33, Code of Federal Regulations, on the date of approval of the vessel response plan; or

(B) by name or reference in the vessel response plan's

geographic-specific appendix on the date of approval of the vessel response plan.

(d) LIMITATIONS.—A vessel exempted under subsection (b) is subject to the following operating limitations:

(1) The voyage of a vessel described in subsection (b)(1)(A) shall—

(A) be less than 12 hours in total duration;

(B) originate and end in the inspection zone of a single Officer in Charge, Marine Inspection; and

(C) occur no further than 10 nautical miles from the Boundary Line.

(2) The voyage of a vessel described in subsection (b)(1)(B) shall—

(A) originate and end in the inspection zone of a single Officer in Charge, Marine Inspection; and

(B) either—

(i) in the case of a voyage in the territorial waters of Alaska, Guam, Hawaii, American Samoa, and the Northern Mariana Islands, have sufficient manning as determined by the Secretary; or

(ii) be less than 12 hours.

(e) SAFETY.—

(1) SAFETY RESTRICTIONS.—The Officer in Charge, Marine Inspection for an inspection zone may restrict operations under the interim exemption provided under subsection (b) for safety purposes.

(2) COMPREHENSIVE LISTS.—The Officer in Charge, Marine Inspection for an inspection zone shall maintain and periodically update a comprehensive list of all towing vessels described in subsection (c) that operate in the inspection zone.

(3) NOTIFICATION.—Not later than 24 hours prior to intended operations outside of the Boundary Line, a towing vessel exempted under subsection (b) shall notify the Office in Charge, Marine Inspection for the inspection zone of such operations. Such notification shall include—

(A) the date, time, and length of voyage;

(B) a crew list, with each crew member's credentials

and work hours; and

(C) an attestation from the master of the towing vessel that the vessel has sufficient manning and lifesaving equipment for all persons on board.

(f) BRIEFING. Not later than 180 days after the date of the enactment of this Act, the Commandant of the Coast Guard shall brief the Committee on Commerce, Science, and Transportation of the Senate and the Committee on Transportation and Infrastructure of the House of Representatives regarding the following:

(1) The impacts of the interim exemption provided under this section.

(2) Any safety concerns regarding the expiration of such interim exemption.

(3) Whether such interim exemption should be extended.

(g) TERMINATION.—The interim exemption provided under subsection (b) shall terminate on the date that is 2 years after the date of the enactment of this Act.

SEC. 8403. SENSE OF CONGRESS REGARDING THE MARITIME INDUSTRY OF THE UNITED STATES.

It is the sense of Congress that the maritime industry of the United States contributes to the Nation's economic prosperity and national security.

SEC. 8404. CARGO PREFERENCE STUDY.

(a) IN GENERAL.—The Comptroller General of the United States shall conduct an audit regarding the enforcement of the United States Cargo Preference Laws set forth in sections 55302, 55303, 55304, and 55305 of title 46, United States Code, and section 2631 of title 10, United States Code (hereinafter in this section referred to as the "United States Cargo Preference Laws").

(b) SCOPE.—The audit conducted under subsection (a) shall include, for the period from October 14, 2008, until the date of the enactment of this Act—

(1) a listing of the agencies and organizations required to comply with the United States Cargo Preference Laws;

(2) an analysis of the compliance or noncompliance of such agencies and organizations with such laws, including—

(A) the total amount of oceangoing cargo that each such agency, organization, or contractor procured for its own account or for which financing was in any way provided with Federal funds, including loan guarantees;

(B) the percentage of such cargo shipped on privately owned commercial vessels of the United States;

(C) an assessment of internal programs and controls used by each such agency or organization to monitor and ensure compliance with the United States Cargo Preference Laws, to include education, training, and supervision of its contracting personnel, and the procedures and controls used to monitor compliance with cargo preference requirements by contractors and subcontractors; and

(D) instances in which cargoes are shipped on foreign-flag vessels under non-availability determinations but not counted as such for purposes of calculating cargo preference compliance; and

(3) an overview of enforcement activities undertaken by the Maritime Administration from October 14, 2008, until the date of the enactment of this Act, including a listing of all bills of lading collected by the Maritime Administration during that period.

(c) REPORT.—Not later than 1 year after the date of enactment of this Act, the Comptroller General shall submit to the Committee on Transportation and Infrastructure of the House of Representatives and the Committee on Commerce, Science, and Transportation of the Senate a report detailing the results of the audit and providing recommendations related to such results, to include—

(1) actions that should be taken by agencies and organizations to fully comply with the United States Cargo Preference Laws; and

(2) Other measures that may compel agencies and organizations, and their contractors and subcontractors, to use United States flag vessels in the international transportation of ocean cargoes as mandated by the United States Cargo Preference Laws.

SEC. 8405. TOWING VESSEL INSPECTION FEES REVIEW.

Not later than 180 days after the date of enactment of this Act, the Commandant shall submit to the Committee on Transportation and Infrastructure of the House of Representatives and the Committee on Commerce, Science, and Transportation of the Senate—

(1) the results of the review required under section 815 of the Frank LoBiondo Coast Guard Authorization Act of 2018 (Public Law 115-282); and

(2) a copy of any regulation required pursuant to section 815(b) of such Act to establish specific inspection fees for such vessels.

Subtitle B—Maritime Domain Awareness

SEC. 8411. [14 U.S.C. 504 note] UNMANNED MARITIME SYSTEMS AND SATELLITE VESSEL TRACKING TECHNOLOGIES.

(a) ASSESSMENT.—The Commandant, acting through the Blue Technology Center of Expertise, shall regularly assess available unmanned maritime systems and satellite vessel tracking technologies for potential use to support missions of the Coast Guard.

(b) REPORT.—

(1) IN GENERAL.—Not later than 1 year after the date of the enactment of this Act, and biennially thereafter, the Commandant shall submit to the Committee on Transportation and Infrastructure of the House of Representatives and the Committee on Commerce, Science, and Transportation of the Senate a report on the actual and potential effects of the use of then-existing unmanned maritime systems and satellite vessel tracking technologies on the mission effectiveness of the Coast Guard.

(2) CONTENTS.—Each report submitted under paragraph (1) shall include the following:

(A) An inventory of current unmanned maritime systems used by the Coast Guard, an overview of such usage, and a discussion of the mission effectiveness of such systems, including any benefits realized or risks or negative aspects of such usage.

(B) An inventory of satellite vessel tracking technologies, and a discussion of the potential mission effectiveness of such technologies, including any benefits or risks or negative aspects of such usage.

(C) A prioritized list of Coast Guard mission requirements that could be met with additional unmanned maritime systems, or with satellite vessel tracking technologies, and the estimated costs of accessing, acquiring, or operating such systems, taking into consideration the interoperability of such systems with the current and future fleet of—

(i) National Security Cutters;

(ii) Fast Response Cutters;

(iii) Offshore Patrol Cutters;

(iv) Polar Security Cutters; and

(v) in-service legacy cutters, including the 210- and 270-foot medium endurance cutters and 225-foot Buoy Tenders.

(c) DEFINITIONS.—In this section:

(1) UNMANNED MARITIME SYSTEMS.—

(A) IN GENERAL.—The term "unmanned maritime systems" means—

(i) remotely operated or autonomous vehicles produced by the commercial sector designed to travel in the air, on or under the ocean surface, on land, or any combination thereof, and that function without an on-board human presence; and

(ii) associated components of such vehicles, including control and communications systems, data transmission systems, and processing systems.

(B) EXAMPLES.—Such term includes the following:

(i) Unmanned undersea vehicles.

(ii) Unmanned surface vehicles.

(iii) Unmanned aerial vehicles.

(iv) Autonomous underwater vehicles.

(v) Autonomous surface vehicles.

(vi) Autonomous aerial vehicles.

(2) AVAILABLE UNMANNED MARITIME SYSTEMS.—The term "available unmanned maritime systems" includes systems that can be purchased commercially or are in use by the Department of Defense or other Federal agencies.

(3) SATELLITE VESSEL TRACKING TECHNOLOGIES.—The term "satellite vessel tracking technologies" means shipboard broadcast systems that use satellites and terrestrial receivers to continually track vessels.

SEC. 8412. [14 U.S.C. 319 note] UNMANNED AIRCRAFT SYSTEMS TESTING.

(a) TRAINING AREA.—The Commandant shall carry out and update, as appropriate, a program for the use of one or more training areas to facilitate the use of unmanned aircraft systems and small unmanned aircraft to support missions of the Coast Guard.

(b) DESIGNATION OF AREA.—

(1) IN GENERAL.—Not later than 180 days after the date of enactment of this Act, the Commandant shall, as part of the program under subsection (a), designate an area for the training, testing, and development of unmanned aircraft systems and small unmanned aircraft.

(2) CONSIDERATIONS.—In designating a training area under paragraph (1), the Commandant shall—

(A) ensure that such training area has or receives all necessary Federal Aviation Administration flight authorization; and

(B) take into consideration all of the following attributes of the training area:

(i) Direct over-water maritime access from the site.

(ii) The availability of existing Coast Guard support facilities, including pier and dock space.

(iii) Proximity to existing and available offshore Warning Area airspace for test and training.

(iv) Existing facilities and infrastructure to support unmanned aircraft system-augmented, and small unmanned aircraft-augmented, training, evaluations, and exercises.

(v) Existing facilities with a proven track record of supporting unmanned aircraft systems and small unmanned aircraft systems flight operations.

(c) DEFINITIONS.—In this section—

(1) the term "existing" means as of the date of enactment of this Act; and

(2) the terms "small unmanned aircraft" and "unmanned aircraft system" have the meanings given those terms in section 44801 of title 49, United States Code.

SEC. 8413. LAND-BASED UNMANNED AIRCRAFT SYSTEM PROGRAM OF COAST GUARD.

(a) FUNDING FOR CERTAIN ENHANCED CAPABILITIES.—Section 319 of title 14, United States Code, is amended by adding at the end the following new subsection:

"(c) FUNDING FOR CERTAIN ENHANCED CAPABILITIES.—In each of fiscal years 2020 and 2021, the Commandant may provide additional funding of $5,000,000 for additional long-range maritime patrol aircraft, acquired through full and open competition."

(b) REPORT ON USE OF UNMANNED AIRCRAFT SYSTEMS FOR CERTAIN SURVEILLANCE.—

(1) REPORT REQUIRED.—Not later than March 31, 2021, the Commandant, in coordination with the Administrator of the Federal Aviation Administration on matters related to aviation safety and civilian aviation and aerospace operations, shall submit to the appropriate committees of Congress a report setting forth an assessment of the feasibility and advisability of using unmanned aircraft systems for surveillance of marine protected areas, the transit zone, and the Arctic in order to—

(A) establish and maintain regular maritime domain awareness of such areas;

(B) ensure appropriate response to illegal activities in such areas; and

(C) collaborate with State, local, and tribal authorities, and international partners, in surveillance missions over their waters in such areas.

(2) APPROPRIATE COMMITTEES OF CONGRESS DEFINED.—In this subsection, the term "appropriate committees of Congress" means—

(A) the Committee on Commerce, Science, and Transportation and the Committee on Homeland Security and Governmental Affairs of the Senate; and

(B) the Committee on Transportation and Infrastructure and the Committee on Homeland Security of the House of Representatives.

SEC. 8414. [14 U.S.C. 1156 note] PROHIBITION ON OPERATION OR PROCUREMENT OF FOREIGN-MADE UNMANNED AIRCRAFT SYSTEMS.

(a) PROHIBITION ON AGENCY OPERATION OR PROCUREMENT.—The Commandant may not operate or enter into or renew a contract for the procurement of—

(1) an unmanned aircraft system that—

(A) is manufactured in a covered foreign country or by an entity domiciled in a covered foreign country;

(B) uses flight controllers, radios, data transmission devices, cameras, or gimbals manufactured in a covered foreign country or by an entity domiciled in a covered foreign country;

(C) uses a ground control system or operating software developed in a covered foreign country or by an entity domiciled in a covered foreign country; or

(D) uses network connectivity or data storage located in or administered by an entity domiciled in a covered foreign country; or

(2) a system manufactured in a covered foreign country or by an entity domiciled in a covered foreign country for the detection or identification of unmanned aircraft systems.

(b) EXEMPTION.—The Commandant is exempt from the restriction under subsection (a) if the operation or procurement is for the purposes of—

(1) counter-UAS system surrogate testing and training; or

(2) intelligence, electronic warfare, and information warfare operations, testing, analysis, and training.

(c) WAIVER.—The Commandant may waive the restriction

under subsection (a) on a case-by-case basis by certifying in writing not later than 15 days after exercising such waiver to the Department of Homeland Security, the Committee on Commerce, Science, and Transportation of the Senate, and the Committee on Transportation and Infrastructure of the House of Representatives that the operation or procurement of a covered unmanned aircraft system is required in the national interest of the United States.

(d) DEFINITIONS.—In this section:

(1) COVERED FOREIGN COUNTRY.—The term "covered foreign country" means any of the following:

(A) The People's Republic of China.

(B) The Russian Federation.

(C) The Islamic Republic of Iran.

(D) The Democratic People's Republic of Korea.

(2) COVERED UNMANNED AIRCRAFT SYSTEM.—The term "covered unmanned aircraft system" means an unmanned aircraft system described in paragraph (1) of subsection (a).

(3) COUNTER-UAS SYSTEM.—The term "counter-UAS system" has the meaning given such term in section 44801 of title 49, United States Code.

(4) UNMANNED AIRCRAFT SYSTEM.—The term "unmanned aircraft system" has the meaning given such term in section 44801 of title 49, United States Code, and any related services and equipment.

(e) REPLACEMENT.—Not later than 90 days after the date of the enactment of the Don Young Coast Guard Authorization Act of 2022, the Commandant shall replace covered unmanned aircraft systems of the Coast Guard with unmanned aircraft systems manufactured in the United States or an allied country (as that term is defined in section 2350f(d)(1) of title 10, United States Code).

SEC. 8415. [14 U.S.C. 504 note] UNITED STATES COMMERCIAL SPACE-BASED RADIO FREQUENCY MARITIME DOMAIN AWARENESS TESTING AND EVALUATION PROGRAM.

(a) TESTING AND EVALUATION PROGRAM.—The Commandant, acting through the Blue Technology Center of Expertise, shall carry out a testing and evaluation program of United States commercial space-based radio frequency geolocation and maritime domain awareness products and services to support the mission objectives of maritime enforcement by the Coast Guard and other components of the Coast Guard. The objectives of this testing and evaluation program shall include—

(1) developing an understanding of how United States commercial space-based radio frequency data products can meet current and future mission requirements;

(2) establishing how United States commercial space-based radio frequency data products should integrate into existing work flows; and

(3) establishing how United States commercial space-based radio frequency data products could be integrated into analytics platforms.

(b) REPORT.—Not later than 240 days after the date of enactment of this Act, the Commandant shall prepare and submit to the Committee on Commerce, Science, and Transportation of the Senate and the Committee on Transportation and Infrastructure of the House of Representatives a report on the results of the testing and evaluation program under subsection (a), including recommendations on how the Coast Guard should fully exploit United States commercial space-based radio frequency data products to meet current and future mission requirements.

SEC. 8416. [47 U.S.C. 303 note] AUTHORIZATION OF USE OF AUTOMATIC IDENTIFICATION SYSTEMS DEVICES TO MARK FISHING EQUIPMENT.

(a) DEFINITIONS.—In this section—

(1) the term "Assistant Secretary" means the Assistant Secretary of Commerce for Communications and Information and the National Telecommunications and Information Administration Administrator;

(2) the term "Automatic Identification System" has the meaning given the term in section 164.46(a) of title 33, Code of Federal Regulations, or any successor regulation;

(3) the term "Automatic Identification System device" means a covered device that operates in radio frequencies assigned for Automatic Identification System stations;

(4) the term "Commission" means the Federal

Communications Commission; and

(5) the term "covered device" means a device used to mark fishing equipment.

(b) RULEMAKING REQUIRED.—Not later than 180 days after the date of enactment of this Act, the Commission, in coordination with the Assistant Secretary, and in consultation with the Commandant and the Secretary of State, shall initiate a rulemaking proceeding to consider whether to authorize covered devices to operate in radio frequencies assigned for Automatic Identification System stations.

(c) CONSIDERATIONS.—In conducting the rulemaking under subsection (b), the Commission shall consider whether imposing requirements with respect to the manner in which Automatic Identification System devices are deployed and used would enable the authorization of covered devices to operate in radio frequencies assigned for Automatic Identification System stations consistent with the core purpose of the Automatic Identification System to prevent maritime accidents.

Subtitle C—Arctic

SEC. 8421. COAST GUARD ARCTIC PRIORITIZATION.

(a) FINDINGS.—Congress makes the following findings:

(1) The strategic importance of the Arctic continues to increase as the United States and other countries recognize the military significance of the sea lanes and choke points within the region and understand the potential for power projection from the Arctic into multiple regions.

(2) Russia and China have conducted military exercises together in the Arctic, have agreed to connect the Northern Sea Route, claimed by Russia, with China's Maritime Silk Road, and are working together in developing natural gas resources in the Arctic.

(3) The economic significance of the Arctic continues to grow as countries around the globe begin to understand the potential for maritime transportation through, and economic and trade development in, the region.

(4) Increases in human, maritime, and resource development activity in the Arctic region may create additional

mission requirements for the Department of Defense and the Department of Homeland Security.

(5) The increasing role of the United States in the Arctic has been highlighted in each of the last four national defense authorization acts.

(6) The United States Coast Guard Arctic Strategic Outlook released in April 2019 states, "Demonstrating commitment to operational presence, Canada, Denmark, and Norway have made strategic investments in ice-capable patrol ships charged with national or homeland security missions. The United States is the only Arctic State that has not made similar investments in ice-capable surface maritime security assets. This limits the ability of the Coast Guard, and the Nation, to credibly uphold sovereignty or respond to contingencies in the Arctic.".

(b) SENSE OF CONGRESS.—It is the sense of Congress that—

(1) the Arctic is a region of strategic importance to the national security interests of the United States, and the Coast Guard must better align its mission prioritization and development of capabilities to meet the growing array of challenges in the region;

(2) the increasing freedom of navigation and expansion of activity in the Arctic must be met with an increasing show of Coast Guard forces capable of exerting influence through persistent presence;

(3) Congress fully supports the needed and important recapitalization of the fleet of cutters and aircraft of the Coast Guard, but, the Coast Guard must avoid overextending operational assets for remote international missions at the cost of dedicated focus on this domestic area of responsibility with significant international interest and activity; and

(4) although some progress has been made to increase awareness of Arctic issues and to promote increased presence in the region, additional measures are needed to protect vital economic, environmental, and national security interests of the United States, and to show the commitment of the United States to this emerging strategic choke point of increasing great power competition.

(c) ARCTIC DEFINED.—In this section, the term "Arctic" has the meaning given that term in section 112 of the Arctic Research and

Policy Act of 1984 (15 U.S.C. 4111).

SEC. 8422. ARCTIC PARS NATIVE ENGAGEMENT.

The Commandant shall—

(1) engage directly with local coastal whaling and fishing communities in the Arctic region when conducting the Alaskan Arctic Coast Port Access Route Study, in accordance with chapter 700 of title 46, United States Code, and as described in the notice of study published in the Federal Register on December 21, 2018 (83 Fed. Reg. 65701); and

(2) consider the concerns of the Arctic coastal community regarding any Alaskan Arctic Coast Port Access Route, including safety needs and concerns.

SEC. 8423. VOTING REQUIREMENT.

Section 305(i)(1)(G)(iv) of the Magnuson-Stevens Fishery Conservation and Management Act (16 U.S.C. 1855(i)(1)(G)(iv)) is amended to read as follows:

"(iv) VOTING REQUIREMENT.—The panel may act only by the affirmative vote of at least 5 of its members, except that any decision made pursuant to the last sentence of subparagraph (C) shall require the unanimous vote of all 6 members of the panel."

SEC. 8424. REPORT ON THE ARCTIC CAPABILITIES OF THE ARMED FORCES.

(a) REPORT REQUIRED.—Not later than 180 days after the date of the enactment of this Act, the Secretary of the department in which the Coast Guard is operating shall submit to the appropriate committees of Congress a report setting forth the results of a study on the Arctic capabilities of the Armed Forces. The Secretary shall enter into a contract with an appropriate federally funded research and development center for the conduct of the study.

(b) ELEMENTS.—The report required by subsection (a) shall include the following:

(1) A comparison of the capabilities of the United States, the Russian Federation, the People's Republic of China, and other countries operating in the Arctic, including an assessment of the ability of the navy of each such country to operate in varying sea-ice conditions.

(2) A description of commercial and foreign military surface forces currently operating in the Arctic in conditions inaccessible to Navy surface forces.

(3) An assessment of the potential security risk posed to Coast Guard forces by military forces of other countries operating in the Arctic in conditions inaccessible to Navy surface or aviation forces in the manner such forces currently operate.

(4) A comparison of the domain awareness capabilities of—

(A) Coast Guard forces operating alone; and

(B) Coast Guard forces operating in tandem with Navy surface and aviation forces and the surface and aviation forces of other allies.

(5) A comparison of the defensive capabilities of—

(A) Coast Guard forces operating alone; and

(B) Coast Guard forces operating in mutual defense with Navy forces, other Armed Forces, and the military forces of allies.

(c) FORM.—The report required under subsection (a) shall be submitted in unclassified form, but may contain a classified annex.

(d) APPROPRIATE COMMITTEES OF CONGRESS DEFINED.—In this section, the term "appropriate committees of Congress" means—

(1) the Committee on Armed Services, the Committee on Commerce, Science, and Transportation, and the Committee on Appropriations of the Senate; and

(2) the Committee on Armed Services, the Committee on Transportation and Infrastructure, and the Committee on Appropriations of the House of Representatives.

SEC. 8425. REPORT ON ARCTIC SEARCH AND RESCUE.

(a) IN GENERAL.—Not later than 180 days after the date of the enactment of this Act, the Commandant shall submit to the Committee on Commerce, Science, and Transportation of the Senate and the Committee on Transportation and Infrastructure of the House of Representatives a report on the search and rescue capabilities of the Coast Guard in Arctic coastal communities.

(b) CONTENTS.—The report under subsection (a) shall include the following:

(1) An identification of ways in which the Coast Guard can more effectively partner with Arctic coastal communities to respond to search and rescue incidents through training, funding, and deployment of assets.

(2) An analysis of the costs of forward deploying on a seasonal basis Coast Guard assets in support of such communities for responses to such incidents.

SEC. 8426. [49 U.S.C. 303a note] ARCTIC SHIPPING FEDERAL ADVISORY COMMITTEE.

(a) PURPOSE.—The purpose of this section is to establish a Federal advisory committee to provide policy recommendations to the Secretary of Transportation on positioning the United States to take advantage of emerging opportunities for Arctic maritime transportation.

(b) DEFINITIONS.—In this section:

(1) ADVISORY COMMITTEE.—The term "Advisory Committee" means the Arctic Shipping Federal Advisory Committee established under subsection (c)(1).

(2) ARCTIC.—The term "Arctic" has the meaning given the term in section 112 of the Arctic Research and Policy Act of 1984 (15 U.S.C. 4111).

(3) ARCTIC SEA ROUTES.—The term "Arctic Sea Routes" means the international Northern Sea Route, the Transpolar Sea Route, and the Northwest Passage.

(c) ESTABLISHMENT OF THE ARCTIC SHIPPING FEDERAL ADVISORY COMMITTEE.—

(1) ESTABLISHMENT OF ADVISORY COMMITTEE.—

(A) IN GENERAL.—The Secretary of Transportation, in coordination with the Secretary of State, the Secretary of Defense acting through the Secretary of the Army and the Secretary of the Navy, the Secretary of Commerce, and the Secretary of the Department in which the Coast Guard is operating, shall establish an Arctic Shipping Federal Advisory Committee in the Department of Transportation to advise the Secretary of Transportation and the Secretary of the Department in which the Coast Guard is operating on matters related to Arctic maritime transportation, including Arctic seaway development.

(B) MEETINGS.—The Advisory Committee shall meet at the call of the Chairperson, and at least once annually in Alaska.

(2) MEMBERSHIP.—

(A) IN GENERAL.—The Advisory Committee shall be composed of 17 members as described in subparagraph (B).

(B) COMPOSITION.—The members of the Advisory Committee shall be—

(i) 1 individual appointed and designated by the Secretary of Transportation to serve as the Chairperson of the Advisory Committee;

(ii) 1 individual appointed and designated by the Secretary of the Department in which the Coast Guard is operating to serve as the Vice Chairperson of the Advisory Committee;

(iii) 1 designee of the Secretary of Commerce;

(iv) 1 designee of the Secretary of State;

(v) 1 designee of the Secretary of Transportation;

(vi) 1 designee of the Secretary of Defense;

(vii) 1 designee from the State of Alaska, nominated by the Governor of Alaska and designated by the Secretary of Transportation;

(viii) 1 designee from the State of Washington, nominated by the Governor of Washington and designated by the Secretary of Transportation;

(ix) 3 Alaska Native Tribal members;

(x) 1 individual representing Alaska Native subsistence co-management groups affected by Arctic maritime transportation;

(xi) 1 individual representing coastal communities affected by Arctic maritime transportation;

(xii) 1 individual representing vessels of the United States (as defined in section 116 of title 46, United States Code) participating in the shipping industry;

(xiii) 1 individual representing the marine safety community;

(xiv) 1 individual representing the Arctic business community; and

(xv) 1 individual representing maritime labor organizations.

(C) TERMS.—

(i) LIMITATIONS.—Each member of the Advisory Committee described in clauses (vii) through (xv) of subparagraph (B) shall serve for a 2-year term and shall not be eligible for more than 2 consecutive term reappointments.

(ii) VACANCIES.—Any vacancy in the membership of the Advisory Committee shall not affect its responsibilities, but shall be filled in the same manner as the original appointment and in accordance with the Federal Advisory Committee Act (5 U.S.C. App.).

(3) FUNCTIONS.—The Advisory Committee shall carry out all of the following functions:

(A) Develop a set of policy recommendations that would enhance the leadership role played by the United States in improving the safety and reliability of Arctic maritime transportation in accordance with customary international maritime law and existing Federal authority. Such policy recommendations shall consider options to establish a United States entity that could perform the following functions in accordance with United States law and customary international maritime law:

(i) Construction, operation, and maintenance of current and future maritime infrastructure necessary for vessels transiting the Arctic Sea Routes, including potential new deep draft and deepwater ports.

(ii) Provision of services that are not widely commercially available in the United States Arctic that would—

(I) improve Arctic maritime safety and environmental protection;

(II) enhance Arctic maritime domain awareness; and

(III) support navigation and incident response

for vessels transiting the Arctic Sea Routes.

(iii) Establishment of rules of measurement for vessels and cargo for the purposes of levying voluntary rates of charges or fees for services.

(B) As an option under subparagraph (A), consider establishing a congressionally chartered seaway development corporation modeled on the Saint Lawrence Seaway Development Corporation, and—

(i) develop recommendations for establishing such a corporation and a detailed implementation plan for establishing such an entity; or

(ii) if the Advisory Committee decides against recommending the establishment of such a corporation, provide a written explanation as to the rationale for the decision and develop an alternative, as practicable.

(C) Provide advice and recommendations, as requested, to the Secretary of Transportation and the Secretary of the Department in which the Coast Guard is operating on Arctic marine transportation, including seaway development, and consider national security interests, where applicable, in such recommendations.

(D) In developing the advice and recommendations under subparagraph (C), engage with and solicit feedback from coastal communities, Alaska Native subsistence co-management groups, and Alaska Native tribes.

(d) REPORT TO CONGRESS.—Not later than 2 years after the date of enactment of this Act, the Advisory Committee shall submit a report with its recommendations under subparagraphs (A) and (B) of subsection (c)(3) to the Committee on Commerce, Science, and Transportation of the Senate and the Committee on Transportation and Infrastructure of the House of Representatives.

(e) TERMINATION OF THE ADVISORY COMMITTEE.—Not later than 8 years after the submission of the report described in subsection (d), the Secretary of Transportation shall dissolve the Advisory Committee.

(f) INTERNATIONAL ENGAGEMENT.—If a Special Representative for the Arctic Region is appointed by the Secretary of State, the duties of that Representative shall include—

(1) coordination of any activities recommended by the implementation plan submitted by the Advisory Committee and approved by the Secretary of Transportation; and

(2) facilitation of multilateral dialogues with member and observer nations of the Arctic Council to encourage cooperation on Arctic maritime transportation.

(g) TRIBAL CONSULTATION.—In implementing any of the recommendations provided under subsection (c)(3)(C), the Secretary of Transportation shall consult with Alaska Native tribes.

Subtitle D—Other Matters

SEC. 8431. PLAN FOR WING-IN-GROUND DEMONSTRATION PLAN.

(a) IN GENERAL.—(1) The Commandant, in coordination with the Administrator of the Federal Aviation Administration with regard to any regulatory or safety matter regarding airspace, air space authorization, or aviation, shall develop plans for a demonstration program that will determine whether wing-in-ground craft, as such term is defined in section 2101 of title 46, United States Code, that is capable of carrying at least one individual, can—

(A) provide transportation in areas in which energy exploration, development or production activity takes place on the Outer Continental Shelf; and

(B) under the craft's own power, safely reach helidecks or platforms located on offshore energy facilities.

(2) REQUIREMENTS.—The plans required under paragraph (1) shall—

(A) examine and explain any safety issues with regard to the operation of the such craft as a vessel, or as an aircraft, or both;

(B) include a timeline and technical milestones for the implementation of such a demonstration program;

(C) outline resource requirements needed to undertake such a demonstration program;

(D) describe specific operational circumstances under which the craft may be used, including distance from United States land, altitude, number of individuals, amount of cargo, and speed and weight of vessel;

(E) describe the operations under which Federal Aviation Administration statutes, regulations, circulars, or orders apply; and

(F) describe the certifications, permits, or authorizations required to perform any operations.

(b) REPORT.—Not later than 1 year after the date of the enactment of this Act, the Commandant, along with the Administrator of the Federal Aviation Administration with regard to any regulatory or safety matter regarding airspace, air space authorization, or aviation, shall brief the Committee on Transportation and Infrastructure of the House of Representatives and the Committee on Commerce, Science and Transportation of the Senate on the plan developed under subsection (a), including—

(1) any regulatory changes needed regarding inspections and manning, to allow such craft to operate between onshore facilities and offshore energy facilities when such craft is operating as a vessel;

(2) any regulatory changes that would be necessary to address potential impacts to air traffic control, the National Airspace System, and other aircraft operations, and to ensure safe operations on or near helidecks and platforms located on offshore energy facilities when such craft are operating as aircraft; and

(3) any other statutory or regulatory changes related to authority of the Federal Aviation Administration over operations of the craft.

SEC. 8432. NORTHERN MICHIGAN OIL SPILL RESPONSE PLANNING.

Notwithstanding any other provision of law, not later than 180 days after the date of the enactment of this Act, the Secretary of the department in which the Coast Guard is operating, in consultation with the Administrator of the Environmental Protection Agency and the Administrator of the Pipeline and Hazardous Materials Safety Administration, shall update the Northern Michigan Area Contingency Plan to include a worst-case discharge from a pipeline in adverse weather conditions.

SEC. 8433. DOCUMENTATION OF LNG TANKERS.

(a) "*SAFARI VOYAGER*".—

(1) IN GENERAL.—Notwithstanding sections 12112 and 12132 of title 46, United States Code, the Secretary of the department in which the Coast Guard is operating shall issue a certificate of documentation with a coastwise endorsement for the vessel *Safari Voyager* (International Maritime Organization number 8963753).

(2) REVOCATION OF EFFECTIVENESS OF CERTIFICATE.—A certificate of documentation issued under paragraph (1) is revoked on the date of the sale of the vessel or the entity that owns the vessel.

(b) "*PACIFIC PROVIDER*".—

(1) IN GENERAL.—Notwithstanding sections 12112 and 12132 of title 46, United States Code, the Secretary of the department in which the Coast Guard is operating may issue a certificate of documentation with a coastwise endorsement for the vessel *Pacific Provider* (United States official number 597967).

(2) REVOCATION OF EFFECTIVENESS OF CERTIFICATE.—A certificate of documentation issued under paragraph (1) is revoked on the date of the sale of the vessel or the entity that owns the vessel.

(c) AMERICA'S CUP ACT OF 2011.—Section 7(b) of the America's Cup Act of 2011 (Public Law 112-61) is amended—

(1) in paragraph (3)—

(A) by striking "of the vessel on the date of enactment of this Act"; and

(B) by inserting before the period the following: ", unless prior to any such sale the vessel has been operated 134 STAT. 4735 in a coastwise trade for not less than 1 year after the date of enactment of the Elijah E. Cummings Coast Guard Authorization Act of 2020 and prior to sale of vessel";

(2) by redesignating paragraphs (2) and (3) as paragraphs (4) and (5), respectively; and

(3) by inserting after paragraph (1) the following:

"(2) LIMITATION ON OWNERSHIP.—The Secretary of the department in which the Coast Guard is operating may only issue a certificate of documentation with a coastwise endorsement to a vessel designated in paragraph (1) if the owner of the vessel is an individual or individuals who are citizens of the United States, or is an entity deemed to be such a citizen under section 50501 of title 46, United States Code.

"(3) LIMITATION ON REPAIR AND MODIFICATION.—

"(A) REQUIREMENT.—Any qualified work shall be performed at a shipyard facility located in the United States.

"(B) EXCEPTIONS.—The requirement in subparagraph (A) does not apply to any qualified work—

"(i) for which the owner or operator enters into a binding agreement no later than 1 year after the date of enactment of the Elijah E. Cummings Coast Guard Authorization Act of 2020; or

"(ii) necessary for the safe towage of the vessel from outside the United States to a shipyard facility in the United States for completion of the qualified work.

"(C) DEFINITION.—In this paragraph, qualified work means repair and modification necessary for the issuance of a certificate of inspection issued as a result of the waiver for which a coastwise endorsement is issued under paragraph (1)."

SEC. 8434. [16 U.S.C. 1851 note] REPLACEMENT VESSEL.

Notwithstanding section 208(g)(5) of the American Fisheries Act (Public Law 105-277; 16 U.S.C. 1851 note), a vessel eligible under section 208(e)(21) of such Act that is replaced under section 208(g) of such Act shall be subject to a sideboard restriction catch limit of zero metric tons in the Bering Sea and Aleutian Islands and in the Gulf of Alaska unless that vessel is also a replacement vessel under section 679.4(o)(4) of title 50, Code of Federal Regulations, in which case such vessel shall not be eligible to be a catcher/processor under section 206(b)(2) of such Act.

SEC. 8435. EDUCATIONAL VESSEL.

(a) IN GENERAL.—Notwithstanding section 12112(a)(2) of title

46, United States Code, the Secretary of the department in which the Coast Guard is operating may issue a certificate of documentation with a coastwise endorsement for the vessel *Oliver Hazard Perry* (IMO number 8775560; United States official number 1257224).

(b) TERMINATION OF EFFECTIVENESS OF ENDORSEMENT.—The coastwise endorsement authorized under subsection (a) for the vessel *Oliver Hazard Perry* (IMO number 8775560; United States official number 1257224) shall expire on the first date on which any of the following occurs:

(1) The vessel is sold to a person, including an entity, that is not related by ownership or control to the person, including an entity, that owned the vessel on the date of the enactment of this Act.

(2) The vessel is rebuilt and not rebuilt in the United States (as defined in section 12101(a) of title 46, United States Code).

(3) The vessel is no longer operating in primary service as a sailing school vessel.

SEC. 8436. [33 U.S.C. 59mm] WATERS DEEMED NOT NAVIGABLE WATERS OF THE UNITED STATES FOR CERTAIN PURPOSES.

The Coalbank Slough in Coos Bay, Oregon, is deemed to not be navigable waters of the United States for all purposes of subchapter J of Chapter I of title 33, Code of Federal Regulations.

SEC. 8437. ANCHORAGES.

(a) IN GENERAL.—The Secretary of the department in which the Coast Guard is operating shall suspend the establishment of new anchorage grounds on the Hudson River between Yonkers, New York, and Kingston, New York, under section 7 of the Rivers and Harbors Appropriations Act of 1915 (33 U.S.C. 471) or chapter 700 of title 46, United States Code.

(b) RESTRICTION.—The Commandant may not establish or expand any anchorage grounds outside of the reach on the Hudson River described in subsection (a) without first providing notice to the Committee on Transportation and Infrastructure of the House of Representatives and the Committee on Commerce, Science, and Transportation of the Senate not later than 180 days prior to the establishment or expansion of any such anchorage grounds.

(c) SAVINGS CLAUSE.—Nothing in this section—

(1) prevents the master or pilot of a vessel operating on the reach of the Hudson River described in subsection (a) from taking actions necessary to maintain the safety of the vessel or to prevent the loss of life or property; or

(2) shall be construed as limiting the authority of the Secretary of the department in which the Coast Guard is operating to exercise authority over the movement of a vessel under section 70002 of title 46, United States Code, or any other applicable laws or regulations governing the safe navigation of a vessel.

(d) STUDY.—The Commandant of the Coast Guard, in consultation with the Hudson River Safety, Navigation, and Operations Committee, shall conduct a study of the Hudson River north of Tarrytown, New York to examine—

(1) the nature of vessel traffic including vessel types, sizes, cargoes, and frequency of transits;

(2) the risks and benefits of historic practices for commercial vessels anchoring; and

(3) the risks and benefits of establishing anchorage grounds on the Hudson River.

(e) REPORT.—Not later than 1 year after the date of the enactment of this Act, the Commandant of the Coast Guard shall submit to the Committee on Transportation and Infrastructure of the House of Representatives and the Committee on Commerce, Science, and Transportation of the Senate a report containing the findings, conclusions, and recommendations from the study required under subsection (d).

SEC. 8438. COMPTROLLER GENERAL OF THE UNITED STATES STUDY AND REPORT ON VERTICAL EVACUATION FOR TSUNAMIS AT COAST GUARD STATIONS IN WASHINGTON AND OREGON.

(a) STUDY.—

(1) IN GENERAL.—The Comptroller General of the United States shall conduct a study that examines the potential use, in the event of a Cascadia subduction zone event, of a vertical evacuation of Coast Guard personnel stationed at United States Coast Guard Station Grays Harbor and Sector Field Office Port Angeles, Washington, and at United States Coast Guard Station Yaquina Bay and United States Coast Guard Motor

Lifeboat Station Coos Bay, Oregon, and the dependents of such Coast Guard personnel housed in Coast Guard housing.

(2) ELEMENTS.—The study required under paragraph (1) shall analyze the following:

(A) The number of such personnel and dependents to be evacuated.

(B) The resources available to conduct an evacuation, and the feasibility of a successful evacuation in a case in which inundation maps and timelines are available.

(C) With the resources available, the amount of time needed to evacuate such personnel and dependents.

(D) Any resource that is otherwise available within a reasonable walking distance to the Coast Guard facilities listed in paragraph (1).

(E) The benefit to the surrounding community of such a vertical evacuation.

(F) The interoperability of the tsunami warning system with the Coast Guard communication systems at the Coast Guard facilities listed in paragraph (1).

(G) Current interagency coordination and communication policies in place for emergency responders to address a Cascadia subduction zone event.

(b) REPORT.—Not later than 1 year after the date of the enactment of this Act, the Comptroller General shall submit to the Committee on Commerce, Science, and Transportation of the Senate and the Committee on Transportation and Infrastructure of the House of Representatives a report containing the findings, conclusions, and recommendations, if any, from the study required under subsection (a).

SEC. 8439. AUTHORITY TO ENTER INTO AGREEMENTS WITH NATIONAL COAST GUARD MUSEUM ASSOCIATION.

(a) IN GENERAL.—Section 316 of title 14, United States Code, is amended to read as follows:

"SEC. 316. National Coast Guard Museum

"(a) ESTABLISHMENT.—The Commandant may establish, accept, operate, maintain and support the Museum, on lands which will be federally owned and administered by the Coast Guard, and are located in New London, Connecticut.

"(b) USE OF FUNDS.—

"(1) The Secretary shall not expend any funds appropriated to the Coast Guard on the construction of any museum established under this section.

"(2) Subject to the availability of appropriations, the Secretary may expend funds appropriated to the Coast Guard on the engineering and design of a Museum.

"(3) The priority for the use of funds appropriated to the Coast Guard shall be to preserve, protect, and display historic Coast Guard artifacts, including the design, fabrication, and installation of exhibits or displays in which such artifacts are included.

"(c) FUNDING PLAN.—Not later than 2 years after the date of the enactment of the Elijah E. Cummings Coast Guard Authorization Act of 2020 and at least 90 days before the date on which the Commandant accepts the Museum under subsection (f), the Commandant shall submit to the Committee on Commerce, Science, and Transportation of the Senate and the Committee on Transportation and Infrastructure of the House of Representatives a plan for constructing, operating, and maintaining such Museum, including—

"(1) estimated planning, engineering, design, construction, operation, and maintenance costs;

"(2) the extent to which appropriated, nonappropriated, and non-Federal funds will be used for such purposes, including the extent to which there is any shortfall in funding for engineering, design, or construction;

"(3) an explanation of any environmental remediation issues related to the land associated with the Museum; and

"(4) a certification by the Inspector General of the department in which the Coast Guard is operating that the estimates provided pursuant to paragraphs (1) and (2) are reasonable and realistic.

"(d) CONSTRUCTION.—

"(1) The Association may construct the Museum described in subsection (a).

"(2) The Museum shall be designed and constructed in

compliance with the International Building Code 2018, and construction performed on Federal land under this section shall be exempt from State and local requirements for building or demolition permits.

"(e) AGREEMENTS.—Under such terms and conditions as the Commandant considers appropriate, notwithstanding section 504, and until the Commandant accepts the Museum under subsection (f), the Commandant may—

"(1) license Federal land to the Association for the purpose of constructing the Museum described in subsection (a); and

"(2)(A) at a nominal charge, lease the Museum from the Association for activities and operations related to the Museum; and

"(B) authorize the Association to generate revenue from the use of the Museum.

"(f) ACCEPTANCE. Not earlier than 90 days after the Commandant submits the plan under subsection (c), the Commandant shall accept the Museum from the Association and all right, title, and interest in and to the Museum shall vest in the United States when—

"(1) the Association demonstrates, in a manner acceptable to the Commandant, that the Museum meets the design and construction requirements of subsection (d); and

"(2) all financial obligations of the Association incident to the National Coast Guard Museum have been satisfied.

"(g) SERVICES.—The Commandant may solicit from the Association and accept services from nonprofit entities, including services related to activities for construction of the Museum.

"(h) AUTHORITY.—The Commandant may not establish a Museum except as set forth in this section.

"(i) DEFINITIONS.—In this section:

"(1) MUSEUM.—The term 'Museum' means the National Coast Guard Museum.

"(2) ASSOCIATION.—The term 'Association' means the National Coast Guard Museum Association."

(b) BRIEFINGS.—Not later than March 1 of the fiscal year after the fiscal year in which the report required under subsection (d) of section 316 of title 14, United States Code, is provided, and not later than March 1 of each year thereafter until 1 year after the year in which the National Coast Guard Museum is accepted pursuant to subsection (f) of such section, the Commandant shall brief the Committee on Commerce, Science, and Transportation of the Senate and the Committee on Transportation and Infrastructure of the House of Representatives on the following issues with respect to the Museum:

(1) The acceptance of gifts.

(2) Engineering.

(3) Design and project status.

(4) Land ownership.

(5) Environmental remediation.

(6) Operation and support issues.

(7) Plans.

SEC. 8440. VIDEO EQUIPMENT; ACCESS AND RETENTION OF RECORDS.

(a) MAINTENANCE AND PLACEMENT OF VIDEO SURVEILLANCE EQUIPMENT.—Section 3507(b)(1) of title 46, United States Code, is amended—

(1) by striking "The owner" and inserting the following:

"(A) IN GENERAL.—The owner"

(2) by striking ", as determined by the Secretary"; and

(3) by adding at the end, the following:

"(B) PLACEMENT OF VIDEO SURVEILLANCE EQUIPMENT.—

"(i) IN GENERAL.—Not later than 18 months after the date of the enactment of the Elijah E. Cummings Coast Guard Authorization Act of 2020, the Commandant in consultation with other relevant Federal agencies or entities as determined by the Commandant, shall establish guidance for performance of the risk assessment described in paragraph (2) regarding the appropriate placement of video surveillance equipment in passenger and crew common areas where there is no reasonable expectation of privacy.

"(ii) RISK ASSESSMENT.—Not later than 1 year after the Commandant establishes the guidance described in paragraph (1), the owner shall conduct the risk assessment required under paragraph (1) and shall—

"(I) evaluate the placement of video surveillance equipment to deter, prevent, and record a sexual assault aboard the vessel considering factors such as: ship layout and design, itinerary, crew complement, number of passengers, passenger demographics, and historical data on the type and location of prior sexual assault incident allegations;

"(II) incorporate to the maximum extent practicable the video surveillance guidance established by the Commandant regarding the appropriate placement of video surveillance equipment;

"(III) arrange for the risk assessment to be conducted by an independent third party with expertise in the use and placement of camera surveillance to deter, prevent and record criminal behavior; and

"(IV) the independent third party referred to in paragraph (C) shall be a company that has been accepted by a classification society that is a member of the International Association of Classification Societies (hereinafter referred to as 'IACS') or another classification society recognized by the Secretary as meeting acceptable standards for such a society pursuant to section 3316(b).

"(C) SURVEILLANCE PLAN.—Not later than 180 days after completion of the risk assessment conducted under subparagraph (B)(ii), the owner of a vessel shall develop a plan to install video surveillance equipment in places determined to be appropriate in accordance with the results of the risk assessment conducted under subparagraph (B)(ii), except in areas where a person has a reasonable expectation of privacy. Such plan shall be evaluated and approved by an independent third party with expertise in the use and placement of camera surveillance to deter, prevent and record criminal behavior that has been accepted as set forth in paragraph (2)(D).

"(D) INSTALLATION.—The owner of a vessel to which this section applies shall, consistent with the surveillance plan approved under subparagraph (C), install appropriate video surveillance equipment aboard the vessel not later than 2 years after approval of the plan, or during the next scheduled drydock, whichever is later.

"(E) ATTESTATION.—At the time of initial installation under subparagraph (D), the vessel owner shall obtain written attestations from—

"(i) an IACS classification society that the video surveillance equipment is installed in accordance with the surveillance plan required under subparagraph (C); and

"(ii) the company security officer that the surveillance equipment and associated systems are operational, which attestation shall be obtained each year thereafter.

"(F) UPDATES.—The vessel owner shall ensure the risk assessment described in subparagraph (B)(ii) and installation plan in subparagraph (C) are updated not later than 5 years after the initial installation conducted under subparagraph (D), and every 5 years thereafter. The updated assessment and plan shall be approved by an independent third party with expertise in the use and placement of camera surveillance to deter, prevent, and record criminal behavior that has been accepted by an IACS classification society. The vessel owner shall implement the updated installation plan not later than 180 days after approval.

"(G) AVAILABILITY.—Each risk assessment, installation plan and attestation shall be protected from disclosure under the Freedom of Information Act, section 552 of title 5 but shall be available to the Coast Guard—

"(i) upon request, and

"(ii) at the time of the certificate of compliance or certificate of inspection examination.

"(H) DEFINITIONS.—For purposes of this section a 'ship security officer' is an individual that, with the master's approval, has full responsibility for vessel security consistent with the International Ship and Port Facility Security Code."

(b) ACCESS TO VIDEO RECORDS; NOTICE OF VIDEO SURVEILLANCE.—Section 3507(b) of title 46, United States Code, is further amended—

(1) by redesignating paragraph (2) as paragraph (3);

(2) by inserting after paragraph (1) the following:

"(2) NOTICE OF VIDEO SURVEILLANCE.—The owner of a vessel to which this section applies shall provide clear and conspicuous signs on board the vessel notifying the public of the presence of video surveillance equipment."

(3) in paragraph (3), as so redesignated—

(A) by striking "The owner" and inserting the following:

"(A) LAW ENFORCEMENT.—The owner"

; and

(B) by adding at the end the following:

"(B) CIVIL ACTIONS.—Except as proscribed by law enforcement authorities or court order, the owner of a vessel to which this section applies shall, upon written request, provide to any individual or the individual's legal representative a copy of all records of video surveillance—

"(i) in which the individual is a subject of the video surveillance; and

"(ii) that may provide evidence of any sexual assault incident in a civil action.

"(C) LIMITED ACCESS.—The owner of a vessel to which this section applies shall ensure that access to records of video surveillance is limited to the purposes described in this paragraph."

(c) RETENTION REQUIREMENTS.—

(1) IN GENERAL.—Section 3507(b) of title 46, United States Code, is further amended by adding at the end the following:

"(4) RETENTION REQUIREMENTS.—The owner of a vessel to which this section applies shall retain all records of video surveillance for not less than 20 days after the footage is obtained. The vessel owner shall include a statement in the security guide required by subsection (c)(1)(A) that the vessel owner is required by law to retain video surveillance footage for the period specified in this paragraph. If an incident described in subsection (g)(3)(A)(i) is alleged and reported to law enforcement, all records of video surveillance from the voyage that the Federal Bureau of Investigation determines are relevant shall—

"(A) be provided to the Federal Bureau of Investigation; and

"(B) be preserved by the vessel owner for not less than 4 years from the date of the alleged incident."

(2) **[46 U.S.C. 3507 note]** ADMINISTRATIVE PROVISIONS.—

(A) STUDY AND REPORT.—Each owner of a vessel to which section 3507 of title 46, United States Code, applies shall, not later than March 1, 2023, submit to the Committee on Transportation and Infrastructure of the House of Representatives and the Committee on Commerce, Science, and Transportation of the Senate a report detailing the total number of voyages for the preceding year and the percentage of those voyages that were 30 days or longer.

(B) INTERIM STANDARDS.—Not later than 180 days after the date of enactment of this Act, the Commandant, in consultation with the Federal Bureau of Investigation, shall promulgate interim standards for the retention of records of video surveillance.

(C) FINAL STANDARDS.—Not later than 1 year after the date of enactment of this Act, the Commandant, in consultation with the Federal Bureau of Investigation, shall promulgate final standards for the retention of records of video surveillance.

(D) CONSIDERATIONS.—In promulgating standards under subparagraphs (B) and (B), the Commandant shall—

(i) consider factors that would aid in the investigation of serious crimes, including the results of the report by the Commandant provided under subparagraph (A), as well as crimes that go unreported until after the completion of a voyage;

(ii) consider the different types of video surveillance systems and storage requirements in creating standards both for vessels currently in operation and for vessels newly built;

(iii) consider privacy, including standards for permissible access to and monitoring and use of the records of video surveillance; and

(iv) consider technological advancements, including requirements to update technology.

SEC. 8441. REGULATIONS FOR COVERED SMALL PASSENGER VESSELS.

(a) IN GENERAL.—Section 3306 of title 46, United States Code, is amended—

(1) in subsection (a)—

(A) in the matter preceding paragraph (1), by inserting ", including covered small passenger vessels (as defined in subsection (n)(5))" after "vessels subject to inspection"; and

(B) in paragraph (5), by inserting before the period at the end ", including rechargeable devices utilized for personal or commercial electronic equipment"; and

(2) by adding at the end the following:

"(n) COVERED SMALL PASSENGER VESSELS.—

"(1) REGULATIONS.—The Secretary shall prescribe additional regulations to secure the safety of individuals and property on board covered small passenger vessels.

"(2) COMPREHENSIVE REVIEW.—In order to prescribe the regulations under paragraph (1), the Secretary shall conduct a comprehensive review of all requirements (including calculations), in existence on the date of enactment of the Elijah E. Cummings Coast Guard Authorization Act of 2020, that apply to covered small passenger vessels, with respect to fire detection, protection, and suppression systems, and avenues of egress, on board such vessels.

"(3) REQUIREMENTS.—

"(A) IN GENERAL.—Subject to subparagraph (B), the regulations prescribed under paragraph (1) shall include, with respect to covered small passenger vessels, regulations for—

"(i) marine firefighting training programs to improve crewmember training and proficiency, including emergency egress training for each member of the crew, to occur for all members on the crew—

"(I) at least monthly while such members are employed on board the vessel; and

"(II) each time a new crewmember joins the crew of such vessel;

"(ii) in all areas on board the vessel where passengers and crew have access, including dining areas, sleeping quarters, and lounges—

"(I) interconnected fire detection equipment, including audible and visual alarms; and

"(II) additional fire extinguishers and other firefighting equipment;

"(iii) the installation and use of monitoring devices to ensure the wakefulness of the required night watch;

"(iv) increased fire detection and suppression systems (including additional fire extinguishers) on board such vessels in unmanned areas with machinery or areas with other potential heat sources;

"(v) all general areas accessible to passengers to have no less than 2 independent avenues of escape that are—

"(I) constructed and arranged to allow for free and unobstructed egress from such areas;

"(II) located so that if one avenue of escape is not available, another avenue of escape is available; and

"(III) not located directly above, or dependent on, a berth;

"(vi) the handling, storage, and operation of flammable items, such as rechargeable batteries, including lithium ion batteries utilized for commercial purposes on board such vessels;

"(vii) passenger emergency egress drills for all areas on the vessel to which passengers have access, which shall occur prior to the vessel beginning each excursion; and

"(viii) all passengers to be provided a copy of the emergency egress plan for the vessel.

"(B) APPLICABILITY TO CERTAIN COVERED SMALL PASSENGER VESSELS.—The requirements described in clauses (iii), (v), (vii), and (viii) of subparagraph (A) shall only apply to a covered small passenger vessel that has overnight passenger accommodations.

"(4) INTERIM REQUIREMENTS.—

"(A) INTERIM REQUIREMENTS.—The Secretary shall, prior to issuing final regulations under paragraph (1), implement interim requirements to enforce the requirements under paragraph (3).

"(B) IMPLEMENTATION.—The Secretary shall implement the interim requirements under subparagraph (A) without regard to chapters 5 and 6 of title 5 and Executive Order Nos. 12866 and 13563 (5 U.S.C. 601 note; relating to regulatory planning and review and relating to improving regulation and regulatory review).

"(5) DEFINITION OF COVERED SMALL PASSENGER VESSEL.—In this subsection, the term 'covered small passenger vessel'—

"(A) except as provided in subparagraph (B), means a small passenger vessel (as defined in section 2101) that—

"(i) has overnight passenger accommodations; or

"(ii) is operating on a coastwise or oceans

route; and

"(B) does not include a ferry (as defined in section 2101) or fishing vessel (as defined in section 2101)."

(b) SECTION 3202.—Section 3202(b) of title 46, United States Code, is amended—

(1) by redesignating paragraphs (1) and (2) as subparagraphs (A) and (B), respectively, and indenting appropriately;

(2) by striking "This chapter" and inserting the following:

"(1) IN GENERAL.—This chapter"

; and

(3) by adding at the end the following:

"(2) SAFETY MANAGEMENT SYSTEM.—Notwithstanding any other provision in this chapter, including paragraph (1)(B), any regulations under section 3203, including the safety management system established by such regulations, issued on or after the date of enactment of the Elijah E. Cummings Coast Guard Authorization Act of 2020, shall apply to all covered small passenger vessels, as defined in section 3306(n)(5)."

(c) SECTION 3203.—Section 3203(a) of title 46, United States Code, is amended by inserting "(including, for purposes of this section, all covered small passenger vessels, as defined in section 3306(n)(5))" after "vessels to which this chapter applies".

TITLE LVXXXV—TECHNICAL, CONFORMING, AND CLARIFYING AMENDMENTS

SEC. 8501. TRANSFERS.

(a) IN GENERAL.—

(1) Section 215 of the Coast Guard and Maritime Transportation Act of 2004 (Public Law 108-293; 14 U.S.C. 504 note) is redesignated as section 322 of title 14, United States Code, transferred to appear after section 321 of such title (as added by this division), and amended so that the enumerator, section heading, typeface, and typestyle conform to those appearing in other sections in title 14, United States Code.

(2) Section 406 of the Maritime Transportation Security Act of 2002 (Public Law 107-295; 14 U.S.C. 501 note) is redesignated as section 720 of title 14, United States Code, transferred to appear after section 719 of such title (as added by this division), and amended so that the enumerator, section heading, typeface, and typestyle conform to those appearing in other sections in title 14, United States Code.

(3) Section 1110 of title 14, United States Code, is redesignated as section 5110 of such title and transferred to appear after section 5109 of such title (as added by this division).

(4) [14 U.S.C. 308 note] Section 401 of the Coast Guard Authorization Act of 2010 (Public Law 111-281) is amended by striking subsection (e).

(5) Subchapter I of chapter 11 of title 14, United States Code, as amended by this division, is amended by inserting after section 1109 the following:

"SEC. 1110. [14 U.S.C. 1110] Elevation of disputes to the Chief Acquisition Officer

If, after 90 days following the elevation to the Chief Acquisition Officer of any design or other dispute regarding level 1 or level 2 acquisition, the dispute remains unresolved, the Commandant shall provide to the appropriate congressional committees a detailed description of the issue and the rationale underlying the decision taken by the Chief Acquisition Officer to resolve the issue."

(6) Section 7 of the Rivers and Harbors Appropriations Act of 1915 (33 U.S.C. 471) is amended—

(A) by transferring such section to appear after section 70005 of title 46, United States Code;

(B) by striking "Sec. 7." and inserting "§70006. Establishment by Secretary of the department in which the Coast Guard is operating of anchorage grounds and regulations generally"; and

(C) by adjusting the margins with respect to subsections (a) and (b) for the presence of a section heading accordingly.

(7) Section 217 of the Coast Guard Authorization Act of 2010 (Public Law 111-281; 14 U.S.C. 504 note)—

(A) is redesignated as section 5112 of title 14, United States Code, transferred to appear after section 5111 of such title (as added by this division), and amended so that the enumerator, section heading, typeface, and typestyle conform to those appearing in other sections in title 14, United States Code; and

(B) is amended—

(i) by striking the heading and inserting the following:

"SEC. 5112. Sexual assault and sexual harassment in the Coast Guard"

; and

(ii) in subsection (b), by adding at the end the following:

"(5)(A) The number of instances in which a covered individual was accused of misconduct or crimes considered collateral to the investigation of a sexual assault committed against the individual.

"(B) The number of instances in which adverse action was taken against a covered individual who was accused of collateral misconduct or crimes as described in subparagraph (A).

"(C) The percentage of investigations of sexual assaults that involved an accusation or adverse action against a covered individual as described in subparagraphs (A) and (B).

"(D) In this paragraph, the term 'covered individual' means an individual who is identified as a victim of a sexual assault in the case files of a military criminal investigative organization."

(b) CLERICAL AMENDMENTS.—

(1) [14 U.S.C. 301] The analysis for chapter 3 of title 14, United States Code, as amended by this division, is further amended by adding at the end the following:

"322. Redistricting notification requirement."

(2) [14 U.S.C. 701] The analysis for chapter 7 of title 14, United States Code, as amended by this division, is further amended by adding at the end the following:

"720. VHF communication services."

(3) [14 U.S.C. 1101] The analysis for chapter 11 of title 14, United States Code, is amended by striking the item relating to section 1110 and inserting the following:

"1110. Elevation of disputes to the Chief Acquisition Officer."

(4) [14 U.S.C. 5101] The analysis for chapter 51 of title 14, United States Code, as amended by this division, is further amended by adding at the end the following:

"5110. Mission need statement.
"5111. Report on diversity at Coast Guard Academy.
"5112. Sexual assault and sexual harassment in the Coast Guard."

(5) [46 U.S.C. 70001] The analysis for chapter 700 of title 46, United States Code, is further amended by inserting after the item relating to section 70005 the following:

"70006. Establishment by the Secretary of the department in which the Coast Guard is operating of anchorage grounds and regulations generally."

SEC. 8502. ADDITIONAL TRANSFERS.

(a) SECTION 204 OF THE MARINE TRANSPORTATION SECURITY

ACT.—

(1) The Maritime Transportation Security Act of 2002 is amended by striking section 204 (33 U.S.C. 1902a).

(2) Section 3 of the Act to Prevent Pollution from Ships (33 U.S.C. 1902)—

(A) is amended by redesignating subsections (e) through (i) as subsections (f) through (j) respectively; and

(B) by inserting after subsection (d) the following:

"(e) DISCHARGE OF AGRICULTURAL CARGO RESIDUE.—Notwithstanding any other provision of law, the discharge from a vessel of any agricultural cargo residue material in the form of hold washings shall be governed exclusively by the provisions of this Act that implement Annex V to the International Convention for the Prevention of Pollution from Ships."

(b) LNG TANKERS.—

(1) [33 U.S.C. 1503 note] The Coast Guard and Maritime Transportation Act of 2006 is amended by striking section 304 (Public Law 109-241; 120 Stat. 527).

(2) Section 5 of the Deepwater Port Act of 1974 (33 U.S.C. 1504) is amended by adding at the end the following:

"(j) LNG TANKERS.—

"(1) PROGRAM.—The Secretary of Transportation shall develop and implement a program to promote the transportation of liquefied natural gas to and from the United States on United States flag vessels.

"(2) INFORMATION TO BE PROVIDED.—When the Coast Guard is operating as a contributing agency in the Federal Energy Regulatory Commission's shoreside licensing process for a liquefied natural gas or liquefied petroleum gas terminal located on shore or within State seaward boundaries, the Coast Guard shall provide to the Commission the information described in section 5(c)(2)(K) of the Deepwater Port Act of 1974 (33 U.S.C. 1504(c)(2)(K)) with respect to vessels reasonably anticipated to be servicing that port."

SEC. 8503. LICENSE EXEMPTIONS; REPEAL OF OBSOLETE

PROVISIONS.

(a) SERVICE UNDER LICENSES ISSUED WITHOUT EXAMINATION.—

(1) [46 U.S.C. 8301] REPEAL.—Section 8303 of title 46, United States Code, and the item relating to that section in the analysis for chapter 83 of that title, are repealed.

(2) CONFORMING AMENDMENT.—Section 14305(a)(10) of title 46, United States Code, is amended by striking “sections 8303 and 8304” and inserting “section 8304”.

(b) STANDARDS FOR TANK VESSELS OF THE UNITED STATES.—Section 9102 of title 46, United States Code, is amended—

(1) by striking “(a)” before the first sentence; and

(2) by striking subsection (b).

SEC. 8504. MARITIME TRANSPORTATION SYSTEM.

(a) MARITIME TRANSPORTATION SYSTEM.—Section 312(b)(4) of title 14, United States Code, is amended by striking “marine transportation system” and inserting “maritime transportation system”.

(b) CLARIFICATION OF REFERENCE TO MARINE TRANSPORTATION SYSTEM PROGRAMS.—Section 50307(a) of title 46, United States Code, is amended by striking “marine transportation” and inserting “maritime transportation”.

SEC. 8505. REFERENCES TO “PERSONS” AND “SEAMEN”.

(a) TECHNICAL CORRECTION OF REFERENCES TO “PERSONS”.—Title 14, United States Code, is amended as follows:

(1) In section 312(d), by striking “persons” and inserting “individuals”.

(2) In section 313(d)(2)(B), by striking “person” and inserting “individual”.

(3) In section 504—

(A) in subsection (a)(19)(B), by striking “a person” and inserting “an individual”; and

(B) in subsection (c)(4), by striking “seamen;” and inserting “mariners;”.

(4) In section 521, by striking “persons” each place it appears and inserting “individuals”.

(5) In section 522—

(A) by striking "a person" and inserting "an individual"; and

(B) by striking "person" the second and third place it appears and inserting "individual".

(6) In section 525(a)(1)(C)(ii), by striking "person" and inserting "individual".

(7) In section 526—

(A) by striking "person" each place it appears and inserting "individual";

(B) by striking "persons" each place it appears and inserting "individuals"; and

(C) in subsection (b), by striking "person's" and inserting "individual's".

(8) In section 709—

(A) by striking "persons" and inserting "individuals"; and

(B) by striking "person" and inserting "individual".

(9) In section 933(b), by striking "Every person" and inserting "An individual".

(10) In section 1102(d), by striking "persons" and inserting "individuals".

(11) In section 1902(b)(3)—

(A) in subparagraph (A), by striking "person or persons" and inserting "individual or individuals"; and

(B) in subparagraph (B), by striking "person" and inserting "individual".

(12) In section 1941(b), by striking "persons" and inserting "individuals".

(13) In section 2101(b), by striking "person" and inserting "individual".

(14) In section 2102(c), by striking "A person" and inserting "An individual".

(15) In section 2104(b)—

(A) by striking "persons" and inserting "individuals"; and

(B) by striking "A person" and inserting "An individual".

(16) In section 2118(d), by striking "person" and inserting "individual who is".

(17) In section 2147(d), by striking "a person" and inserting "an individual".

(18) In section 2150(f), by striking "person" and inserting "individual who is".

(19) In section 2161(b), by striking "person" and inserting "individual".

(20) In section 2317—

(A) by striking "persons" and inserting "individuals";

(B) by striking "person" each place it appears and inserting "individual"; and

(C) in subsection (c)(2), by striking "person's" and inserting "individual's".

(21) In section 2531—

(A) by striking "person" each place it appears and inserting "individual"; and

(B) by striking "persons" each place it appears and inserting "individuals".

(22) In section 2709, by striking "persons" and inserting "individuals".

(23) In section 2710—

(A) by striking "persons" and inserting "individuals"; and

(B) by striking "person" each place it appears and inserting "individual".

(24) In section 2711(b), by striking "person" and inserting "individual".

(25) In section 2732, by striking "a person" and inserting "an individual".

(26) In section 2733—

(A) by striking "A person" and inserting "An individual"; and

(B) by striking "that person" and inserting "that

individual".

(27) In section 2734, by striking "person" each place it appears and inserting "individual".

(28) In section 2735, by striking "a person" and inserting "an individual".

(29) In section 2736, by striking "person" and inserting "individual".

(30) In section 2737, by striking "a person" and inserting "an individual".

(31) In section 2738, by striking "person" and inserting "individual".

(32) In section 2739, by striking "person" and inserting "individual".

(33) In section 2740—

(A) by striking "person" and inserting "individual"; and

(B) by striking "one" the second place it appears.

(34) In section 2741—

(A) in subsection (a), by striking "a person" and inserting "an individual";

(B) in subsection (b)(1), by striking "person's" and inserting "individual's"; and

(C) in subsection (b)(2), by striking "person" and inserting "individual".

(35) In section 2743, by striking "person" each place it appears and inserting "individual".

(36) In section 2744—

(A) in subsection (b), by striking "a person" and inserting "an individual"; and

(B) in subsections (a) and (c), by striking "person" each place it appears and inserting "individual".

(37) In section 2745, by striking "person" and inserting "individual".

(38)(A) In section 2761—

(i) in the section heading, by striking "Persons" and inserting "Individuals";

(ii) by striking "persons" and inserting "individuals";

and

(iii) by striking "person" and inserting "individual".

(B) [14 U.S.C. 2710] In the analysis for chapter 27, by striking the item relating to section 2761 and inserting the following:

"2761. Individuals discharged as result of court-martial; allowances to."

(39)(A) In the heading for section 2767, by striking "persons" and inserting "individuals".

(B) In the analysis for chapter 27, by striking the item relating to section 2767 and inserting the following:

"2767. Reimbursement for medical-related travel expenses for certain individuals residing on islands in the continental United States."

(40) In section 2769—

(A) by striking "a person's" and inserting "an individual's"; and

(B) in paragraph (1), by striking "person" and inserting "individual".

(41) In section 2772(a)(2), by striking "person" and inserting "individual".

(42) In section 2773—

(A) in subsection (b), by striking "persons" each place it appears and inserting "individuals"; and

(B) in subsection (d), by striking "a person" and inserting "an individual".

(43) In section 2775, by striking "person" each place it appears and inserting "individual".

(44) In section 2776, by striking "person" and inserting "individual".

(45)(A) In section 2777—

(i) in the heading, by striking "persons" and inserting "individuals"; and

(ii) by striking "persons" each place it appears and inserting "individuals".

(B) In the analysis for chapter 27, by striking the item

relating to section 2777 and inserting the following:

"2777. Clothing for destitute shipwrecked individuals."

(46) In section 2779, by striking "persons" each place it appears and inserting "individuals".

(47) In section 2902(c), by striking "person" and inserting "individual".

(48) In section 2903(b), by striking "person" and inserting "individual".

(49) In section 2904(b)(1)(B), by striking "a person" and inserting "an individual".

(50) In section 3706—

(A) by striking "a person" and inserting "an individual"; and

(B) by striking "person's" and inserting "individual's".

(51) In section 3707—

(A) in subsection (c)—

(i) by striking "person" and inserting "individual"; and

(ii) by striking "person's" and inserting "individual's"; and

(B) in subsection (e), by striking "a person" and inserting "an individual".

(52) In section 3708, by striking "person" each place it appears and inserting "individual".

(53) In section 3738—

(A) by striking "a person" each place it appears and inserting "an individual";

(B) by striking "person's" and inserting "individual's"; and

(C) by striking "A person" and inserting "An individual".

(b) CORRECTION OF REFERENCES TO PERSONS AND SEAMEN.—

(1) Section 2303a(a) of title 46, United States Code, is amended by striking "persons" and inserting "individuals".

(2) Section 2306(a)(3) of title 46, United States Code, is

amended to read as follows:

"(3) An owner, charterer, managing operator, or agent of a vessel of the United States notifying the Coast Guard under paragraph (1) or (2) shall—

"(A) provide the name and identification number of the vessel, the names of individuals on board, and other information that may be requested by the Coast Guard; and

"(B) submit written confirmation to the Coast Guard within 24 hours after nonwritten notification to the Coast Guard under such paragraphs."

(3) Section 7303 of title 46, United States Code, is amended by striking "seaman" each place it appears and inserting "individual".

(4) Section 7319 of title 46, United States Code, is amended by striking "seaman" each place it appears and inserting "individual".

(5) Section 7501(b) of title 46, United States Code, is amended by striking "seaman" and inserting "holder".

(6) Section 7508(b) of title 46, United States Code, is amended by striking "individual seamen or a specifically identified group of seamen" and inserting "an individual or a specifically identified group of individuals".

(7) Section 7510 of title 46, United States Code, is amended—

(A) in subsection (c)(8)(B), by striking "merchant seamen" and inserting "merchant mariner"; and

(B) in subsection (d), by striking "merchant seaman" and inserting "merchant mariner".

(8) Section 8103(k)(3)(C) of title 46, United States Code, is amended by striking "merchant mariners" each place it appears and inserting "merchant mariner's".

(9) Section 8104 of title 46, United States Code, is amended—

(A) in subsection (c), by striking "a licensed individual or seaman" and inserting "an individual";

(B) in subsection (d), by striking "A licensed individual or seaman" and inserting "An individual";

(C) in subsection (e), by striking "a seaman" each place it appears and inserting "an individual"; and

(D) in subsection (j), by striking "seaman" and inserting "individual".

(10) Section 8302(d) of title 46, United States Code, is amended by striking "3 persons" and inserting "3 individuals".

(11) Section 11201 of title 46, United States Code, is amended by striking "a person" each place it appears and inserting "an individual".

(12) Section 11202 of title 46, United States Code, is amended—

(A) by striking "a person" and inserting "an individual"; and

(B) by striking "the person" each place it appears and inserting "the individual".

(13) Section 11203 of title 46, United States Code, is amended—

(A) by striking "a person" each place it appears and inserting "an individual"; and

(B) in subsection (a)(2), by striking "that person" and inserting "that individual".

(14) Section 15109(i)(2) of title 46, United States Code, is amended by striking "additional persons" and inserting "additional individuals".

SEC. 8506. REFERENCES TO "HIMSELF" AND "HIS".

(a) Section 1927 of title 14, United States Code, is amended by—

(1) striking "of his initial" and inserting "of an initial"; and

(2) striking "from his pay" and inserting "from the pay of such cadet".

(b) Section 2108(b) of title 14, United States Code, is amended by striking "himself" and inserting "such officer".

(c) Section 2732 of title 14, United States Code, as amended by this division, is further amended—

(1) by striking "distinguishes himself conspicuously by" and inserting "displays conspicuous"; and

(2) by striking "his" and inserting "such individual's".

(d) Section 2736 of title 14, United States Code, as amended by this division, is further amended by striking "distinguishes himself by" and inserting "performs".

(e) Section 2738 of title 14, United States Code, as amended by this division, is further amended by striking "distinguishes himself by" and inserting "displays".

(f) Section 2739 of title 14, United States Code, as amended by this division, is further amended by striking "distinguishes himself by" and inserting "displays".

(g) Section 2742 of title 14, United States Code, is amended by striking "he distinguished himself" and inserting "of the acts resulting in the consideration of such award".

(h) Section 2743 of title 14, United States Code, as amended by this division, is further amended—

(1) by striking "distinguishes himself"; and

(2) by striking "he" and inserting "such individual".

SEC. 8507. MISCELLANEOUS TECHNICAL CORRECTIONS.

(a) MISCELLANEOUS TECHNICAL CORRECTIONS.—

(1) Section 3305(d)(3)(B) of title 46, United States Code, is amended by striking "Coast Guard Authorization Act of 2017" and inserting "Frank LoBiondo Coast Guard Authorization Act of 2018".

(2) Section 4312 of title 46, United States Code, is amended by striking "Coast Guard Authorization Act of 2017" each place it appears and inserting "Frank LoBiondo Coast Guard Authorization Act of 2018 (Public Law 115-282)".

(3) **[46 U.S.C. 70001]** The analysis for chapter 700 of title 46, United States Code, is amended—

(A) by striking the item relating to the heading for the first subchapter and inserting the following:

"subchapter i— vessel operations"

(B) by striking the item relating to the heading for the second subchapter and inserting the following:

"subchapter ii— ports and waterways safety"

(C) by striking the item relating to the heading for the third subchapter and the item relating to section 70021 of such chapter and inserting the following:

"subchapter iii— conditions for entry into ports in the united states

"70021. Conditions for entry into ports in the United States."

(D) by striking the item relating to the heading for the fourth subchapter and inserting the following:

"subchapter iv— definitions regulations, enforcement, investigatory powers, applicability"

(E) by striking the item relating to the heading for the fifth subchapter and inserting the following:

"subchapter v— regattas and marine parades"

and

(F) by striking the item relating to the heading for the sixth subchapter and inserting the following:

"subchapter vi— regulation of vessels in territorial waters of the united states"

(4) Section 70031 of title 46, United States Code, is amended by striking "A through C" and inserting "I through III".

(5) Section 70032 of title 46, United States Code, is amended by striking "A through C" and inserting "I through III".

(6) Section 70033 of title 46, United States Code, is amended by striking "A through C" and inserting "I through III".

(7) Section 70034 of title 46, United States Code, is amended by striking "A through C" each place it appears and inserting "I through III".

(8) Section 70035(a) of title 46, United States Code, is amended by striking "A through C" and inserting "I through III".

(9) Section 70036 of title 46, United States Code, is amended by—

(A) striking "A through C" each place it appears and inserting "I through III"; and

(B) striking "A, B, or C" each place it appears and inserting "I, II, or III".

(10) Section 70051 of title 46, United States Code, is amended—

(A) by striking "immediate Federal response," and all that follows through "subject to the approval" and inserting "immediate Federal response, the Secretary of the department in which the Coast Guard is operating may make, subject to the approval"; and

(B) by striking "authority to issue such rules" and all that follows through "Any appropriation" and inserting "authority to issue such rules and regulations to the Secretary of the department in which the Coast Guard is operating. Any appropriation".

(11) Section 70052(e) of title 46, United States Code, is amended by striking "Secretary" and inserting "Secretary of the department in which the Coast Guard is operating" each place it appears.

(b) ALTERATION OF BRIDGES; TECHNICAL CHANGES.—The Act of June 21, 1940 (33 U.S.C. 511 et seq.), popularly known as the Truman-Hobbs Act, is amended by striking section 12 (33 U.S.C. 522).

(c) REPORT OF DETERMINATION; TECHNICAL CORRECTION.—Section 105(f)(2) of the Pribilof Islands Transition Act (16 U.S.C. 1161 note; Public Law 106-562) is amended by striking "subsection (a)," and inserting "paragraph (1),".

(d) TECHNICAL CORRECTIONS TO FRANK LOBIONDO COAST GUARD AUTHORIZATION ACT OF 2018.—

(1) [33 U.S.C. 1226;46] Section 408 of the Frank LoBiondo Coast Guard Authorization Act of 2018 (Public Law 115-282) and the item relating to such section in section 2 of such Act are repealed, and the provisions of law redesignated, transferred, or otherwise amended by section 408 are amended to read as if such section were not enacted.

(2) Section 514(b) of the Frank LoBiondo Coast Guard Authorization Act of 2018 (Public Law 115-282) is amended by striking "Chapter 30" and inserting "Chapter 3".

(3) Section 810(d) of the Frank LoBiondo Coast Guard Authorization Act of 2018 (Public Law 115-282) is amended by striking "within 30 days after receiving the notice under subsection (a)(1), the Secretary shall, by not later than 60 days after transmitting such notice," and inserting "in accordance within subsection (a)(2), the Secretary shall".

(4) Section 820(a) of the Frank LoBiondo Coast Guard Authorization Act of 2018 (Public Law 115-282) is amended by striking "years 2018 and" and inserting "year".

(5) Section 820(b)(2) of the Frank LoBiondo Coast Guard Authorization Act of 2018 (Public Law 115-282) is amended by inserting "and the Consolidated Appropriations Act, 2018 (Public Law 115-141)" after "(Public Law 115-31)".

(6) Section 821(a)(2) of the Frank LoBiondo Coast Guard Authorization Act of 2018 (Public Law 115-282) is amended by striking "Coast Guard Authorization Act of 2017" and inserting "Frank LoBiondo Coast Guard Authorization Act of 2018".

(7) [33 U.S.C. 1226 note] This section shall take effect on the date of the enactment of the Frank LoBiondo Coast Guard Authorization Act of 2018 (Public Law 115-282) and apply as if included therein.

(e) TECHNICAL CORRECTION.—Section 533(d)(2)(A) of the Coast Guard Authorization Act of 2016 (Public Law 114-120) is amended by striking "Tract 6" and inserting "such Tract".

(f) [46 U.S.C. 8103 note] DISTANT WATER TUNA FLEET; TECHNICAL CORRECTIONS.—Section 421 of the Coast Guard and Maritime Transportation Act of 2006 (Public Law 109-241) is amended—

(1) in subsection (a)—

(A) by striking "Notwithstanding" and inserting the following:

"(1) IN GENERAL.—Notwithstanding"

; and

(B) by adding at the end the following:

"(2) DEFINITION.—In this subsection, the term 'treaty area' has the meaning given the term in the Treaty on Fisheries Between the Governments of Certain Pacific Island States and the Government of the United States of America as in effect on the date of the enactment of the Coast Guard and Maritime Transportation Act of 2006 (Public Law 109-241).”

; and

(2) in subsection (c)—

(A) by striking “12.6 or 12.7” and inserting “13.6”; and

(B) by striking “and Maritime Transportation Act of 2012” and inserting “Authorization Act of 2020”.

SEC. 8508. TECHNICAL CORRECTIONS RELATING TO CODIFICATION OF PORTS AND WATERWAYS SAFETY ACT.

Effective upon the enactment of section 401 of the Frank LoBiondo Coast Guard Authorization Act of 2018 (Public Law 115-282), and notwithstanding section 402(e) of such Act—

(1) [33 U.S.C. 1232c] section 16 of the Ports and Waterways Safety Act, as added by section 315 of the Countering America’s Adversaries Through Sanctions Act (Public Law 115-44; 131 Stat. 947)—

(A) is redesignated as section 70022 of title 46, United States Code, transferred to appear after section 70021 of that title, and amended so that the enumerator, section heading, typeface, and typestyle conform to those appearing in other sections in title 46, United States Code; and

(B) as so redesignated and transferred, is amended—

(i) in subsections (b) and (e), by striking “section 4(a)(5)” each place it appears and inserting “section 70001(a)(5)”;

(ii) in subsection (c)(2), by striking “not later than” and all that follows through “thereafter,” and inserting “periodically”; and

(iii) by striking subsection (h); and

(2) chapter 700 of title 46, United States Code, is amended—

(A) in section 70002(2), by inserting “or 70022” after “section 70021”;

(B) in section 70036(e), by inserting “or 70022” after “section 70021”; and

(C) [46 U.S.C. 70001] in the analysis for such chapter—

(i) by inserting "Sec." above the section items, in accordance with the style and form of such an entry in other chapter analyses of such title; and

(ii) by adding at the end the following:

"70022. Prohibition on entry and operation."

SEC. 8509. AIDS TO NAVIGATION.

(a) Section 541 of title 14, United States Code, is amended—

(1) by striking "In" and inserting "(a) In"; and

(2) by adding at the end the following:

"(b) In the case of pierhead beacons, the Commandant may—

"(1) acquire, by donation or purchase in behalf of the United States, the right to use and occupy sites for pierhead beacons; and

"(2) properly mark all pierheads belonging to the United States situated on the northern and northwestern lakes, whenever the Commandant is duly notified by the department charged with the construction or repair of pierheads that the construction or repair of any such pierheads has been completed."

(b) Subchapter III of chapter 5 of title 14, United States Code, is amended by adding at the end the following:

"SEC. 548. [14 U.S.C. 548] Prohibition against officers and employees being interested in contracts for materials

No officer, enlisted member, or civilian member of the Coast Guard in any manner connected with the construction, operation, or maintenance of lighthouses, shall be interested, either directly or indirectly, in any contract for labor, materials, or supplies for the construction, operation, or maintenance of lighthouses, or in any patent, plan, or mode of construction or illumination, or in any article of supply for the construction, operation, or maintenance of lighthouses.

"SEC. 549. [14 U.S.C. 549] Lighthouse and other sites; necessity and sufficiency of cession by State of jurisdiction

"(a) No lighthouse, beacon, public pier, or landmark, shall be built or erected on any site until cession of jurisdiction over the same has been made to the United States.

"(b) For the purposes of subsection (a), a cession by a State of jurisdiction over a place selected as the site of a lighthouse, or other structure or work referred to in subsection (a), shall be deemed sufficient if the cession contains a reservation that process issued under authority of such State may continue to be served within such place.

"(c) If no reservation of service described in subsection (b) is contained in a cession, all process may be served and executed within the place ceded, in the same manner as if no cession had been made.

"SEC. 550. [14 U.S.C. 550] Marking pierheads in certain lakes

The Commandant of the Coast Guard shall properly mark all pierheads belonging to the United States situated on the northern and northwestern lakes, whenever he is duly notified by the department charged with the construction or repair of pierheads that the construction or repair of any such pierhead has been completed."

(c) [14 U.S.C. 501] CLERICAL AMENDMENT.—The analysis for chapter 5 of title 14, United States Code, is amended by inserting after the item relating to section 547 the following:

"548.	Prohibition against officers and employees being interested in contracts for materials.
"549.	Lighthouse and other sites; necessity and sufficiency of cession by State of jurisdiction.
"550.	Marking pierheads in certain lakes."

SEC. 8510. TRANSFERS RELATED TO EMPLOYEES OF LIGHTHOUSE SERVICE.

(a) Section 6 of chapter 103 of the Act of June 20, 1918 (33 U.S.C. 763) is repealed.

(b) Chapter 25 of title 14, United States Code, is amended by inserting after section 2531 the following:

"SEC. 2532. [14 U.S.C. 2532] Retirement of employees

"(a) OPTIONAL RETIREMENT.—Except as provided in subsections (d) and (e), a covered employee may retire from further performance of duty if such officer or employee—

"(1) has completed 30 years of active service in the

Government and is at least 55 years of age;

"(2) has completed 25 years of active service in the Government and is at least 62 years of age; or

"(3) is involuntarily separated from further performance of duty, except by removal for cause on charges of misconduct or delinquency, after completing 25 years of active service in the Government, or after completing 20 years of such service and if such employee is at least 50 years of age.

"(b) COMPULSORY RETIREMENT.—A covered employee who becomes 70 years of age shall be compulsorily retired from further performance of duty.

"(c) RETIREMENT FOR DISABILITY.—

"(1) IN GENERAL.—A covered employee who has completed 15 years of active service in the Government and is found, after examination by a medical officer of the United States, to be disabled for useful and efficient service by reason of disease or injury not due to vicious habits, intemperance, or willful misconduct of such officer or employee, shall be retired.

"(2) RESTORATION TO ACTIVE DUTY.—Any individual retired under paragraph (1) may, upon recovery, be restored to active duty, and shall from time to time, before reaching the age at which such individual may retire under subsection (a), be reexamined by a medical officer of the United States upon the request of the Secretary of the department in which the Coast Guard is operating.

"(d) ANNUAL COMPENSATION.—

"(1) IN GENERAL.—Except as provided in paragraph (2), The annual compensation of a person retired under this section shall be a sum equal to one-fortieth of the average annual pay received for the last 3 years of service for each year of active service in the Lighthouse Service, or in a department or branch of the Government having a retirement system, not to exceed thirty-fortieths of such average annual pay received.

"(2) RETIREMENT BEFORE 55.—The retirement pay computed under paragraph (1) for any officer or employee retiring under this section shall be reduced by one-sixth of 1 percent for each full month the officer or employee is under 55 years of age at the date of retirement.

"(3) NO ALLOWANCE OR SUBSISTENCE.—Retirement pay

under this section shall not include any amount on account of subsistence or other allowance.

"(e) EXCEPTION.—The retirement and pay provision in this section shall not apply to—

"(1) any person in the field service of the Lighthouse Service whose duties do not require substantially all their time; or

"(2) persons of the Coast Guard.

"(f) WAIVER.—Any person entitled to retirement pay under this section may decline to accept all or any part of such retirement pay by a waiver signed and filed with the Secretary of the Treasury. Such waiver may be revoked in writing at any time, but no payment of the retirement pay waived shall be made covering the period during which such waiver was in effect.

"(g) DEFINITION.—For the purposes of this section, the term 'covered employee' means an officer or employee engaged in the field service or on vessels of the Lighthouse Service, except a person continuously employed in district offices or shop."

(c) [14 U.S.C. 2501] CLERICAL AMENDMENT.—The analysis for chapter 25 of title 14, United States Code, is amended by inserting after the item relating to section 2531 the following:

"2532. Retirement of employees."

SEC. 8511. TRANSFERS RELATED TO SURVIVING SPOUSES OF LIGHTHOUSE SERVICE EMPLOYEES.

(a) BENEFIT TO SURVIVING SPOUSES.—Chapter 25 of title 14, United States Code, is further amended by inserting after section 2532 (as added by this division) the following:

"SEC. 2533. [14 U.S.C. 2533] Surviving spouses

"The Secretary of the department in which the Coast Guard is operating shall pay $100 per month to the surviving spouse of a current or former employee of the Lighthouse Service in accordance with section 2532 if such employee dies—

"(1) at a time when such employee was receiving or was entitled to receive retirement pay under this subchapter; or

"(2) from non-service-connected causes after fifteen or more years of employment in such service."

(b) TRANSFERS RELATED TO SURVIVING SPOUSES OF

LIGHTHOUSE SERVICE EMPLOYEES.—

(1) Chapter 25 of title 14, United States Code, is amended by inserting after section 2533 (as added by this division) the following:

"SEC. 2534. [14 U.S.C. 2534] Application for benefits"

(2)(A) Section 3 of chapter 761 of the Act of August 19, 1950 (33 U.S.C. 773), is redesignated as section 2534(a) of title 14, United States Code, transferred to appear after the heading of section 2534 of that title, and amended so that the enumerator, section heading, typeface, and typestyle conform to those appearing in other sections in title 14, United States Code.

(B) Section 2534(a), as so redesignated, transferred, and amended is further amended by striking "this Act" and inserting "section 2533".

(3)(A) Section 4 of chapter 761 of the Act of August 19, 1950 (33 U.S.C. 774), is redesignated as section 2534(b) of title 14, United States Code, transferred to appear after section 2534(a) of that title, and amended so that the enumerator, section heading, typeface, and typestyle conform to those appearing in other sections in title 14, United States Code.

(B) Section 2534(b), as so redesignated, transferred, and amended is further amended by striking "the provisions of this Act" and inserting "section 2533".

(4)(A) The proviso under the heading "Payment to Civil Service Retirement and Disability Fund" of title V of division C of Public Law 112-74 (33 U.S.C. 776) is redesignated as section 2534(c) of title 14, United States Code, transferred to appear after section 2534(b) of that title, and amended so that the enumerator, section heading, typeface, and typestyle conform to those appearing in other sections in title 14, United States Code.

(B) Section 2534(c), as so redesignated, transferred, and amended is further amended by striking "the Act of May 29, 1944, and the Act of August 19, 1950 (33 U.S.C. 771-775)," and inserting "section 2533".

(c) [14 U.S.C. 2501] CLERICAL AMENDMENT.—The analysis for chapter 25 of title 14, United States Code, is further amended by inserting after the item relating to section 2532 (as added by this division) the following:

"2533.	Surviving spouses.
"2534.	Application for benefits."

SEC. 8512. REPEALS RELATED TO LIGHTHOUSE STATUTES.

(a) IN GENERAL.—The following provisions are repealed:

(1) Section 4680 of the Revised Statutes of the United States (33 U.S.C. 725).

(2) Section 4661 of the Revised Statutes of the United States (33 U.S.C. 727).

(3) Section 4662 of the Revised Statutes of the United States (33 U.S.C. 728).

(4) The final paragraph in the account "For Life-Saving and Life-Boat Stations" under the heading Treasury Department in the first section of chapter 130 of the Act of March 3, 1875 (33 U.S.C. 730a).

(5) [33 U.S.C. 717] Section 11 of chapter 301 of the Act of June 17, 1910 (33 U.S.C. 743).

(6) The first section of chapter 215 of the Act of May 13, 1938 (33 U.S.C. 745a).

(7) The first section of chapter 313 of the Act of February 25, 1929 (33 U.S.C. 747b).

(8) Section 2 of chapter 103 of the Act of June 20, 1918 (33 U.S.C. 748).

(9) Section 4 of chapter 371 of the Act of May 22, 1926 (33 U.S.C. 754a).

(10) Chapter 642 of the Act of August 10, 1939 (33 U.S.C. 763a-1).

(11) Chapter 788 of the Act of October 29, 1949 (33 U.S.C. 763-1).

(12) Chapter 524 of the Act of July 9, 1956 (33 U.S.C. 763-2).

(13) The last 2 provisos under the heading Lighthouse Service, under the heading Department of Commerce, in the first section of chapter 161 of the Act of March 4, 1921 (41 Stat. 1417, formerly 33 U.S.C. 764).

(14) Section 3 of chapter 215 of the Act of May 13, 1938 (33 U.S.C. 770).

(15) The first section and section 2 of chapter 761 of the Act

of August 19, 1950 (33 U.S.C. 771 and 772).

(b) SAVINGS.—

(1) [33 U.S.C. 725 note] Notwithstanding any repeals made by this section, any individual beneficiary currently receiving payments under the authority of any provisions repealed in this section shall continue to receive such benefits.

(2) [33 U.S.C. 763-1 note] Notwithstanding the repeals made under paragraphs (10) and (11) of subsection (a), any pay increases made under chapter 788 of the Act of October 29, 1949, and chapter 524 of the Act of July 9, 1956, as in effect prior to their repeal shall remain in effect.

SEC. 8513. COMMON APPROPRIATION STRUCTURE.

(a) COMMON APPROPRIATIONS STRUCTURE.—

(1) PROSPECTIVE PAYMENT OF FUNDS NECESSARY TO PROVIDE MEDICAL CARE.—Section 506 of title 14, United States Code, is amended—

(A) in subsection (a)(1), by inserting "as established under chapter 56 of title 10" after "Medicare-Eligible Retiree Health Care Fund"; and

(B) in subsection (b)(1), by striking "operating expenses" and inserting "operations and support".

(2) USE OF CERTAIN APPROPRIATED FUNDS.—Section 903 of title 14, United States Code, is amended—

(A) in subsection (a), by striking "acquisition, construction, and improvement of facilities, for research, development, test, and evaluation; and for the alteration of bridges over the navigable waters" and inserting "procurement, construction, and improvement of facilities and for research and development"; and

(B) in subsection (d)(1), amended by section 241(b)(1), by striking "operating expenses" and inserting "operations and support".

(3) CONFIDENTIAL INVESTIGATIVE EXPENSES.—Section 944 of title 14, United States Code, is amended—

(A) by striking "necessary expenses for the operation" and inserting "the operations and support"; and

(B) by striking "his" each place it appears and inserting

"the Commandant's".

(4) PROCUREMENT OF PERSONNEL.—Section 2701 of title 14, United States Code, is amended—

(A) by striking "operating expense" and inserting "operations and support";

(B) by striking "but not limited to"; and

(C) by striking "in order".

(5) REQUIREMENT FOR PRIOR AUTHORIZATION OF APPROPRIATIONS.—Section 4901 of title 14, United States Code, is amended—

(A) in paragraph (1), by striking "maintenance" and inserting "support";

(B) in paragraph (2), by striking "acquisition" and inserting "procurement";

(C) by striking paragraphs (3), (4), and (6);

(D) by redesignating paragraph (5) as paragraph (3); and

(E) in paragraph (3), as redesignated by subparagraph (D), by striking "research, development, test, and evaluation" and inserting "research and development.".

(b) TITLE 46.—Sections 3317(b), 7504, 80301(c), and 80505(b)(3) of title 46, United States Code, are each amended by striking "operating expenses" and inserting "operations and support".

(c) OIL SPILL LIABILITY TRUST FUND.—Section 1012(a)(5)(A) of the Oil Pollution Act of 1990 (33 U.S.C. 2712(a)(5)(A)) is amended by striking "operating expenses" and inserting "operations and support".

TITLE LVXXXVI—FEDERAL MARITIME COMMISSION

SEC. 8601. SHORT TITLE.

This title may be cited as the "Federal Maritime Commission Authorization Act of 2020".

SEC. 8602. AUTHORIZATION OF APPROPRIATIONS.

Section 308 of title 46, United States Code, is amended by striking "$28,012,310 for fiscal year 2018 and $28,544,543 for fiscal year 2019" and inserting "$29,086,888 for fiscal year 2020 and $29,639,538 for fiscal year 2021".

SEC. 8603. UNFINISHED PROCEEDINGS.

Section 305 of title 46, United States Code, is amended—

(1) by striking "The Federal" and inserting "(a) In General.—The Federal"; and

(2) by adding at the end the following:

"(b) TRANSPARENCY.—

"(1) IN GENERAL.—In conjunction with the transmittal by the President to the Congress of the Budget of the United States for fiscal year 2021 and biennially thereafter, the Federal Maritime Commission shall submit to the Committee on Commerce, Science, and Transportation of the Senate and the Committee on Transportation and Infrastructure of the House of Representatives reports that describe the Commission's progress toward addressing the issues raised in each unfinished regulatory proceeding, regardless of whether the proceeding is subject to a statutory or regulatory deadline.

"(2) FORMAT OF REPORTS.—Each report under paragraph (1) shall, among other things, clearly identify for each unfinished regulatory proceeding—

"(A) the popular title;

"(B) the current stage of the proceeding;

"(C) an abstract of the proceeding;

"(D) what prompted the action in question;

"(E) any applicable statutory, regulatory, or judicial deadline;

"(F) the associated docket number;

"(G) the date the rulemaking was initiated;

"(H) a date for the next action; and

"(I) if a date for the next action identified in the previous report is not met, the reason for the delay."

SEC. 8604. NATIONAL SHIPPER ADVISORY COMMITTEE.

(a) IN GENERAL.—Part B of subtitle IV of title 46, United States

Code, is amended by adding at the end the following:

"CHAPTER 425—[46 U.S.C. 42501] NATIONAL SHIPPER ADVISORY COMMITTEE

"SEC. 42501. [46 U.S.C. 42501] Definitions

"In this chapter:

"(1) COMMISSION.—The term 'Commission' means the Federal Maritime Commission.

"(2) COMMITTEE.—The term 'Committee' means the National Shipper Advisory Committee established under section 42502.

"SEC. 42502. [46 U.S.C. 42502] National Shipper Advisory Committee

"(a) ESTABLISHMENT.—There is established a National Shipper Advisory Committee.

"(b) FUNCTION.—The Committee shall advise the Federal Maritime Commission on policies relating to the competitiveness, reliability, integrity, and fairness of the international ocean freight delivery system.

"(c) MEMBERSHIP.—

"(1) IN GENERAL.—The Committee shall consist of 24 members appointed by the Commission in accordance with this section.

"(2) EXPERTISE.—Each member of the Committee shall have particular expertise, knowledge, and experience in matters relating to the function of the Committee.

"(3) REPRESENTATION.—REPRESENTATION.—Members of the Committee shall be appointed as follows: —

"(A) Twelve members shall represent entities who import cargo to the United States using ocean common carriers.

"(B) Twelve members shall represent entities who export cargo from the United States using ocean common carriers.

"SEC. 42503. [46 U.S.C. 42503] Administration

"(a) MEETINGS.—The Committee shall, not less than once each year, meet at the call of the Commission or a majority of the members of the Committee.

"(b) EMPLOYEE STATUS.—A member of the Committee shall not be considered an employee of the Federal Government by reason of service on such Committee, except for the purposes of the following:

"(1) Chapter 81 of title 5.

"(2) Chapter 171 of title 28 and any other Federal law relating to tort liability.

"(c) VOLUNTEER SERVICES AND COMPENSATION.—

"(1) Notwithstanding any other provision of law, a member of the Committee may serve on such committee on a voluntary basis without pay.

"(2) No member of the Committee shall receive compensation for service on the Committee.

"(d) STATUS OF MEMBERS.—

"(1) IN GENERAL.—Except as provided in paragraph (2), with respect to a member of the Committee whom the Commission appoints to represent an entity or group—

"(A) the member is authorized to represent the interests of the applicable entity or group; and

"(B) requirements under Federal law that would interfere with such representation and that apply to a special Government employee (as defined in section 202(a) of title 18), including requirements relating to employee conduct, political activities, ethics, conflicts of interest, and corruption, do not apply to the member.

"(2) EXCEPTION.—Notwithstanding subsection (b), a member of the Committee shall be treated as a special Government employee for purposes of the committee service of the member if the member, without regard to service on the Committee, is a special Government employee.

"(e) SERVICE ON COMMITTEE.—

"(1) SOLICITATION OF NOMINATIONS.—Before appointing an individual as a member of the Committee, the Commission shall publish a timely notice in the Federal Register soliciting nominations for membership on such Committee.

"(2) APPOINTMENTS.—

"(A) IN GENERAL.—After considering nominations received pursuant to a notice published under paragraph (1), the Commission may appoint a member to the Committee.

"(B) PROHIBITION.—The Commission shall not seek, consider, or otherwise use information concerning the political affiliation of a nominee in making an appointment to the Committee.

"(3) SERVICE AT PLEASURE OF COMMISSION.—Each member of the Committee shall serve at the pleasure of the Commission.

"(4) SECURITY BACKGROUND EXAMINATIONS.—The Commission may require an individual to have passed an appropriate security background examination before appointment to the Committee.

"(5) PROHIBITION.—A Federal employee may not be appointed as a member of the Committee.

"(6) TERMS.—

"(A) IN GENERAL.—The term of each member of the Committee shall expire on December 31 of the third full year after the effective date of the appointment.

"(B) CONTINUED SERVICE AFTER TERM.—When the term of a member of the Committee ends, the member, for a period not to exceed 1 year, may continue to serve as a member until a successor is appointed.

"(7) VACANCIES.—A vacancy on the Committee shall be filled in the same manner as the original appointment.

"(8) SPECIAL RULE FOR REAPPOINTMENTS.—Notwithstanding paragraphs (1) and (2), the Commission may reappoint a member of a committee for any term, other than the first term of the member, without soliciting, receiving, or considering nominations for such appointment.

"(f) STAFF SERVICES.—The Commission shall furnish to the Committee any staff and services considered by the Commission to be necessary for the conduct of the Committee's functions.

"(g) CHAIR; VICE CHAIR.—

"(1) IN GENERAL.—The Committee shall elect a Chair and

Vice Chair from among the committee's members.

"(2) VICE CHAIRMAN ACTING AS CHAIRMAN.—The Vice Chair shall act as Chair in the absence or incapacity of, or in the event of a vacancy in the office of, the Chair.

"(h) SUBCOMMITTEES AND WORKING GROUPS.—

"(1) IN GENERAL.—The Chair of the Committee may establish and disestablish subcommittees and working groups for any purpose consistent with the function of the Committee.

"(2) PARTICIPANTS.—Subject to conditions imposed by the Chair, members of the Committee may be assigned to subcommittees and working groups established under paragraph (1).

"(i) CONSULTATION, ADVICE, REPORTS, AND RECOMMENDATIONS.—

"(1) CONSULTATION.—Before taking any significant action, the Commission shall consult with, and consider the information, advice, and recommendations of, the Committee if the function of the Committee is to advise the Commission on matters related to the significant action.

"(2) ADVICE, REPORTS, AND RECOMMENDATIONS.—The Committee shall submit, in writing, to the Commission its advice, reports, and recommendations, in a form and at a frequency determined appropriate by the Committee.

"(3) EXPLANATION OF ACTIONS TAKEN.—Not later than 60 days after the date on which the Commission receives recommendations from the Committee under paragraph (2), the Commission shall—

"(A) publish the recommendations on a public website; and

"(B) respond, in writing, to the Committee regarding the recommendations, including by providing an explanation of actions taken regarding the recommendations.

"(4) SUBMISSION TO CONGRESS.—The Commission shall submit to the Committee on Transportation and Infrastructure of the House of Representatives and the Committee on Commerce, Science, and Transportation of the Senate the advice, reports, and recommendations received from the

Committee under paragraph (2).

"(j) OBSERVERS.—The Commission may designate a representative to—

"(1) attend any meeting of the Committee; and

"(2) participate as an observer at such meeting.

"(k) TERMINATION.—The Committee shall terminate on September 30, 2029."

(b) NO ADDITIONAL FUNDS AUTHORIZED.—No funds in addition to the funds authorized in section 308 of title 46, United States Code, are authorized to carry out this title or the amendments made by this section.

(c) [46 U.S.C. 40101] CLERICAL AMENDMENT.—The analysis for subtitle IV of title 46, United States Code, is amended by inserting after the item related to chapter 423 the following:

"Chapter 425— National Shipper Advisory Committee"

SEC. 8605. TRANSFER OF FEDERAL MARITIME COMMISSION PROVISIONS.

(a) TRANSFER.—

(1) Subtitle IV of title 46, United States Code, is amended by adding at the end the following:

"PART D—[46 U.S.C. 46101] FEDERAL MARITIME COMMISSION

"CHAPTER 461—[46 U.S.C. 46101] FEDERAL MARITIME COMMISSION" "

(2) [46 U.S.C. 46101] Chapter 3 of title 46, United States Code, is redesignated as chapter 461 of part D of subtitle IV of such title and transferred to appear in such part.

(3) Sections 301 through 308 of such title are redesignated as sections 46101 through 46108, respectively, of such title.

(b) CONFORMING AMENDMENTS.—

(1) Section 46101(c)(3)(A)(v) of title 46, United States Code, as so redesignated, is amended by striking "304" and inserting "46104".

(2) section 322(b) of the Coast Guard Personnel and Maritime Safety Act of 2002 (31 U.S.C. 1113 note) is amended by striking "208 of the Merchant Marine Act, 1936 (46 App. U.S.C. 1118)" and inserting "46106(a) of title 46, United States Code".

(3) Section 1031(23) of the National Defense Authorization Act for Fiscal Year 2000 (31 U.S.C. 1113 note) is amended by striking "208, 901(b)(2), and 1211 of the Merchant Marine Act, 1936 (46 App. U.S.C. 1118, 1241(b)(2), 1291)" and inserting "44106(a) and 55305(d) of title 46, United States Code".

(4) [46 U.S.C. 101] The analysis for subtitle I of title 46, United States Code, is amended by striking the item relating to chapter 3.

(5) [46 U.S.C. 40101] The analysis for subtitle IV of such title is amended by adding at the end the following:

"PART D— **Federal Maritime Commission**

"461.	**Federal Maritime Commission**	**46101"."**

(6) [46 U.S.C. 46101] The analysis for chapter 461 of part D of subtitle IV of such title, as so redesignated, is amended to read as follows:

"46101.	General organization.
"46102.	Quorum.
"46103.	Meetings.
"46104.	Delegation of authority.
"46105.	Regulations.
"46106.	Annual report.
"46107.	Expenditures.
"46108.	Authorization of appropriations."

(c) TECHNICAL CORRECTION.—Section 46103(c)(3) of title 46, United States Code, as so redesignated, is amended by striking "555b(c)" and inserting "552b(c)".

* * * * * * *

Maritime Security and Fisheries Enforcement Act – Title XXXV-Maritime Matters

Public Law 116-92

As amended through P.L.118-159

National Defense Authorization Act for Fiscal Year 2020

[(Public Law 116–92)]

[As Amended Through P.L. 118–159, Enacted December 23, 2024]

AN ACT To authorize appropriations for fiscal year 2020 for military activities of the Department of Defense, for military construction, and for defense activities of the Department of Energy, to prescribe military personnel strengths for such fiscal year, and for other purposes.

Be it enacted by the Senate and House of Representatives of the United States of America in Congress assembled,

SECTION 1. SHORT TITLE.

This Act may be cited as the "National Defense Authorization Act for Fiscal Year 2020".

SEC. 2. ORGANIZATION OF ACT INTO DIVISIONS; TABLE OF CONTENTS.

(a) DIVISIONS.—This Act is organized into four divisions as follows:

(1) Division A—Department of Defense Authorizations.

(2) Division B—Military Construction Authorizations.

(3) Division C—Department of Energy National Security Authorizations and Other Authorizations.

(4) Division D—Funding Tables.

(5) Division E—Intelligence Authorizations for Fiscal Years 2018, 2019, and 2020.

(6) Division F—Other Matters.

(b) TABLE OF CONTENTS.—The table of contents for this Act is as follows:

* * * * * * *

* * * * * * *

DIVISION C—DEPARTMENT OF ENERGY NATIONAL SECURITY AUTHORIZATIONS AND OTHER AUTHORIZATIONS

TITLE XXXI—DEPARTMENT OF ENERGY NATIONAL SECURITY PROGRAMS

Subtitle A—National Security Programs and Authorizations

Subtitle B—Program Authorizations, Restrictions, and Limitations

* * * * * * *

TITLE XXXV—MARITIME MATTERS

Subtitle A—Maritime Administration

SEC. 3501. AUTHORIZATION OF THE MARITIME ADMINISTRATION.

(a) IN GENERAL.—There are authorized to be appropriated to the Department of Transportation for fiscal year 2020, to be available without fiscal year limitation if so provided in appropriations Acts, for programs associated with maintaining the United States Merchant Marine, the following amounts:

(1) For expenses necessary for operations of the United States Merchant Marine Academy, $95,944,000, of which—

(A) $77,944,000 shall remain available until September 30, 2021 for Academy operations; and

(B) $18,000,000 shall remain available until expended for capital asset management at the Academy.

(2) For expenses necessary to support the State maritime academies, $50,280,000, of which—

(A) $2,400,000 shall remain available until September 30, 2021, for the Student Incentive Program;

(B) $6,000,000 shall remain available until expended for direct payments to such academies;

(C) $30,080,000 shall remain available until expended for maintenance and repair of State maritime academy training vessels;

(D) $3,800,000 shall remain available until expended for training ship fuel assistance; and

(E) $8,000,000 shall remain available until expended for offsetting the costs of training ship sharing.

(3) For expenses necessary to support the National Security Multi-Mission Vessel Program, $600,000,000, which shall remain available until expended.

(4) For expenses necessary to support Maritime Administration operations and programs, $60,442,000, of which $5,000,000 shall remain available until expended for activities authorized under section 50307 of title 46, United States Code.

(5) For expenses necessary to dispose of vessels in the National Defense Reserve Fleet, $5,000,000, which shall

remain available until expended.

(6) For expenses necessary to maintain and preserve a United States flag Merchant Marine to serve the national security needs of the United States under chapter 531 of title 46, United States Code, $300,000,000, which shall remain available until expended.

(7) For expenses necessary for the loan guarantee program authorized under chapter 537 of title 46, United States Code, $33,000,000, of which—

(A) $30,000,000 may be used for the cost (as defined in section 502(5) of the Federal Credit Reform Act of 1990 (2 U.S.C. 661a(5)) of loan guarantees under the program, which shall remain available until expended; and

(B) $3,000,000 may be used for administrative expenses relating to loan guarantee commitments under the program.

(8) For expenses necessary to provide assistance to small shipyards and for maritime training programs under section 54101 of title 46, United States Code, $40,000,000, which shall remain available until expended.

(9) For expenses necessary to implement the Port and Intermodal Improvement Program, $500,000,000, except that no funds shall be used for a grant award to purchase fully automated cargo handling equipment that is remotely operated or remotely monitored with or without the exercise of human intervention or control, if the Secretary determines such equipment would result in a net loss of jobs within a port or port terminal.

SEC. 3502. REAUTHORIZATION OF MARITIME SECURITY PROGRAM.

(a) AWARD OF OPERATING AGREEMENTS.—Section 53103 of title 46, United States Code, is amended by striking “2025” each place it appears and inserting “2035”.

(b) EFFECTIVENESS OF OPERATING AGREEMENTS.—Section 53104(a) of title 46, United States Code, is amended by striking “2025” and inserting “2035”.

(c) PAYMENTS.—Section 53106(a)(1) of title 46, United States Code, is amended—

(1) in subparagraph (B), by striking "and";

(2) in subparagraph (C), by striking "$3,700,000 for each of fiscal years 2022, 2023, 2024, and 2025." and inserting "$5,300,000 for each of fiscal years 2022, 2023, 2024, and 2025;"; and

(3) by adding at the end the following new subparagraphs:

"(D) $5,800,000 for each of fiscal years 2026, 2027, and 2028;

"(E) $6,300,000 for each of fiscal years 2029, 2030, and 2031; and

"(F) $6,800,000 for each of fiscal years 2032, 2033, 2034, and 2035."

(d) AUTHORIZATION OF APPROPRIATIONS.—Section 53111 of title 46, United States Code, is amended—

(1) in paragraph (2), by striking "and";

(2) in paragraph (3), by striking "$222,000,000 for each fiscal year thereafter through fiscal year 2025." and inserting "$318,000,000 for each of fiscal years 2022, 2023, 2024, and 2025;"; and

(3) by adding at the end the following new paragraphs:

"(4) $348,000,000 for each of fiscal years 2026, 2027, and 2028;

"(5) $378,000,000 for each of fiscal years 2029, 2030, and 2031; and

"(6) $408,000,000 for each of fiscal years 2032, 2033, 2034, and 2035."

SEC. 3503. MARITIME TECHNICAL ASSISTANCE PROGRAM.

Section 50307 of title 46, United States Code, is amended—

(1) in subsection (a), by striking "The Secretary of Transportation may engage in the environmental study" and inserting "The Secretary of Transportation, acting through the Maritime Administrator, shall engage in the study";

(2) in subsection (b)—

(A) by striking "may—" and all that follows through "improvements by—" and inserting "shall identify, study, evaluate, test, demonstrate, or improve emerging marine technologies and practices to improve—";

(B) by inserting before subparagraph (A) the following:

"(1) environmental performance to meet United States Federal and international standards and guidelines, including—"

(C) in subparagraph (C), by striking "species; and" and all that follows through the end of the subsection and inserting"species; or

"(D) reducing propeller cavitation; and

"(2) the efficiency and safety of domestic maritime industries."

(3) in subsection (c)(2), by striking "benefits" and inserting "or other benefits to domestic maritime industries"; and

(4) by adding at the end the following:

"(e) LIMITATIONS ON THE USE OF FUNDS.—Not more than three percent of the funds appropriated to carry out this section may be used for administrative purposes."

SEC. 3504. APPOINTMENT OF CANDIDATES ATTENDING SPONSORED PREPARATORY SCHOOL.

Section 51303 of title 46, United States Code, is amended—

(1) by striking "The Secretary" and inserting the following:

"(a) IN GENERAL.—The Secretary"

; and

(2) by adding at the end the following:

"(b) APPOINTMENT OF CANDIDATES SELECTED FOR PREPARATORY SCHOOL SPONSORSHIP.—The Secretary of Transportation may appoint each year as cadets at the United States Merchant Marine Academy not more than 40 qualified individuals sponsored by the Academy to attend preparatory school during the academic year prior to entrance in the Academy, and who have successfully met the terms and conditions of sponsorship set by the Academy."

SEC. 3505. GENERAL SUPPORT PROGRAM.

Section 51501 of title 46, United States Code, is amended by adding at the end the following:

"(c) AMERICAN MARITIME CENTERS OF EXCELLENCE.—The Secretary shall designate each State maritime academy as an American Maritime Center of Excellence."

SEC. 3506. IMPROVEMENTS TO THE MARITIME GUARANTEED LOAN PROGRAM.

(a) DEFINITIONS.—Section 53701 of title 46, United States Code, is amended—

(1) by striking paragraph (5);

(2) by redesignating paragraphs (6) through (15) as paragraphs (5) through (14), respectively; and

(3) by adding at the end the following:

"(15) VESSEL OF NATIONAL INTEREST.—The term 'Vessel of National Interest' means a vessel deemed to be of national interest that meets characteristics determined by the Administrator, in consultation with the Secretary of Defense, the Secretary of the Department in which the Coast Guard is operating when it is not operating as a service in the Department of the Navy, or the heads of other Federal agencies, as described in section 53703(d)."

(b) PREFERRED LENDER.—Subsection (a) of section 53702 of title 46, United States Code, is amended to read as follows:

"(a) IN GENERAL.—

"(1) GUARANTEE OF PAYMENTS.—The Secretary or Administrator, on terms the Secretary or Administrator may prescribe, may guarantee or make a commitment to guarantee the payment of the principal of and interest on an obligation eligible to be guaranteed under this chapter. A guarantee or commitment to guarantee shall cover 100 percent of the principal and interest.

"(2) PREFERRED ELIGIBLE LENDER.—The Federal Financing Bank shall be the preferred eligible lender of the principal and interest of the guaranteed obligations issued under this chapter."

(c) APPLICATION AND ADMINISTRATION.—Section 53703 of title 46, United States Code, is amended—

(1) in the section heading, by striking "procedures" and

inserting “and administration”; and

(2) by adding at the end the following:

“(c) INDEPENDENT ANALYSIS.—

“(1) IN GENERAL.—To assess and mitigate the risks due to factors associated with markets, technology, financial, or legal structures related to an application or guarantee under this chapter, the Secretary or Administrator may utilize third party experts, including legal counsel, to—

“(A) process and review applications under this chapter, including conducting independent analysis and review of aspects of an application;

“(B) represent the Secretary or Administrator in structuring and documenting the obligation guarantee;

“(C) analyze and review aspects of, structure, and document the obligation guarantee during the term of the guarantee;

“(D) recommend financial covenants or financial ratios to be met by the applicant during the time a guarantee under this chapter is outstanding that are—

“(i) based on the financial covenants or financial ratios, if any, that are then applicable to the obligor under private sector credit agreements; and

“(ii) in lieu of other financial covenants applicable to the obligor under this chapter with respect to requirements regarding long-term debt-to-equity, minimum working capital, or minimum amount of equity; and

“(E) represent the Secretary or Administrator to protect the security interests of the Government relating to an obligation guarantee.

“(2) PRIVATE SECTOR EXPERT.—Independent analysis, review, and representation conducted under this subsection shall be performed by a private sector expert in the applicable field who is selected by the Secretary or Administrator.

“(d) VESSELS OF NATIONAL INTEREST.—

“(1) NOTICE OF FUNDING.—The Secretary or

Administrator may post a notice in the Federal Register regarding the availability of funding for obligation guarantees under this chapter for the construction, reconstruction, or reconditioning of a Vessel of National Interest and include a timeline for the submission of applications for such vessels.

"(2) VESSEL CHARACTERISTICS.—

"(A) IN GENERAL.—The Secretary or Administrator, in consultation with the Secretary of Defense, the Secretary of the Department in which the Coast Guard is operating when it is not operating as service in the Department of the Navy, or the heads of other Federal agencies, shall develop and publish a list of vessel types that would be considered Vessels of National Interest.

"(B) REVIEW.—Such list shall be reviewed and revised every four years or as necessary, as determined by the Administrator."

(d) FUNDING LIMITS.—Section 53704 of title 46, United States Code, is amended—

(1) in subsection (a)—

(A) by striking "that amount" and all the follows through "$850,000,000" and inserting "that amount, $850,000,000"; and

(B) by striking "facilities" and all that follows through the end of the subsection and inserting "facilities."; and

(2) in subsection (c)(4)—

(A) by striking subparagraph (A); and

(B) by redesignating subparagraphs (B) through (K), as subparagraphs (A) through (J), respectively.

(e) ELIGIBLE PURPOSES OF OBLIGATIONS.—Section 53706 of title 46, United States Code, is amended—

(1) in subsection (a)(1)(A)—

(A) in the matter preceding clause (i), by striking "(including an eligible export vessel)";

(B) in clause (iv) by inserting "or" after the semicolon;

(C) in clause (v), by striking "; or" and inserting a

period; and

(D) by striking clause (vi); and

(2) in subsection (c)(1)—

(A) in subparagraph (A), by striking "and" after the semicolon;

(B) in subparagraph (B)(ii), by striking the period at the end and inserting "; and"; and

(C) by adding at the end the following:

"(C) after applying subparagraphs (A) and (B), Vessels of National Interest."

(f) AMOUNT OF OBLIGATIONS.—Section 53709(b) of title 46, United States Code, is amended—

(1) by striking paragraphs (3) and (6); and

(2) by redesignating paragraphs (4) and (5) as paragraphs (3) and (4), respectively.

(g) CONTENTS OF OBLIGATIONS.—Section 53710 of title 46, United States Code, is amended—

(1) in subsection (a)(4)—

(A) in subparagraph (A)—

(i) by striking "or, in the case of" and all that follows through "party"; and

(ii) by striking "and" after the semicolon; and

(B) in subparagraph (B), by striking the period at the end and inserting "; and"; and

(C) by adding at the end the following:

"(C) documented under the laws of the United States for the term of the guarantee of the obligation or until the obligation is paid in full, whichever is sooner."

; and

(2) in subsection (c)—

(A) in the subsection heading, by inserting "and Provide for the Financial Stability of the Obligor" after "Interests";

(B) by striking "provisions for the protection of" and inserting"provisions, which shall include—

"(1) provisions for the protection of"

(C) by striking ", and other matters that the Secretary or Administrator may prescribe." and inserting, "; and"; and

(D) by adding at the end the following:

"(2) any other provisions that the Secretary or Administrator may prescribe."

(h) ADMINISTRATIVE FEES.—Section 53713 of title 46, United States Code, is amended—

(1) in subsection (a)—

(A) in the matter preceding paragraph (1), by striking "reasonable for—" and inserting " reasonable for processing the application and monitoring the loan guarantee, including for—";

(B) in paragraph (4), by striking "; and" and inserting "or a deposit fund under section 53716 of this title;";

(C) in paragraph (5), by striking the period at the end and inserting "; and"; and

(D) by adding at the end the following:

"(6) monitoring and providing services related to the obligor's compliance with any terms related to the obligations, the guarantee, or maintenance of the Secretary or Administrator's security interests under this chapter."

; and

(2) in subsection (c)—

(A) in paragraph (1), by striking "under section 53708(d) of this title" and inserting "under section 53703(c) of this title";

(B) by redesignating paragraphs (1) through (3) as subparagraphs (A) through (C), respectively, and adjusting the margins accordingly;

(C) by striking "The Secretary" and inserting the following:

"(1) IN GENERAL.—The Secretary"

; and

(D) by adding at the end the following:

"(2) FEE LIMITATION INAPPLICABLE.—Fees

collected under this subsection are not subject to the limitation of subsection (b)."

(i) BEST PRACTICES; ELIGIBLE EXPORT VESSELS.—Chapter 537 of title 46, United States Code, is further amended—

(1) in subchapter I, by adding at the end the following new section:

"SEC. 53719. [46 U.S.C. 53719] Best practices

The Secretary or Administrator shall ensure that all standard documents and agreements that relate to loan guarantees made pursuant to this chapter are reviewed and updated every four years to ensure that such documents and agreements meet the current commercial best practices to the extent permitted by law."

; and

(2) in subchapter III, by striking section 53732.

(j) EXPEDITED CONSIDERATION OF LOW-RISK APPLICATIONS.—

(1) IN GENERAL.—In accordance with the requirements of this subsection, the Administrator shall establish an administrative process and issue guidance for the expedited consideration of low-risk applications submitted under chapter 537 of title 46, United States Code.

(2) [46 U.S.C. 53703 note] STAKEHOLDER COMMENT.—Not later than 180 days after the date of enactment of this section, the Administrator of the Maritime Administration shall publish in the Federal Register a notice of a 45-day public comment period to request stakeholder input and recommendations to establish the administrative process required under this subsection, including proposals to assist applicants—

(A) in the development and submission of initial applications;

(B) in meeting requests for supplemental information made by the Administrator; and

(C) to comply with other requirements made by the Administrator to ensure the expedited consideration of applications.

(3) INDUSTRY BEST PRACTICES.—The administrative process established under this subsection shall utilize, to the extent practicable, relevant Federal and industry best practices found

in the maritime and shipbuilding industries.

(4) FINAL GUIDANCE.—Not later than 90 days after the conclusion of the public comment period required under paragraph (2), the Administrator shall publish in the Federal Register final guidance to assist applicants in the preparation and filing of applications under this subsection.

(k) CONGRESSIONAL NOTIFICATION.—

(1) NOTIFICATION.—Not less than 60 days before reorganizing or consolidating the activities or personnel covered under chapter 537 of title 46, United States Code, the Secretary of Transportation shall notify, in writing, the Committee on Commerce, Science, and Transportation of the Senate and the Committee on Transportation and Infrastructure of the House of Representatives of the proposed reorganization or consolidation.

(2) CONTENTS.—Each notification under paragraph (1) shall include an evaluation of, and justification for, the reorganization or consolidation.

(l) [46 U.S.C. 53701] CLERICAL AMENDMENTS.—The table of sections at the beginning of chapter 537 of title 46, United States Code,is amended—

(1) by inserting after the item relating to section 53718 the following new item:

"53719. Best practices."

; and

(2) by striking the item relating to section 53732.

SEC. 3507. REQUIREMENT FOR SMALL SHIPYARD GRANTEES.

(a) IN GENERAL.—Section 54101(d) of title 46, United States Code, is amended—

(1) by striking "Grants awarded" and inserting the following:

"(1) IN GENERAL.—Grants awarded"

; and

(2) by adding at the end the following:

"(2) BUY AMERICA.—

"(A) IN GENERAL.—Subject to subparagraph (B), no

funds may be obligated by the Administrator of the Maritime Administration under this section, unless each product and material purchased with those funds (including products and materials purchased by a grantee), and including any commercially available off-the-shelf item, is—

"(i) an unmanufactured article, material, or supply that has been mined or produced in the United States; or

"(ii) a manufactured article, material, or supply that has been manufactured in the United States substantially all from articles, materials, or supplies mined, produced, or manufactured in the United States.

"(B) EXCEPTIONS.—

"(i) IN GENERAL.—Notwithstanding subparagraph (A), the requirements of that subparagraph shall not apply with respect to a particular product or material if the Administrator determines—

"(I) that the application of those requirements would be inconsistent with the public interest;

"(II) that such product or material is not available in the United States in sufficient and reasonably available quantities, of a satisfactory quality, or on a timely basis; or

"(III) that inclusion of a domestic product or material will increase the cost of that product or material by more than 25 percent, with respect to a certain contract between a grantee and that grantee's supplier.

"(ii) FEDERAL REGISTER.—A determination made by the Administrator under this subparagraph shall be published in the Federal Register.

"(C) DEFINITIONS.—In this paragraph:

"(i) The term 'commercially available off-the-shelf item' means—

"(I) any item of supply (including construction material) that is—

"(aa) a commercial item, as defined by section 2.101 of title 48, Code of Federal Regulations (as in effect on the date of the enactment of the National Defense Authorization Act for Fiscal Year 2020); and

"(bb) sold in substantial quantities in the commercial marketplace; and

"(II) does not include bulk cargo, as defined in section 40102(4) of this title, such as agricultural products and petroleum products.

"(ii) The term 'product or material' means an article, material, or supply brought to the site by the recipient for incorporation into the building, work, or project. The term also includes an item brought to the site preassembled from articles, materials, or supplies. However, emergency life safety systems, such as emergency lighting, fire alarm, and audio evacuation systems, that are discrete systems incorporated into a public building or work and that are produced as complete systems, are evaluated as a single and distinct construction material regardless of when or how the individual parts or components of those systems are delivered to the construction site.

"(iii) The term 'United States' includes the District of Columbia, the Commonwealth of Puerto Rico, the Northern Mariana Islands, Guam, American Samoa, and the Virgin Islands."

(b) AUTHORIZATION OF APPROPRIATIONS.—Section 54101(i) of title 46, United States Code, is amended—

(1) by striking "2018, 2019, and 2020" and inserting "2020 and 2021"; and

(2) by striking "$35,000,000" and inserting "$40,000,000".

(c) NOTIFICATION OF COMMITTEES OF CERTAIN PROPOSED OBLIGATIONS.—The first section of Public Law 85-804 (50 U.S.C.

1431) is amended, in the third sentence, by inserting "and in addition, the Committee on Transportation and Infrastructure of the House of Representatives and the Committee on Commerce, Science, and Transportation of the Senate with respect to contracts, or modifications or amendments to contracts, or advance payments proposed to be made under this section by the Secretary of the Department in which the Coast Guard is operating with respect to the acquisition of Coast Guard cutters or aircraft," after "House of Representatives".

SEC. 3508. SALVAGE RECOVERIES OF CARGOES.

Section 57107 of title 46, United States Code, is amended by adding at the end the following:

"(c) SALVAGING CARGOES.—

"(1) REIMBURSABLE AGREEMENTS.—The Secretary of Transportation, acting through the Administrator of the Maritime Administration, may enter into reimbursable agreements with other Federal entities to provide legal services to such entities relating to the salvaging of cargoes for which such entities have custody, or control, or for which for such entities have trustee responsibilities from vessels in the custody or control of the Maritime Administration or its predecessor agencies. The Secretary may receive and retain reimbursement from such entities for all costs incurred related to the provision of such services.

"(2) AMOUNTS RECEIVED.—Amounts received as reimbursements under this subsection shall be credited to the fund or account that was used to cover the costs incurred by the Secretary or, if the period of availability of obligations for that appropriation has expired, to the appropriation of funds that is currently available to the Secretary for substantially the same purpose. Amounts so credited shall be merged with amounts in such fund or account and shall be available for the same purposes, and subject to the same conditions and limitations, as amounts in such fund or account.

"(3) ADVANCE PAYMENTS.—Payments made in advance shall be for any part of the estimated cost as determined by the Secretary of Transportation. Adjustments to the amounts paid in advance shall be made as agreed to by the Secretary of Transportation and the head of the ordering agency or unit based on the actual cost of goods or services provided."

SEC. 3509. SALVAGE RECOVERIES FOR SUBROGATED OWNERSHIP OF VESSELS AND CARGOES.

(a) IN GENERAL.—Chapter 571 of title 46, United States Code, as amended by this title, is further amended by adding at the end the following new section:

"SEC. 57111. [46 U.S.C. 57111] SALVAGE RECOVERIES FOR SUBROGATED OWNERSHIP OF VESSELS AND CARGOES

"(a) SALVAGE AGREEMENTS.—The Secretary of Transportation is authorized to enter into marine salvage agreements for the recoveries, sale, and disposal of sunken or damaged vessels, cargoes, or properties owned or insured by or on behalf of the Maritime Administration, the United States Shipping Board, the U.S. Shipping Bureau, the United States Maritime Commission, or the War Shipping Administration.

"(b) MILITARY CRAFT.—The Secretary of Transportation shall consult with the Secretary of the military department concerned prior to engaging in or authorizing any activity under subsection (a) that will disturb sunken military craft, as such term is defined in section 1408(3) of the Ronald W. Reagan National Defense Authorization Act for Fiscal Year 2005 (Public Law 108-375; 10 U.S.C. 113 note).

"(c) RECOVERIES.—Notwithstanding any other provision of law, the net proceeds from salvage agreements entered into as authorized in subsection (a) shall remain available until expended and be distributed as follows:

"(1) Fifty percent shall be available to the Administrator of the Maritime Administration for the payment or reimbursement of expenses incurred by or on behalf of State maritime academies or the United States Merchant Marine Academy for facility and training ship maintenance, repair, and modernization, and for the purchase of simulators and fuel.

"(2) The remainder shall be distributed for maritime heritage preservation to the Department of the Interior for grants as authorized by section 308703 of title 54."

(b) [46 U.S.C. 57100] CLERICAL AMENDMENT.—The table of sections at the beginning of such chapter, as amended by this title, is further amended by adding at the end the following new item:

"57111. Salvage recoveries for subrogated ownership of vessels and cargoes."

SEC. 3510. MARITIME OCCUPATIONAL SAFETY AND HEALTH ADVISORY COMMITTEE.

Section 7 of the Occupational Safety and Health Act of 1970 (29 U.S.C. 656) is amended by adding at the end the following:

"(d) There is established a Maritime Occupational Safety and Health Advisory Committee, which shall be a continuing body and shall provide advice to the Secretary in formulating maritime industry standards and regarding matters pertaining to the administration of this Act related to the maritime industry. The composition of such advisory committee shall be consistent with the advisory committees established under subsection (b). A member of the advisory committee who is otherwise qualified may continue to serve until a successor is appointed. The Secretary may promulgate or amend regulations as necessary to implement this subsection."

SEC. 3511. [46 U.S.C. 3702 note] MILITARY TO MARINER.

(a) CREDENTIALING SUPPORT.—Not later than one year after the date of enactment of this title, the Secretary of Defense, the Secretary of the Department in which the Coast Guard is operating when it is not operating as a service in the Department of the Navy, the Secretary of Commerce, and the Secretary of Health and Human Services, with respect to the applicable services in their respective departments, and in coordination with one another and with the United States Committee on the Marine Transportation System, and in consultation with the Merchant Marine Personnel Advisory Committee, shall, consistent with applicable law, identify all training and experience within the applicable service that may qualify for merchant mariner credentialing and submit a list of all identified training and experience to the United States Coast Guard National Maritime Center for a determination of whether such training and experience counts for credentialing purposes.

(b) REVIEW OF APPLICABLE SERVICE.—The United States Coast Guard Commandant shall make a determination of whether training and experience counts for credentialing purposes, as described in subsection (a), not later than 6 months after the date on which the United States Coast Guard National Maritime Center receives a submission under subsection (a) identifying a training or experience and requesting such a determination.

(c) FEES AND SERVICES.—The Secretary of Defense, the Secretary of the Department in which the Coast Guard is operating when it is not operating as a service in the Department of the Navy, and the Secretary of Commerce, with respect to the applicable services in their respective departments, shall—

(1) take all necessary and appropriate actions to provide for the waiver of fees through the National Maritime Center license evaluation, issuance, and examination for members of the uniformed services on active duty, if a waiver is authorized and appropriate, and, if a waiver is not granted, take all necessary and appropriate actions to provide for the payment of fees for members of the uniformed services on active duty by the applicable service to the fullest extent permitted by law;

(2) direct the applicable services to take all necessary and appropriate actions to provide for Transportation Worker Identification Credential cards for members of the uniformed services on active duty pursuing or possessing a mariner credential, such as implementation of an equal exchange process for members of the uniformed services on active duty at no or minimal cost;

(3) ensure that members of the applicable services who are to be discharged or released from active duty and who request certification or verification of sea service be provided such certification or verification no later than one month after discharge or release;

(4) ensure the applicable services have developed, or continue to operate, as appropriate, the online resource known as Credentialing Opportunities On-Line to support separating members of the uniformed services who are seeking information and assistance on merchant mariner credentialing; and

(5) not later than 1 year after the date of enactment of this section, take all necessary and appropriate actions to review and implement service-related medical certifications to merchant mariner credential requirements.

(d) ADVANCING MILITARY TO MARINER WITHIN THE EMPLOYER AGENCIES.—

(1) IN GENERAL.—The Secretary of Defense, the Secretary of the Department in which the Coast Guard is operating when

it is not operating as a service in the Department of the Navy, and the Secretary of Commerce shall have direct hiring authority to employ separated members of the uniformed services with valid merchant mariner licenses or sea service experience in support of United States national maritime needs, including the Army Corps of Engineers, U.S. Customs and Border Protection, and the National Oceanic and Atmospheric Administration.

(2) APPOINTMENTS OF RETIRED MEMBERS OF THE ARMED FORCES.—Except in the case of positions in the Senior Executive Service, the requirements of section 3326(b) of title 5, United States Code, shall not apply with respect to the hiring of a separated member of the uniformed services under paragraph (1).

(e) SEPARATED MEMBER OF THE UNIFORMED SERVICES.—In this section, the term "separated member of the uniformed services" means an individual who—

(1) is retiring or is retired as a member of the uniformed services;

(2) is voluntarily separating or voluntarily separated from the uniformed services at the end of enlistment or service obligation; or

(3) is administratively separating or has administratively separated from the uniformed services with an honorable or general discharge characterization.

SEC. 3512. DEPARTMENT OF TRANSPORTATION INSPECTOR GENERAL REPORT.

The Inspector General of the Department of Transportation shall—

(1) not later than 180 days after the date of enactment of this title, initiate an audit of the Maritime Administration's actions to address only those recommendations from Chapter 3 and recommendations 5-1, 5-2, 5-3, 5-4, 5-5, and 5-6 identified by a National Academy of Public Administration panel in the November 2017 report entitled "Maritime Administration: Defining its Mission, Aligning its Programs, and Meeting its Objectives"; and

(2) submit to the Committee on Commerce, Science, and

Transportation of the Senate and the Committee on Transportation and Infrastructure of the House of Representatives a report containing the results of that audit once the audit is completed.

SEC. 3513. INDEPENDENT STUDY ON THE UNITED STATES MERCHANT MARINE ACADEMY.

(a) IN GENERAL.—Not later than 180 days after the date of enactment of this title, the Secretary of Transportation shall seek to enter into an agreement with the National Academy of Public Administration (referred to in this section as the "Academy") to carry out the activities described in this section.

(b) STUDY ELEMENTS.—In accordance with the agreement described in subsection (a), the Academy shall conduct a study of the United States Merchant Marine Academy that consists of the following:

(1) A comprehensive assessment of the United States Merchant Marine Academy's systems, training, facilities, infrastructure, information technology, and stakeholder engagement.

(2) Identification of needs and opportunities for modernization to help the United States Merchant Marine Academy keep pace with more modern campuses.

(3) Development of an action plan for the United States Merchant Marine Academy with specific recommendations for—

(A) improvements or updates relating to the opportunities described in paragraph (2); and

(B) systemic changes needed to help the United States Merchant Marine Academy achieve its mission of inspiring and educating the next generation of the mariner workforce on a long-term basis.

(c) DEADLINE AND REPORT.—Not later than 1 year after the date of the agreement described in subsection (a), the Academy shall prepare and submit to the Administrator of the Maritime Administration a report containing the action plan described in subsection (b)(3), including specific findings and recommendations.

SEC. 3514. PORT OPERATIONS, RESEARCH, AND TECHNOLOGY.

(a) **[46 U.S.C. 101 note]** SHORT TITLE.—This section may be cited as the "Ports Improvement Act".

(b) PORT AND INTERMODAL IMPROVEMENT PROGRAM.—Section **50302** of title **46**, United States Code, is amended by striking subsection (c) and inserting the following:

"(c) PORT AND INTERMODAL IMPROVEMENT PROGRAM.—

"(1) GENERAL AUTHORITY.—Subject to the availability of appropriations, the Secretary of Transportation shall make grants, on a competitive basis, to eligible applicants to assist in funding eligible projects for the purpose of improving the safety, efficiency, or reliability of the movement of goods through ports and intermodal connections to ports.

"(2) ELIGIBLE APPLICANT.—The Secretary may make a grant under this subsection to the following:

"(A) A State.

"(B) A political subdivision of a State, or a local government.

"(C) A public agency or publicly chartered authority established by 1 or more States.

"(D) A special purpose district with a transportation function.

"(E) An Indian Tribe (as defined in section 4 of the Indian Self-Determination and Education Assistance Act (25 U.S.C. 5304), without regard to capitalization), or a consortium of Indian Tribes.

"(F) A multistate or multijurisdictional group of entities described in this paragraph.

"(G) A lead entity described in subparagraph (A), (B), (C), (D), (E), or (F) jointly with a private entity or group of private entities.

"(3) ELIGIBLE PROJECTS.—The Secretary may make a grant under this subsection—

"(A) for a project, or package of projects, that—

"(i) is either—

"(I) within the boundary of a port; or

"(II) outside the boundary of a port, but is directly related to port operations or to an intermodal connection to a port; and

"(ii) will be used to improve the safety, efficiency, or reliability of—

"(I) the loading and unloading of goods at the port, such as for marine terminal equipment;

"(II) the movement of goods into, out of, around, or within a port, such as for highway or rail infrastructure, intermodal facilities, freight intelligent transportation systems, and digital infrastructure systems; or

"(III) environmental mitigation measures and operational improvements directly related to enhancing the efficiency of ports and intermodal connections to ports; or

"(B) notwithstanding paragraph (6)(A)(v), to provide financial assistance to 1 or more projects under subparagraph (A) for development phase activities, including planning, feasibility analysis, revenue forecasting, environmental review, permitting, and preliminary engineering and design work.

"(4) PROHIBITED USES.—A grant award under this subsection may not be used—

"(A) to finance or refinance the construction, reconstruction, reconditioning, or purchase of a vessel that is eligible for such assistance under chapter 537, unless the Secretary determines such vessel—

"(i) is necessary for a project described in paragraph (3)(A)(ii)(III) of this subsection; and

"(ii) is not receiving assistance under chapter 537; or

"(B) for any project within a small shipyard (as defined in section 54101).

"(5) APPLICATIONS AND PROCESS.—

"(A) APPLICATIONS.—To be eligible for a grant under this subsection, an eligible applicant shall submit to the Secretary an application in such form, at such time, and containing such information as the Secretary considers appropriate.

"(B) SOLICITATION PROCESS.—Not later than 60 days after the date that amounts are made available for grants under this subsection for a fiscal year, the Secretary shall solicit grant applications for eligible projects in accordance with this subsection.

"(6) PROJECT SELECTION CRITERIA.—

"(A) IN GENERAL.—The Secretary may select a project described in paragraph (3) for funding under this subsection if the Secretary determines that—

"(i) the project improves the safety, efficiency, or reliability of the movement of goods through a port or intermodal connection to a port;

"(ii) the project is cost effective;

"(iii) the eligible applicant has authority to carry out the project;

"(iv) the eligible applicant has sufficient funding available to meet the matching requirements under paragraph (8);

"(v) the project will be completed without unreasonable delay; and

"(vi) the project cannot be easily and efficiently completed without Federal funding or financial assistance available to the project sponsor.

"(B) ADDITIONAL CONSIDERATIONS.—In selecting projects described in paragraph (3) for funding under this subsection, the Secretary shall give substantial weight to—

"(i) the utilization of non-Federal contributions; and

"(ii) the net benefits of the funds awarded under this subsection, considering the cost-benefit analysis of the project, as applicable.

"(C) SMALL PROJECTS.—The Secretary may waive the cost-benefit analysis under subparagraph (A)(ii), and establish a simplified, alternative basis for determining whether a project is cost effective, for a small project described in paragraph (7)(B).

"(7) ALLOCATION OF FUNDS.—

"(A) GEOGRAPHIC DISTRIBUTION.—Not more than 25

percent of the amounts made available for grants under this subsection for a fiscal year may be used to make grants for projects in any 1 State.

"(B) SMALL PROJECTS.—The Secretary shall reserve 25 percent of the amounts made available for grants under this subsection each fiscal year to make grants for eligible projects described in paragraph (3)(A) that request the lesser of—

"(i) 10 percent of the amounts made available for grants under this subsection for a fiscal year; or

"(ii) $10,000,000.

"(C) DEVELOPMENT PHASE ACTIVITIES.—Not more than 10 percent of the amounts made available for grants under this subsection for a fiscal year may be used to make grants for development phase activities under paragraph (3)(B).

"(8) FEDERAL SHARE OF TOTAL PROJECT COSTS.—

"(A) TOTAL PROJECT COSTS.—To be eligible for a grant under this subsection, an eligible applicant shall submit to the Secretary an estimate of the total costs of a project under this subsection based on the best available information, including any available engineering studies, studies of economic feasibility, environmental analyses, and information on the expected use of equipment or facilities.

"(B) FEDERAL SHARE.—

"(i) IN GENERAL.—Except as provided in clause (ii), the Federal share of the total costs of a project under this subsection shall not exceed 80 percent.

"(ii) RURAL AREAS.—The Secretary may increase the Federal share of costs above 80 percent for a project located in a rural area.

"(9) PROCEDURAL SAFEGUARDS.—The Secretary shall issue guidelines to establish appropriate accounting, reporting, and review procedures to ensure that—

"(A) grant funds are used for the purposes for which those funds were made available;

"(B) each grantee properly accounts for all expenditures of grant funds; and

"(C) grant funds not used for such purposes and amounts not obligated or expended are returned.

"(10) GRANT CONDITIONS.—

"(A) IN GENERAL.—The Secretary shall require as a condition of making a grant under this subsection that a grantee—

"(i) maintain such records as the Secretary considers necessary;

"(ii) make the records described in clause (i) available for review and audit by the Secretary; and

"(iii) periodically report to the Secretary such information as the Secretary considers necessary to assess progress.

"(B) ADDITIONAL REQUIREMENT.—The Secretary shall apply the same requirements of section 117(k) of title 23, United States Code, to a port project assisted in whole or in part under this section as the Secretary does a port-related freight project under section 117 of title 23, United States Code.

"(C) CONSTRUCTION, REPAIR, OR ALTERATION OF VESSELS.—With regard to the construction, repair, or alteration of vessels, the same requirements of section 117(k) of title 23, United States Code, shall apply regardless of whether the location of contract performance is known when bids for such work are solicited.

"(11) ADMINISTRATION.—

"(A) ADMINISTRATIVE AND OVERSIGHT COSTS.—The Secretary may retain not more than 2 percent of the amounts appropriated for each fiscal year under this subsection for the administrative and oversight costs incurred by the Secretary to carry out this subsection.

"(B) AVAILABILITY.—

"(i) IN GENERAL.—Amounts appropriated for carrying out this subsection shall remain available until expended.

"(ii) UNEXPENDED FUNDS.—Amounts awarded as a grant under this subsection that are not expended by the grantee during the 5-year period following the date of the award shall remain available to the Secretary for use for grants under this subsection in a subsequent fiscal year.

"(12) DEFINITIONS.—In this subsection:

"(A) APPROPRIATE COMMITTEES OF CONGRESS.—The term 'appropriate committees of Congress' means—

"(i) the Committee on Commerce, Science, and Transportation of the Senate; and

"(ii) the Committee on Transportation and Infrastructure of the House of Representatives.

"(B) PORT.—The term 'port' includes—

"(i) any port on the navigable waters of the United States; and

"(ii) any harbor, marine terminal, or other shore side facility used principally for the movement of goods on inland waters.

"(C) PROJECT.—The term 'project' includes construction, reconstruction, environmental rehabilitation, acquisition of property, including land related to the project and improvements to the land, equipment acquisition, and operational improvements.

"(D) RURAL AREA.—The term 'rural area' means an area that is outside an urbanized area.

"(d) ADDITIONAL AUTHORITY OF THE SECRETARY.—In carrying out this section, the Secretary may—

"(1) coordinate with other Federal agencies to expedite the process established under the National Environmental Policy Act of 1969 (42 U.S.C. 4321 et seq.) for the improvement of port facilities to improve the efficiency of the transportation system, to increase port security, or to provide greater access to port facilities;

"(2) seek to coordinate all reviews or requirements with appropriate Federal, State, and local agencies; and

"(3) in addition to any financial assistance provided under subsection (c), provide such technical assistance to port authorities or commissions or their subdivisions and agents."

(c) **[46 U.S.C. 50302 note]** SAVINGS CLAUSE.—A repeal made by subsection (b) of this section shall not affect amounts apportioned or allocated before the effective date of the repeal. Such apportioned or allocated funds shall continue to be subject to the requirements to which the funds were subject under—

(1) section 50302(c) of title 46, United States Code, as in effect on the day before the date of enactment of this title;

(2) section 9008 of the SAFETEA-LU Act (Public Law 109-59; 119 Stat. 1926);

(3) section 10205 of the SAFETEA-LU Act (Public Law 109-59; 119 Stat. 1934); and

(4) section 3512 of the Duncan Hunter National Defense Authorization Act for Fiscal Year 2009 (48 U.S.C. 1421r).

(d) REMEDIAL ACTIONS.—Section 533 of the Coast Guard Authorization Act of 2016 (Public Law 114-120; 130 Stat. 74) is amended by adding at the end the following:

"(f) REMEDIAL ACTIONS.—For purposes of the conveyances under this section, the remedial actions required under section 120(h) of the Comprehensive Environmental Response, Compensation, and Liability Act of 1980 (42 U.S.C. 9620(h)) may be completed by the United States Coast Guard after the date of such conveyance and a deed entered into for such conveyance shall include a clause granting the United States Coast Guard access to the property in any case in which remedial action or corrective action is found to be necessary after the date of such conveyance."

(e) ENVIRONMENTAL COMPLIANCE.—Section 534(a) of the Coast Guard Authorization Act of 2016 (Public Law 114-120; 42 U.S.C. 9620 note) is amended—

(1) by striking "Nothing" and inserting "After the date on which the Secretary of the Interior conveys land under section 533 of this Act, nothing"; and

(2) by inserting ", with respect to contaminants on such land prior to the date on which the land is conveyed" before the period.

SEC. 3515. ASSESSMENT AND REPORT ON STRATEGIC SEAPORTS.

(a) IN GENERAL.—Not later than 90 days after the date of the enactment of this title, the Secretary of Defense shall submit to the Committee on Armed Services and the Committee on Transportation and Infrastructure of the House of Representatives and the Committee on Armed Services and the Committee on

Commerce, Science, and Transportation of the Senate a report on port facilities used for military purposes at ports designated by the Department of Defense as strategic seaports.

(b) ELEMENTS.—The report required by subsection (a) shall include, with respect to port facilities included in the report, the following:

(1) An assessment of whether there are structural integrity or other deficiencies in such facilities.

(2) If there are such deficiencies—

(A) an assessment of infrastructure improvements to such facilities that would be needed to meet, directly or indirectly, national security and readiness requirements;

(B) an assessment of the impact on operational readiness of the Armed Forces if such improvements are not undertaken; and

(C) an identification of, to the maximum extent practical, all potential funding sources for such improvements from existing authorities.

(3) An identification of the support that would be appropriate for the Department of Defense to provide in the execution of the responsibilities of the Secretary of Transportation under section 50302 of title 46, United States Code, with respect to such facilities.

(4) If additional statutory or administrative authorities would be required for the provision of support as described in paragraph (3), recommendations for legislative or administrative action to establish such authorities.

(c) CONSULTATION.—The Secretary of Defense shall prepare the report required by subsection (a) in consultation with the Maritime Administrator and the individual responsible for each port facility described in such subsection.

SEC. 3516. TECHNICAL CORRECTIONS.

(a) OFFICE OF PERSONNEL MANAGEMENT GUIDANCE.—Not later than 120 days after the date of the enactment of this title, the Director of the Office of Personnel Management, in consultation with the Administrator of the Maritime Administration, shall identify key skills and competencies necessary to maintain a balance of expertise in merchant marine seagoing service and strategic sealift military service in each of the following positions within the Office of the Commandant of the Merchant Marine Academy:

(1) Commandant.

(2) Deputy Commandant.

(3) Tactical company officers.

(4) Regimental officers.

(b) SEA YEAR COMPLIANCE.—Section 3514(a)(1)(A) of the National Defense Authorization Act for Fiscal Year 2017 (Public Law 114-328; 46 U.S.C. 51318 note) is amended by inserting “domestic and international” after “criteria that”.

SEC. 3517. [46 U.S.C. 51318 note] UNITED STATES MERCHANT MARINE ACADEMY SEXUAL ASSAULT PREVENTION AND RESPONSE PROGRAM.

(a) IMPLEMENTATION OF RECOMMENDATIONS.—The Secretary of Transportation shall ensure that, not later than 180 days after the date of the enactment of this title, the recommendations in report of the Inspector General of the Department of Transportation on the effectiveness sexual assault prevention and response program of the United States Merchant Marine Academy (mandated under section 3512 of the National Defense Authorization Act for Fiscal Year 2017 (Public Law 114-328; 130 Stat. 2786)), are fully implemented.

(b) REPORT.—Not later than 180 days after the date of the enactment of this title, the Secretary of Transportation shall submit to Congress a report that includes—

(1) confirmation that the recommendations described in subsection (a) have been fully implemented, and explaining how those recommendations have been implemented; or

(2) if such recommendations have not been fully implemented as of the date of the report, an explanation of why such recommendations have not been fully implemented and a description of the resources that are needed to fully implement such recommendations.

SEC. 3518. REPORT ON VESSELS FOR EMERGING OFFSHORE ENERGY INFRASTRUCTURE.

(a) IN GENERAL.—Not later than six months after the date of the enactment of this Act, the Comptroller General of the United

States shall submit to the Committee on Commerce, Science, and Transportation of the Senate, the Committee on Energy and Natural Resources of the Senate, and the Committee on Transportation and Infrastructure of the House of Representatives a report on the need for vessels documented under chapter 121 of title 46, United States Code, to install, operate, and maintain emerging offshore energy infrastructure, including offshore wind energy.

(b) CONTENTS.—The report required by subsection (a) shall include—

(1) an inventory of vessels documented under chapter 121 of title 46, United States Code, (including existing vessels and vessels that have the potential to be refurbished) to install, operate, and maintain such emerging offshore energy infrastructure;

(2) a projection of existing vessels needed to meet such emerging offshore energy needs over the next 10 years;

(3) a summary of actions taken or proposed by offshore energy developers and producers, the United States domestic shipbuilding industry, and United States coastwise qualified operators to ensure sufficient vessel capacity in compliance with United States coastwise laws; and

(4) a description of the potential benefits to the United States maritime and shipbuilding industries and to the United States economy associated with the use of United States coastwise qualified vessels to support offshore energy development and production.

SEC. 3519. REPORT ON UNITED STATES FLAGGED FUEL TANKER VESSEL CAPACITY.

(a) REPORT REQUIRED.—Concurrent with the budget of the President for fiscal year 2021, as submitted to Congress under section 1105 of title 31, United States Code, the Secretary of Defense shall, in consultation with the Secretary of Transportation, submit to the appropriate committees of Congress a report on the capabilities of the United States to maintain adequate United States-flagged fuel tanker vessel capacity to support the full range of anticipated military operations over each period as follows:

(1) In 2020.

(2) Between 2020 and 2025.

(3) Between 2020 and 2030.

(b) ELEMENTS.—The report required by subsection (a) shall include, for each period specified in that subsection, the following:

(1) A description of current and projected United States-flagged fuel tanker vessel capacity.

(2) A description of current and projected United States military needs for United States-flagged fuel tanker vessel capacity, including the most stressing peacetime and wartime requirements.

(3) A description and assessment of the number of foreign-flagged tanker vessels required to address United States military needs described pursuant to paragraph (2), including the most stressing peacetime and wartime requirements.

(4) An identification and assessment of any gaps in the capacity described pursuant to paragraph (1) to meet the United States military needs described pursuant to paragraph (2), including quantities of tanker vessels, as well as an assessment of the risk to military objectives due to reliance on foreign-flagged tanker vessels described pursuant to paragraph (3).

(5) A description and assessment of options to address the gaps identified pursuant to paragraph (4), including the establishment of a program for United States-flagged fuel tanker vessels modeled on the Maritime Security Program.

(6) Such recommendations as the Secretary of Defense considers appropriate in light of the matters set forth in the report.

(c) FORM.—The report required by subsection (a) shall be submitted in unclassified form, but may include a classified annex.

(d) DEFINITIONS.—In this section:

(1) The term "appropriate committees of Congress" means—

(A) the Committee on Commerce, Science, and Transportation and the Committee on Armed Services of the Senate; and

(B) the Committee on Transportation and Infrastructure and the Committee on Armed Services of the House of Representatives.

(2) The term "Maritime Security Program" means the program in connection with the Maritime Security Fleet under chapter 531 of title 46, United States Code.

Subtitle B—Cable Security Fleet

SEC. 3521. ESTABLISHMENT OF CABLE SECURITY FLEET.

(a) IN GENERAL.—Title 46, United States Code, is amended by inserting before chapter 533 the following new chapter:

"CHAPTER 532—CABLE SECURITY FLEET

"SEC. 53201. [46 U.S.C. 53201] Definitions

In this chapter:

"(1) CABLE SERVICES.—The term "'cable services"' means the installation, maintenance, or repair of submarine cables and related equipment, and related cable vessel operations.

"(2) CABLE VESSEL.—The term "'cable vessel"' means a vessel—

"(A) classed as a cable ship or cable vessel by, and designed in accordance with the rules of, the American Bureau of Shipping, or another classification society accepted by the Secretary; and

"(B) capable of installing, maintaining, and repairing submarine cables.

"(3) CABLE FLEET.—The term "'Cable Fleet"' means the Cable Security Fleet established under section 53202(a).

"(4) CONTINGENCY AGREEMENT.—The term "'Contingency Agreement'" means the agreement required by section 53207.

"(5) CONTRACTOR.—The term "'Contractor'" means an owner or operator of a vessel that enters into an Operating Agreement for a cable vessel with the Secretary under section 53203.

"(6) FISCAL YEAR.—The term "'fiscal year'" means any annual period beginning on October 1 and ending on September 30.

"(7) OPERATING AGENCY.—The term "'Operating Agency'" means that agency or component of the Department of Defense so designated by the Secretary of Defense under this chapter.

"(8) OPERATING AGREEMENT OR AGREEMENT.—The terms 'Operating Agreement' or 'Agreement' mean the agreement required by section 53203.

"(9) PERSON.—The term "'person'" includes corporations, partnerships, and associations existing under or authorized by the laws of the United States, or any State, Territory, District, or possession thereof, or of any foreign country.

"(10) SECRETARY.—The term "'Secretary'" means the Secretary of Transportation.

"(11) UNITED STATES.—The term "'United States'" includes the States, the District of Columbia, the Commonwealth of Puerto Rico, the Northern Mariana Islands, Guam, American Samoa, and the Virgin Islands.

"(12) UNITED STATES CITIZEN TRUST.—

"(A) Subject to paragraph (C), the term "'United States citizen trust'" means a trust that is qualified under this paragraph.

"(B) A trust is qualified under this paragraph with respect to a vessel only if—

"(i) it was created under the laws of a state of the United States;

"(ii) each of the trustees is a citizen of the United States; and

"(iii) the application for documentation of the vessel under chapter 121 of this title includes the affidavit of each trustee stating that the trustee is not aware of any reason involving a beneficiary of the trust that is not a citizen of the United States, or involving any other person that is not a citizen of the United States, as a result of which the beneficiary or other person would hold more than 25 percent of the aggregate power to influence, or limit the exercise of the authority of, the trustee with respect to matters involving any ownership or operation of the vessel that may adversely affect the interests of the United States.

"(C) If any person that is not a citizen of the United States has authority to direct, or participate in directing, the trustee for a trust in matters involving any ownership or operation of the vessel that may adversely affect the interests of the United States or in removing a trustee for a trust without cause, either directly or indirectly through the control of another person, the trust is not qualified under this paragraph unless the trust instrument provides that persons who are not citizens of the United States may not hold more than 25 percent of the aggregate authority to direct or remove a trustee.

"(D) This paragraph shall not be considered to prohibit a person who is not a citizen of the United States from holding more than 25 percent of the beneficial interest in a trust.

"SEC. 53202. [46 U.S.C. 53202] Establishment of the Cable Security Fleet

"(a) IN GENERAL.—(1) The Secretary, in consultation with the Operating Agency, shall establish a fleet of active, commercially viable, cable vessels to meet national security requirements. The fleet shall consist of privately owned, United States-documented cable vessels for which there are in effect Operating Agreements under this chapter, and shall be known as the Cable Security Fleet.

"(2) The Fleet described under this section shall include two vessels.

"(b) VESSEL ELIGIBILITY.—A cable vessel is eligible to be included in the Fleet if—

"(1) the vessel meets the requirements of paragraph (1), (2), (3), or (4) of subsection (c);

"(2) the vessel is operated (or in the case of a vessel to be constructed, will be operated) in commercial service providing cable services;

"(3) the vessel is 40 years of age or less on the date the vessel is included in the Fleet;

"(4) the vessel is—

"(A) determined by the Operating Agency to be suitable for engaging in cable services by the United States in the interest of national security; and

"(B) determined by the Secretary to be commercially viable, whether independently or taking any payments which are the consequence of participation in the Cable Fleet into account; and

"(5) the vessel—

"(A) is a United States-documented vessel; or

"(B) is not a United States-documented vessel, but—

"(i) the owner of the vessel has demonstrated an intent to have the vessel documented under chapter 121 of this title if it is included in the Cable Fleet; and

"(ii) at the time an Operating Agreement is entered into under this chapter, the vessel is eligible for documentation under chapter 121 of this title.

"(c) REQUIREMENTS REGARDING CITIZENSHIP OF OWNERS AND OPERATORS.—

"(1) VESSELS OWNED AND OPERATED BY SECTION 50501 CITIZENS.—A vessel meets the requirements of this paragraph if, during the period of an Operating Agreement under this chapter that applies to the vessel, the vessel will be owned and operated by one or more persons that are citizens of the United states under section 50501 of this title.

"(2) VESSELS OWNED BY A SECTION 50501 CITIZEN, OR UNITED STATES CITIZEN TRUST, AND CHARTERED TO A DOCUMENTATION CITIZEN.—A vessel meets the requirements of this paragraph if—

"(A) during the period of an Operating Agreement under this chapter that applies to the vessel, the vessel will be—

"(i) owned by a person that is a citizen of the

United States under section 50501 of this title or that is a United States citizen trust; and

"(ii) demise chartered to and operated by a person—

"(I) that is eligible to document the vessel under chapter 121 of this title;

"(II) the chairman of the board of directors, chief executive officer, and a majority of the members of the board of directors of which are citizens of the United States under section 50501 of this title, and are appointed and subject to removal only upon approval by the Secretary; and

"(III) that certifies to the Secretary that there are no treaties, statutes, regulations, or other laws that would prohibit the Contractor for the vessel from performing its obligations under an Operating Agreement under this chapter;

"(B) in the case of a vessel that will be demise chartered to a person that is owned or controlled by another person that is not a citizen of the United States under section 50501 of this title, the other person enters into an agreement with the Secretary not to influence the operation of the vessel in a manner that will adversely affect the interests of the United States; and

"(C) the Secretary and the Operating Agency notify the Committee on Armed Services and the Committee on Commerce, Science and Transportation of the Senate, and the Committee on Armed Services of the House of Representatives that they concur, and have reviewed the certification required under subparagraph (A)(ii)(III) and determined that there are no legal, operational, or other impediments that would prohibit the Contractor for the vessel from performing its obligations under an Operating Agreement under this chapter.

"(3) VESSEL OWNED AND OPERATED BY A DEFENSE CONTRACTOR.—A vessel meets the requirements of this paragraph if—

"(A) during the period of an Operating Agreement under this chapter that applies to the vessel, the vessel will be owned and operated by a person that—

"(i) is eligible to document a vessel under chapter 121 of this title;

"(ii) operates or manages other United States-documented vessels for the Secretary of Defense, or charters other vessels to the Secretary of Defense;

"(iii) has entered into a special security agreement for purposes of this paragraph with the Secretary of Defense;

"(iv) makes the certification described in paragraph (2)(A)(ii)(III); and

"(v) in the case of a vessel described in paragraph (2)(B), enters into an agreement referred to in that paragraph; and

"(B) the Secretary and the Secretary of Defense notify the Committee on Armed Services and Committee on Commerce, Science, and Transportation of the Senate and the Committee on Armed Services of the House of Representatives that they have reviewed the certification required by subparagraph (A)(iv) and determined that there are no other legal, operational, or other impediments that would prohibit the Contractor for the vessel from performing its obligations under an Operating Agreement under this chapter.

"(4) VESSEL OWNED BY A DOCUMENTATION CITIZEN AND CHARTERED TO A SECTION 50501 CITIZEN.—A vessel meets the requirements of this paragraph if, during the period of an Operating Agreement under this chapter that applies to the vessel, the vessel will be—

"(A) owned by a person that is eligible to document a vessel under chapter 121 of this title; and

"(B) demise chartered to a person that is a citizen of the United States under section 50501 of this title.

"(d) VESSEL STANDARDS.—

"(1) CERTIFICATE OF INSPECTION.—A cable vessel which the Secretary of the Department in which the Coast Guard is operating determines meets the criteria of subsection (b) of this section but which, on the date of enactment of the Act, is not documented under chapter 121 of this title, shall be eligible for a certificate of inspection if that Secretary determines that—

"(A) the vessel is classed by, and designed in accordance with the rules of, the American Bureau of Shipping, or another classification society accepted by that Secretary;

"(B) the vessel complies with applicable international agreements and associated guidelines, as determined by the country in which the vessel was documented immediately before becoming documented under chapter 121; and

"(C) that country has not been identified by that Secretary as inadequately enforcing international vessel regulations as to that vessel.

"(2) CONTINUED ELIGIBILITY FOR CERTIFICATE.—Paragraph (1) does not apply to a vessel after any date on which the vessel fails to comply with the applicable international agreements and associated guidelines referred to in paragraph (1)(B).

"(3) RELIANCE ON CLASSIFICATION SOCIETY.—

"(A) IN GENERAL.—The Secretary of the Department in which the Coast Guard is operating may rely on a certification from the American Bureau of Shipping or, subject to subparagraph (B), another classification society accepted by that Secretary to establish that a vessel is in compliance with the requirements of paragraphs (1) and (2).

"(B) FOREIGN CLASSIFICATION SOCIETY.—The Secretary of the Department in which the Coast Guard is operating may accept certification from a foreign classification society under subparagraph (A) only—

"(i) to the extent that the government of the foreign country in which the society is headquartered provides access on a reciprocal basis to the American Bureau of Shipping; and

"(ii) if the foreign classification society has offices and maintains records in the United States.

"(e) WAIVER OF AGE REGISTRATION.—The Secretary, in conjunction with the Operating Agency, may waive the application of the age restriction under subsection (b)(3) if they jointly determine that the waiver—

"(1) is in the national interest;

"(2) the subject cable vessel and any associated operating network is and will continue to be economically viable; and

"(3) is necessary due to the lack of availability of other vessels and operators that comply with the requirements of this chapter.

"SEC. 53203. [46 U.S.C. 53203] Award of operating agreements

"(a) IN GENERAL.—The Secretary shall require, as a condition of including any vessel in the Cable Fleet, that the person that is the owner or operator of the vessel for purposes of section 53202(c) enter into an Operating Agreement with the Secretary under this section.

"(b) PROCEDURE FOR APPLICATIONS.—

"(1) ACCEPTANCE OF APPLICATIONS.—Beginning no later than 60 days after the effective date of this chapter, the Secretary shall accept applications for enrollment of vessels in the Cable Fleet.

"(2) ACTION ON APPLICATIONS.—Within 120 days after receipt of an application for enrollment of a vessel in the Cable Fleet, the Secretary shall approve the application in conjunction with the Operating Agency, and shall enter into an Operating Agreement with the applicant, or provide in writing the reason for denial of that application.

"(c) PRIORITY FOR AWARDING AGREEMENTS.—Subject to the availability of appropriations, the Secretary shall enter into Operating Agreements with those vessels determined by the Operating Agency, in its sole discretion, to best meet the national security requirements of the United States. After consideration of national security requirements, priority shall be given to an applicant that is a United States citizen under section 50501 of this title.

"SEC. 53204. [46 U.S.C. 53204] Effectiveness of operating agreements

"(a) EFFECTIVENESS GENERALLY.—The Secretary may enter into an Operating Agreement under this chapter for fiscal year 2021. Except as provided in subsection (d), the agreement shall be effective only for one fiscal year, but shall be renewable, subject to available appropriations, for each subsequent year.

"(b) VESSELS UNDER CHARTER TO THE UNITED STATES.—Vessels under charter to the United States are eligible to receive payments pursuant to their Operating Agreements.

"(c) TERMINATION.—

"(1) TERMINATION BY THE SECRETARY.—If the Contractor with respect to an Operating Agreement materially fails to comply with the terms of the Agreement—

"(A) the Secretary shall notify the Contractor and provide a reasonable opportunity for it to comply with the Operating Agreement;

"(B) the Secretary shall terminate the Operating Agreement if the Contractor fails to achieve such compliance; and

"(C) upon such termination, any funds obligated by the Agreement shall be available to the Secretary to carry out this chapter.

"(2) EARLY TERMINATION BY A CONTRACTOR.—An Operating Agreement under this chapter shall terminate on a date specified by the Contractor if the Contractor notifies the Secretary, not fewer than 60 days prior to the effective date of the termination, that the Contractor intends to terminate the Agreement.

"(d) NONRENEWAL FOR LACK OF FUNDS.—If, by the first day of a fiscal year, sufficient funds have not been appropriated under the authority provided by this chapter for that fiscal year for all Operating Agreements, then the Secretary shall notify the Committee on Armed Services and the Committee on Commerce, Science, and Transportation of the Senate and the Committee on Armed Services of the House of Representatives that Operating Agreements authorized under this chapter for which sufficient funds are not available will not be renewed for that fiscal year if sufficient funds are not appropriated by the 60th day of that fiscal year. If only partial funding is appropriated by the 60th day of such fiscal year, then the Secretary, in consultation with the Operating Agency, shall select the vessels to retain under Operating Agreements, based on their determinations of which vessels are most useful for national security. In the event that no funds are appropriated, then no Operating Agreements shall be renewed and each Contractor shall be released from its obligations under the

Operating Agreement. Final payments under an Operating Agreement that is not renewed shall be made in accordance with section 53206. To the extent that sufficient funds are appropriated in a subsequent fiscal year, an Operating Agreement that has not been renewed pursuant to this subsection may be reinstated if mutually acceptable to the Secretary, in consultation with the Operating Agency, and the Contractor, provided the vessel remains eligible for participation pursuant to section 53202, without regard to subsection 53202 (b)(3).

"(e) RELEASE OF VESSELS FROM OBLIGATIONS.—If funds are not appropriated for payments under an Operating Agreement under this chapter for any fiscal year by the 60th day of a fiscal year, and the Secretary, in consultation with the Operating Agency determines to not renew a Contractor's Operating Agreement for a vessel, then—

"(1) each vessel covered by the Operating Agreement that is not renewed is thereby released from any further obligation under the Operating Agreement;

"(2) the owner or operator of the vessel whose Operating Agreement was not renewed may transfer and register such vessel under a foreign registry that is acceptable to the Secretary and the Operating Agency, notwithstanding section 56101 of this title; and

"(3) if chapter 563 of this title is applicable to such vessel after registration, then the vessel is available to be requisitioned by the Secretary pursuant to chapter 563.

"SEC. 53205. [46 U.S.C. 53205] Obligations and rights under operating agreements

"(a) OPERATION OF VESSEL.—An Operating Agreement under this chapter shall require that, during the period the vessel is operating under the Agreement, the vessel—

"(1) shall be operated in the trade for Cable Services, or under a charter to the United States; and

"(2) shall be documented under chapter 121 of this title.

"(b) ANNUAL PAYMENTS BY THE SECRETARY.—

"(1) IN GENERAL.—An Operating Agreement under this chapter shall require, subject to the availability of appropriations, that the Secretary make payment to the

Contractor in accordance with section 53206.

"(2) OPERATING AGREEMENT IS AN OBLIGATION OF THE UNITED STATES GOVERNMENT.—An Operating Agreement under this chapter constitutes a contractual obligation of the United States Government to pay the amounts provided for in the Operating Agreement to the extent of actual appropriations.

"(c) DOCUMENTATION REQUIREMENT.—Each vessel covered by an Operating Agreement (including an Agreement terminated under section 53204(c)(2)) shall remain documented under chapter 121 of this title, until the date the Operating Agreement would terminate according to its own terms.

"(d) NATIONAL SECURITY REQUIREMENTS.—

"(1) IN GENERAL.—A Contractor with respect to an Operating Agreement (including an Agreement terminated under section 53204(c)(2)) shall continue to be bound by the provisions of section 53207 until the date the Operating Agreement would terminate according to its terms.

"(2) CONTINGENCY AGREEMENT WITH OPERATING AGENCY.—All terms and conditions of a Contingency Agreement entered into under section 53207 shall remain in effect until a date the Operating Agreement would terminate according to its terms, except that the terms of such Contingency Agreement may be modified by the mutual consent of the Contractor, and the Operating Agency.

"(e) TRANSFER OF OPERATING AGREEMENTS.—Operating Agreements shall not be transferrable by the Contractor.

"(f) REPLACEMENT VESSEL.—A Contractor may replace a vessel under an Operating Agreement with another vessel that is eligible to be included in the Fleet under section 53202(b), if the Secretary and the Operating Agency jointly determine that the replacement vessel meets national security requirements and approve the replacement.

"SEC. 53206. [46 U.S.C. 53206] Payment

"(a) ANNUAL PAYMENT.—

"(1) IN GENERAL.—The Secretary, subject to availability of appropriations and other provisions of this section, shall pay to the Contractor for an operating agreement, for each vessel that is covered by the operating agreement, an amount equal to

$5,000,000 for each fiscal year 2021 through 2035.

"(2) TIMING.—This amount shall be paid in equal monthly installments at the end of each month. The amount shall not be reduced except as provided by this section.

"(b) CERTIFICATION REQUIRED FOR PAYMENT.—As a condition of receiving payment under this section for a fiscal year for a vessel, the Contractor for the vessel shall certify that the vessel has been and will be operated in accordance with section 53205(a)(1) for 365 days in each fiscal year. Up to thirty (30) days during which the vessel is drydocked, surveyed, inspected, or repaired shall be considered days of operation for purposes of this subsection.

"(c) GENERAL LIMITATIONS.—The Secretary shall not make any payment under this chapter for a vessel with respect to any days for which the vessel is—

"(1) not operated or maintained in accordance with an Operating Agreement under this chapter; or

"(2) more than 40 years of age.

"(d) REDUCTIONS IN PAYMENTS.—With respect to payments under this chapter for a vessel covered by an Operating Agreement, the Secretary shall make a pro rata reduction for each day less than 365 in a fiscal year that the vessel is not operated in accordance with section 53205(a)(1), with days during which the vessel is drydocked or undergoing survey, inspection or repair to be considered days on which the vessel is operated as provided in subsection (b).

"SEC. 53207. [46 U.S.C. 53207] National security requirements

"(a) CONTINGENCY AGREEMENT REQUIRED.—The Secretary shall include in each Operating Agreement under this chapter a requirement that the Contractor enter into a Contingency Agreement with the Operating Agency. The Operating Agency shall negotiate and enter into a Contingency Agreement with each Contractor as promptly as practicable after the Contractor has entered into an Operating Agreement under this chapter.

"(b) TERMS OF CONTINGENCY AGREEMENT.—

"(1) IN GENERAL.—A Contingency Agreement under this section shall require that a Contractor for a vessel covered by an Operating Agreement under this chapter make the vessel, including all necessary resources to engage in Cable Services required by the Operating Agency, available upon request by the Operating Agency.

"(2) TERMS.—

"(A) IN GENERAL.—The basic terms of a Contingency Agreement shall be established (subject to subparagraph (B)) by the Operating Agency.

"(B) ADDITIONAL TERMS.—The Operating Agency and a Contractor may agree to additional or modifying terms appropriate to the Contractor's circumstances.

"(c) DEFENSE MEASURES AGAINST UNAUTHORIZED SEIZURES.—(1) The Contingency Agreement shall require that any vessel operating under the direction of the Operating Agency operating in area that is designated by the Coast Guard as an area of high risk of piracy shall be equipped with, at a minimum, appropriate non-lethal defense measures to protect the vessel and crew from unauthorized seizure at sea.

"(2) The Secretary of Defense and the Secretary of the department in which the Coast Guard is operating shall jointly prescribe the non-lethal defense measures that are required under this paragraph.

"(d) PARTICIPATION AFTER EXPIRATION OF OPERATING AGREEMENT.—Except as provided by section 53205(d), the Operating Agency may not require, through a Contingency Agreement or an Operating Agreement, that a Contractor continue to participate in a Contingency Agreement after the Operating Agreement with the Contractor has expired according to its terms or is otherwise no longer in effect.

"(e) RESOURCES MADE AVAILABLE.—The resources to be made available in addition to the vessel under a Contingency Agreement shall include all equipment, personnel, supplies, management services, and other related services as the Operating Agency may determine to be necessary to provide the Cable Services required by the Operating Agency.

"(f) COMPENSATION.—

"(1) IN GENERAL.—The Operating Agency shall include in each Contingency Agreement provisions under which the Operating Agency shall pay fair and reasonable compensation for use of the vessel and all Cable Services provided pursuant to this section and the Contingency Agreement.

"(2) SPECIFIC REQUIREMENTS.—Compensation under this subsection—

"(A) shall be at the rate specified in the Contingency Agreement;

"(B) shall be provided from the time that a vessel is required by the Operating Agency under the Contingency Agreement until the time it is made available by the Operating Agency available to reenter commercial service; and

"(C) shall be in addition to and shall not in any way reflect amounts payable under section 53206.

"(g) LIABILITY OF THE UNITED STATES FOR DAMAGES.—

"(1) LIMITATION ON THE LIABILITY OF THE U.S.—Except as otherwise provided by law, the Government shall not be liable for disruption of a Contractor's commercial business or other consequential damages to a Contractor arising from the activation of the Contingency Agreement.

"(2) AFFIRMATIVE DEFENSE.—In any action in any Federal or State court for breach of third-party contract, there shall be available as an affirmative defense that the alleged breach of contract was caused predominantly by action taken to carry out a Contingent Agreement. Such defense shall not release the party asserting it from any obligation under applicable law to mitigate damages to the greatest extent possible.

"SEC. 53208. [46 U.S.C. 53208] Regulatory relief

The telecommunications and other electronic equipment on an existing vessel that is redocumented under the laws of the United States for operation under an Operating Agreement under this chapter shall be deemed to satisfy all Federal Communication Commission equipment certification requirements, if—

"(1) such equipment complies with all applicable international agreements and associated guidelines as determined by the country in which the vessel was documented immediately before becoming documented under the laws of the United States;

"(2) that country has not been identified by the Secretary of the Department in which the Coast Guard is operating as inadequately enforcing international regulations as to that vessel; and

"(3) at the end of its useful life, such equipment shall be replaced with equipment that meets Federal Communication Commission equipment certification standards.

"SEC. 53209. [46 U.S.C. 53209] Authorization of appropriations

There are authorized to be appropriated for payments under section 53206, $10,000,000 for each of the fiscal years 2021 through 2035."

(b) [46 U.S.C. 50101] CONFORMING AMENDMENT.—The table of chapters at the beginning of subtitle V of title 46, United States Code, is amended by inserting before the item relating to chapter 533 the following new item:

"532. Cable Security Fleet"

Subtitle C—Maritime SAFE Act

SEC. 3531. [16 U.S.C. 8001 note] SHORT TITLES.

This subtitle may be cited as the "Maritime Security and Fisheries Enforcement Act" or the "Maritime SAFE Act".

SEC. 3532. [16 U.S.C. 8001] DEFINITIONS.

In this subtitle:

(1) AIS.—The term "AIS" means Automatic Identification System (as defined in section 164.46 of title 33, Code of Federal Regulations, or a similar successor regulation).

(2) COMBINED MARITIME FORCES.—The term "Combined Maritime Forces" means the 33-nation naval partnership, originally established in February 2002, which promotes security, stability, and prosperity across approximately 3,200,000 square miles of international waters.

(3) EXCLUSIVE ECONOMIC ZONE.—

(A) IN GENERAL.—Unless otherwise specified by the President as being in the public interest in a writing published in the Federal Register, the term "exclusive economic zone" means—

(i) the area within a zone established by a maritime boundary that has been established by a treaty in force or a treaty that is being provisionally applied by the United States; or

(ii) in the absence of a treaty described in clause (i)—

(I) a zone, the outer boundary of which is 200 nautical miles from the baseline from which the breadth of the territorial sea is measured; or

(II) if the distance between the United States and another country is less than 400 nautical miles, a zone, the outer boundary of which is represented by a line equidistant between the United States and the other country.

(B) INNER BOUNDARY.—Without affecting any Presidential Proclamation with regard to the establishment of the United States territorial sea or exclusive economic zone, the inner boundary of the exclusive economic zone is—

(i) in the case of coastal States, a line coterminous with the seaward boundary of each such State (as described in section 4 of the Submerged Lands Act (43 U.S.C. 1312));

(ii) in the case of the Commonwealth of Puerto Rico, a line that is 3 marine leagues from the coastline of the Commonwealth of Puerto Rico;

(iii) in the case of American Samoa, the United States Virgin Islands, Guam, and the Northern Mariana Islands, a line that is 3 geographic miles from the coastlines of American Samoa, the United States Virgin Islands, Guam, or the Northern Mariana Islands, respectively; or

(iv) for any possession of the United States not referred to in clause (ii) or (iii), the coastline of such possession.

(C) RULE OF CONSTRUCTION.—Nothing in this paragraph may be construed to diminish the authority of the Department of Defense, the Department of the Interior, or any other Federal department or agency.

(4) FOOD SECURITY.—The term "food security" means access to, and availability, utilization, and stability of, sufficient food to meet caloric and nutritional needs for an

active and healthy life.

(5) GLOBAL RECORD OF FISHING VESSELS, REFRIGERATED TRANSPORT VESSELS, AND SUPPLY VESSELS.—The term "global record of fishing vessels, refrigerated transport vessels, and supply vessels" means the Food and Agriculture Organization of the United Nations' initiative to rapidly make available certified data from state authorities about vessels and vessel related activities.

(6) IUU FISHING.—The term "IUU fishing" means illegal fishing, unreported fishing, or unregulated fishing (as such terms are defined in paragraph 3 of the International Plan of Action to Prevent, Deter, and Eliminate Illegal, Unreported and Unregulated Fishing, adopted at the 24th Session of the Committee on Fisheries in Rome on March 2, 2001).

(7) PORT STATE MEASURES AGREEMENT.—The term "Port State Measures Agreement" means the Agreement on Port State Measures to Prevent, Deter, and Eliminate Illegal, Unreported, and Unregulated Fishing set forth by the Food and Agriculture Organization of the United Nations, done at Rome, Italy November 22, 2009, and entered into force June 5, 2016, which offers standards for reporting and inspecting fishing activities of foreign-flagged fishing vessels at port.

(8) PRIORITY FLAG STATE.—The term "priority flag state" means a country selected in accordance with section 3552 (b)(3)—

(A) whereby the flagged vessels of which actively engage in, knowingly profit from, or are complicit in IUU fishing; and

(B) that is willing, but lacks the capacity, to monitor or take effective enforcement action against its fleet.

(9) PRIORITY REGION.—The term "priority region" means a region selected in accordance with section 3552 (b)(2)—

(A) that is at high risk for IUU fishing activity or the entry of illegally caught seafood into the markets of countries in the region; and

(B) in which countries lack the capacity to fully address the illegal activity described in subparagraph (A).

(10) REGIONAL FISHERIES MANAGEMENT ORGANIZATION.—The term "Regional Fisheries Management

Organization" means an intergovernmental fisheries organization or arrangement, as appropriate, that has the competence to establish conservation and management measures.

(11) SEAFOOD.—The term "seafood"—

(A) means marine finfish, mollusks, crustaceans, and all other forms of marine animal and plant life, including those grown, produced, or reared through marine aquaculture operations or techniques; and

(B) does not include marine mammals, turtles, or birds.

(12) TRANSNATIONAL ORGANIZED ILLEGAL ACTIVITY.—The term "transnational organized illegal activity" means criminal activity conducted by self-perpetuating associations of individuals who operate transnationally for the purpose of obtaining power, influence, or monetary or commercial gains, wholly or in part by illegal means, while protecting their activities through a pattern of corruption or violence or through a transnational organizational structure and the exploitation of transnational commerce or communication mechanisms.

(13) TRANSSHIPMENT.—The term "transshipment" means the use of refrigerated vessels that—

(A) collect catch from multiple fishing boats;

(B) carry the accumulated catches back to port; and

(C) deliver supplies to fishing boats, which allows fishing vessels to remain at sea for extended periods without coming into port.

SEC. 3533. [16 U.S.C. 8002] PURPOSES.

The purposes of this subtitle are—

(1) to support a whole-of-government approach across the Federal Government to counter IUU fishing and related threats to maritime security;

(2) to improve data sharing that enhances surveillance, enforcement, and prosecution against IUU fishing and related activities at a global level;

(3) to support coordination and collaboration to counter IUU fishing within priority regions;

(4) to increase and improve global transparency and traceability across the seafood supply chain as—

(A) a deterrent to IUU fishing; and

(B) a tool for strengthening fisheries management and food security;

(5) to improve global enforcement operations against IUU fishing through a whole-of-government approach by the United States; and

(6) to prevent the use of IUU fishing as a financing source for transnational organized groups that undermine United States and global security interests.

SEC. 3534. [16 U.S.C. 8003] STATEMENT OF POLICY.

It is the policy of the United States_

(1) to take action to curtail the global trade in seafood and seafood products derived from IUU fishing, including its links to forced labor and transnational organized illegal activity;

(2) to develop holistic diplomatic, military, law enforcement, economic, and capacity-building tools to counter IUU fishing;

(3) to provide technical assistance to countries in priority regions and priority flag states to combat IUU fishing, including assistance—

(A) to increase local, national, and regional level capacities to counter IUU fishing through the engagement of law enforcement and security forces;

(B) to enhance port capacity and security, including by supporting other countries in working toward the adoption and implementation of the Port State Measures Agreement;

(C) to combat corruption and increase transparency and traceability in fisheries management and trade;

(D) to enhance information sharing within and across governments and multilateral organizations through the development and use of agreed standards for information sharing; and

(E) to support effective, science-based fisheries management regimes that promote legal and safe fisheries and act as a deterrent to IUU fishing;

(4) to promote global maritime security through improved capacity and technological assistance to support improved maritime domain awareness;

(5) to engage with priority flag states to encourage the use of high quality vessel tracking technologies where existing enforcement tools are lacking;

(6) to engage with multilateral organizations working on fisheries issues, including Regional Fisheries Management Organizations and the Food and Agriculture Organization of the United Nations, to combat and deter IUU fishing;

(7) to advance information sharing across governments and multilateral organizations in areas that cross multiple jurisdictions, through the development and use of an agreed standard for information sharing;

(8) to continue to use existing and future trade agreements to combat IUU fishing;

(9) to employ appropriate assets and resources of the United States Government in a coordinated manner to disrupt the illicit networks involved in IUU fishing;

(10) to continue to declassify and make available, as appropriate and practicable, technologies developed by the United States Government that can be used to help counter IUU fishing;

(11) to recognize the ties of IUU fishing to transnational organized illegal activity, including human trafficking and illegal trade in narcotics and arms, and as applicable, to focus on illicit activity in a coordinated, cross-cutting manner;

(12) to recognize and respond to poor working conditions, labor abuses, and other violent crimes in the fishing industry;

(13) to increase and improve global transparency and traceability along the seafood supply chain as—

(A) a deterrent to IUU fishing; and

(B) an approach for strengthening fisheries management and food security; and

(14) to promote technological investment and innovation to combat IUU fishing.

PART I—PROGRAMS TO COMBAT IUU FISHING AND INCREASE MARITIME SECURITY

SEC. 3541. [16 U.S.C. 8011] COORDINATION WITH INTERNATIONAL ORGANIZATIONS.

The Secretary of State, in consultation with the Secretary of Commerce, shall coordinate with Regional Fisheries Management Organizations and the Food and Agriculture Organization of the United Nations, and may coordinate with other relevant international governmental or nongovernmental organizations, or the private sector, as appropriate, to enhance regional responses to IUU fishing and related transnational organized illegal activities.

SEC. 3542. [16 U.S.C. 8012] ENGAGEMENT OF DIPLOMATIC MISSIONS OF THE UNITED STATES.

Not later than 1 year after the date of the enactment of this title, each chief of mission (as defined in section 102 of the Foreign Service Act of 1980 (22 U.S.C. 3902)) to a relevant country in a priority region or to a priority flag state may, if the Secretary of State determines such action is appropriate—

(1) convene a working group, led by Department of State officials, to examine IUU fishing, which may include stakeholders such as—

(A) United States officials from relevant agencies participating in the interagency Working Group identified in section 3551, foreign officials, nongovernmental organizations, the private sector, and representatives of local fishermen in the region; and

(B) experts on IUU fishing, law enforcement, criminal justice, transnational organized illegal activity, defense, intelligence, vessel movement monitoring, and international development operating in or with knowledge of the region; and

(2) designate a counter-IUU Fishing Coordinator from among existing personnel at the mission if the chief of mission determines such action is appropriate.

SEC. 3543. [16 U.S.C. 8013] ASSISTANCE BY FEDERAL AGENCIES TO IMPROVE LAW ENFORCEMENT WITHIN PRIORITY REGIONS AND

PRIORITY FLAG STATES.

(a) IN GENERAL.—The Secretary of State, in consultation with the Secretary of Commerce and the Commandant of the Coast Guard when the Coast Guard is not operating as a service in the Department of the Navy, as well as any other relevant department or agency, shall provide assistance, as appropriate, in accordance with this section.

(b) LAW ENFORCEMENT TRAINING AND COORDINATION ACTIVITIES.—The officials referred to in subsection (a) shall evaluate opportunities to provide assistance, as appropriate, to countries in priority regions and priority flag states to improve the effectiveness of IUU fishing enforcement, with clear and measurable targets and indicators of success, including—

(1) by assessing and using existing resources, enforcement tools, and legal authorities to coordinate efforts to combat IUU fishing with efforts to combat other illegal trade, including weapons, drugs, and human trafficking;

(2) by expanding existing IUU fishing enforcement training;

(3) by providing targeted, country- and region-specific training on combating IUU fishing, including in those countries that have not adopted the Port State Measures Agreement;

(4) by supporting increased effectiveness and transparency of the fisheries enforcement sectors of the governments of such countries; and

(5) by supporting increased outreach to stakeholders in the affected communities as key partners in combating and prosecuting IUU fishing.

(c) IMPLEMENTATION OF PORT STATE MEASURES.—The officials referred to in subsection (a) shall evaluate opportunities to provide assistance, as appropriate, to countries in priority regions and priority flag states to help those states implement programs related to port security and capacity for the purposes of preventing IUU fishing products from entering the global seafood market, including by supporting other countries in working toward the adoption and implementation of the Port State Measures Agreement.

(d) CAPACITY BUILDING FOR INVESTIGATIONS AND PROSECUTIONS.—The officials referred to in subsection (a), in collaboration with the governments of countries in priority regions and of priority flag states, shall evaluate opportunities to assist those countries in designing and implementing programs in such countries, to increase the capacity of IUU fishing enforcement and customs and border security officers to improve their ability—

(1) to conduct effective investigations, including using law enforcement techniques such as undercover investigations and the development of informer networks and actionable intelligence;

(2) to conduct vessel boardings and inspections at sea and associated enforcement actions;

(3) to exercise existing shiprider agreements and to enter into and implement new shiprider agreements, for all priority regions identified by the Working Group, including in those countries that have not adopted the Port State Measures Agreement;

(4) to conduct vessel inspections at port and associated enforcement actions;

(5) to assess technology needs and promote the use of technology to improve monitoring, enforcement, and prosecution of IUU fishing;

(6) to conduct DNA-based and forensic identification of seafood used in trade;

(7) to conduct training on techniques, such as collecting electronic evidence and using computer forensics, for law enforcement personnel involved in complex investigations related to international matters, financial issues, and government corruption that include IUU fishing;

(8) to assess financial flows and the use of financial institutions to launder profits related to IUU fishing;

(9) to conduct training on the legal mechanisms that can be used to prosecute those identified in the investigations as alleged perpetrators of IUU fishing and other associated crimes such as trafficking and forced labor; and

(10) to conduct training to raise awareness of the use of whistleblower information and ways to incentivize whistleblowers to come forward with original information related to IUU fishing.

(e) CAPACITY BUILDING FOR INFORMATION SHARING.—The

officials referred to in subsection (a) shall evaluate opportunities to provide assistance, as appropriate, to key countries in priority regions and priority flag states in the form of training, equipment, and systems development to build capacity for information sharing related to maritime enforcement and port security.

(f) COORDINATION WITH OTHER RELEVANT AGENCIES.—The Secretary of State shall coordinate, as appropriate, with the Secretary of Commerce, the Commandant of the Coast Guard when the Coast Guard is not operating as a service in the Department of the Navy, and with other relevant Federal agencies in accordance with this section.

SEC. 3544. [16 U.S.C. 8014] EXPANSION OF EXISTING MECHANISMS TO COMBAT IUU FISHING.

(a) MECHANISMS TO COMBAT IUU FISHING.—The Secretary of State, the Administrator of the United States Agency for International Development, the Secretary of the Department in which the Coast Guard is operating when it is not operating as a service in the Department of the Navy, the Secretary of Defense, the Secretary of Commerce, the Attorney General, and the heads of other appropriate Federal agencies shall assess opportunities to combat IUU fishing by expanding, as appropriate, the use of the following mechanisms:

(1) Including counter-IUU fishing in existing shiprider agreements in which the United States is a party.

(2) Entering into shiprider agreements that include counter-IUU fishing with priority flag states and countries in priority regions with which the United States does not already have such an agreement.

(3) Including counter-IUU fishing as part of the mission of the Combined Maritime Forces.

(4) Including counter-IUU fishing exercises in the annual at-sea exercises conducted by the Department of Defense, in coordination with the United States Coast Guard.

(5) Creating partnerships similar to the Oceania Maritime Security Initiative and the Africa Maritime Law Enforcement Partnership in other priority regions.

(b) INFORMATION SHARING.—The Director of National Intelligence, in conjunction with other agencies, as appropriate, shall develop an enterprise approach to appropriately share information and data within the United States Government or with other countries or nongovernmental organizations, or the private sector, as appropriate, on IUU fishing and other connected transnational organized illegal activity occurring in priority regions and elsewhere, including big data analytics and machine learning.

SEC. 3545. [16 U.S.C. 8015] IMPROVEMENT OF TRANSPARENCY AND TRACEABILITY PROGRAMS.

The Secretary of State, the Administrator of the United States Agency for International Development, the Secretary of the Department in which the Coast Guard is operating when it is not operating as a service in the Department of the Navy, the Secretary of Commerce, and the heads of other Federal agencies, if merited, shall work, as appropriate, with priority flag states and key countries in priority regions—

(1) to increase knowledge within such countries about the United States transparency and traceability standards for imports of seafood and seafood products;

(2) to improve the capacity of seafood industries within such countries through information sharing and training to meet the requirements of transparency and traceability standards for seafood and seafood product imports, including catch documentation and trade tracking programs adopted by relevant regional fisheries management organizations; and

(3) to improve the capacities of government, industry, and civil society groups to develop and implement comprehensive traceability systems that—

(A) deter IUU fishing;

(B) strengthen fisheries management; and

(C) enhance maritime domain awareness.

SEC. 3546. [16 U.S.C. 8016] TECHNOLOGY PROGRAMS.

The Secretary of State, the Administrator of the United States Agency for International Development, the Secretary of the Department in which the Coast Guard is operating when it is not operating as a service in the Department of the Navy, the Secretary of Defense, the Secretary of Commerce, and the heads of other Federal agencies, if merited, shall pursue programs, as appropriate, to expand the role of technology for combating IUU fishing, including by—

(1) promoting the use of technology to combat IUU fishing;

(2) assessing the technology needs, including vessel tracking technologies and data sharing, in priority regions and priority flag states;

(3) engaging with priority flag states to encourage the mandated use of vessel tracking technologies, including vessel monitoring systems, AIS, or other vessel movement monitoring technologies on fishing vessels and transshipment vessels at all times, as appropriate, while at sea as a means to identify IUU fishing activities and the shipment of illegally caught fish products; and

(4) building partnerships with the private sector, including universities, nonprofit research organizations, the seafood industry, and the technology, transportation and logistics sectors, to leverage new and existing technologies and data analytics to address IUU fishing.

SEC. 3547. [16 U.S.C. 8017] SAVINGS CLAUSE.

No provision of section 3532 or of this part shall impose, or be interpreted to impose, any duty, responsibility, requirement, or obligation on the Department of Defense, the Department of the Navy, the United States Coast Guard when operating as a service in the Department of Homeland Security, or any official or component of either.

PART II—ESTABLISHMENT OF INTERAGENCY WORKING GROUP ON IUU FISHING

SEC. 3551. [16 U.S.C. 8031] INTERAGENCY WORKING GROUP ON IUU FISHING.

(a) In General.—There is established a collaborative interagency working group on maritime security and IUU fishing (referred to in this subtitle as the "Working Group").

(b) Members.—The members of the Working Group shall be composed of—

(1) 1 chair, who shall rotate between the Secretary of the Department in which the Coast Guard is operating, acting through the Commandant of the Coast Guard, the Secretary

of State, and the National Oceanographic and Atmospheric Administration, acting through the Administrator, on a 3-year term;

(2) 2 deputy chairs, who shall be appointed by their respective agency heads and shall be from a different Department than that of the chair, from—

(A) the Coast Guard;

(B) the Department of State; and

(C) the National Oceanic and Atmospheric Administration;

(3) 12 members, who shall be appointed by their respective agency heads, from—

(A) the Department of Defense;

(B) the United States Navy;

(C) the United States Agency for International Development;

(D) the United States Fish and Wildlife Service;

(E) the Department of Justice;

(F) the Department of the Treasury;

(G) U.S. Customs and Border Protection;

(H) U.S. Immigration and Customs Enforcement;

(I) the Federal Trade Commission;

(J) the Department of Agriculture;

(K) the Food and Drug Administration; and

(L) the Department of Labor;

(4) 1 or more members from the intelligence community (as defined in section 3 of the National Security Act of 1947 (50 U.S.C. 3003)), who shall be appointed by the Director of National Intelligence; and

(5) 5 members, who shall be appointed by the President, from—

(A) the National Security Council;

(B) the Council on Environmental Quality;

(C) the Office of Management and Budget;

(D) the Office of Science and Technology Policy; and

(E) the Office of the United States Trade Representative.

(c) RESPONSIBILITIES.—The Working Group shall ensure an integrated, Federal Government-wide response to IUU fishing globally, including by—

(1) improving the coordination of Federal agencies to identify, interdict, investigate, prosecute, and dismantle IUU fishing operations and organizations perpetrating and knowingly benefitting from IUU fishing;

(2) assessing areas for increased interagency information sharing on matters related to IUU fishing and related crimes;

(3) establishing standards for information sharing related to maritime enforcement;

(4) maximizing the utility of the import data collected by the members of the Working Group by harmonizing data standards and entry fields;

(5) developing a strategy to determine how military assets and intelligence can contribute to enforcement strategies to combat IUU fishing;

(6) increasing maritime domain awareness relating to IUU fishing and related crimes and developing a strategy to leverage awareness for enhanced enforcement and prosecution actions against IUU fishing;

(7) supporting the adoption and implementation of the Port State Measures Agreement in relevant countries and assessing the capacity and training needs in such countries;

(8) outlining a strategy to coordinate, increase, and use shiprider agreements between the Department of Defense or the Coast Guard and relevant countries;

(9) enhancing cooperation with partner governments to combat IUU fishing;

(10) identifying opportunities for increased information sharing between Federal agencies and partner governments working to combat IUU fishing;

(11) consulting and coordinating with the seafood industry and nongovernmental stakeholders that work to combat IUU fishing;

(12) supporting the work of collaborative international

initiatives to make available certified data from state authorities about vessel and vessel-related activities related to IUU fishing;

(13) supporting the identification and certification procedures to address IUU fishing in accordance with the High Seas Driftnet Fishing Moratorium Protection Act (16 U.S.C. 1826d et seq.); and

(14) publishing annual reports summarizing nonsensitive information about the Working Group's efforts to investigate, enforce, and prosecute groups and individuals engaging in IUU fishing.

SEC. 3552. [16 U.S.C. 8032] STRATEGIC PLAN.

(a) STRATEGIC PLAN.—Not later than 2 years after the date of the enactment of this title, the Working Group, after consultation with the relevant stakeholders, shall submit to the Committee on Commerce, Science, and Transportation of the Senate, the Committee on Foreign Relations of the Senate, the Committee on Appropriations of the Senate, the Committee on Transportation and Infrastructure of the House of Representatives, the Committee on Natural Resources of the House of Representatives, the Committee on Foreign Affairs of the House of Representatives, and the Committee on Appropriations of the House of Representatives a 5-year integrated strategic plan on combating IUU fishing and enhancing maritime security, including specific strategies with monitoring benchmarks for addressing IUU fishing in priority regions.

(b) IDENTIFICATION OF PRIORITY REGIONS AND PRIORITY FLAG STATES.—

(1) IN GENERAL.—The strategic plan submitted under subsection (a) shall identify priority regions and priority flag states to be the focus of assistance coordinated by the Working Group under section 3551.

(2) PRIORITY REGION SELECTION CRITERIA.—In selecting priority regions under paragraph (1), the Working Group shall select regions that—

(A) are at high risk for IUU fishing activity or the entry of illegally caught seafood into their markets; and

(B) lack the capacity to fully address the issues

described in subparagraph (A).

(3) PRIORITY FLAG STATES SELECTION CRITERIA.—In selecting priority flag states under paragraph (1), the Working Group shall select countries—

(A) the flagged vessels of which actively engage in, knowingly profit from, or are complicit in IUU fishing; and

(B) that lack the capacity to police their fleet.

SEC. 3553. [16 U.S.C. 8033] REPORTS.

Not later than 5 years after the submission of the 5-year integrated strategic plan under section 3552, and 5 years after, the Working Group shall submit a report to the Committee on Commerce, Science, and Transportation of the Senate, the Committee on Foreign Relations of the Senate, the Committee on Appropriations of the Senate, the Committee on the Judiciary of the Senate, the Select Committee on Intelligence of the Senate, the Committee on Agriculture, Nutrition, and Forestry of the Senate, the Committee on Transportation and Infrastructure of the House of Representatives, the Committee on Natural Resources of the House of Representatives, the Committee on Foreign Affairs of the House of Representatives, and the Committee on Appropriations of the House of Representatives that contains—

(1) a summary of global and regional trends in IUU fishing;

(2) an assessment of the extent of the convergence between transnational organized illegal activity, including human trafficking and forced labor, and IUU fishing;

(3) an assessment of the topics, data sources, and strategies that would benefit from increased information sharing and recommendations regarding harmonization of data collection and sharing;

(4) an assessment of assets, including military assets and intelligence, which can be used for either enforcement operations or strategies to combat IUU fishing;

(5) summaries of the situational threats with respect to IUU fishing in priority regions and an assessment of the capacity of countries within such regions to respond to those threats;

(6) an assessment of the progress of countries in priority regions in responding to those threats as a result of assistance

by the United States pursuant to the strategic plan developed under section 3552, including—

(A) the identification of—

(i) relevant supply routes, ports of call, methods of landing and entering illegally caught product into legal supply chains, and financial institutions used in each country by participants engaging in IUU fishing; and

(ii) indicators of IUU fishing that are related to money laundering;

(B) an assessment of the adherence to, or progress toward adoption of, international treaties related to IUU fishing, including the Port State Measures Agreement, by countries in priority regions;

(C) an assessment of the implementation by countries in priority regions of seafood traceability or capacity to apply traceability to verify the legality of catch and strengthen fisheries management;

(D) an assessment of the capacity of countries in priority regions to implement shiprider agreements;

(E) an assessment of the capacity of countries in priority regions to increase maritime domain awareness; and

(F) an assessment of the capacity of governments of relevant countries in priority regions to sustain the programs for which the United States has provided assistance under this subtitle;

(7) an assessment of the capacity of priority flag states to track the movement of and police their fleet, prevent their flagged vessels from engaging in IUU fishing, and enforce applicable laws and regulations;

(8) an assessment of the extent of involvement in IUU fishing of organizations designated as foreign terrorist organizations under section 219 of the Immigration and Nationality Act (8 U.S.C. 1189); and

(9) the status of work with global enforcement partners.

SEC. 3554. [16 U.S.C. 8034] GULF OF MEXICO IUU FISHING SUBWORKING GROUP.

(a) IN GENERAL.—Not later than 90 days after the date of the enactment of this title, the Administrator of the National Oceanic and Atmospheric Administration, in coordination with the Commandant of the Coast Guard and the Secretary of State, shall establish a subworking group to address IUU fishing in the exclusive economic zone of the United States in the Gulf of Mexico.

(b) FUNCTIONS.—The subworking group established under subsection (a) shall identify—

(1) Federal actions taken and policies established during the 5-year period immediately preceding the date of the enactment of this title with respect to IUU fishing in the exclusive economic zone of the United States in the Gulf of Mexico, including such actions and policies related to—

(A) the surveillance, interdiction, and prosecution of any foreign nationals engaged in such fishing; and

(B) the application of the provisions of the High Seas Driftnet Fishing Moratorium Protection Act (16 U.S.C. 1826d et seq.) to any relevant nation, including the status of any past or ongoing consultations and certification procedures;

(2) actions and policies, in addition to the actions and policies described in paragraph (1), each of the Federal agencies described in subsection (a) can take, using existing resources, to combat IUU fishing in the exclusive economic zone of the United States in the Gulf of Mexico; and

(3) any additional authorities that could assist each such agency in more effectively addressing such IUU fishing.

(c) REPORT.—Not later than 1 year after the IUU Fishing Subworking Group is established under subsection (a), the group shall submit a report to the Committee on Commerce, Science, and Transportation of the Senate, the Committee on Transportation and Infrastructure of the House of Representatives, and the Committee on Natural Resources of the House of Representatives that contains—

(1) the findings identified pursuant to subsection (b); and

(2) a timeline for each of the Federal agencies described in subsection (a) to implement each action or policy identified pursuant to subsection (b)(2).

PART III—COMBATING HUMAN TRAFFICKING IN CONNECTION WITH THE CATCHING AND PROCESSING OF SEAFOOD PRODUCTS

SEC. 3561. FINDING.

Congress finds that human trafficking, including forced labor, is a pervasive problem in the catching and processing of certain seafood products imported into the United States, particularly seafood products obtained through illegal, unreported, and unregulated fishing.

SEC. 3562. ADDING THE SECRETARY OF COMMERCE TO THE INTERAGENCY TASK FORCE TO MONITOR AND COMBAT TRAFFICKING.

Section 105(b) of the Victims of Trafficking and Violence Protection Act of 2000 (22 U.S.C. 7103(b)) is amended by inserting "the Secretary of Commerce," after "the Secretary of Education,".

SEC. 3563. HUMAN TRAFFICKING IN THE SEAFOOD SUPPLY CHAIN REPORT.

(a) IN GENERAL.—Not later than 1 year after the date of the enactment of this title, the Secretary of State and the Administrator of the National Oceanic and Atmospheric Administration shall jointly submit a report to the Committee on Commerce, Science, and Transportation of the Senate, the Committee on Foreign Relations of the Senate, the Committee on Appropriations of the Senate, the Committee on Natural Resources of the House of Representatives, the Committee on Foreign Affairs of the House of Representatives, and the Committee on Appropriations of the House of Representatives that describes the existence of human trafficking, including forced labor, in the supply chains of seafood products imported into the United States.

(b) REPORT ELEMENTS.—The report required under subsection (a) shall include—

(1) a list of the countries at risk for human trafficking, including forced labor, in their seafood catching and processing industries, and an assessment of such risk for each listed country;

(2) a description of the quantity and economic value of

seafood products imported into the United States from the countries on the list compiled pursuant to paragraph (1);

(3) a description and assessment of the methods, if any, in the countries on the list compiled pursuant to paragraph (1) to trace and account for the manner in which seafood is caught;

(4) a description of domestic and international enforcement mechanisms to deter illegal practices in the catching of seafood in the countries on the list compiled pursuant to paragraph (1); and

(5) such recommendations as the Secretary of State and the Administrator of the National Oceanic and Atmospheric Administration jointly consider appropriate for administrative action to enhance and improve actions against human trafficking, including forced labor, in the catching and processing of seafood products outside of United States waters.

PART IV—AUTHORIZATION OF APPROPRIATIONS

SEC. 3571. AUTHORIZATION OF APPROPRIATIONS.

(a) [16 U.S.C. 8041] FUNDING.—Amounts made available to carry out this subtitle shall be derived from amounts appropriated to the relevant agencies and departments.

(b) NO INCREASE IN CONTRIBUTIONS.—Nothing in this subtitle shall be construed to authorize an increase in required or voluntary contributions paid by the United States to any multilateral or international organization.

SEC. 3572. ACCOUNTING OF FUNDS.

By not later than 180 days after the date of enactment of this title, the head of each Federal agency receiving or allocating funds to carry out activities under this subtitle shall, to the greatest extent practicable, prepare and submit to Congress a report that provides an accounting of all funds made available under this subtitle to the Federal agency.

* * * * * * *

National Defense Authorization Act for Fiscal Year 2022
Title XXXV-Maritime Security

Public Law 117-81

As amended through P.L. 118-159

National Defense Authorization Act for Fiscal Year 2022

[(Public Law 117–81)]

[As Amended Through P.L. 118–159, Enacted December 23, 2024]

AN ACT To authorize appropriations for fiscal year 2022 for military activities of the Department of Defense, for military construction, and for defense activities of the Department of Energy, to prescribe military personnel strengths for such fiscal year, and for other purposes.

Be it enacted by the Senate and House of Representatives of the United States of America in Congress assembled,

SECTION 1. SHORT TITLE.

This Act may be cited as the "National Defense Authorization Act for Fiscal Year 2022".

SEC. 2. ORGANIZATION OF ACT INTO DIVISIONS; TABLE OF CONTENTS.

(a) DIVISIONS.—This Act is organized into six divisions as follows:

(1) Division A—Department of Defense Authorizations.

(2) Division B—Military Construction Authorizations.

(3) Division C—Department of Energy National Security Authorizations and Other Authorizations.

(4) Division D—Funding Tables.

(5) Division E—Department of State Authorization

(6) Division F—Other Non-Department of Defense Matters.

(b) TABLE OF CONTENTS.—The table of contents for this Act is as follows:

Sec. 2. Organization of Act into divisions; table of contents.

* * * * * * *

DIVISION C— DEPARTMENT OF ENERGY NATIONAL SECURITY AUTHORIZATIONS AND OTHER AUTHORIZATIONS

* * * * * * *

TITLE XXXV—MARITIME SECURITY

Subtitle A—Maritime Administration

Subtitle B—Other Matters

* * * * * * *

DIVISION C—DEPARTMENT OF ENERGY NATIONAL SECURITY AUTHORIZATIONS AND OTHER AUTHORIZATIONS

* * * * * * *

TITLE XXXV—MARITIME SECURITY

Subtitle A—Maritime Administration

Subtitle B—Other Matters

Subtitle A—Maritime Administration

SEC. 3501. AUTHORIZATION OF THE MARITIME ADMINISTRATION.

(a) IN GENERAL.—There are authorized to be appropriated to the Department of Transportation for fiscal year 2022 for programs associated with maintaining the United States merchant marine, the following amounts:

(1) For expenses necessary for operations of the United States Merchant Marine Academy, $90,532,000, of which—

(A) $85,032,000 shall be for Academy operations, which may be used to hire personnel pursuant to subsection (d) and to implement any recommendations of the Merchant Marine Academy Advisory Council established under subsection (c); and

(B) $5,500,000 shall remain available until expended for capital asset management at the Academy.

(2) For expenses necessary to support the State maritime academies, $50,780,000, of which—

(A) $2,400,000 is for the Student Incentive Program;

(B) $6,000,000 is for direct payments;

(C) $3,800,000 is for training ship fuel assistance;

(D) $8,080,000 is for offsetting the costs of training ship sharing; and

(E) $30,500,000 is for maintenance and repair of State maritime academy training vessels.

(3) For expenses necessary to support the National Security Multi-Mission Vessel Program, $315,600,000.

(4) For expenses necessary to support Maritime Administration operations and programs, $60,853,000.

(5) For expenses necessary to dispose of vessels in the National Defense Reserve Fleet, $10,000,000.

(6) For expenses necessary to maintain and preserve a United States flag merchant marine to serve the national

security needs of the United States under chapter 531 of title 46, United States Code, $318,000,000.

(7) For expenses necessary for the loan guarantee program authorized under chapter 537 of title 46, United States Code, $33,000,000, of which—

(A) $30,000,000 may be used for the cost (as defined in section 502(5) of the Federal Credit Reform Act of 1990 (2 U.S.C. 661a(5))) of loan guarantees under the program; and

(B) $3,000,000 may be used for administrative expenses relating to loan guarantee commitments under the program.

(8) For expenses necessary to provide for the Tanker Security Fleet, as authorized under chapter 534 of title 46, United States Code, $60,000,000.

(9) For expenses necessary to support maritime environmental and technical assistance activities authorized under section 50307 of title 46, United States Code, $10,000,000.

(10) For expenses necessary to support marine highway program activities authorized under chapter 556 of such title, $11,000,000.

(11) For expenses necessary to provide assistance to small shipyards and for the maritime training program authorized under section 54101 of title 46, United States Code, $40,000,000.

(12) For expenses necessary to implement the Port and Intermodal Improvement Program, $750,000,000, to remain available until expended, except that no such funds may be used to provide a grant to purchase fully automated cargo handling equipment that is remotely operated or remotely monitored with or without the exercise of human intervention or control, if the Secretary determines such equipment would result in a net loss of jobs within a port of port terminal.

(b) AVAILABILITY OF AMOUNTS.—The amounts authorized to be appropriated under subsection (a) shall remain available as follows:

(1) The amounts authorized to be appropriated under paragraphs (1)(A), (2)(A), and (4)(A) shall remain available until September 30, 2022.

(2) The amounts authorized to be appropriated under paragraphs (1)(B), (2)(B), (D), and (E), (3), (4)(B), (5), (6), (7)(A), (8), and (9) shall remain available until expended without fiscal year limitation.

(c) UNITED STATES MERCHANT MARINE ACADEMY ADVISORY COUNCIL; UNFILLED VACANCIES.—

(1) IN GENERAL.—Chapter 513 of title 46, United States Code, is amended by adding at the end the following new sections:

"SEC. 51323. [46 U.S.C. 51323] United States Merchant Marine Academy Advisory Council

"(a) ESTABLISHMENT.—The Secretary of Transportation shall establish an advisory council, to be known as the 'United States Merchant Marine Academy Advisory Council' (in this section referred to as the 'Council').

"(b) MEMBERSHIP.—

"(1) IN GENERAL.—The Secretary shall select not fewer than 8 and not more than 14 individuals to serve as members of the Council. Such individuals shall have such expertise as the Secretary determines necessary and appropriate for providing advice and guidance on improving the Academy.

"(2) GOVERNMENTAL EXPERTS.—The number of members of the Council who are employees of the Federal Government may not exceed the number of members of the Council who are not employees of the Federal Government.

"(3) EMPLOYEE STATUS.—Members of the Council shall not be considered employees of the United States Government by reason of their membership on the Council for any purpose and shall not receive compensation other than reimbursement of travel expenses and per diem allowance in accordance with section 5703 of title 5.

"(c) RESPONSIBILITIES.—The Council shall provide advice to the Secretary at the time and in the manner requested by the Secretary.

"(d) PERSONALLY IDENTIFIABLE INFORMATION.—In carrying out its responsibilities under this subsection, the Council shall comply with the obligations of the Department of Transportation to protect personally identifiable information.

"SEC. 51324. [46 U.S.C. 51301] Unfilled vacancies

"(a) IN GENERAL.—In the event of an unfilled vacancy for any critical position at the United States Merchant Marine Academy, the Secretary of Transportation may appoint, without regard to the provisions of subchapter I of chapter 33 of title 5, other than sections 3303 and 3328 of that title, a qualified candidate for the purposes of filling up to 20 of such positions.

"(b) CRITICAL POSITION DEFINED.—In this section, the term 'critical position' means a position that contributes to the improvement of—

"(1) the culture or infrastructure of the Academy;

"(2) student health and well being;

"(3) Academy governance; or

"(4) any other priority areas identified by the Council."

(2) CLERICAL AMENDMENT.—The table of sections at the beginning of such chapter is amended by adding at the end the following new items:

"51323. United States Merchant Marine Academy Advisory Council.
"51324. Unfilled vacancies."

Subtitle B—Other Matters

SEC. 3511. EFFECTIVE PERIOD FOR ISSUANCE OF DOCUMENTATION FOR RECREATIONAL VESSELS.

Section 12105(e)(2) of title 46, United States Code, is amended—

(1) by striking subparagraphs (A) and (B) and inserting the following:

"(A) IN GENERAL.—The owner or operator of a recreational vessel may choose a period of effectiveness of between 1 and 5 years for a certificate of documentation for a recreational vessel or the renewal thereof."

; and

(2) by redesignating subparagraph (C) as subparagraph (B).

SEC. 3512. COMMITTEES ON MARITIME MATTERS.

(a) IN GENERAL.—

(1) [46 U.S.C. 50401] Chapter 555 of title 46, United States Code, is redesignated as chapter 504 of such title and transferred to appear after chapter 503 of such title.

(2) Chapter 504 of such title, as redesignated by paragraph (1), is amended in the chapter heading by striking "MISCELLANEOUS" and inserting "COMMITTEES".

(3) [46 U.S.C. 55502 note] Sections 55501 and 55502 of such title are redesignated as section 50401 and section 50402, respectively, of such title and transferred to appear in chapter 504 of such title (as redesignated by paragraph (1)).

(4) The section heading for section 50401 of such title, as redesignated by paragraph (3), is amended to read as follows: "united states committee on the marine transportation system".

(b) [46 U.S.C. 50402 note] CONFORMING AMENDMENT.—Section 8332(b)(1) of the Elijah E. Cummings Coast Guard Authorization Act of 2020 (division G of the William M. (Mac) Thornberry National Defense Authorization Act for Fiscal Year 2021 (Public Law 116-283)) is amended by striking "section 55502" and inserting "section 50402".

(c) CLERICAL AMENDMENTS.—

(1) [46 U.S.C. 50101] The analysis for chapter 504 of title 46, United States Code, as redesignated by subsection (a)(1), is amended to read as follows:

"Chapter 504—	Committees
"Sec.	
"50401.	United States Committee on the Marine Transportation System.
"50402.	Maritime Transportation System National Advisory Committee."

(2) The table of chapters for subtitle V of title 46, United States Code, is amended—

(A) by inserting after the item relating to chapter 503 the following:

"504.	**Committees**	**50401"**

; and

(B) by striking the item relating to chapter 555.

SEC. 3513. PORT INFRASTRUCTURE DEVELOPMENT PROGRAM.

(a) IN GENERAL.—

(1) Part C of subtitle V of title 46, United States Code, is amended by adding at the end the following:

"CHAPTER 543—[46 U.S.C. 54301] PORT INFRASTRUCTURE DEVELOPMENT PROGRAM

"SEC. 54301. [46 U.S.C. 54301] Port infrastructure development program"

(2) Subsections (c), (d), and (e) of section 50302 of such title are redesignated as subsections (a), (b), and (c) of section 54301 of such title, respectively, and transferred to appear in chapter 543 of such title (as added by paragraph (1)).

(b) AMENDMENTS TO SECTION 54301.—Section 54301 of such title, as redesignated by subsection (a)(2), is amended—

(1) in subsection (a)—

(A) in paragraph (2) by striking "or subsection (d)" and inserting "or subsection (b)";

(B) in paragraph (3)(A)(ii)—

(i) in subclause (II) by striking "; or" and inserting a semicolon;

(ii) by striking subclause (III); and

(iii) by adding at the end the following:

"(III) operational improvements, including projects to improve port resilience; or

"(IV) environmental and emission mitigation measures; including projects for—

"(aa) port electrification or electrification master planning;

"(bb) harbor craft or equipment

replacements or retrofits;

"(cc) development of port or terminal microgrids;

"(dd) providing idling reduction infrastructure;

"(ee) purchase of cargo handling equipment and related infrastructure;

"(ff) worker training to support electrification technology;

"(gg) installation of port bunkering facilities from oceangoing vessels for fuels;

"(hh) electric vehicle charge or hydrogen refueling infrastructure for drayage and medium or heavy duty trucks and locomotives that service the port and related grid upgrades; or

"(ii) other related port activities, including charging infrastructure, electric rubber-tired gantry cranes, and anti-idling technologies."

(C) in paragraph (5)—

(i) in subparagraph (A) by striking "or subsection (d)" and inserting "or subsection (b)"; and

(ii) in subparagraph (B) by striking "subsection (d)" and inserting "subsection (b)";

(D) in paragraph (6)(B)—

(i) in clause (i) by striking "; and" and inserting a semicolon;

(ii) in clause (ii) by striking the period and inserting "; and"; and

(iii) by adding at the end the following:

"(iii) a port's increased resilience as a result of the project."

(E) in paragraph (7)—

(i) in subparagraph (B)—

(I) by striking "subsection (d)" in each place it appears and inserting "subsection (b)"; and

(II) by striking "18 percent" and inserting "25 percent";

(ii) in subparagraph (C) by striking "subsection (d)(3)(A)(ii)(III)" and inserting "subsection (b)(3)(A)(ii)(III)";

(F) in paragraph (8)—

(i) in subparagraph (A) by striking "or subsection (d)" and inserting "or subsection (b)"; and

(ii) in subparagraph (B)—

(I) in clause (i) by striking "subsection (d)" and inserting "subsection (b)"; and

(II) in clause (ii) by striking "subsection (d)" and inserting "subsection (b)";

(G) in paragraph (9) by striking "subsection (d)" and inserting "subsection (b)";

(H) in paragraph (10)—

(i) in subparagraph (A), by striking "subsection (d)" and inserting "subsection (b)";

(ii) by redesignating subparagraphs (B) and (C) as subparagraphs (C) and (D), respectively; and

(iii) by inserting after subparagraph (A) the following new subparagraph (B):

"(B) EFFICIENT USE OF NON-FEDERAL FUNDS.—

"(i) IN GENERAL.—Notwithstanding any other provision of law ans subject to approval by the Secretary, in the case of any grant for a project under this section, during the period beginning on the date on which the grant recipient is selected and ending on the date on which the grant agreement is signed—

"(I) the grant recipient may obligate and expend non-Federal funds with respect to the project for which the grant is provided; and

"(II) any non-Federal funds obligated or expended in accordance with subclause (I) shall be credited toward the non-

Federal cost share for the project for which the grant is provided.

"(ii) REQUIREMENTS.—

"(I) APPLICATION.—In order to obligate and expend non-Federal funds under clause (i), the grant recipient shall submit to the Secretary a request to obligate and expend non- Federal funds under that clause, including—

"(aa) a description of the activities the grant recipient intends to fund;

"(bb) a justification for advancing the activities described in item (aa), including an assessment of the effects to the project scope, schedule, and budget if the request is not approved; and

"(cc) the level of risk of the activities described in item (aa).

"(II) APPROVAL.—The Secretary shall approve or disapprove each request submitted under subclause (I).

"(III) COMPLIANCE WITH APPLICABLE REQUIREMENTS.—Any obligation or expenditure of non-Federal funds under clause (i) shall be in compliance with all applicable requirements, including any requirements included in the grant agreement.

"(iii) EFFECT.—The obligation or expenditure of any non-Federal funds in accordance with this subparagraph shall not—

"(I) affect the signing of a grant agreement or other applicable grant procedures with respect to the applicable grant;

"(II) create an obligation on the part

of the Federal Government to repay any non-Federal funds if the grant agreement is not signed; or

"(III) affect the ability of the recipient of the grant to obligate or expend non-Federal funds to meet the non-Federal cost share for the project for which the grant is provided after the period described in clause (i)."

; and

(I) in paragraph (12)—

(i) by striking "subsection (d)" and inserting "subsection (b)"; and

(ii) by adding at the end the following:

"(D) RESILIENCE.—The term 'resilience' means the ability to anticipate, prepare for, adapt to, withstand, respond to, and recover from operational disruptions and sustain critical operations at ports, including disruptions caused by natural or manmade hazards, such as sea level rise, flooding, earthquakes, hurricanes, tsunami inundation or other extreme weather events."

(2) in subsection (b)—

(A) in the subsection heading by striking "Inland" and inserting "Inland River";

(B) in paragraph (1) by striking "subsection (c)(7)(B)" and inserting "subsection (a)(7)(B)";

(C) in paragraph (3)(A)(ii)(III) by striking "subsection (c)(3)(B)" and inserting "subsection (a)(3)(B)"; and

(D) in paragraph (5)(A) by striking "subsection (c)(8)(B)" and inserting "subsection (a)(8)(B)"; and

(3) in subsection (c)—

(A) by striking "subsection (c) or subsection (d)" and inserting "subsection (a) or subsection (b)"; and

(B) by striking "subsection (c)(2)" and inserting "subsection (a)(2)".

(c) GRANTS FOR EMISSION MITIGATION MEASURES.—For fiscal

year 2022, the Secretary may make grants under section 54301(a) of title 46, United States Code, as redesignated by subsection (a)(2) and amended by subsection (b), to provide for emission mitigation measures that provide for the use of shore power for vessels to which sections 3507 and 3508 of such title apply, if such grants meet the other requirements set out in such section 54301(a).

(d) [46 U.S.C. 50101] CLERICAL AMENDMENTS.—The table of chapters for subtitle V of title 46, United States Code, as amended by this title, is further amended by inserting after the item relating to chapter 541 the following:

"543. Port Infrastructure Development Program 54301"".

SEC. 3514. USES OF EMERGING MARINE TECHNOLOGIES AND PRACTICES.

Section 50307 of title 46, United States Code, is amended—

(1) by redesignating subsection (e) as subsection (f); and

(2) by inserting after subsection (d) the following new subsection (e):

"(e) USES.—The results of activities conducted under subsection (b)(1) shall be used to inform—

"(1) the policy decisions of the United States related to domestic regulations; and

"(2) the position of the United States on matters before the International Maritime Organization."

SEC. 3515. PROHIBITION ON PARTICIPATION OF LONG TERM CHARTERS IN TANKER SECURITY FLEET.

(a) DEFINITION OF LONG TERM CHARTER.—Section 53401 of title 46, United States Code, is amended by adding at the end the following new paragraph:

"(8) LONG TERM CHARTER.—The term 'long term charter' means any time charter of a product tank vessel to the United States Government that, together with options, occurs for a continuous period of more than 180 days."

(b) PARTICIPATION OF LONG TERM CHARTERS IN TANKER SECURITY FLEET.—Section 53404(b) of such title is amended—

(1) by striking "The program participant of a" and inserting "Any";

(2) by inserting "long term" before "charter";

(3) by inserting "not" before "eligible"; and

(4) by striking "receive payments pursuant to any operating agreement that covers such vessel" and inserting "participate in the Fleet".

SEC. 3516. COASTWISE ENDORSEMENT.

Notwithstanding section 12112 of title 46, United States Code, the Secretary of the department in which the Coast Guard is operating may issue a certificate of documentation with a coastwise endorsement for the vessel WIDGEON (United States official number 1299656).

SEC. 3517. REPORT ON EFFORTS OF COMBATANT COMMANDS TO COMBAT THREATS POSED BY ILLEGAL, UNREPORTED, AND UNREGULATED FISHING.

(a) REPORT REQUIRED.—Not later than 180 days after the date of the enactment of this Act, the Secretary of the Navy, in consultation with the Director of the Office of Naval Research, the co-chairs of the collaborative interagency working group on maritime security and IUU fishing established under section 3551 of the Maritime Security and Fisheries Enforcement Act (16 U.S.C. 8031), and the heads of other relevant agencies, as determined by the Secretary, shall submit to the appropriate congressional committees a report on the combatant commands' maritime domain awareness efforts to combat the threats posed by illegal, unreported, and unregulated fishing.

(b) CONTENTS OF REPORT.—The report required by subsection (a) shall include a detailed summary of each of the following for each combatant command:

(1) The activities undertaken to date to combat the threats posed by illegal, unreported, and unregulated fishing in the geographic area of the combatant command, including the steps taken to build partner capacity to combat such threats.

(2) Coordination with the Armed Forces of the United States, partner nations, and public-private partnerships to combat such threats.

(3) Efforts undertaken to support unclassified data integration, analysis, and delivery with regional partners to combat such threats.

(4) Information sharing and coordination with efforts of the collaborative interagency working group on maritime security and IUU fishing established under section 3551 of the Maritime Security and Fisheries Enforcement Act (16 U.S.C. 8031).

(5) Best practices and lessons learned from existing and previous efforts relating to such threats, including strategies for coordination and success in public-private partnerships.

(6) Limitations related to affordability, resource constraints, or other gaps or factors that affect the success or expansion of efforts related to such threats.

(7) Any new authorities needed to support efforts to combat such threats.

(c) FORM OF REPORT.—The report required by subsection (a) shall be submitted in unclassified form, but may include a classified annex.

(d) APPROPRIATE CONGRESSIONAL COMMITTEES.—In this section, the term "appropriate congressional committees" means—

(1) the Committee on Armed Services, the Committee on Commerce, Science, and Transportation, the Committee on Foreign Relations, and the Committee on Appropriations of the Senate; and

(2) the Committee on Armed Services, the Committee on Natural Resources, the Committee on Transportation and Infrastructure, the Committee on Foreign Affairs, and the Committee on Appropriations of the House of Representatives.

SEC. 3518. AUTHORIZATION TO PURCHASE DUPLICATE MEDALS.

(a) IN GENERAL.—The Secretary of Transportation, acting through the Administrator of the Maritime Administration, may use funds appropriated for the fiscal year in which the date of the enactment of this Act occurs, or funds appropriated for any prior fiscal year, for the Maritime Administration to purchase duplicate medals authorized under the Merchant Mariners of World War II Congressional Gold Medal Act of 2020 (Public Law 116-125) and provide such medals to eligible individuals who engaged in qualified service who submit an application under subsection (b) and were United States merchant mariners of World War II.

(b) APPLICATION.—To be eligible to receive a medal described in subsection (a), an eligible individual who engaged in qualified service shall submit to the Administrator an application containing such information and assurances as the Administrator may require.

(c) ELIGIBLE INDIVIDUAL WHO ENGAGED IN QUALIFIED SERVICE.—In this section, the term “eligible individual who engaged in qualified service” means an individual who, between December 7, 1941, and December 31, 1946—

(1) was a member of the United States merchant marine, including the Army Transport Service and the Navy Transport Service, serving as a crewmember of a vessel that was—

(A) operated by the War Shipping Administration, the Office of Defense Transportation, or an agent of such departments;

(B) operated in waters other than inland waters, the Great Lakes, and other lakes, bays, or harbors of the United States;

(C) under contract or charter to, or property of, the Government of the United States; and

(D) serving in the Armed Forces; and

(2) while so serving, was licensed or otherwise documented for service as a crewmember of such a vessel by an officer or employee of the United States authorized to license or document the person for such service.

* * * * * * *

Don Young Coast Guard

Authorization Act of 2022 Division K of the James M. Inhofe National Defense Authorization Act for Fiscal Year 2023

Public Law 117-263

As amended through P.L. 118-172

James M. Inhofe National Defense Authorization Act for Fiscal Year 2023

[(Public Law 117–263)]

[As Amended Through P.L. 118–172, Enacted December 23, 2024]

AN ACT To authorize appropriations for fiscal year 2023 for military activities of the Department of Defense, for military construction, and for defense activities of the Department of Energy, to prescribe military personnel strengths for such fiscal year, and for other purposes.

Be it enacted by the Senate and House of Representatives of the United States of America in Congress assembled,

SECTION 1. SHORT TITLE.

(a) IN GENERAL.—This Act may be cited as the "James M. Inhofe National Defense Authorization Act for Fiscal Year 2023".

(b) **[**10 U.S.C. 101 note**]** REFERENCES.—Any reference in this or any other Act to the "National Defense Authorization Act for Fiscal Year 2023" shall be deemed to be a reference to the "James M. Inhofe National Defense Authorization Act for Fiscal Year 2023".

SEC. 2. ORGANIZATION OF ACT INTO DIVISIONS; TABLE OF CONTENTS.

(a) DIVISIONS.—This Act is organized into 11 divisions as follows:

* * * * * * *

(11) Division K—Don Young Coast Guard Authorization Act of 2022.

(b) TABLE OF CONTENTS.—The table of contents for this Act is as follows:

* * * * * * *

DIVISION K—DON YOUNG COAST GUARD AUTHORIZATION ACT OF 2022

SEC. 11001. SHORT TITLE; TABLE OF CONTENTS.

(a) SHORT TITLE.—This division may be cited as the "Don Young Coast Guard Authorization Act of 2022".

(b) TABLE OF CONTENTS.—The table of contents for this division is as follows:

SEC. 11002. [14 U.S.C. 106 note] DEFINITIONS.

In this division:

(1) COMMANDANT.—The term "Commandant" means the

Commandant of the Coast Guard.

(2) SECRETARY.—Except as otherwise provided, the term "Secretary" means the Secretary of the department in which the Coast Guard is operating.

SEC. 11003. [6 U.S.C. 245 note] RULE OF CONSTRUCTION.

(a) IN GENERAL.—Nothing in this division may be construed—

(1) to satisfy any requirement for government-to-government consultation with Tribal governments; or

(2) to affect or modify any treaty or other right of any Tribal government.

(b) TRIBAL GOVERNMENT DEFINED.—In this section, the term "Tribal government" means the recognized governing body of any Indian or Alaska Native Tribe, band, nation, pueblo, village, community, component band, or component reservation, individually identified (including parenthetically) in the list published most recently as of the date of the enactment of this Act pursuant to section 104 of the Federally Recognized Indian Tribe List Act of 1994 (25 U.S.C. 5131).

TITLE CXI—AUTHORIZATIONS

SEC. 11101. AUTHORIZATION OF APPROPRIATIONS.

Section 4902 of title 14, United States Code, is amended—

(1) in the matter preceding paragraph (1) by striking "fiscal years 2020 and 2021" and inserting "fiscal years 2022 and 2023";

(2) in paragraph (1)—

(A) in subparagraph (A) by striking clauses (i) and (ii) and inserting the following:

"(i) $10,000,000,000 for fiscal year 2022; and

"(ii) $10,750,000,000 for fiscal year 2023."

(B) in subparagraph (B) by striking "$17,035,000" and inserting "$23,456,000"; and

(C) in subparagraph (C) by striking ", (A)(ii) $17,376,000" and inserting "(A)(ii), $24,353,000";

(3) in paragraph (2)—

(A) in subparagraph (A) by striking clauses (i) and (ii)

and inserting the following:

"(i) $3,312,114,000 for fiscal year 2022; and

"(ii) $3,477,600,000 for fiscal year 2023."

; and

(B) in subparagraph (B) by striking clauses (i) and (ii) and inserting the following:

"(i) $20,400,000 for fiscal year 2022; and

"(ii) $20,808,000 for fiscal year 2023."

(4) in paragraph (3) by striking subparagraphs (A) and (B) and inserting the following:

"(A) $7,476,000 for fiscal year 2022; and

"(B) $14,681,084 for fiscal year 2023."

; and

(5) in paragraph (4) by striking subparagraphs (A) and (B) and inserting the following:

"(A) $240,577,000 for fiscal year 2022; and

"(B) $252,887,000 for fiscal year 2023."

SEC. 11102. AUTHORIZED LEVELS OF MILITARY STRENGTH AND TRAINING.

Section 4904 of title 14, United States Code, is amended—

(1) in subsection (a) by striking "fiscal years 2020 and 2021" and inserting "fiscal years 2022 and 2023"; and

(2) in subsection (b) by striking "fiscal years 2020 and 2021" and inserting "fiscal years 2022 and 2023".

SEC. 11103. AUTHORIZATION FOR CERTAIN PROGRAMS AND SERVICES.

Of the amounts authorized to be appropriated under section 4902(1)(A) of title 14, United States Code, there are authorized to the Commandant for each of fiscal years 2022 and 2023—

(1) $25,000,000 for the child care subsidy program as established under section 11401and any additional eligible uses established by the Commandant under the amendment made by subsection (c) of section 11401;

(2) $1,300,000 for expansion of behavioral health services in the Coast Guard under section 11412;

(3) $3,000,000 for the Aqua Alert Notification System pilot program established under section 11207; and

(4) $1,000,000 to prepare the evaluation of requirements for the Arctic Security Cutter.

SEC. 11104. AVAILABILITY OF AMOUNTS FOR ACQUISITION OF ADDITIONAL VESSELS.

(a) IN GENERAL.—Of the amounts authorized to be appropriated under section 4902(2)(A)(ii) of title 14, United States Code, as amended by section 11101, for fiscal year 2023—

(1) $300,000,000 shall be authorized for the acquisition of a twelfth National Security Cutter;

(2) $420,000,000 shall be authorized for the acquisition of 6 Fast Response Cutters;

(3) $172,500,000 is authorized for the program management, design, and acquisition of 12 Pacific Northwest heavy weather boats that are at least as capable as the Coast Guard 52-foot motor surfboat;

(4) $167,200,000 is authorized for the third Polar Security Cutter;

(5) $150,000,000 is authorized for the acquisition or procurement of an available icebreaker (as such term is defined under section 11223);

(6) for fiscal year 2022, $350,000,000 shall be authorized for the acquisition of a Great Lakes icebreaker at least as capable as Coast Guard cutter Mackinaw (WLBB-30);

(7) in addition to amounts authorized under paragraph (6), $20,000,000 shall be authorized for the design and selection of icebreaking cutters for operation in the Great Lakes, the Northeastern United States, and the Arctic as appropriate, that are at least as capable as the Coast Guard 140-foot icebreaking tugs; and

(8) $650,000,000 is authorized for the continued acquisition of Offshore Patrol Cutters.

(b) TREATMENT OF ACQUIRED CUTTER.—Any cutter acquired using amounts authorized under subsection (a) shall be in addition to the National Security Cutters and Fast Response Cutters approved under the existing acquisition baseline in the program of record for the National Security Cutter and Fast Response Cutter.

SEC. 11105. SHORESIDE INFRASTRUCTURE AND FACILITIES.

(a) IN GENERAL.—Of the amounts authorized to be appropriated under section 4902(2)(A) of title 14, United States Code—

(1) for each of fiscal years 2022 and 2023, $1,000,000,000 is authorized to fund maintenance, construction, and repairs for Coast Guard shoreside infrastructure; and

(2) for fiscal year 2023, $127,000,000 is authorized for improvements to facilities of the Coast Guard Yard.

(b) SET-ASIDES.—Of the amounts authorized under subsection (a)(1)—

(1) up to $60,000,000 is authorized to fund Phase I, in fiscal year 2022, and $60,000,000 is authorized to fund Phase II, in fiscal year 2023, for the recapitalization of the barracks at the United States Coast Guard Training Center Cape May in Cape May, New Jersey;

(2) $67,500,000 is authorized for the construction of additional new child care development centers not constructed using funds authorized by title V of the Infrastructure Investment and Jobs Act (Public Law 117-58); and

(3) up to $1,200,000 is authorized to—

(A) complete repairs to the United States Coast Guard Station, New York, waterfront, including repairs to the concrete pier; and

(B) replace floating piers Alpha and Bravo, the South Breakwater and Ice Screen, the North Breakwater and Ice Screen and the seawall.

(c) MITIGATION OF HAZARD RISKS.—In carrying out projects with funds authorized under subsection (a), the Coast Guard shall mitigate, to the greatest extent practicable, natural hazard risks identified in any Shore Infrastructure Vulnerability Assessment for Phase I related to such projects.

SEC. 11106. COAST GUARD YARD RESILIENT INFRASTRUCTURE AND CONSTRUCTION IMPROVEMENT.

There is authorized to appropriated for the period of fiscal years 2023 through 2028 for the Secretary—

(1) $273,000,000 for the purposes of improvements to facilities of the Coast Guard Yard; and

(2) $236,000,000 for the acquisition of a new floating drydock at the Yard.

TITLE CXII—COAST GUARD

Subtitle A—Infrastructure and Assets

SEC. 11201. [14 U.S.C. 5102 note] REPORT ON SHORESIDE INFRASTRUCTURE AND FACILITIES PROJECTS.

(a) IN GENERAL.—Not less frequently than annually, the Commandant shall submit to the Committee on Commerce, Science, and Transportation of the Senate and the Committee on Transportation and Infrastructure of the House of Representatives a report that includes—

(1) a detailed list of Coast Guard shoreside infrastructure projects contemplated in each Coast Guard Sector area of responsibility and planned within the 7 years following the submission of the annual report for all Coast Guard facilities located within each Coast Guard Sector area of responsibility in the order of priority, including recapitalization, maintenance needs in excess of $100,000, dredging, and other shoreside infrastructure needs of the Coast Guard;

(2) the estimated cost of projects to fulfill each project, to the extent available; and

(3) a general description of the state of planning, including design and engineering, for each such project.

(b) CONTENTS.—The report submitted under subsection (a) shall include all unfunded shoreside infrastructure and facility priorities meeting the criteria under subsection (a) recommended to the Commandant for consideration for inclusion in the unfunded priority list report to Congress under section 5108 of title 14, United States Code, regardless of whether the unfunded shoreside infrastructure project is included in the final annual unfunded priority list to Congress.

SEC. 11202. REPORT AND BRIEFING ON RESOURCING STRATEGY FOR WESTERN PACIFIC REGION.

(a) REPORT.—

(1) IN GENERAL.—Not later than 1 year after the date of enactment of this Act, the Commandant, in consultation with the Coast Guard Commander of the Pacific Area, the Commander of United States Indo-Pacific Command, and the Under Secretary of Commerce for Oceans and Atmosphere, shall submit to the Committee on Commerce, Science, and Transportation of the Senate and the Committee on Transportation and Infrastructure of the House of Representatives a report outlining the resourcing needs of the Coast Guard to achieve optimum operations in the Western Pacific region.

(2) ELEMENTS.—The report required under paragraph (1) shall include the following:

(A) An assessment of the risks and associated needs—

(i) to United States strategic maritime interests, in particular such interests in areas west of the International Date Line, including risks to bilateral maritime partners of the United States, posed by not fully staffing and equipping Coast Guard operations in the Western Pacific region;

(ii) to the Coast Guard mission and force posed by not fully staffing and equipping Coast Guard operations in the Western Pacific region; and

(iii) to support the call of the President, as set forth in the Indo-Pacific Strategy, to expand Coast Guard presence and cooperation in Southeast Asia, South Asia, and the Pacific Islands, with a focus on advising, training, deployment, and capacity building.

(B) A description of the additional resources, including shoreside resources, required to fully implement the needs described in subparagraph (A), including the United States commitment to bilateral fisheries law enforcement in the Pacific Ocean.

(C) A description of the operational and personnel assets required and a dispersal plan for available and projected future Coast Guard cutters and aviation forces to conduct optimum operations in the Western Pacific region.

(D) An analysis with respect to whether a national

security cutter or fast response cutter located at a United States military installation in a foreign country in the Western Pacific region would enhance United States national security, partner country capacity building, and prevention and effective response to illegal, unreported, and unregulated fishing.

(E) An assessment of the benefits and associated costs involved in—

(i) increasing staffing of Coast Guard personnel within the command elements of United States Indo-Pacific Command or subordinate commands; and

(ii) designating a Coast Guard patrol force under the direct authority of the Commander of the United States Indo-Pacific Command with associated forward-based assets and personnel.

(F) An identification of any additional authority necessary, including proposals for legislative change, to meet the needs identified in accordance with subparagraphs (A) through (E) and any other mission requirement in the Western Pacific region.

(3) FORM.—The report required under paragraph (1) shall be submitted in unclassified form but may include a classified annex.

(b) BRIEFING.—Not later than 60 days after the date on which the Commandant submits the report under subsection (a), the Commandant, or a designated individual, shall provide to the Committee on Commerce, Science, and Transportation of the Senate and the Committee on Transportation and Infrastructure of the House of Representatives a briefing on the findings and conclusions of such report.

SEC. 11203. STUDY AND REPORT ON NATIONAL SECURITY AND DRUG TRAFFICKING THREATS IN FLORIDA STRAITS, CUBA, AND CARIBBEAN REGION.

(a) IN GENERAL.—The Commandant shall conduct a study on threats to national security, drug trafficking, and other relevant threats the Commandant considers appropriate in the Florida Straits and Caribbean region, including Cuba.

(b) ELEMENTS.—The study required under subsection (a) shall

include the following:

(1) An assessment of—

(A) new technology and evasive maneuvers used by transnational criminal organizations to evade detection and interdiction by Coast Guard law enforcement units and interagency partners; and

(B) capability gaps of the Coast Guard with respect to—

(i) the detection and interdiction of illicit drugs in the Florida Straits and Caribbean region, including Cuba; and

(ii) the detection of national security threats in such region.

(2) An identification of—

(A) the critical technological advancements required for the Coast Guard to meet current and anticipated threats in such region;

(B) the capabilities required to enhance information sharing and coordination between the Coast Guard and interagency partners, foreign governments, and related civilian entities; and

(C) any significant developing threats to the United States posed by illicit actors in such region.

(c) REPORT.—Not later than 2 years after the date of enactment of this Act, the Commandant shall submit to the Committee on Commerce, Science, and Transportation of the Senate and the Committee on Transportation and Infrastructure of the House of Representatives a report on the results of the study under subsection (a).

SEC. 11204. COAST GUARD YARD.

(a) IN GENERAL.—With respect to the Coast Guard Yard, the uses of the amounts authorized under sections 11105(a)(2) and 11106 are to—

(1) improve resilience and capacity;

(2) maintain and expand Coast Guard organic manufacturing capacity;

(3) expand training and recruitment;

(4) enhance safety;

(5) improve environmental compliance; and

(6) ensure that the Coast Guard Yard is prepared to meet the growing needs of the modern Coast Guard fleet.

(b) INCLUSIONS.—The Secretary shall ensure that the Coast Guard Yard receives improvements that include the following:

(1) Facilities upgrades needed to improve resilience of the shipyard, its facilities, and associated infrastructure.

(2) Acquisition of a large-capacity drydock.

(3) Improvements to piers and wharves, drydocks, and capital equipment utilities.

(4) Environmental remediation.

(5) Construction of a new warehouse and paint facility.

(6) Acquisition of a new travel lift.

(7) Dredging necessary to facilitate access to the Coast Guard Yard.

(c) WORKFORCE DEVELOPMENT PLAN.—Not later than 180 days after the date of enactment of this Act, the Commandant shall submit to the Committee on Commerce, Science, and Transportation of the Senate and the Committee on Transportation and Infrastructure of the House of Representatives, a workforce development plan that—

(1) outlines the workforce needs of the Coast Guard Yard with respect to civilian employees and active duty members of the Coast Guard, including engineers, individuals engaged in trades, cyber specialists, and other personnel necessary to meet the evolving mission set of the Coast Guard Yard; and

(2) includes recommendations for Congress with respect to the authorities, training, funding, and civilian and active-duty recruitment, including the recruitment of women and underrepresented minorities, necessary to meet workforce needs of the Coast Guard Yard for the 10-year period beginning on the date of submission of the plan.

SEC. 11205. AUTHORITY TO ENTER INTO TRANSACTIONS OTHER THAN CONTRACTS AND GRANTS TO PROCURE COST-EFFECTIVE TECHNOLOGY FOR MISSION NEEDS.

(a) IN GENERAL.—Subchapter III of chapter 11 of title 14,

United States Code, is amended by adding at the end the following:

"SEC. 1158. [14 U.S.C. 1158] Authority to enter into transactions other than contracts and grants to procure cost-effective, advanced technology for mission-critical needs

"(a) IN GENERAL.—Subject to subsections (b) and (c), the Commandant may enter into transactions (other than contracts, cooperative agreements, and grants) to operate, test, and acquire cost-effective technology for the purpose of meeting the mission needs of the Coast Guard.

"(b) OPERATION, TESTING, AND ACQUISITION.—Operation, testing, and acquisition of technologies under subsection (a) shall be—

"(1) carried out in accordance with Coast Guard policies and guidance; and

"(2) consistent with the operational requirements of the Coast Guard.

"(c) LIMITATIONS.—The Commandant may not enter into a transaction under subsection (a) with respect to a technology that—

"(1) does not comply with the cybersecurity standards of the Coast Guard; or

"(2) is sourced from an entity domiciled in the People's Republic of China, unless the Commandant determines that the prototype or procurement of such a technology is for the purpose of—

"(A) counter-UAS or surrogate testing; or

"(B) intelligence, electronic warfare, and information warfare, testing, and analysis.

"(d) EDUCATION AND TRAINING.—The Commandant shall ensure that management, technical, and contracting personnel of the Coast Guard involved in the award or administration of transactions under this section are provided adequate education and training with respect to the authority under this section.

"(e) REGULATIONS.—The Commandant shall prescribe regulations as necessary to carry out this section.

"(f) COUNTER-UAS DEFINED.—In this section, the term 'counter-UAS' has the meaning given such term in section 44801 of title 49."

(b) CLERICAL AMENDMENT.—The analysis for chapter 11 of title

14, United States Code, is amended by inserting after the item relating to section 1157 the following:

"1158. Authority to enter into transactions other than contracts and grants to procure cost-effective, advanced technology for mission-critical needs."

(c) REPORT.—

(1) IN GENERAL.—Not later than 5 years after the date of the enactment of this Act, the Commandant shall submit to the appropriate committees of Congress a report that—

(A) describes the use of the authority pursuant to section 1158 of title 14, United States Code (as added by this section); and

(B) assesses the mission and operational benefits of such authority.

(2) APPROPRIATE COMMITTEES OF CONGRESS DEFINED.—In this subsection, the term "appropriate committees of Congress" means—

(A) the Committee on Commerce, Science, and Transportation of the Senate; and

(B) the Committee on Transportation and Infrastructure of the House of Representatives.

SEC. 11206. IMPROVEMENTS TO INFRASTRUCTURE AND OPERATIONS PLANNING.

(a) IN GENERAL.—Not later than 1 year after the date of enactment of this Act, the Commandant shall incorporate the most recent oceanic and atmospheric data relating to the increasing rates of extreme weather, including flooding, into planning scenarios for Coast Guard infrastructure and mission deployments with respect to all Coast Guard Missions.

(b) COORDINATION WITH NATIONAL OCEANIC AND ATMOSPHERIC ADMINISTRATION.—In carrying out subsection (a), the Commandant shall—

(1) coordinate with the Under Secretary of Commerce for Oceans and Atmosphere to ensure the incorporation of the most recent environmental and climatic data; and

(2) request technical assistance and advice from the Under Secretary in planning scenarios, as appropriate.

(c) BRIEFING.—Not later than 1 year after the date of enactment of this Act, the Commandant shall provide to the Committee on Commerce, Science, and Transportation of the Senate and the Committee on Transportation and Infrastructure of the House of Representatives a briefing on the manner in which the best-available science from the National Oceanic and Atmospheric Administration has been incorporated into at least 1 key mission area of the Coast Guard, and the lessons learned from incorporating such science.

SEC. 11207. [14 U.S.C. 521 note] AQUA ALERT NOTIFICATION SYSTEM PILOT PROGRAM.

(a) IN GENERAL.—Not later than 2 years after the date of enactment of this Act, the Commandant shall, subject to the availability of appropriations, establish a pilot program to improve the issuance of alerts to facilitate cooperation with the public to render aid to distressed individuals under section 521 of title 14, United States Code.

(b) PILOT PROGRAM CONTENTS.—In carrying out the pilot program established under subsection (a), the Commandant shall, to the maximum extent possible—

(1) include a voluntary opt-in program under which members of the public, as appropriate, and the entities described in subsection (c), may receive notifications on cellular devices regarding Coast Guard activities to render aid to distressed individuals under section 521 of title 14, United States Code;

(2) cover areas located within the area of responsibility of 3 different Coast Guard sectors in diverse geographic regions; and

(3) provide that the dissemination of an alert shall be limited to the geographic areas most likely to facilitate the rendering of aid to distressed individuals.

(c) CONSULTATION.—In developing the pilot program under subsection (a), the Commandant shall consult—

(1) the head of any relevant Federal agency;

(2) the government of any relevant State;

(3) any Tribal Government;

(4) the government of any relevant territory or possession

of the United States; and

(5) any relevant political subdivision of an entity described in paragraph (2), (3), or (4).

(d) REPORT TO CONGRESS.—

(1) IN GENERAL.—Not later than 2 years after the date of enactment of this Act, and annually thereafter through 2026, the Commandant shall submit to the Committee on Commerce, Science, and Transportation of the Senate and the Committee on Transportation and Infrastructure of the House of Representatives a report on the implementation of this section.

(2) PUBLIC AVAILABILITY.—The Commandant shall make the report submitted under paragraph (1) available to the public.

SEC. 11208. [14 U.S.C. 504 note] PILOT PROJECT FOR ENHANCING COAST GUARD CUTTER READINESS THROUGH CONDITION-BASED MAINTENANCE.

(a) IN GENERAL.—Not later than 3 years after the date of enactment of this Act, the Commandant shall conduct a pilot project to enhance cutter readiness and reduce lost patrol days through the deployment of condition-based program standards for cutter maintenance, in accordance with the criteria set forth in subsection (b).

(b) CRITERIA FOR CONDITION-BASED MAINTENANCE EVALUATION.—In conducting the pilot project under subsection (a), the Commandant, in cooperation with government and industry partners, shall—

(1) select at least 1 class of cutters under construction with respect to which the application of the pilot project would enhance readiness;

(2) use condition-based program standards which incorporate artificial, intelligence, prognostic based maintenance planning;

(3) create and model a full ship digital twin for the cutters selected under paragraph (1);

(4) install or modify instrumentation capable of producing full hull, mechanical, and electrical data necessary to analyze cutter operational conditions with active maintenance alerts; and

(5) evaluate and weight efficacy of potential emergent repairs as well as planned depot maintenance activities.

(c) CONSIDERATION.—Prior to developing the pilot project in this section, the Commandant shall evaluate commercially available products, technology, applications, standards, and technology for development and implementation of the pilot program.

(d) REPORT TO CONGRESS.—The Commandant shall submit to the Committee on Commerce, Science, and Transportation of the Senate and the Committee on Transportation and Infrastructure of the House of Representatives—

(1) an interim report not later than 12 months after the date of enactment of this Act on the progress in carrying out the pilot project described in subsection (a); and

(2) a final report not later than 3 years after the date of enactment of this Act on the results of the pilot project described in subsection (a) that includes—

(A) options to integrate condition-based program standards with prognostic based maintenance planning to Coast Guard cutters; and

(B) plans to deploy condition-based program standards with prognostic based maintenance planning to Coast Guard cutters.

SEC. 11209. STUDY ON LAYDOWN OF COAST GUARD CUTTERS.

Not later than 120 days after the date of enactment of this Act, the Secretary shall conduct a study on the laydown of Coast Guard Fast Response Cutters to assess Coast Guard mission readiness and to identify areas of need for asset coverage.

SEC. 11210. ACQUISITION LIFE-CYCLE COST ESTIMATES.

Section 1132(e) of title 14, United States Code, is amended by striking paragraphs (2) and (3) and inserting the following:

"(2) TYPES OF ESTIMATES.—For each Level 1 or Level 2 acquisition project or program, in addition to life-cycle cost estimates developed under paragraph (1), the Commandant shall require that—

"(A) life-cycle cost estimates developed under paragraph (1) be updated before—

"(i) each milestone decision is concluded; and

"(ii) the project or program enters a new acquisition phase; and

"(B) an independent cost estimate or independent cost assessment, as appropriate, be developed to validate life-cycle cost estimates developed under paragraph (1)."

SEC. 11211. DISPOSITION OF INFRASTRUCTURE RELATED TO E-LORAN.

Section 914 of title 14, United States Code, is amended to read as follows:

"SEC. 914. Disposition of infrastructure related to E-LORAN

"(a) IN GENERAL.—Notwithstanding any other provision of law, the Commandant may dismantle or dispose of any real or personal property under the administrative control of the Coast Guard and used for the LORAN-C system.

"(b) RESTRICTION.—No action described in subsection (a) may be taken unless and until—

"(1) the Commandant notifies the Secretary of Transportation and the Secretary of Defense in writing of the proposed dismantling or disposal of a LORAN-C system; and

"(2) a period of 90 calendar days expires following the day on which the notice has been submitted.

"(c) RECEIPT OF NOTIFICATION.—If, not later than 90 calendar days of receipt of the written notification under subsection (b), the Secretary of Transportation or the Secretary of Defense notifies the Commandant, in writing, of a determination under section 312(d) of title 49 that the property is required to provide a positioning, navigation, and timing system to provide redundant capability in the event the Global Positioning System signals are disrupted, the Commandant shall transfer the property to the Department of Transportation without any consideration.

"(d) NOTIFICATION EXPIRATION.—If, at the end of the 90 calendar day period no notification under subsection (b) has been received, the Commandant shall notify the Committee on Transportation and Infrastructure and the Committee on Appropriations in the House of Representatives and the Committee on Commerce, Science, and Transportation and the Committee on Appropriations of the Senate that the period in subsection (b)(2) has expired, and may proceed with the dismantling and disposal of the personal property, and disposing of the real property in accordance with section 2945 of this title.

"(e) EXCEPTION.—The prohibition on actions in subsection (b) does not apply to actions necessary for the safety of human life."

Subtitle B—Great Lakes

SEC. 11212. GREAT LAKES WINTER COMMERCE.

(a) GREAT LAKES ICEBREAKING OPERATIONS.—

(1) GOVERNMENT ACCOUNTABILITY OFFICE REPORT.—

(A) IN GENERAL.—Not later than 1 year after the date of enactment of this Act, the Comptroller General of the United States shall submit to the Committee on Commerce, Science, and Transportation of the Senate and the Committee on Transportation and Infrastructure of the House of Representatives a report on Coast Guard icebreaking in the Great Lakes.

(B) ELEMENTS.—The report required under subparagraph (A) shall evaluate—

(i) the economic impact of vessel delays or cancellations associated with ice coverage on the Great Lakes;

(ii) mission needs of the Coast Guard Great Lakes icebreaking program;

(iii) the impact that the proposed standards described in paragraph (2) would have on—

(I) Coast Guard operations in the Great Lakes;

(II) Northeast icebreaking missions; and

(III) inland waterway operations;

(iv) a fleet mix analysis for meeting such proposed standards;

(v) a description of the resources necessary to support the fleet mix resulting from such fleet mix analysis, including billets for crew and operating costs; and

(vi) recommendations to the Commandant for

Improvements to the Great Lakes icebreaking program, including with respect to facilitating commerce and meeting all Coast Guard mission needs.

(2) PROPOSED STANDARDS FOR ICEBREAKING OPERATIONS.—The proposed standards described in this subsection are the following:

(A) Except as provided in subparagraph (B), the Commandant shall keep ice-covered waterways in the Great Lakes open to navigation during not less than 90 percent of the hours that commercial vessels and ferries attempt to transit such ice-covered waterways.

(B) In a year in which the Great Lakes are not open to navigation, because of ice of a thickness that occurs on average only once every 10 years, the Commandant shall keep ice-covered waterways in the Great Lakes open to navigation during not less than 70 percent of the hours that commercial vessels and ferries attempt to transit such ice-covered waterways.

(3) REPORT BY COMMANDANT.—Not later than 90 days after the date on which the Comptroller General submits the report under paragraph (1), the Commandant shall submit to the Committee on Commerce, Science, and Transportation of the Senate and the Committee on Transportation and Infrastructure of the House of Representatives a report that includes the following:

(A) A plan for Coast Guard implementation of any recommendation made by the Comptroller General under paragraph (1)(B)(ii) that the Commandant considers appropriate.

(B) With respect to any recommendation made under such paragraph that the Commandant declines to implement and a justification for such decision.

(C) A review of, and a proposed implementation plan for, the results of the fleet mix analysis under paragraph (1)(B)(iv).

(D) Any proposed modifications to the standards for icebreaking operations in the Great Lakes.

(b) DEFINITIONS.—In this section:

(1) COMMERCIAL VESSEL.—The term "commercial vessel"

means any privately owned cargo vessel operating in the Great Lakes during the winter season of at least 500 tons, as measured under section 14502 of title 46, or an alternate tonnage measured under section 14302 of such title, as prescribed by the Secretary under section 14104 of such title.

(2) GREAT LAKES.—The term "Great Lakes" means the United States waters of Lake Superior, Lake Michigan, Lake Huron (including Lake St. Clair), Lake Erie, and Lake Ontario, their connecting waterways, and their adjacent harbors, and the connecting channels (including the following rivers and tributaries of such rivers: Saint Mary's River, Saint Clair River, Detroit River, Niagara River, Illinois River, Chicago River, Fox River, Grand River, St. Joseph River, St. Louis River, Menominee River, Muskegon River, Kalamazoo River, and Saint Lawrence River to the Canadian border).

(3) ICE-COVERED WATERWAY.—The term "ice-covered waterway" means any portion of the Great Lakes in which commercial vessels or ferries operate that is 70 percent or greater covered by ice, but does not include any waters adjacent to piers or docks for which commercial icebreaking services are available and adequate for the ice conditions.

(4) OPEN TO NAVIGATION.—The term "open to navigation" means navigable to the extent necessary, in no particular order of priority, to meet the reasonable demands of commerce, minimize delays to passenger ferries, extricate vessels and individuals from danger, prevent damage due to flooding, and conduct other Coast Guard missions (as required).

(5) REASONABLE DEMANDS OF COMMERCE.—The term "reasonable demands of commerce" means the safe movement of commercial vessels and ferries transiting ice-covered waterways in the Great Lakes, regardless of type of cargo, at a speed consistent with the design capability of Coast Guard icebreakers operating in the Great Lakes and appropriate to the ice capability of the commercial vessel.

SEC. 11213. [14 U.S.C. 504 note] DATABASE ON ICEBREAKING OPERATIONS IN GREAT LAKES.

(a) IN GENERAL.—The Commandant shall establish and maintain a database for collecting, archiving, and disseminating data on icebreaking operations and commercial vessel and ferry transit in the Great Lakes during ice season.

(b) ELEMENTS.—The database required under subsection (a) shall include the following:

(1) Attempts by commercial vessels and ferries to transit ice-covered waterways in the Great Lakes that are unsuccessful because of inadequate icebreaking.

(2) The period of time that each commercial vessel or ferry was unsuccessful at transit described in paragraph (1) due to inadequate icebreaking.

(3) The amount of time elapsed before each such commercial vessel or ferry was successfully broken out of the ice and whether it was accomplished by the Coast Guard or by commercial icebreaking assets.

(4) Relevant communications of each such commercial vessel or ferry with the Coast Guard and with commercial icebreaking services during such period.

(5) A description of any mitigating circumstance, such as Coast Guard icebreaker diversions to higher priority missions, that may have contributed to the amount of time described in paragraph (3).

(c) VOLUNTARY REPORTING.—Any reporting by operators of commercial vessels or ferries under this section shall be voluntary.

(d) PUBLIC AVAILABILITY.—The Commandant shall make the database available to the public on a publicly accessible website of the Coast Guard.

(e) CONSULTATION WITH INDUSTRY.—With respect to the Great Lakes icebreaking operations of the Coast Guard and the development of the database required under subsection (a), the Commandant shall consult operators of commercial vessels and ferries.

(f) PUBLIC REPORT.—Not later than July 1 after the first winter in which the Commandant is subject to the requirements of section 564 of title 14, United States Code, the Commandant shall publish on a publicly accessible website of the Coast Guard a report on the cost to the Coast Guard of meeting the requirements of such section.

(g) DEFINITIONS.—In this section:

(1) COMMERCIAL VESSEL.—The term "commercial vessel" means any privately owned cargo vessel operating in the Great

Lakes during the winter season of at least 500 tons, as measured under section 14502 of title 46, United States Code, or an alternate tonnage measured under section 14302 of such title, as prescribed by the Secretary under section 14104 of such title.

(2) GREAT LAKES.—The term "Great Lakes" means the United States waters of Lake Superior, Lake Michigan, Lake Huron (including Lake St. Clair), Lake Erie, and Lake Ontario, their connecting waterways, and their adjacent harbors, and the connecting channels (including the following rivers and tributaries of such rivers: Saint Mary's River, Saint Clair River, Detroit River, Niagara River, Illinois River, Chicago River, Fox River, Grand River, St. Joseph River, St. Louis River, Menominee River, Muskegon River, Kalamazoo River, and Saint Lawrence River to the Canadian border).

(3) ICE-COVERED WATERWAY.—The term "ice-covered waterway" means any portion of the Great Lakes in which commercial vessels or ferries operate that is 70 percent or greater covered by ice, but does not include any waters adjacent to piers or docks for which commercial icebreaking services are available and adequate for the ice conditions.

(4) OPEN TO NAVIGATION.—The term "open to navigation" means navigable to the extent necessary to—

(A) extricate vessels and individuals from danger;

(B) prevent damage due to flooding;

(C) meet the reasonable demands of commerce;

(D) minimize delays to passenger ferries; and

(E) conduct other Coast Guard missions as required.

(5) REASONABLE DEMANDS OF COMMERCE.—The term "reasonable demands of commerce" means the safe movement of commercial vessels and ferries transiting ice-covered waterways in the Great Lakes, regardless of type of cargo, at a speed consistent with the design capability of Coast Guard icebreakers operating in the Great Lakes and appropriate to the ice capability of the commercial vessel.

SEC. 11214. CENTER OF EXPERTISE FOR GREAT LAKES OIL SPILL SEARCH AND RESPONSE.

Section 807(d) of the Frank LoBiondo Coast Guard

Authorization Act of 2018 (14 U.S.C. 313 note) is amended to read as follows:

"(d) DEFINITION.—In this section, the term 'Great Lakes' means—

"(1) Lake Ontario;

"(2) Lake Erie;

"(3) Lake Huron (including Lake St. Clair);

"(4) Lake Michigan;

"(5) Lake Superior; and

"(6) the connecting channels (including the following rivers and tributaries of such rivers: Saint Mary's River, Saint Clair River, Detroit River, Niagara River, Illinois River, Chicago River, Fox River, Grand River, St. Joseph River, St. Louis River, Menominee River, Muskegon River, Kalamazoo River, and Saint Lawrence River to the Canadian border)."

SEC. 11215. GREAT LAKES SNOWMOBILE ACQUISITION PLAN.

(a) IN GENERAL.—The Commandant shall develop a plan to expand snowmobile procurement for Coast Guard units for which snowmobiles may improve ice rescue response times while maintaining the safety of Coast Guard personnel engaged in ice search and rescue. The plan shall include consideration of input from Officers in Charge, commanding officers, and commanders of such units.

(b) ELEMENTS.—The plan required under subsection (a) shall include—

(1) a consideration of input from Officers in Charge, commanding officers, and commanders of Coast Guard units described in subsection (a);

(2) a detailed description of the estimated costs of procuring, maintaining, and training members of the Coast Guard at such units to use snowmobiles; and

(3) an assessment of—

(A) the degree to which snowmobiles may improve ice rescue response times while maintaining the safety of Coast Guard personnel engaged in ice search and rescue;

(B) the operational capabilities of a snowmobile, as compared to an airboat, and a force laydown assessment with respect to the assets needed for effective operations at Coast Guard units conducting ice search and rescue activities; and

(C) the potential risks to members of the Coast Guard and members of the public posed by the use of snowmobiles by members of the Coast Guard for ice search and rescue activities.

(c) PUBLIC AVAILABILITY.—Not later than 1 year after the date of enactment of this Act, the Commandant shall finalize the plan required under subsection (a) and make the plan available on a publicly accessible website of the Coast Guard.

SEC. 11216. GREAT LAKES BARGE INSPECTION EXEMPTION.

Section 3302(m) of title 46, United States Code, is amended—

(1) in the matter preceding paragraph (1) by inserting "or a Great Lakes barge" after "seagoing barge"; and

(2) by striking "section 3301(6) of this title" and inserting "paragraph (6) or (13) of section 3301 of this title".

SEC. 11217. STUDY ON SUFFICIENCY OF COAST GUARD AVIATION ASSETS TO MEET MISSION DEMANDS.

(a) IN GENERAL.—Not later than 1 year after the date of enactment of this Act, the Commandant shall submit to the Committee on Commerce, Science, and Transportation of the Senate and the Committee on Transportation and Infrastructure of the House of Representatives a report on—

(1) the force laydown of Coast Guard aviation assets; and

(2) any geographic gaps in coverage by Coast Guard assets in areas in which the Coast Guard has search and rescue responsibilities.

(b) ELEMENTS.—The report required under subsection (a) shall include the following:

(1) The distance, time, and weather challenges that MH-65 and MH-60 units may face in reaching the outermost limits of the area of operation of Coast Guard District 8 and Coast Guard District 9 for which such units are responsible.

(2) An assessment of the advantages that Coast Guard fixed-wing assets, or an alternate rotary wing asset, would offer to the outermost limits of any area of operation for purposes

of search and rescue, law enforcement, ice operations, and logistical missions.

(3) A comparison of advantages and disadvantages of the manner in which each of the Coast Guard fixed-wing aircraft would operate in the outermost limits of any area of operation.

(4) A specific assessment of the coverage gaps, including gaps in fixed-wing coverage, and potential solutions to address such gaps in the area of operation of Coast Guard District 8 and Coast Guard District 9, including the eastern region of such area of operation with regard to Coast Guard District 9 and the southern region of such area of operation with regard to Coast Guard District 8.

Subtitle C—Arctic

SEC. 11218. [14 U.S.C. 561 note] ESTABLISHMENT OF MEDIUM ICEBREAKER PROGRAM OFFICE.

(a) IN GENERAL.—Not later than 180 days after the date of enactment of this Act, the Commandant, in consultation with the heads of the other Federal agencies as appropriate, shall submit to the Committee on Commerce, Science, and Transportation of the Senate and the Committee on Transportation and Infrastructure of the House of Representatives a report to establish a fleet mix analysis with respect to polar icebreakers and icebreaking tugs.

(b) CONTENTS.—The report required under subsection (a) shall include—

(1) a full fleet mix of heavy and medium icebreaker and 140-foot icebreaking tug replacements, including cost and timelines for the acquisition of such vessels;

(2) a revised time table showing the construction, commissioning, and acceptance of planned Polar Security Cutters 1 through 3, as of the date of report;

(3) a comparison and alternatives analysis of the costs and timeline of constructing 2 Polar Security Cutters beyond the construction of 3 such vessels rather than constructing 3 Arctic Security Cutters, including the cost of planning, design, and engineering of a new class of ships, which shall include the increased costs resulting from the delays in building a new class of cutters rather than building 2 additional cutters from an

ongoing production line;

(4) the operational benefits, limitations, and risks of a common hull design for polar icebreaking cutters for operation in the polar regions;

(5) the operational benefits, limitations, and risks of a common hull design for icebreaking tugs for operation in the Northeastern United States; and

(6) the cost and timetable for replacing the Coast Guard Cutter *Healy* (WAGB 20) as—

(A) a Polar Security Cutter;

(B) an Arctic Security Cutter; or

(C) other platform as determined by the Commandant.

(c) QUARTERLY BRIEFINGS.—As part of quarterly acquisition briefings provided by the Commandant to the Committee on Commerce, Science, and Transportation of the Senate and the Committee on Transportation and Infrastructure of the House of Representatives, the Commandant shall include an update on the status of—

(1) all acquisition activities related to the Polar Security Cutter;

(2) the performance of the entity which the Coast Guard has contracted with for detailed design and construction of the Polar Security Cutter; and

(3) the requirements for the planning, detailed design, engineering, and construction of the—

(A) Arctic Security Cutter; and

(B) Great Lakes Icebreaker.

(d) LIMITATION.—The report required to be submitted under subsection (a) shall not include an analysis of the Great Lakes Icebreaker authorized under section 11104.

(e) ESTABLISHMENT OF THE ARCTIC SECURITY CUTTER PROGRAM OFFICE.—

(1) DETERMINATION.—Not later than 90 days after the submission of the report under subsection (a), the Commandant shall determine if constructing additional Polar Security Cutters is more cost effective and efficient than constructing 3 Arctic Security Cutters.

(2) ESTABLISHMENT.—If the Commandant determines under paragraph (1) that it is more cost effective to build 3 Arctic Security Cutters than to build additional Polar Security Cutters or if the Commandant fails to make a determination under paragraph (1) by June 1, 2024, the Commandant shall establish a program office for the acquisition of the Arctic Security Cutter not later than January 1, 2025.

(3) REQUIREMENTS AND DESIGN PHASE.—Not later than 270 days after the date on which the Commandant establishes a program office under paragraph (2), the Commandant shall complete the evaluation of requirements for the Arctic Security Cutter and initiate the design phase of the Arctic Security Cutter vessel class.

(f) QUARTERLY BRIEFINGS.—Not less frequently than quarterly until the date on which a contract for acquisition of the Arctic Security Cutter is awarded under chapter 11 of title 14, United States Code, the Commandant shall provide to the Committee on Commerce, Science, and Transportation of the Senate and the Committee on Transportation and Infrastructure of the House of Representatives a briefing on the status of requirements evaluations, design of the vessel, and schedule of the program.

SEC. 11219. ARCTIC ACTIVITIES.

(a) ARCTIC OPERATIONAL IMPLEMENTATION REPORT.—Not later than 1 year after the date of enactment of this Act, the Secretary shall submit to the appropriate committees of Congress a report that describes the ability and timeline to conduct a transit of the Northern Sea Route and periodic transits of the Northwest Passage.

(b) DEFINITIONS.—In this section:

(1) APPROPRIATE COMMITTEES OF CONGRESS.—The term "appropriate committees of Congress" means—

(A) the Committee on Commerce, Science, and Transportation of the Senate; and

(B) the Committee on Transportation and Infrastructure of the House of Representatives.

(2) ARCTIC.—The term "Arctic" has the meaning given such term in section 112 of the Arctic Research and Policy Act of 1984 (15 U.S.C. 4111).

SEC. 11220. STUDY ON ARCTIC OPERATIONS AND INFRASTRUCTURE.

(a) IN GENERAL.—Not later than 1 year after the date of enactment of this Act, the Comptroller General of the United States shall commence a study on the Arctic operations and infrastructure of the Coast Guard.

(b) ELEMENTS.—The study required under subsection (a) shall assess the following:

(1) The extent of the collaboration between the Coast Guard and the Department of Defense to assess, manage, and mitigate security risks in the Arctic region.

(2) Actions taken by the Coast Guard to manage risks to Coast Guard operations, infrastructure, and workforce planning in the Arctic.

(3) The plans the Coast Guard has in place for managing and mitigating the risks to commercial maritime operations and the environment in the Arctic region.

(c) REPORT.—Not later than 1 year after commencing the study required under subsection (a), the Comptroller General shall submit to the Committee on Commerce, Science, and Transportation of the Senate and the Committee on Transportation and Infrastructure of the House of Representatives a report on the findings of the study.

SEC. 11221. PRIBILOF ISLAND TRANSITION COMPLETION ACTIONS.

(a) ACTUAL USE AND OCCUPANCY REPORTS.—Not later than 90 days after enactment of this Act, and quarterly thereafter, the Secretary shall submit to the Committee on Transportation and Infrastructure of the House of Representatives and the Committee on Commerce, Science, and Transportation of the Senate a report describing—

(1) the degree to which Coast Guard personnel and equipment are deployed to St. Paul Island, Alaska, in actual occupancy of the facilities, as required under section 524 of the Pribilof Island Transition Completion Act of 2016 (Public Law 114-120); and

(2) the status of the activities described in subsections (c) and (d) until such activities have been completed.

(b) AIRCRAFT HANGER.—The Secretary may—

(1) enter into a lease for a hangar to house deployed Coast Guard aircraft if such hanger was previously under lease by the Coast Guard for purposes of housing such aircraft; and

(2) enter into an agreement with the lessor of such a hanger in which the Secretary may carry out repairs necessary to support the deployment of such aircraft and the cost of such repairs may be offset under the terms of the lease.

(c) FUEL TANK.—

(1) IN GENERAL.—Not later than 30 days after the date of enactment of this Act, the Commandant shall notify the Alaska Native Village Corporation for St. Paul Island, Alaska of the availability of any fuel tank—

(A) which is located on property on St. Paul Island, Alaska, which is leased by the Coast Guard for the purpose of housing such a fuel tank; and

(B) for which the Commandant has determined that the Coast Guard no longer has an operational need.

(2) TRANSFER.—If not later than 30 days after a notification under subsection (a), the Alaska Native Village Corporation for St. Paul Island, Alaska requests that the ownership of the tank be transferred to such corporation then the Commandant shall—

(A) after conducting any necessary environmental remediation pursuant to the lease referred to in paragraph (1)(A), transfer ownership of such fuel tank to such corporation; and

(B) upon the date of such transfer, terminate the lease referred to in paragraph (1)(A).

(d) SAVINGS CLAUSE.—Nothing in this section shall be construed to limit any rights of the Alaska Native Village Corporation for St. Paul to receive conveyance of all or part of the lands and improvements related to Tract 43 under the same terms and conditions as prescribed in section 524 of the Pribilof Island Transition Completion Act of 2016 (Public Law 114-120).

SEC. 11222. REPORT ON SHIPYARDS OF FINLAND AND SWEDEN.

Not later than 2 years after the date of enactment of this Act, the Commandant, in consultation with the Comptroller General of the United States, shall submit to Congress a report that analyzes the shipyards of Finland and Sweden to assess future opportunities for technical assistance related to engineering to aid the Coast Guard in fulfilling its future mission needs.

SEC. 11223. [14 U.S.C. 561 note] ACQUISITION OF ICEBREAKER.

(a) IN GENERAL.—The Commandant may acquire or procure 1 United States built available icebreaker.

(b) EXEMPTIONS FROM REQUIREMENTS.—

(1) IN GENERAL.—Sections 1131, 1132(2), 1132(c), 1133, and 1171 of title 14, United States Code, shall not apply to an acquisition or procurement under subsection (a).

(2) ADDITIONAL EXCEPTIONS.—Paragraphs (1), (3), (4), and (5) of subsection (a) and subsections (b), (d), and (e) of section 1132 of title 14, United States Code, shall apply to an acquisition or procurement under subsection (a) until the first phase of the initial acquisition or procurement is complete and initial operating capacity is achieved.

(c) SCIENCE MISSION REQUIREMENTS.—For any available icebreaker acquired or procured under subsection (a), the Commandant shall ensure scientific research capacity comparable to the Coast Guard Cutter *Healy* (WAGB 20), for the purposes of hydrographic, bathymetric, oceanographic, weather, atmospheric, climate, fisheries, marine mammals, genetic and other data related to the Arctic, and other research as the Under Secretary determines appropriate.

(d) OPERATIONS AND AGREEMENTS.—

(1) COAST GUARD.—With respect to any available icebreaker acquired or procured under subsection (a), the Secretary shall be responsible for any acquisition, retrofitting, operation, and maintenance costs necessary to achieve full operational capability, including testing, installation, and acquisition, including for the suite of hull-mounted, ship-provided scientific instrumentation and equipment for data collection.

(2) NATIONAL OCEANIC AND ATMOSPHERIC ADMINISTRATION.—The Under Secretary shall not be responsible for the costs of retrofitting any available icebreaker acquired or procured under subsection (a), including costs relating to—

(A) vessel maintenance, construction, operations, and crewing other than the science party; and

(B) making such icebreaker capable of conducting the research described in subsection (c), including design, procurement of laboratory space and equipment, and modification of living quarters.

(3) RESPONSIBILITY OF UNDER SECRETARY.—The Under Secretary shall be responsible for costs related to—

(A) the science party;

(B) the scientific mission; and

(C) other scientific assets and equipment that augment such icebreaker beyond full operational capacity as determined by the Under Secretary and Commandant.

(4) MEMORANDUM OF AGREEMENT.—The Commandant and the Under Secretary shall enter into a memorandum of agreement to facilitate science activities, data collection, and other procedures necessary to meet the requirements of this section.

(e) RESTRICTION AND BRIEFING.—Not later than 60 days after the date of enactment of this Act, the Commandant shall brief the appropriate congressional committees with respect to available icebreaker acquired or procured under subsection (a) on—

(1) a proposed concept of operations of such icebreaker;

(2) a detailed cost estimate for such icebreaker, including estimated costs for acquisition, modification, shoreside infrastructure, crewing, and maintaining such an icebreaker by year for the estimated service life of such icebreaker; and

(3) the expected capabilities of such icebreaker as compared to the capabilities of a fully operational Coast Guard built Polar Security Cutter for each year in which such an icebreaker is anticipated to serve in lieu of such a cutter and the projected annual costs to achieve such anticipated capabilities.

(f) INTERIM REPORT.—Not later than 30 days after the date of enactment of this Act, and not later than every 90 days thereafter until any available icebreaker acquired or procured under subsection (a) has reached full operational capability, the Commandant shall provide to the appropriate Committees of Congress an interim report of the status and progress of all elements under subsection (d).

(g) RULE OF CONSTRUCTION.—Nothing in this section shall effect acquisitions of vessels by the Under Secretary.

(h) SAVINGS CLAUSE.—

(1) IN GENERAL.—Any operations necessary for the saving of life or property at sea, response to environmental pollution, national security, defense readiness, or other missions as determined by the Commandant shall take priority over any scientific or economic missions under subsection (c).

(2) AUGMENTATION.—Any available icebreaker acquired or procured under subsection (a) shall augment the Coast Guard mission in the Arctic, including by conducting operations and missions that are in addition to missions conducted by the Coast Guard Cutter *Healy* (WAGB 20) in the region.

(i) DEFINITIONS.—In this section:

(1) APPROPRIATE CONGRESSIONAL COMMITTEES.—The term "appropriate congressional committees" means the Committee on Transportation and Infrastructure and the Committee on Appropriations of the House of Representatives and the Committee on Commerce, Science, and Transportation and the Committee on Appropriations of the Senate.

(2) ARCTIC.—The term "Arctic" has the meaning given such term in section 112 of the Arctic Research and Policy Act of 1984 (15 U.S.C. 4111).

(3) AVAILABLE ICEBREAKER.—The term "available icebreaker" means a vessel that—

(A) is capable of—

(i) supplementing United States Coast Guard polar icebreaking capabilities in the Arctic region of the United States;

(ii) projecting United States sovereignty;

(iii) ensuring a continuous operational capability in the Arctic region of the United States;

(iv) carrying out the primary duty of the Coast Guard described in section 103(7) of title 14, United States Code; and

(v) collecting hydrographic, environmental, and climate data; and

(B) is documented with a coastwise endorsement under chapter 121 of title 46, United States Code.

(4) UNDER SECRETARY.—The term "Under Secretary" means the Under Secretary of Commerce for Oceans and Atmosphere.

(j) SUNSET.—The authority under subsections (a) through (c) shall expire on the date that is 3 years after the date of enactment of this Act.

Subtitle D—Maritime Cyber and Artificial Intelligence

SEC. 11224. [14 U.S.C. 504 note] ENHANCING MARITIME CYBERSECURITY.

(a) DEFINITIONS.—In this section:

(1) CYBER INCIDENT.—The term "cyber incident" means an occurrence that actually or imminently jeopardizes, without lawful authority, the integrity, confidentiality, or availability of information on an information system, or actually or imminently jeopardizes, without lawful authority, an information system.

(2) MARITIME OPERATORS.—The term "maritime operators" means the owners or operators of vessels engaged in commercial service, the owners or operators of facilities, and port authorities.

(3) FACILITIES.—The term "facilities" has the meaning given the term "facility" in section 70101 of title 46, United States Code.

(b) PUBLIC AVAILABILITY OF CYBERSECURITY TOOLS AND RESOURCES.—

(1) IN GENERAL.—Not later than 2 years after the date of enactment of this Act, the Commandant, in coordination with the Administrator of the Maritime Administration, the Director of the Cybersecurity and Infrastructure Security Agency, and the Director of the National Institute of Standards and Technology, shall identify and make available to the public a list of tools and resources, including the resources of the Coast Guard and the Cybersecurity and Infrastructure Security

Agency, designed to assist maritime operators in identifying, detecting, protecting against, mitigating, responding to, and recovering from cyber incidents.

(2) IDENTIFICATION.—In carrying out paragraph (1), the Commandant, the Administrator of the Maritime Administration, the Director of the Cybersecurity and Infrastructure Security Agency, and the Director of the National Institute of Standards and Technology shall identify tools and resources that—

(A) comply with the cybersecurity framework for improving critical infrastructure established by the National Institute of Standards and Technology; or

(B) use the guidelines on maritime cyber risk management issued by the International Maritime Organization on July 5, 2017 (or successor guidelines).

(3) CONSULTATION.—The Commandant, the Administrator of the Maritime Administration, the Director of the Cybersecurity and Infrastructure Security Agency, and the Director of the National Institute of Standards and Technology may consult with maritime operators, other Federal agencies, industry stakeholders, and cybersecurity experts to identify tools and resources for purposes of this section.

SEC. 11225. ESTABLISHMENT OF UNMANNED SYSTEM PROGRAM AND AUTONOMOUS CONTROL AND COMPUTER VISION TECHNOLOGY PROJECT.

(a) IN GENERAL.—Section 319 of title 14, United States Code, is amended to read as follows:

"SEC. 319. Unmanned system program and autonomous control and computer vision technology project

"(a) UNMANNED SYSTEM PROGRAM.—Not later than 2 years after the date of enactment of this section, the Secretary shall establish, under the control of the Commandant, an unmanned system program for the use by the Coast Guard of land-based, cutter-based, and aircraft-based unmanned systems for the purpose of increasing effectiveness and efficiency of mission execution.

"(b) AUTONOMOUS CONTROL AND COMPUTER VISION TECHNOLOGY PROJECT.—

"(1) IN GENERAL.—The Commandant shall conduct a

project to retrofit 2 or more existing Coast Guard small boats deployed at operational units with—

"(A) commercially available autonomous control and computer vision technology; and

"(B) such sensors and methods of communication as are necessary to control, and technology to assist in conducting, search and rescue, surveillance, and interdiction missions.

"(2) DATA COLLECTION.—As part of the project required under paragraph (1), the Commandant shall collect and evaluate field-collected operational data from the retrofit described in such paragraph to inform future requirements.

"(3) BRIEFING.—Not later than 180 days after the date on which the project required under paragraph (1) is completed, the Commandant shall provide to the Committee on Commerce, Science, and Transportation of the Senate and the Committee on Transportation and Infrastructure of the House of Representatives a briefing on the project that includes an evaluation of the data collected from the project.

"(c) UNMANNED SYSTEM DEFINED.—In this section, the term 'unmanned system' means—

"(1) an unmanned aircraft system (as such term is defined in section 44801 of title 49);

"(2) an unmanned marine surface system; and

"(3) an unmanned marine subsurface system."

(b) CLERICAL AMENDMENT.—The analysis for chapter 3 of title 14, United States Code, is amended by striking the item relating to section 319 and inserting the following:

"319. Unmanned system program and autonomous control and computer vision technology project."

(c) SUBMISSION TO CONGRESS.—Not later than 180 days after the date of enactment of this Act, the Commandant shall submit to the Committee on Transportation and Infrastructure of the House of Representatives and the Committee on Commerce, Science, and Transportation of the Senate a detailed description of the strategy of the Coast Guard to implement unmanned systems across mission areas, including—

(1) the steps taken to implement actions recommended in

the consensus study report of the National Academies of Sciences, Engineering, and Medicine titled "Leveraging Unmanned Systems for Coast Guard Missions: A Strategic Imperative", published on November 12, 2020;

(2) the strategic goals and acquisition strategies for proposed uses and procurements of unmanned systems;

(3) a strategy to sustain competition and innovation for procurement of unmanned systems and services for the Coast Guard, including defining opportunities for new and existing technologies; and

(4) an estimate of the timeline, costs, staff resources, technology, or other resources necessary to accomplish the strategy.

(d) COST ASSESSMENT.—Not later than 1 year after the date of the enactment of this Act, the Commandant shall provide to Congress an estimate of the costs associated with implementing the amendments made by this section.

SEC. 11226. [14 U.S.C. 504 note] ARTIFICIAL INTELLIGENCE STRATEGY.

(a) COORDINATION OF DATA AND ARTIFICIAL INTELLIGENCE ACTIVITIES RELATING TO IDENTIFYING, DEMONSTRATING, AND WHERE APPROPRIATE TRANSITIONING TO OPERATIONAL USE.—

(1) IN GENERAL.—The Commandant shall coordinate data and artificial intelligence activities relating to identifying, demonstrating and where appropriate transitioning to operational use of artificial intelligence technologies when such technologies enhance mission capability or performance.

(2) EMPHASIS.—The set of activities established under paragraph (1) shall—

(A) apply data analytics, artificial intelligence, and machine-learning solutions to operational and mission-support problems; and

(B) coordinate activities involving artificial intelligence and artificial intelligence-enabled capabilities within the Coast Guard.

(b) DESIGNATED OFFICIAL.—

(1) IN GENERAL.—Not later than 1 year after the date of

enactment of this Act, the Commandant shall designate a senior official of the Coast Guard (referred to in this section as the "designated official") with the principal responsibility for the coordination of data and artificial intelligence activities relating to identifying, demonstrating, and, where appropriate, transitioning to operational use artificial intelligence and machine learning for the Coast Guard.

(2) GOVERNANCE AND OVERSIGHT OF ARTIFICIAL INTELLIGENCE AND MACHINE LEARNING POLICY.—The designated official shall regularly convene appropriate officials of the Coast Guard—

(A) to integrate the functional activities of the Coast Guard with respect to data, artificial intelligence, and machine learning;

(B) to ensure that there are efficient and effective data, artificial intelligence, and machine-learning capabilities throughout the Coast Guard, where appropriate; and

(C) to develop and continuously improve research, innovation, policy, joint processes, and procedures to facilitate the coordination of data and artificial intelligence activities relating to identification, demonstration, and, where appropriate, transition into operational use artificial intelligence and machine learning throughout the Coast Guard.

(c) STRATEGIC PLAN.—

(1) IN GENERAL.—The designated official shall develop a strategic plan to coordinate activities relating to identifying, demonstrating, and transitioning artificial intelligence technologies into operational use where appropriate.

(2) ELEMENTS.—The plan required by paragraph (1) shall include the following:

(A) A strategic roadmap for the coordination of data and artificial intelligence activities for the identification, demonstration, and transition to operational use, where appropriate, artificial intelligence technologies and key enabling capabilities.

(B) The continuous identification, evaluation, and adaptation of relevant artificial intelligence capabilities adopted by the Coast Guard and developed and adopted by other organizations for military missions and business operations.

(C) Consideration of the identification, adoption, and procurement of artificial intelligence technologies for use in operational and mission support activities.

(3) SUBMISSION TO COMMANDANT.—Not later than 2 years after the date of enactment of this Act, the designated official shall submit to the Commandant the plan developed under paragraph (1).

(4) SUBMISSION TO CONGRESS.—Not later than 2 years after the date of enactment of this Act, the Commandant shall submit to the Committee on Commerce, Science, and Transportation of the Senate and the Committee on Transportation and Infrastructure of the House of Representatives the plan developed under paragraph (1).

SEC. 11227. REVIEW OF ARTIFICIAL INTELLIGENCE APPLICATIONS AND ESTABLISHMENT OF PERFORMANCE METRICS.

(a) IN GENERAL.—Not later than 2 years after the date of enactment of this Act, the Commandant shall—

(1) review the potential applications of artificial intelligence and digital technology to the platforms, processes, and operations of the Coast Guard;

(2) identify the resources necessary to improve the use of artificial intelligence and digital technology in such platforms, processes, and operations; and

(3) establish performance objectives and accompanying metrics for the incorporation of artificial intelligence and digital readiness into such platforms, processes, and operations.

(b) PERFORMANCE OBJECTIVES AND ACCOMPANYING METRICS.—

(1) SKILL GAPS.—In carrying out subsection (a), the Commandant shall—

(A) conduct a comprehensive review and assessment of—

(i) skill gaps in the fields of software development, software engineering, data science, and artificial intelligence;

(ii) the qualifications of civilian personnel needed

for both management and specialist tracks in such fields; and

(iii) the qualifications of military personnel (officer and enlisted) needed for both management and specialist tracks in such fields; and

(B) establish recruiting, training, and talent management performance objectives and accompanying metrics for achieving and maintaining staffing levels needed to fill identified gaps and meet the needs of the Coast Guard for skilled personnel.

(2) AI MODERNIZATION ACTIVITIES.—In carrying out subsection (a), the Commandant shall—

(A) assess investment by the Coast Guard in artificial intelligence innovation, science and technology, and research and development;

(B) assess investment by the Coast Guard in test and evaluation of artificial intelligence capabilities;

(C) assess the integration of, and the resources necessary to better use artificial intelligence in wargames, exercises, and experimentation;

(D) assess the application of, and the resources necessary to better use, artificial intelligence in logistics and sustainment systems;

(E) assess the integration of, and the resources necessary to better use, artificial intelligence for administrative functions;

(F) establish performance objectives and accompanying metrics for artificial intelligence modernization activities of the Coast Guard; and

(G) identify the resources necessary to effectively use artificial intelligence to carry out the missions of the Coast Guard.

(c) REPORT TO CONGRESS.—Not later than 180 days after the completion of the review required under subsection (a)(1), the Commandant shall submit to the Committee on Commerce, Science, and Transportation and the Committee on Appropriations of the Senate and the Committee on Transportation and Infrastructure and the Committee on Appropriations of the House of

Representatives a report on—

(1) the findings of the Commandant with respect to such review and any action taken or proposed to be taken by the Commandant, and the resources necessary to address such findings;

(2) the performance objectives and accompanying metrics established under subsections (a)(3) and (b)(1)(B); and

(3) any recommendation with respect to proposals for legislative change necessary to successfully implement artificial intelligence applications within the Coast Guard.

SEC. 11228. [14 U.S.C. 504 note] CYBER DATA MANAGEMENT.

(a) IN GENERAL.—The Commandant and the Director of the Cybersecurity and Infrastructure Security Agency shall—

(1) develop policies, processes, and operating procedures governing—

(A) access to and the ingestion, structure, storage, and analysis of information and data relevant to the Coast Guard Cyber Mission, including—

(i) intelligence data relevant to Coast Guard missions;

(ii) internet traffic, topology, and activity data relevant to such missions; and

(iii) cyber threat information relevant to such missions; and

(B) data management and analytic platforms relating to such missions; and

(2) evaluate data management platforms referred to in paragraph (1)(B) to ensure that such platforms operate consistently with the Coast Guard Data Strategy.

(b) REPORT.—Not later than 1 year after the date of enactment of this Act, the Commandant shall submit to the Committee on Commerce, Science, and Transportation and the Committee on Homeland Security and Governmental Affairs of the Senate and the Committee on Transportation and Infrastructure and the Committee on Homeland Security of the House of Representatives a report that includes—

(1) an assessment of the progress on the activities required

by subsection (a); and

(2) any recommendation with respect to funding or additional authorities necessary, including proposals for legislative change, to improve Coast Guard cyber data management.

SEC. 11229. DATA MANAGEMENT.

Section 504(a) of title 14, United States Code, is amended—

(1) in paragraph (24) by striking "; and" and inserting a semicolon;

(2) in paragraph (25) by striking the period and inserting "; and"; and

(3) by adding at the end the following:

"(26) develop data workflows and processes for the leveraging of mission-relevant data by the Coast Guard to enhance operational effectiveness and efficiency."

SEC. 11230. STUDY ON CYBER THREATS TO UNITED STATES MARINE TRANSPORTATION SYSTEM.

(a) IN GENERAL.—Not later than 1 year after the date of enactment of this Act, the Comptroller General of the United States shall commence a study on cyber threats to the United States marine transportation system.

(b) ELEMENTS.—The study required under paragraph (1) shall assess the following:

(1) The extent to which the Coast Guard, in collaboration with other Federal agencies, sets standards for the cybersecurity of facilities and vessels regulated under part 104, 105, or 106 of title 33, Code of Federal Regulations, as in effect on the date of enactment of this Act.

(2) The manner in which the Coast Guard ensures cybersecurity standards are followed by port, vessel, and facility owners and operators.

(3) The extent to which maritime sector-specific planning addresses cybersecurity, particularly for vessels and offshore platforms.

(4) The manner in which the Coast Guard, other Federal agencies, and vessel and offshore platform operators exchange information regarding cyber risks.

(5) The extent to which the Coast Guard is developing and deploying cybersecurity specialists in port and vessel systems and collaborating with the private sector to increase the expertise of the Coast Guard with respect to cybersecurity.

(6) The cyber resource and workforce needs of the Coast Guard necessary to meet future mission demands.

(c) REPORT.—Not later than 1 year after commencing the study required under subsection (a), the Comptroller General shall submit to the Committee on Commerce, Science, and Transportation of the Senate and the Committee on Transportation and Infrastructure of the House of Representatives a report on the findings of the study.

(d) FACILITY DEFINED.—In this section, the term "facility" has the meaning given the term in section 70101 of title 46, United States Code.

Subtitle E—Aviation

SEC. 11231. SPACE-AVAILABLE TRAVEL ON COAST GUARD AIRCRAFT: PROGRAM AUTHORIZATION AND ELIGIBLE RECIPIENTS.

(a) IN GENERAL.—Subchapter I of chapter 5 of title 14, United States Code, is amended by adding at the end the following:

"SEC. 509. [14 U.S.C. 509] Space-available travel on Coast Guard aircraft

"(a) ESTABLISHMENT.—

"(1) IN GENERAL.—The Commandant may establish a program to provide transportation on Coast Guard aircraft on a space-available basis to the categories of eligible individuals described in subsection (c) (in this section referred to as the 'program').

"(2) POLICY DEVELOPMENT.—Not later than 1 year after the date on which the program is established, the Commandant shall develop a policy for the operation of the program.

"(b) OPERATION OF PROGRAM.—

"(1) IN GENERAL.—The Commandant shall operate the program in a budget-neutral manner.

"(2) LIMITATIONS.—

"(A) IN GENERAL.—Except as provided in

subparagraph (B), no additional funds may be used, or flight hours performed, for the purpose of providing transportation under the program.

"(B) DE MINIMIS EXPENDITURES.—The Commandant may make de minimis expenditures of resources required for the administrative aspects of the program.

"(3) REIMBURSEMENT NOT REQUIRED.—Eligible individuals described in subsection (c) shall not be required to reimburse the Coast Guard for travel provided under this section.

"(c) CATEGORIES OF ELIGIBLE INDIVIDUALS.—Subject to subsection (d), the categories of eligible individuals described in this subsection are the following:

"(1) Members of the armed forces on active duty.

"(2) Members of the Selected Reserve who hold a valid Uniformed Services Identification and Privilege Card.

"(3) Retired members of a regular or reserve component of the armed forces, including retired members of reserve components who, but for being under the eligibility age applicable under section 12731 of title 10, would be eligible for retired pay under chapter 1223 of title 10.

"(4) Subject to subsection (f), veterans with a permanent service-connected disability rated as total.

"(5) Such categories of dependents of individuals described in paragraphs (1) through (3) as the Commandant shall specify in the policy under subsection (a)(2), under such conditions and circumstances as the Commandant shall specify in such policy.

"(6) Such other categories of individuals as the Commandant considers appropriate.

"(d) REQUIREMENTS.—In operating the program, the Commandant shall—

"(1) in the sole discretion of the Commandant, establish an order of priority for transportation for categories of eligible individuals that is based on considerations of military necessity, humanitarian concerns, and enhancement of morale;

"(2) give priority in consideration of transportation to the demands of members of the armed forces in the regular components and in the reserve components on active duty and to the need to provide such members, and their dependents, a means of respite from such demands; and

"(3) implement policies aimed at ensuring cost control (as required under subsection (b)) and the safety, security, and efficient processing of travelers, including limiting the benefit under the program to 1 or more categories of otherwise eligible individuals, as the Commandant considers necessary.

"(e) TRANSPORTATION.—

"(1) IN GENERAL.—Notwithstanding subsection (d)(1), in establishing space-available transportation priorities under the program, the Commandant shall provide transportation for an individual described in paragraph (2), and a single dependent of the individual if needed to accompany the individual, at a priority level in the same category as the priority level for an unaccompanied dependent over the age of 18 years traveling on environmental and morale leave.

"(2) INDIVIDUALS COVERED.—Subject to paragraph (3), paragraph (1) applies with respect to an individual described in subsection (c)(3) who—

"(A) resides in or is located in a Commonwealth or possession of the United States; and

"(B) is referred by a military or civilian primary care provider located in that Commonwealth or possession to a specialty care provider for services to be provided outside of such Commonwealth or possession.

"(3) APPLICATION TO CERTAIN RETIRED INDIVIDUALS.—If an individual described in subsection (c)(3) is a retired member of a reserve component who is ineligible for retired pay under chapter 1223 of title 10 by reason of being under the eligibility age applicable under section 12731 of title 10, paragraph (1) applies to the individual only if the individual is also enrolled in the TRICARE program for certain members of the Retired Reserve authorized under section 1076e of title 10.

"(4) PRIORITY.—The priority for space-available transportation required by this subsection applies with respect to—

"(A) the travel from the Commonwealth or possession of the United States to receive the specialty care services; and

"(B) the return travel.

"(5) PRIMARY CARE PROVIDER AND SPECIALTY CARE PROVIDER DEFINED.—In this subsection, the terms 'primary care provider' and 'specialty care provider' refer to a medical or dental professional who provides health care services under chapter 55 of title 10.

"(f) LIMITATIONS ON TRAVEL.—

"(1) IN GENERAL.—Travel may not be provided under this section to a veteran eligible for travel pursuant to paragraph (4) of subsection (c) in priority over any member eligible for travel under paragraph (1) of that subsection or any dependent of such a member eligible for travel under this section.

"(2) RULE OF CONSTRUCTION.—Subsection (c)(4) may not be construed as—

"(A) affecting or in any way imposing on the Coast Guard, any armed force, or any commercial entity with which the Coast Guard or an armed force contracts, an obligation or expectation that the Coast Guard or such armed force will retrofit or alter, in any way, military aircraft or commercial aircraft, or related equipment or facilities, used or leased by the Coast Guard or such armed force to accommodate passengers provided travel under such authority on account of disability; or

"(B) preempting the authority of an aircraft commander to determine who boards the aircraft and any other matters in connection with safe operation of the aircraft.

"(g) APPLICATION OF SECTION.—The authority to provide transportation under the program is in addition to any other authority under law to provide transportation on Coast Guard aircraft on a space-available basis."

(b) CLERICAL AMENDMENT.—The analysis for chapter 5 of title 14, United States Code, is amended by inserting after the item relating to section 508 the following:

"509. Space-available travel on Coast Guard aircraft."

SEC. 11232. REPORT ON COAST GUARD AIR STATION BARBERS POINT HANGAR.

(a) IN GENERAL.—Not later than 180 days after the date of enactment of this Act, the Commandant shall submit to the

Committee on Commerce, Science, and Transportation and the Committee on Appropriations of the Senate and the Committee on Transportation and Infrastructure and the Committee on Appropriations of the House of Representatives a report on facilities requirements for constructing a hangar at Coast Guard Air Station Barbers Point at Oahu, Hawaii.

(b) ELEMENTS.—The report required by subsection (a) shall include the following:

(1) A description of the—

(A) $45,000,000 phase one design for the hangar at Coast Guard Air Station Barbers Point funded by the Consolidated Appropriations Act, 2021 (Public Law 116-260; 134 Stat. 1132); and

(B) phase two facility improvements referenced in the U.S. Coast Guard Unfunded Priority List for fiscal year 2023.

(2) An evaluation of the full facilities requirements for such hangar and maintenance facility improvements to house, maintain, and operate the MH-65 and HC-130J, including—

(A) storage and provision of fuel; and

(B) maintenance and parts storage facilities.

(3) An evaluation of facilities growth requirements for possible future basing of the MH-60 with the C-130J at Coast Guard Air Station Barbers Point.

(4) A description of and cost estimate for each project phase for the construction of such hangar and maintenance facility improvements.

(5) A description of the plan for sheltering in the hangar during extreme weather events aircraft of the Coast Guard and partner agencies, such as the National Oceanic and Atmospheric Administration.

(6) A description of the risks posed to operations at Coast Guard Air Station Barbers Point if future project phases for the construction of such hangar are not funded.

SEC. 11233. STUDY ON OPERATIONAL AVAILABILITY OF COAST GUARD AIRCRAFT AND STRATEGY FOR COAST GUARD AVIATION.

(a) STUDY.—

(1) IN GENERAL.—Not later than 1 year after the date of enactment of this Act, the Comptroller General of the United States shall commence a study on the operational availability of Coast Guard aircraft.

(2) ELEMENTS.—The study required under paragraph (1) shall include the following:

(A) An assessment of—

(i) the extent to which the fixed-wing and rotary-wing aircraft of the Coast Guard have met annual operational availability targets in recent years;

(ii) the challenges the Coast Guard may face with respect to such aircraft meeting operational availability targets, and the effects of such challenges on the ability of the Coast Guard to meet mission requirements; and

(iii) the status of Coast Guard efforts to upgrade or recapitalize its fleet of such aircraft to meet growth in future mission demands globally, such as in the Western Hemisphere, the Arctic region, and the Western Pacific region.

(B) Any recommendation with respect to the operational availability of Coast Guard aircraft.

(C) The resource and workforce requirements necessary for Coast Guard Aviation to meet current and future mission demands specific to each rotary-wing and fixed-wing airframe type in the current inventory of the Coast Guard.

(3) REPORT.—On completion of the study required under paragraph (1), the Comptroller General shall submit to the Commandant a report on the findings of the study.

(b) COAST GUARD AVIATION STRATEGY.—

(1) IN GENERAL.—Not later than 180 days after the date on which the study under subsection (a) is completed, the Commandant shall develop a comprehensive strategy for Coast Guard Aviation that is informed by the relevant recommendations and findings of the study.

(2) ELEMENTS.—The strategy required under paragraph (1) shall include the following:

(A) With respect to aircraft of the Coast Guard—

(i) an analysis of—

(I) the current and future operations and future resource needs, including the potential need for a second rotary wing airframe to carry out cutter-based operations and National Capital Region air interdiction mission; and

(II) the manner in which such future needs are integrated with the Future Vertical Lift initiatives of the Department of Defense; and

(ii) an estimated timeline with respect to when such future needs will arise.

(B) The projected number of aviation assets, the locations at which such assets are to be stationed, the cost of operation and maintenance of such assets, and an assessment of the capabilities of such assets as compared to the missions they are expected to execute, at the completion of major procurement and modernization plans.

(C) A procurement plan, including an estimated timetable and the estimated appropriations necessary for all platforms, including unmanned aircraft.

(D) A training plan for pilots and aircrew that addresses—

(i) the use of simulators owned and operated by the Coast Guard, and simulators that are not owned or operated by the Coast Guard, including any such simulators based outside the United States; and

(ii) the costs associated with attending training courses.

(E) Current and future requirements for cutter and land-based deployment of aviation assets globally, including in the Arctic, the Eastern Pacific, the Western Pacific, the Caribbean, the Atlantic Basin, and any other area the Commandant considers appropriate.

(F) A description of the feasibility of deploying, and the resource requirements necessary to deploy, rotary-winged assets onboard all future Arctic cutter patrols.

(G) An evaluation of current and future facilities needs

for Coast Guard aviation units.

(H) An evaluation of pilot and aircrew training and retention needs, including aviation career incentive pay, retention bonuses, and any other workforce tools the Commandant considers necessary.

(3) BRIEFING.—Not later than 180 days after the date on which the strategy required under paragraph (1) is completed, the Commandant shall provide to the Committee on Commerce, Science, and Transportation of the Senate and the Committee on Transportation and Infrastructure of the House of Representatives a briefing on the strategy.

Subtitle F—Workforce Readiness

SEC. 11234. AUTHORIZED STRENGTH.

Section 3702 of title 14, United States Code, is amended by adding at the end the following:

"(c) The Secretary may vary the authorized end strength of the Coast Guard Selected Reserves for a fiscal year by a number equal to not more than 3 percent of such end strength upon a determination by the Secretary that varying such authorized end strength is in the national interest.

"(d) The Commandant may increase the authorized end strength of the Coast Guard Selected Reserves by a number equal to not more than 2 percent of such authorized end strength upon a determination by the Commandant that such increase would enhance manning and readiness in essential units or in critical specialties or ratings."

SEC. 11235. CONTINUATION OF OFFICERS WITH CERTAIN CRITICAL SKILLS ON ACTIVE DUTY.

(a) IN GENERAL.—Chapter 21 of title 14, United States Code, is amended by inserting after section 2165 the following:

"SEC. 2166. [14 U.S.C. 2166] Continuation on active duty; Coast Guard officers with certain critical skills

"(a) IN GENERAL.—The Commandant may authorize an officer in a grade above grade O-2 to remain on active duty after the date otherwise provided for the retirement of such officer in section 2154 of this title, if the officer possesses a critical skill, or specialty, or is in a career field designated pursuant to subsection (b).

"(b) CRITICAL SKILLS, SPECIALTY, OR CAREER FIELD.—The Commandant shall designate any critical skill, specialty, or career field eligible for continuation on active duty as provided in subsection (a).

"(c) DURATION OF CONTINUATION.—An officer continued on active duty pursuant to this section shall, if not earlier retired, be retired on the first day of the month after the month in which the officer completes 40 years of active service.

"(d) POLICY.—The Commandant shall carry out this section by prescribing policy which shall specify the criteria to be used in designating any critical skill, specialty, or career field for purposes of subsection (b)."

(b) CLERICAL AMENDMENT.—The analysis for chapter 21 of title 14, United States Code, is amended by inserting after the item relating to section 2165 the following:

"2166.	Continuation on active duty; Coast Guard officers with certain critical skills."

SEC. 11236. NUMBER AND DISTRIBUTION OF OFFICERS ON ACTIVE DUTY PROMOTION LIST.

(a) MAXIMUM NUMBER OF OFFICERS.—Section 2103(a) of title 14, United States Code, is amended to read as follows:

"(a) MAXIMUM TOTAL NUMBER.—

"(1) IN GENERAL.—The total number of Coast Guard commissioned officers on the active duty promotion list, excluding warrant officers, shall not exceed—

"(A) 7,100 in fiscal year 2022;

"(B) 7,200 in fiscal year 2023;

"(C) 7,300 in fiscal year 2024; and

"(D) 7,400 in fiscal year 2025 and each subsequent fiscal year.

"(2) TEMPORARY INCREASE.—Notwithstanding paragraph (1), the Commandant may temporarily increase the total number of commissioned officers permitted under such paragraph by up to 4 percent for not more than 60 days after the date of the commissioning of a Coast Guard Academy class.

"(3) NOTIFICATION.—Not later than 30 days after exceeding

the total number of commissioned officers permitted under paragraphs (1) and (2), and each 30 days thereafter until the total number of commissioned officers no longer exceeds the number of such officers permitted under paragraphs (1) and (2), the Commandant shall notify the Committee on Transportation and Infrastructure of the House of Representatives and the Committee on Commerce, Science, and Transportation of the Senate of the number of officers on the active duty promotion list on the last day of the preceding 30-day period."

(b) OFFICERS NOT ON ACTIVE DUTY PROMOTION LIST.—

(1) IN GENERAL.—Chapter 51 of title 14, United States Code, is amended by adding at the end the following:

"SEC. 5113. [14 U.S.C. 5113] Officers not on active duty promotion list

"Not later than 60 days after the date on which the President submits to Congress a budget pursuant to section 1105 of title 31, the Commandant shall submit to the Committee on Transportation and Infrastructure of the House of Representatives and the Committee on Commerce, Science, and Transportation of the Senate the number of Coast Guard officers serving at other Federal entities on a reimbursable basis, and the number of Coast Guard officers who are serving at other Federal agencies on a non-reimbursable basis, but not on the active duty promotion list."

(2) CLERICAL AMENDMENT.—The analysis for chapter 51 of title 14, United States Code, is amended by adding at the end the following:

"5113. Officers not on active duty promotion list."

SEC. 11237. [37 U.S.C. 352 note] CAREER INCENTIVE PAY FOR MARINE INSPECTORS.

(a) AUTHORITY TO PROVIDE ASSIGNMENT PAY OR SPECIAL DUTY PAY.—The Secretary may provide assignment pay or special duty pay under section 352 of title 37, United States Code, to a member of the Coast Guard serving in a prevention position and assigned as a marine inspector or marine investigator pursuant to section 312 of title 14, United States Code.

(b) ANNUAL BRIEFING.—

(1) IN GENERAL.—Not later than 180 days after the date of

enactment of this Act, and annually thereafter, the Secretary shall provide to the Committee on Commerce, Science, and Transportation of the Senate and the Committee on Transportation and Infrastructure of the House of Representatives a briefing on any uses of the authority under subsection (a) during the preceding year.

(2) ELEMENTS.—Each briefing required under paragraph (1) shall include the following:

(A) The number of members of the Coast Guard serving as marine inspectors or marine investigators pursuant to section 312 of title 14, United States Code, who are receiving assignment pay or special duty pay under section 352 of title 37, United States Code.

(B) An assessment of the impact of the use of the authority under this section on the effectiveness and efficiency of the Coast Guard in administering the laws and regulations for the promotion of safety of life and property on and under the high seas and waters subject to the jurisdiction of the United States.

(C) An assessment of the effects of assignment pay and special duty pay on retention of marine inspectors and investigators.

(D) If the authority provided in subsection (a) is not exercised, a detailed justification for not exercising such authority, including an explanation of the efforts the Secretary is taking to ensure that the Coast Guard workforce contains an adequate number of qualified marine inspectors.

(c) STUDY.—

(1) IN GENERAL.—Not later than 2 years after the date of enactment of this Act, the Secretary, in coordination with the Director of the National Institute for Occupational Safety and Health, shall conduct a study on the health of marine inspectors and marine investigators who have served as such inspectors or investigators for a period of not less than 10 years.

(2) ELEMENTS.—The study required under paragraph (1) shall include the following:

(A) An evaluation of—

(i) the daily vessel inspection duties of marine

inspectors and marine investigators, including the examination of internal cargo tanks and voids and new construction activities;

(ii) major incidents to which marine inspectors and marine investigators have had to respond, and any other significant incident, such as a vessel casualty, that has resulted in the exposure of marine inspectors and marine investigators to hazardous chemicals or substances; and

(iii) the types of hazardous chemicals or substances to which marine inspectors and marine investigators have been exposed relative to the effects such chemicals or substances have had on marine inspectors and marine investigators.

(B) A review and analysis of the current Coast Guard health and safety monitoring systems, and recommendations for improving such systems, specifically with respect to the exposure of members of the Coast Guard to hazardous substances while carrying out inspections and investigation duties.

(C) Any other element the Secretary considers appropriate.

(3) REPORT.—Upon completion of the study required under paragraph (1), the Secretary shall submit to the Committee on Commerce, Science, and Transportation of the Senate and the Committee on Transportation and Infrastructure of the House of Representatives a report on the findings of the study and recommendations for actions the Commandant should take to improve the health and exposure of marine inspectors and marine investigators.

(d) TERMINATION.—The authority provided by subsection (a) shall terminate on December 31, 2028.

SEC. 11238. EXPANSION OF ABILITY FOR SELECTION BOARD TO RECOMMEND OFFICERS OF PARTICULAR MERIT FOR PROMOTION.

Section 2116(c)(1) of title 14, United States Code, is amended, in the second sentence, by inserting “three times” after “may not exceed”.

SEC. 11239. MODIFICATION TO EDUCATION LOAN REPAYMENT

PROGRAM.

(a) IN GENERAL.—Section 2772 of title 14, United States Code, is amended to read as follows:

"SEC. 2772. Education loan repayment program for members on active duty in specified military specialties

"(a) IN GENERAL.—

"(1) REPAYMENT.—Subject to the provisions of this section, the Secretary may repay—

"(A) any loan made, insured, or guaranteed under part B of title IV of the Higher Education Act of 1965 (20 U.S.C. 1071 et seq.);

"(B) any loan made under part D of such title (the William D. Ford Federal Direct Loan Program, 20 U.S.C. 1087a et seq.);

"(C) any loan made under part E of such title (20 U.S.C. 1087aa et seq.); or

"(D) any loan incurred for educational purposes made by a lender that is—

"(i) an agency or instrumentality of a State;

"(ii) a financial or credit institution (including an insurance company) that is subject to examination and supervision by an agency of the United States or any State;

"(iii) a pension fund approved by the Secretary for purposes of this section; or

"(iv) a nonprofit private entity designated by a State, regulated by such State, and approved by the Secretary for purposes of this section.

"(2) REQUIREMENT.—Repayment of any such loan shall be made on the basis of each complete year of service performed by the borrower.

"(3) ELIGIBILITY.—The Secretary may repay loans described in paragraph (1) in the case of any person for service performed on active duty as a member in an officer program or military specialty specified by the Secretary.

"(b) AMOUNT.—The portion or amount of a loan that may be repaid under subsection (a) is 33⅓ percent or $1,500, whichever is greater, for each year of service.

"(c) INTEREST ACCRUAL.—If a portion of a loan is repaid under this section for any year, interest on the remainder of such loan shall accrue and be paid in the same manner as is otherwise required.

"(d) RULE OF CONSTRUCTION.—Nothing in this section shall be construed to authorize refunding any repayment of a loan.

"(e) FRACTIONAL CREDIT FOR TRANSFER.—An individual who transfers from service making the individual eligible for repayment of loans under this section (as described in subsection (a)(3)) to service making the individual eligible for repayment of loans under section 16301 of title 10 (as described in subsection (a)(2) or (g) of that section) during a year shall be eligible to have repaid a portion of such loan determined by giving appropriate fractional credit for each portion of the year so served, in accordance with regulations of the Secretary concerned.

"(f) SCHEDULE FOR ALLOCATION.—The Secretary shall prescribe a schedule for the allocation of funds made available to carry out the provisions of this section and section 16301 of title 10 during any year for which funds are not sufficient to pay the sum of the amounts eligible for repayment under subsection (a) and section 16301(a) of title 10.

"(g) FAILURE TO COMPLETE PERIOD OF SERVICE.—Except an individual described in subsection (e) who transfers to service making the individual eligible for repayment of loans under section 16301 of title 10, a member of the Coast Guard who fails to complete the period of service required to qualify for loan repayment under this section shall be subject to the repayment provisions of section 303a(e) or 373 of title 37.

"(h) AUTHORITY TO ISSUE REGULATIONS.—The Secretary may prescribe procedures for implementing this section, including standards for qualified loans and authorized payees and other terms and conditions for making loan repayments. Such regulations may include exceptions that would allow for the payment as a lump sum of any loan repayment due to a member under a written agreement that existed at the time of a member's death or disability."

(b) CLERICAL AMENDMENT.—The analysis for chapter 27 of title 14, United States Code, is amended by striking the item relating to section 2772 and inserting the following:

"2772.	Education loan repayment program for members on active duty in specified military specialties."

SEC. 11240. RETIREMENT OF VICE COMMANDANT.

Section 303 of title 14, United States Code, is amended—

(1) by amending subsection (a)(2) to read as follows:

"(2) A Vice Commandant who is retired while serving as Vice Commandant, after serving not less than 2 years as Vice Commandant, shall be retired with the grade of admiral, except as provided in section 306(d)."

; and

(2) in subsection (c) by striking "or Vice Commandant" and inserting "or as an officer serving as Vice Commandant who has served less than 2 years as Vice Commandant".

SEC. 11241. [14 U.S.C. 2502 note] REPORT ON RESIGNATION AND RETIREMENT PROCESSING TIMES AND DENIAL.

(a) IN GENERAL.—Not later than 30 days after the date of enactment of this Act, and annually thereafter, the Commandant shall submit to the Committee on Commerce, Science, and Transportation of the Senate and the Committee on Transportation and Infrastructure of the House of Representatives a report that evaluates resignation and retirement processing timelines.

(b) ELEMENTS.—The report required under subsection (a) shall include, for the preceding calendar year—

(1) statistics on the number of resignations, retirements, and other separations that occurred;

(2) the processing time for each action described in paragraph (1);

(3) the percentage of requests for such actions that had a command endorsement;

(4) the percentage of requests for such actions that did not have a command endorsement; and

(5) for each denial of a request for a command endorsement and each failure to take action on such a request, a detailed description of the rationale for such denial or failure to take such action.

SEC. 11242. CALCULATION OF ACTIVE SERVICE.

(a) IN GENERAL.—Subchapter I of chapter 25 of title 14, United States Code, is amended by adding at the end the following:

"SEC. 2515. [14 U.S.C. 2515] Calculation of active service

"Any service described, including service described prior to the date of enactment of the Don Young Coast Guard Authorization Act of 2022, in writing, including by electronic communication, by a representative of the Coast Guard Personnel Service Center as service that counts toward total active service for regular retirement under section 2152 or section 2306 shall be considered by the President as active service for purposes of applying section 2152 or section 2306 with respect to the determination of the retirement qualification for any officer or enlisted member to whom a description was provided."

(b) CLERICAL AMENDMENT.—The analysis for chapter 25 of title 14, United States Code, is amended by inserting after the item relating to section 2515 the following:

"2515. Calculation of active service."

(c) [14 U.S.C. 2515 note] RULE OF CONSTRUCTION.—The amendment made by subsection (a)—

(1) shall only apply to officers of the Coast Guard that entered active service after January 1, 1997, temporarily separated for a period of time, and have retired from the Coast Guard before January 1, 2024; and

(2) shall not apply to any member of any other uniformed service, or to any Coast Guard member regarding active service of the member in any other uniformed service.

SEC. 11243. PHYSICAL DISABILITY EVALUATION SYSTEM PROCEDURE REVIEW.

(a) STUDY.—

(1) IN GENERAL.—Not later than 3 years after the date of enactment of this Act, the Comptroller General of the United States shall complete a study on the Coast Guard Physical Disability Evaluation System and medical retirement procedures.

(2) ELEMENTS.—In completing the study required under paragraph (1), the Comptroller General shall review, and

provide recommendations to address, the following:

(A) Coast Guard compliance with all applicable laws, regulations, and policies relating to the Physical Disability Evaluation System and the Medical Evaluation Board.

(B) Coast Guard compliance with timelines set forth in—

(i) the instruction of the Commandant entitled "Physical Disability Evaluation System" issued on May 19, 2006 (COMDTNST M1850.2D); and

(ii) the Physical Disability Evaluation System Transparency Initiative (ALCGPSC 030/20).

(C) An evaluation of Coast Guard processes in place to ensure the availability, consistency, and effectiveness of counsel appointed by the Coast Guard Office of the Judge Advocate General to represent members of the Coast Guard undergoing an evaluation under the Physical Disability Evaluation System.

(D) The extent to which the Coast Guard has and uses processes to ensure that such counsel may perform the functions of such counsel in a manner that is impartial, including being able to perform such functions without undue pressure or interference by the command of the affected member of the Coast Guard, the Personnel Service Center, and the Coast Guard Office of the Judge Advocate General.

(E) The frequency, including the frequency aggregated by member pay grade, with which members of the Coast Guard seek private counsel in lieu of counsel appointed by the Coast Guard Office of the Judge Advocate General.

(F) The timeliness of determinations, guidance, and access to medical evaluations necessary for retirement or rating determinations and overall well-being of the affected member of the Coast Guard.

(G) The guidance, formal or otherwise, provided by the Personnel Service Center and the Coast Guard Office of the Judge Advocate General, other than the counsel directly representing affected members of the Coast Guard, in communication with medical personnel examining members.

(H) The guidance, formal or otherwise, provided by the medical professionals reviewing cases within the Physical Disability Evaluation System to affected members of the Coast Guard, and the extent to which such guidance is disclosed to the commanders, commanding officers, or other members of the Coast Guard in the chain of command of such affected members.

(I) The feasibility of establishing a program to allow members of the Coast Guard to select an expedited review to ensure completion of the Medical Evaluation Board report not later than 180 days after the date on which such review was initiated.

(b) REPORT.—The Comptroller General shall submit to the Committee on Commerce, Science, and Transportation of the Senate and the Committee on Transportation and Infrastructure of the House of Representatives a report on the findings of the study conducted under subsection (a) and recommendations for improving the Physical Disability Evaluation System process.

(c) UPDATED POLICY GUIDANCE.—

(1) IN GENERAL.—Not later than 180 days after the date on which the report under subsection (b) is submitted, the Commandant shall issue updated policy guidance in response to the findings and recommendations contained in the report.

(2) ELEMENTS.—The updated policy guidance required under paragraph (1) shall include the following:

(A) A requirement that a member of the Coast Guard, or the counsel of such a member, shall be informed of the contents of, and afforded the option to be present for, any communication between the member's command and the Personnel Service Center, or other Coast Guard entity, with respect to the duty status of the member.

(B) An exception to the requirement described in subparagraph (A) that such a member, or the counsel of the member, is not required to be informed of the contents of such a communication if it is demonstrated that there is a legitimate health or safety need for the member to be excluded from such communications, supported by a medical opinion that such exclusion is necessary for the health or safety of the member, command, or any other individual.

(C) An option to allow a member of the Coast Guard to initiate an evaluation by a Medical Evaluation Board if a Coast Guard healthcare provider, or other military healthcare provider, has raised a concern about the ability of the member to continue serving in the Coast Guard, in accordance with existing medical and physical disability policy.

(D) An updated policy to remove the command endorsement requirement for retirement or separation unless absolutely necessary for the benefit of the United States.

SEC. 11244. EXPANSION OF AUTHORITY FOR MULTIRATER ASSESSMENTS OF CERTAIN PERSONNEL.

(a) IN GENERAL.—Section 2182(a) of title 14, United States Code, is amended by striking paragraph (2) and inserting the following:

"(2) OFFICERS.—Each officer of the Coast Guard shall undergo a multirater assessment before promotion to—

"(A) the grade of O-4;

"(B) the grade of O-5; and

"(C) the grade of O-6.

"(3) ENLISTED MEMBERS.—Each enlisted member of the Coast Guard shall undergo a multirater assessment before advancement to—

"(A) the grade of E-7;

"(B) the grade of E-8;

"(C) the grade of E-9; and

"(D) the grade of E-10.

"(4) SELECTION.—An individual assessed shall not be permitted to select the peers and subordinates who provide opinions for the multirater assessment of such individual.

"(5) POST-ASSESSMENT ELEMENTS.—

"(A) IN GENERAL.—Following an assessment of an individual pursuant to paragraphs (1) through (3), the individual shall be provided appropriate post-assessment counseling and leadership coaching.

"(B) AVAILABILITY OF RESULTS.—The supervisor of the individual assessed shall be provided with the results of the multirater assessment."

(b) COST ASSESSMENT.—

(1) IN GENERAL.—Not later than 1 year after the date of enactment of this Act, the Commandant shall provide to the appropriate committees of Congress an estimate of the costs associated with implementing the amendment made by subsection (a).

(2) APPROPRIATE COMMITTEES OF CONGRESS DEFINED.—In this subsection, the term "appropriate committees of Congress" means—

(A) the Committee on Commerce, Science, and Transportation and the Committee on Appropriations of the Senate; and

(B) the Committee on Transportation and Infrastructure and the Committee on Appropriations of the House of Representatives.

SEC. 11245. PROMOTION PARITY.

(a) INFORMATION TO BE FURNISHED.—Section 2115(a) of title 14, United States Code, is amended—

(1) in paragraph (1) by striking "; and" and inserting a semicolon;

(2) in paragraph (2) by striking the period at the end and inserting "; and"; and

(3) by adding at the end the following:

"(3) in the case of an eligible officer considered for promotion to a rank above lieutenant, any credible information of an adverse nature, including any substantiated adverse finding or conclusion from an officially documented investigation or inquiry and any information placed in the personnel service record of the officer under section 1745(a) of the National Defense Authorization Act for Fiscal Year 2014 (Public Law 113-66; 10 U.S.C. 1561 note), shall be furnished to the selection board in accordance with standards and procedures set out in the regulations prescribed by the Secretary."

(b) SPECIAL SELECTION REVIEW BOARDS.—

(1) IN GENERAL.—Subchapter I of chapter 21 of title 14, United States Code, is amended by inserting after section 2120 the following:

"SEC. 2120a. [14 U.S.C. 2120a] Special selection review boards

"(a) IN GENERAL.—(1) If the Secretary determines that a person recommended by a promotion board for promotion to a grade at or below the grade of rear admiral is the subject of credible information of an adverse nature, including any substantiated adverse finding or conclusion described in section 2115(a)(3) of this title that was not furnished to the promotion board during its consideration of the person for promotion as otherwise required by such section, the Secretary shall convene a special selection review board under this section to review the person and recommend whether the recommendation for promotion of the person should be sustained.

"(2) If a person and the recommendation for promotion of the person is subject to review under this section by a special selection review board convened under this section, the name of the person—

"(A) shall not be disseminated or publicly released on the list of officers recommended for promotion by the promotion board recommending the promotion of the person; and

"(B) shall not be forwarded to the President or the Senate, as applicable, or included on a promotion list under section 2121 of this title.

"(b) CONVENING.—(1) Any special selection review board convened under this section shall be convened in accordance with the provisions of section 2120(c) of this title.

"(2) Any special selection review board convened under this section may review such number of persons, and recommendations for promotion of such persons, as the Secretary shall specify in convening such special selection review board.

"(c) INFORMATION CONSIDERED.—(1) In reviewing a person and recommending whether the recommendation for promotion of the person should be sustained under this section, a special selection review board convened under this section shall be furnished and consider the following:

"(A) The record and information concerning the person furnished in accordance with section 2115 of this title to the promotion board that recommended the person for promotion.

"(B) Any credible information of an adverse nature on the person, including any substantiated adverse finding or conclusion from an officially documented investigation or inquiry described in section 2115(a)(3) of this title.

"(2) The furnishing of information to a special selection review board under paragraph (1)(B) shall be governed by the standards and procedures referred to in section 2115 of this title.

"(3)(A) Before information on a person described in paragraph (1)(B) is furnished to a special selection review board for purposes of this section, the Secretary shall ensure that—

"(i) such information is made available to the person; and

"(ii) subject to subparagraphs (C) and (D), the person is afforded a reasonable opportunity to submit comments on such information to the special selection review board before its review of the person and the recommendation for promotion of the person under this section.

"(B) If information on a person described in paragraph (1)(B) is not made available to the person as otherwise required by subparagraph (A)(i) due to the classification status of such information, the person shall, to the maximum extent practicable, be furnished a summary of such information appropriate to the person's authorization for access to classified information.

"(C)(i) An opportunity to submit comments on information is not required for a person under subparagraph (A)(ii) if—

"(I) such information was made available to the person in connection with the furnishing of such information under section 2115(a) of this title to the promotion board that recommended the promotion of the person subject to review under this section; and

"(II) the person submitted comments on such information to that promotion board.

"(ii) The comments on information of a person described in clause (i)(II) shall be furnished to the special selection review board.

"(D) A person may waive either or both of the following:

"(i) The right to submit comments to a special selection review board under subparagraph (A)(ii).

"(ii) The furnishing of comments to a special selection review board under subparagraph (C)(ii).

"(d) CONSIDERATION.—(1) In considering the record and information on a person under this section, the special selection review board shall compare such record and information with an appropriate sampling of the records of those officers who were recommended for promotion by the promotion board that recommended the person for promotion, and an appropriate sampling of the records of those officers who were considered by and not recommended for promotion by that promotion board.

"(2) Records and information shall be presented to a special selection review board for purposes of paragraph (1) in a manner that does not indicate or disclose the person or persons for whom the special selection review board was convened.

"(3) In considering whether the recommendation for promotion of a person should be sustained under this section, a special selection review board shall, to the greatest extent practicable, apply standards used by the promotion board that recommended the person for promotion.

"(4) The recommendation for promotion of a person may be sustained under this section only if the special selection review board determines that the person—

"(A) ranks on an order of merit created by the special selection review board as better qualified for promotion than the sample officer highest on the order of merit list who was considered by and not recommended for promotion by the promotion board concerned; and

"(B) is comparable in qualification for promotion to those sample officers who were recommended for promotion by that promotion board.

"(5) A recommendation for promotion of a person may be sustained under this section only by a vote of a majority of the members of the special selection review board.

"(6) If a special selection review board does not sustain a recommendation for promotion of a person under this section, the person shall be considered to have failed of selection for promotion.

"(e) REPORTS.—(1) Each special selection review board convened under this section shall submit to the Secretary a written report, signed by each member of the board, containing the name of each person whose recommendation for promotion it recommends for sustainment and certifying that the board has carefully considered the record and information of each person whose name was referred to it.

"(2) The provisions of sections 2117(a) of this title apply to the report and proceedings of a special selection review board convened under this section in the same manner as they apply to the report and proceedings of a promotion board convened under section 2106 of this title.

"(f) APPOINTMENT OF PERSONS.—(1) If the report of a special selection review board convened under this section recommends the sustainment of the recommendation for promotion to the next higher grade of a person whose name was referred to it for review under this section, and the President approves the report, the person shall, as soon as practicable, be appointed to that grade in accordance with section 2121 of this title.

"(2) A person who is appointed to the next higher grade as described in paragraph (1) shall, upon that appointment, have the same date of rank, the same effective date for the pay and allowances of that grade, and the same position on the active-duty list as the person would have had pursuant to the original recommendation for promotion of the promotion board concerned.

"(g) REGULATIONS.—The Secretary shall prescribe regulations to carry out this section.

"(h) PROMOTION BOARD DEFINED.—In this section, the term 'promotion board' means a selection board convened by the Secretary under section 2106 of this title."

(2) CLERICAL AMENDMENT.—The analysis for chapter 21 of title 14, United States Code, is amended by inserting after the item relating to section 2120 the following:

"2120a. Special selection review boards."

(c) AVAILABILITY OF INFORMATION.—Section 2118 of title 14, United States Code, is amended by adding at the end the following:

"(e) If the Secretary makes a recommendation under this section that the name of an officer be removed from a report of a selection board and the recommendation is accompanied by information that was not presented to that selection board, that information shall be made available to that officer. The officer shall then be afforded a reasonable opportunity to submit comments on that information to the officials making the recommendation and the officials reviewing the recommendation. If an eligible officer cannot be given access to such information because of its classification status, the officer shall, to the maximum extent practicable, be provided with an appropriate summary of the information."

(d) DELAY OF PROMOTION.—Section 2121(f) of title 14, United States Code, is amended to read as follows:

"(f)(1) The promotion of an officer may be delayed without prejudice if any of the following applies:

"(A) The officer is under investigation or proceedings of a court-martial or a board of officers are pending against the officer.

"(B) A criminal proceeding in a Federal or State court is pending against the officer.

"(C) The Secretary determines that credible information of an adverse nature, including a substantiated adverse finding or conclusion described in section 2115(a)(3), with respect to the officer will result in the convening of a special selection review board under section 2120a of this title to review the officer and recommend whether the recommendation for promotion of the officer should be sustained.

"(2)(A) Subject to subparagraph (B), a promotion may be delayed under this subsection until, as applicable—

"(i) the completion of the investigation or proceedings described in subparagraph (A);

"(ii) a final decision in the proceeding described in subparagraph (B) is issued; or

"(iii) the special selection review board convened under section 2120a of this title issues recommendations with respect to the officer.

"(B) Unless the Secretary determines that a further delay is necessary in the public interest, a promotion may not be delayed under this subsection for more than one year after the date the officer would otherwise have been promoted.

"(3) An officer whose promotion is delayed under this subsection and who is subsequently promoted shall be given the date of rank and position on the active duty promotion list in the grade to which promoted that he would have held had his promotion not been so delayed."

SEC. 11246. [14 U.S.C. 2301 note] PARTNERSHIP PROGRAM TO DIVERSIFY COAST GUARD.

(a) ESTABLISHMENT.—The Commandant shall establish a program for the purpose of increasing the number of individuals in the enlisted ranks of the Coast Guard who are—

(1) underrepresented minorities; or

(2) from rural areas.

(b) PARTNERSHIPS.—In carrying out the program established under subsection (a), the Commandant shall—

(1) seek to enter into 1 or more partnerships with eligible institutions—

(A) to increase the visibility of Coast Guard careers;

(B) to promote curriculum development—

(i) to enable acceptance into the Coast Guard; and

(ii) to improve success on relevant exams, such as the Armed Services Vocational Aptitude Battery; and

(C) to provide mentoring for students entering and beginning Coast Guard careers; and

(2) enter into a partnership with an existing Junior Reserve Officers' Training Corps for the purpose of promoting Coast Guard careers.

(c) DEFINITIONS.—In this section:

(1) ELIGIBLE INSTITUTION.—The term "eligible institution" means an institution—

(A) that is—

(i) an institution of higher education (as such term is defined in section 101 of the Higher Education Act of 1965 (20 U.S.C. 1001)); or

(ii) a junior or community college (as such term is defined in section 312 of the Higher Education Act of 1965 (20 U.S.C. 1058); and

(B) that is—

(i) a part B institution (as such term is defined in section 322 of the Higher Education Act of 1965 (20 U.S.C. 1061));

(ii) a Tribal College or University (as such term is defined in section 316(b) of such Act (20 U.S.C. 1059c(b)));

(iii) a Hispanic-serving institution (as such term is defined in section 502 of such Act (20 U.S.C. 1101a));

(iv) an Alaska Native-serving institution or a Native Hawaiian-serving institution (as such term is defined in section 317(b) of such Act (20 U.S.C. 1059d(b)));

(v) a Predominantly Black institution (as such term is defined in section 371(c) of that Act (20 U.S.C. 1067q(c)));

(vi) an Asian American and Native American Pacific Islander-serving institution (as defined in section 320(b) of such Act (20 U.S.C. 1059g(b))); or

(vii) a Native American-serving nontribal

institution (as defined in section 319(b) of such Act (20 U.S.C. 1059f(b)).

(2) RURAL AREA.—The term "rural area" means an area that is outside of an urbanized area, as determined by the Bureau of the Census.

SEC. 11247. EXPANSION OF COAST GUARD JUNIOR RESERVE OFFICERS' TRAINING CORPS.

(a) IN GENERAL.—Section 320 of title 14, United States Code, is amended—

(1) by redesignating subsection (c) as subsection (d);

(2) in subsection (b) by striking "subsection (c)" and inserting "subsection (d)"; and

(3) by inserting after subsection (b) the following:

"(c) SCOPE.—Beginning on December 31, 2025, the Secretary of the department in which the Coast Guard is operating shall maintain at all times a Junior Reserve Officers' Training Corps program with not fewer than 1 such program established in each Coast Guard district."

(b) COST ASSESSMENT.—Not later than 1 year after the date of enactment of this Act, the Secretary shall provide to Congress an estimate of the costs associated with implementing the amendments made by this section.

SEC. 11248. [14 U.S.C. 504 note] IMPROVING REPRESENTATION OF WOMEN AND RACIAL AND ETHNIC MINORITIES AMONG COAST GUARD ACTIVE-DUTY MEMBERS.

(a) IN GENERAL.—Not later than 180 days after the date of enactment of this Act, in consultation with the Advisory Board on Women at the Coast Guard Academy established under section 1904 of title 14, United States Code, and the minority outreach team program established by section 1905 of such title, the Commandant shall—

(1) determine which recommendations in the RAND representation report may practicably be implemented to promote improved representation in the Coast Guard of—

(A) women; and

(B) racial and ethnic minorities; and

(2) submit to the Committee on Commerce, Science, and Transportation of the Senate and the Committee on Transportation and Infrastructure of the House of Representatives a report on the actions the Commandant has taken, or plans to take, to implement such recommendations.

(b) CURRICULUM AND TRAINING.—In the case of any action the Commandant plans to take to implement recommendations described in subsection (a)(1) that relate to modification or development of curriculum and training, such modified curriculum and trainings shall be provided at—

(1) officer accession points, including the Coast Guard Academy and the Leadership Development Center;

(2) enlisted member accession at the United States Coast Guard Training Center Cape May in Cape May, New Jersey; and

(3) the officer, enlisted member, and civilian leadership courses managed by the Leadership Development Center.

(c) DEFINITION OF RAND REPRESENTATION REPORT.—In this section, the term "RAND representation report" means the report of the Homeland Security Operational Analysis Center of the RAND Corporation entitled "Improving the Representation of Women and Racial/Ethnic Minorities Among U.S. Coast Guard Active-Duty Members", issued on August 11, 2021.

SEC. 11249. STRATEGY TO ENHANCE DIVERSITY THROUGH RECRUITMENT AND ACCESSION.

(a) IN GENERAL.—The Commandant shall develop a 10-year strategy to enhance Coast Guard diversity through recruitment and accession—

(1) at educational institutions at the high school and higher education levels; and

(2) for the officer and enlisted ranks.

(b) REPORT.—

(1) IN GENERAL.—Not later than 180 days after the date of enactment of this Act, the Commandant shall submit to the Committee on Commerce, Science, and Transportation of the Senate and the Committee on Transportation and Infrastructure of the House of Representatives a report on the strategy developed under subsection (a).

(2) ELEMENTS.—The report required under paragraph (1) shall include the following:

(A) A description of existing Coast Guard recruitment and accession programs at educational institutions at the high school and higher education levels.

(B) An explanation of the manner in which the strategy supports the overall diversity and inclusion action plan of the Coast Guard.

(C) A description of the manner in which existing programs and partnerships will be modified or expanded to enhance diversity in recruiting in high school and institutions of higher education (as such term is defined in section 101 of the Higher Education Act of 1965 (20 U.S.C. 1001)) and accession.

SEC. 11250. SUPPORT FOR COAST GUARD ACADEMY.

(a) IN GENERAL.—Subchapter II of chapter 9 of title 14, United States Code, is amended by adding at the end the following:

"SEC. 953. [14 U.S.C. 953] Support for Coast Guard Academy

"(a) AUTHORITY.—

"(1) CONTRACTS AND COOPERATIVE AGREEMENTS.—

"(A) IN GENERAL.—The Commandant may enter contract and cooperative agreements with 1 or more qualified organizations for the purpose of supporting the athletic programs of the Coast Guard Academy.

"(B) AUTHORITY.—Notwithstanding section 3201(e) of title 10, the Commandant may enter into such contracts and cooperative agreements on a sole source basis pursuant to section 3204(a) of title 10.

"(C) ACQUISITIONS.—Notwithstanding chapter 63 of title 31, a cooperative agreement under this section may be used to acquire property or services for the direct benefit or use of the Coast Guard Academy.

"(2) FINANCIAL CONTROLS.—

"(A) IN GENERAL.—Before entering into a contract or cooperative agreement under paragraph (1), the Commandant shall ensure that the contract or agreement includes appropriate financial controls to account for the resources of the Coast Guard Academy and the qualified organization concerned in accordance with accepted accounting principles.

"(B) CONTENTS.—Any such contract or cooperative agreement shall contain a provision that allows the Commandant to review, as the Commandant considers necessary, the financial accounts of the qualified organization to determine whether the operations of the qualified organization—

"(i) are consistent with the terms of the contract or cooperative agreement; and

"(ii) would compromise the integrity or appearance of integrity of any program of the Department of Homeland Security.

"(3) LEASES.—For the purpose of supporting the athletic programs of the Coast Guard Academy, the Commandant may, consistent with section 504(a)(13), rent or lease real property located at the Coast Guard Academy to a qualified organization, except that proceeds from such a lease shall be retained and expended in accordance with subsection (f).

"(b) SUPPORT SERVICES.—

"(1) AUTHORITY.—To the extent required by a contract or cooperative agreement under subsection (a), the Commandant may provide support services to a qualified organization while the qualified organization conducts support activities at the Coast Guard Academy only if the Commandant determines that the provision of such services is essential for the support of the athletic programs of the Coast Guard Academy.

"(2) NO LIABILITY OF THE UNITED STATES.—Support services may only be provided without any liability of the United States to a qualified organization.

"(3) SUPPORT SERVICES DEFINED.—In this subsection, the term 'support services' includes utilities, office furnishings and equipment, communications services, records staging and archiving, audio and video support, and security systems, in conjunction with the leasing or licensing of property.

"(c) TRANSFERS FROM NONAPPROPRIATED FUND OPERATION.—

"(1) IN GENERAL.—Except as provided in paragraph (2), the Commandant may, subject to the acceptance of the qualified organization concerned, transfer to the qualified organization all title to and ownership of the assets and liabilities of the Coast Guard nonappropriated fund instrumentality, the function of which includes providing support for the athletic programs of the Coast Guard Academy, including bank accounts and financial reserves in the accounts of such fund instrumentality, equipment, supplies, and other personal property.

"(2) LIMITATION.—The Commandant may not transfer under paragraph (1) any interest in real property.

"(d) ACCEPTANCE OF SUPPORT FROM QUALIFIED ORGANIZATION.—

"(1) IN GENERAL.—Notwithstanding section 1342 of title 31, the Commandant may accept from a qualified organization funds, supplies, and services for the support of the athletic programs of the Coast Guard Academy.

"(2) EMPLOYEES OF QUALIFIED ORGANIZATION.—For purposes of this section, employees or personnel of the qualified organization may not be considered to be employees of the United States.

"(3) FUNDS RECEIVED FROM NCAA.—The Commandant may accept funds from the National Collegiate Athletic Association to support the athletic programs of the Coast Guard Academy.

"(4) LIMITATION.—The Commandant shall ensure that contributions under this subsection and expenditure of funds pursuant to subsection (f) do not—

"(A) reflect unfavorably on the ability of the Coast Guard, any employee of the Coast Guard, or any member of the armed forces (as such term is defined in section 101(a) of title 10) to carry out any responsibility or duty in a fair and objective manner; or

"(B) compromise the integrity or appearance of integrity of any program of the Coast Guard, or any individual involved in such a program.

"(e) TRADEMARKS AND SERVICE MARKS.—

"(1) LICENSING, MARKETING, AND SPONSORSHIP AGREEMENTS.—An agreement under subsection (a) may, consistent with section 2260 of title 10 (other than subsection (d) of such section), authorize a qualified organization to enter into licensing, marketing, and sponsorship agreements relating to trademarks and service marks identifying the Coast Guard Academy, subject to the approval of the Commandant.

"(2) LIMITATIONS.—A licensing, marketing, or sponsorship agreement may not be entered into under paragraph (1) if—

"(A) such agreement would reflect unfavorably on the ability of the Coast Guard, any employee of the Coast Guard, or any member of the armed forces to carry out any responsibility or duty in a fair and objective manner; or

"(B) the Commandant determines that the use of the trademark or service mark would compromise the integrity or appearance of integrity of any program of the Coast Guard or any individual involved in such a program.

"(f) RETENTION AND USE OF FUNDS.—Funds received by the Commandant under this section may be retained for use to support the athletic programs of the Coast Guard Academy and shall remain available until expended.

"(g) CONDITIONS.—The authority provided in this section with respect to a qualified organization is available only so long as the qualified organization continues—

"(1) to operate in accordance with this section, the law of the State of Connecticut, and the constitution and bylaws of the qualified organization; and

"(2) to operate exclusively to support the athletic programs of the Coast Guard Academy.

"(h) QUALIFIED ORGANIZATION DEFINED.—In this section, the term 'qualified organization' means an organization—

"(1) that operates as an organization under subsection (c)(3) of section 501 of the Internal Revenue Code of 1986 and exempt from taxation under subsection (a) of that section;

"(2) for which authorization under sections 1033(a) and 1589(a) of title 10 may be provided; and

"(3) established by the Coast Guard Academy Alumni Association solely for the purpose of supporting Coast Guard athletics.

"SEC. 954. [14 U.S.C. 954] Mixed-funded athletic and recreational extracurricular programs

"(a) AUTHORITY.—In the case of a Coast Guard Academy mixed-funded athletic or recreational extracurricular program, the Commandant may designate funds appropriated to the Coast Guard and available for that program to be treated as nonappropriated funds and expended for that program in accordance with laws applicable to the expenditure of nonappropriated funds. Appropriated funds so designated shall be considered to be nonappropriated funds for all purposes and shall remain available until expended.

"(b) COVERED PROGRAMS.—In this section, the term 'Coast Guard Academy mixed-funded athletic or recreational extracurricular program' means an athletic or recreational extracurricular program of the Coast Guard Academy to which each of the following applies:

"(1) The program is not considered a morale, welfare, or recreation program.

"(2) The program is supported through appropriated funds.

"(3) The program is supported by a nonappropriated fund instrumentality.

"(4) The program is not a private organization and is not operated by a private organization."

(b) CLERICAL AMENDMENT.—The analysis for chapter 9 of title 14, United States Code, is amended by inserting after the item relating to section 952 the following:

"953.	Support for Coast Guard Academy.
"954.	Mixed-funded athletic and recreational extracurricular programs."

SEC. 11251. TRAINING FOR CONGRESSIONAL AFFAIRS PERSONNEL.

(a) IN GENERAL.—Section 315 of title 14, United States Code, is amended to read as follows:

"SEC. 315. Training for congressional affairs personnel

"(a) IN GENERAL.—The Commandant shall develop a training course, which shall be administered in person, on the workings of Congress for any member of the Coast Guard selected for a position as a fellow, liaison, counsel, or administrative staff for the Coast Guard Office of Congressional and Governmental Affairs or as any Coast Guard district or area governmental affairs officer.

"(b) COURSE SUBJECT MATTER.—

"(1) IN GENERAL.—The training course required under this section shall provide an overview and introduction to Congress and the Federal legislative process, including—

"(A) the congressional budget process;

"(B) the congressional appropriations process;

"(C) the congressional authorization process;

"(D) the Senate advice and consent process for Presidential nominees;

"(E) the Senate advice and consent process for treaty ratification;

"(F) the roles of Members of Congress and congressional staff in the legislative process;

"(G) the concept and underlying purposes of congressional oversight within the governance framework of separation of powers;

"(H) the roles of Coast Guard fellows, liaisons, counsels, governmental affairs officers, the Coast Guard Office of Program Review, the Coast Guard Headquarters program offices, and any other entity the Commandant considers relevant; and

"(I) the roles and responsibilities of Coast Guard public affairs and external communications personnel with respect to Members of Congress and the staff of such Members necessary to enhance communication between Coast Guard units, sectors, and districts and Member offices and committees of jurisdiction so as to ensure visibility of Coast Guard activities.

"(2) DETAIL WITHIN COAST GUARD OFFICE OF BUDGET AND PROGRAMS.—

"(A) IN GENERAL.—At the written request of a receiving congressional office, the training course required under this section shall include a multi-day detail within the Coast Guard Office of Budget and Programs to ensure adequate exposure to Coast Guard policy, oversight, and requests from Congress.

"(B) NONCONSECUTIVE DETAIL PERMITTED.—A detail under this paragraph is not required to be consecutive with the balance of the training.

"(c) COMPLETION OF REQUIRED TRAINING.—A member of the Coast Guard selected for a position described in subsection (a) shall complete the training required by this section before the date on which such member reports for duty for such position."

(b) CLERICAL AMENDMENT.—The analysis for chapter 3 of title 14, United States Code, is amended by striking the item relating to section 315 and inserting the following:

"315. Training for congressional affairs personnel."

SEC. 11252. STRATEGY FOR RETENTION OF CUTTERMEN.

(a) IN GENERAL.—Not later than 180 days after the date of enactment of this Act, the Commandant shall publish a strategy to improve incentives to attract and retain a qualified workforce serving on Coast Guard cutters that includes underrepresented minorities, and servicemembers from rural areas, as such term is defined in section 54301(a)(12)(C) of title 46, United States Code.

(b) ELEMENTS.—The strategy required by subsection (a) shall include the following:

(1) Policies to improve flexibility in the afloat career path, including a policy that enables members of the Coast Guard serving on Coast Guard cutters to transition between operations afloat and operations ashore assignments without detriment to the career progression of a member.

(2) A review of current officer requirements for afloat assignments at each pay grade, and an assessment as to whether such requirements are appropriate or present undue limitations.

(3) Strategies to improve crew comfort afloat, such as berthing modifications to accommodate all crewmembers.

(4) Actionable steps to improve access to highspeed internet capable of video conference for the purposes of medical, educational, and personal use by members of the Coast Guard serving on Coast Guard cutters.

(5) An assessment of the effectiveness of bonuses to attract members to serve at sea and retain talented members of the Coast Guard serving on Coast Guard cutters to serve as leaders in senior enlisted positions, department head positions, and command positions.

(6) Policies to ensure that high-performing members of the Coast Guard serving on Coast Guard cutters are competitive for special assignments, postgraduate education, senior service schools, and other career-enhancing positions.

(c) RULE OF CONSTRUCTION.—The Commandant shall ensure that the elements described in subsection (b) do not result in discrimination based on race, color, religion, sexual orientation, national origin, or gender.

SEC. 11253. STUDY ON PERFORMANCE OF COAST GUARD FORCE READINESS COMMAND.

(a) IN GENERAL.—Not later than 1 year after the date of enactment of this Act, the Comptroller General of the United States shall commence a study on the performance of the Coast Guard Force Readiness Command.

(b) ELEMENTS.—The study required under subsection (a) shall include an assessment of the following:

(1) The actions the Force Readiness Command has taken to develop and implement training for the Coast Guard workforce.

(2) The extent to which the Force Readiness Command—

(A) has made an assessment of performance, policy, and training compliance across Force Readiness Command headquarters and field units, and the results of any such assessment; and

(B) is modifying and expanding Coast Guard training to match the future demands of the Coast Guard with respect to growth in workforce numbers, modernization of assets and infrastructure, and increased global mission demands relating to the Arctic and Western Pacific regions and cyberspace.

(c) REPORT.—Not later than 1 year after the study required by subsection (a) commences, the Comptroller General shall submit to the Committee on Commerce, Science, and Transportation of the Senate and the Committee on Transportation and Infrastructure of the House of Representatives a report on the findings of the study.

SEC. 11254. STUDY ON FREQUENCY OF WEAPONS TRAINING FOR COAST GUARD PERSONNEL.

(a) IN GENERAL.—The Commandant shall conduct a study to

assess whether current weapons training required for Coast Guard law enforcement and other relevant personnel is sufficient.

(b) ELEMENTS.—The study required under subsection (a) shall—

(1) assess whether there is a need to improve weapons training for Coast Guard law enforcement and other relevant personnel; and

(2) identify—

(A) the frequency of such training most likely to ensure adequate weapons training, proficiency, and safety among such personnel;

(B) Coast Guard law enforcement and other applicable personnel who should be prioritized to receive such improved training; and

(C) any challenge posed by a transition to improving such training and offering such training more frequently, and the resources necessary to address such a challenge.

(c) REPORT.—Not later than 1 year after the date of enactment of this Act, the Commandant shall submit to the Committee on Commerce, Science, and Transportation of the Senate and the Committee on Transportation and Infrastructure of the House of Representatives a report on the findings of the study conducted under subsection (a).

Subtitle G—Miscellaneous Provisions

SEC. 11255. MODIFICATION OF PROHIBITION ON OPERATION OR PROCUREMENT OF FOREIGN-MADE UNMANNED AIRCRAFT SYSTEMS.

Section 8414 of the William M. (Mac) Thornberry National Defense Authorization Act for Fiscal Year 2021 (Public Law 116-283; 14 U.S.C. 1156 note) is amended—

(1) by amending subsection (b) to read as follows:

"(b) EXEMPTION.—The Commandant is exempt from the restriction under subsection (a) if the operation or procurement is for the purposes of—

"(1) counter-UAS system surrogate testing and training; or

"(2) intelligence, electronic warfare, and information

warfare operations, testing, analysis, and training."

(2) by amending subsection (c) to read as follows:

"(c) WAIVER.—The Commandant may waive the restriction under subsection (a) on a case-by-case basis by certifying in writing not later than 15 days after exercising such waiver to the Department of Homeland Security, the Committee on Commerce, Science, and Transportation of the Senate, and the Committee on Transportation and Infrastructure of the House of Representatives that the operation or procurement of a covered unmanned aircraft system is required in the national interest of the United States."

(3) in subsection (d)—

(A) by amending paragraph (1) to read as follows:

"(1) COVERED FOREIGN COUNTRY.—The term 'covered foreign country' means any of the following:

"(A) The People's Republic of China.

"(B) The Russian Federation.

"(C) The Islamic Republic of Iran.

"(D) The Democratic People's Republic of Korea."

(B) by redesignating paragraphs (2) and (3) as paragraphs (3) and (4), respectively;

(C) by inserting after paragraph (1) the following:

"(2) COVERED UNMANNED AIRCRAFT SYSTEM.—The term 'covered unmanned aircraft system' means an unmanned aircraft system described in paragraph (1) of subsection (a)."

; and

(D) in paragraph (4), as so redesignated, by inserting ", and any related services and equipment" after "United States Code"; and

(4) by adding at the end the following:

"(e) REPLACEMENT.—Not later than 90 days after the date of the enactment of the Don Young Coast Guard Authorization Act of 2022, the Commandant shall replace covered unmanned aircraft systems of the Coast Guard with unmanned aircraft systems manufactured in the United States or an allied country (as that term is defined in section 2350f(d)(1) of title 10, United States Code).”

SEC. 11256. BUDGETING OF COAST GUARD RELATING TO CERTAIN OPERATIONS.

(a) IN GENERAL.—Chapter 51 of title 14, United States Code, is further amended by adding at the end the following:

“SEC. 5114. Expenses of performing and executing defense readiness missions

“Not later than 1 year after the date of enactment of this section, and every February 1 thereafter, the Commandant shall submit to the Committee on Commerce, Science, and Transportation of the Senate and the Committee on Transportation and Infrastructure of the House of Representatives a report that adequately represents a calculation of the annual costs and expenditures of performing and executing all defense readiness mission activities, including—

“(1) all expenses related to the Coast Guard’s coordination, training, and execution of defense readiness mission activities in the Coast Guard’s capacity as an armed force (as such term is defined in section 101 of title 10) in support of Department of Defense national security operations and activities or for any other military department or Defense Agency (as such terms are defined in such section);

“(2) costs associated with Coast Guard detachments assigned in support of the defense readiness mission of the Coast Guard; and

“(3) any other related expenses, costs, or matters the Commandant considers appropriate or otherwise of interest to Congress.”

(b) CLERICAL AMENDMENT.—The analysis for chapter 51 of title 14, United States Code, as amended by section 252(b), is further amended by adding at the end the following:

“5114. Expenses of performing and executing defense readiness missions.”

SEC. 11257. REPORT ON SAN DIEGO MARITIME DOMAIN AWARENESS.

Not later than 180 days after the date of enactment of this Act, the Commandant shall submit to the Committee on Transportation and Infrastructure of the House of Representatives and the Committee on Commerce, Science, and Transportation of the Senate a report containing—

(1) an overview of the maritime domain awareness in the area of responsibility of the Coast Guard sector responsible for San Diego, California, including—

(A) the average volume of known maritime traffic that transited the area during fiscal years 2020 through 2022;

(B) current sensor platforms deployed by such sector to monitor illicit activity occurring at sea in such area;

(C) the number of illicit activity incidents at sea in such area that the sector responded to during fiscal years 2020 through 2022;

(D) an estimate of the volume of traffic engaged in illicit activity at sea in such area and the type and description of any vessels used to carry out illicit activities that such sector responded to during fiscal years 2020 through 2022; and

(E) the maritime domain awareness requirements to effectively meet the mission of such sector;

(2) a description of current actions taken by the Coast Guard to partner with Federal, regional, State, and local entities to meet the maritime domain awareness needs of such area;

(3) a description of any gaps in maritime domain awareness within the area of responsibility of such sector resulting from an inability to meet the enduring maritime domain awareness requirements of the sector or adequately respond to maritime disorder;

(4) an identification of current technology and assets the Coast Guard has to mitigate the gaps identified in paragraph (3);

(5) an identification of capabilities needed to mitigate such gaps, including any capabilities the Coast Guard currently possesses that can be deployed to the sector;

(6) an identification of technology and assets the Coast Guard does not currently possess and are needed to acquire in order to address such gaps; and

(7) an identification of any financial obstacles that prevent the Coast Guard from deploying existing commercially available sensor technology to address such gaps.

SEC. 11258. CONVEYANCE OF COAST GUARD VESSELS FOR PUBLIC PURPOSES.

(a) [14 U.S.C. 510] TRANSFER.—Section 914 of the Coast Guard Authorization Act of 2010 (14 U.S.C. 501 note; Public Law 111-281) is—

(1) transferred to subchapter I of chapter 5 of title 14, United States Code;

(2) added at the end so as to follow section 509 of such title, as added by this Act;

(3) redesignated as section 510 of such title; and

(4) amended so that the enumerator, the section heading, typeface, and typestyle conform to those appearing in other sections of title 14, United States Code.

(b) CLERICAL AMENDMENTS.—

(1) COAST GUARD AUTHORIZATION ACT OF 2010.—The table of contents in section 1(b) of the Coast Guard Authorization Act of 2010 (Public Law 111-281) is amended by striking the item relating to section 914.

(2) TITLE 14.—The analysis for subchapter I of chapter 5 of title 14, United States Code, is further amended by adding at the end the following:

"510. Conveyance of Coast Guard vessels for public purposes."

(c) CONVEYANCE OF COAST GUARD VESSELS FOR PUBLIC PURPOSES.—Section 510 of title 14, United States Code, as transferred and redesignated by subsection (a), is amended—

(1) by amending subsection (a) to read as follows:

"(a) IN GENERAL.—On request by the Commandant, the Administrator of the General Services Administration may transfer ownership of a Coast Guard vessel or aircraft to an eligible entity for educational, cultural, historical, charitable, recreational, or other public purposes if such transfer is authorized by law."

; and

(2) in subsection (b)—

(A) in paragraph (1)—

(i) by inserting "as if the request were being processed" after "vessels"; and

(ii) by inserting ", as in effect on the date of the enactment of the Don Young Coast Guard Authorization Act of 2022" after "Code of Federal Regulations";

(B) in paragraph (2) by inserting ", as in effect on the date of the enactment of the Don Young Coast Guard Authorization Act of 2022" after "such title"; and

(C) in paragraph (3) by striking "of the Coast Guard".

SEC. 11259. NATIONAL COAST GUARD MUSEUM FUNDING PLAN.

Section 316(c)(4) of title 14, United States Code, is amended by striking "the Inspector General of the department in which the Coast Guard is operating" and inserting "a third party entity qualified to undertake such a certification process".

SEC. 11260. REPORT ON COAST GUARD EXPLOSIVE ORDNANCE DISPOSAL.

(a) IN GENERAL.—Not later than 1 year after the date of enactment of this Act, the Commandant shall submit to the Committee on Transportation and Infrastructure of the House of Representatives and the Committee on Commerce, Science, and Transportation of the Senate a report on the viability of establishing an explosive ordnance disposal program (in this section referred to as the "Program") in the Coast Guard.

(b) CONTENTS.—The report required under subsection (a) shall contain, at a minimum, an explanation of the following with respect to such a Program:

(1) Where within the organizational structure of the Coast Guard the Program would be located, including a discussion of whether the Program should reside in—

(A) Maritime Safety and Security Teams;

(B) Maritime Security Response Teams;

(C) a combination of the teams described under subparagraphs (A) and (B); or

(D) elsewhere within the Coast Guard.

(2) The vehicles and dive craft that are Coast Guard airframe and vessel transportable that would be required for the transportation of explosive ordnance disposal elements.

(3) The Coast Guard stations at which—

(A) portable explosives storage magazines would be available for explosive ordnance disposal elements; and

(B) explosive ordnance disposal elements equipment would be pre-positioned.

(4) How the Program would support other elements within the Department of Homeland Security, the Department of Justice, and, in wartime, the Department of Defense to—

(A) counter improvised explosive devices;

(B) counter unexploded ordnance;

(C) combat weapons of destruction;

(D) provide service in support of the President; and

(E) support national security special events.

(5) The career progression of members of the Coast Guard participating in the Program from—

(A) Seaman Recruit to Command Master Chief Petty Officer;

(B) Chief Warrant Officer 2 to that of Chief Warrant Officer 4; and

(C) Ensign to that of Rear Admiral.

(6) Initial and annual budget justification estimates on a single program element of the Program for—

(A) civilian and military pay with details on military pay, including special and incentive pays such as—

(i) officer responsibility pay;

(ii) officer SCUBA diving duty pay;

(iii) officer demolition hazardous duty pay;

(iv) enlisted SCUBA diving duty pay;

(v) enlisted demolition hazardous duty pay;

(vi) enlisted special duty assignment pay at level special duty-5;

(vii) enlisted assignment incentive pays;

(viii) enlistment and reenlistment bonuses;

(ix) officer and enlisted full civilian clothing allowances;

(x) an exception to the policy allowing a third hazardous duty pay for explosive ordnance disposal-qualified officers and enlisted; and

(xi) parachutist hazardous duty pay;

(B) research, development, test, and evaluation;

(C) procurement;

(D) other transaction agreements;

(E) operations and support; and

(F) overseas contingency operations.

SEC. 11261. TRANSFER AND CONVEYANCE.

(a) IN GENERAL.—

(1) REQUIREMENT.—In accordance with section 120(h) of the Comprehensive Environmental Response, Compensation, and Liability Act (42 U.S.C. 9620(h)), the Commandant shall, without consideration, transfer in accordance with subsection (b) and convey in accordance with subsection (c) a parcel of the real property described in paragraph (2), including any improvements thereon.

(2) PROPERTY.—The property described in this paragraph is real property at Dauphin Island, Alabama, located at 100 Agassiz Street, and consisting of a total of approximately 35.63 acres. The exact acreage and legal description of the parcel of such property to be transferred or conveyed in accordance with subsection (b) or (c), respectively, shall be determined by a survey satisfactory to the Commandant.

(b) TO THE SECRETARY OF HEALTH AND HUMAN SERVICES.—The Commandant shall transfer, as described in subsection (a), to the Secretary of Health and Human Services (in this section referred to as the "Secretary"), for use by the Food and Drug Administration, custody and control of a portion, consisting of approximately 4 acres, of the parcel of real property described in such subsection, to be identified by agreement between the Commandant and the Secretary.

(c) TO THE STATE OF ALABAMA.—The Commandant shall convey, as described in subsection (a), to the Marine Environmental Sciences Consortium, a unit of the government of the State of Alabama, located at Dauphin Island, Alabama, all rights, title, and interest of the United States in and to such portion of the parcel described in such subsection that is not transferred to the Secretary under subsection (b).

(d) PAYMENTS AND COSTS OF TRANSFER AND CONVEYANCE.—

(1) PAYMENTS.—

(A) IN GENERAL.—The Secretary shall pay costs to be incurred by the Coast Guard, or reimburse the Coast Guard for such costs incurred by the Coast Guard, to carry out the transfer and conveyance required by this section, including survey costs, appraisal costs, costs for environmental documentation related to the transfer and conveyance, and any other necessary administrative costs related to the transfer and conveyance.

(B) FUNDS.—Notwithstanding section 780 of division B of the Further Consolidated Appropriations Act, 2020 (Public Law 116-94), any amounts that are made available to the Secretary under such section and not obligated on the date of enactment of this Act shall be available to the Secretary for the purpose described in subparagraph (A).

(2) TREATMENT OF AMOUNTS RECEIVED.—Amounts received by the Commandant as reimbursement under paragraph (1) shall be credited to the Coast Guard Housing Fund established under section 2946 of title 14, United States Code, or the account that was used to pay the costs incurred by the Coast Guard in carrying out the transfer or conveyance under this section, as determined by the Commandant, and shall be made available until expended. Amounts so credited shall be merged with amounts in such fund or account and shall be available for the same purposes, and subject to the same conditions and limitations, as amounts in such fund or account.

SEC. 11262. TRANSPARENCY AND OVERSIGHT.

(a) IN GENERAL.—Chapter 51 of title 14, United States Code, is further amended by adding at the end the following:

"SEC. 5115. [14 U.S.C. 5115] Major grants, contracts, or other

transactions

"(a) NOTIFICATION.—

"(1) IN GENERAL.—Subject to subsection (b), the Commandant shall notify the appropriate committees of Congress and the Coast Guard Office of Congressional and Governmental Affairs not later than 3 full business days in advance of the Coast Guard—

"(A) making or awarding a grant allocation or grant in excess of $1,000,000;

"(B) making or awarding a contract, other transaction agreement, or task or delivery order for the Coast Guard on the multiple award contract, or issuing a letter of intent totaling more than $4,000,000;

"(C) awarding a task or delivery order requiring an obligation of funds in an amount greater than $10,000,000 from multi-year Coast Guard funds;

"(D) making a sole-source grant award; or

"(E) announcing publicly the intention to make or award an item described in subparagraph (A), (B), (C), or (D), including a contract covered by the Federal Acquisition Regulation.

"(2) ELEMENT.—A notification under this subsection shall include—

"(A) the amount of the award;

"(B) the fiscal year for which the funds for the award were appropriated;

"(C) the type of contract;

"(D) an identification of the entity awarded the contract, such as the name and location of the entity; and

"(E) the account from which the funds are to be drawn.

"(b) EXCEPTION.—If the Commandant determines that compliance with subsection (a) would pose a substantial risk to human life, health, or safety, the Commandant—

"(1) may make an award or issue a letter described in such subsection without the notification required under such subsection; and

"(2) shall notify the appropriate committees of Congress not later than 5 full business days after such an award is made or letter issued.

"(c) APPLICABILITY.—Subsection (a) shall not apply to funds that are not available for obligation.

"(d) APPROPRIATE COMMITTEES OF CONGRESS DEFINED.—In this section, the term 'appropriate committees of Congress' means—

"(1) the Committee on Commerce, Science, and Transportation and the Committee on Appropriations of the Senate; and

"(2) the Committee on Transportation and Infrastructure and the Committee on Appropriations of the House of Representatives."

(b) CLERICAL AMENDMENT.—The analysis for chapter 51 of title 14, United States Code, is further amended by adding at the end the following:

"5115. Major grants, contracts, or other transactions."

SEC. 11263. STUDY ON SAFETY INSPECTION PROGRAM FOR CONTAINERS AND FACILITIES.

(a) IN GENERAL.—Not later than 1 year after the date of enactment of this Act, the Commandant shall complete a study on the safety inspection program for containers (as such term is defined in section 80501 of title 46, United States Code) and designated waterfront facilities receiving containers.

(b) ELEMENTS.—The study required under subsection (a) shall include the following:

(1) An evaluation and review of such safety inspection program.

(2) A determination of—

(A) the number of container inspections conducted annually by the Coast Guard during the preceding 10-year period, as compared to the number of containers moved through United States ports annually during such period; and

(B) the number of qualified Coast Guard container and facility inspectors, and an assessment as to whether, during the preceding 10-year period, there have been a sufficient number of such inspectors to carry out the mission of the Coast Guard.

(3) An evaluation of the training programs available to such inspectors and the adequacy of such training programs during the preceding 10-year period.

(4) An identification of areas of improvement for such program in the interest of commerce and national security, and the costs associated with such improvements.

(c) REPORT TO CONGRESS.—Not later than 180 days after the completion of the study required under subsection (a), the Commandant shall submit to the Committee on Commerce, Science, and Transportation of the Senate and the Committee on Transportation and Infrastructure of the House of Representatives a report on the findings of the study required by subsection (a), including the personnel and resource requirements necessary for such program.

SEC. 11264. [6 U.S.C. 245] OPERATIONAL DATA SHARING CAPABILITY.

(a) IN GENERAL.—Not later than 18 months after the date of enactment of this Act, the Secretary shall, consistent with the ongoing Integrated Multi-Domain Enterprise joint effort by the Department of Homeland Security and the Department of Defense, establish a secure, centralized capability to allow real-time, or near real-time, data and information sharing between Customs and Border Protection and the Coast Guard for purposes of maritime boundary domain awareness and enforcement activities along the maritime boundaries of the United States, including the maritime boundaries in the northern and southern continental United States and Alaska.

(b) PRIORITY.—In establishing the capability under subsection (a), the Secretary shall prioritize enforcement areas experiencing the highest levels of enforcement activity.

(c) REQUIREMENTS.—The capability established under subsection (a) shall be sufficient for the secure sharing of data, information, and surveillance necessary for operational missions, including data from governmental assets, irrespective of whether an asset located in or around mission operation areas belongs to the Coast Guard, Customs and Border Protection, or any other partner agency.

(d) ELEMENTS.—The Commissioner of Customs and Border Protection and the Commandant shall jointly—

(1) assess and delineate the types of data and quality of data sharing needed to meet the respective operational missions of Customs and Border Protection and the Coast Guard, including video surveillance, seismic sensors, infrared detection, space-based remote sensing, and any other data or information necessary;

(2) develop appropriate requirements and processes for the credentialing of personnel of Customs and Border Protection and personnel of the Coast Guard to access and use the capability established under subsection (a); and

(3) establish a cost-sharing agreement for the long-term operation and maintenance of the capability and the assets that provide data to the capability.

(e) REPORT.—Not later than 2 years after the date of enactment of this Act, the Secretary shall submit to the Committee on Commerce, Science, and Transportation and the Committee on Homeland Security and Governmental Affairs of the Senate and the Committee on Transportation and Infrastructure and the Committee on Homeland Security of the House of Representatives a report on the establishment of the capability under this section.

(f) RULE OF CONSTRUCTION.—Nothing in this section may be construed to authorize the Coast Guard, Customs and Border Protection, or any other partner agency to acquire, share, or transfer personal information relating to an individual in violation of any Federal or State law or regulation.

SEC. 11265. FEASIBILITY STUDY ON CONSTRUCTION OF COAST GUARD STATION AT PORT MANSFIELD.

(a) STUDY.—

(1) IN GENERAL.—Not later than 180 days after the date of the enactment of this Act, the Commandant shall commence a feasibility study on construction of a Coast Guard station at Port Mansfield, Texas.

(2) ELEMENTS.—The study required under paragraph (1) shall include the following:

(A) An assessment of the resources and workforce requirements necessary for a new Coast Guard station at

Port Mansfield.

(B) An identification of the enhancements to the missions and capabilities of the Coast Guard that a new Coast Guard station at Port Mansfield would provide.

(C) An estimate of the life-cycle costs of such a facility, including the costs of construction, maintenance costs, and staffing costs.

(D) A cost-benefit analysis of the enhancements and capabilities provided, as compared to the costs of construction, maintenance, and staffing.

(b) REPORT.—Not later than 180 days after commencing the study required by subsection (a), the Commandant shall submit to the Committee on Commerce, Science, and Transportation of the Senate and the Committee on Transportation and Infrastructure of the House of Representatives a report on the findings of the study.

SEC. 11266. PROCUREMENT OF TETHERED AEROSTAT RADAR SYSTEM FOR COAST GUARD STATION SOUTH PADRE ISLAND.

Subject to the availability of appropriations, the Secretary shall procure not fewer than 1 tethered aerostat radar system, or similar technology, for use by the Coast Guard at and around Coast Guard Station South Padre Island.

SEC. 11267. PROHIBITION ON MAJOR ACQUISITION CONTRACTS WITH ENTITIES ASSOCIATED WITH CHINESE COMMUNIST PARTY.

(a) IN GENERAL.—The Commandant may not award any major acquisition contract until the Commandant receives a certification from the party that it has not, during the 10-year period preceding the planned date of award, directly or indirectly held an economic interest in an entity that is—

(1) owned or controlled by the People's Republic of China; and

(2) part of the defense industry of the Chinese Communist Party.

(b) INAPPLICABILITY TO TAIWAN.—Subsection (a) shall not apply with respect to an economic interest in an entity owned or controlled by Taiwan.

SEC. 11268. [14 U.S.C. 522 note] REVIEW OF DRUG INTERDICTION EQUIPMENT AND STANDARDS; TESTING FOR FENTANYL DURING

INTERDICTION OPERATIONS.

(a) REVIEW.—

(1) IN GENERAL.—The Commandant, in consultation with the Administrator of the Drug Enforcement Administration and the Secretary of Health and Human Services, shall—

(A) conduct a review of—

(i) the equipment, testing kits, and rescue medications used to conduct Coast Guard drug interdiction operations; and

(ii) the safety and training standards, policies, and procedures with respect to such operations; and

(B) determine whether the Coast Guard is using the latest equipment and technology and up-to-date training and standards for recognizing, handling, testing, and securing illegal drugs, fentanyl and other synthetic opioids, and precursor chemicals during such operations.

(2) REPORT.—Not later than 180 days after the date of enactment of this Act, the Commandant shall submit to the appropriate committees of Congress a report on the results of the review conducted under paragraph (1).

(3) APPROPRIATE COMMITTEES OF CONGRESS DEFINED.—In this subsection, the term "appropriate committees of Congress" means—

(A) the Committee on Commerce, Science, and Transportation and the Committee on Appropriations of the Senate; and

(B) the Committee on Transportation and Infrastructure and the Committee on Appropriations of the House of Representatives.

(b) REQUIREMENT.—If, as a result of the review required by subsection (a), the Commandant determines that the Coast Guard is not using the latest equipment and technology and up-to-date training and standards for recognizing, handling, testing, and securing illegal drugs, fentanyl and other synthetic opioids, and precursor chemicals during drug interdiction operations, the Commandant shall ensure that the Coast Guard acquires and uses such equipment and technology, carries out such training, and implements such standards.

(c) TESTING FOR FENTANYL.—The Commandant shall ensure that Coast Guard drug interdiction operations include the testing of substances encountered during such operations for fentanyl, as appropriate.

SEC. 11269. [14 U.S.C. 522 note] PUBLIC AVAILABILITY OF INFORMATION ON MONTHLY MIGRANT INTERDICTIONS.

Not later than the 15th day of each month, the Commandant shall make available to the public on the website of the Coast Guard the number of migrant interdictions carried out by the Coast Guard during the preceding month.

SEC. 11270. CARGO WAITING TIME REDUCTION.

Not later than 90 days after the date of enactment of this Act, the Commandant shall submit to the Committee on Transportation and Infrastructure of the House of Representatives and the Committee on Commerce, Science, and Transportation of the Senate a report that includes—

(1) an explanation of the extent to which vessels carrying cargo are complying with the requirements of chapter 700 of title 46, United States Code;

(2) the status of the investigation on the cause of the oil spill that occurred in October 2021 on the waters over the San Pedro Shelf related to an anchor strike, including the expected date on which the Marine Casualty Investigation Report with respect to such spill will be released; and

(3) with respect to such vessels, a summary of actions taken or planned to be taken by the Commandant to provide additional protections against oil spills or other hazardous discharges caused by anchor strikes.

SEC. 11271. STUDY ON COAST GUARD OVERSIGHT AND INVESTIGATIONS.

(a) IN GENERAL.—Not later than 2 years after the date of enactment of this Act, the Comptroller General of the United States shall commence a study to assess the oversight over Coast Guard activities, including investigations, personnel management, whistleblower protection, and other activities carried out by the Department of Homeland Security Office of Inspector General.

(b) ELEMENTS.—The study required under subsection (a) shall

include the following:

(1) An analysis of the ability of the Department of Homeland Security Office of Inspector General to ensure timely, thorough, complete, and appropriate oversight over the Coast Guard, including oversight over both civilian and military activities.

(2) An assessment of—

(A) the best practices with respect to such oversight; and

(B) the ability of the Department of Homeland Security Office of Inspector General and the Commandant to identify and achieve such best practices.

(3) An analysis of the methods, standards, and processes employed by the Department of Defense Office of Inspector General and the inspectors generals of the armed forces (as such term is defined in section 101 of title 10, United States Code), other than the Coast Guard, to conduct oversight and investigation activities.

(4) An analysis of the methods, standards, and processes of the Department of Homeland Security Office of Inspector General with respect to oversight over the civilian and military activities of the Coast Guard, as compared to the methods, standards, and processes described in paragraph (3).

(5) An assessment of the extent to which the Coast Guard Investigative Service completes investigations or other disciplinary measures after referral of complaints from the Department of Homeland Security Office of Inspector General.

(6) A description of the staffing, expertise, training, and other resources of the Department of Homeland Security Office of Inspector General, and an assessment as to whether such staffing, expertise, training, and other resources meet the requirements necessary for meaningful, timely, and effective oversight over the activities of the Coast Guard.

(c) REPORT.—Not later than 1 year after commencing the study required under subsection (a), the Comptroller General shall submit to the Committee on Commerce, Science, and Transportation of the Senate and the Committee on Transportation and Infrastructure of the House of Representatives a report on the findings of the study, including recommendations with respect to oversight over Coast

Guard activities.

(d) OTHER REVIEWS.—The study required under subsection (a) may rely upon recently completed or ongoing reviews by the Comptroller General or other entities, as applicable.

Subtitle H—Sexual Assault and Sexual Harassment Response and Prevention

SEC. 11272. ADMINISTRATION OF SEXUAL ASSAULT FORENSIC EXAMINATION KITS.

(a) IN GENERAL.—Subchapter IV of chapter 5 of title 14, United States Code, is amended by adding at the end the following:

"SEC. 564. [14 U.S.C. 564] Administration of sexual assault forensic examination kits

"(a) SEXUAL ASSAULT FORENSIC EXAM PROCEDURE.—

"(1) IN GENERAL.—Before embarking on any prescheduled voyage, a Coast Guard vessel shall have in place a written operating procedure that ensures that an embarked victim of sexual assault shall have access to a sexual assault forensic examination—

"(A) as soon as possible after the victim requests an examination; and

"(B) that is treated with the same level of urgency as emergency medical care.

"(2) REQUIREMENTS.—The written operating procedure required by paragraph (1), shall, at a minimum, account for—

"(A) the health, safety, and privacy of a victim of sexual assault;

"(B) the proximity of ashore or afloat medical facilities, including coordination as necessary with the Department of Defense, including other military departments (as defined in section 101 of title 10);

"(C) the availability of aeromedical evacuation;

"(D) the operational capabilities of the vessel concerned;

"(E) the qualifications of medical personnel onboard;

"(F) coordination with law enforcement and the preservation of evidence;

"(G) the means of accessing a sexual assault forensic examination and medical care with a restricted report of sexual assault;

"(H) the availability of nonprescription pregnancy prophylactics; and

"(I) other unique military considerations."

(b) CLERICAL AMENDMENT.—The analysis for chapter 5 of title 14, United States Code, is amended by inserting after the item relating to section 563 the following:

"564. Administration of sexual assault forensic examination kits."

(c) STUDY.—

(1) IN GENERAL.—Not later than 1 year after the date of the enactment of this Act, the Secretary shall seek to enter into an agreement with the National Academy of Sciences under which the National Academy of Sciences shall conduct a study to assess challenges and prospective solutions associated with sexual assault at sea, to include the provision of survivor care, forensic examination of the victim, and evidence collection.

(2) CONTENTS.—The study under paragraph (1) shall, at a minimum, address the feasibility of crisis response services and physical evaluation through telemedicine and other options concerning immediate access to care whether onboard the vessel or at the nearest shore side facility, including best practices for administering sexual assault forensic examinations.

(3) ELEMENTS.—The study under paragraph (1) shall—

(A) take into account—

(i) the safety and security of the alleged victim of sexual assault;

(ii) the ability to properly identify, document, and preserve any evidence relevant to the allegation of sexual assault;

(iii) the applicable criminal procedural laws relating to authenticity, relevance, preservation of evidence, chain of custody, and any other matter relating to evidentiary admissibility; and

(iv) best practices of conducting sexual assault forensic examinations, as such term is defined in section 40723 of title 34, United States Code;

(B) provide any appropriate recommendation for changes to existing laws, regulations, or employer policies;

(C) solicit public stakeholder input from individuals and organizations with relevant expertise in sexual assault response including healthcare, advocacy services, law enforcement, and prosecution;

(D) evaluate the operational capabilities of the Coast Guard since 2013 in providing alleged victims of sexual assault immediate access to care onboard a vessel undertaking a prescheduled voyage that, at any point during such voyage, would require the vessel to travel 3 consecutive days or longer to reach a land-based or afloat medical facility, including—

(i) the average of and range in the reported hours taken to evacuate an individual with any medical emergency to a land-based or afloat medical facility; and

(ii) the number of alleged victims, subjects, and total incidents of sexual assault and sexual harassment occurring while underway reported annually; and

(E) summarize the financial cost, required operational adjustments, and potential benefits to the Coast Guard to provide sexual assault forensic examination kits onboard Coast Guard vessels undertaking a prescheduled voyage that, at any point during such voyage, would require the vessel to travel 3 consecutive days or longer to reach a land-based or afloat medical facility.

(4) REPORT.—Upon completion of the study under paragraph (1), the National Academy of Sciences shall submit to the Committee on Commerce, Science, and Transportation of the Senate, the Committee on Transportation and Infrastructure of the House of Representatives, and the Secretary a report on the findings of the study.

(5) [14 U.S.C. 564 note] ANNUAL REPORT.—The

Commandant shall submit to the Transportation and Infrastructure Committee of the House and the Commerce, Science, and Transportation Committee of the Senate a report containing the number of sexual assault forensic examinations that were requested by, but not administered within 3 days to, alleged victims of sexual assault when such victims were onboard a vessel.

(6) SAVINGS CLAUSE.—In collecting the information required under paragraphs (2) and (3), the Commandant shall collect such information in a manner which protects the privacy rights of individuals who are subjects of such information.

SEC. 11273. POLICY ON REQUESTS FOR PERMANENT CHANGES OF STATION OR UNIT TRANSFERS BY PERSONS WHO REPORT BEING THE VICTIM OF SEXUAL ASSAULT.

(a) INTERIM UPDATE.—Not later than 30 days after the date of enactment of this Act, the Commandant, in consultation with the Director of the Health, Safety, and Work Life Directorate, shall issue an interim update to Coast Guard policy guidance to allow a member of the Coast Guard who has reported being the victim of a sexual assault, or any other offense covered by section 920, 920c, or 930 of title 10, United States Code (article 120, 120c, or 130 of the Uniform Code of Military Justice), to request an immediate change of station or an immediate unit transfer.

(b) FINAL POLICY.—The Commandant shall issue a final policy based on the interim updates issued under the preceding sentence not later than 1 year after the date of enactment of this Act.

SEC. 11274. SEX OFFENSES AND PERSONNEL RECORDS.

Not later than 180 days after the date of enactment of this Act, the Commandant shall issue final regulations or policy guidance required to fully implement section 1745 of the National Defense Authorization Act for Fiscal Year 2014 (Public Law 113-66; 10 U.S.C. 1561 note) with respect to members of the Coast Guard.

SEC. 11275. STUDY ON SPECIAL VICTIMS' COUNSEL PROGRAM.

(a) IN GENERAL.—Not later than 30 days after the date of enactment of this Act, the Secretary shall enter into an agreement with a federally funded research and development center for the conduct of a study on—

(1) the Special Victims' Counsel program of the Coast Guard;

(2) Coast Guard investigations of sexual assault offenses for cases in which the subject of the investigation is no longer under jeopardy for the alleged misconduct for reasons including the death of the accused, a lapse in the statute of limitations for the alleged offense, and a fully adjudicated criminal trial of the alleged offense in which all appeals have been exhausted; and

(3) legal support and representation provided to members of the Coast Guard who are victims of sexual assault, including in instances in which the accused is a member of the Army, Navy, Air Force, Marine Corps, or Space Force.

(b) ELEMENTS.—The study required by subsection (a) shall assess the following:

(1) The Special Victims' Counsel program of the Coast Guard, including training, effectiveness, capacity to handle the number of cases referred, and experience with cases involving members of the Coast Guard or members of another armed force (as defined in section 101 of title 10, United States Code).

(2) The experience of Special Victims' Counsels in representing members of the Coast Guard during a court-martial.

(3) Policies concerning the availability and detailing of Special Victims' Counsels for sexual assault allegations, in particular such allegations in which the accused is a member of another armed force (as defined in section 101 of title 10, United States Code), and the impact that the cross-service relationship had on—

(A) the competence and sufficiency of services provided to the alleged victim; and

(B) the interaction between—

(i) the investigating agency and the Special Victims' Counsels; and

(ii) the prosecuting entity and the Special Victims' Counsels.

(4) Training provided to, or made available for, Special Victims' Counsels and paralegals with respect to Department of Defense processes for conducting sexual assault investigations

and Special Victims' Counsel representation of sexual assault victims.

(5) The ability of Special Victims' Counsels to operate independently without undue influence from third parties, including the command of the accused, the command of the victim, the Judge Advocate General of the Coast Guard, and the Deputy Judge Advocate General of the Coast Guard.

(6) The skill level and experience of Special Victims' Counsels, as compared to special victims' counsels available to members of the Army, Navy, Air Force, Marine Corps, and Space Force.

(7) Policies regarding access to an alternate Special Victims' Counsel, if requested by the member of the Coast Guard concerned, and potential improvements for such policies.

(c) REPORT.—Not later than 180 days after entering into an agreement under subsection (a), the federally funded research and development center shall submit to the Committee on Commerce, Science, and Transportation of the Senate and the Committee on Transportation and Infrastructure of the House of Representatives a report that includes—

(1) the findings of the study required by such subsection;

(2) recommendations to improve the coordination, training, and experience of Special Victims' Counsels of the Coast Guard so as to improve outcomes for members of the Coast Guard who have reported sexual assault; and

(3) any other recommendation the federally funded research and development center considers appropriate.

TITLE CXIII—ENVIRONMENT

Subtitle A—Marine Mammals

SEC. 11301. [16 U.S.C. 1390 note] DEFINITIONS.

In this subtitle:

(1) APPROPRIATE CONGRESSIONAL COMMITTEES.—The term "appropriate congressional committees" means—

(A) the Committee on Commerce, Science, and Transportation of the Senate; and

(B) the Committees on Transportation and Infrastructure and Natural Resources of the House of Representatives.

(2) CORE FORAGING HABITATS.—The term "core foraging habitats" means areas—

(A) with biological and physical oceanographic features that aggregate *Calanusfinmarchicus*; and

(B) where North Atlantic right whales foraging aggregations have been well documented.

(3) EXCLUSIVE ECONOMIC ZONE.—The term "exclusive economic zone" has the meaning given that term in section 107 of title 46, United States Code.

(4) INSTITUTION OF HIGHER EDUCATION.—The term "institution of higher education" has the meaning given that term in section 101(a) of the Higher Education Act of 1965 (20 U.S.C. 1001(a)).

(5) LARGE CETACEAN.—The term "large cetacean" means all endangered or threatened species within—

(A) the suborder Mysticeti;

(B) the genera *Physeter*; or

(C) the genera *Orcinus*

(6) NEAR REAL-TIME.—The term "near real-time", with respect to monitoring of whales, means that visual, acoustic, or other detections of whales are processed, transmitted, and reported as close to the time of detection as is technically feasible.

(7) NONPROFIT ORGANIZATION.—The term "nonprofit organization" means an organization that is described in section 501(c) of the Internal Revenue Code of 1986 and exempt from tax under section 501(a) of such Code.

(8) PUGET SOUND REGION.—The term "Puget Sound region" means the Vessel Traffic Service Puget Sound area described in section 161.55 of title 33, Code of Federal Regulations (as of the date of enactment of this Act).

(9) TRIBAL GOVERNMENT.—The term "Tribal government" means the recognized governing body of any Indian or Alaska Native Tribe, band, nation, pueblo, village, community, component band, or component reservation, individually

identified (including parenthetically) in the list published most recently as of the date of enactment of this Act pursuant to section 104 of the Federally Recognized Indian Tribe List Act of 1994 (25 U.S.C. 5131).

(10) UNDER SECRETARY.—The term "Under Secretary" means the Under Secretary of Commerce for Oceans and Atmosphere.

SEC. 11302. [16 U.S.C. 1390] ASSISTANCE TO PORTS TO REDUCE IMPACTS OF VESSEL TRAFFIC AND PORT OPERATIONS ON MARINE MAMMALS.

(a) IN GENERAL.—Not later than 180 days after the date of enactment of this Act, the Under Secretary, in consultation with the Director of the United States Fish and Wildlife Service, the Secretary, the Secretary of Defense, and the Administrator of the Maritime Administration, shall establish a grant program to provide assistance to eligible entities to develop and implement mitigation measures that will lead to a quantifiable reduction in threats to marine mammals from vessel traffic, including shipping activities and port operations.

(b) ELIGIBLE USES.—Assistance provided under subsection (a) may be used to develop, assess, and carry out activities that reduce threats to marine mammals by—

(1) reducing underwater stressors related to marine traffic;

(2) reducing mortality and serious injury from vessel strikes and other physical disturbances;

(3) monitoring sound;

(4) reducing vessel interactions with marine mammals;

(5) conducting other types of monitoring that are consistent with reducing the threats to, and enhancing the habitats of, marine mammals; or

(6) supporting State agencies and Tribal governments in developing the capacity to receive assistance under this section through education, training, information sharing, and collaboration to participate in the grant program under this section.

(c) PRIORITY.—The Under Secretary shall prioritize providing assistance under subsection (a) for projects that—

(1) are based on the best available science with respect to methods to reduce threats to marine mammals;

(2) collect data on the effects of such methods and the reduction of such threats;

(3) assist ports that pose a higher relative threat to marine mammals listed as threatened or endangered under the Endangered Species Act of 1973 (16 U.S.C. 1531 et seq.);

(4) are in close proximity to areas in which threatened or endangered cetaceans are known to experience other stressors; or

(5) allow eligible entities to conduct risk assessments and to track progress toward threat reduction.

(d) OUTREACH.—The Under Secretary, in coordination with the Secretary, the Administrator of the Maritime Administration, and the Director of the United States Fish and Wildlife Service, as appropriate, shall conduct coordinated outreach to ports to provide information with respect to—

(1) how to apply for assistance under subsection (a);

(2) the benefits of such assistance; and

(3) facilitation of best practices and lessons, including the best practices and lessons learned from activities carried out using such assistance.

(e) REPORT REQUIRED.—Not less frequently than annually, the Under Secretary shall make available to the public on a publicly accessible website of the National Oceanic and Atmospheric Administration a report that includes the following information:

(1) The name and location of each entity to which assistance was awarded under subsection (a) during the year preceding submission of the report.

(2) The amount of each such award.

(3) A description of the activities carried out with each such award.

(4) An estimate of the likely impact of such activities on the reduction of threats to marine mammals.

(f) DEFINITION OF ELIGIBLE ENTITY.—In this section, the term “eligible entity” means—

(1) a port authority for a port;

(2) a State, regional, local, or Tribal government, or an Alaska Native or Native Hawaiian entity that has jurisdiction over a maritime port authority or a port;

(3) an academic institution, research institution, or nonprofit organization working in partnership with a port; or

(4) a consortium of entities described in paragraphs (1) through (3).

(g) FUNDING.—From funds otherwise appropriated to the Under Secretary, $10,000,000 is authorized to carry out this section for each of fiscal years 2023 through 2028.

(h) SAVINGS CLAUSE.—An activity may not be carried out under this section if the Secretary of Defense, in consultation with the Under Secretary, determines that the activity would negatively impact the defense readiness or the national security of the United States.

SEC. 11303. [16 U.S.C. 1391] NEAR REAL-TIME MONITORING AND MITIGATION PROGRAM FOR LARGE CETACEANS.

(a) ESTABLISHMENT.—The Under Secretary, in coordination with the heads of other relevant Federal agencies, shall design and deploy a cost-effective, efficient, and results-oriented near real-time monitoring and mitigation program (referred to in this section as the "Program") for threatened or endangered cetaceans.

(b) PURPOSE.—The purpose of the Program shall be to reduce the risk to large cetaceans posed by vessel collisions and to minimize other impacts on large cetaceans through the use of near real-time location monitoring and location information.

(c) REQUIREMENTS.—The Program shall—

(1) prioritize species of large cetaceans for which impacts from vessel collisions are of particular concern;

(2) prioritize areas where such impacts are of particular concern;

(3) be capable of detecting and alerting ocean users and enforcement agencies of the probable location of large cetaceans on an actionable real-time basis, including through real-time data whenever possible;

(4) inform sector-specific mitigation protocols to effectively reduce takes (as defined in section 216.3 of title 50, Code of

Federal Regulations, or successor regulations) of large cetaceans;

(5) integrate technology improvements; and

(6) be informed by technologies, monitoring methods, and mitigation protocols developed under the pilot project required under subsection (d).

(d) PILOT PROJECT.—

(1) ESTABLISHMENT.—In carrying out the Program, the Under Secretary shall first establish a pilot monitoring and mitigation project (referred to in this section as the "pilot project") for North Atlantic right whales for the purposes of informing the Program.

(2) REQUIREMENTS.—In designing and deploying the pilot project, the Under Secretary, in coordination with the heads of other relevant Federal agencies, shall, using the best available scientific information, identify and ensure coverage of—

(A) core foraging habitats; and

(B) important feeding, breeding, calving, rearing, or migratory habitats of North Atlantic right whales that co-occur with areas of high risk of mortality or serious injury of such whales from vessels, vessel strikes, or disturbance.

(3) COMPONENTS.—Not later than 3 years after the date of enactment of this Act, the Under Secretary, in consultation with relevant Federal agencies and Tribal governments, and with input from affected stakeholders, shall design and deploy a near real-time monitoring system for North Atlantic right whales that—

(A) comprises the best available detection power, spatial coverage, and survey effort to detect and localize North Atlantic right whales within habitats described in paragraph (2);

(B) is capable of detecting North Atlantic right whales, including visually and acoustically;

(C) uses dynamic habitat suitability models to inform the likelihood of North Atlantic right whale occurrence habitats described in paragraph (2) at any given time;

(D) coordinates with the Integrated Ocean Observing System of the National Oceanic and Atmospheric

Administration and Regional Ocean Partnerships to leverage monitoring assets;

(E) integrates historical data;

(F) integrates new near real-time monitoring methods and technologies as such methods and technologies become available;

(G) accurately verifies and rapidly communicates detection data to appropriate ocean users;

(H) creates standards for contributing, and allows ocean users to contribute, data to the monitoring system using comparable near real-time monitoring methods and technologies;

(I) communicates the risks of injury to large cetaceans to ocean users in a manner that is most likely to result in informed decision-making regarding the mitigation of those risks; and

(J) minimizes additional stressors to large cetaceans as a result of the information available to ocean users.

(4) REPORTS.—

(A) PRELIMINARY REPORT.—

(i) IN GENERAL.—Not later than 2 years after the date of enactment of this Act, the Under Secretary shall submit to the Committee on Commerce, Science, and Transportation of the Senate and the Committee on Natural Resources of the House of Representatives, and make available to the public, a preliminary report on the pilot project.

(ii) ELEMENTS.—The report required under clause (i) shall include the following:

(I) A description of the monitoring methods and technology in use or planned for deployment under the pilot project.

(II) An analysis of the efficacy of the methods and technology in use or planned for deployment for detecting North Atlantic right whales.

(III) An assessment of the manner in which the monitoring system designed and deployed under this subsection is directly informing and improving the management, health, and survival of North Atlantic right whales.

(IV) A prioritized identification of technology or research gaps.

(V) A plan to communicate the risks of injury to large cetaceans to ocean users in a manner that is most likely to result in informed decision making regarding the mitigation of such risks.

(VI) Any other information on the potential benefits and efficacy of the pilot project the Under Secretary considers appropriate.

(B) FINAL REPORT.—

(i) IN GENERAL.—Not later than 6 years after the date of enactment of this Act, the Under Secretary, in coordination with the heads of other relevant Federal agencies, shall submit to the Committee on Commerce, Science, and Transportation of the Senate and the Committee on Natural Resources of the House of Representatives, and make available to the public, a final report on the pilot project.

(ii) ELEMENTS.—The report required under clause (i) shall—

(I) address the preliminary report required under subparagraph (A); and

(II) include—

(aa) an assessment of the benefits and efficacy of the pilot project;

(bb) a strategic plan to expand the pilot project to provide near real-time monitoring and mitigation measures—

(AA) to additional large cetaceans of concern for which such measures would reduce risk of serious injury or death; and

(BB) in important feeding, breeding, calving, rearing, or migratory habitats of large cetaceans that co-occur with areas of high risk of mortality or serious injury from vessel strikes or disturbance;

(cc) a budget and description of funds necessary to carry out such plan;

(dd) a prioritized plan for acquisition, deployment, and maintenance of monitoring technologies; and

(ee) the locations or species to which such plan would apply.

(e) MITIGATION PROTOCOLS.—The Under Secretary, in consultation with the Secretary, the Secretary of Defense, the Secretary of Transportation, and the Secretary of the Interior, and with input from affected stakeholders, shall develop and deploy mitigation protocols that make use of any monitoring system designed and deployed under this section to direct sector-specific mitigation measures that avoid and significantly reduce risk of serious injury and mortality to North Atlantic right whales.

(f) ACCESS TO DATA.—The Under Secretary shall provide access to data generated by any monitoring system designed and deployed under this section for purposes of scientific research and evaluation and public awareness and education, including through the Right Whale Sighting Advisory System of the National Oceanic and Atmospheric Administration and WhaleMap or other successor public website portals, subject to review for national security considerations.

(g) ADDITIONAL AUTHORITY.—The Under Secretary may enter into and perform such contracts, leases, grants, or cooperative agreements as may be necessary to carry out this section on such terms as the Under Secretary considers appropriate, consistent with the Federal Acquisition Regulation.

(h) SAVINGS CLAUSE.—An activity may not be carried out under this section if the Secretary of Defense, in consultation with the Under Secretary, determines that the activity would negatively impact the defense readiness or the national security of the United States.

(i) FUNDING.—From funds otherwise appropriated to the Under Secretary $5,000,000 is authorized to support development, deployment, application, and ongoing maintenance of the Program and to otherwise carry out this section for each of fiscal years 2023 through 2027.

SEC. 11304. [16 U.S.C. 1390 note] PILOT PROGRAM TO ESTABLISH A CETACEAN DESK FOR PUGET SOUND REGION.

(a) ESTABLISHMENT.—

(1) IN GENERAL.—Not later than 1 year after the date of enactment of this Act, the Secretary, with the concurrence of the Under Secretary, shall carry out a pilot program to establish a Cetacean Desk, which shall be—

(A) located and manned within the Puget Sound Vessel Traffic Service; and

(B) designed—

(i) to improve coordination with the maritime industry to reduce the risk of vessel impacts on large cetaceans, including impacts from vessel strikes, disturbances, and other sources; and

(ii) to monitor the presence and location of large cetaceans during the months during which such large cetaceans are present in Puget Sound, the Strait of Juan de Fuca, and the United States portion of the Salish Sea.

(2) DURATION AND STAFFING.—The pilot program required under paragraph (1)—

(A) shall—

(i) be for a duration of 4 years; and

(ii) require not more than 1 full-time equivalent position, who shall also contribute to other necessary Puget Sound Vessel Traffic Service duties and responsibilities as needed; and

(B) may be supported by other existing Federal employees, as appropriate.

(b) ENGAGEMENT WITH VESSEL OPERATORS.—

(1) IN GENERAL.—In carrying out the pilot program required under subsection (a), the Secretary shall require personnel of the Cetacean Desk to engage with vessel operators in areas where large cetaceans have been seen or could reasonably be present to ensure compliance with applicable laws, regulations, and voluntary guidance, to reduce the impact of vessel traffic on large cetaceans.

(2) CONTENTS.—In engaging with vessel operators as

required under paragraph (1), personnel of the Cetacean Desk shall communicate where and when sightings of large cetaceans have occurred.

(c) MEMORANDUM OF UNDERSTANDING.—The Secretary and the Under Secretary may enter into a memorandum of understanding to facilitate real-time sharing of data relating to large cetaceans between the Quiet Sound program of the State of Washington, the National Oceanic and Atmospheric Administration, the Puget Sound Vessel Traffic Service, and other relevant entities, as appropriate.

(d) DATA.—The Under Secretary shall leverage existing data collection methods, the program required by section 11303, and public data to ensure accurate and timely information on the sighting of large cetaceans.

(e) CONSULTATIONS.—

(1) IN GENERAL.—In carrying out the pilot program required under subsection (a), the Secretary shall consult with Tribal governments, the State of Washington, institutions of higher education, the maritime industry, ports in the Puget Sound region, and nongovernmental organizations.

(2) COORDINATION WITH CANADA.—When appropriate, the Secretary shall coordinate with the Government of Canada, consistent with policies and agreements relating to management of vessel traffic in Puget Sound.

(f) PUGET SOUND VESSEL TRAFFIC SERVICE LOCAL VARIANCE AND POLICY.—The Secretary, with the concurrence of the Under Secretary and in consultation with the Captain of the Port for the Puget Sound region—

(1) shall implement local variances, as authorized by subsection (c) of section 70001 of title 46, United States Code, to reduce the impact of vessel traffic on large cetaceans; and

(2) may enter into cooperative agreements, in accordance with subsection (d) of such section, with Federal, State, Tribal, and local officials to reduce the likelihood of vessel interactions with protected large cetaceans, which may include—

(A) communicating marine mammal protection guidance to vessels;

(B) training on requirements imposed by local, State, Tribal, and Federal laws and regulations and guidelines concerning—

(i) vessel buffer zones;

(ii) vessel speed;

(iii) seasonal no-go zones for vessels;

(iv) protected areas, including areas designated as critical habitat, as applicable to marine operations; and

(v) any other activities to reduce the direct and indirect impact of vessel traffic on large cetaceans;

(C) training to understand, utilize, and communicate large cetacean location data; and

(D) training to understand and communicate basic large cetacean detection, identification, and behavior, including—

(i) cues of the presence of large cetaceans such as spouts, water disturbances, breaches, or presence of prey;

(ii) important feeding, breeding, calving, and rearing habitats that co-occur with areas of high risk of vessel strikes;

(iii) seasonal large cetacean migration routes that co-occur with areas of high risk of vessel strikes; and

(iv) areas designated as critical habitat for large cetaceans.

(g) REPORT REQUIRED.—Not later than 1 year after the date of enactment of this Act, and every 2 years thereafter for the duration of the pilot program, the Commandant, in coordination with the Under Secretary and the Administrator of the Maritime Administration, shall submit to the appropriate congressional committees a report that—

(1) evaluates the functionality, utility, reliability, responsiveness, and operational status of the Cetacean Desk established under this section, including a quantification of reductions in vessel strikes to large cetaceans as a result of the pilot program;

(2) assesses the efficacy of communication between the Cetacean Desk and the maritime industry and provides recommendations for improvements;

(3) evaluates the integration and interoperability of existing data collection methods, as well as public data, into the Cetacean Desk operations;

(4) assesses the efficacy of collaboration and stakeholder engagement with Tribal governments, the State of Washington, institutions of higher education, the maritime industry, ports in the Puget Sound region, and nongovernmental organizations; and

(5) evaluates the progress, performance, and implementation of guidance and training procedures for Puget Sound Vessel Traffic Service personnel, as required under subsection (f).

SEC. 11305. [16 U.S.C. 1392] MONITORING OCEAN SOUNDSCAPES.

(a) IN GENERAL.—The Under Secretary shall maintain and expand an ocean soundscape development program to—

(1) award grants to expand the deployment of Federal and non-Federal observing and data management systems capable of collecting measurements of underwater sound for purposes of monitoring and analyzing baselines and trends in the underwater soundscape to protect and manage marine life;

(2) continue to develop and apply standardized forms of measurements to assess sounds produced by marine animals, physical processes, and anthropogenic activities; and

(3) after coordinating with the Secretary of Defense, coordinate and make accessible to the public the datasets, modeling and analysis, and user-driven products and tools resulting from observations of underwater sound funded through grants awarded under paragraph (1).

(b) COORDINATION.—The program described in subsection (a) shall—

(1) include the Ocean Noise Reference Station Network of the National Oceanic and Atmospheric Administration and the National Park Service;

(2) use and coordinate with the Integrated Ocean Observing System; and

(3) coordinate with the Regional Ocean Partnerships and the Director of the United States Fish and Wildlife Service, as appropriate.

(c) PRIORITY.—In awarding grants under subsection (a), the Under Secretary shall consider the geographic diversity of the recipients of such grants.

(d) SAVINGS CLAUSE.—An activity may not be carried out under this section if the Secretary of Defense, in consultation with the Under Secretary, determines that the activity would negatively impact the defense readiness or the national security of the United States.

(e) FUNDING.—From funds otherwise appropriated to the Under Secretary, $1,500,000 is authorized for each of fiscal years 2023 through 2028 to carry out this section.

Subtitle B—Oil Spills

SEC. 11306. REPORT ON CHANGING SALVORS.

Section 311(c)(3) of the Federal Water Pollution Control Act (33 U.S.C. 1321(c)(3)) is amended by adding at the end the following:

"(C) In any case in which the President or the Federal On-Scene Coordinator authorizes a deviation from the salvor as part of a deviation under subparagraph (B) from the applicable response plan required under subsection (j), the Commandant of the Coast Guard shall submit to the Committee on Transportation and Infrastructure of the House of Representatives and the Committee on Commerce, Science, and Transportation of the Senate a report describing the deviation and the reasons for such deviation not less than 3 days after such deviation is authorized."

SEC. 11307. [33 U.S.C. 1321 note] LIMITED INDEMNITY PROVISIONS IN STANDBY OIL SPILL RESPONSE CONTRACTS.

(a) IN GENERAL.—Subject to subsections (b) and (c), a contract with the Coast Guard for the containment or removal of a discharge entered into by the President under section 311(c) of the Federal Water Pollution Control Act (33 U.S.C. 1321(c)) shall contain a provision to indemnify a contractor for liabilities and expenses incidental to the containment or removal arising out of the performance of the contract that is substantially identical to the terms contained in subsections (d) through (h) of section H.4 (except for paragraph (1) of subsection (d)) of the contract offered by the Coast Guard in the solicitation numbered DTCG89-98- A-68F953, dated November 17, 1998.

(b) REQUIREMENTS.—

(1) SOURCE OF FUNDS.—The provision required under subsection (a) shall include a provision that the obligation to indemnify is limited to funds available in the Oil Spill Liability Trust Fund established by section 9509(a) of the Internal Revenue Code of 1986 at the time the claim for indemnity is made.

(2) UNCOMPENSATED REMOVAL.—A claim for indemnity under a contract described in subsection (a) shall be made as a claim for uncompensated removal costs under section 1012(a)(4) of the Oil Pollution Act of 1990 (33 U.S.C. 2712(a)(4)).

(3) LIMITATION.—The total indemnity for a claim under a contract described in subsection (a) may not be more than $50,000 per incident.

(c) APPLICABILITY OF EXEMPTIONS.—Notwithstanding subsection (a), the United States shall not be obligated to indemnify a contractor for any act or omission of the contractor carried out pursuant to a contract entered into under this section where such act or omission is grossly negligent or which constitutes willful misconduct.

SEC. 11308. [33 U.S.C. 2761 note] IMPROVING OIL SPILL PREPAREDNESS.

The Under Secretary of Commerce for Oceans and Atmosphere shall include in the Automated Data Inquiry for Oil Spills database (or a successor database) used by National Oceanic and Atmospheric Administration oil weathering models new data, including peer-reviewed data, on properties of crude and refined oils, including data on diluted bitumen, as such data becomes publicly available.

SEC. 11309. WESTERN ALASKA OIL SPILL PLANNING CRITERIA.

(a) ALASKA OIL SPILL PLANNING CRITERIA PROGRAM.—

(1) IN GENERAL.—Chapter 3 of title 14, United States Code, is amended by adding at the end the following:

"SEC. 323. [14 U.S.C. 323] Western Alaska Oil Spill Planning Criteria Program

"(a) ESTABLISHMENT.—There is established within the Coast Guard a Western Alaska Oil Spill Planning Criteria Program (referred to in this section as the 'Program') to develop and administer the Western Alaska oil spill planning criteria.

"(b) PROGRAM MANAGER.—

"(1) IN GENERAL.—Not later than 1 year after the date of enactment of this section, the Commandant shall select a permanent civilian career employee through a competitive search process for a term of not less than 5 years to serve as the Western Alaska Oil Spill Criteria Program Manager (referred to in this section as the 'Program Manager')—

"(A) the primary duty of whom shall be to administer the Program; and

"(B) who shall not be subject to frequent or routine reassignment.

"(2) CONFLICTS OF INTEREST.—The individual selected to serve as the Program Manager shall not have conflicts of interest relating to entities regulated by the Coast Guard.

"(3) DUTIES.—

"(A) DEVELOPMENT OF GUIDANCE.—The Program Manager shall develop guidance for—

"(i) approval, drills, and testing relating to the Western Alaska oil spill planning criteria; and

"(ii) gathering input concerning such planning criteria from Federal agencies, State and local governments, Tribes, and relevant industry and nongovernmental entities.

"(B) ASSESSMENTS.—Not less frequently than once every 5 years, the Program Manager shall—

"(i) assess whether such existing planning criteria adequately meet the needs of vessels operating in the geographic area; and

"(ii) identify methods for advancing response capability so as to achieve, with respect to a vessel, compliance with national planning criteria.

"(C) ONSITE VERIFICATIONS.—The Program Manager shall address the relatively small number and limited nature of verifications of response capabilities for vessel response plans by increasing, within the Seventeenth Coast Guard District, the quantity and frequency of onsite verifications of the providers identified in vessel response plans.

"(c) TRAINING.—The Commandant shall enhance the knowledge and proficiency of Coast Guard personnel with respect to the Program by—

"(1) developing formalized training on the Program that, at a minimum—

"(A) provides in-depth analysis of—

"(i) the national planning criteria described in part 155 of title 33, Code of Federal Regulations (as in effect on the date of enactment of this section);

"(ii) alternative planning criteria;

"(iii) Western Alaska oil spill planning criteria;

"(iv) Captain of the Port and Federal On-Scene Coordinator authorities related to activation of a vessel response plan;

"(v) the responsibilities of vessel owners and operators in preparing a vessel response plan for submission; and

"(vi) responsibilities of the Area Committee, including risk analysis, response capability, and development of alternative planning criteria;

"(B) explains the approval processes of vessel response plans that involve alternative planning criteria or Western Alaska oil spill planning criteria; and

"(C) provides instruction on the processes involved in carrying out the actions described in paragraphs (9)(D) and (9)(F) of section 311(j) of the Federal Water Pollution Control Act (33 U.S.C. 1321(j)), including instruction on carrying out such actions—

"(i) in any geographic area in the United States; and

"(ii) specifically in the Seventeenth Coast

Guard District; and

"(2) providing such training to all Coast Guard personnel involved in the Program.

"(d) DEFINITIONS.—In this section:

"(1) ALTERNATIVE PLANNING CRITERIA.—The term 'alternative planning criteria' means criteria submitted under section 155.1065 or 155.5067 of title 33, Code of Federal Regulations (as in effect on the date of enactment of this section), for vessel response plans.

"(2) TRIBE.—The term 'Tribe' has the meaning given the term 'Indian Tribe' in section 4 of the Indian Self-Determination and Education Assistance Act (25 U.S.C. 5304).

"(3) VESSEL RESPONSE PLAN.—The term 'vessel response plan' means a plan required to be submitted by the owner or operator of a tank vessel or a nontank vessel under regulations issued by the President under section 311(j)(5) of the Federal Water Pollution Control Act (33 U.S.C. 1321(j)(5)).

"(4) WESTERN ALASKA OIL SPILL PLANNING CRITERIA.—The term 'Western Alaska oil spill planning criteria' means the criteria required to be established under paragraph (9) of section 311(j) of the Federal Water Pollution Control Act (33 U.S.C. 1321(j))."

(2) CLERICAL AMENDMENT.—The analysis for chapter 3 of title 14, United States Code, is amended by adding at the end the following:

"323. Western Alaska Oil Spill Planning Criteria Program."

(b) WESTERN ALASKA OIL SPILL PLANNING CRITERIA.—

(1) AMENDMENT.—Section 311(j) of the Federal Water Pollution Control Act (33 U.S.C. 1321(j)) is amended by adding at the end the following:

"(9) WESTERN ALASKA OIL SPILL PLANNING CRITERIA PROGRAM.—

"(A) DEFINITIONS.—In this paragraph:

"(i) ALTERNATIVE PLANNING CRITERIA.—The term 'alternative planning criteria' means criteria submitted under section 155.1065 or 155.5067 of title 33, Code of Federal Regulations (as in effect on the date of enactment of this paragraph), for vessel response plans.

"(ii) PRINCE WILLIAM SOUND CAPTAIN OF THE PORT ZONE.—The term 'Prince William Sound Captain of the Port Zone' means the area described in section 3.85-15(b) of title 33, Code of Federal Regulations (or successor regulations).

"(iii) SECRETARY.—The term 'Secretary' means the Secretary of the department in which the Coast Guard is operating.

"(iv) VESSEL RESPONSE PLAN.—The term 'vessel response plan' means a plan required to be submitted by the owner or operator of a tank vessel or a nontank vessel under regulations issued by the President under paragraph (5).

"(v) WESTERN ALASKA CAPTAIN OF THE PORT ZONE.—The term 'Western Alaska Captain of the Port Zone' means the area described in section 3.85-15(a) of title 33, Code of Federal Regulations (as in effect on the date of enactment of this paragraph).

"(B) REQUIREMENT.—Except as provided in subparagraph (I), for any part of the area of responsibility of the Western Alaska Captain of the Port Zone or the Prince William Sound Captain of the Port Zone for which the Secretary has determined that the national planning criteria established pursuant to this subsection are inappropriate for a vessel operating in such area, a vessel response plan with respect to a discharge of oil for such a vessel shall comply with the Western Alaska oil spill planning criteria established under subparagraph (D)(i).

"(C) RELATION TO NATIONAL PLANNING CRITERIA.—The Western Alaska oil spill planning criteria established under subparagraph (D)(i) shall, with respect to a discharge of oil from a vessel described in subparagraph (B), apply in lieu of any alternative planning criteria accepted for vessels operating, prior to the date on which the Western Alaska oil spill planning criteria are established, in any part of the area of responsibility of the Western Alaska Captain of the Port Zone or the Prince William Sound Captain of the Port Zone for which the Secretary has determined that the national planning criteria established pursuant to this subsection are inappropriate for a vessel operating in such area.

"(D) ESTABLISHMENT OF WESTERN ALASKA OIL SPILL PLANNING CRITERIA.—

"(i) IN GENERAL.—The President, acting through the Commandant, in consultation with the Western Alaska Oil Spill Criteria Program Manager selected under section 323 of title 14, United States Code, shall establish—

"(I) Western Alaska oil spill planning criteria for a worst case discharge of oil, and a substantial threat of such a discharge, within any part of the area of responsibility of the Western Alaska Captain of the Port Zone or Prince William Sound Captain of the Port Zone for which the Secretary has determined that the national planning criteria established pursuant to this subsection are inappropriate for a vessel operating in such area; and

"(II) standardized submission, review, approval, and compliance verification processes for the Western Alaska oil spill planning criteria established under this clause, including the quantity and frequency of drills and on-site verifications of vessel response plans approved pursuant to such planning criteria.

"(ii) DEVELOPMENT OF SUBREGIONS.—

"(I) DEVELOPMENT.—After establishing the Western Alaska oil spill planning criteria under clause (i), and if necessary to adequately reflect the needs and capabilities of various locations within the Western

Alaska Captain of the Port Zone, the President, acting through the Commandant, and in consultation with the Western Alaska Oil Spill Criteria Program Manager selected under section 323 of title 14, United States Code, may develop subregions for which planning criteria may differ from planning criteria for other subregions in the Western Alaska Captain of the Port Zone.

"(II) LIMITATION.—Any planning criteria for a subregion developed under this clause may not be less stringent than the Western Alaska oil spill planning criteria established under clause (i).

"(iii) ASSESSMENT.—

"(I) IN GENERAL.—Prior to developing a subregion, the President, acting through the Commandant, shall conduct an assessment on any potential impacts to the entire Western Alaska Captain of the Port Zone to include quantity and availability of response resources in the proposed subregion and in surrounding areas and any changes or impacts to surrounding areas resulting in the development of a subregion with different standards.

"(II) CONSULTATION.—In conducting an assessment under this clause, the President, acting through the Commandant, shall consult with State and local governments, Tribes (as defined in section 323 of title 14, United States Code), the owners and operators that would operate under the proposed subregions, oil spill removal organizations, Alaska Native organizations, and environmental nongovernmental organizations, and shall take into account any experience with the prior use of subregions within the State of Alaska.

"(III) SUBMISSION.—The President, acting

through the Commandant, shall submit the results of an assessment conducted under this clause to the Committee on Transportation and Infrastructure of the House of Representatives and the Committee on Commerce, Science, and Transportation of the Senate.

"(E) INCLUSIONS.—

"(i) REQUIREMENTS.—The Western Alaska oil spill planning criteria established under subparagraph (D)(i) shall include planning criteria for the following:

"(I) Mechanical oil spill response resources that are required to be located within any part of the area of responsibility of the Western Alaska Captain of the Port Zone or the Prince William Sound Captain of the Port Zone for which the Secretary has determined that the national planning criteria established pursuant to this subsection are inappropriate for a vessel operating in such area.

"(II) Response times for mobilization of oil spill response resources and arrival on the scene of a worst case discharge of oil, or substantial threat of such a discharge, occurring within such part of such area.

"(III) Pre-identified vessels for oil spill response that are capable of operating in the ocean environment.

"(IV) Ensuring the availability of at least 1 oil spill removal organization that is classified by the Coast Guard and that—

"(aa) is capable of responding in all operating environments in such part of such area;

"(bb) controls oil spill response resources of dedicated and nondedicated resources within such part of such area, through ownership, contracts, agreements, or other means approved by the President, sufficient—

"(AA) to mobilize and sustain a response to a worst case discharge of oil; and

"(BB) to contain, recover, and temporarily store discharged oil;

"(cc) has pre-positioned oil spill response resources in strategic locations throughout such part of such area in a manner that ensures the ability to support response personnel, marine operations, air cargo, or other related logistics infrastructure;

"(dd) has temporary storage capability using both dedicated and non-dedicated assets located within such part of such area;

"(ee) has non-mechanical oil spill response resources capable of responding to a discharge of persistent oil and a discharge of nonpersistent oil, whether the discharged oil was carried by a vessel as fuel or cargo; and

"(ff) has wildlife response resources for primary, secondary, and tertiary responses to support carcass collection, sampling, deterrence, rescue, and rehabilitation of birds, sea turtles, marine mammals, fishery resources, and other wildlife.

"(V) With respect to tank barges carrying nonpersistent oil in bulk as cargo, oil spill response resources that are required to be carried on board.

"(VI) Specifying a minimum length of time that approval of a vessel response plan under this paragraph is valid.

"(VII) Managing wildlife protection and rehabilitation, including identified wildlife protection and rehabilitation resources in that area.

"(ii) ADDITIONAL CONSIDERATIONS.—The Western Alaska oil spill planning criteria established under subparagraph (D)(i) may include planning criteria for the following:

"(I) Vessel routing measures consistent with international routing measure deviation protocols.

"(II) Maintenance of real-time continuous vessel tracking, monitoring, and engagement protocols with the ability to detect and address vessel operation anomalies.

"(F) REQUIREMENT FOR APPROVAL.—The President may approve a vessel response plan for a vessel under this paragraph only if the owner or operator of the vessel demonstrates the availability of the oil spill response resources required to be included in the vessel response plan under the Western Alaska oil spill planning criteria established under subparagraph (D)(i).

"(G) PERIODIC AUDITS.—The Secretary shall conduct periodic audits to ensure compliance of vessel response plans and oil spill removal organizations within the Western Alaska Captain of the Port Zone and the Prince William Sound Captain of the Port Zone with the Western Alaska oil spill planning criteria established under subparagraph (D)(i).

"(H) REVIEW OF DETERMINATION.—Not less frequently than once every 5 years, the Secretary shall review each determination of the Secretary under subparagraph (B) that the national planning criteria established pursuant to this subsection are inappropriate for a vessel operating in the area of responsibility of the Western Alaska Captain of the Port Zone and the Prince William Sound Captain of the Port Zone.

"(I) VESSELS IN COOK INLET.—Unless otherwise authorized by the Secretary, a vessel may only operate in Cook Inlet, Alaska, under a vessel response plan approved under paragraph (5) that meets the requirements of the national planning criteria established pursuant to this subsection.

"(J) SAVINGS PROVISIONS.—Nothing in this paragraph affects—

"(i) the requirements under this subsection applicable to vessel response plans for vessels operating within the area of responsibility of the Western Alaska Captain of the Port Zone, within Cook Inlet, Alaska;

"(ii) the requirements under this subsection applicable to vessel response plans for vessels operating within the area of responsibility of the Prince William Sound Captain of the Port Zone that are subject to section 5005 of the Oil Pollution Act of 1990 (33 U.S.C. 2735); or

"(iii) the authority of a Federal On-Scene Coordinator to use any available resources when responding to an oil spill."

(2) [33 U.S.C. 1321 note] ESTABLISHMENT OF WESTERN ALASKA OIL SPILL PLANNING CRITERIA.—

(A) DEADLINE.—Not later than 2 years after the date of enactment of this Act, the President shall establish the Western Alaska oil spill planning criteria required to be established under paragraph (9)(D)(i) of section 311(j) of the Federal Water Pollution Control Act (33 U.S.C. 1321(j)).

(B) CONSULTATION.—In establishing the Western Alaska oil spill planning criteria described in subparagraph (A), the President shall consult with the Federal agencies, State and local governments, Tribes (as defined in section 323 of title 14, United States Code), the owners and operators that would be subject to such planning criteria, oil spill removal organizations, Alaska Native organizations, and environmental nongovernmental organizations.

(C) CONGRESSIONAL REPORT.—Not later than 2 years after the date of enactment of this Act, the Secretary shall submit to Congress a report describing the status of implementation of paragraph (9) of section 311(j) of the Federal Water Pollution Control Act (33 U.S.C. 1321(j)).

SEC. 11310. COAST GUARD CLAIMS PROCESSING COSTS.

Section 1012(a)(4) of the Oil Pollution Act of 1990 (33 U.S.C. 2712(a)(4)) is amended by striking "damages;" and inserting "damages, including, in the case of a spill of national significance that results in extraordinary Coast Guard claims processing activities, the administrative and personnel costs of the Coast Guard to process such claims (including the costs of commercial claims processing, expert services, training, and technical services), subject 136 STAT. 4086 to the condition that the Coast Guard shall submit to Congress a report describing each spill of national significance not later than 30 days after the date on which the Coast Guard determines it necessary to process such claims;".

SEC. 11311. CALCULATION OF INTEREST ON DEBT OWED TO NATIONAL POLLUTION FUND.

Section 1005(b)(4) of the Oil Pollution Act of 1990 (33 U.S.C. 2705(b)(4)) is amended—

(1) by striking "The interest paid" and inserting the following:

"(A) IN GENERAL.—The interest paid for claims, other than Federal Government cost recovery claims,"

; and

(2) by adding at the end the following:

"(B) FEDERAL COST RECOVERY CLAIMS.—The interest paid for Federal Government cost recovery claims under this section shall be calculated in accordance with section 3717 of title 31, United States Code."

SEC. 11312. [26 U.S.C. 9509] PER-INCIDENT LIMITATION.

Subparagraph (A) of section 9509(c)(2) of the Internal Revenue Code of 1986 is amended—

(1) in clause (i) by striking "$1,000,000,000" and inserting "$1,500,000,000";

(2) in clause (ii) by striking "$500,000,000" and inserting

"$750,000,000"; and

(3) in the heading by striking "$1,000,000,000" and inserting "$1,500,000,000".

SEC. 11313. ACCESS TO OIL SPILL LIABILITY TRUST FUND.

Section 6002 of the Oil Pollution Act of 1990 (33 U.S.C. 2752) is amended by striking subsection (b) and inserting the following:

"(b) EXCEPTIONS.—

"(1) IN GENERAL.—Subsection (a) shall not apply to—

"(A) section 1006(f), 1012(a)(4), or 5006; or

"(B) an amount, which may not exceed $50,000,000 in any fiscal year, made available by the President from the Fund—

"(i) to carry out section 311(c) of the Federal Water Pollution Control Act (33 U.S.C. 1321(c)); and

"(ii) to initiate the assessment of natural resources damages required under section 1006.

"(2) FUND ADVANCES.—

"(A) IN GENERAL.—To the extent that the amount described in subparagraph (B) of paragraph (1) is not adequate to carry out the activities described in such subparagraph, the Coast Guard may obtain 1 or more advances from the Fund as may be necessary, up to a maximum of $100,000,000 for each advance, with the total amount of advances not to exceed the amounts available under section 9509(c)(2) of the Internal Revenue Code of 1986.

"(B) NOTIFICATION TO CONGRESS.—Not later than 30 days after the date on which the Coast Guard obtains an advance under subparagraph (A), the Coast Guard shall notify Congress of—

"(i) the amount advanced; and

"(ii) the facts and circumstances that necessitated the advance.

"(C) REPAYMENT.—Amounts advanced under this paragraph shall be repaid to the Fund when, and to the extent that, removal costs are recovered by the Coast Guard from responsible parties for the discharge or substantial threat of discharge.

"(3) AVAILABILITY.—Amounts to which this subsection applies shall remain available until expended."

SEC. 11314. COST-REIMBURSABLE AGREEMENTS.

Section 1012 of the Oil Pollution Act of 1990 (33 U.S.C. 2712) is amended—

(1) in subsection (a)(1)(B) by striking "by a Governor or designated State official" and inserting "by a State, a political subdivision of a State, or an Indian tribe, pursuant to a cost-reimbursable agreement";

(2) by striking subsections (d) and (e) and inserting the following:

"(d) COST-REIMBURSABLE AGREEMENT.—

"(1) IN GENERAL.—In carrying out section 311(c) of the Federal Water Pollution Control Act (33 U.S.C. 1321(c)), the President may enter into cost-reimbursable agreements with a State, a political subdivision of a State, or an Indian tribe to obligate the Fund for the payment of removal costs consistent with the National Contingency Plan.

"(2) INAPPLICABILITY.—Chapter 63 and section 1535 of title 31, United States Code shall not apply to a cost-reimbursable agreement entered into under this subsection."

; and

(3) by redesignating subsections (f), (h), (i), (j), (k), and (l) as subsections (e), (f), (g), (h), (i), and (j), respectively.

SEC. 11315. [33 U.S.C. 1321 note] OIL SPILL RESPONSE REVIEW.

(a) IN GENERAL.—Subject to the availability of appropriations, the Commandant shall develop and carry out a program—

(1) to increase collection and improve the quality of incident data on oil spill location and response capability by periodically evaluating the data, documentation, and analysis of—

(A) Coast Guard-approved vessel response plans, including vessel response plan audits and assessments;

(B) oil spill response drills conducted under section

311(j)(7) of the Federal Water Pollution Control Act (33 U.S.C. 1321(j)(7)) that occur within the Marine Transportation System; and

(C) responses to oil spill incidents that require mobilization of contracted response resources;

(2) to improve the effectiveness of vessel response plans by—

(A) systematically reviewing the capacity of an oil spill response organization identified in a vessel response plan to provide the specific response resources, such as private personnel, equipment, other vessels identified in such vessel response plan; and

(B) approving a vessel response plan only after confirming the identified oil spill response organization has the capacity to provide such response resources;

(3) to update, not less frequently than annually, information contained in the Coast Guard Response Resource Inventory and other Coast Guard tools used to document the availability and status of oil spill response equipment, so as to ensure that such information remains current; and

(4) subject to section 552 of title 5, United States Code (commonly known as the "Freedom of Information Act"), to make data collected under paragraph (1) available to the public.

(b) POLICY.—Not later than 1 year after the date of enactment of this Act, the Commandant shall issue a policy—

(1) to establish processes to maintain the program under subsection (a) and support Coast Guard oil spill prevention and response activities, including by incorporating oil spill incident data from after-action oil spill reports and data ascertained from vessel response plan exercises and audits into—

(A) review and approval process standards and metrics;

(B) alternative planning criteria review processes;

(C) Area Contingency Plan development;

(D) risk assessments developed under section 70001 of title 46, United States Code, including lessons learned from reportable marine casualties;

(E) processes and standards which mitigate the impact

of military personnel rotations in Coast Guard field units on knowledge and awareness of vessel response plan requirements, including knowledge relating to the evaluation of proposed alternatives to national planning requirements; and

(F) processes and standards which evaluate the consequences of reporting inaccurate data in vessel response plans submitted to the Commandant pursuant to part 300 of title 40, Code of Federal Regulations, and submitted for storage in the Marine Information for Safety and Law Enforcement database pursuant to section 300.300 of such title (or any successor regulation);

(2) to standardize and develop tools, training, and other relevant guidance that may be shared with vessel owners and operators to assist with accurately calculating and measuring the performance and viability of proposed alternatives to national planning criteria requirements and Area Contingency Plans administered by the Coast Guard;

(3) to improve training of Coast Guard personnel to ensure continuity of planning activities under this section, including by identifying ways in which civilian staffing may improve the continuity of operations; and

(4) to increase Federal Government engagement with State, local, and Tribal governments and stakeholders so as to strengthen coordination and efficiency of oil spill responses.

(c) PERIODIC UPDATES.—Not less frequently than every 5 years, the Commandant shall update the processes established under subsection (b)(1) to incorporate relevant analyses of—

(1) incident data on oil spill location and response quality;

(2) oil spill risk assessments;

(3) oil spill response effectiveness and the effects of such response on the environment;

(4) oil spill response drills conducted under section 311(j)(7) of the Federal Water Pollution Control Act (33 U.S.C. 1321(j)(7));

(5) marine casualties reported to the Coast Guard; and

(6) near miss incidents documented by a vessel traffic service center (as such terms are defined in sections 70001(m)

of title 46, United States Code).

(d) REPORT.—

(1) IN GENERAL.—Not later than 1 year after the date of enactment of this Act, and annually thereafter for 5 years, the Commandant shall provide to the Committee on Commerce, Science, and Transportation of the Senate and the Committee on Transportation and Infrastructure of the House of Representatives a briefing on the status of ongoing and planned efforts to improve the effectiveness and oversight of the program established under subsection (a) and vessel response plan approvals.

(2) PUBLIC AVAILABILITY.—The Commandant shall publish the briefing required under paragraph (1) on a publicly accessible website of the Coast Guard.

SEC. 11316. [46 U.S.C. 3306 note] ADDITIONAL EXCEPTIONS TO REGULATIONS FOR TOWING VESSELS.

(a) IN GENERAL.—Not later than 180 days after the date of enactment of this Act, the Secretary shall review existing Coast Guard policies with respect to exceptions to the applicability of subchapter M of chapter I of title 46, Code of Federal Regulations (or successor regulations), for—

(1) an oil spill response vessel, or a vessel of opportunity, while such vessel is—

(A) towing boom for oil spill response; or

(B) participating in an oil response exercise; and

(2) a fishing vessel while that vessel is operating as a vessel of opportunity.

(b) POLICY.—Not later than 180 days after the conclusion of the review required under subsection (a), the Secretary shall revise or issue any necessary policy to clarify the applicability of subchapter M of chapter I of title 46, Code of Federal Regulations (or successor regulations) to the vessels described in subsection (a). Such a policy shall ensure safe and effective operation of such vessels.

(c) DEFINITIONS.—In this section:

(1) FISHING VESSEL; OIL SPILL RESPONSE VESSEL.—The terms "fishing vessel" and "oil spill response vessel" have the meanings given such terms in section 2101 of title 46, United

States Code.

(2) VESSEL OF OPPORTUNITY.—The term "vessel of opportunity" means a vessel engaged in spill response activities that is normally and substantially involved in activities other than spill response and not a vessel carrying oil as a primary cargo.

SEC. 11317. PORT COORDINATION COUNCIL FOR POINT SPENCER.

Section 541 of the Coast Guard Authorization Act of 2016 (Public Law 114-120) is amended—

(1) in subsection (b)(2) by striking "BSNC" and inserting the following:"BSNC (to serve as Council Chair).

"(3) The Denali Commission.

"(4) An oil spill removal organization that serves the area in which such Port is located.

"(5) A salvage and marine firefighting organization that serves the area in which such Port is located."

; and

(2) in subsection (c)—

(A) in paragraph (1)—

(i) in subparagraph (B) by striking the semicolon and inserting "; and";

(ii) by striking "; and" and inserting the following: "at Point Spencer in support of the activities for which Congress finds a compelling need in section 531 of this subtitle."; and

(iii) by striking subparagraph (D); and

(B) by striking paragraph (3) and inserting the following:

"(3) Facilitate coordination among members of the Council on the development and use of the land and coastline of Point Spencer, as such development and use relate to activities of the Council at the Port of Point Spencer."

Subtitle C—Environmental Compliance

SEC. 11318. PROVIDING REQUIREMENTS FOR VESSELS ANCHORED IN ESTABLISHED ANCHORAGE GROUNDS.

(a) IN GENERAL.—Subchapter I of chapter 700 of title 46, United States Code, is amended by adding at the end the following:

"SEC. 70007. [46 U.S.C. 70007] Anchorage grounds

"(a) ANCHORAGE GROUNDS.—

"(1) ESTABLISHMENT.—The Secretary of the department in which the Coast Guard is operating shall define and establish anchorage grounds in the navigable waters of the United States for vessels operating in such waters.

"(2) RELEVANT FACTORS FOR ESTABLISHMENT.—In carrying out paragraph (1), the Secretary shall take into account all relevant factors concerning navigational safety, protection of the marine environment, proximity to undersea pipelines and cables, safe and efficient use of Marine Transportation System, and national security.

"(b) VESSEL REQUIREMENTS.—Vessels, of certain sizes or type determined by the Secretary, shall—

"(1) set and maintain an anchor alarm for the duration of an anchorage;

"(2) comply with any directions or orders issued by the Captain of the Port; and

"(3) comply with any applicable anchorage regulations.

"(c) PROHIBITIONS.—A vessel may not—

"(1) anchor in any Federal navigation channel unless authorized or directed to by the Captain of the Port;

"(2) anchor in near proximity, within distances determined by the Coast Guard, to an undersea pipeline or cable, unless authorized or directed to by the Captain of the Port; and

"(3) anchor or remain anchored in an anchorage ground during any period in which the Captain of the Port orders closure of the anchorage ground due to inclement weather, navigational hazard, a threat to the environment, or other safety or security concern.

"(d) SAFETY EXCEPTION.—Nothing in this section shall be construed to prevent a vessel from taking actions necessary to maintain the safety of the vessel or to prevent the loss of life or property."

(b) REGULATORY REVIEW.—

(1) REVIEW REQUIRED.—Not later than 1 year after the date of enactment of this Act, the Secretary shall review existing policies, final agency actions, regulations, or other rules relating to anchorage promulgated under section 70006 of title 46, United States Code and—

(A) identify any such regulations or rules that may need modification or repeal—

(i) in the interest of marine safety, security, and environmental concerns, taking into account undersea pipelines, cables, or other infrastructure; or

(ii) to implement the amendments made by this section; and

(B) complete a cost-benefit analysis for any modification or repeal identified under paragraph (1).

(2) BRIEFING.—Upon completion of the review under paragraph (1), but not later than 2 years after the date of enactment of this Act, the Secretary shall provide a briefing to the Committee on Commerce, Science, and Transportation of the Senate and the Committee on Transportation and Infrastructure of the House of Representatives that summarizes such review.

(c) [46 U.S.C. 70007 note] SAVINGS CLAUSE.—Nothing in this section shall limit any authority available, as of the date of enactment of this Act, to the captain of a port with respect to safety measures or any other authority as necessary for the safety of vessels located in anchorage grounds in the navigable waters of the United States.

(d) CLERICAL AMENDMENT.—The analysis for chapter 700 of title 46, United States Code, is amended by inserting after the item relating to section 70006 the following:

"70007. Anchorage grounds."

(e) [46 U.S.C. 70007 note] APPLICABILITY OF REGULATIONS.—The amendments made by subsection (a) may not be construed to alter any existing rules, regulations, or final agency actions issued under section 70006 of title 46, United States Code, as in effect on the day before the date of enactment of this Act, until all regulations required under subsection (b) take effect.

SEC. 11319. STUDY ON IMPACTS ON SHIPPING AND COMMERCIAL, TRIBAL, AND RECREATIONAL FISHERIES FROM DEVELOPMENT OF RENEWABLE ENERGY ON WEST COAST.

(a) STUDY.—Not later than 180 days after the date of enactment of this Act, the Secretary, the Secretary of the Interior, and the Under Secretary of Commerce for Oceans and Atmosphere, shall seek to enter into an agreement with the National Academies of Science, Engineering, and Medicine under which the National Academy of Sciences, Engineering, and Medicine shall carry out a study to—

(1) identify, document, and analyze—

(A) historic and current, as of the date of the study, Tribal, commercial, and recreational fishing grounds, as well as areas where fish stocks are likely to shift in the future in all covered waters;

(B) usual and accustomed fishing areas in all covered waters;

(C) historic, current, and potential future shipping lanes, based on projected growth in shipping traffic in all covered waters;

(D) current and expected Coast Guard operations relevant to commercial fishing activities, including search and rescue, radar, navigation, communications, and safety within and near renewable energy sites; and

(E) key types of data needed to properly site renewable energy sites on the West Coast, with regard to assessing and mitigating conflicts;

(2) analyze—

(A) methods used to manage fishing, shipping, and other maritime activities; and

(B) potential future interactions between such activities and the placement of renewable energy infrastructure and the associated construction, maintenance, and operation of such infrastructure, including potential benefits and methods of mitigating adverse impacts; and

(3) review the current decision-making process for offshore wind in covered waters, and outline recommendations for

governmental consideration of all impacted coastal communities, particularly Tribal governments and fisheries communities, in the decision-making process for offshore wind in covered waters, including recommendations for—

(A) ensuring the appropriate governmental consideration of potential benefits of offshore wind in covered waters; and

(B) risk reduction and mitigation of adverse impacts on Coast Guard operations relevant to commercial fishing activities.

(b) SUBMISSION.—Not later than 1 year after commencing the study under subsection (a), the Secretary shall—

(1) submit the study to the Committees on Commerce, Science, and Transportation, and Energy and Natural Resources of the Senate and the Committees on Transportation and Infrastructure, Natural Resources, and Energy and Commerce of the House of Representatives, including the review and outline provided under subsection (a)(3); and

(2) make the study publicly available.

(c) DEFINITIONS.—In this section:

(1) COVERED WATERS.—The term "covered waters" means Federal or State waters off of the Canadian border and out to the furthest extent of the exclusive economic zone along the West Coast of the United States.

(2) EXCLUSIVE ECONOMIC ZONE.—The term "exclusive economic zone" has the meaning given such term in section 107 of title 46, United States Code.

SEC. 11320. USE OF DEVICES BROADCASTING ON AIS FOR PURPOSES OF MARKING FISHING GEAR.

The Secretary shall, within the Eleventh Coast Guard District, Thirteenth Coast Guard District, Fourteenth Coast Guard District, and Seventeenth Coast Guard District, suspend enforcement of individuals using automatic identification systems devices to mark fishing equipment during the period beginning on the date of enactment of this Act and ending on the earlier of—

(1) the date that is 2 years after such date of enactment; or

(2) the date on which the Federal Communications Commission promulgates a final rule to authorize a device used

to mark fishing equipment to operate in radio frequencies assigned for Automatic Identification System stations.

Subtitle D—Environmental Issues

SEC. 11321. NOTIFICATION OF COMMUNICATION OUTAGES.

(a) UPGRADES TO RESCUE 21 SYSTEM IN ALASKA.—Not later than August 30, 2023, the Commandant shall ensure the timely upgrade of the Rescue 21 system in Alaska so as to achieve 98 percent operational availability of remote fixed facility sites.

(b) PLAN TO REDUCE OUTAGES.—

(1) IN GENERAL.—Not later than 180 days after the date of enactment of this Act, the Commandant shall develop an operations and maintenance plan for the Rescue 21 system in Alaska that anticipates maintenance needs so as to reduce Rescue 21 system outages to the maximum extent practicable.

(2) PUBLIC AVAILABILITY.—The plan required under paragraph (1) shall be made available to the public on a publicly accessible website.

(c) REPORT REQUIRED.—Not later than 180 days after the date of enactment of this Act, the Commandant shall submit to the Committee on Commerce, Science, and Transportation of the Senate and the Committee on Transportation and Infrastructure of the House of Representatives a report that—

(1) contains a plan for the Coast Guard to notify mariners of radio outages for towers owned and operated by the Seventeenth Coast Guard District;

(2) addresses in such plan how the Seventeenth Coast Guard will—

(A) disseminate updates regarding outages on social media not less frequently than every 48 hours;

(B) provide updates on a publicly accessible website not less frequently than every 48 hours;

(C) develop methods for notifying mariners in areas in which cellular connectivity does not exist; and

(D) develop and advertise a web based communications update hub on AM/FM radio for mariners; and

(3) identifies technology gaps that need to be mitigated in order to implement the plan and provides a budgetary assessment necessary to implement the plan.

(d) CONTINGENCY PLAN.—

(1) IN GENERAL.—Not later than 180 days after the date of enactment of this Act, the Commandant shall, in collaboration with relevant Federal, State, Tribal, and other relevant entities (including the North Pacific Fishery Management Council, the National Oceanic and Atmospheric Administration Weather Service, the National Oceanic and Atmospheric Administration Fisheries Service, agencies of the State of Alaska, local radio stations, and stakeholders), establish a contingency plan to ensure that notifications of an outage of the Rescue 21 system in Alaska are broadly disseminated in advance of such an outage.

(2) ELEMENTS.—The contingency plan required under paragraph (1) shall require the Coast Guard to—

(A) disseminate updates regarding outages of the Rescue 21 system in Alaska on social media not less frequently than every 48 hours during an outage;

(B) provide updates on a publicly accessible website not less frequently than every 48 hours during an outage;

(C) notify mariners in areas in which cellular connectivity does not exist;

(D) develop and advertise a web-based communications update hub on AM/FM radio for mariners; and

(E) identify technology gaps necessary to implement the plan and provides a budgetary assessment necessary to implement the plan.

SEC. 11322. [46 U.S.C. 4502 note] IMPROVEMENTS TO COMMUNICATION WITH FISHING INDUSTRY AND RELATED STAKEHOLDERS.

(a) IN GENERAL.—The Commandant, in coordination with the National Commercial Fishing Safety Advisory Committee established by section 15102 of title 46, United States Code, shall develop a publicly accessible website that contains all information related to fishing industry activities, including vessel safety, inspections, enforcement, hazards, training, regulations (including proposed regulations), outages of the Rescue 21 system in Alaska and similar outages, and any other fishing-related activities.

(b) AUTOMATIC COMMUNICATIONS.—The Commandant shall provide methods for regular and automatic email communications with stakeholders who elect, through the website developed under subsection (a), to receive such communications.

SEC. 11323. [14 U.S.C. 504 note] ADVANCE NOTIFICATION OF MILITARY OR OTHER EXERCISES.

In consultation with the Secretary of Defense, the Secretary of State, and commercial fishing industry participants, the Commandant shall develop and publish on a publicly available website a plan for notifying United States mariners and the operators of United States fishing vessels in advance of—

(1) military exercises in the exclusive economic zone (as defined in section 3 of the Magnuson-Stevens Fishery Conservation and Management Act (16 U.S.C. 1802)); or

(2) other military activities that will impact recreational or commercial activities.

SEC. 11324. MODIFICATIONS TO SPORT FISH RESTORATION AND BOATING TRUST FUND ADMINISTRATION.

(a) DINGELL-JOHNSON SPORT FISH RESTORATION ACT AMENDMENTS.—

(1) AVAILABLE AMOUNTS.—Section 4(b)(1)(B)(i) of the Dingell-Johnson Sport Fish Restoration Act (16 U.S.C. 777c(b)(1)(B)(i)) is amended to read as follows:

"(i) for the fiscal year that includes November 15, 2021, the product obtained by multiplying—

"(I) $12,786,434; and

"(II) the change, relative to the preceding fiscal year, in the Consumer Price Index for All Urban Consumers published by the Department of Labor; and"

(2) AUTHORIZED EXPENSES.—Section 9(a) of the Dingell-Johnson Sport Fish Restoration Act (16 U.S.C. 777h(a)) is amended

(A) in paragraph (7) by striking "full-time"; and

(B) in paragraph (9) by striking "on a full-time basis".

(b) PITTMAN-ROBERTSON WILDLIFE RESTORATION ACT AMENDMENTS.—

(1) AVAILABLE AMOUNTS.—Section 4(a)(1)(B)(i) of the Pittman-Robertson Wildlife Restoration Act (16 U.S.C. 669c(a)(1)(B)(i)) is amended to read as follows:

"(i) for the fiscal year that includes November 15, 2021, the product obtained by multiplying—

"(I) $12,786,434; and

"(II) the change, relative to the preceding fiscal year, in the Consumer Price Index for All Urban Consumers published by the Department of Labor; and"

(2) AUTHORIZED EXPENSES.—Section 9(a) of the Pittman-Robertson Wildlife Restoration Act (16 U.S.C. 669h(a)) is amended—

(A) in paragraph (7) by striking "full-time"; and

(B) in paragraph (9) by striking "on a full-time basis".

SEC. 11325. LOAD LINES.

(a) APPLICATION TO CERTAIN VESSELS.—During the period beginning on the date of enactment of this Act and ending on the date that is 3 years after the date on which the report required under subsection (b) is submitted, the load line requirements of chapter 51 of title 46, United States Code, shall not apply to covered fishing vessels.

(b) GAO REPORT.—

(1) IN GENERAL.—Not later than 12 months after the date of enactment of this Act, the Comptroller General of the United States shall submit to the Committee on Commerce, Science, and Transportation of the Senate and the Committee on Transportation and Infrastructure of the House of Representatives—

(A) a report on the safety and seaworthiness of vessels described in section 5102(b)(5) of title 46, United States Code; and

(B) recommendations for exempting certain vessels from the load line requirements under chapter 51 of title 46 of such Code.

(2) ELEMENTS.—The report required under paragraph (1) shall include the following:

(A) An assessment of stability requirements of vessels referenced in section 5102(b)(5) of title 46, United States Code.

(B) An analysis of vessel casualties, mishaps, or other safety information relevant to load line requirements when a vessel is operating part-time as a fish tender vessel.

(C) An assessment of any other safety information as the Comptroller General determines appropriate.

(D) A list of all vessels that, as of the date of the report—

(i) are covered under section 5102(b)(5) of title 46, United States Code;

(ii) are acting as part-time fish tender vessels; and

(iii) are subject to any captain of the port zone subject to the oversight of the Commandant.

(3) CONSULTATION.—In preparing the report required under paragraph (1), the Comptroller General shall consider consultation with, at a minimum, the maritime industry, including—

(A) relevant Federal, State, and Tribal maritime associations and groups; and

(B) relevant federally funded research institutions, nongovernmental organizations, and academia.

(c) SAVINGS CLAUSE.—Nothing in this section shall limit any authority available, as of the date of enactment of this Act, to the captain of a port with respect to safety measures or any other authority as necessary for the safety of covered fishing vessels.

(d) DEFINITION OF COVERED FISHING VESSEL.—In this section, the term "covered fishing vessel" means a vessel that operates exclusively in one, or both, of the Thirteenth and Seventeenth Coast Guard Districts and that—

(1) was constructed, under construction, or under contract to be constructed as a fish tender vessel before January 1, 1980;

(2) was converted for use as a fish tender vessel before

January 1, 2022, and—

(A) has a valid stability letter issued in accordance with regulations prescribed under chapter 51 of title 46, United States Code; and

(B) the hull and internal structure of the vessel has been verified as suitable for intended service as examined by a marine surveyor of an organization accepted by the Secretary two times in the past five years with no interval of more than three years between such examinations; or

(3) operates part-time as a fish tender vessel for a period of less than 180 days.

SEC. 11326. ACTIONS BY NATIONAL MARINE FISHERIES SERVICE TO INCREASE ENERGY PRODUCTION.

(a) IN GENERAL.—The National Marine Fisheries Service shall, immediately upon the enactment of this Act, take action to address the outstanding backlog of letters of authorization for the Gulf of Mexico.

(b) SENSE OF CONGRESS.—It is the sense of Congress that the National Marine Fisheries Service should—

(1) take immediate action to issue a rule that allows the Service to approve outstanding and future applications for letters of authorization consistent with the permitting activities of the Service; and

(2) on or after the effective date of such rule, prioritize the consideration of applications in a manner that is consistent with applicable Federal law.

SEC. 11327. AQUATIC NUISANCE SPECIES TASK FORCE.

(a) RECREATIONAL VESSEL DEFINED.—Section 1003 of the Nonindigenous Aquatic Nuisance Prevention and Control Act of 1990 (16 U.S.C. 4702) is amended—

(1) by redesignating paragraphs (13) through (17) as paragraphs (15) through (19), respectively; and

(2) by inserting after paragraph (12) the following:

"(13) 'State' means each of the several States, the District of Columbia, American Samoa, Guam, Puerto Rico, the Northern Mariana Islands, and the Virgin Islands of the United States;

"(14) 'recreational vessel' has the meaning given that term in section 502 of the Federal Water Pollution Control Act (33 U.S.C. 1362);"

(b) OBSERVERS.—Section 1201 of the Nonindigenous Aquatic Nuisance Prevention and Control Act of 1990 (16 U.S.C. 4721) is amended by adding at the end the following:

"(g) OBSERVERS.—The chairpersons designated under subsection (d) may invite representatives of nongovernmental entities to participate as observers of the Task Force."

(c) AQUATIC NUISANCE SPECIES TASK FORCE.—Section 1201(b) of the Nonindigenous Aquatic Nuisance Prevention and Control Act of 1990 (16 U.S.C. 4721(b)) is amended—

(1) in paragraph (6) by striking "and" at the end;

(2) by redesignating paragraph (7) as paragraph (10); and

(3) by inserting after paragraph (6) the following:

"(7) the Director of the National Park Service;

"(8) the Director of the Bureau of Land Management;

"(9) the Commissioner of Reclamation; and"

(d) AQUATIC NUISANCE SPECIES PROGRAM.—Section 1202 of the Nonindigenous Aquatic Nuisance Prevention and Control Act of 1990 (16 U.S.C. 4722) is amended—

(1) in subsection (e) by adding at the end the following:

"(4) TECHNICAL ASSISTANCE AND RECOMMENDATIONS.—The Task Force may provide technical assistance and recommendations for best practices to an agency or entity engaged in vessel inspections or decontaminations for the purpose of—

"(A) effectively managing and controlling the movement of aquatic nuisance species into, within, or out of water of the United States; and

"(B) inspecting recreational vessels in a manner that minimizes disruptions to public access for boating and recreation in non-contaminated vessels.

"(5) CONSULTATION AND INPUT.—In carrying out paragraph (4), including the development of recommendations, the Task Force may consult with Indian Tribes and solicit input from—

"(A) State and Tribal fish and wildlife management agencies;

"(B) other State and Tribal agencies that manage fishery resources of the State or sustain fishery habitat; and

"(C) relevant nongovernmental entities."

; and

(2) in subsection (k) by adding at the end the following:

"(3) Not later than 90 days after the date of enactment of the Don Young Coast Guard Authorization Act of 2022, the Task Force shall submit a report to Congress recommending legislative, programmatic, or regulatory changes to eliminate remaining gaps in authorities between members of the Task Force to effectively manage and control the movement of aquatic nuisance species."

(e) TECHNICAL CORRECTIONS AND CONFORMING AMENDMENTS.—The Nonindigenous Aquatic Nuisance Prevention and Control Act of 1990 (16 U.S.C. 4701 et seq.) is further amended—

(1) in section 1002(b)(2) by inserting a comma after "funded";

(2) in section 1003 in paragraph (7) by striking "Canandian" and inserting "Canadian";

(3) in section 1203(a)—

(A) in paragraph (1)(F) by inserting "and" after "research,"; and

(B) in paragraph (3) by striking "encourage" and inserting "encouraged";

(4) in section 1204(b)(4) in the paragraph heading by striking "Adminisrative" and inserting "Administrative"; and

(5) in section 1209 by striking "subsection (a)" and inserting "section 1202(a)".

SEC. 11328. SAFETY STANDARDS.

(a) IN GENERAL.—Section 4502 of title 46, United States Code, is amended—

(1) in subsection (i)(4) by striking "each of fiscal years 2018

through 2021" and inserting "fiscal year 2023"; and

(2) in subsection (j)(4) by striking "each of fiscal years 2018 through 2021" and inserting "fiscal year 2023".

(b) AUTHORIZATION OF APPROPRIATIONS.—Section 9 of the Marine Debris Act (33 U.S.C. 1958) is amended—

(1) in subsection (a) by striking "each of fiscal years 2018 through 2022" and inserting "fiscal year 2023"; and

(2) in subsection (b) by striking "2702(1)" and inserting "4902(1)".

Subtitle E—Illegal Fishing and Forced Labor Prevention

SEC. 11329. [16 U.S.C. 1885a note] DEFINITIONS.

In this subtitle:

(1) FORCED LABOR.—The term "forced labor" means any labor or service provided for or obtained by any means described in section 1589(a) of title 18, United States Code.

(2) HUMAN TRAFFICKING.—The term "human trafficking" has the meaning given the term "severe forms of trafficking in persons" in section 103 of the Trafficking Victims Protection Act of 2000 (22 U.S.C. 7102).

(3) ILLEGAL, UNREPORTED, OR UNREGULATED FISHING.—The term "illegal, unreported, or unregulated fishing" has the meaning given such term in the implementing regulations or any subsequent regulations issued pursuant to section 609(e) of the High Seas Driftnet Fishing Moratorium Protection Act (16 U.S.C. 1826j(e)).

(4) OPPRESSIVE CHILD LABOR.—The term "oppressive child labor" has the meaning given such term in section 3 of the Fair Labor Standards Act of 1938 (29 U.S.C. 203).

(5) SEAFOOD.—The term "seafood" means all marine animal and plant life meant for consumption as food other than marine mammals and birds, including fish, shellfish, shellfish products, and processed fish.

(6) SEAFOOD IMPORT MONITORING PROGRAM.—The term "Seafood Import Monitoring Program" means the Seafood

Traceability Program established in subpart Q of part 300 of title 50, Code of Federal Regulations (or any successor regulation).

(7) SECRETARY.—The term "Secretary" means the Secretary of Commerce, acting through the Under Secretary of Commerce for Oceans and Atmosphere.

CHAPTER 1—COMBATING HUMAN TRAFFICKING THROUGH SEAFOOD IMPORT MONITORING

SEC. 11330. ENHANCEMENT OF SEAFOOD IMPORT MONITORING PROGRAM MESSAGE SET IN AUTOMATED COMMERCIAL ENVIRONMENT SYSTEM.

The Secretary, in coordination with the Commissioner of U.S. Customs and Border Protection, shall, not later than 6 months after the date of enactment of this Act, develop a strategy to improve the quality and verifiability of already collected Seafood Import Monitoring Program Message Set data elements in the Automated Commercial Environment system. Such strategy shall prioritize the use of enumerated data types, such as checkboxes, dropdown menus, or radio buttons, and any additional elements the Administrator of the National Oceanic and Atmospheric Administration finds appropriate.

SEC. 11331. DATA SHARING AND AGGREGATION.

(a) INTERAGENCY WORKING GROUP ON ILLEGAL, UNREPORTED, OR UNREGULATED FISHING.—Section 3551(c) of the Maritime SAFE Act (16 U.S.C. 8031(c)) is amended—

(1) by redesignating paragraphs (4) through (13) as paragraphs (5) through (14), respectively; and

(2) by inserting after paragraph (3) the following:

"(4) maximizing the utility of the import data collected by the members of the Working Group by harmonizing data standards and entry fields;"

(b) [16 U.S.C. 8031 note] PROHIBITION ON AGGREGATED CATCH DATA FOR CERTAIN SPECIES. Beginning not later than 1 year after the date of enactment of this Act, for the purposes of compliance with respect to Northern red snapper under the Seafood Import

Monitoring Program, the Secretary may not allow an aggregated harvest report of such species, regardless of vessel size.

SEC. 11332. [16 U.S.C. 1885 note] IMPORT AUDITS.

(a) AUDIT PROCEDURES.—The Secretary shall, not later than 1 year after the date of enactment of this Act, implement procedures to audit information and supporting records of sufficient numbers of imports of seafood and seafood products subject to the Seafood Import Monitoring Program to support statistically robust conclusions that the samples audited are representative of all seafood imports covered by the Seafood Import Monitoring Program with respect to a given year.

(b) EXPANSION OF MARINE FORENSICS LABORATORY.—The Secretary shall, not later than 1 year after the date of enactment of this Act, begin the process of expanding the National Oceanic and Atmospheric Administration's Marine Forensics Laboratory, including by establishing sufficient capacity for the development and deployment of rapid, and follow-up, analysis of field-based tests focused on identifying Seafood Import Monitoring Program species, and prioritizing such species at high risk of illegal, unreported, or unregulated fishing and seafood fraud.

(c) ANNUAL REVISION.—In developing the procedures required in subsection (a), the Secretary shall use predictive analytics to inform whether to revise such procedures to prioritize for audit those imports originating from nations—

(1) identified pursuant to section 609(a) or 610(a) of the High Seas Driftnet Fishing Moratorium Protection Act (16 U.S.C. 1826j(a) or 1826k(a)) that have not yet received a subsequent positive certification pursuant to section 609(d) or 610(c) of such Act, respectively;

(2) identified by an appropriate regional fishery management organization as being the flag state or landing location of vessels identified by other nations or regional fisheries management organizations as engaging in illegal, unreported, or unregulated fishing;

(3) identified as having human trafficking or forced labor in any part of the seafood supply chain, including on vessels flagged in such nation, and including feed for cultured production, in the most recent Trafficking in Persons Report issued by the Department of State in accordance with the

Trafficking Victims Protection Act of 2000 (22 U.S.C. 7101 et seq.);

(4) identified as producing goods that contain seafood using forced labor or oppressive child labor in the most recent List of Goods Produced by Child Labor or Forced Labor in accordance with the Trafficking Victims Protection Act (22 U.S.C. 7101 et seq.); and

(5) identified as at risk for human trafficking, including forced labor, in their seafood catching and processing industries by the report required under section 3563 of the Maritime SAFE Act (Public Law 116-92).

SEC. 11333. AVAILABILITY OF FISHERIES INFORMATION.

Section 402(b)(1) of the Magnuson-Stevens Fishery Conservation and Management Act (16 U.S.C. 1881a(b)(1)) is amended—

(1) in subparagraph (G) by striking "or" after the semicolon;

(2) in subparagraph (H) by striking the period at the end of such subparagraph and inserting "; or"; and

(3) by adding at the end the following:

"(I) to Federal agencies, to the extent necessary and appropriate, to administer Federal programs established to combat illegal, unreported, or unregulated fishing or forced labor (as such terms are defined in section 11329 of the Don Young Coast Guard Authorization Act of 2022), which shall not include an authorization for such agencies to release data to the public unless such release is related to enforcement."

SEC. 11334. [16 U.S.C. 1885a] REPORT ON SEAFOOD IMPORT MONITORING PROGRAM.

(a) REPORT TO CONGRESS AND PUBLIC AVAILABILITY OF REPORTS. The Secretary shall, not later than 120 days after the end of each fiscal year, submit to the Committee on Commerce, Science, and Transportation and the Committee on Finance of the Senate and the Committee on Natural Resources and the Committee on Financial Services of the House of Representatives a report that summarizes the National Marine Fisheries Service's efforts to prevent the importation of seafood harvested through illegal, unreported, or unregulated fishing, particularly with respect to seafood harvested, produced, processed, or manufactured by forced labor. Each such report shall be made publicly available on the website of the National Oceanic and Atmospheric Administration.

(b) CONTENTS.—Each report submitted under subsection (a) shall include—

(1) the volume and value of seafood species subject to the Seafood Import Monitoring Program, reported by 10-digit Harmonized Tariff Schedule of the United States codes, imported during the previous fiscal year;

(2) the enforcement activities and priorities of the National Marine Fisheries Service with respect to implementing the requirements under the Seafood Import Monitoring Program;

(3) the percentage of import shipments subject to the Seafood Import Monitoring Program selected for inspection or the information or records supporting entry selected for audit, as described in section 300.324(d) of title 50, Code of Federal Regulations;

(4) the number and types of instances of noncompliance with the requirements of the Seafood Import Monitoring Program;

(5) the number and types of instances of violations of State or Federal law discovered through the Seafood Import Monitoring Program;

(6) the seafood species with respect to which violations described in paragraphs (4) and (5) were most prevalent;

(7) the location of catch or harvest with respect to which violations described in paragraphs (4) and (5) were most prevalent;

(8) the additional tools, such as high performance computing and associated costs, that the Secretary needs to improve the efficacy of the Seafood Import Monitoring Program; and

(9) such other information as the Secretary considers appropriate with respect to monitoring and enforcing compliance with the Seafood Import Monitoring Program.

SEC. 11335. AUTHORIZATION OF APPROPRIATIONS.

There is authorized to be appropriated to the Commissioner of U.S. Customs and Border Protection to carry out enforcement actions pursuant to section 307 of the Tariff Act of 1930 (19 U.S.C. 1307) $20,000,000 for each of fiscal years 2023 through 2027.

CHAPTER 2—STRENGTHENING INTERNATIONAL FISHERIES MANAGEMENT TO COMBAT HUMAN TRAFFICKING

SEC. 11336. DENIAL OF PORT PRIVILEGES.

Section 101(a)(2) of the High Seas Driftnet Fisheries Enforcement Act (16 U.S.C. 1826a(a)(2)) is amended to read as follows:

"(2) DENIAL OF PORT PRIVILEGES.—The Secretary of Homeland Security shall, in accordance with international law—

"(A) withhold or revoke the clearance required by section 60105 of title 46, United States Code, for any large-scale driftnet fishing vessel of a nation that receives a negative certification under section 609(d) or 610(c) of the High Seas Driftnet Fishing Moratorium Protection Act (16 U.S.C. 1826j(d) or 1826k(c)), or fishing vessels of a nation that has been listed pursuant to section 609(b) or section 610(a) of such Act (16 U.S.C. 1826j(b) or 1826k(a)) in 2 or more consecutive reports for the same type of fisheries activity, as described under section 607 of such Act (16 U.S.C. 1826h), until a positive certification has been received;

"(B) withhold or revoke the clearance required by section 60105 of title 46, United States Code, for fishing vessels of a nation that has been listed pursuant to section 609(a) or 610(a) of the High Seas Driftnet Fishing Moratorium Protection Act (16 U.S.C. 1826j(a) or 1826k(a)) in 2 or more consecutive reports as described under section 607 of such Act (16 U.S.C. 1826h); and

"(C) deny entry of that vessel to any place in the United States and to the navigable waters of the United States, except for the purposes of inspecting such vessel, conducting an investigation, or taking other appropriate enforcement action."

SEC. 11337. IDENTIFICATION AND CERTIFICATION CRITERIA.

(a) DENIAL OF PORT PRIVILEGES.—Section 609(a) of the High Seas Driftnet Fishing Moratorium Protection Act (16 U.S.C. 1826j(a)) is amended—

(1) by striking paragraph (2) and inserting the following:

"(2) FOR ACTIONS OF A NATION.—The Secretary shall identify, and list in such report, a nation engaging in or endorsing illegal, unreported, or unregulated fishing. In determining which nations to list in such report, the Secretary shall consider the following:

"(A) Any nation that is violating, or has violated at any point during the 3 years preceding the date of the determination, conservation and management measures, including catch and other data reporting obligations and requirements, required under an international fishery management agreement to which the United States is a party.

"(B) Any nation that is failing, or has failed in the 3-year period preceding the date of the determination, to effectively address or regulate illegal, unreported, or unregulated fishing within its fleets in any areas where its vessels are fishing.

"(C) Any nation that fails to discharge duties incumbent upon it under international law or practice as a flag, port, or coastal state to take action to prevent, deter, and eliminate illegal, unreported, or unregulated fishing.

"(D) Any nation that has been identified as producing for export to the United States seafood-related goods through forced labor or oppressive child labor (as those terms are defined in section 11329 of the Don Young Coast Guard Authorization Act of 2022) in the most recent List of Goods Produced by Child Labor or Forced Labor in accordance with the Trafficking Victims Protection Act of 2000 (22 U.S.C. 7101 et seq.)."

; and

(2) by adding at the end the following:

"(4) TIMING.—The Secretary shall make an

identification under paragraph (1) or (2) at any time that the Secretary has sufficient information to make such identification."

(b) ILLEGAL, UNREPORTED, OR UNREGULATED CERTIFICATION DETERMINATION.—Section 609 of the High Seas Driftnet Fishing Moratorium Protection Act (16 U.S.C. 1826j) is amended—

(1) in subsection (d) by striking paragraph (3) and inserting the following:

"(3) EFFECT OF CERTIFICATION DETERMINATION.—

"(A) EFFECT OF NEGATIVE CERTIFICATION.—The provisions of subsection (a) and paragraphs (3) and (4) of subsection (b) of section 101 of the High Seas Driftnet Fisheries Enforcement Act (16 U.S.C. 1826a(a)and (b)(3) and (4)) shall apply to any nation that, after being identified and notified under subsection (b) has failed to take the appropriate corrective actions for which the Secretary has issued a negative certification under this subsection.

"(B) EFFECT OF POSITIVE CERTIFICATION.—The provisions of subsection (a) and paragraphs (3) and (4) of subsection (b) of section 101 of the High Seas Driftnet Fisheries Enforcement Act (16 U.S.C. 1826a(a)and (b)(3) and (4)) shall not apply to any nation identified under subsection (a) for which the Secretary has issued a positive certification under this subsection."

(2) by redesignating subsections (e) and (f) as subsections (f) and (g), respectively; and

(3) by inserting after subsection (d) the following:

"(e) RECORDKEEPING REQUIREMENTS.—The Secretary shall ensure that seafood or seafood products authorized for entry under this section are imported consistent with the reporting and the recordkeeping requirements of the Seafood Import Monitoring Program described in part 300.324(b) of title 50, Code of Federal Regulations (or any successor regulation)."

SEC. 11338. EQUIVALENT CONSERVATION MEASURES.

(a) IDENTIFICATION.—Section 610(a) of the High Seas Driftnet Fishing Moratorium Protection Act (16 U.S.C. 1826k(a)) is amended to read as follows:

"(a) IDENTIFICATION.—

"(1) IN GENERAL.—The Secretary shall identify and list in the report under section 607—

"(A) a nation if—

"(i) any fishing vessel of that nation is engaged, or has been engaged during the 3 years preceding the date of the determination, in fishing activities or practices on the high seas or within the exclusive economic zone of any nation, that have resulted in bycatch of a protected living marine resource; and

"(ii) the vessel's flag state has not adopted, implemented, and enforced a regulatory program governing such fishing designed to end or reduce such bycatch that is comparable in effectiveness to the regulatory program of the United States, taking into account differing conditions; and

"(B) a nation if—

"(i) any fishing vessel of that nation is engaged, or has engaged during the 3 years preceding the date of the determination, in fishing activities on the high seas or within the exclusive economic zone of another nation that target or incidentally catch sharks; and

"(ii) the vessel's flag state has not adopted, implemented, and enforced a regulatory program to provide for the conservation of sharks, including measures to prohibit removal of any of the fins of a shark, including the tail, before landing the shark in port, that is comparable to that of the United States.

"(2) TIMING.—The Secretary shall make an identification under paragraph (1) at any time that the Secretary has sufficient information to make such identification."

(b) CONSULTATION AND NEGOTIATION.—Section 610(b) of the High Seas Driftnet Fishing Moratorium Protection Act (16 U.S.C. 1826k(b)) is amended to read as follows:

"(b) CONSULTATION AND NEGOTIATION.—The Secretary of State, acting in consultation with the Secretary, shall—

"(1) notify, as soon as practicable, the President and

nations that are engaged in, or that have any fishing vessels engaged in, fishing activities or practices described in subsection (a), about the provisions of this Act;

"(2) initiate discussions as soon as practicable with all foreign nations that are engaged in, or a fishing vessel of which has engaged in, fishing activities described in subsection (a), for the purpose of entering into bilateral and multilateral treaties with such nations to protect such species and to address any underlying failings or gaps that may have contributed to identification under this Act;

"(3) seek agreements calling for international restrictions on fishing activities or practices described in subsection (a) through the United Nations, the Committee on Fisheries of the Food and Agriculture Organization of the United Nations, and appropriate international fishery management bodies; and

"(4) initiate the amendment of any existing international treaty for the protection and conservation of such species to which the United States is a party in order to make such treaty consistent with the purposes and policies of this section."

(c) CONSERVATION CERTIFICATION PROCEDURE.—Section 610(c) of the High Seas Driftnet Fishing Moratorium Protection Act (16 U.S.C. 1826k(c)) is amended—

(1) in paragraph (2) by inserting "the public and" after "comment by";

(2) in paragraph (4)—

(A) in subparagraph (A) by striking "and" after the semicolon;

(B) in subparagraph (B) by striking the period at the end and inserting "; and"; and

(C) by adding at the end the following:

"(C) ensure that any such fish or fish products authorized for entry under this section are imported consistent with the reporting and the recordkeeping requirements of the Seafood Import Monitoring Program established in subpart Q of part 300 of title 50, Code of Federal Regulations (or any successor regulation)."

; and

(3) in paragraph (5) by striking "(except to the extent that such provisions apply to sport fishing equipment or fish or fish products not caught by the vessels engaged in illegal, unreported, or unregulated fishing)".

(d) DEFINITION OF PROTECTED LIVING MARINE RESOURCE.—Section 610(e) of the High Seas Driftnet Fishing Moratorium Protection Act (16 U.S.C. 1826k(e)) is amended by striking paragraph (1) and inserting the following:

"(1) except as provided in paragraph (2), means nontarget fish, sea turtles, or marine mammals that are protected under United States law or international agreement, including—

"(A) the Marine Mammal Protection Act of 1972 (16 U.S.C. 1361 et seq.);

"(B) the Endangered Species Act of 1973 (16 U.S.C. 1531 et seq.);

"(C) the Shark Finning Prohibition Act (16 U.S.C. 1822 note); and

"(D) the Convention on International Trade in Endangered Species of Wild Fauna and Flora, done at Washington March 3, 1973 (27 UST 1087; TIAS 8249); but"

SEC. 11339. CAPACITY BUILDING IN FOREIGN FISHERIES.

(a) [16 U.S.C. 8018] IN GENERAL.—The Secretary, in consultation with the heads of other Federal agencies, as appropriate, shall develop and carry out with partner governments and civil society—

(1) multi-year international environmental cooperation agreements and projects; and

(2) multi-year capacity-building projects for implementing measures to address illegal, unreported, or unregulated fishing, fraud, forced labor, bycatch, and other conservation measures.

(b) CAPACITY BUILDING.—Section 3543(d) of the Maritime SAFE Act (16 U.S.C. 8013(d)) is amended—

(1) in the matter preceding paragraph (1) by striking "as appropriate,"; and

(2) in paragraph (3) by striking "as appropriate" and inserting "for all priority regions identified by the Working Group".

(c) REPORTS.—Section 3553 of the Maritime SAFE Act (16 U.S.C. 8033) is amended—

(1) in paragraph (7) by striking "and" after the semicolon;

(2) in paragraph (8) by striking the period at the end and inserting "; and"; and

(3) by adding at the end the following:

"(9) the status of work with global enforcement partners."

SEC. 11340. TRAINING OF UNITED STATES OBSERVERS.

Section 403(b) of the Magnuson-Stevens Fishery Conservation and Management Act (16 U.S.C. 1881b(b)) is amended—

(1) in paragraph (3) by striking "and" after the semicolon;

(2) by redesignating paragraph (4) as paragraph (5); and

(3) by inserting after paragraph (3) the following:

"(4) ensure that each observer has received training to identify indicators of forced labor and human trafficking (as such terms are defined in section 11329 of the Don Young Coast Guard Authorization Act of 2022) and refer this information to appropriate authorities; and"

SEC. 11341. [16 U.S.C. 1826a note] REGULATIONS.

Not later than 1 year after the date of enactment of this Act, the Secretary shall promulgate such regulations as may be necessary to carry out this subtitle and the amendments made by this subtitle.

TITLE CXIV—SUPPORT FOR COAST GUARD WORKFORCE

Subtitle A—Support for Coast Guard Members and Families

SEC. 11401. COAST GUARD CHILD CARE IMPROVEMENTS.

(a) FAMILY DISCOUNT FOR CHILD DEVELOPMENT SERVICES.—Section 2922(b)(2) of title 14, United States Code, is amended by adding at the end the following:

"(D) In the case of an active duty member with two or more

children attending a Coast Guard child development center, the Commandant may modify the fees to be charged for attendance for the second and any subsequent child of such member by an amount that is 15 percent less than the amount of the fee otherwise chargeable for the attendance of the first such child enrolled at the center, or another fee as the Commandant determines appropriate, consistent with multiple children."

(b) CHILD DEVELOPMENT CENTER STANDARDS AND INSPECTIONS.—Section 2923(a) of title 14, United States Code, is amended to read as follows:

"(a) STANDARDS.—The Commandant shall require each Coast Guard child development center to meet standards of operation—

"(1) that the Commandant considers appropriate to ensure the health, safety, and welfare of the children and employees at the center; and

"(2) necessary for accreditation by an appropriate national early childhood programs accrediting entity."

(c) CHILD CARE SUBSIDY PROGRAM.—

(1) AUTHORIZATION.—

(A) IN GENERAL.—Subchapter II of chapter 29 of title 14, United States Code, is amended by adding at the end the following:

"SEC. 2927. [14 U.S.C. 2927] Child care subsidy program

"(a) IN GENERAL.—

"(1) AUTHORITY.—The Commandant may operate a child care subsidy program to provide financial assistance to eligible providers that provide child care services or youth program services to members of the Coast Guard, members of the Coast Guard with dependents who are participating in the child care subsidy program, and any other individual the Commandant considers appropriate, if—

"(A) providing such financial assistance—

"(i) is in the best interests of the Coast Guard; and

"(ii) enables supplementation or expansion of the provision of Coast Guard child care services, while not supplanting or replacing Coast Guard child care services; and

"(B) the Commandant ensures, to the extent practicable, that the eligible provider is able to comply, and does comply, with the regulations, policies, and standards applicable to Coast Guard child care services.

"(2) ELIGIBLE PROVIDERS.—A provider of child care services or youth program services is eligible for financial assistance under this section if the provider—

"(A) is licensed to provide such services under applicable State and local law or meets all applicable State and local health and safety requirements if licensure is not required;

"(B) is either—

"(i) is a family home daycare; or

"(ii) is a provider of family child care services that—

"(I) otherwise provides federally funded or federally sponsored child development services;

"(II) provides such services in a child development center owned and operated by a private, not-for-profit organization;

"(III) provides a before-school or after-school child care program in a public school facility;

"(IV) conducts an otherwise federally funded or federally sponsored school-age child care or youth services program; or

"(V) conducts a school-age child care or youth services program operated by a not-for-profit organization; or

"(C) is a provider of another category of child care services or youth program services the Commandant considers appropriate for meeting the needs of members or civilian employees of the Coast Guard.

"(3) FINANCIAL ASSISTANCE FOR IN-HOME CHILD

CARE.—

"(A) IN GENERAL.—The Commandant may provide financial assistance to members of the Coast Guard who pay for services provided by in-home child care providers.

"(B) REQUIREMENTS.—In carrying out such program, the Commandant shall establish a policy and procedures to—

"(i) support the needs of families who request services provided by in-home childcare providers;

"(ii) provide the appropriate amount of financial assistance to provide to families described in paragraph, that is at minimum consistent with the program authorized in subsection (a)(1); and

"(iii) ensure the appropriate qualifications for such in-home child care provider, which shall at minimum—

"(I) take into consideration qualifications for available in-home child care providers in the private sector; and

"(II) ensure that the qualifications the Commandant determines appropriate under this paragraph are comparable to the qualifications for a provider of child care services in a Coast Guard child development center or family home day care.

"(b) DIRECT PAYMENT.—

"(1) IN GENERAL.—In carrying out a child care subsidy program under subsection (a)(1), subject to paragraph (3), the Commandant shall provide financial assistance under the program to an eligible member or individual the Commandant considers appropriate by direct payment to such eligible member or individual through monthly pay, direct deposit, or other direct form of payment.

"(2) POLICY.—Not later than 180 days after the

date of the enactment of this section, the Commandant shall establish a policy to provide direct payment as described in paragraph (1).

"(3) ELIGIBLE PROVIDER FUNDING CONTINUATION.—With the approval of an eligible member or an individual the Commandant considers appropriate, which shall include the written consent of such member or individual, the Commandant may continue to provide financial assistance under the child care subsidy program directly to an eligible provider on behalf of such member or individual.

"(4) RULE OF CONSTRUCTION.—Nothing in this subsection may be construed to affect any preexisting reimbursement arrangement between the Coast Guard and a qualified provider."

(B) CLERICAL AMENDMENT.—The analysis for chapter 29 of title 14, United States Code, is amended by inserting after the item relating to section 2926 the following:

"2927. Child care subsidy program."

(2) **[14 U.S.C. 2927 note]** EXPANSION OF CHILD CARE SUBSIDY PROGRAM.—

(A) IN GENERAL.—The Commandant shall—

(i) evaluate potential eligible uses for the child care subsidy program established under section 2927 of title 14, United States Code (referred to in this paragraph as the "program");

(ii) expand the eligible uses of funds for the program to accommodate the child care needs of members of the Coast Guard (including such members with nonstandard work hours and surge or other deployment cycles), including in-home care as described in section 2927(a)(3) of title 14, United States Code, and including by providing funds directly to such members instead of care providers; and

(iii) streamline enrollment policies, practices, paperwork, and requirements for eligible child care providers to reduce barriers for members to enroll in such providers.

(B) CONSIDERATIONS.—In evaluating potential eligible uses under subparagraph (A), the Commandant shall consider in-home child care services, care services such as supplemental care for children with disabilities, and any other child care delivery method the Commandant considers appropriate.

(C) REQUIREMENTS.—In establishing expanded eligible uses of funds for the program, the Commandant shall ensure that such uses—

(i) are in the best interests of the Coast Guard;

(ii) provide flexibility for members of the Coast Guard, including such members and employees with nonstandard work hours; and

(iii) ensure a safe environment for dependents of such members and employees.

(D) PUBLICATION.—Not later than 18 months after the date of the enactment of this Act, the Commandant shall publish an updated Commandant Instruction Manual (referred to in this paragraph as the "manual") that describes the expanded eligible uses of the program.

(E) REPORT.—

(i) IN GENERAL.—Not later than 18 months after the date of the enactment of this Act, the Commandant shall submit to the Committee on Commerce, Science, and Transportation of the Senate and the Committee on Transportation and Infrastructure of the House of Representatives a report outlining the expansion of the program.

(ii) ELEMENTS.—The report required by clause (i) shall include the following:

(I) An analysis of the considerations described in subparagraph (B).

(II) A description of the analysis used to identify eligible uses that were evaluated and incorporated into the manual under subparagraph (D).

(III) A full analysis and justification with respect to the forms of care that were ultimately not included in the manual.

(IV) Any recommendation with respect to funding or additional authorities necessary, including proposals for legislative change, to meet the current and anticipated future child care subsidy demands of the Coast Guard.

(V) A description of the steps taken to streamline enrollment policies, practices, and requirements for eligible child care providers in accordance with paragraph (2)(A)(iii).

SEC. 11402. ARMED FORCES ACCESS TO COAST GUARD CHILD DEVELOPMENT SERVICES.

Section 2922(a) of title 14, United States Code, is amended to read as follows:

"(a)(1) The Commandant may make child development services available, in such priority as the Commandant considers to be appropriate and consistent with readiness and resources and in the best interests of dependents of members and civilian employees of the Coast Guard, for—

"(A) members and civilian employees of the Coast Guard;

"(B) surviving dependents of service members who have died on active duty, if such dependents were beneficiaries of a Coast Guard child development service at the time of the death of such members;

"(C) members of the armed forces (as defined in section 101(a) of title 10); and

"(D) Federal civilian employees.

"(2) Child development service benefits provided under the authority of this section shall be in addition to benefits provided under other laws."

SEC. 11403. [14 U.S.C. 1901 note] CADET PREGNANCY POLICY IMPROVEMENTS.

(a) REGULATIONS REQUIRED.—Not later than 18 months after the date of enactment of this Act, the Secretary, in consultation with the Secretary of Defense, shall prescribe regulations for the Coast Guard Academy consistent with regulations required to be promulgated by section 559(a) of the National Defense

Authorization Act of 2022 (Public Law 117-81).

(b) BRIEFING.—Not later than 180 days after the date of the enactment of this Act, the Secretary shall provide to the Committee on Commerce, Science, and Transportation of the Senate and the Committee on Transportation and Infrastructure of the House of Representatives a briefing on the development of the regulations required by subsection (a).

SEC. 11404. COMBAT-RELATED SPECIAL COMPENSATION.

(a) REPORT AND BRIEFING.—Not later than 90 days after the date of enactment of this Act, and every 180 days thereafter until the date that is 5 years after the date on which the initial report is submitted under this subsection, the Commandant shall submit a report and provide an in-person briefing to the Committee on Commerce, Science, and Transportation of the Senate and the Committee on Transportation and Infrastructure of the House of Representatives on the implementation of section 221 of the Coast Guard Authorization Act of 2016 (Public Law 114-120; 10 U.S.C. 1413a note).

(b) ELEMENTS.—Each report and briefing required by subsection (a) shall include the following:

(1) A description of methods to educate members and retirees on the combat-related special compensation program.

(2) Statistics regarding enrollment in such program for members of the Coast Guard and Coast Guard retirees.

(3) A summary of each of the following:

(A) Activities carried out relating to the education of members of the Coast Guard participating in the Transition Assistance Program with respect to the combat-related special compensation program.

(B) Activities carried out relating to the education of members of the Coast Guard who are engaged in missions in which they are susceptible to injuries that may result in qualification for combat-related special compensation, including flight school, the National Motor Lifeboat School, deployable special forces, and other training programs as the Commandant considers appropriate.

(C) Activities carried out relating to training physicians and physician assistants employed by the Coast

Guard, or otherwise stationed in Coast Guard clinics, sickbays, or other locations at which medical care is provided to members of the Coast Guard, for the purpose of ensuring, during medical examinations, appropriate counseling and documentation of symptoms, injuries, and the associated incident that resulted in such injuries.

(D) Activities relating to the notification of heath service officers with respect to the combat-related special compensation program.

(4) The written guidance provided to members of the Coast Guard regarding necessary recordkeeping to ensure eligibility for benefits under such program.

(5) Any other matter relating to combat-related special compensation the Commandant considers appropriate.

(c) DISABILITY DUE TO CHEMICAL OR HAZARDOUS MATERIAL EXPOSURE.—Section 221(a) of the Coast Guard Authorization Act of 2016 (Public Law 114-120; 10 U.S.C. 1413a note) is amended—

(1) in paragraph (1) by striking "department is" and inserting "department in"; and

(2) in paragraph (2)—

(A) in the matter preceding subparagraph (A)—

(i) by striking "and hazardous" and inserting "hazardous"; and

(ii) by inserting ", or a duty in which chemical or other hazardous material exposure has occurred (such as during marine inspections or pollution response activities)" after "surfman)"; and

(B) in subparagraph (B)—

(i) by striking "paragraph (1) or paragraph (2) of"; and

(ii) by striking ", including—" and all that follows through "search and rescue; or" and inserting "; or".

SEC. 11405. STUDY ON FOOD SECURITY.

(a) STUDY.—

(1) IN GENERAL.—The Commandant shall conduct a study on food insecurity among members of the Coast Guard.

(2) ELEMENTS.—The study required under paragraph (1) shall include the following:

(A) An analysis of the impact of food deserts on members of the Coast Guard and their dependents who live in areas with high costs of living, including areas with high-density populations and rural areas.

(B) A comparison of—

(i) the current method used by the Commandant to determine which areas are considered to be high cost-of-living areas;

(ii) local-level indicators used by the Bureau of Labor Statistics to determine a cost of living that indicates buying power and consumer spending in specific geographic areas; and

(iii) indicators of the cost of living used by the Department of Agriculture in market basket analyses and other measures of the local or regional cost of food.

(C) An assessment of the accuracy of the method and indicators described in subparagraph (B) in quantifying high cost of living in low-data and remote areas.

(D) An assessment of the manner in which data accuracy and availability affect the accuracy of cost-of-living allowance calculations and other benefits, as the Commandant considers appropriate.

(E) Recommendations—

(i) to improve access to high-quality, affordable food within a reasonable distance of Coast Guard units located in areas identified as food deserts;

(ii) to reduce transit costs for members of the Coast Guard and their dependents who are required to travel to access high-quality, affordable food; and

(iii) for improving the accuracy of the calculations referred to in subparagraph (D).

(F) The estimated costs of implementing each recommendation made under subparagraph (E).

(b) PLAN.—

(1) IN GENERAL.—The Commandant shall develop a detailed plan to implement the recommendations of the study

conducted under subsection (a).

(2) REPORT.—Not later than 1 year after date of the enactment of this Act, the Commandant shall provide to the Committee on Commerce, Science, and Transportation of the Senate and the Committee on Transportation and Infrastructure of the House of Representatives a briefing on the plan required under paragraph (1), including the cost of implementation, proposals for legislative change, and any other result of the study the Commandant considers appropriate.

(c) FOOD DESERT DEFINED.—In this section, the term "food desert" means an area, as determined by the Commandant, in which it is difficult, even with a vehicle or an otherwise-available mode of transportation, to obtain affordable, high-quality fresh food in the immediate area in which members of the Coast Guard serve and reside.

Subtitle B—Healthcare

SEC. 11406. [14 U.S.C. 504 note] DEVELOPMENT OF MEDICAL STAFFING STANDARDS FOR COAST GUARD.

(a) IN GENERAL.—Not later than 180 days after the date of enactment of this Act, the Commandant, in consultation with the Defense Health Agency and any healthcare expert the Commandant considers appropriate, shall develop medical staffing standards for the Coast Guard that are consistent with the recommendations of the Comptroller General of the United States set forth in the report titled "Coast Guard Health Care: Improvements Needed for Determining Staffing Needs and Monitoring Access to Care" and published in February 2022.

(b) INCLUSIONS.—In developing the standards under subsection (a), the Commandant shall address and take into consideration the following:

(1) Current and future operations of healthcare personnel in support of Department of Homeland Security missions, including surge deployments for incident response.

(2) Staffing standards for specialized providers, including flight surgeons, dentists, behavioral health specialists, and physical therapists.

(3) Staffing levels of medical, dental, and behavioral health

providers for the Coast Guard who are—

(A) members of the Coast Guard;

(B) assigned to the Coast Guard from the Public Health Service;

(C) Federal civilian employees; or

(D) contractors hired by the Coast Guard to fill vacancies.

(4) Staffing levels at medical facilities for Coast Guard units in remote locations.

(5) Any discrepancy between medical staffing standards of the Department of Defense and medical staffing standards of the Coast Guard.

(c) REVIEW BY COMPTROLLER GENERAL.—Not later than 90 days after the Commandant completes the staffing standards required by subsection (a), the Commandant shall submit the standards to the Comptroller General, who shall review the standards and provide recommendations to the Commandant.

(d) REPORT TO CONGRESS.—Not later than 180 days after developing the standards developed under subsection (a), the Commandant shall submit to the Committee on Commerce, Science, and Transportation of the Senate and the Committee on Transportation and Infrastructure of the House of Representatives a report on the standards developed under subsection (a) and the recommendations provided under subsection (c) that includes a plan and a description of the resources and budgetary needs required to implement the standards.

(e) MODIFICATION, IMPLEMENTATION, AND PERIODIC UPDATES.—The Commandant shall—

(1) modify such standards, as necessary, based on the recommendations under subsection (c);

(2) implement the standards; and

(3) review and update the standards not less frequently than every 4 years.

SEC. 11407. HEALTHCARE SYSTEM REVIEW AND STRATEGIC PLAN.

(a) IN GENERAL.—Not later than 270 days after the completion of the studies conducted by the Comptroller General of the United

States under sections 8259 and 8260 of the William M. (Mac) Thornberry National Defense Authorization Act of Fiscal Year 2021 (Public Law 116-283; 134 Stat. 4679), the Commandant shall—

(1) conduct a comprehensive review of the Coast Guard healthcare system; and

(2) develop a strategic plan for improvements to, and the modernization of, such system to ensure access to high-quality, timely healthcare for members of the Coast Guard, their dependents, and applicable Coast Guard retirees.

(b) PLAN.—

(1) IN GENERAL.—The strategic plan developed under subsection (a) shall seek to—

(A) maximize the medical readiness of members of the Coast Guard;

(B) optimize delivery of healthcare benefits;

(C) ensure high-quality training of Coast Guard medical personnel; and

(D) prepare for the future needs of the Coast Guard.

(2) ELEMENTS.—The plan shall address, at a minimum, the following:

(A) Improving access to healthcare for members of the Coast Guard, their dependents, and applicable Coast Guard retirees.

(B) Quality of healthcare.

(C) The experience and satisfaction of members of the Coast Guard and their dependents with the Coast Guard healthcare system.

(D) The readiness of members of the Coast Guard and Coast Guard medical personnel.

(c) REVIEW COMMITTEE.—

(1) ESTABLISHMENT.—The Commandant shall establish a review committee to conduct a comprehensive analysis of the Coast Guard healthcare system (referred to in this section as the "Review Committee").

(2) MEMBERSHIP.—The Review Committee shall be composed of members selected by the Commandant, including—

(A) 1 or more members of the uniformed services (as defined in section 101 of title 10, United States Code) or Federal employees, either of which have expertise in—

(i) the medical, dental, pharmacy, or behavioral health fields; or

(ii) any other field the Commandant considers appropriate;

(B) 1 representative of the Defense Health Agency; and

(C) 1 medical representative from each Coast Guard district.

(3) CHAIRPERSON.—The chairperson of the Review Committee shall be the Director of the Health, Safety, and Work Life Directorate of the Coast Guard.

(4) STAFF.—The Review Committee shall be staffed by employees of the Coast Guard.

(5) REPORT TO COMMANDANT.—Not later than 1 year after the Review Committee is established, the Review Committee shall submit to the Commandant a report that—

(A) assesses, taking into consideration the medical staffing standards developed under section 11406, the recommended medical staffing standards set forth in the Comptroller General study required by section 8260 of the William M. (Mac) Thornberry National Defense Authorization Act for Fiscal Year 2021 (Public Law 116-283; 134 Stat. 4679), and compares such standards to the medical staffing standards of the Department of Defense and the private sector;

(B) addresses improvements needed to ensure continuity of care for members of the Coast Guard, including by evaluating the feasibility of having a dedicated primary care manager for each such member while the member is stationed at a duty station;

(C) evaluates the effects of increased surge deployments of medical personnel on staffing needs at Coast Guard clinics;

(D) identifies ways to improve access to care for members of the Coast Guard and their dependents who are stationed in remote areas, including methods to expand access to providers in the available network;

(E) identifies ways the Coast Guard may better use Department of Defense Military Health System resources for members of the Coast Guard, their dependents, and applicable Coast Guard retirees;

(F) identifies barriers to participation in the Coast Guard healthcare system and ways the Coast Guard may better use patient feedback to improve quality of care at Coast Guard-owned facilities, military treatment facilities, and specialist referrals;

(G) includes recommendations to improve the Coast Guard healthcare system; and

(H) any other matter the Commandant or the Review Committee considers appropriate.

(6) TERMINATION.—The Review Committee shall terminate on the date that is 1 year after the date on which the Review Committee submits the report required under paragraph (5).

(7) INAPPLICABILITY OF FEDERAL ADVISORY COMMITTEE ACT.—The Federal Advisory Committee Act (5 U.S.C. App.) shall not apply to the Review Committee.

(d) REPORT TO CONGRESS.—Not later than 2 years after the date of enactment of this Act, the Commandant shall submit to the Committee on Commerce, Science, and Transportation of the Senate and the Committee on Transportation and Infrastructure of the House of Representatives—

(1) the strategic plan for the Coast Guard medical system required under subsection (a);

(2) the report of the Review Committee submitted to the Commandant under subsection (c)(5); and

(3) a description of the manner in which the Commandant plans to implement the recommendations of the Review Committee.

SEC. 11408. [14 U.S.C. 504 note] DATA COLLECTION AND ACCESS TO CARE.

(a) IN GENERAL.—Not later than 180 days after the date of enactment of this Act, the Commandant, in consultation with the Defense Health Agency and any healthcare expert the Commandant considers appropriate, shall develop, and make publicly available, a policy to require the collection of data regarding access by members of the Coast Guard and their dependents to medical, dental, and behavioral healthcare as recommended by the Comptroller General of the United States in the report entitled "Coast Guard Health Care: Improvements Needed for Determining Staffing Needs and Monitoring Access to Care", published in February 2022.

(b) ELEMENTS.—The policy required by subsection (a) shall address the following:

(1) Methods to collect data on access to care for—

(A) routine annual physical health assessments;

(B) flight physicals for aviators or prospective aviators;

(C) sick call;

(D) injuries;

(E) dental health; and

(F) behavioral health conditions.

(2) Collection of data on access to care for referrals.

(3) Collection of data on access to care for members of the Coast Guard stationed at remote units, aboard Coast Guard cutters, and on deployments.

(4) Use of the electronic health record system to improve data collection on access to care.

(5) Use of data for addressing the standards of care, including time between requests for appointments and actual appointments, including appointments made with referral services.

(c) PUBLICATION AND REPORT TO CONGRESS.—Not later than 90 days after the policy under subsection (a) is completed, or any subsequent updates to such policy, the Commandant shall—

(1) publish the policy on a publicly accessible internet website of the Coast Guard; and

(2) submit to the Committee on Commerce, Science, and Transportation of the Senate and the Committee on Transportation and Infrastructure of the House of Representatives a report on the policy and the manner in which the Commandant plans to address access-to-care deficiencies.

(d) PERIODIC UPDATES.—Not less frequently than every 5 years, the Commandant shall review and update the policy required under subsection (a).

SEC. 11409. [14 U.S.C. 504 note] BEHAVIORAL HEALTH POLICY.

(a) INTERIM BEHAVIORAL HEALTH POLICY.—

(1) IN GENERAL.—Not later than 180 days after the date of enactment of this Act, the Commandant shall establish an interim behavioral health policy for members of the Coast Guard that is in parity with section 5.28 (relating to behavioral health) of Department of Defense Instruction 6130.03, volume 2, "Medical Standards for Military Service: Retention".

(2) TERMINATION.—The interim policy established under paragraph (1) shall remain in effect until the date on which the Commandant issues a permanent behavioral health policy for members of the Coast Guard.

(b) PERMANENT POLICY.—In developing a permanent policy with respect to retention and behavioral health, the Commandant shall ensure that, to the extent practicable, the policy of the Coast Guard is in parity with section 5.28 (relating to behavioral health) of Department of Defense Instruction 6130.03, volume 2, "Medical Standards for Military Service: Retention".

SEC. 11410. MEMBERS ASSERTING POST-TRAUMATIC STRESS DISORDER OR TRAUMATIC BRAIN INJURY.

(a) IN GENERAL.—Subchapter I of chapter 25 of title 14, United States Code, is further amended by adding at the end the following:

"SEC. 2516. [14 U.S.C. 2516] Members asserting post-traumatic stress disorder or traumatic brain injury

"(a) MEDICAL EXAMINATION REQUIRED.—

"(1) IN GENERAL.—The Secretary shall ensure that a member of the Coast Guard who has performed Coast Guard operations or has been sexually assaulted during the preceding 2-year period, and who is diagnosed by an appropriate licensed or certified healthcare professional as experiencing post-traumatic stress disorder or traumatic brain injury or who otherwise alleges, based on the service of the member or based on such sexual assault, the influence of such a condition, receives a medical examination to evaluate a diagnosis of post-traumatic stress disorder or traumatic brain injury.

"(2) RESTRICTION ON ADMINISTRATIVE SEPARATION.—A member described in paragraph (1) shall not be administratively separated under conditions other than honorable, including an administrative separation in lieu of a court-martial, until the results of the medical examination have been reviewed by appropriate authorities responsible for evaluating, reviewing, and approving the separation case, as determined by the Secretary.

"(3) POST-TRAUMATIC STRESS DISORDER.—In a case involving post-traumatic stress disorder under this subsection, a medical examination shall be—

"(A) performed by—

"(i) a board-certified or board-eligible psychiatrist; or

"(ii) a licensed doctorate-level psychologist; or

"(B) performed under the close supervision of—

"(i) a board-certified or board-eligible psychiatrist; or

"(ii) a licensed doctorate-level psychologist, a doctorate-level mental health provider, a psychiatry resident, or a clinical or counseling psychologist who has completed a 1-year internship or residency.

"(4) TRAUMATIC BRAIN INJURY.—In a case involving traumatic brain injury under this subsection, a medical examination shall be performed by a physiatrist, psychiatrist, neurosurgeon, or neurologist.

"(b) PURPOSE OF MEDICAL EXAMINATION.—The medical examination required under subsection (a) shall assess whether the effects of mental or neurocognitive disorders, including post-traumatic stress disorder and traumatic brain injury, constitute matters in extenuation that relate to the basis for administrative separation under conditions other than honorable or the overall characterization of the service of the member as other than honorable.

"(c) INAPPLICABILITY TO PROCEEDINGS UNDER UNIFORM CODE OF MILITARY JUSTICE.—The medical examination and procedures required by this section do not apply to courts-martial or other proceedings conducted pursuant to the Uniform Code of Military Justice.

"(d) COAST GUARD OPERATIONS DEFINED.—In this section, the term 'Coast Guard operations' has the meaning given that term in section 888(a) of the Homeland Security Act of 2002 (6 U.S.C. 468(a))."

(b) CLERICAL AMENDMENT.—The analysis for chapter 25 of title 14, United States Code, is amended by inserting after the item relating to section 2515 (as added by this Act) the following:

"2516. Members asserting post-traumatic stress disorder or traumatic brain injury."

SEC. 11411. IMPROVEMENTS TO PHYSICAL DISABILITY EVALUATION SYSTEM AND TRANSITION PROGRAM.

(a) TEMPORARY POLICY.—Not later than 60 days after the date of enactment of this Act, the Commandant shall develop a temporary policy that—

(1) improves timeliness, communication, and outcomes for members of the Coast Guard undergoing the Physical Disability Evaluation System, or a related formal or informal process;

(2) affords maximum career transition benefits to members of the Coast Guard determined by a Medical Evaluation Board to be unfit for retention in the Coast Guard; and

(3) maximizes the potential separation and career transition benefits for members of the Coast Guard undergoing the Physical Disability Evaluation System, or a related formal or informal process.

(b) ELEMENTS.—The policy required under subsection (a) shall include the following:

(1) A requirement that any member of the Coast Guard who is undergoing the Physical Disability Evaluation System, or a related formal or informal process, shall be placed in a duty status that allows the member the opportunity to attend necessary medical appointments and other activities relating to the Physical Disability Evaluation System, including completion of any application of the Department of Veterans Affairs and career transition planning.

(2) In the case of a Medical Evaluation Board report that is not completed not later than 120 days after the date on which

an evaluation by the Medical Evaluation Board was initiated, the option for such a member to enter permissive duty status.

(3) A requirement that the date of initiation of an evaluation by a Medical Evaluation Board shall include the date on which any verbal or written affirmation is made to the member, command, or medical staff that the evaluation by the Medical Evaluation Board has been initiated.

(4) An option for such member to seek an internship under the SkillBridge program established under section 1143(e) of title 10, United States Code, and outside employment aimed at improving the transition of the member to civilian life, only if such an internship or employment does not interfere with necessary medical appointments required for the member's physical disability evaluation.

(5) A requirement that not less than 21 days notice shall be provided to such a member for any such medical appointment, to the maximum extent practicable, to ensure that the appointment timeline is in the best interests of the immediate health of the member.

(6) A requirement that the Coast Guard shall provide such a member with a written separation date upon the completion of a Medical Evaluation Board report that finds the member unfit to continue active duty.

(7) To provide certainty to such a member with respect to a separation date, a policy that ensures—

(A) that accountability measures are in place with respect to Coast Guard delays throughout the Physical Disability Evaluation System, including—

(i) placement of the member in an excess leave status after 270 days have elapsed since the date of initiation of an evaluation by a Medical Evaluation Board by any competent authority; and

(ii) a calculation of the costs to retain the member on active duty, including the pay, allowances, and other associated benefits of the member, for the period beginning on the date that is 90 days after the date of initiation of an evaluation by a Medical Evaluation Board by any competent authority and ending on the date on which the member is separated from the Coast

Guard; and

(B) the availability of administrative solutions to any such delay.

(8) With respect to a member of the Coast Guard on temporary limited duty status, an option to remain in the member's current billet, to the maximum extent practicable, or to be transferred to a different active-duty billet, so as to minimize any negative impact on the member's career trajectory.

(9) A requirement that each respective command shall report to the Coast Guard Personnel Service Center any delay of more than 21 days between each stage of the Physical Disability Evaluation System for any such member, including between stages of the processes, the Medical Evaluation Board, the Informal Physical Evaluation Board, and the Formal Physical Evaluation Board.

(10) A requirement that, not later than 7 days after receipt of a report of a delay described in paragraph (9), the Personnel Service Center shall take corrective action, which shall ensure that the Coast Guard exercises maximum discretion to continue the Physical Disability Evaluation System of such a member in a timely manner, unless such delay is caused by the member.

(11) A requirement that—

(A) a member of the Coast Guard shall be allowed to make a request for a reasonable delay in the Physical Disability Evaluation System to obtain additional input and consultation from a medical or legal professional; and

(B) any such request for delay shall be approved by the Commandant based on a showing of good cause by the member.

(c) REPORT ON TEMPORARY POLICY.—Not later than 60 days after the date of enactment of this Act, the Commandant shall submit to the Committee on Commerce, Science, and Transportation of the Senate and the Committee on Transportation and Infrastructure of the House of Representatives a copy of the policy developed under subsection (a).

(d) PERMANENT POLICY.—Not later than 180 days after the date of enactment of this Act, the Commandant shall publish a Commandant Instruction making the policy developed under subsection (a) a permanent policy of the Coast Guard.

(e) BRIEFING.—Not later than 1 year after the date of enactment of this Act, the Commandant shall provide to the Committee on Commerce, Science, and Transportation of the Senate and the Committee on Transportation and Infrastructure of the House of Representatives a briefing on, and a copy of, the permanent policy.

(f) ANNUAL REPORT ON COSTS.—

(1) IN GENERAL.—Not less frequently than annually, the Commandant shall submit to the Committee on Commerce, Science, and Transportation of the Senate and the Committee on Transportation and Infrastructure of the House of Representatives a report that, for the preceding fiscal year—

(A) details the total aggregate service-wide costs described in subsection (b)(7)(A)(ii) for members of the Coast Guard whose Physical Disability Evaluation System process has exceeded 90 days; and

(B) includes for each such member—

(i) an accounting of such costs; and

(ii) the number of days that elapsed between the initiation and completion of the Physical Disability Evaluation System process.

(2) PERSONALLY IDENTIFIABLE INFORMATION.—A report under paragraph (1) shall not include the personally identifiable information of any member of the Coast Guard.

SEC. 11412. [14 U.S.C. 504 note] EXPANSION OF ACCESS TO COUNSELING.

(a) IN GENERAL.—Not later than 180 days after the date of enactment of this Act, the Commandant shall hire, train, and deploy not fewer than an additional 5 behavioral health specialists.

(b) REQUIREMENT.—Through the hiring process required under subsection (a), the Commandant shall ensure that at least 35 percent of behavioral health specialists employed by the Coast Guard have experience in behavioral healthcare for the purpose of supporting members of the Coast Guard with needs for perinatal mental health care and counseling service for miscarriage, child loss, and postpartum depression.

(c) ACCESSIBILITY.—The support provided by the behavioral

health specialists described in subsection (a)—

(1) may include care delivered via telemedicine; and

(2) shall be made widely available to members of the Coast Guard.

SEC. 11413. EXPANSION OF POSTGRADUATE OPPORTUNITIES FOR MEMBERS OF COAST GUARD IN MEDICAL AND RELATED FIELDS.

(a) [14 U.S.C. 2770 note] IN GENERAL.—The Commandant shall expand opportunities for members of the Coast Guard to secure postgraduate degrees in medical and related professional disciplines for the purpose of supporting Coast Guard clinics and operations.

(b) APPLICATION OF LAW.—Individuals who receive assistance pursuant to subsection (a) shall be subject to the service obligations required under section 2114 of title 10, United States Code.

(c) MILITARY TRAINING STUDENT LOADS.—Section 4904(b)(3) of title 14, United States Code, is amended by striking "350" and inserting "385".

SEC. 11414. STUDY ON COAST GUARD MEDICAL FACILITIES NEEDS.

(a) IN GENERAL.—Not later than 270 days after the date of enactment of this Act, the Comptroller General of the United States shall commence a study on Coast Guard medical facilities needs.

(b) ELEMENTS.—The study required by subsection (a) shall include the following:

(1) A list of Coast Guard medical facilities, including clinics, sickbays, and shipboard facilities.

(2) A summary of capital needs for Coast Guard medical facilities, including construction and repair.

(3) A summary of equipment upgrade backlogs of Coast Guard medical facilities.

(4) An assessment of improvements to Coast Guard medical facilities, including improvements to information technology infrastructure, required to enable the Coast Guard to fully use telemedicine and implement other modernization initiatives.

(5) An evaluation of the process used by the Coast Guard to identify, monitor, and construct Coast Guard medical facilities.

(6) A description of the resources necessary to fully address all Coast Guard medical facilities needs.

(c) REPORT.—Not later than 1 year after commencing the study required by subsection (a), the Comptroller General shall submit to the Committee on Commerce, Science, and Transportation of the Senate and the Committee on Transportation and Infrastructure of the House of Representatives a report on the findings of the study.

SEC. 11415. STUDY ON COAST GUARD TELEMEDICINE PROGRAM.

(a) IN GENERAL.—Not later than 180 days after the date of enactment of this Act, the Comptroller General of the United States shall commence a study on the Coast Guard telemedicine program.

(b) ELEMENTS.—The study required under subsection (a) shall include the following:

(1) An assessment of—

(A) the current capabilities and limitations of the Coast Guard telemedicine program;

(B) the degree of integration of such program with existing electronic health records;

(C) the capability and accessibility of such program, as compared to the capability and accessibility of the telemedicine programs of the Department of Defense and commercial medical providers;

(D) the manner in which the Coast Guard telemedicine program may be expanded to provide better clinical and behavioral medical services to members of the Coast Guard, including such members stationed at remote units or onboard Coast Guard cutters at sea; and

(E) the costs savings associated with the provision of—

(i) care through telemedicine; and

(ii) preventative care.

(2) An identification of barriers to full use or expansion of such program.

(3) A description of the resources necessary to expand such program to its full capability.

(c) REPORT.—Not later than 1 year after commencing the study required by subsection (a), the Comptroller General shall submit to the Committee on Commerce, Science, and Transportation of the

Senate and the Committee on Transportation and Infrastructure of the House of Representatives a report on the findings of the study.

Subtitle C—Housing

SEC. 11416. STUDY ON COAST GUARD HOUSING ACCESS, COST, AND CHALLENGES.

(a) IN GENERAL.—Not later than 90 days after the date of enactment of this Act, the Comptroller General of the United States shall commence a study on housing access, cost, and associated challenges facing members of the Coast Guard.

(b) ELEMENTS.—The study required under subsection (a) shall include the following:

(1) An assessment of—

(A) the extent to which—

(i) the Commandant has evaluated the sufficiency, availability, and affordability of housing options for members of the Coast Guard and their dependents; and

(ii) the Coast Guard owns and leases housing for members of the Coast Guard and their dependents;

(B) the methods used by the Commandant to manage housing data, and the manner in which the Commandant uses such data—

(i) to inform Coast Guard housing policy; and

(ii) to guide investments in Coast Guard-owned housing capacity and other investments in housing, such as long-term leases and other housing options; and

(C) the process used by the Commandant to gather and provide information used to calculate housing allowances for members of the Coast Guard and their dependents, including whether the Commandant has established best practices to manage low-data areas.

(2) An assessment as to whether the Department of Defense basic allowance for housing is sufficient for members of the Coast Guard.

(3) Recommendations for actions the Commandant should take to improve the availability and affordability of housing for members of the Coast Guard and their dependents who are stationed in—

(A) remote units located in areas in which members of the Coast Guard and their dependents are eligible for TRICARE Prime Remote; or

(B) units located in areas with a high number of vacation rental properties.

(c) REPORT.—Not later than 1 year after commencing the study required under subsection (a), the Comptroller General shall submit to the Committee on Commerce, Science, and Transportation of the Senate and the Committee on Transportation and Infrastructure of the House of Representatives a report on the findings of the study.

(d) STRATEGY.—Not later than 180 days after the submission of the report required under subsection (c), the Commandant shall publish a Coast Guard housing strategy that addresses the findings set forth in the report. Such strategy shall, at a minimum—

(1) address housing inventory shortages and affordability; and

(2) include a Coast Guard-owned housing infrastructure investment prioritization plan.

SEC. 11417. AUDIT OF CERTAIN MILITARY HOUSING CONDITIONS OF ENLISTED MEMBERS OF COAST GUARD IN KEY WEST, FLORIDA.

(a) IN GENERAL.—Not later than 30 days after the date of enactment of this Act, the Commandant, in coordination with the Secretary of the Navy, shall commence an audit to assess—

(1) the conditions of housing units of enlisted members of the Coast Guard located at Naval Air Station Key West Sigsbee Park Annex;

(2) the percentage of such units that are considered unsafe or unhealthy housing units for enlisted members of the Coast Guard and their families;

(3) the process used by enlisted members of the Coast Guard and their families to report housing concerns;

(4) the extent to which enlisted members of the Coast Guard and their families experience unsafe or unhealthy

housing units, relocate, receive a per diem, or expend similar expenses as a direct result of displacement that are not covered by a landlord, insurance, or claims process;

(5) the feasibility of providing reimbursement for uncovered expenses described in paragraph (4); and

(6) what resources are needed to provide appropriate and safe housing for enlisted members of the Coast Guard and their families in Key West, Florida.

(b) REPORT.—Not later than 120 days after the date of enactment of this section , the Commandant shall submit to the appropriate committees of Congress a report on the results of the audit.

(c) DEFINITIONS.—In this section:

(1) APPROPRIATE COMMITTEES OF CONGRESS.—The term “appropriate committees of Congress” means—

(A) the Committee on Commerce, Science, and Transportation and the Committee on Homeland Security and Governmental Affairs of the Senate; and

(B) the Committee on Transportation and Infrastructure and the Committee on Homeland Security of the House of Representatives.

(2) UNSAFE OR UNHEALTHY HOUSING UNIT.—The term “unsafe or unhealthy housing unit” means a unit of housing unit in which is present, at levels exceeding relevant governmental health or housing standards or guidelines, at least 1 of the following hazards:

(A) Physiological hazards, including the following:

(i) Dampness or microbial growth.

(ii) Lead-based paint.

(iii) Asbestos or manmade fibers.

(iv) Ionizing radiation.

(v) Biocides.

(vi) Carbon monoxide.

(vii) Volatile organic compounds.

(viii) Infectious agents.

(ix) Fine particulate matter.

(B) Psychological hazards, including the following:

(i) Ease of access by unlawful intruders.

(ii) Lighting issues.

(iii) Poor ventilation.

(iv) Safety hazards.

(v) Other hazards similar to the hazards specified in clauses (i) through (iv).

SEC. 11418. STUDY ON COAST GUARD HOUSING AUTHORITIES AND PRIVATIZED HOUSING.

(a) STUDY.—

(1) IN GENERAL.—Not later than 180 days after the date of enactment of this Act, the Comptroller General of the United States shall commence a study that—

(A) evaluates the authorities of the Coast Guard relating to construction, operation, and maintenance of housing provided to members of the Coast Guard and their dependents; and

(B) assesses other options to meet Coast Guard housing needs in rural and urban housing markets, including public-private partnerships, long-term lease agreements, privately owned housing, and any other housing option the Comptroller General identifies.

(2) ELEMENTS.—The study required under paragraph (1) shall include the following:

(A) A review of authorities, regulations, and policies available to the Secretary with respect to construction, maintenance, and operation of housing for members of the Coast Guard and their dependents, including unaccompanied member housing, that considers—

(i) housing that is owned and managed by the Coast Guard;

(ii) long-term leasing or extended-rental housing;

(iii) public-private partnerships or other privatized housing options for which the Secretary may enter into 1 or more contracts with a private entity to build, maintain, and manage privatized housing for members of the Coast Guard and their dependents;

(iv) on-installation and off-installation housing options, and the availability of, and authorities relating to, such options; and

(v) housing availability near Coast Guard units, readiness needs, and safety.

(B) A review of the housing-related authorities, regulations, and policies available to the Secretary of Defense, and an identification of the differences between such authorities afforded to the Secretary of Defense and the housing-related authorities, regulations, and policies afforded to the Secretary.

(C) A description of lessons learned, or recommendations for, the Coast Guard based on the use of private housing by the Department of Defense, including the recommendations set forth in the report of the Government Accountability Office titled "Privatized Military Housing: Update on DOD's Efforts to Address Oversight Challenges" (GAO-22-105866), issued in March 2022.

(D) An assessment of the extent to which the Secretary uses the authorities provided in subchapter IV of chapter 169 of title 10, United States Code.

(E) An analysis of immediate and long-term costs associated with housing owned and operated by the Coast Guard, as compared to opportunities for long-term leases, private housing, and other public-private partnerships in urban and remote locations.

(b) REPORT.—Not later than 1 year after the date of enactment of this Act, the Comptroller General shall submit to the appropriate committees of Congress a report on the results of the study conducted under subsection (a).

(c) BRIEFING.—Not later than 180 days after the date on which the report required under subsection (b) is submitted, the Commandant or the Secretary shall provide a briefing to the appropriate committees of Congress on—

(1) the actions the Commandant has, or has not, taken with respect to the results of the study;

(2) a plan for addressing areas identified in the report

that present opportunities for improving the housing options available to members of the Coast Guard and their dependents; and

(3) the need for, or potential manner of use of, any authorities the Coast Guard does not have with respect to housing, as compared to the Department of Defense.

(d) APPROPRIATE COMMITTEES OF CONGRESS.—In this section, the term "appropriate committees of Congress" means the Committee on Commerce, Science, and Transportation of the Senate and the Committee on Transportation and Infrastructure of the House of Representatives.

SEC. 11419. STRATEGY TO IMPROVE QUALITY OF LIFE AT REMOTE UNITS.

(a) IN GENERAL.—Not more than 180 days after the date of enactment of this Act, the Commandant shall develop a strategy to improve the quality of life for members of the Coast Guard and their dependents who are stationed in remote units.

(b) ELEMENTS.—The strategy developed under subsection (a) shall address the following:

(1) Methods to improve the availability or affordability of housing options for such members and their dependents through—

(A) Coast Guard-owned housing; or

(B) Coast Guard-facilitated housing.

(2) A review of whether current methods for determining the amount of basic housing allowances received by such members of the Coast Guard accurately reflect the costs of privately owned or privately rented housing in such areas.

(3) Methods to improve access by such members and their dependents to—

(A) medical, dental, and pediatric care; and

(B) behavioral health care that is covered under the TRICARE program (as defined in section 1072 of title 10, United States Code).

(4) Methods to increase access to child care services in such areas, including recommendations for increasing child care capacity and opportunities for care within the Coast Guard and

in the private sector.

(5) Methods to improve non-Coast Guard network internet access at remote units—

(A) to improve communications between members of the Coast Guard on active duty who are assigned or attached to a remote unit and the family members of such members who are not located in the same location as such member; and

(B) for other purposes such as education and training.

(6) Methods to support spouses and other dependents of members serving in such areas who face challenges specific to remote locations.

(7) Any other matter the Commandant considers appropriate.

(c) BRIEFING.—Not later than 180 days after the strategy developed under subsection (a) is completed, the Commandant shall provide to the Committee on Commerce, Science, and Transportation of the Senate and the Committee on Transportation and Infrastructure of the House of Representatives a briefing on the strategy.

(d) REMOTE UNIT DEFINED.—In this section, the term "remote unit" means a unit located in an area in which members of the Coast Guard and their dependents are eligible for TRICARE Prime Remote.

Subtitle D—Other Matters

SEC. 11420. REPORT ON AVAILABILITY OF EMERGENCY SUPPLIES FOR COAST GUARD PERSONNEL.

(a) IN GENERAL.—Not later than 180 days after the date of enactment of this Act, the Comptroller General of the United States shall submit to the Committee on Commerce, Science, and Transportation of the Senate and the Committee on Transportation and Infrastructure of the House of Representatives a report on the availability of appropriate emergency supplies at Coast Guard units.

(b) ELEMENTS.—The report required under subsection (a) shall include the following:

(1) An assessment of the extent to which—

(A) the Commandant ensures that Coast Guard units assess risks and plan accordingly to obtain and maintain appropriate emergency supplies; and

(B) Coast Guard units have emergency food and water supplies available according to local emergency preparedness needs.

(2) A description of any challenge the Commandant faces in planning for and maintaining adequate emergency supplies for Coast Guard personnel.

(c) PUBLICATION.—Not later than 90 days after the date of submission of the report required by subsection (a), the Commandant shall publish a strategy and recommendations in response to the report that includes—

(1) a plan for improving emergency preparedness and emergency supplies for Coast Guard units; and

(2) a process for periodic review and engagement with Coast Guard units to ensure emerging emergency response supply needs are achieved and maintained.

SEC. 11421. FLEET MIX ANALYSIS AND SHORE INFRASTRUCTURE INVESTMENT PLAN.

(a) FLEET MIX ANALYSIS.—

(1) IN GENERAL.—The Commandant shall conduct an updated fleet mix analysis that provides for a fleet mix sufficient, as determined by the Commandant—

(A) to carry out—

(i) the missions of the Coast Guard; and

(ii) emerging mission requirements; and

(B) to address—

(i) national security threats; and

(ii) the global deployment of the Coast Guard to counter great power competitors.

(2) REPORT.—Not later than 1 year after the date of enactment of this Act, the Commandant shall submit to Congress a report on the results of the updated fleet mix analysis required under paragraph (1).

(b) SHORE INFRASTRUCTURE INVESTMENT PLAN.—

(1) IN GENERAL.—The Commandant shall develop an updated shore infrastructure investment plan that includes—

(A) the construction of additional facilities to accommodate the updated fleet mix described in subsection (a)(1);

(B) improvements necessary to ensure that existing facilities meet requirements and remain operational for the lifespan of such fleet mix, including necessary improvements to information technology infrastructure;

(C) a timeline for the construction and improvement of the facilities described in subparagraphs (A) and (B); and

(D) a cost estimate for construction and life-cycle support of such facilities, including for necessary personnel.

(2) REPORT.—Not later than 1 year after the date on which the report under subsection (a)(2) is submitted, the Commandant shall submit to Congress a report on the plan required under paragraph (1).

TITLE CXV—MARITIME

Subtitle A—Vessel Safety

SEC. 11501. RESPONSES TO SAFETY RECOMMENDATIONS.

(a) IN GENERAL.—Chapter 7 of title 14, United States Code, is amended by adding at the end the following:

"SEC. 721. [14 U.S.C. 721] Responses to safety recommendations

"(a) IN GENERAL.—Not later than 90 days after the National Transportation Safety Board submits to the Commandant a recommendation, and supporting justification for such recommendation, relating to transportation safety, the Commandant shall submit to the National Transportation Safety Board a written response to the recommendation, including whether the Commandant—

"(1) concurs with the recommendation;

"(2) partially concurs with the recommendation; or

"(3) does not concur with the recommendation.

"(b) EXPLANATION OF CONCURRENCE.—The Commandant shall include in a response submitted under subsection (a)—

"(1) with respect to a recommendation with which the Commandant concurs or partially concurs, an explanation of the actions the Commandant intends to take to implement such recommendation or part of such recommendation; and

"(2) with respect to a recommendation with which the Commandant does not concur, the reasons the Commandant does not concur.

"(c) FAILURE TO RESPOND.—If the National Transportation Safety Board has not received the written response required under subsection (a) by the end of the time period described in such subsection, the National Transportation Safety Board shall notify the Committee on Commerce, Science, and Transportation of the Senate and the Committee on Transportation and Infrastructure of the House of Representatives that such response has not been received."

(b) CLERICAL AMENDMENT.—The analysis for chapter 7 of title 14, United States Code, is amended by adding at the end the following:

"721. Responses to safety recommendations."

SEC. 11502. [46 U.S.C. 3306 note] REQUIREMENTS FOR DUKW AMPHIBIOUS PASSENGER VESSELS.

(a) RULEMAKING REQUIRED.—

(1) IN GENERAL.—Not later than 6 months after the date of enactment of this Act, the Commandant shall initiate a rulemaking to establish additional safety standards for DUKW amphibious passenger vessels.

(2) DEADLINE FOR REGULATIONS.—The regulations issued under paragraph (1) shall take effect not later than 18 months after the Commandant promulgates a final rule pursuant to such paragraph.

(b) REQUIREMENTS.—The regulations required under subsection (a) shall include the following:

(1) A requirement that operators of DUKW amphibious passenger vessels provide reserve buoyancy for such vessels

through passive means, including watertight compartmentalization, built-in flotation, or such other means as determined appropriate by the Commandant, in order to ensure that such vessels remain afloat and upright in the event of flooding, including when carrying a full complement of passengers and crew.

(2) An identification, in consultation with the Under Secretary of Commerce for Oceans and Atmosphere, of limiting environmental conditions, such as weather, in which DUKW amphibious passenger vessels may safely operate and a requirement that such limiting conditions be described in the certificate of inspection of each DUKW amphibious passenger vessel.

(3) Requirements that an operator of a DUKW amphibious passenger vessel—

(A) proceed to the nearest harbor or safe refuge in any case in which a watch or warning is issued for wind speeds exceeding the wind speed equivalent used to certify the stability of such DUKW amphibious passenger vessel; and

(B) maintain and monitor a weather monitor radio receiver at the operator station of the vessel that is automatically activated by the warning alarm device of the National Weather Service.

(4) A requirement that—

(A) operators of DUKW amphibious passenger vessels inform passengers that seat belts may not be worn during waterborne operations;

(B) before the commencement of waterborne operations, a crew member shall visually check that the seatbelt of each passenger is unbuckled; and

(C) operators or crew maintain a log recording the actions described in subparagraphs (A) and (B).

(5) A requirement for annual training for operators and crew of DUKW amphibious passenger vessels, including—

(A) training for personal flotation and seat belt requirements, verifying the integrity of the vessel at the onset of each waterborne departure, identification of weather hazards, and use of National Weather Service resources prior to operation; and

(B) training for crew to respond to emergency situations, including flooding, engine compartment fires, man-overboard situations, and in water emergency egress procedures.

(c) CONSIDERATION.—In issuing the regulations required under subsection (a), the Commandant shall consider whether personal flotation devices should be required for the duration of the waterborne transit of a DUKW amphibious passenger vessel.

(d) WAIVER.—The Commandant may waive the reserve buoyancy requirements described in subsection (b)(1) for a DUKW amphibious passenger vessel if the Commandant certifies in writing, using the best available science, to the appropriate congressional committees that such requirement is not practicable or technically or practically achievable for such vessel.

(e) NOTICE TO PASSENGERS.—A DUKW amphibious passenger vessel that receives a waiver under subsection (d) shall provide a prominently displayed notice on its website, ticket counter, and each ticket for passengers that the vessel is exempt from meeting Coast Guard safety compliance standards concerning reserve buoyancy.

(f) INTERIM REQUIREMENTS.—Prior to issuing final regulations pursuant to subsection (a) and not later than 180 days after the date of enactment of this Act, the Commandant shall require that operators of DUKW amphibious passenger vessels implement the following requirements:

(1) Remove the canopies and any window coverings of such vessels for waterborne operations, or install in such vessels a canopy that does not restrict horizontal or vertical escape by passengers in the event of flooding or sinking.

(2) If a canopy and window coverings are removed from any such vessel pursuant to paragraph (1), require that all passengers wear a personal flotation device approved by the Coast Guard before the onset of waterborne operations of such vessel.

(3) Reengineer such vessels to permanently close all unnecessary access plugs and reduce all through-hull penetrations to the minimum number and size necessary for operation.

(4) Install in such vessels independently powered electric

bilge pumps that are capable of dewatering such vessels at the volume of the largest remaining penetration in order to supplement an operable Higgins pump or a dewatering pump of equivalent or greater capacity.

(5) Install in such vessels not fewer than 4 independently powered bilge alarms.

(6) Conduct an in-water inspection of any such vessel after each time a through-hull penetration of such vessel has been removed or uncovered.

(7) Verify through an in-water inspection the watertight integrity of any such vessel at the outset of each waterborne departure of such vessel.

(8) Install underwater LED lights that activate automatically in an emergency.

(9) Otherwise comply with any other provisions of relevant Coast Guard guidance or instructions in the inspection, configuration, and operation of such vessels.

(g) IMPLEMENTATION.—The Commandant shall implement the interim requirements under subsection (f) without regard to chapters 5 and 6 of title 5, United States Code, and Executive Order Nos. 12866 and 13563 (5 U.S.C. 601 note).

(h) DEFINITIONS.—In this section:

(1) APPROPRIATE CONGRESSIONAL COMMITTEES.—The term "appropriate congressional committees" means the Committee Transportation and Infrastructure of the House of Representatives and the Committee on Commerce, Science, and Transportation of the Senate.

(2) DUKW AMPHIBIOUS PASSENGER VESSEL.—The term "DUKW amphibious passenger vessel" means a vessel that uses, modifies, or is derived from the GMC DUKW-353 design, and which is operating as a small passenger vessel in waters subject to the jurisdiction of the United States, as defined in section 2.38 of title 33, Code of Federal Regulations (or a successor regulation).

SEC. 11503. EXONERATION AND LIMITATION OF LIABILITY FOR SMALL PASSENGER VESSELS.

(a) RESTRUCTURING.—Chapter 305 of title 46, United States Code, is amended—

(1) by inserting before section 30501 the following:

SUBCHAPTER "Subchapter I—General Provisions"

(2) by inserting before section 30503 the following:

SUBCHAPTER "Subchapter II—Exoneration and Limitation of Liability"

; and

(3) by redesignating sections 30503 through 30512 as sections 30521 through 30530, respectively.

(b) DEFINITIONS.—Section 30501 of title 46, United States Code, is amended to read as follows:

"SEC. 30501. Definitions

"In this chapter:

"(1) COVERED SMALL PASSENGER VESSEL.—The term '"covered small passenger vessel"'—

"(A) means a small passenger vessel, as defined in section 2101, that is—

"(i) not a wing-in-ground craft; and

"(ii) carrying—

"(I) not more than 49 passengers on an overnight domestic voyage; and

"(II) not more than 150 passengers on any voyage that is not an overnight domestic voyage; and

"(B) includes any wooden vessel constructed prior to March 11, 1996, carrying at least 1 passenger for hire.

"(2) OWNER.—The term '"owner"' includes a charterer that mans, supplies, and navigates a vessel at the charterer's own expense or by the charterer's own procurement."

(c) APPLICABILITY.—Section 30502 of title 46, United States Code, is amended to read as follows:

"SEC. 30502. Application

"(a) IN GENERAL.—Except as otherwise provided, this chapter (except section 30521) applies to seagoing vessels and vessels used on lakes or rivers or in inland navigation, including canal boats, barges, and lighters.

"(b) EXCEPTION.—This chapter (except for section 30526) shall not apply to covered small passenger vessels."

(d) PROVISIONS REQUIRING NOTICE OF CLAIM OR LIMITING TIME FOR BRINGING ACTION.—Section 30526(b) of title 46, United States Code, as redesignated by subsection (a), is amended—

(1) in paragraph (1)—

(A) by inserting ", in the case of seagoing vessels," after "personal injury or death"; and

(B) by inserting ", or in the case of covered small passenger vessels, to less than two years after the date of the injury or death" after "date of the injury or death"; and

(2) in paragraph (2)—

(A) by inserting ", in the case of seagoing vessels," after "personal injury or death"; and

(B) by inserting ", or in the case of covered small passenger vessels, to less than two years after the date of the injury or death" after "date of the injury or death".

(e) CHAPTER ANALYSIS.—The analysis for chapter 305 of title 46, United States Code, is amended—

(1) by inserting before the item relating to section 30501 the following:

"subchapter i— general provisions"

(2) by inserting after the item relating to section 30502 the following:

"subchapter ii— exoneration and limitation of liability"

(3) by striking the item relating to section 30501 and inserting the following:

"30501. Definitions."

; and

(4) by redesignating the items relating to sections 30503 through 30512 as items relating to sections 30521 through 30530, respectively.

(f) CONFORMING AMENDMENTS.—Title 46, United States Code,

is further amended—

(1) in section 14305(a)(5) by striking "section 30506" and inserting "section 30524";

(2) in section 30523(a), as redesignated by subsection (a), by striking "section 30506" and inserting "section 30524";

(3) in section 30524(b), as redesignated by subsection (a), by striking "section 30505" and inserting "section 30523"; and

(4) in section 30525, as redesignated by subsection (a)—

(A) in the matter preceding paragraph (1) by striking "sections 30505 and 30506" and inserting "sections 30523 and 30524";

(B) in paragraph (1) by striking "section 30505" and inserting "section 30523"; and

(C) in paragraph (2) by striking "section 30506(b)" and inserting "section 30524(b)".

SEC. 11504. [14 U.S.C. 501 note] AT-SEA RECOVERY OPERATIONS PILOT PROGRAM.

(a) IN GENERAL.—The Secretary shall conduct a pilot program to evaluate the potential use of remotely controlled or autonomous operation and monitoring of certain vessels for the purposes of—

(1) better understanding the complexities of such at-sea operations and potential risks to navigation safety, vessel security, maritime workers, the public, and the environment;

(2) gathering observational and performance data from monitoring the use of remotely-controlled or autonomous vessels; and

(3) assessing and evaluating regulatory requirements necessary to guide the development of future occurrences of such operations and monitoring activities.

(b) DURATION AND EFFECTIVE DATE.—The duration of the pilot program established under this section shall be not more than 5 years beginning on the date on which the pilot program is established, which shall be not later than 180 days after the date of enactment of this Act.

(c) AUTHORIZED ACTIVITIES.—The activities authorized under this section include—

(1) remote over-the-horizon monitoring operations related

to the active at-sea recovery of spaceflight components on an unmanned vessel or platform;

(2) procedures for the unaccompanied operation and monitoring of an unmanned spaceflight recovery vessel or platform; and

(3) unmanned vessel transits and testing operations without a physical tow line related to space launch and recovery operations, except within 12 nautical miles of a port.

(d) INTERIM AUTHORITY.—In recognition of potential risks to navigation safety, vessel security, maritime workers, the public, and the environment, and the unique circumstances requiring the use of remotely operated or autonomous vessels, the Secretary, in the pilot program established under subsection (a), may—

(1) allow remotely controlled or autonomous vessel operations to proceed consistent to the extent practicable under the proposed title 33, United States Code, and 46, United States Code, including navigation and manning laws and regulations;

(2) modify or waive applicable regulations and guidance as the Secretary considers appropriate to—

(A) allow remote and autonomous vessel at-sea operations and activities to occur while ensuring navigation safety; and

(B) ensure the reliable, safe, and secure operation of remotely-controlled or autonomous vessels; and

(3) require each remotely operated or autonomous vessel to be at all times under the supervision of 1 or more individuals—

(A) holding a merchant mariner credential which is suitable to the satisfaction of the Coast Guard; and

(B) who shall practice due regard for the safety of navigation of the autonomous vessel, to include collision avoidance.

(e) RULE OF CONSTRUCTION.—Nothing in this section shall be construed to authorize the Secretary to—

(1) permit foreign vessels to participate in the pilot program established under subsection (a);

(2) waive or modify applicable laws and regulations under the proposed title 33, United States Code, and title 46, United States Code, except to the extent authorized under subsection

(d)(2);

(3) waive or modify applicable laws and regulations under titles 49 and 51 of the United States Code; or

(4) waive or modify any regulations arising under international conventions.

(f) SAVINGS PROVISION.—Nothing in this section may be construed to authorize the employment in the coastwise trade of a vessel or platform that does not meet the requirements of sections 12112, 55102, 55103, and 55111 of title 46, United States Code.

(g) AUTHORITY UNAFFECTED.—Nothing in this section shall be construed to affect, impinge, or alter any authority of the Secretary of Transportation under titles 49 and 51, United States Code.

(h) BRIEFINGS.—The Secretary or the designee of the Secretary shall brief the Committee on Commerce, Science, and Transportation of the Senate and the Committee on Transportation and Infrastructure and the Committee on Science, Space, and Technology of the House of Representatives on the program established under subsection (a) on a quarterly basis.

(i) REPORT.—Not later than 180 days after the expiration of the pilot program established under subsection (a), the Secretary shall submit to the Committee on Commerce, Science, and Transportation of the Senate and the Committee on Transportation and Infrastructure and the Committee on Science, Space, and Technology of the House of Representatives a final report regarding an assessment of the execution of the pilot program and implications for maintaining navigation safety, the safety of maritime workers, and the preservation of the environment.

(j) GAO REPORT.—

(1) IN GENERAL.—Not later than 18 months after the date of enactment of this section, the Comptroller General of the United States shall submit to the Committee on Commerce, Science, and Transportation of the Senate and the Committee on Transportation and Infrastructure of the House of Representatives a report on the state of autonomous and remote technologies in the operation of shipboard equipment and the safe and secure navigation of vessels in Federal waters of the United States.

(2) ELEMENTS.—The report required under paragraph (1) shall include the following:

(A) An assessment of commercially available autonomous and remote technologies in the operation of shipboard equipment and the safe and secure navigation of vessels during the 10 years immediately preceding the date of the report.

(B) An analysis of the safety, physical security, cybersecurity, and collision avoidance risks and benefits associated with autonomous and remote technologies in the operation of shipboard equipment and the safe and secure navigation of vessels, including environmental considerations.

(C) An assessment of the impact of such autonomous and remote technologies, and all associated technologies, on labor, including—

(i) roles for credentialed and noncredentialed workers regarding such autonomous, remote, and associated technologies; and

(ii) training and workforce development needs associated with such technologies.

(D) An assessment and evaluation of regulatory requirements necessary to guide the development of future autonomous, remote, and associated technologies in the operation of shipboard equipment and safe and secure navigation of vessels.

(E) An assessment of the extent to which such technologies are being used in other countries and how such countries have regulated such technologies.

(F) Recommendations regarding authorization, infrastructure, and other requirements necessary for the implementation of such technologies in the United States.

(3) CONSULTATION.—The report required under paragraph (1) shall include, at a minimum, consultation with the maritime industry including—

(A) vessel operators, including commercial carriers, entities engaged in exploring for, developing, or producing resources, including non-mineral energy resources in its offshore areas, and supporting entities in the maritime industry;

(B) shipboard personnel impacted by any change to

autonomous vessel operations, in order to assess the various benefits and risks associated with the implementation of autonomous, remote, and associated technologies in the operation of shipboard equipment and safe and secure navigation of vessels and the impact such technologies would have on maritime jobs and maritime manpower;

(C) relevant federally funded research institutions, non-governmental organizations, and academia; and

(D) the commercial space industry.

(k) MERCHANT MARINER CREDENTIAL DEFINED.—In this section, the term "merchant mariner credential" means a merchant mariner license, certificate, or document that the Secretary is authorized to issue pursuant to title 46, United States Code.

SEC. 11505. [46 U.S.C. 3306 note] HISTORIC WOOD SAILING VESSELS.

(a) REPORT ON HISTORIC WOOD SAILING VESSELS.—

(1) IN GENERAL.—Not later than 1 year after the date of enactment of this Act, the Comptroller General of the United States shall submit to the Committee on Commerce, Science, and Transportation of the Senate and the Committee on Transportation and Infrastructure of the House of Representatives a report evaluating the practicability of the application of section 3306(n)(3)(A)(v) of title 46, United States Code, to historic wood sailing vessels.

(2) ELEMENTS.—The report required under paragraph (1) shall include the following:

(A) An assessment of the compliance, as of the date on which the report is submitted under paragraph (1), of historic wood sailing vessels with section 3306(n)(3)(A)(v) of title 46, United States Code.

(B) An assessment of the safety record of historic wood sailing vessels.

(C) An assessment of any risk that modifying the requirements under such section would have on the safety of passengers and crew of historic wood sailing vessels.

(D) An evaluation of the economic practicability of requiring the compliance of historic wood sailing vessels with such section and whether such compliance would meaningfully improve safety of passengers and crew in a manner that is both feasible and economically practicable.

(E) Any recommendations to improve safety in addition to, or in lieu of, applying such section to historic wood sailing vessels.

(F) Any other recommendations as the Comptroller General determines are appropriate with respect to the applicability of such section to historic wood sailing vessels.

(G) An assessment to determine if historic wood sailing vessels could be provided an exemption to such section and the changes to legislative or rulemaking requirements, including modifications to section 177.500(q) of title 46, Code of Federal Regulations (as in effect on the date of enactment of this Act), that are necessary to provide the Commandant the authority to make such exemption or to otherwise provide for such exemption.

(b) CONSULTATION.—In completing the report required under subsection (a), the Comptroller General may consult with—

(1) the National Transportation Safety Board;

(2) the Coast Guard; and

(3) the maritime industry, including relevant federally funded research institutions, nongovernmental organizations, and academia.

(c) WAIVER FOR COVERED HISTORIC VESSELS.—The captain of a port may waive the requirements of section 3306(n)(3)(A)(v) of title 46, United States Code, with respect to covered historic vessels for not more than 2 years after the date on which the report required under subsection (a) is submitted.

(d) WAIVER FOR OTHER HISTORIC WOOD SAILING VESSELS.—

(1) IN GENERAL.—The captain of a port may, upon the request of the owner or operator of a historic wood sailing vessel that is not a covered historic vessel, waive the requirements of section 3306(n)(3)(A)(v) of title 46, United States Code, with respect to the historic wood sailing vessel for not more than 2 years after date on which the report required under subsection (a) is submitted, if the captain of the port—

(A) determines that it is technically infeasible for the

historic wood sailing vessel to comply with the requirements described in section 3306(n)(3)(A)(v) of title 46, United States Code, due to its age; and

(B) approves the alternative arrangements proposed for the historic wood sailing vessel in accordance with paragraph (2).

(2) REQUEST AND ALTERNATIVE ARRANGEMENTS.—An owner or operator of a historic wood sailing vessel requesting a waiver under paragraph (1) shall submit such a request to the captain of a port that includes the alternative arrangements the owner or operator will take to ensure an equivalent level of safety, to the maximum extent practicable, to the requirements under section 3306(n)(3)(A)(v) of title 46, United States Code.

(e) SAVINGS CLAUSE.—Nothing in this section shall limit any authority available, as of the date of enactment of this Act, to the captain of a port with respect to safety measures or any other authority as necessary for the safety of historic wood sailing vessels.

(f) NOTICE TO PASSENGERS.—Any vessel that receives a waiver under subsection (c) or subsection (d) shall, beginning on the date on which the requirements under section 3306(n)(3)(v) of title 46, United States Code, take effect, provide a prominently displayed notice on its website, ticket counter, and each ticket for a passenger that the vessel is exempt from meeting the Coast Guard safety compliance standards concerning egress as described under such section.

(g) DEFINITIONS.—In this section:

(1) COVERED HISTORIC VESSELS.—The term "covered historic vessels" means each of the following:

(A) Adventuress (Official Number 210877).

(B) American Eagle (Official Number 229913).

(C) Angelique (Official Number 623562).

(D) Heritage (Official Number 649561).

(E) J & E Riggin (Official Number 226422).

(F) Ladona (Official Number 222228).

(G) Lady Washington (Official Number 944970).

(H) Lettie G. Howard (Official Number 222838).

(I) Lewis R. French (Official Number 015801).

(J) Mary Day (Official Number 288714).

(K) Stephen Taber (Official Number 115409).

(L) Victory Chimes (Official Number 136784).

(M) Grace Bailey (Official Number 085754).

(N) Mercantile (Official Number 214388).

(O) Mistress (Official Number 509004).

(P) Wendameen (Official Number 210173).

(2) HISTORIC WOOD SAILING VESSEL.—The term "historic wood sailing vessel" means a covered small passenger vessel, as defined in section 3306(n)(5) of title 46, United States Code, that—

(A) has overnight passenger accommodations;

(B) is a wood sailing vessel;

(C) has a hull constructed of wood;

(D) is principally equipped for propulsion by sail, even if the vessel has an auxiliary means of production;

(E) has no fewer than three masts; and

(F) was constructed before 1986.

SEC. 11506. CERTIFICATES OF NUMBERS FOR UNDOCUMENTED VESSELS.

Section 12304(a) of title 46, United States Code, is amended—

(1) by striking "shall be pocketsized,"; and

(2) by inserting "in hard copy or digital form. Any certificate issued in hard copy under this section shall be pocketsized. The certificate shall be" after "and may be".

SEC. 11507. COMPTROLLER GENERAL REVIEW AND REPORT ON COAST GUARD OVERSIGHT OF THIRD-PARTY ORGANIZATIONS.

(a) IN GENERAL.—Not later than 1 year after the date of enactment of this Act, the Comptroller General of the United States shall initiate a review that assesses the oversight of the Coast Guard of third-party organizations.

(b) ELEMENTS.—In carrying out the review required under subsection (a), the Comptroller General shall analyze the following:

(1) Coast Guard use of third-party organizations in the prevention mission of the Coast Guard and the extent to which

the Coast Guard plans to increase such use to enhance prevention mission performance, including resource use and specialized expertise.

(2) The extent to which the Coast Guard has assessed the potential risks and benefits of using third-party organizations to support prevention mission activities.

(3) The extent to which the Coast Guard provides oversight of third-party organizations authorized to support prevention mission activities.

(c) REPORT.—Not later than 1 year after initiating the review required under subsection (a), the Comptroller General shall submit to the Committee on Commerce, Science, and Transportation of the Senate and the Committee on Transportation and Infrastructure of the House of Representatives the results of such review.

SEC. 11508. [46 U.S.C. 8104 note] ARTICULATED TUG-BARGE MANNING.

(a) IN GENERAL.—Notwithstanding the watch setting requirements set forth in section 8104 of title 46, United States Code, the Secretary shall authorize an Officer in Charge, Marine Inspection to issue an amended certificate of inspection that does not require engine room watch setting to inspected towing vessels certificated prior to July 19, 2022, forming part of an articulated tug-barge unit, provided that such vessels are equipped with engineering control and monitoring systems of a type accepted for no engine room watch setting under a previously approved minimum safe manning document or certificate of inspection for articulated tug-barge units.

(b) DEFINITIONS.—In this section:

(1) CERTIFICATE OF INSPECTION.—The term "certificate of inspection" means a certificate of inspection under subchapter M of chapter I of title 46, Code of Federal Regulations.

(2) INSPECTED TOWING VESSEL.—The term "inspected towing vessel" means a vessel issued a certificate of inspection.

SEC. 11509. FISHING VESSEL SAFETY.

(a) IN GENERAL.—Chapter 45 of title 46, United States Code, is amended—

(1) in section 4502(f)(2) by striking "certain vessels

described in subsection (b) if requested by the owner or operator; and" and inserting the following:"vessels described in subsection (b) if—

"(A) requested by an owner or operator; or

"(B) the vessel is—

"(i) at least 50 feet overall in length;

"(ii) built before July 1, 2013; and

"(iii) 25 years of age or older; and"

(2) in section 4503(b) by striking "Except as provided in section 4503a, subsection (a)" and inserting "Subsection (a)"; and

(3) by repealing section 4503a.

(b) [46 U.S.C. 4502 note] ALTERNATIVE SAFETY COMPLIANCE AGREEMENTS.—Nothing in this section or the amendments made by this section shall be construed to affect or apply to any alternative compliance and safety agreement entered into by the Coast Guard that is in effect on the date of enactment of this Act.

(c) CONFORMING AMENDMENTS.—The analysis for chapter 45 of title 46, United States Code, is amended by striking the item relating to section 4503a.

SEC. 11510. [46 U.S.C. 3508 note] EXEMPTIONS FOR CERTAIN PASSENGER VESSELS.

Notwithstanding any other provision of law, requirements authorized under sections 3508 and 3509 of title 46, United States Code, shall not apply to any passenger vessel, as defined in section 2101 of such title —

(1) that carries in excess of 250 passengers;

(2) that is, or was, in operation exclusively within the inland rivers and internal waters of the United States on voyages inside the Boundary Line, as defined in section 103 of such title, on or before July 27, 2030; and

(3) the operators or charterers of which operated any documented vessels with a coastwise endorsement prior to January 1, 2024.

Subtitle B—Merchant Mariner

Credentialing

SEC. 11511. [46 U.S.C. 7502 note] MODERNIZING MERCHANT MARINER CREDENTIALING SYSTEM.

(a) REPORT.—

(1) IN GENERAL.—Not later than 90 days after the date of enactment of this Act, the Commandant shall submit to the Committees on Commerce, Science, and Transportation and Appropriations of the Senate, and the Committees on Transportation and Infrastructure and Appropriations of the House of Representatives, a report on the financial, human, and information technology infrastructure resources needed to establish an electronic merchant mariner licensing and documentation system.

(2) LEGISLATIVE AND REGULATORY SUGGESTIONS.—In preparing the report described in paragraph (1), the Commandant—

(A) shall include recommendations for any legislative or administrative actions as the Commandant determines necessary to establish the electronic merchant mariner licensing and documentation system described in paragraph (1) as soon as possible; and

(B) may include findings, conclusions, or recommendations from the study conducted under subsection (b).

(b) STUDY.—

(1) IN GENERAL.—In preparing the report required under subsection (a), the Commandant and the Administrator of the Maritime Administration, in coordination with the Commander of the United States Transportation Command, shall conduct a study on the feasibility of developing and maintaining a database as part of an electronic merchant mariner licensing and documentation system that—

(A) contains records with respect to each credentialed mariner, including credential validity, drug and alcohol testing results, and information on any final adjudicated agency action involving a credentialed mariner or regarding any involvement in a marine casualty; and

(B) maintains such records in a manner that allows data to be readily accessed by the Federal Government for the purpose of assessing workforce needs and for the purpose of the economic and national security of the United States.

(2) CONTENTS.—The study required under paragraph (1) shall—

(A) include an assessment of the resources, including information technology, and authorities necessary to develop and maintain the database described in such paragraph;

(B) specifically address ways to protect the privacy interests of any individual whose information may be contained within such database, which shall include limiting access to the database or having access to the database be monitored by, or accessed through, a member of the Coast Guard; and

(C) address the feasibility of incorporating in such database a reporting mechanism to alert the Administrator of the Maritime Administration each time a mariner's credential is reinstated upon completion of a period of suspension as the result of a suspension and revocation proceeding under section 7702 of title 46, United States Code, with details about the violation that led to such suspension.

(c) ELECTRONIC MERCHANT MARINER LICENSING AND DOCUMENTATION SYSTEM.—Notwithstanding any other provision of law, not later than 2 years after the date of enactment of this Act, the Secretary shall implement an electronic merchant mariner licensing and documentation system.

SEC. 11512. ASSESSMENT REGARDING APPLICATION PROCESS FOR MERCHANT MARINER CREDENTIALS.

(a) IN GENERAL.—The Secretary shall conduct an assessment to determine the resources, including personnel and computing resources, required to reduce the amount of time necessary to process an application for a merchant mariner credential to not more than 2 weeks after the date of receipt of such application.

(b) BRIEFING REQUIRED.—Not later than 180 days after the date of enactment of this Act, the Secretary shall provide a briefing to the Committee on Commerce, Science, and Transportation of the Senate and the Committee on Transportation and Infrastructure of the House of Representatives with the results of the assessment required under subsection (a).

SEC. 11513. GAO REPORT.

(a) IN GENERAL.—Not later than 180 days after the date of enactment of this Act, the Comptroller General of the United States shall prepare and submit a report to Congress that evaluates the processes of the National Maritime Center for processing and approving merchant mariner credentials, as of the date of enactment of this Act.

(b) CONTENTS.—In preparing the report required under subsection (a), the Comptroller General shall—

(1) analyze the effectiveness of the merchant mariner credentialing process, as of the date of enactment of this Act;

(2) analyze the backlogs relating to the merchant mariner credentialing process and the reasons for such backlogs; and

(3) provide recommendations for improving and expediting the merchant mariner credentialing process, including funding needed to support improved processing times.

SEC. 11514. [46 U.S.C. 7302 note] MILITARY TO MARINERS ACT OF 2022.

(a) SHORT TITLE.—This section may be cited as the "Military to Mariners Act of 2022".

(b) MODIFICATION OF SEA SERVICE REQUIREMENTS FOR MERCHANT MARINER CREDENTIALS FOR VETERANS AND MEMBERS OF THE UNIFORMED SERVICES.—

(1) REVIEW AND REGULATIONS.—Notwithstanding any other provision of law, not later than 2 years after the date of enactment of this Act, the Secretary shall—

(A) review and examine—

(i) the timeframes and impediments for veterans and members of the uniformed services to receive a merchant mariner credential;

(ii) the classifications of sea service acquired through training and service as a member of the

Uniformed Services and level of equivalence such service has with respect to sea service on merchant vessels; and

(iii) the amount of sea service, including percent of the total time onboard for purposes of equivalent underway service, that will be accepted as required experience for all endorsements for applicants for a merchant mariner credential who are veterans or members of the Uniformed Services; and

(B) issue new regulations to—

(i) streamline, ensure the accuracy of, and expedite the transfer, review and acceptance of information pertaining to training and sea time for applicants for a merchant mariner credential who are veterans or members of the Uniformed Services;

(ii) increase the acceptable percentages of time equivalent to sea service for such applicants pursuant to findings of the review and examination conducted under subparagraph (A); and

(iii) reduce burdens and create a means of alternative compliance to demonstrate instructor competency for Standards of Training, Certification and Watchkeeping for Seafarers courses.

(2) CONSULTATION.—In carrying out paragraph (2), the Secretary shall consult with the National Merchant Marine Personnel Advisory Committee and shall take into account the present and future needs of the United States Merchant Marine labor workforce.

(3) REPORT.—Not later than 180 days after the date of enactment of this Act, the United States Committee on the Marine Transportation System shall submit to the Committees on Commerce, Science, and Transportation and Armed Services of the Senate and the Committees on Transportation and Infrastructure and Armed Services of the House of Representatives, a report that contains an update on the activities carried out to implement—

(A) the July 2020 report by the Committee on the Marine Transportation System to the White House Office of Trade and Manufacturing Policy on the implementation of Executive Order 13860 (84 Fed. Reg. 8407; relating to supporting the transition of active duty servicemembers and military veterans into the Merchant Marine); and

(B) section 3511 of the National Defense Authorization Act for Fiscal Year 2020 (46 U.S.C. 3702 note).

(c) ASSESSMENT OF SKILLBRIDGE FOR EMPLOYMENT AS A MERCHANT MARINER.—The Secretary, in collaboration with the Secretary of Defense, shall assess the use of the SkillBridge program of the Department of Defense as a means for transitioning active duty sea service personnel to employment as merchant mariners.

SEC. 11515. [46 U.S.C. 7302 note] DEFINITIONS.

In this subtitle:

(1) CREDENTIALED MARINER.—The term "credentialed mariner" means an individual with a merchant mariner credential.

(2) MERCHANT MARINER CREDENTIAL.—The term "merchant mariner credential" has the meaning given such term in section 7510(d) of title 46, United States Code.

(3) UNIFORMED SERVICES.—The term "uniformed services" has the meaning given the term "uniformed services" in section 2101 of title 5, United States Code.

Subtitle C—Other Matters

SEC. 11516. [46 U.S.C. 8701 note] NONOPERATING INDIVIDUAL.

Section 8313(b) of the William M. (Mac) Thornberry National Defense Authorization Act for Fiscal Year 2021 (Public Law 116-283) is amended by striking "the date that is 2 years after the date of the enactment of this Act" and inserting "January 1, 2025".

SEC. 11517. OCEANOGRAPHIC RESEARCH VESSELS.

(a) REPORT REQUIRED.—Not later than 180 days after the date of enactment of this Act, the Secretary of Transportation, in consultation with the Secretary, shall submit to the Committee on Transportation and Infrastructure of the House of Representatives and the Committee on Commerce, Science, and Transportation of the Senate a report detailing the total number of vessels known or estimated to operate or to have operated under section 50503 of title 46, United States Code, during each of the past 10 fiscal years.

(b) CONTENTS.—The report required under subsection (a) shall include the following elements:

(1) The total number of foreign-flagged vessels known or estimated to operate or to have operated as oceanographic research vessels (as such term is defined in section 2101 of title 46, United States Code) during each of the past 10 fiscal years.

(2) The total number of United States-flagged vessels known or estimated to operate or to have operated as oceanographic research vessels (as such term is defined section 2101 of title 46, United States Code) during each of the past 10 fiscal years.

SEC. 11518. PORT ACCESS ROUTES BRIEFING.

(a) ATLANTIC COAST PORT ACCESS ROUTE.—Not later than 30 days after the date of enactment of this Act, and not less than every 30 days thereafter until the requirements of section 70003 of title 46, United States Code, are fully executed with respect to the Atlantic Coast Port Access Route, the Secretary shall brief the Committee on Transportation and Infrastructure of the House of Representatives and the Committee on Commerce, Science, and Transportation of the Senate on any progress made to execute such requirements.

(b) OTHER COAST PORT ACCESS ROUTES.—Not later than 180 days after the date of enactment of this Act, and not less than every 180 days thereafter until the requirements of section 70003 of title 46, United States Code, are fully executed with respect to each of the Alaskan Arctic, Gulf of Mexico and Pacific Coast port access route studies, the Secretary shall brief the Committee on Transportation and Infrastructure of the House of Representatives and the Committee on Commerce, Science, and Transportation of the Senate on the status of each study and the implementation of any recommendations made in each such study.

SEC. 11519. DEFINITION OF STATELESS VESSEL.

Section 70502(d)(1) of title 46, United States Code, is amended—

(1) in subparagraph (B) by striking "and" after the semicolon;

(2) in subparagraph (C) by striking the period at the end and inserting "; and"; and

(3) by adding at the end the following new subparagraph:

"(D) a vessel aboard which no individual, on request of an officer of the United States authorized to enforce applicable provisions of United States law, claims to be the master or is identified as the individual in charge, and that has no other claim of nationality or registry under paragraph (1) or (2) of subsection (e)."

SEC. 11520. LIMITATION ON RECOVERY FOR CERTAIN INJURIES INCURRED IN AQUACULTURE ACTIVITIES.

(a) IN GENERAL.—Section 30104 of title 46, United States Code, is amended—

(1) by inserting "(a) In General.—" before the first sentence; and

(2) by adding at the end the following:

"(b) LIMITATION ON RECOVERY BY AQUACULTURE WORKERS.—

"(1) IN GENERAL.—For purposes of subsection (a), the term 'seaman' does not include an individual who—

"(A) is an aquaculture worker if State workers' compensation is available to such individual; and

"(B) was, at the time of injury, engaged in aquaculture in a place where such individual had lawful access.

"(2) AQUACULTURE WORKER DEFINED.—In this subsection, the term 'aquaculture worker' means an individual who—

"(A) is employed by a commercial enterprise that is involved in the controlled cultivation and harvest of aquatic plants and animals, including—

"(i) the cleaning, processing, or canning of fish and fish products;

"(ii) the cultivation and harvesting of shellfish; and

"(iii) the controlled growing and harvesting of other aquatic species;

"(B) does not hold a license issued under section 7101(c); and

"(C) is not required to hold a merchant mariner credential under part F of subtitle II."

(b) [46 U.S.C. 30104 note] APPLICABILITY.—The amendments made by this section shall apply to an injury incurred on or after the date of enactment of this Act.

SEC. 11521. REPORT ON SECURING VESSELS AND CARGO.

(a) IN GENERAL.—Not later than 1 year after the date of enactment of this Act, the Comptroller General of the United States shall conduct a study that assesses the efforts of the Coast Guard with respect to securing vessels and maritime cargo bound for the United States from national security related risks and threats.

(b) ELEMENTS.—In conducting the study under subsection (a), the Comptroller General shall assess the following:

(1) Programs of the Coast Guard to secure vessels and maritime cargo bound for the United States from national security related risks and threats and the extent to which such programs cover the critical components of the global supply chain.

(2) The extent to which the Coast Guard has implemented leading practices in such programs, including the extent to which the Coast Guard has collaborated with foreign countries or foreign ports that ship goods to the United States to implement such leading practices.

(3) The extent to which the Coast Guard has assessed the effectiveness of such programs.

(c) REPORT.—Upon completion of the study conducted under subsection (a), the Comptroller General shall submit to the Committee on Commerce, Science, and Transportation of the Senate and the Committee on Transportation and Infrastructure of the House of Representatives the results of the study conducted under this section.

SEC. 11522. REPORT ON ENFORCEMENT OF COASTWISE LAWS.

Not later than 1 year of the date of enactment of this Act, the Commandant shall submit to Congress a report describing any changes to the enforcement of chapters 121 and 551 of title 46,

United States Code, as a result of the amendments to section 4(a)(1) of the Outer Continental Shelf Lands Act (43 U.S.C. 1333(a)(1)) made by section 9503 of the William M. (Mac) Thornberry National Defense Authorization Act for Fiscal Year 2021 (Public Law 116-283).

SEC. 11523. LAND CONVEYANCE, SHARPE ARMY DEPOT, LATHROP, CALIFORNIA.

Not later than 1 year after the date of enactment of this Act, the Administrator of the Maritime Administration shall complete the land conveyance required under section 2833 of the William M. (Mac) Thornberry National Defense Authorization Act for Fiscal Year 2021 (Public Law 116-283).

SEC. 11524. [46 U.S.C. 70022 note] PROHIBITION ON ENTRY AND OPERATION.

(a) PROHIBITION.—

(1) IN GENERAL.—Except as otherwise provided in this section, during the period in which Executive Order 14065 (87 Fed. Reg. 10293, relating to blocking certain Russian property or transactions), or any successor Executive Order is in effect, no vessel described in subsection (b) may enter or operate in the navigable waters of the United States or transfer cargo in any port or place under the jurisdiction of the United States.

(2) LIMITATIONS ON APPLICATION.—

(A) IN GENERAL.—The prohibition under paragraph (1) shall not apply with respect to a vessel described in subsection (b) if the Secretary of State determines that—

(i) the vessel is owned or operated by a Russian national or operated by the government of the Russian Federation; and

(ii) it is in the national security interest not to apply the prohibition to such vessel.

(B) NOTICE.—Not later than 15 days after making a determination under subparagraph (A), the Secretary of State shall submit to the Committee on Foreign Affairs and the Committee on Transportation and Infrastructure of the House of Representatives and the Committee on Foreign Relations and the Committee on Commerce, Science, and Transportation of the Senate written notice of the determination and the basis upon which the determination was made.

(C) PUBLICATION.—The Secretary of State shall publish a notice in the Federal Register of each determination made under subparagraph (A).

(3) SAVINGS CLAUSE.—The prohibition under paragraph (1) shall not apply with respect to vessels engaged in passage permitted under international law.

(b) VESSELS DESCRIBED.—A vessel referred to in subsection (a) is a vessel owned or operated by a Russian national or operated by the government of the Russian Federation.

(c) INFORMATION AND PUBLICATION.—The Secretary, with the concurrence of the Secretary of State, shall—

(1) maintain timely information on the registrations of all foreign vessels owned or operated by or on behalf of the Government of the Russian Federation, a Russian national, or a entity organized under the laws of the Russian Federation or any jurisdiction within the Russian Federation; and

(2) periodically publish in the Federal Register a list of the vessels described in paragraph (1).

(d) NOTIFICATION OF GOVERNMENTS.—

(1) IN GENERAL.—The Secretary of State shall notify each government, the agents or instrumentalities of which are maintaining a registration of a foreign vessel that is included on a list published under subsection (c)(2), not later than 30 days after such publication, that all vessels registered under such government's authority are subject to subsection (a).

(2) ADDITIONAL NOTIFICATION.—In the case of a government that continues to maintain a registration for a vessel that is included on such list after receiving an initial notification under paragraph (1), the Secretary shall issue an additional notification to such government not later than 120 days after the publication of a list under subsection (c)(2).

(e) NOTIFICATION OF VESSELS.—Upon receiving a notice of arrival under section 70001(a)(5) of title 46, United States Code, from a vessel described in subsection (b), the Secretary shall notify the master of such vessel that the vessel may not enter or operate in the navigable waters of the United States or transfer cargo in any port or place under the jurisdiction of the United States, unless—

(1) the Secretary of State has made a determination under subsection (a)(2); or

(2) the Secretary allows provisional entry of the vessel, or transfer of cargo from the vessel, under subsection (f).

(f) PROVISIONAL ENTRY OR CARGO TRANSFER.—Notwithstanding any other provision of this section, the Secretary may allow provisional entry of, or transfer of cargo from, a vessel, if such entry or transfer is necessary for the safety of the vessel or persons aboard.

SEC. 11525. FLOATING DRY DOCKS.

Section 55122(a) of title 46, United States Code, is amended—

(1) in paragraph (1)(C)—

(A) by striking "2015; and" and inserting "2015; or";

(B) by striking "(C) was" and inserting the following:

"(C)(i) was"

; and

(C) by adding at the end the following:

"(ii) had a letter of intent for purchase by such shipyard or affiliate signed prior to such date of enactment; and"

; and

(2) in paragraph (2) by inserting "or, in the case of a dry dock described in paragraph (1)(C)(ii), occurs between Honolulu, Hawaii, and Pearl Harbor, Hawaii" before the period at the end.

SEC. 11526. UPDATED REQUIREMENTS FOR FISHING CREW AGREEMENTS.

Section 10601(b) of title 46, United States Code, is amended—

(1) in paragraph (2) by striking "and" after the semicolon;

(2) by redesignating paragraph (3) as paragraph (4); and

(3) by inserting after paragraph (2) the following:

"(3) in the case of a seaman employed on a vessel that is a catcher processor or fish processing vessel that employs more than 25 crewmembers, include a requirement that each crewmember shall be served not less than three meals a day that—

"(A) total not less than 3,100 calories; and

"(B) include adequate water and minerals in accordance with the United States Recommended Daily Allowances; and"

TITLE CXVI—SEXUAL ASSAULT AND SEXUAL HARASSMENT PREVENTION AND RESPONSE

SEC. 11601. DEFINITIONS.

(a) IN GENERAL.—Section 2101 of title 46, United States Code, is amended—

(1) by redesignating paragraphs (45) through (54) as paragraphs (47) through (56), respectively; and

(2) by inserting after paragraph (44) the following:

"(45) 'sexual assault' means any form of abuse or contact as defined in chapter 109A of title 18, or a substantially similar offense under State, local, or Tribal law.

"(46) 'sexual harassment' means—

"(A) conduct that—

"(i) involves unwelcome sexual advances, requests for sexual favors, or deliberate or repeated offensive comments or gestures of a sexual nature if any—

"(I) submission to such conduct is made either explicitly or implicitly a term or condition of employment, pay, career, benefits, or entitlements of the individual;

"(II) submission to, or rejection, of such conduct by an individual is used as a basis for decisions affecting that individual's job, pay, career, benefits, or entitlements;

"(III) such conduct has the purpose or effect of unreasonably interfering with an individual's work performance or creates an intimidating, hostile, or offensive work environment; or

"(IV) conduct may have been by an individual's supervisor, a supervisor in another area, a co-worker, or another credentialed mariner; and

"(ii) is so severe or pervasive that a reasonable person would perceive, and the victim does perceive, the environment as hostile or offensive;

"(B) any use or condonation associated with first-hand or personal knowledge, by any individual in a supervisory or command position, of any form of sexual behavior to control, influence, or affect the career, pay, benefits, entitlements, or employment of a subordinate; and

"(C) any intentional or repeated unwelcome verbal comment or gesture of a sexual nature towards or about an individual by the individual's supervisor, a supervisor in another area, a coworker, or another credentialed mariner."

(b) REPORT.—The Commandant shall submit to the Committee on Transportation and Infrastructure of the House of Representatives and the Committee on Commerce, Science, and Transportation of the Senate a report describing any changes the Commandant may propose to the definitions added by the amendments in subsection (a).

(c) CONFORMING AMENDMENTS.—

(1) AUTHORITY TO EXEMPT CERTAIN VESSELS.—Section 2113(3) of title 46, United States Code, is amended by striking "section 2101(51)(A)" and inserting "section 2101(53)(A)"

(2) UNINSPECTED PASSENGER VESSELS.—Section 4105 of title 46, United States Code, is amended—

(A) in subsections (b)(1) and (c) by striking "section 2101(51)" each place it appears and inserting "section 2101"; and

(B) in subsection (d) by striking "section 2101(51)(A)" and inserting "section 2101(53)(A)"

(3) GENERAL AUTHORITY.—Section 1131(a)(1)(E) of title 49, United States Code, is amended by striking "section 2101(46)"

and inserting "section 116"

SEC. 11602. CONVICTED SEX OFFENDER AS GROUNDS FOR DENIAL.

(a) IN GENERAL.—Chapter 75 of title 46, United States Code, is amended by adding at the end the following:

"SEC. 7511. [46 U.S.C. 7511] Convicted sex offender as grounds for denial

"(a) SEXUAL ABUSE.—A license, certificate of registry, or merchant mariner's document authorized to be issued under this part shall be denied to an individual who has been convicted of a sexual offense prohibited under—

"(1) chapter 109A of title 18, except for subsection (b) of section 2244 of title 18; or

"(2) a substantially similar offense under State, local, or Tribal law.

"(b) ABUSIVE SEXUAL CONTACT.—A license, certificate of registry, or merchant mariner's document authorized to be issued under this part may be denied to an individual who within 5 years before applying for the license, certificate, or document, has been convicted of a sexual offense prohibited under subsection (b) of section 2244 of title 18, or a substantially similar offense under State, local, or Tribal law."

(b) CLERICAL AMENDMENT.—The analysis for chapter 75 of title 46, United States Code, is amended by adding at the end the following:

"7511. Convicted sex offender as grounds for denial."

SEC. 11603. SEXUAL HARASSMENT OR SEXUAL ASSAULT AS GROUNDS FOR SUSPENSION OR REVOCATION.

(a) IN GENERAL.—Chapter 77 of title 46, United States Code, is amended by inserting after section 7704 the following:

"SEC. 7704a. [46 U.S.C. 7704a] Sexual harassment or sexual assault as grounds for suspension or revocation

"(a) SEXUAL HARASSMENT.—If it is shown at a hearing under this chapter that a holder of a license, certificate of registry, or merchant mariner's document issued under this part, within 5 years before the beginning of the suspension and revocation proceedings, is the subject of an official finding of sexual harassment, then the license, certificate of registry, or merchant mariner's document may be suspended or revoked.

"(b) SEXUAL ASSAULT.—If it is shown at a hearing under this chapter that a holder of a license, certificate of registry, or merchant mariner's document issued under this part, within 10 years before the beginning of the suspension and revocation proceedings, is the subject of an official finding of sexual assault, then the license, certificate of registry, or merchant mariner's document shall be revoked.

"(c) OFFICIAL FINDING.—

"(1) IN GENERAL.—In this section, the term 'official finding' means—

"(A) a legal proceeding or agency finding or decision that determines the individual committed sexual harassment or sexual assault in violation of any Federal, State, local, or Tribal law or regulation; or

"(B) a determination after an investigation by the Coast Guard that, by a preponderance of the evidence, the individual committed sexual harassment or sexual assault if the investigation affords appropriate due process rights to the subject of the investigation.

"(2) ADMINISTRATIVE LAW JUDGE REVIEW.—

"(A) COAST GUARD INVESTIGATION.—A determination under paragraph (1)(B) shall be reviewed and affirmed by an administrative law judge within the same proceeding as any suspension or revocation of a license, certificate of registry, or merchant mariner's document under subsection (a) or (b).

"(B) LEGAL PROCEEDING.—A determination under paragraph (1)(A) that an individual committed sexual harassment or sexual assault is conclusive in suspension and revocation proceedings."

(b) CLERICAL AMENDMENT.—The analysis for chapter 77 of title 46, United States Code, is amended by inserting after the item relating to section 7704 the following:

"7704a. Sexual harassment or sexual assault as grounds for suspension or revocation."

SEC. 11604. ACCOMMODATION; NOTICES.

Section 11101 of title 46, United States Code, is amended—

(1) in subsection (a)(3) by striking "and" at the end;

(2) in subsection (a)(4) by striking the period at the end and inserting "; and";

(3) in subsection (a) by adding at the end the following:

"(5) each crew berthing area shall be equipped with information regarding—

"(A) vessel owner or company policies prohibiting sexual assault and sexual harassment, retaliation, and drug and alcohol usage; and

"(B) procedures and resources to report crimes, including sexual assault and sexual harassment, including information—

"(i) on the telephone number, website address, and email address for reporting allegations of sexual assault and sexual harassment to the Coast Guard;

"(ii) on vessel owner or company procedures to report violations of company policy and access resources;

"(iii) on resources provided by outside organizations such as sexual assault hotlines and counseling;

"(iv) on the retention period for surveillance video recording after an incident of sexual harassment or sexual assault is reported; and

"(v) additional items specified in regulations issued by, and at the discretion of, the Secretary of the department in which the Coast Guard is operating."

; and

(4) in subsection (d) by adding at the end the following: "In each washing space in a visible location there shall be information regarding procedures and resources to report crimes upon the vessel, including sexual assault and sexual harassment, and vessel owner or company policies prohibiting sexual assault and sexual harassment, retaliation, and drug

and alcohol usage.".

SEC. 11605. PROTECTION AGAINST DISCRIMINATION.

Section 2114(a) of title 46, United States Code, is amended—

(1) in paragraph (1)—

(A) by redesignating subparagraphs (B) through (G) as subparagraphs (C) through (H), respectively; and

(B) by inserting after subparagraph (A) the following:

"(B) the seaman in good faith has reported or is about to report to the vessel owner, Coast Guard or other appropriate Federal agency or department sexual harassment or sexual assault against the seaman or knowledge of sexual harassment or sexual assault against another seaman;"

; and

(2) in paragraphs (2) and (3) by striking "paragraph (1)(B)" and inserting "paragraph (1)(C)".

SEC. 11606. [46 U.S.C. 3306 note] ALCOHOL AT SEA.

(a) IN GENERAL.—The Commandant shall seek to enter into an agreement with the National Academy of Sciences not later than 1 year after the date of enactment of this Act under which the National Academy of Sciences shall prepare an assessment to determine safe levels of alcohol consumption and possession by crew members aboard vessels of the United States engaged in commercial service, except when such possession is associated with the commercial sale to individuals aboard the vessel who are not crew members.

(b) ASSESSMENT.—The assessment prepared pursuant to subsection (a) shall—

(1) take into account the safety and security of every individual on the vessel;

(2) take into account reported incidences of sexual harassment or sexual assault, as defined in section 2101 of title 46, United States Code; and

(3) provide any appropriate recommendations for any changes to laws, regulations, or employer policies.

(c) SUBMISSION.—Upon completion of the assessment under

this section, the National Academy of Sciences shall submit to the Committee on Commerce, Science, and Transportation of the Senate, the Committee on Transportation and Infrastructure of the House of Representatives, the Commandant, and the Secretary the assessment prepared pursuant to subsection (a).

(d) REGULATIONS.—The Commandant—

(1) shall, not later than 180 days after receiving the submission of the assessment under subsection (c), review the changes to regulations recommended in such assessment; and

(2) taking into account the safety and security of every individual on vessels of the United States engaged in commercial service, may issue regulations relating to alcohol consumption on such vessels.

(e) SAVINGS CLAUSE.—To the extent the Commandant issues regulations establishing safe levels of alcohol consumption in accordance with subsection (d), the Commandant may not issue regulations which prohibit—

(1) the owner or operator of a vessel from imposing additional restrictions on the consumption of alcohol, including the prohibition of the consumption of alcohol on such vessels; and

(2) possession of alcohol associated with the commercial sale to individuals aboard the vessel who are not crew members.

(f) REPORT REQUIRED.—If, by the date that is 2 years after the receipt of the assessment under subsection (c), the Commandant does not issue regulations under subsection (d), the Commandant shall provide a report by such date to the committees described in subsection (c)—

(1) containing the rationale for not issuing such regulations; and

(2) providing other recommendations as necessary to ensure safety at sea.

SEC. 11607. SURVEILLANCE REQUIREMENTS.

(a) IN GENERAL.—Part B of subtitle II of title 46, United States Code, is amended by adding at the end the following:

"CHAPTER 49—OCEANGOING NON-PASSENGER COMMERCIAL VESSELS

"SEC. 4901. [46 U.S.C. 4901] Surveillance requirements

"(a) IN GENERAL.—A vessel engaged in commercial service that does not carry passengers, shall maintain a video surveillance system.

"(b) APPLICABILITY.—The requirements in this section shall apply to—

"(1) documented vessels with overnight accommodations for at least 10 individuals on board that are—

"(A) on a voyage of at least 600 miles and crosses seaward of the Boundary Line; or

"(B) at least 24 meters (79 feet) in overall length and required to have a load line under chapter 51;

"(2) documented vessels of at least 500 gross tons as measured under section 14502, or an alternate tonnage measured under section 14302 as prescribed by the Secretary under section 14104 on an international voyage; and

"(3) vessels with overnight accommodations for at least 10 individuals on board that are operating for no less than 72 hours on waters superjacent to the outer Continental Shelf (as defined in section 2(a) of the Outer Continental Shelf Lands Act (43 U.S.C. 1331(a)).

"(c) PLACEMENT OF VIDEO AND AUDIO SURVEILLANCE EQUIPMENT.—

"(1) IN GENERAL.—The owner of a vessel to which this section applies shall install video and audio surveillance equipment aboard the vessel not later than 2 years after enactment of the Don Young Coast Guard Authorization Act of 2022, or during the next scheduled drydock, whichever is later.

"(2) LOCATIONS.—Video and audio surveillance equipment shall be placed in passageways on to which doors from staterooms open. Such equipment shall be placed in a manner ensuring the visibility of every door in each such passageway.

"(d) NOTICE OF VIDEO AND AUDIO SURVEILLANCE.—The owner

of a vessel to which this section applies shall provide clear and conspicuous signs on board the vessel notifying the crew of the presence of video and audio surveillance equipment.

"(e) ACCESS TO VIDEO AND AUDIO RECORDS.—The owner of a vessel to which this section applies shall ensure that access to records of video and audio surveillance is not used as part of a labor action against a crew member or employment dispute unless used in a criminal or civil action.

"(f) RETENTION REQUIREMENTS.—The owner of a vessel to which this section applies shall retain all records of audio and video surveillance for not less than 1 year after the footage is obtained. Any video and audio surveillance found to be associated with an alleged incident should be preserved for not less than 5 years from the date of the alleged incident.

"(g) PERSONNEL TRAINING.—A vessel owner or employer of a seafarer shall provide training for all individuals employed by the owner or employer for the purpose of responding to incidents of sexual assault or sexual harassment, including—

"(1) such training to ensure the individuals—

"(A) retain audio and visual records and other evidence objectively; and

"(B) act impartially without influence from the company or others; and

"(2) training on applicable Federal, State, Tribal, and local laws and regulations regarding sexual assault and sexual harassment investigations and reporting requirements.

"(g) DEFINITION OF OWNER.—In this section, the term 'owner' means the owner, charterer, managing operator, master, or other individual in charge of a vessel.

"(h) EXEMPTION.—Fishing vessels, fish processing vessels, and fish tender vessels are exempt from this section."

(b) CLERICAL AMENDMENT.—The table of chapters for subtitle II of title 46, United States Code, is amended by adding after the item related to chapter 47 the following:

"49. Oceangoing Non-Passenger Commercial Vessels 4901""

SEC. 11608. MASTER KEY CONTROL.

(a) IN GENERAL.—Chapter 31 of title 46, United States Code, is amended by adding at the end the following:

"SEC. 3106. [46 U.S.C. 3106] Master key control system

"(a) IN GENERAL.—The owner of a vessel subject to inspection under section 3301 shall—

"(1) ensure that such vessel is equipped with a vessel master key control system, manual or electronic, which provides controlled access to all copies of the vessel's master key of which access shall only be available to the individuals described in paragraph (2);

"(2) establish a list of all crew, identified by position, allowed to access and use the master key and maintain such list upon the vessel, within owner records and included in the vessel safety management system;

"(3) record in a log book information on all access and use of the vessel's master key, including—

"(A) dates and times of access;

"(B) the room or location accessed; and

"(C) the name and rank of the crew member that used the master key; and

"(4) make the list under paragraph (2) and the log book under paragraph (3) available upon request to any agent of the Federal Bureau of Investigation, any member of the Coast Guard, and any law enforcement officer performing official duties in the course and scope of an investigation.

"(b) PROHIBITED USE.—Crew not included on the list described in subsection (a)(2) shall not have access to or use the master key unless in an emergency and shall immediately notify the master and owner of the vessel following use of such key.

"(c) REQUIREMENTS FOR LOG BOOK.—The log book described in subsection (a)(3) and required to be included in a safety management system under section 3203(a)(6)—

"(1) may be electronic; and

"(2) shall be located in a centralized location that is readily accessible to law enforcement personnel.

"(d) PENALTY.—Any crew member who uses the master key without having been granted access pursuant to subsection (a)(2) shall be liable to the United States Government for a civil penalty of not more than $1,000 and may be subject to suspension or revocation under section 7703.

"(e) EXEMPTION.—This section shall not apply to vessels subject to section 3507(f)."

(b) CLERICAL AMENDMENT.—The analysis for chapter 31 of title 46, United States Code, is amended by adding at the end the following:

"3106. Master key control system."

SEC. 11609. REQUIREMENT TO REPORT SEXUAL ASSAULT AND HARASSMENT.

Section 10104 of title 46, United States Code, is amended by striking subsections (a) and (b) and inserting the following:

"(a) MANDATORY REPORTING BY RESPONSIBLE ENTITY OF A VESSEL.—

"(1) IN GENERAL.—The responsible entity of a vessel shall report to the Commandant any complaint or incident of harassment, sexual harassment, or sexual assault in violation of employer policy or law, of which such entity is made aware.

"(2) PENALTY.—A responsible entity of a vessel who knowingly fails to report in compliance with paragraph (1) is liable to the United States Government for a civil penalty of not more than $50,000.

"(b) REPORTING PROCEDURES.—

"(1) RESPONSIBLE ENTITY OF A VESSEL REPORTING.—A report required under subsection (a) shall be made immediately after the responsible entity of a vessel gains knowledge of a sexual assault or sexual harassment incident by the fastest telecommunication channel available to—

"(A) a single entity in the Coast Guard designated by the Commandant to receive such reports; and

"(B) the appropriate officer or agency of the government of the country in whose waters the incident occurs.

"(2) CONTENTS.—Such shall include, to the best of the knowledge of the individual making the report—

"(A) the name, official position or role in relation to the vessel, and contact information of such individual;

"(B) the name and official number of the documented

vessel;

"(C) the time and date of the incident;

"(D) the geographic position or location of the vessel when the incident occurred; and

"(E) a brief description of the alleged sexual harassment or sexual assault being reported.

"(3) RECEIVING REPORTS; COLLECTION OF INFORMATION.—

"(A) RECEIVING REPORTS.—With respect to reports submitted under subsection (a), the Commandant—

"(i) may establish additional reporting procedures, including procedures for receiving reports through—

"(I) a single telephone number that is continuously manned at all times; and

"(II) a single email address that is continuously monitored; and

"(ii) shall use procedures that include preserving evidence in such reports and providing emergency service referrals.

"(B) COLLECTION OF INFORMATION.—After receipt of the report made under subsection (a), the Coast Guard shall collect information related to the identity of each alleged victim, alleged perpetrator, and any witnesses identified in the report through means designed to protect, to the extent practicable, the personal identifiable information of such individuals.

"(c) SUBPOENA AUTHORITY.—

"(1) IN GENERAL.—The Commandant may compel the testimony of witnesses and the production of any evidence by subpoena to determine compliance with this section.

"(2) JURISDICTIONAL LIMITS.—The jurisdictional limits of a subpoena issued under this section are the same as, and are enforceable in the same manner as, subpoenas issued under chapter 63 of this title.

"(d) COMPANY AFTER-ACTION SUMMARY.—

"(1) A responsible entity of a vessel that makes a report under subsection (a) shall—

"(A) submit to the Commandant a document with

detailed information to describe the actions taken by such entity after becoming aware of the sexual assault or sexual harassment incident, including the results of any investigation into the complaint or incident and any action taken against the offending individual; and

"(B) make such submission not later than 10 days after such entity made the report under subsection (a).

"(2) CIVIL PENALTY.—A responsible entity of a vessel that fails to comply with paragraph (1) is liable to the United States Government for a civil penalty of $25,000 and $500 shall be added for each day of noncompliance, except that the total amount of a penalty with respect to a complaint or incident shall not exceed $50,000 per violation.

"(e) INVESTIGATORY AUDIT.—The Commandant shall periodically perform an audit or other systematic review of the submissions made under this section to determine if there were any failures to comply with the requirements of this section.

"(f) APPLICABILITY; REGULATIONS.—

"(1) REGULATIONS.—The Secretary may issue regulations to implement the requirements of this section.

"(2) INTERIM REPORTS.—Any report required to be made to the Commandant under this section shall be made to the Coast Guard National Command Center, until regulations implementing the procedures required by this section are issued.

"(g) DEFINITION OF RESPONSIBLE ENTITY OF A VESSEL.—In this section, the term 'responsible entity of a vessel' means—

"(1) the owner, master, or managing operator of a documented vessel engaged in commercial service; or

"(2) the employer of a seafarer on such a vessel."

SEC. 11610. SAFETY MANAGEMENT SYSTEM.

(a) SAFETY MANAGEMENT SYSTEM.—Section 3203 of title 46, United States Code, is amended—

(1) in subsection (a)—

(A) by redesignating paragraphs (5) and (6) as paragraphs (7) and (8); and

(B) by inserting after paragraph (4) the following:

"(5) with respect to sexual harassment and sexual assault, procedures for, and annual training requirements for all responsible persons and vessels to which this chapter applies on—

"(A) prevention;

"(B) bystander intervention;

"(C) reporting;

"(D) response; and

"(E) investigation;

"(6) the list required under section 3106(a)(2) and the log book required under section 3106(a)(3);"

(2) by redesignating subsections (b) and (c) as subsections (d) and (e), respectively; and

(3) by inserting after subsection (a) the following:

"(b) PROCEDURES AND TRAINING REQUIREMENTS.—In prescribing regulations for the procedures and training requirements described in subsection (a)(5), such procedures and requirements shall be consistent with the requirements to report sexual harassment or sexual assault under section 10104.

"(c) AUDITS.—

"(1) CERTIFICATES.—

"(A) SUSPENSION.—During an audit of a safety management system of a vessel required under section 10104(e), the Secretary may suspend the Safety Management Certificate issued for the vessel under section 3205 and issue a separate Safety Management Certificate for the vessel to be in effect for a 3-month period beginning on the date of the issuance of such separate certificate.

"(B) REVOCATION.—At the conclusion of an audit of a safety management system required under section 10104(e), the Secretary shall revoke the Safety Management Certificate issued for the vessel under section 3205 if the Secretary determines—

"(i) that the holder of the Safety Management Certificate knowingly, or repeatedly, failed to comply with section 10104; or "(ii) other failure of the safety management system resulted in the failure to comply with such section.

"(2) DOCUMENTS OF COMPLIANCE.—

"(A) IN GENERAL.—Following an audit of the safety management system of a vessel required under section 10104(e), the Secretary may audit the safety management system of the responsible person for the vessel.

"(B) SUSPENSION.—During an audit under subparagraph (A), the Secretary may suspend the Document of Compliance issued to the responsible person under section 3205 and issue a separate Document of Compliance to such person to be in effect for a 3-month period beginning on the date of the issuance of such separate document.

"(C) REVOCATION.—At the conclusion of an assessment or an audit of a safety management system under subparagraph (A), the Secretary shall revoke the Document of Compliance issued to the responsible person if the Secretary determines—

"(i) that the holder of the Document of Compliance knowingly, or repeatedly, failed to comply with section 10104; or

"(ii) that other failure of the safety management system resulted in the failure to comply with such section."

(b) VERIFICATION OF COMPLIANCE.—Section 3205(c)(1) of title 46, United States Code, is amended by inserting ", or upon discovery from other sources of information acquired by the Coast Guard, including a discovery made during an audit or systematic review conducted under section 10104(e) of a failure of a responsible person or vessel to comply with a requirement of a safety management system for which a Safety Management Certificate and a Document of compliance has been issued under this section, including a failure to comply with regulations prescribed under section 3203(a)(7) and (8)," after "periodically".

SEC. 11611. REPORTS TO CONGRESS.

(a) IN GENERAL.—Chapter 101 of title 46, United States Code, is amended by adding at the end the following:

"SEC. 10105. [46 U.S.C. 10105] Reports to Congress

"(a) IN GENERAL.—Not later than 1 year after the date of enactment of the Don Young Coast Guard Authorization Act of 2022, and on an annual basis thereafter, the Commandant shall submit to the Committee on Commerce, Science, and Transportation of the Senate and the Committee on Transportation and Infrastructure of the House of Representatives a report that includes—

"(1) the number of reports received under section 10104;

"(2) the number of penalties issued under such section;

"(3) the number of open investigations under such section, completed investigations under such section, and the outcomes of such open or completed investigations;

"(4) the number of assessments or audits conducted under section 3203 and the outcome of those assessments or audits;

"(5) a statistical analysis of compliance with the safety management system criteria under section 3203;

"(6) the number of credentials denied or revoked due to sexual harassment, sexual assault, or related offenses; and

"(7) recommendations to support efforts of the Coast Guard to improve investigations and oversight of sexual harassment and sexual assault in the maritime sector, including funding requirements and legislative change proposals necessary to ensure compliance with title CXVI of the Don Young Coast Guard Authorization Act of 2022 and the amendments made by such title.

"(b) PRIVACY.—In collecting the information required under subsection (a), the Commandant shall collect such information in a manner that protects the privacy rights of individuals who are subjects of such information."

(b) CLERICAL AMENDMENT.—The analysis for chapter 101 of title 46, United States Code, is amended by adding at the end the following:

"10105. Reports to Congress."

TITLE CXVII—NATIONAL OCEANIC AND

ATMOSPHERIC ADMINISTRATION

Subtitle A—National Oceanic and Atmospheric Administration Commissioned Officer Corps

SEC. 11701. DEFINITIONS.

Section 212(b) of the National Oceanic and Atmospheric Administration Commissioned Officer Corps Act of 2002 (33 U.S.C. 3002(b)) is amended by adding at the end the following:

"(8) UNDER SECRETARY.—The term "'Under Secretary"' means the Under Secretary of Commerce for Oceans and Atmosphere."

SEC. 11702. REQUIREMENT FOR APPOINTMENTS.

Section 221(c) of the National Oceanic and Atmospheric Administration Commissioned Officer Corps Act of 2002 (33 U.S.C. 3021(c)) is amended by striking "may not be given" and inserting the following:"may—

"(1) be given only to an individual who is a citizen of the United States; and

"(2) not be given."

SEC. 11703. REPEAL OF REQUIREMENT TO PROMOTE ENSIGNS AFTER 3 YEARS OF SERVICE.

(a) IN GENERAL.—Section 223 of the National Oceanic and Atmospheric Administration Commissioned Officer Corps Act of 2002 (33 U.S.C. 3023) is amended to read as follows:

"SEC. 223. SEPARATION OF ENSIGNS FOUND NOT FULLY QUALIFIED

"If an officer in the permanent grade of ensign is at any time found not fully qualified, the officer's commission shall be revoked and the officer shall be separated from the commissioned service."

(b) CLERICAL AMENDMENT.—The table of contents in section 1 of the Act entitled "An Act to reauthorize the Hydrographic Services Improvement Act of 1998, and for other purposes" (Public Law 107-372) is amended by striking the item relating to section 223 and inserting the following:

SEC. 11704. AUTHORITY TO PROVIDE AWARDS AND DECORATIONS.

(a) IN GENERAL.—Subtitle A of the National Oceanic and Atmospheric Administration Commissioned Officer Corps Act of 2002 (33 U.S.C. 3001 et seq.) is amended by adding at the end the following:

"SEC. 220. [33 U.S.C. 3010] AWARDS AND DECORATIONS

"The Under Secretary may provide ribbons, medals, badges, trophies, and similar devices to members of the commissioned officer corps of the Administration and to members of other uniformed services for service and achievement in support of the missions of the Administration."

(b) CLERICAL AMENDMENT.—The table of contents in section 1 of the Act entitled "An Act to reauthorize the Hydrographic Services Improvement Act of 1998, and for other purposes" (Public Law 107-372) is amended by inserting after the item relating to section 219 the following:

SEC. 11705. RETIREMENT AND SEPARATION.

(a) INVOLUNTARY RETIREMENT OR SEPARATION.—Section 241(a)(1) of the National Oceanic and Atmospheric Administration Commissioned Officer Corps Act of 2002 (33 U.S.C. 3041(a)(1)) is amended to read as follows:

"(1) an officer in the permanent grade of captain or commander may—

"(A) except as provided by subparagraph (B), be transferred to the retired list; or

"(B) if the officer is not qualified for retirement, be separated from service; and"

(b) RETIREMENT FOR AGE.—Section 243(a) of that Act (33 U.S.C. 3043(a)) is amended by striking "be retired" and inserting "be retired or separated (as specified in section 1251(e) of title 10, United States Code)".

(c) RETIREMENT OR SEPARATION BASED ON YEARS OF CREDITABLE SERVICE.—Section 261(a) of that Act (33 U.S.C. 3071(a)) is amended—

(1) by redesignating paragraphs (17) through (26) as paragraphs (18) through (27), respectively; and

(2) by inserting after paragraph (16) the following:

"(17) Section 1251(e), relating to retirement or separation based on years of creditable service."

SEC. 11706. IMPROVING PROFESSIONAL MARINER STAFFING.

(a) IN GENERAL.—Subtitle E of the National Oceanic and Atmospheric Administration Commissioned Officer Corps Act of 2002 (33 U.S.C. 3071 et seq.) is amended by adding at the end the following:

"SEC. 269B. [33 U.S.C. 3079b] SHORE LEAVE FOR PROFESSIONAL MARINERS

"(a) IN GENERAL.—The Under Secretary may prescribe regulations relating to shore leave for professional mariners without regard to the requirements of section 6305 of title 5, United States Code.

"(b) REQUIREMENTS.—The regulations prescribed under subsection (a) shall—

"(1) require that a professional mariner serving aboard an ocean-going vessel be granted a leave of absence of 4 days per pay period; and

"(2) provide that a professional mariner serving in a temporary promotion position aboard a vessel may be paid the difference between such mariner's temporary and permanent rates of pay for leave accrued while serving in the temporary promotion position.

"(c) PROFESSIONAL MARINER DEFINED.—In this section, the term 'professional mariner' means an individual employed on a vessel of the Administration who has the necessary expertise to serve in the engineering, deck, steward, electronic technician, or survey department."

(b) CLERICAL AMENDMENT.—The table of contents in section 1 of the Act entitled "An Act to reauthorize the Hydrographic Services Improvement Act of 1998, and for other purposes" (Public Law 107-372) is amended by inserting after the item relating to section 269A the following:

"Sec. 269B. Shore leave for professional mariners."

SEC. 11707. LEGAL ASSISTANCE.

Section 1044(a)(3) of title 10, United States Code, is amended by inserting "or the commissioned officer corps of the National Oceanic and Atmospheric Administration" after "Public Health Service".

SEC. 11708. ACQUISITION OF AIRCRAFT FOR AGENCY AIR, ATMOSPHERE, AND WEATHER RECONNAISSANCE AND RESEARCH MISSION.

(a) INCREASED FLEET CAPACITY.—

(1) IN GENERAL.—The Under Secretary of Commerce for Oceans and Atmosphere shall acquire adequate aircraft platforms with the necessary observation and modification requirements—

(A) to meet agency-wide air reconnaissance and research mission requirements, particularly with respect to hurricanes and tropical cyclones, and also for atmospheric chemistry, climate, air quality for public health, full-season fire weather research and operations, full-season atmospheric river air reconnaissance observations, and other mission areas; and

(B) to ensure data and information collected by the aircraft are made available to all users for research and operations purposes.

(2) CONTRACTS.—In carrying out paragraph (1), the Under Secretary shall negotiate and enter into 1 or more contracts or other agreements, to the extent practicable and necessary, with 1 or more governmental or nongovernmental entities.

(b) ACQUISITION OF AIRCRAFT TO REPLACE WP-3D AIRCRAFT.—Subject to the availability of appropriations, the Under Secretary may enter into a contract for the acquisition of up to 6 aircraft to replace the WP-3D aircraft that provides for—

(1) the first newly acquired aircraft to be fully operational before the retirement of the last WP-3D aircraft operated by the National Oceanic and Atmospheric Administration; and

(2) the second newly acquired aircraft to be fully operational not later than 1 year after the first such aircraft is required to be fully operational under subparagraph (A).

(c) ACQUISITION OF AIRCRAFT TO REPLACE END OF LIFE-CYCLE

AIRCRAFT.—Subject to the availability of appropriations, the Under Secretary shall maintain the ability of the National Oceanic and Atmospheric Administration to meet agency air reconnaissance and research mission requirements by acquiring new aircraft prior to the end of the service life of the aircraft being replaced with sufficient lead time that the replacement aircraft is fully operation prior to the retirement of the aircraft it is replacing.

(d) AUTHORIZATION OF APPROPRIATIONS.—For fiscal year 2023, there is authorized to be appropriated to the Under Secretary $800,000,000 for the acquisition of aircraft under this section.

SEC. 11709. REPORT ON PROFESSIONAL MARINER STAFFING MODELS.

(a) IN GENERAL.—Not later than 18 months after the date of the enactment of this Act, the Comptroller General of the United States shall submit to the Committee on Commerce, Science, and Transportation of the Senate and the Committee on Transportation and Infrastructure and the Committee on Natural Resources of the House of Representatives a report on staffing issues relating to professional mariners within the Office of Marine and Aviation Operations of the National Oceanic and Atmospheric Administration.

(b) ELEMENTS.—In conducting the report required under subsection (a), the Comptroller General shall consider—

(1) the challenges the Office of Marine and Aviation Operations faces in recruiting and retaining qualified professional mariners;

(2) workforce planning efforts to address such challenges; and

(3) other models or approaches that exist, or are under consideration, to provide incentives for the retention of qualified professional mariners.

(c) PROFESSIONAL MARINER DEFINED.—In this section, the term "professional mariner" means an individual employed on a vessel of the National Oceanic and Atmospheric Administration who has the necessary expertise to serve in the engineering, deck, steward, or survey department.

Subtitle B—Other Matters

SEC. 11710. CONVEYANCE OF CERTAIN PROPERTY OF NATIONAL OCEANIC AND ATMOSPHERIC ADMINISTRATION IN JUNEAU, ALASKA.

(a) DEFINITIONS.—In this section:

(1) CITY.—The term “City” means the City and Borough of Juneau, Alaska.

(2) MASTER PLAN.—The term “Master Plan” means the Juneau Small Cruise Ship Infrastructure Master Plan released by the Docks and Harbors Board and Port of Juneau for the City and dated March 2021.

(3) PROPERTY.—The term “Property” means the parcel of real property consisting of approximately 2.4 acres, including tidelands, owned by the United States and under administrative custody and control of the National Oceanic and Atmospheric Administration and located at 250 Egan Drive, Juneau, Alaska, including any improvements thereon that are not authorized or required by another provision of law to be conveyed to a specific individual or entity.

(4) SECRETARY.—The term “Secretary” means the Secretary of Commerce, acting through the Under Secretary of Commerce for Oceans and Atmosphere and the Administrator of the National Oceanic and Atmospheric Administration.

(b) CONVEYANCE AUTHORIZED.—

(1) IN GENERAL.—The Secretary may convey, at fair market value, all right, title, and interest of the United States in and to the Property, subject to the restrictions in subsections (b)(2) and (c) and the requirements of this section.

(2) RESTRICTION.—The Secretary may not take action under this section until the Commandant notifies the Secretary in writing that the Coast Guard does not have an interest in acquiring the property, or a period of 180 calendar days expires following the date of enactment of this section.

(3) NOTIFICATION EXPIRATION.—If, the Secretary has not received notification under paragraph (2) at the end of the 180 calendar day period, the Secretary and the Commandant shall notify the Committee on Transportation and Infrastructure and the Committee on Appropriations of the House of Representatives and the Committee on Commerce, Science, and Transportation and the Committee on Appropriations of the Senate in writing that no notification has been received.

(4) TERMINATION OF AUTHORITY.—The authority provided under paragraph (1) shall terminate on the date that is 3 years after the date of the enactment of this Act.

(c) TRANSFER OF PROPERTY TO COAST GUARD.—

(1) IN GENERAL.—If not later than 180 calendar days after the date of enactment of this Act the Commandant notifies the Secretary that the Coast Guard has an interest in the Property, the Secretary shall transfer the Property to the Coast Guard.

(2) TRANSFER.—Any transfer performed pursuant to this subsection shall—

(A) occur not later than 1 year of any written notification required under paragraph (1);

(B) include within the transfer from the Department of Commerce to the Coast Guard all legal obligations attached to ownership or administrative control of the Property, interest therein, or improvements thereto, including environmental compliance and restoration liabilities and historical preservation liabilities and responsibilities;

(C) be at no cost to the Department of Commerce, to include all land survey costs;

(D) not affect or limit any remaining real property interests held by the Department of Commerce on any real property subject to such transfer; and

(E) be accompanied by a memorandum of agreement between the Coast Guard and the Department of Commerce to require the Commandant to allow—

(i) future access to, and use of, the Property, including use of available pier space, to accommodate the reasonable expectations of the Secretary for future operational and logistical needs in southeast Alaska; and

(ii) continued access to, and use of, existing facilities on the Property, including a warehouse and machine shop, unless the Commandant determines that the Property on which the facilities are located is needed to support polar operations, at which time the Coast Guard shall provide the Department of Commerce access to and use of comparable space in reasonable proximity to the existing facilities.

(d) RIGHT OF FIRST REFUSAL.—If the Coast Guard does not transfer the Property under subsection (c), the City shall have the right of first refusal with respect to the purchase, at fair market value, of the Property.

(e) SURVEY.—The exact acreage and legal description of the Property shall be determined by a survey satisfactory to the Secretary.

(f) CONDITION; QUITCLAIM DEED.—If the Property is conveyed under subsection (b)(1), the Property shall be conveyed—

(1) in an "as is, where is" condition; and

(2) via a quitclaim deed.

(g) FAIR MARKET VALUE.—

(1) IN GENERAL.—The fair market value of the Property shall be—

(A) determined by an appraisal that—

(i) is conducted by an independent appraiser selected by the Secretary; and

(ii) meets the requirements of paragraph (2); and

(B) adjusted, at the Secretary's discretion, based on the factors described in paragraph (3).

(2) APPRAISAL REQUIREMENTS.—An appraisal conducted under paragraph (1)(A) shall be conducted in accordance with nationally recognized appraisal standards, including the Uniform Standards of Professional Appraisal Practice.

(3) FACTORS.—The factors described in this paragraph are—

(A) matters of equity and fairness;

(B) actions taken by the City regarding the Property, if the City exercises the right of first refusal under subsection (d), including—

(i) comprehensive waterfront planning, site development, and other redevelopment activities supported by the City in proximity to the Property in furtherance of the Master Plan;

(ii) in-kind contributions made to facilitate and support use of the Property by governmental agencies; and

(iii) any maintenance expenses, capital improvement, or emergency expenditures made necessary to ensure public safety and access to and from the Property; and

(C) such other factors as the Secretary considers appropriate.

(h) COSTS OF CONVEYANCE.—If the City exercises the right of first refusal under subsection (d), all reasonable and necessary costs, including real estate transaction and environmental documentation costs, associated with the conveyance of the Property to the City under this section may be shared equitably by the Secretary and the City, as determined by the Secretary, including with the City providing in-kind contributions for any or all of such costs.

(i) PROCEEDS.—Any proceeds from a conveyance of the Property under subsection (b)(1) shall—

(1) be credited as discretionary offsetting collections to the applicable appropriations accounts or funds of the National Oceanic and Atmospheric Administration that exists as of the date of enactment of this Act; and

(2) be used to cover costs associated with the conveyance of the Property, related relocation efforts, and other facility and infrastructure projects in Alaska and shall be made available for such purposes only to the extent and in the amounts provided in advance in appropriations Acts.

(j) MEMORANDUM OF AGREEMENT.—If the City exercises the right of first refusal under subsection (d), before finalizing a conveyance to the City under this section, the Secretary and the City shall enter into a memorandum of agreement to establish the terms under which the Secretary shall have future access to, and use of, the Property to accommodate the reasonable expectations of the Secretary for future operational and logistical needs in southeast Alaska.

(k) RESERVATION OR EASEMENT FOR ACCESS AND USE.—The conveyance authorized under subsection (b)(1) shall be subject to a reservation providing, or an easement granting, the Secretary, at no cost to the United States, a right to access and use the Property that—

(1) is compatible with the Master Plan; and

(2) authorizes future operational access and use by other Federal, State, and local government agencies that have customarily used the Property.

(l) LIABILITY.—In the event that the Property is conveyed to the City of Juneau the following shall apply:

(1) AFTER CONVEYANCE.—An individual or entity to which a conveyance is made under this section shall hold the United States harmless from any liability with respect to activities carried out on or after the date and time of the conveyance of the Property.

(2) BEFORE CONVEYANCE.—The United States shall remain responsible for any liability the United States incurred with respect to activities carried out by the United States on the Property before the date and time of the conveyance of the Property.

(m) ADDITIONAL TERMS AND CONDITIONS.—The Secretary may require such additional terms and conditions in connection with a conveyance under this section as the Secretary considers appropriate and reasonable to protect the interests of the United States.

(n) ENVIRONMENTAL COMPLIANCE.—Nothing in this section shall be construed to affect or limit the application of or obligation to comply with any applicable environmental law, including—

(1) the National Environmental Policy Act of 1969 (42 U.S.C. 4321 et seq.); or

(2) section 120(h) of the Comprehensive Environmental Response, Compensation, and Liability Act of 1980 (42 U.S.C. 9620(h)).

(o) CONVEYANCE NOT A MAJOR FEDERAL ACTION.—A conveyance under this section shall not be considered a major Federal action for purposes of section 102(2) of the National Environmental Policy Act of 1969 (42 U.S.C. 4332(2)).

TITLE CXVIII—TECHNICAL, CONFORMING, AND CLARIFYING AMENDMENTS

SEC. 11801. TERMS AND VACANCIES.

(a) IN GENERAL.—Section 46101(b) of title 46, United States Code, is amended by—

(1) in paragraph (2)—

(A) by striking "one year" and inserting "2 years"; and

(B) by striking "2 terms" and inserting "3 terms"; and

(2) in paragraph (3)—

(A) by striking "of the individual being succeeded" and inserting "to which such individual is appointed";

(B) by striking "2 terms" and inserting "3 terms"; and

(C) by striking "the predecessor of that" and inserting "such".

(b) [46 U.S.C. 46101 note] APPLICABILITY.—The amendments made by this section shall not apply to Commissioners to whom section 403(b) of the Howard Coble Coast Guard and Maritime Transportation Act of 2014 (Public Law 113-281) applies.

SEC. 11802. PASSENGER VESSEL SECURITY AND SAFETY REQUIREMENTS.

Section 3507(k)(1) of title 46, United States Code, is amended—

(1) in subparagraph (A) by striking "at least 250" and inserting "250 or more"; and

(2) by striking subparagraph (B) and inserting the following:

"(B) has overnight accommodations for 250 or more passengers; and"

SEC. 11803. TECHNICAL CORRECTIONS.

(a) Section 319(b) of title 14, United States Code, is amended by striking "section 331 of the FAA Modernization and Reform Act of 2012 (49 U.S.C. 40101 note)" and inserting "section 44801 of title 49".

(b) Section 1156(c) of title 14, United States Code, is amended by striking "section 331 of the FAA Modernization and Reform Act of 2012 (49 U.S.C. 40101 note)" and inserting "section 44801 of title 49".

SEC. 11804. TRANSPORTATION WORKER IDENTIFICATION CREDENTIAL TECHNICAL AMENDMENTS.

(a) IN GENERAL.—Section 70105 of title 46, United States Code, is amended—

(1) in the section heading by striking "security cards" and inserting "worker identification credentials";

(2) by striking "transportation security card" each place it appears and inserting "transportation worker identification credential";

(3) by striking "transportation security cards" each place it appears and inserting "transportation worker identification credentials";

(4) by striking "card" each place it appears and inserting "credential";

(5) in the heading for subsection (b) by striking "Cards" and inserting "Credentials";

(6) in subsection (g) by striking "Assistant Secretary of Homeland Security for" and inserting "Administrator of";

(7) by striking subsection (i) and redesignating subsections (j) and (k) as subsections (i) and (j), respectively;

(8) by striking subsection (l) and redesignating subsections (m) through (q) as subsections (k) through (o), respectively;

(9) in subsection (j), as so redesignated—

(A) in the subsection heading by striking "Security Card" and inserting "Worker Identification Credential"; and

(B) in the heading for paragraph (2) by striking "security cards" and inserting "worker identification credential";

(10) in subsection (k)(1), as so redesignated, by striking "subsection (k)(3)" and inserting "subsection (j)(3)";

(11) by striking paragraph (4) of subsection (k), as so redesignated; and

(12) in subsection (o), as so redesignated—

(A) in the subsection heading by striking "Security Card" and inserting "Worker Identification Credential";

(B) in paragraph (1)—

(i) by striking "subsection (k)(3)" and inserting "subsection (j)(3)"; and

(ii) by striking "This plan shall" and inserting "Such receipt and activation shall"; and

(C) in paragraph (2) by striking "on-site activation capability" and inserting "on-site receipt and activation of transportation worker identification credentials".

(b) CLERICAL AMENDMENT.—The analysis for chapter 701 of title 46, United States Code, is amended by striking the item related to section 70105 and inserting the following:

"70105. Transportation worker identification credentials."

(c) [46 U.S.C. 70105 note] LIMITATION ON IMPLEMENTATION.—The Secretary may not implement the rule entitled "Transportation Worker Identification Credential (TWIC)-Reader Requirements" (81 Fed. Reg. 57651) for covered facilities before May 8, 2026.

(d) COVERED FACILITIES DEFINED.—In this section, the term "covered facilities" means—

(1) facilities that handle Certain Dangerous Cargoes in bulk and transfer such cargoes from or to a vessel;

(2) facilities that handle Certain Dangerous Cargoes in bulk, but do not transfer it from or to a vessel; and

(3) facilities that receive vessels carrying Certain Dangerous Cargoes in bulk but, during the vessel-to-facility interface, do not transfer it from or to the vessel.

SEC. 11805. REINSTATEMENT.

(a) REINSTATEMENT.—The text of section 12(a) of the Act of June 21, 1940 (33 U.S.C. 522(a)), popularly known as the "Truman-Hobbs Act", is—

(1) reinstated as it appeared on the day before the date of the enactment of section 8507(b) of the William M. (Mac) Thornberry National Defense Authorization Act for Fiscal Year 2021 (Public Law 116-283; 134 Stat. 4754); and

(2) redesignated as the sole text of section 12 of the Act of June 21, 1940 (33 U.S.C. 522).

(b) [33 U.S.C. 522 note] EFFECTIVE DATE.—The provision reinstated under subsection (a) shall be treated as if such section 8507(b) had never taken effect.

(c) CONFORMING AMENDMENT.—The provision reinstated under subsection (a) is amended by striking ", except to the extent provided in this section".

SEC. 11806. DETERMINATION OF BUDGETARY EFFECTS.

The budgetary effects of this Act, for the purpose of complying with the Statutory Pay-As-You-Go Act of 2010, shall be determined by reference to the latest statement titled "Budgetary Effects of PAYGO Legislation for this Act", submitted for printing in the Congressional Record by the Chairman of the House Budget Committee, provided that such statement has been submitted prior to the vote on passage.

SEC. 11807. TECHNICAL AMENDMENT.

(a) IN GENERAL.—Section 6304 of title 46, United States Code, is amended—

(1) by striking "subpena" and inserting "subpoena" each place it appears; and

(2) in subsection (d) by striking "subpenas" and inserting "subpoenas".

(b) CLERICAL AMENDMENT.—The analysis for chapter 63 of title 46, United States Code, is amended by striking the item relating to section 6304 and inserting the following:

"6304. Subpoena authority."

SEC. 11808. LIGHTHOUSE SERVICE AMENDMENTS.

(a) REPEALS.—The following provisions are repealed:

(1) Sections 1, 2, and 3 of the Act of March 6, 1896 (33 U.S.C. 474).

(2) Section 4 of the Act of June 17, 1910 (33 U.S.C. 711; 721).

(3) The first sentence of section 2 of the Act of July 27, 1912 (33 U.S.C. 712).

(4) Section 10 of the Act of June 17, 1910 (33 U.S.C. 713).

(5) Section 6 of the Act of June 17, 1910 (33 U.S.C. 714).

(6) Section 5 of the Act of June 17, 1910 (33 U.S.C. 715).

(7) **[33 U.S.C. 719]** Section 4679 of the Revised Statutes.

(8) Section 4 of the Act of May 14, 1908 (33 U.S.C. 737).

(9) The first sentence of the sixteenth paragraph of the section entitled "Coast Guard" under the heading "Treasury Department" of the Act of June 5, 1920 (33 U.S.C. 738).

(10) Section 7 of the Act of June 20, 1918 (33 U.S.C. 744).

(11) Section 2 of the Act of May 13, 1938 (33 U.S.C. 748a).

(12) The Act of June 15, 1938 (33 U.S.C. 752b).

(13) The last proviso of the second paragraph of the section entitled "Lighthouse Service" under the heading "Department of Commerce" of the Act of November 4, 1918 (33 U.S.C. 763).

(14) Section 7 of the Act of June 6, 1940 (33 U.S.C. 763a-2).

(15) The last paragraph of the section entitled "Lighthouse Service" under the heading "Department of Commerce" of the Act of March 4, 1921 (33 U.S.C. 764).

(16) Sections 1 and 2 of the Act of March 4, 1925 (33 U.S.C. 765; 766).

(17) Section 5 of the Act of August 19, 1950 (33 U.S.C. 775).

(18) Subchapter III of chapter 25 of title 14, United States Code, and the items relating to such subchapter in the analysis for chapter 25 of such title.

(b) [33 U.S.C. 714 note] OPERATION OF REPEALS.—The repeals under paragraphs (5) and (6) of subsection (a) shall not affect the operation of section 103 of title 14, United States Code.

(c) [33 U.S.C. 472;14] TRANSFER.—Chapter 313 of the Act of September 15, 1922 is transferred to appear at the end of subchapter III of chapter 5 of title 14, United States Code, redesignated as section 548 of such title, and amended—

(1) by striking "That hereafter the Commissioner of Lighthouses" and insert "The Commandant of the Coast Guard"; and

(2) by striking "Lighthouse Service" and inserting "Coast Guard".

NATIONAL DEFENSE AUTHORIZATION ACT FOR FISCAL YEAR 2024
TITLE XXXV-MARITIME SECURITY

PUBLIC LAW 118-31

National Defense Authorization Act for Fiscal Year 2024

[(Public Law 118–31)]

[As Amended Through P.L. 118–159, Enacted December 23, 2024]

AN ACT To authorize appropriations for fiscal year 2024 for military activities of the Department of Defense and for military construction, and for defense activities of the Department of Energy, to prescribe military personnel strengths for such fiscal year, and for other purposes.

Be it enacted by the Senate and House of Representatives of the United States of America in Congress assembled,

SECTION 1. SHORT TITLE.

This Act may be cited as the "National Defense Authorization Act for Fiscal Year 2024".

SEC. 2. ORGANIZATION OF ACT INTO DIVISIONS; TABLE OF CONTENTS.

(a) DIVISIONS.—This Act is organized into seven divisions as follows:

* * * * * * *

(3) Division C—Department of Energy National Security Authorizations and Other Authorizations.

* * * * * * *

(5) Division E—Other Matters.

(b) TABLE OF CONTENTS.—The table of contents for this Act is as follows:

* * * * * * *

TITLE XXXV—MARITIME ADMINISTRATION

Subtitle A—Maritime Administration

Sec. 3501. Authorization of appropriations for Maritime Administration.

Subtitle B—Maritime Infrastructure

Sec. 3511. Port infrastructure development program eligible projects.
Sec. 3512. Assistance for small inland river and coastal ports and terminals.
Sec. 3513. Port infrastructure development program: eligibility of shore power projects; selection criteria.
Sec. 3514. Codification of existing language; technical amendments.

Subtitle C—Reports

Sec. 3521. Reports on maritime industry, policies, and programs.
Sec. 3522. Reports on availability of used sealift vessels and the scrapping and recycling of imported vessels.
Sec. 3523. Study on foreign ownership and control of marine terminals.
Sec. 3524. Reports to Congress.

Subtitle D—Other Matters

Sec. 3531. Cargoes procured, furnished, or financed by the United States Government.
Sec. 3532. Recapitalization of National Defense Reserve Fleet.
Sec. 3533. United States Merchant Marine Academy and Coast Guard Academy matters; Maritime Administration requirements.
Sec. 3534. Maritime workforce working group.
Sec. 3535. Consideration of life-cycle cost estimates for acquisition and procurement of vessels.
Sec. 3536. Loans for retrofitting to qualify as a vessel of the United States.
Sec. 3537. Accountability for National Maritime Strategy.
DIVISION D— DEPARTMENT OF DEFENSE AUTHORIZATIONS

* * * * * * *

TITLE LVI—TRANSPORTATION AND INFRASTRUCTURE MATTERS

* * * * * * *

Sec. 5603. International Port Security Enforcement Act.

* * * * * * *

* * * * * * *

DIVISION C—DEPARTMENT OF ENERGY NATIONAL SECURITY AUTHORIZATIONS AND OTHER AUTHORIZATIONS

* * * * * * *

TITLE XXXV—MARITIME ADMINISTRATION

Subtitle A—Maritime Administration

SEC. 3501. AUTHORIZATION OF APPROPRIATIONS FOR MARITIME ADMINISTRATION.

(a) In General.—There are authorized to be appropriated to the Department of Transportation for fiscal year 2024, for programs associated with maintaining the United States Merchant Marine, the following amounts:

(1) For expenses necessary to support the United States Merchant Marine Academy, $198,500,000, of which—

(A) $103,500,000 shall be for Academy operations;

(B) $70,000,000 shall be for United States Merchant Marine Academy capital improvement projects;

(C) $22,000,000 shall be for facilities maintenance and repair and equipment; and

(D) $3,000,000 shall be for training, staffing, retention, recruiting, and contract management for United States Merchant Marine Academy capital improvement projects.

(2) For expenses necessary to support the State maritime academies, $66,580,000, of which—

(A) $4,480,000 shall be for the Student Incentive Payment Program;

(B) $6,000,000 shall be for direct payments for State maritime academies;

(C) $17,600,000 shall be for training ship fuel assistance;

(D) $8,000,000 shall be for offsetting the costs of training ship sharing; and

(E) $30,500,000 shall be for maintenance and repair of State maritime academy training vessels.

(3) For expenses necessary to support the National Security Multi-Mission Vessel program, including funds for construction and necessary expenses to construct shoreside infrastructure to support such vessels, $75,000,000.

(4) For expenses necessary to support Maritime Administration operations and programs, $105,573,000, of which—

(A) $15,000,000 shall be for the maritime environmental and technical assistance under section 50307 of title 46, United States Code;

(B) $15,000,000 shall be for the United States marine highways program, including to make grants authorized under section 55601 of title 46, United States Code;

(C) $74,773,000 shall be for headquarters operations expenses; and

(D) $800,000 shall be for expenses necessary to provide for National Defense Reserve Fleet resiliency.

(5) For expenses necessary for the disposal of obsolete vessels in the National Defense Reserve Fleet of the Maritime Administration, $6,021,000.

(6) For expenses necessary to maintain and preserve a United States flag merchant marine to serve the national security needs of the United States under chapter 531 of title 46, United States Code, $318,000,000.

(7) For expenses necessary for the loan guarantee program authorized under chapter 537 of title 46, United States Code, $43,020,000, of which—

(A) $40,000,000 may be for the cost (as such term is defined in section 502(5) of the Federal Credit Reform Act of 1990 (2 U.S.C. 661a(5)) of loan guarantees under the program; and

(B) $3,020,000 may be used for administrative expenses relating to loan guarantee commitments under the program.

(8) For expenses necessary to provide assistance to small shipyards and for maritime training programs authorized under section 54101 of title 46, United States Code, $30,000,000.

(9) For expenses necessary to implement the port infrastructure development program, as authorized under section 54301 of title 46, United States Code, $500,000,000, to remain available until expended, except that no such funds authorized under this title for this program may be used to provide a grant to purchase fully automated cargo handling equipment that is remotely operated or remotely monitored with or without the exercise of human intervention or control, if the Secretary of Transportation determines such equipment would result in a net loss of jobs within a port or port terminal. If such a determination is made, the data and analysis for such determination shall be reported to the Committee on Commerce, Science, and Transportation of the Senate and the Committee on Transportation and Infrastructure of the House

of Representatives not later than 3 days after the date of the determination.

(10) For expenses necessary to implement the development of a national maritime strategy, as required by section 3542 of the James M. Inhofe National Defense Authorization Act for Fiscal Year 2023 (Public Law 117-263; 136 Stat. 3094), $2,000,000, to remain available until expended.

(11) For expenses necessary for the design of a vessel for the National Defense Reserve Fleet, as required by section 3546 of the James M. Inhofe National Defense Authorization Act for Fiscal Year 2023 (Public Law 117-263; 46 U.S.C. 57100 note), $6,000,000, to remain available until expended.

(b) STUDENT INCENTIVE PAYMENT AGREEMENTS.—Section 51509(b) of title 46, United States Code, is amended—

(1) in paragraph (1), by striking "$8,000" and inserting "$16,000"; and

(2) in paragraph (2), by striking "$32,000" and inserting "$64,000".

Subtitle B—Maritime Infrastructure

SEC. 3511. PORT INFRASTRUCTURE DEVELOPMENT PROGRAM ELIGIBLE PROJECTS.

Section 54301(a)(3)(A)(ii) of title 46, United States Code, is amended—

(1) in subclause (III), by striking "or" at the end;

(2) in subclause (IV)(ii), by striking the period and inserting "; or"; and

(3) by adding at the end the following new subclause:

"(V) port and port-related infrastructure that supports seafood and seafood-related businesses, including the loading and unloading of commercially harvested fish and fish products, seafood processing, cold storage, and other related infrastructure."

SEC. 3512. ASSISTANCE FOR SMALL INLAND RIVER AND COASTAL PORTS AND TERMINALS.

(a) IN GENERAL.—Section 54301(b) of title 46, United States

Code, is amended—

(1) in paragraph (1), by striking "the findings of which are acceptable to the Secretary";

(2) by redesignating paragraphs (2) through (5) as paragraphs (4) through (7), respectively; and

(3) by inserting after paragraph (1) the following new paragraph (2):

"(2) INDEPENDENT AUDIT.—

"(A) IN GENERAL. If an eligible applicant provides data by an independent audit for purposes of paragraph (1), the Secretary shall use such data to make a tonnage determination if the Secretary determines that it is acceptable to use such data instead of using Corps of Engineers data.

"(B) ACCEPTABLE USE OF DATA.—For purposes of subparagraph (A), an acceptable use of data means that the Secretary has determined such data is a reasonable substitute for Army Corps data.

"(C) JUSTIFICATION.—If the Secretary makes a determination pursuant to subparagraph (A) that it is not acceptable to use independent audit data provided by an eligible applicant, the Secretary shall provide the eligible applicant with notification of, and justification for, such determination.

"(3) TONNAGE DETERMINATION.—In making a determination of the average annual tonnage of cargo using Corps of Engineers data for purposes of evaluating an application of an eligible applicant pursuant to paragraph (1), the Secretary shall use data that is specific to the eligible applicant."

(b) CONFORMING AMENDMENT.—Section 54301(a)(7)(C)(ii) of title 46, United States Code, is amended by striking "subsection (b)(3)(A)(ii)(III)" and inserting "subsection (b)(5)(A)(ii)(III)".

SEC. 3513. PORT INFRASTRUCTURE DEVELOPMENT PROGRAM: ELIGIBILITY OF SHORE POWER PROJECTS; SELECTION CRITERIA.

(a) ELIGIBILITY OF SHORE POWER PROJECTS.—

(1) IN GENERAL.—In making port infrastructure

development grants under section 54301 of title 46, United States Code, for fiscal year 2024, the Secretary of Transportation shall treat a project described in paragraph (2) as—

(A) having met the requirements of paragraphs (1) and (6)(A)(i) of section 54301(a) of such title; and

(B) being an eligible project under section 54301(a)(3) of such title.

(2) PROJECT DESCRIBED.—A project described in this paragraph is a project to provide shore power at a port that services both of the following:

(A) Passenger vessels described in section 3507(k) of title 46, United States Code.

(B) Vessels that move goods or freight.

(b) SELECTION CRITERIA.—Section 54301(a)(6) of title 46, United States Code, is amended—

(1) in subparagraph (A)(ii), by inserting "(except in the case of a project described under subparagraph (C))" after "effective";

(2) in subparagraph (B)(ii), by inserting "(except in the case of a project described under subparagraph (C))" after "as applicable"; and

(3) by adding at the end, the following:

"(C) NONCONTIGUOUS STATES AND TERRITORIES.—The requirements under subparagraphs (A)(ii) and (B)(ii) shall not apply in the case of a project described in paragraph (3) in a noncontiguous State or territory."

SEC. 3514. CODIFICATION OF EXISTING LANGUAGE; TECHNICAL AMENDMENTS.

(a) PORT INFRASTRUCTURE DEVELOPMENT PROGRAM.—

(1) STRATEGIC SEAPORTS.—

(A) IN GENERAL.—Section 3505(a)(1) of the National Defense Authorization Act for Fiscal Year 2014 (Public Law 113-66; 46 U.S.C. 50302 note) is—

(i) transferred to appear after section 54301(a)(6)(B) of title 46, United States Code;

(ii) redesignated as subparagraph (C); and

(iii) [46 U.S.C. 54301] amended by striking "Under the port infrastructure development grant program established under section 50302(c) of title 46, United States Code" and inserting "In selecting projects described in paragraph (3)".

(B) [46 U.S.C. 50302 note] STRATEGIC SEAPORT DEFINED.—Section 3505(a)(2) of such Act is transferred to appear after section 54301(a)(12)(D) of title 46, United States Code, and redesignated as subparagraph (E).

(C) REPEAL.—Section 3505(a) of such Act is repealed.

(2) DETERMINATION OF EFFECTIVENESS.—Section 54301(b)(5)(B) of title 46, United States Code, is amended by striking "subsection (c)(6)(A)" and inserting "subsection (a)(6)(A)".

(b) TRANSFER OF IMPROVEMENTS TO PROCESS FOR WAIVING NAVIGATION AND INSPECTION LAWS.—Section 3502(b) of the William M. (Mac) Thornberry National Defense Authorization Act for Fiscal Year 2021 is—

(1) [46 U.S.C. 56101 note] amended—

(A) by striking "For fiscal year 2020 and each subsequent fiscal year, the" and inserting "The"; and

(B) by striking "section 56101 of title 46, United States Code," and inserting "this section";

(2) [46 U.S.C. 56101 note] transferred to appear after section 56101(e) of title 46, United States Code; and

(3) redesignated as subsection (f).

(c) CHAPTER ANALYSIS.—The analysis for chapter 503 of title 46, United States Code, is amended in the item relating to section 50308 by striking "Port development; maritime transportation system emergency relief program" and inserting "Maritime transportation system emergency relief program".

(d) VESSEL OPERATIONS REVOLVING FUND.—Section 50301(b) of title 46, United States Code, is amended by striking "(50 App. 137 STAT. 811 U.S.C. 1291(a), (c), 1293(c), 1294)"and inserting "(50 U.S.C. 4701(a), (c), 4703(c), 4704)".

(e) MARITIME TRANSPORTATION SYSTEM EMERGENCY RELIEF PROGRAM.—Section 50308 of title 46, United States Code, is amended—

(1) in subsection (a)(2)(B), by striking "Federal Emergency Management Administration" and inserting "Federal Emergency Management Agency"; and

(2) in subsection (j)(4)(A), by striking "Federal Emergency Management Administration" and inserting "Federal Emergency Management Agency".

(f) MARINE HIGHWAYS.—The analysis for subtitle V of title 46, United States Code, is amended in the item relating to chapter 556 by striking "SHORT SEA TRANSPORTATION" and inserting "MARINE HIGHWAYS".

(g) CHAPTER 537.—The analysis for chapter 537 of title 46, United States Code, is amended by striking the item relating to section 53703 and inserting the following:

"53703. Application and administration."

(h) CHAPTER 541.—The analysis for chapter 541 of title 46, United States Code, is amended to read as follows:

"Chapter 541— MISCELLANEOUS

"54101. Assistance for small shipyards."

(i) **[33 U.S.C. 1958]** TECHICAL AMENDMENT.—Section 11328(b) of the James M. Inhofe National Defense Authorization Act for Fiscal Year 2023 (Public Law 117-263) is amended by striking "Maritime" and inserting "Marine".

(j) NATIONAL DEFENSE RESERVE FLEET OBSOLETE VESSEL.—

(1) DEFINITION OF OBSOLETE VESSELS.—Chapter 571 of title 46, United States Code, is amended—

(A) by redesignating section 57111 as section 57110; and

(B) by adding at the end the following:

"SEC. 57111. [46 U.S.C. 57111] Definition of obsolete vessel

"In this chapter, the term 'obsolete vessel' means a vessel that—

"(1) is or will be in the custody and control of the Maritime Administration for purposes of disposing of the vessel; and

"(2) has been determined by the Secretary of Transportation to be of insufficient value, with respect to the programs of the Maritime Administration, to warrant—

"(A) preserving for future use or spare parts harvesting; or

"(B) retaining in the National Defense Reserve Fleet."

(2) NATIONAL DEFENSE RESERVE FLEET VESSEL STATUS.—Section 57100(g) of title 46, United States Code, is amended by striking "of insufficient value to remain in the National Defense Reserve Fleet" and inserting "an obsolete vessel".

(3) PLACEMENT OF VESSELS IN NATIONAL DEFENSE RESERVE FLEET.—Section 57101(b) of title 46, United States Code, is amended by inserting ", or section 308704 of title 54" before the period at the end.

(4) DISPOSITION OF VESSELS.—Section 57102 of title 46, United States Code, is amended—

(A) in the heading, by striking "not worth preserving";

(B) in subsection (a), by striking "owned by the Maritime Administration" and all that follows through the period at the end and inserting "is an obsolete vessel, the Secretary may dispose of such vessel (by sale or by purchase of disposal services)."; and

(C) in subsection (b), by striking "on the basis of competitive sealed bids, after an appraisal and due advertisement" and inserting "on a best value basis".

(5) DONATION OF VESSELS IN THE NATIONAL DEFENSE RESERVE FLEET.—Section 57103 of title 46, United States Code, is amended—

(A) in the heading, by striking "nonretention"; and

(B) in subsection (a), by striking "of insufficient value to warrant its further preservation".

(6) TECHNICAL AND CONFORMING AMENDMENTS.—The analysis for chapter 571 of title 46, United States Code, is amended—

(A) by striking the item relating to section 57102 and inserting the following:

"Disposition of vessels."

(B) by striking the item relating to section 57103 and inserting the following:

"Donation of vessels in the National Defense Reserve Fleet."

(C) by redesignating the item relating to section 57111 as the item relating to section 57110; and

(D) by adding at the end the following:

"57111. Definition of obsolete vessel."

(k) DEEPWATER PORTS.—

(1) DECLARATION OF POLICY.—Section 2 of the Deepwater Port Act of 1974 (33 U.S.C. 1501) is amended—

(A) in subsection (a)—

(i) in the matter preceding paragraph (1), by striking "(a) It" and all that follows through "to—" and inserting the following:

"(a) PURPOSES.—The purposes of this Act are—"

(ii) in each of paragraphs (1) through (6)—

(I) by inserting "to" after the paragraph designation; and

(II) by indenting the paragraphs appropriately;

(iii) in paragraph (2), by striking "such ports" and inserting "deepwater ports";

(iv) in paragraph (5)—

(I) by striking "continental shelf" and inserting "Continental Shelf"; and

(II) by striking "attendant thereto" and inserting "associated with that traffic"; and

(v) in paragraph (6), by striking "continental shelf" each place it appears and inserting "Continental Shelf"; and

(B) in subsection (b), by striking the subsection designation and all that follows through "to affect" and inserting the following:

"(b) EFFECT OF ACT.—Nothing in this Act affects"

(2) DEFINITIONS.—Section 3 of the Deepwater Port Act of 1974 (33 U.S.C. 1502) is amended—

(A) by striking the section designation and heading and all that follows through "the term—" in the matter preceding paragraph (1) and inserting the following:

"SEC. 3. DEFINITIONS

"In this Act:"

(B) in each of paragraphs (1) through (17)—

(i) by inserting "The term" after the paragraph designation;

(ii) by inserting a paragraph heading, the text of which comprises the term defined in that paragraph; and

(iii) by striking the semicolon at the end of the paragraph and inserting a period;

(C) in paragraph (2), by striking "section 5(c)(2)(A) or (B)" and inserting "subparagraph (A) or (B) of section 5(c)(2)";

(D) in each of paragraphs (18) and (19)—

(i) by inserting "The term" after the paragraph designation; and

(ii) by inserting a paragraph heading, the text of which comprises the term defined in that paragraph; and

(E) in paragraph (18), by striking "; and" at the end and inserting a period.

(3) LICENSES FOR OWNERSHIP, CONSTRUCTION, AND OPERATION OF DEEPWATER PORTS.—Section 4 of the Deepwater Port Act of 1974 (33 U.S.C. 1503) is amended—

(A) in subsection (c)—

(i) in each of paragraphs (1) through (7), by striking "he" after the paragraph designation and inserting "the Secretary";

(ii) in paragraph (1), by adding a semicolon at the end; and

(iii) in paragraph (8)—

(I) by striking "the adjacent" and inserting

"each adjacent";

(II) by striking "of States, pursuant to section 9 of this Act,";

(III) by inserting "the" before "issuance"; and

(IV) by inserting "pursuant to section 9(b)(1), if applicable" before "; and";

(B) in subsection (e)—

(i) in paragraph (1), in the second sentence—

(I) by striking "requirements of this title" and inserting "requirements of this Act";

(II) by striking "section 10(a) of this title" and inserting "section 10(a)"; and

(III) by striking the semicolon and inserting a comma;

(ii) in paragraph (2)(B), by striking "he will comply" and inserting "the licensee or transferee will comply"; and

(iii) in paragraph (3)—

(I) in the first sentence, by striking "he deems necessary to assure" and inserting "the Secretary determines to be necessary to ensure";

(II) in the second sentence, by striking "he finds" and inserting "the Secretary finds"; and

(III) in the third sentence—

(aa) by striking "he determines" and inserting "the Secretary determines";

(bb) by striking "(67 Stat. 462)"and inserting "(43 U.S.C. 1331 et seq.)"; and

(cc) by striking "terms" and all that follows through the period at the end and inserting "terms of that Act."; and

(C) in subsection (f), by striking "this title" and inserting "this Act".

(4) PROCEDURE.—Section 5 of the Deepwater Port Act of 1974 (33 U.S.C. 1504) is amended—

(A) in subsection (c)—

(i) by striking the subsection designation and all that follows through the end of paragraph (1) and inserting the following:

"(c) APPLICATIONS.—

"(1) REQUIREMENTS.—

"(A) IN GENERAL. Each person that submits to the Secretary an application shall include in the application a detailed plan that contains all information required under paragraph (2).

"(B) ACTION BY SECRETARY. Not later than 21 days after the date of receipt of an application, the Secretary shall—

"(i) determine whether the application contains all information required under paragraph (2); and

"(ii)(I) if the Secretary determines that such information is contained in the application, not later than 5 days after making the determination, publish in the Federal Register—

"(aa) a notice of the application; and

"(bb) a summary of the plans; or

"(II) if the Secretary determines that all required information is not contained in the application—

"(aa) notify the applicant of the applicable deficiencies; and

"(bb) take no further action with respect to the application until those deficiencies have been remedied.

"(C) APPLICABILITY.—On publication of a notice relating to an application under subparagraph (B)(ii)(I), the Secretary shall be subject to subsection (f)."

; and

(ii) in paragraph (2)—

(I) by striking "of this paragraph" each place it appears;

(II) by striking the paragraph designation and all that follows through "to—" in the matter preceding subparagraph (A) and inserting the following:

"(2) INCLUSIONS.—Each application shall include such financial, technical, and other information as the Secretary determines to be necessary or appropriate, including—"

; and

(III) by indenting subparagraphs (A) through (M) appropriately;

(B) in subsection (g), in the last sentence, by striking "section 5(c) of this Act" and inserting "subsection (c)";

(C) in subsection (h)—

(i) by striking "(h)(1) Each" and inserting the following:

"(h) FEES.—

"(1) REQUIREMENT.—

"(A) IN GENERAL.—Each"

(ii) in subparagraph (A) of paragraph (1) (as so designated), in the second sentence, by striking "In addition" and inserting the following:

"(B) REIMBURSEMENT.—In addition to a fee under subparagraph (A)"

; and

(iii) in paragraph (2)—

(I) by striking the last sentence;

(II) by striking "(2) Notwithstanding" and inserting the following:

"(2) USAGE FEES.—

"(A) DEFINITION OF DIRECTLY RELATED LAND-BASED FACILITY.—In this paragraph, the term 'directly related land-based facility', with respect to a deepwater port facility, means an onshore tank farm and any pipelines connecting the tank farm to the deepwater port facility.

"(B) AUTHORIZATION.—Notwithstanding"

; and

(III) in subparagraph (B) (as so designated)—

(aa) in the fourth sentence, by striking "Such fees" and inserting the following:

"(E) APPROVAL.—A fee established under this paragraph"

(bb) in the third sentence—

(AA) by striking "such" each place it appears and inserting "the applicable"; and

(BB) by striking "Fees under" and inserting the following:

"(D) AMOUNT.—The amount of a fee established under"

; and

(cc) in the second sentence—

(AA) by striking "such" each place it appears and inserting "the applicable"; and

(BB) by striking "Fees may be fixed under authority of this paragraph" and inserting the following:

"(C) TREATMENT.—A fee may be established pursuant to this paragraph"

; and

(iv) in paragraph (3)—

(I) by striking "Outer" and inserting "outer"; and

(II) by striking "(3) A licensee" and inserting

the following:

"(3) RENTAL PAYMENT.—A licensee"

(D) in subsection (i)—

(i) in paragraph (2)—

(I) in subparagraph (A)—

(aa) by inserting "First," after the subparagraph designation; and

(bb) by striking the semicolon at the end and inserting a period;

(II) in subparagraph (B)—

(aa) by inserting "Second," after the subparagraph designation; and

(bb) by striking the semicolon at the end and inserting a period; and

(III) in subparagraph (C), by inserting "Third," after the subparagraph designation;

(ii) in paragraph (3)—

(I) in subparagraph (C), by striking "(C) any" and inserting the following:

"(D) Any"

(II) in subparagraph (B)—

(aa) by striking "; and" at the end and inserting a period; and

(bb) by striking "(B) any" and inserting the following:

"(C) Any"

(III) in subparagraph (A)—

(aa) by striking "section 6 of this Act;" and inserting "section 6."; and

(bb) by striking "(A) the degree" and inserting the following:

"(A) The degree"

; and

(IV) by inserting after subparagraph (A) the following:

"(B) National security, including an assessment of the implications for the national security of the United States or an allied country (as that term is defined in section 2350f(d)(1) of title 10, United States Code) of the United States."

; and

(iii) in paragraph (4)—

(I) by striking the second sentence and inserting the following:

"(B) EFFECT OF FAILURE TO DETERMINE.—If the Secretary fails to approve or deny an application for a deepwater port for natural gas by the applicable deadline under subparagraph (A), the reporting requirements under paragraphs (1), (2), and (3) shall not apply to the application."

; and

(II) in the matter preceding subparagraph (B) (as so added), by striking "(4) The Secretary" and inserting the following:

"(4) APPLICATIONS FOR DEEPWATER PORTS FOR NATURAL GAS.—

"(A) DEADLINE FOR DETERMINATION.—The Secretary"

(E) in subsection (j)(1), by striking "of Transportation"; and

(F) by adding at the end the following:

"(k) TRANSPARENCY IN ISSUANCE OF LICENSES AND PERMITS.—

"(1) DEFINITION OF APPLICABLE DEADLINE.—In this subsection, the term 'applicable deadline', with respect to an applicant, means the deadline or date applicable to the applicant under any of the following:

"(A) Section 4(c)(6).

"(B) Section 4(d)(3).

"(C) Subsection (c)(1)(B) (including clause

(ii)(I) of that subsection).

"(D) Subsection (d)(3).

"(E) Paragraph (1) or (2) of subsection (e).

"(F) Subsection (g).

"(G) Paragraph (1) or (4)(A) of subsection (i).

"(2) SUSPENSIONS AND DELAYS. If the Secretary suspends or delays an applicable deadline, the Secretary shall submit to the applicant, and publish in the Federal Register, a written statement—

"(A) describing the reasons for the suspension or delay;

"(B) describing and requesting any information necessary to issue the applicable license or permit and the status of applicable license or permit application at the lead agency and any cooperating agencies; and

"(C) identifying the applicable deadline with respect to the statement.

"(3) APPLICANT RIGHTS TO TECHNICAL ASSISTANCE.—

"(A) IN GENERAL. An applicant that receives a statement under paragraph (2) may submit to the Secretary a request for a meeting with appropriate personnel of the Department of Transportation and representatives of each cooperating Federal agency, as appropriate, determined by the Secretary to be relevant with respect to the application, including such officials as are appropriate, who shall provide technical assistance, status, process, and timeline updates and additional information as necessary.

"(B) TIMING.—A meeting requested under clause (i) shall be held not later than 30 days after the date on which the Secretary receives the request under that clause.

"(4) REQUIREMENTS.—On receipt of a request under paragraph (3)(A), and not less frequently than once every 30 days thereafter until the date on which the application process is no longer suspended or delayed, the Secretary shall submit a notice of the delay, including a description of the time elapsed since the applicable deadline and the nature and circumstances of the applicable suspension or delay, to—

"(A) the Committee on Commerce, Science, and Transportation of the Senate; and

"(B) the Committee on Transportation and Infrastructure of the House of Representatives.

"(5) BRIEFING. If the Secretary suspends or delays an applicable deadline, not later than 120 days after that applicable deadline, and not less frequently than once every 120 days thereafter until the date on which the application process is no longer suspended or delayed, the Secretary (or a designee of the Secretary) shall provide a briefing regarding the time elapsed since the applicable deadline and the nature and circumstances of the applicable suspension or delay to—

"(A) the Committee on Commerce, Science, and Transportation of the Senate; and

"(B) the Committee on Transportation and Infrastructure of the House of Representatives."

(5) REVIEW CRITERIA.—Section 6 of the Deepwater Port Act of 1974 (33 U.S.C. 1505) is amended—

(A) in subsection (a), by striking "(a) The Secretary" and inserting the following:

"(a) ESTABLISHMENT.—The Secretary"

(B) in subsection (b)—

(i) by striking "of this section"; and

(ii) by striking "(b) The Secretary" and inserting the following:

"(b) REVIEW AND REVISION.—The Secretary"

; and

(C) in subsection (c)—

(i) by striking "concurrently with the regulations

in section 5(a) of this Act and in accordance with the provisions of that subsection" and inserting "concurrently with the regulations promulgated pursuant to section 5(a) and in accordance with that section"; and

(ii) by striking "(c) Criteria" and inserting the following:

"(c) REQUIREMENT.—The criteria"

(6) ADJACENT COASTAL STATES.—Section 9 of the Deepwater Port Act of 1974 (33 U.S.C. 1508) is amended—

(A) by striking subsection (a) and inserting the following:

"(a) DESIGNATION.—In issuing a notice relating to an application for a deepwater port under section 5(c)(1)(B)(ii)(I), the Secretary shall designate as an adjacent coastal State, with respect to the deepwater port, any coastal State that would be—

"(1) directly connected by pipeline to that deepwater port; or

"(2) located within 15 miles of that deepwater port."

; and

(B) in subsection (b)—

(i) by striking "(b)(1) Not later than 10 days after the designation of adjacent coastal States pursuant to this Act" and inserting the following:

"(b) INPUT FROM ADJACENT COASTAL STATES AND OTHER INTERESTED STATES.—

"(1) SUBMISSION OF APPLICATIONS TO GOVERNORS FOR APPROVAL.—

"(A) IN GENERAL. Not later than 10 days after the date on which the Secretary designates adjacent coastal States under subsection (a) with respect to a deepwater port proposed in an application"

(ii) in paragraph (1)(A) (as so designated)—

(I) in the fourth sentence, by striking "If the

Governor" and inserting the following:

"(D) INCONSISTENCY WITH CERTAIN STATE PROGRAMS.—If the Governor of an adjacent coastal State"

(II) in the third sentence, by striking "If the Governor fails to transmit his" and inserting the following:

"(C) PRESUMED APPROVAL.—If the Governor of an adjacent coastal State fails to transmit a required"

; and

(III) in the second sentence, by striking "The Secretary" and inserting the following:

"(B) PROHIBITION.—The Secretary"

; and

(iii) in paragraph (2)—

(I) by striking "(2) Any other interested State" and inserting the following:

"(2) OTHER INTERESTED STATES.—Any other State with an interest relating to a deepwater port proposed in an application"

; and

(II) by striking "a deepwater port" and inserting "the deepwater port".

Subtitle C—Reports

SEC. 3521. REPORTS ON MARITIME INDUSTRY, POLICIES, AND PROGRAMS.

(a) REPORT ON ADMINISTRATION OF PROGRAMS.—

(1) IN GENERAL.—Chapter 553 of title 46, United States Code, is amended by inserting before section 55302 the following:

"SEC. 55301. [46 U.S.C. 55301] Report on administration of programs by other Federal departments and agencies

"(a) IN GENERAL.—The Administrator of the Maritime

Administration shall annually submit to Congress a report on the administration by—

"(1) the Department of Defense of section 2631 of title 10; and

"(2) other Federal departments and agencies of programs the Administrator determines are subject to section 55305 of this title.

"(b) CONTENTS.—Each annual report required under subsection (a) shall include, for each Federal department or agency that administers a program covered by the report—

"(1) the gross tonnage of cargo (equipment, materials, or agricultural products), expressed by type of cargo, transported on United States flag vessels as compared to on foreign vessels; and

"(2) the total number of United States flag vessels and total number of foreign vessels contracted by each department or agency.

"(c) AGENCY REPORTING REQUIREMENTS.—Not later than January 31 of each year, the head of each Federal department or agency that administers a program covered by a report required under subsection (a) shall submit to the Administrator of the Maritime Administration the information described in subsection (b) for that department or agency."

(2) CLERICAL AMENDMENT.—The analysis for chapter 553 of title 46, United States Code, is amended by inserting before the item relating to section 55302 the following new item:

"55301. Report on administration of programs by other Federal departments and agencies."

(b) REPORT ON SURVEY OF UNITED STATES SHIPBUILDING AND REPAIR FACILITIES.—

(1) IN GENERAL.—Not later than 180 days after the date of enactment of this Act, and annually thereafter for each of the subsequent four fiscal years, the Secretary of Transportation, in consultation with the Secretary of Defense, the Administrator of the Maritime Administration, and the Commandant of the Coast Guard, shall submit to the appropriate committees of Congress a report that includes a survey of United States shipbuilding and repair facilities.

(2) CONTENTS.—Each report required under paragraph (1) shall include an identification of all requirements for a survey of United States shipbuilding and repair facilities in accordance with sections 50102 and 50103 of title 46, United States Code, and section 502(f) of the Merchant Marine Act of 1936 (46 U.S.C. 53101 note).

(3) PUBLIC AVAILABILITY.—At the time the Secretary of Transportation submits to the appropriate congressional committees a report under paragraph (1), the Secretary shall make the report, and all report data, publicly available on an appropriate website.

(4) DEFINITION.—In this subsection, the term “appropriate congressional committees” means—

(A) the Committee on Commerce, Science, and Transportation of the Senate; and

(B) the Committee on Transportation and Infrastructure and the Committee on Armed Services of the House of Representatives.

(c) REPORT ON PORT PREFERENCES FOR US-FLAG VESSELS.—Not later than one year after the date of the enactment of this Act, the Administrator of the Maritime Administration shall submit to Congress a report on the preference, if any, afforded by each port authority or marine terminal operator, as applicable, to vessels documented under the laws of the United States, including such vessels—

(1) operated by an armed force (as such term is defined in section 101(4) of title 10, United States Code);

(2) participating in the Maritime Security Program or the Emergency Preparedness Program under chapter 531 of title 46, United States Code, the Cable Security Fleet under chapter 532 of such title, the Tanker Security Fleet under chapter 534 of such title, or the National Defense Reserve Fleet under section 57100 of such title; or

(3) with a coastwise endorsement under chapter 121 of title 46, United States Code.

(d) [46 U.S.C. 55601 note] REPORT ON INCREASING EFFECTIVENESS OF MARINE HIGHWAYS.—

(1) IN GENERAL.—Not later than one year after the date of the enactment of this Act, the Administrator of the Maritime

Administration shall complete and make publicly available on an appropriate website a study that identifies opportunities for, and barriers to, increasing the effectiveness of marine highways designated under section 55601 of title 46, United States Code, in addressing two or more of the components described in clauses (i), (ii), and (iv) of subparagraphs (A) and subparagraph (B) of section 50307(a)(2) of title 46, United States Code.

(2) PILOT PROGRAM. Beginning on the date that is 120 days after the date of the completion of the study required under paragraph (1), the Administrator shall carry out a one-year pilot program under which the Administrator shall select one marine highway project and implement the findings of the study with respect to that project.

(3) FINAL REPORT. Not later than 90 days after the completion of the pilot program under paragraph (3), the Administrator shall provide to the Committee on Commerce, Science, and Transportation of the Senate and the Committee on Transportation and Infrastructure of the House of Representatives, a briefing on the lessons learned from the pilot program, any recommendations based on feedback from maritime stakeholders, States, Indian Tribes, nonprofit organizations, and other stakeholders, and recommendations for establishing future marine highways in the United States.

(e) STUDY ON AVAILABILITY OF FEDERAL STUDENT AID FOR MARINER TRAINING.—

(1) IN GENERAL.—The Comptroller General of the United States shall conduct a study of the availability of Federal financial assistance for licensed and unlicensed mariners, as applicable, for mariner training and the effectiveness of coordination with respect to such assistance of—

(A) Federal agencies;

(B) Federal agencies and States; and

(C) Federal agencies and Indian Tribes.

(2) MATTERS EVALUATED.—The study conducted under paragraph (1) shall include an evaluation of the following:

(A) The availability of Federal financial assistance for mariner training provided by the Department of Education, the Department of Veterans Affairs, the Department of Labor, the Maritime Administration, or other agencies to the full range of prospective mariners, and an identification of any gaps in financial assistance.

(B) The extent to which the Maritime Administration has effectively coordinated with the Department of Education, the Department of Veterans Affairs, the Department of Labor, or other relevant Federal agencies to align Federal financial assistance with the education and training needs of mariners.

(C) The extent to which the Maritime Administration has effectively communicated with prospective and current mariners about the availability of Federal financial assistance to facilitate their training and education needs.

(3) SCOPE.—The study conducted under paragraph (1) shall include an examination of the availability of Federal financial assistance, and the service obligations related to such financial assistance, if applicable, at mariner training institutions within the United States, including for students attending, or participating in—

(A) the United States Merchant Marine Academy;

(B) a State maritime academy;

(C) an institution described in subparagraphs (B) and (C) of section 51706(c)(1) of title 46, United States Code;

(D) an Indian Tribe apprenticeship or other training program; or

(E) an educational program carried out by a Federal agency.

(4) REPORT.—Not later than two years after the date of the enactment of this Act, the Comptroller General shall submit to the Committee on Commerce, Science, and Transportation of the Senate and the Committee on Transportation and Infrastructure and the Committee on Armed Services of the House of Representatives a report containing the findings of the Comptroller General with respect to the study conducted under paragraph (1).

SEC. 3522. REPORTS ON AVAILABILITY OF USED SEALIFT VESSELS AND THE SCRAPPING AND RECYCLING OF IMPORTED VESSELS.

(a) REPORT ON AVAILABILITY OF USED SEALIFT VESSELS.—

(1) IN GENERAL.—The Commander of the United States Transportation Command, in consultation with the Administrator of the Maritime Administration, shall conduct a market analysis to determine the availability of used sealift vessels that—

(A) meet military requirements; and

(B) may be purchased using the authority provided under section 2218 of title 10, United States Code, within the period of five years following the date of the enactment of this Act.

(2) REPORT.—Not later than 180 days after the date of the enactment of this Act, the Commander of the United States Transportation Command shall submit to the congressional defense committees and the Committee on Commerce, Science, and Transportation of the Senate a report on the results of the market analysis conducted under paragraph (1).

(b) STUDY ON THE SCRAPPING AND RECYCLING OF IMPORTED VESSELS.—

(1) IN GENERAL.—The Administrator of the Maritime Administration and the Deputy Under Secretary for International Affairs of the Department of Labor shall jointly conduct a study to review domestic United States ship scrapping capacity and capability.

(2) ELEMENTS.—The study required under paragraph (1) shall include the following:

(A) An assessment of—

(i) the capabilities of United States shipyards to recycle and dispose of domestic and foreign vessels and their component parts;

(ii) the capacity of United States shipyards to complete ship recycling and disposal of domestic and foreign vessels and their component parts and related activities; and

(iii) the infrastructure, regulatory, economic, or other barriers to domestic ship recycling and disposal of vessels of the United States (as defined in section 116 of title 46, United States Code) and foreign vessels and their component parts.

(B) An identification of—

(i) the estimated number of vessels over 1,000 tons that were recycled or scrapped globally each year for the ten-year period preceding the date of the enactment of this Act;

(ii) the country in which such vessels were scrapped or recycled;

(iii) the component parts of a vessel that require additional processing after ship recycling;

(iv) best practices and methods used globally, including in the United States, at the time of the study, to recycle or dispose of the components described in clause (iii); and

(v) for the 15 foreign countries with the highest global market share for ship recycling and disposal, and for any countries with documented labor exploitation or environmental concerns (as determined by the Administrator and the Deputy Under Secretary)—

(I) the practices used at the time of the study for ship recycling and disposal, including for the component parts described in clause (iii); and

(II) to the extent such information is available, environmental and labor practices used in such recycling and disposal.

(3) REPORT.—Not later than one year after the date of the enactment of this Act, the Administrator shall submit to the Committee on Commerce, Science, and Transportation of the Senate and the Committee on Transportation and Infrastructure of the House of Representatives a report containing the findings of the study required under paragraph (1).

(4) DEFINITIONS OF COMPONENT PARTS.—In this subsection, the term "component parts" means an item or items on a ship that require additional processing after removal from the ship, such as cable insulation, rubber and felt gaskets, electronic equipment, caulking, or paint.

SEC. 3523. STUDY ON FOREIGN OWNERSHIP AND CONTROL OF

MARINE TERMINALS.

(a) IN GENERAL. Not later than 90 days after the date of the enactment of this Act, the Secretary of Transportation, in consultation with the Secretary of Commerce, shall seek to enter into an agreement with a federally funded research and development center under which the center shall evaluate how foreign state-owned enterprises with leases, long term concessions, partial ownership, or ownership of marine terminals (including marine terminal operators) at the 15 largest United States container ports affect, or could affect, United States national and economic security.

(b) CONTENTS.—An agreement entered into pursuant to subsection (a) shall provide that the center shall—

(1) consider—

(A) foreign ownership or state-owned enterprises with leases, long-term concessions, partial ownership, or ownership of marine terminals (including marine terminal operators) at 15 largest United States container ports over the 30-year period preceding the date of enactment of this Act;

(B) instances of ownership in individual marine terminals and cumulative ownership by Chinese or Russian entities, state-owned enterprises, or nationals;

(C) instances of ownership in individual marine terminals and partial or complete ownership by any foreign entity;

(D) the amount of Federal funds that have been distributed to ports and marine terminals that are wholly or partially foreign-owned, including Chinese and Russian state-owned enterprises;

(E) where any stake in foreign ownership, or other vectors of control, exists (including any level of equity stake in joint ventures with United States or foreign marine terminal operators), including Chinese or Russian state-owned enterprises, a detailed description of foreign operational control, including both affirmative and negative control; and

(F) the degree to which transactions for leases, long-term concessions, partial ownership, or ownership of marine terminals referred to in subparagraph (A) were considered covered transactions by the Committee on Foreign Investment in the United States and subsequently subject to review during the 30-year period preceding the date of the enactment of this Act; and

(2) offer recommendations on—

(A) policies by ports and marine terminal operators with respect to foreign ownership or control to prevent any degree of threats to United States national security and economic security;

(B) whether foreign ownership, a positional relationship, or state-owned enterprises with leases, long term concessions, partial ownership, or ownership of marine terminals (including marine terminal operators) affords the foreign entity access to operational technology and information unique to the United States and otherwise unavailable;

(C) whether foreign ownership or state-owned enterprises with leases, long term concessions, partial ownership, or ownership of marine terminals (including marine terminal operators) has or could affect the supply chain and policies related to the prioritization of certain cargoes; and

(D) legislative or other policy changes needed to secure and advance United States national and economic security of the United States.

(c) REPORT.—Not later than one year after the initiation of an evaluation carried out pursuant to an agreement entered into under subsection (a), the Secretary of Transportation shall submit to the Committee on Commerce, Science, and Transportation of the Senate and the Committee on Transportation and Infrastructure of the House of Representatives a report containing the results of such evaluation.

(d) FORM.—The report required under subsection (c) shall be submitted in unclassified form, but may include a classified annex.

SEC. 3524. REPORTS TO CONGRESS.

Not later than 180 days after the date of the enactment of this Act, the Secretary of Defense shall submit to Congress a report on the implementation by the Department of Defense of the amendments to section 2631 of title 10, United States Code, made by section 1024 of the William M. (Mac) Thornberry National Defense Authorization Act for Fiscal Year 2021 (Public Law 116-283).

Subtitle D—Other Matters

SEC. 3531. CARGOES PROCURED, FURNISHED, OR FINANCED BY THE UNITED STATES GOVERNMENT.

(a) IN GENERAL.—Section 55305 of title 46, United States Code, is amended—

(1) by striking subsection (a);

(2) by redesignating—

(A) subsection (b) as subsection (a); and

(B) subsections (c), (d), and (e), as subsections (d), (e), and (f), respectively;

(3) in subsection (a), as so redesignated, by striking "privately-owned commercial vessels of the United States," and inserting "privately-owned commercial vessels of the United States, as provided under subsection (b),";

(4) by inserting after subsection (a), as so redesignated, the following:

"(b) ELIGIBLE VESSELS.—To be eligible to carry cargo as provided under subsection (a), a privately-owned commercial vessel shall be documented under the laws of the United States—

"(1) for not less than three years; or

"(2) after January 1, 2030, for less than three years, if the vessel owner signs an agreement with the Secretary providing that—

"(A) the vessel shall remain documented under the laws of the United States for not less than three years; and

"(B) the vessel owner shall, upon request of the Secretary, agree to enroll the vessel in an emergency preparedness agreement or voluntary agreement authorized under section 708 of the Defense Production Act of 1950 (50 U.S.C. 4558) and shall ensure the vessel remains so enrolled until the vessel ceases to be documented under the laws of the United States.

"(c) VIOLATION OF AGREEMENT.—A vessel under an agreement executed pursuant to subsection (b)(2) may be seized by, and forfeited to, the United States if, in violation of that agreement—

"(1) the vessel owner places the vessel under foreign registry; or

"(2) a person operates the vessel under the authority of a foreign country."

; and

(5) by striking subsection (d), as so redesignated, and inserting the following:

"(d) WAIVERS.—(1) Notwithstanding any other provision of law, when the President, the Secretary of Defense, or the Secretary of Transportation declares the existence of an emergency justifying a temporary waiver of this section or section 55314 of this title, the President, the Secretary of Defense, or the Secretary of Transportation, following a determination by the Maritime Administrator, acting in the Administrator's capacity as Director, National Shipping Authority, of the non-availability of qualified United States flag capacity at fair and reasonable rates for commercial vessels of the United States to meet the requirements of this section or section 55314 of this title, may waive compliance with such section to the extent, in the manner, and on the terms the Maritime Administrator, acting in such capacity, prescribes, and no other waivers of the requirements of this section or section 55314 of this title shall be authorized.

"(2)(A) Subject to subparagraphs (B) and (C), a waiver issued under this subsection shall be for a period of not more than 60 days.

"(B) Upon termination of the period of a waiver issued under this subsection, the Maritime Administrator may extend the waiver for an additional period of not more than 30 days, if the Maritime

Administrator makes the determinations described in paragraph (1).

"(C) The aggregate duration of the period of all waivers and extensions of waivers under this subsection with respect to any one set of events shall not exceed three months in a fiscal year.

"(3) The Maritime Administrator shall—

"(A) for each determination referred to in paragraph (1), identify any actions that could be taken to enable qualified United States flag capacity to meet the requirements of this section or section 55314 at fair and reasonable rates for commercial vessels of the United States;

"(B) provide notice of each determination referred to in paragraph (1) to the Secretary of Transportation and, as applicable, the President or the Secretary of Defense; and

"(C) publish each determination referred to in paragraph (1)—

"(i) on the website of the Maritime Administration not later than 24 hours after notice of the determination is provided to the Secretary of Transportation; and

"(ii) in the Federal Register.

"(4) The Maritime Administrator shall notify—

"(A) the Committee on Commerce, Science, and Transportation of the Senate and the Committee on Transportation and Infrastructure of the House of Representatives of—

"(i) any request for a waiver (or an extension thereof) made by the Secretary of Transportation of this section or section 55314(a) of this title by not later than 72 hours after receiving such a request; and

"(ii) the issuance of any such waiver (or an extension thereof), and why such waiver or extension was necessary, by not later than 72 hours after such issuance; and

"(B) the Committee on Commerce, Science, and Transportation and the Committee on Armed Services of the Senate and the Committee on Transportation and Infrastructure and the Committee on Armed Services of the House of Representatives of—

"(i) any request for a waiver (or an extension thereof) made by the Secretary of Defense of this section or section 55314(a) of this title by not later than 72 hours after receiving such a request; and

"(ii) the issuance of any such waiver (or an extension thereof), and why such waiver or extension was necessary, by not later than 72 hours after such issuance."

(b) [46 U.S.C. 3306 note] SMALL PASSENGER VESSELS WITH OVERNIGHT ACCOMMODATIONS.—

(1) EXTENSION AUTHORITY.—

(A) IN GENERAL.—The Commandant of the Coast Guard shall not enforce the requirements of section 3306(n)(3)(A)(v) of title 46, United States Code, against an operator of an overnight fishing charter before April 1, 2024.

(B) PLAN REQUIRED.—Not later than April 1, 2024, an operator of an overnight fishing charter not in compliance with such section 3306(n)(3)(A)(v) shall submit to the Commandant a plan for complying with such requirements.

(C) EXTENSION. On and after April 1, 2024, with respect to an operator of an overnight fishing charter which has submitted a plan for compliance in accordance with subparagraph (B), a captain of the port may extend the period described under subparagraph (A) until a date not later than January 1, 2026.

(2) LIMITATION.—Without further Congressional action, a captain of the port may not extend the period of nonenforcement of the requirements of section 3306(n)(3)(A)(v) of title 46, United States Code, with respect to an overnight fishing charter, to a date later than January 1, 2026.

(3) NOTICE TO PASSENGERS. Beginning on the date on which the requirements under section 3306(n)(3)(A)(v) of title 46,

United States Code, take effect, the owner or operator of a vessel for which an extension is granted under paragraph (1)(C) shall provide on the website of such owner or operator of the vessel, the vessel, and each ticket for a passenger a prominently displayed notice that the vessel is exempt from meeting the Coast Guard safety compliance standards concerning egress as described in such section.

(4) OVERNIGHT FISHING CHARTER DEFINED.—In this section, the term "overnight fishing charter" means a vessel that—

(A) is engaged in "charter fishing" as such term is defined in section 3 of the Magnuson-Stevens Fishery Conservation and Management Act (16 U.S.C. 1802); and

(B) has overnight accommodations for passengers.

SEC. 3532. RECAPITALIZATION OF NATIONAL DEFENSE RESERVE FLEET.

Section 3546 of the James M. Inhofe National Defense Authorization Act for Fiscal Year 2023 (Public Law 117-263; 46 U.S.C. 57100 note) is amended—

(1) in subsection (a)—

(A) in the matter preceding paragraph (1)—

(i) by striking "Subject to the availability of appropriations" and inserting "Subject to the availability of appropriations made specifically available for reimbursements to the Ready Reserve Force, Maritime Administration account of the Department of Transportation for programs, projects, activities, and expenses related to the National Defense Reserve Fleet"; and

(ii) by striking "of Transportation" and inserting "of the Navy"; and

(B) in paragraph (1)—

(i) by striking "roll-on, roll-off cargo" and inserting "sealift"; and

(ii) by striking "2024" and inserting "2025";

(2) in subsection (d), by striking "The Secretary of Transportation shall consult and coordinate with the Secretary of the 137 STAT. 828 Navy"and inserting "The Secretary of

the Navy shall consult and coordinate with the Secretary of Transportation"; and

(3) by adding at the end the following new subsection:

"(f) LIMITATION. Of the amounts authorized to be appropriated by this Act or otherwise made available for fiscal year 2024 for the Secretary of the Navy for travel expenses, not more than 50 percent may be obligated or expended until the Secretary of the Navy submits to the congressional defense committees a report that includes a detailed description of the acquisition strategy for the execution of the authority under subsection (a)."

SEC. 3533. UNITED STATES MERCHANT MARINE ACADEMY AND COAST GUARD ACADEMY MATTERS; MARITIME ADMINISTRATION REQUIREMENTS.

(a) [46 U.S.C. 51301 note] TRAINING COURSE ON WORKINGS OF CONGRESS.—

(1) IN GENERAL.—Not later than 180 days after the date of the enactment of this section, the Secretary of Transportation, in consultation with the Maritime Administrator, the Superintendent of the United States Merchant Marine Academy, and such other individuals and organizations as the Secretary of Transportation considers appropriate, shall develop a training course on the workings of Congress and offer that training course at least once each year. This course shall be similar in design to the training course required under section 315 of title 14, United States Code, as practicable.

(2) COURSE SUBJECT MATTER.—The training course required by paragraph (1) shall provide an overview and introduction to Congress and the Federal legislative process, including—

(A) the history and structure of Congress and the committee systems of the Senate and the House of Representatives, including the functions and responsibilities of the Committee on Commerce, Science, and Transportation of the Senate and the Committee on Transportation and Infrastructure and the Committee on Armed Services of the House of Representatives;

(B) the documents produced by Congress, including

bills, resolutions, committee reports, and conference reports, and the purposes and functions of those documents;

(C) the legislative processes and rules of the Senate and the House of Representatives, including similarities and differences between the processes and rules of each chamber, including—

(i) the congressional budget process;

(ii) the congressional authorization and appropriations processes;

(iii) the Senate advice and consent process for Presidential nominees; and

(iv) the Senate advice and consent process for treaty ratification;

(D) the roles of Members of Congress and congressional staff in the legislative process; and

(E) the concept and underlying purposes of congressional oversight within the governance framework of separation of powers of the United States.

(3) LECTURERS AND PANELISTS.—

(A) OUTSIDE EXPERTS.—The Secretary of Transportation shall ensure that not less than 60 percent of the lecturers, panelists, and other individuals providing education and instruction as part of the training course required by this subsection are bipartisan subject matter experts on Congress and the Federal legislative process who are not employed by the executive branch of the Federal Government.

(B) AUTHORITY TO ACCEPT PRO BONO SERVICES.—In satisfying the requirement under subparagraph (A), the Secretary of Transportation shall seek, and may accept, educational and instructional services of lecturers, panelists, and other individuals and organizations provided to the Department of Transportation on a pro bono basis.

(4) COMPLETION OF REQUIRED TRAINING.—

(A) IN GENERAL.—Not later than 60 days after the date on which the Secretary of Transportation completes the development of the training course described in this section, and annually thereafter while serving in applicable positions, the covered individuals described in subparagraph (B) shall complete the training course described in this subsection.

(B) COVERED INDIVIDUALS.—The covered individuals in this subsection are the following:

(i) The Administrator of the Maritime Administration and the Deputy Administrator of the Maritime Administration.

(ii) Any official of the Maritime Administration whose appointment is subject to the advice and consent of the Senate and Maritime Administration employees that are serving in a Senior Executive Service position (as defined in section 3132(a) of title 5, United States Code).

(iii) Any Maritime Administration employees whose duties consist of engagement with congressional, governmental, or public affairs, who are appointed or assigned to a billet in the National Capital Region on the date on which the Secretary of Transportation completes the development of the training course described in this section.

(iv) The Superintendent, Deputy Superintendent, Provost, Commandant of Midshipmen, Counsel, and Director of Public Affairs of the United States Merchant Marine Academy.

(C) NEW OFFICIALS AND EMPLOYEES.—Any Maritime Administration official or employee or United States Merchant Marine Academy official or employee who is a covered individual described in subparagraph (B) who is newly appointed, newly employed in the National Capital Region, or newly employed by the United States Merchant Marine Academy after the date on which the Secretary of Transportation completes the development of the training course described in this subsection, shall complete a training course that meets the requirements of this subsection not later than 60 days after reporting for duty, and annually thereafter, while serving in applicable positions.

(b) GOVERNMENT ACCOUNTABILITY OFFICE REPORT ON MARITIME ADMINISTRATION STAFFING REQUIREMENTS.—

(1) IN GENERAL. Not later than six months after the date of the enactment of this Act, the Comptroller General of the United States shall submit to the Committee on Commerce, Science, and Transportation of the Senate and the Committee on Transportation and Infrastructure of the House of Representatives, a report that includes an analysis of the staffing requirements for effectively executing the mission of the Maritime Administration and an identification of any existing gaps that could impede its operations.

(2) CONTENTS.—The report under paragraph (1) shall include—

(A) an evaluation of the personnel requirements for the successful execution of the mission of the Maritime Administration, including such requirements for—

(i) those offices that deal with infrastructure, shipbuilding, or student safety;

(ii) those offices that have significant delays in meeting constituent needs, including offices involved in the processing of permits and grants, or which preform a communication or outreach function to the public, constituents, or Congress (including the Office of Public Affairs of the Maritime Administration);

(iii) the United States Merchant Marine Academy; and

(iv) other activities carried out by the Maritime Administration;

(B) a thorough analysis of any deficiencies or inadequacies in staffing levels, at the time the report is submitted, that could hinder the efficient functioning of the Maritime Administration; and

(C) recommendations for integrating the findings of the report into the policies and planning processes of the Maritime Administration, with the aim of addressing the identified gaps and enhancing the overall effectiveness of the Maritime Administration.

(c) COAST GUARD ACADEMY IMPROVEMENT BRIEFING.—Not later than 30 days after the date of the enactment of this Act, the

Commandant of the Coast Guard shall provide to the Committee on Transportation and Infrastructure of the House of Representatives and the Committee on Commerce, Science, and Transportation of the Senate a briefing on—

(1) a plan, which shall include timelines and cost estimates, to—

(A) remediate asbestos, lead, and mold from the Chase Hall of the Coast Guard Academy;

(B) house not more than two students to a room in Chase Hall; and

(C) upgrade electric outlet availability and storage space in student rooms at Chase Hall; and

(2) the increased student housing capacity necessary to allow the Coast Guard to put through sufficient officers to eliminate the current portion of the officer shortfall due to space constraints at the Coast Guard Academy, including the Officer Candidate School and direct Commission Officer Program housed at the Academy.

SEC. 3534. MARITIME WORKFORCE WORKING GROUP.

(a) IN GENERAL.—Not later than 120 days after the date of the enactment of this Act, the Maritime Administrator, in consultation with the National Merchant Marine Personnel Advisory Committee, the National Offshore Safety Advisory Committee, the National Towing Safety Advisory Committee, and the Committee on the Marine Transportation System, shall convene a working group to examine and assess the size of the pool of mariners with covered credentials necessary to support the United States flag fleet.

(b) MEMBERSHIP.—The Maritime Administrator shall designate individuals to serve as members of the working group convened under subsection (a). The working group shall consist of—

(1) the Maritime Administrator, who shall serve as chairperson of the working group;

(2) the Superintendent of the United States Merchant Marine Academy;

(3) the Commandant of the Coast Guard;

(4) the Commander of the United States Transportation Command;

(5) the Secretary of the Navy; and

(6) at least one representative from each of—

(A) the State maritime academies;

(B) the owners and operators of United States-flagged vessels engaged in offshore oil and gas exploration, development, and production;

(C) the owners and operators of United States-flagged vessels engaged in inland river transportation;

(D) the owners and operators of United States-flagged vessels engaged in inland river transportation;

(E) a nonprofit labor organization representing a class of licensed or unlicensed engine department mariners who are employed on vessels operating in the United States flag fleet;

(F) a nonprofit labor organization representing a class of licensed or unlicensed mariners who are employed on vessels operating in the United States flag fleet;

(G) the owners of vessels operating in the United States flag fleet, or their private contracting parties, that are primarily operating in international transportation;

(H) Centers of Excellence for Maritime Training designated under section 51706 of title 46, United States Code; and

(I) private maritime training providers.

(c) NO QUORUM REQUIREMENT.—The Maritime Administrator may convene the working group virtually and without all members present.

(d) RESPONSIBILITIES.—The working group shall carry out the following responsibilities:

(1) Reviewing the report required by section 3525(b), and the study required by section 3542(a), of the James Inhofe National Defense Authorization Act for Fiscal Year 2023 (Public Law 117-263), if available.

(2) Identifying the number of mariners with covered credentials in each of the following categories:

(A) All such mariners.

(B) Such mariners who have a valid Coast Guard

merchant mariner credential with the necessary endorsements for service on unlimited tonnage vessels that are subject to the International Convention on Standards of Training, Certification and Watchkeeping for Seafarers, 1978, as amended.

(C) Such mariners who are participating in a Federal program that supports the United States merchant marine and the United States flag fleet.

(D) Such mariners who are available to crew the United States flag fleet and the surge sealift fleet in times of a national emergency.

(E) Such mariners who are full-time.

(F) Such mariners who are merchant mariner credentialed officers in the United States Navy Reserve.

(G) Such licensed and unlicensed mariners—

(i) required to maintain, mobilize, and operate the entire Ready Reserve Force for periods of 30 days, 90 days, 180 days, and one year including separate totals for merchant mariners employed to maintain the Ready Reserve Force in a reduced operating status; and

(ii) required to submit documentation of sea service to the National Maritime Center, including such mariners that have acquired sea service during the prior year and such mariners that have not acquired sea service during the prior year.

(3) Evaluating potential gaps or surpluses of credentialed merchant mariners, by rating and qualification, required to maintain, mobilize, and operate the Ready Reserve Force for periods of 30 days, 90 days, 180 days, and one year and the potential impacts such mobilization and operation will have on the commercial maritime industry's capability to operate during such periods.

(4) Identifying a list of all actively operating documented vessels of at least 500 gross registered tons, as measured under section 14502 of title 46, United States Code, or an alternate tonnage measured under section 14302 of such title as prescribed by the Secretary under section 14104, of such title, with the tonnage of each such vessel.

(5) Assessing the effect on the United States merchant marine and United States Merchant Marine Academy if graduates from State maritime academies and the United States Merchant Marine Academy were assigned to, or required to fulfill, certain maritime positions based on the overall needs of the United States merchant marine.

(6) Assessing the effectiveness of marketing and outreach efforts, including recruitment and retention strategy and methods of publicizing opportunities, for new mariner accession into the maritime industry.

(7) Assessing the accessibility of Coast Guard Merchant Mariner Licensing and Documentation System data for mariners with covered credentials, the maritime industry, and the Maritime Administration for the purposes of evaluating the pool of mariners with covered credentials.

(8) Assessing the impediments to the credentialing of United States merchant mariners, including training capacity, credentialing system delays, costs to merchant mariners, statutory or regulatory requirements, and other factors.

(9) Making recommendations to—

(A) enhance the availability and quality of interagency data, including data from the United States Transportation Command, the Coast Guard, the Navy, and the Bureau of Transportation Statistics, for use by the Maritime Administration in evaluating the pool of mariners with covered credentials;

(B) close any gaps identified in the evaluation described in paragraph (3), including specific policy, legislative change proposals, and funding requests; and

(C) improve United States merchant mariner recruitment and retention.

(e) PROVISION OF INFORMATION.—All members of the working group convened under subsection (a) shall provide to the Maritime Administrator, in a timely manner and in a suitable format agreed to by members, any information that is needed to carry out the responsibilities under subsection (d).

(f) REPORT.—Not later than one year after the date of the enactment of this Act, the Secretary of Transportation shall submit to the Committee on Commerce, Science, and Transportation of the Senate, the Committee on Armed Services of the House of Representatives, and the Committee on Transportation and Infrastructure of the House of Representatives a report that contains the findings and conclusions of the working group gathered in the course of performing the responsibilities under subsection (d). Such report shall include each of the following:

(1) The number of mariners with covered credentials identified for each category described in subparagraphs (A) through (G) of subsection (d)(2).

(2) The results of the evaluation under subsection (d)(3).

(3) The list identified under subsection (d)(4).

(4) The results of the assessments conducted under paragraphs (5) and (8) of subsection (d).

(5) The recommendations made under paragraphs (5) and (9) of subsection (d).

(6) Such other information as the working group determines appropriate.

(g) CLASSIFIED ANNEX.—The report required under this section shall be submitted in unclassified form, but shall include a classified annex including the results from subsection (d)(2)(G) and subsection (d)(3).

(h) DEFINITIONS.—In this section:

(1) The term "covered credential" means any credential issued under part E of subtitle II of title 46, United States Code.

(2) The term "documented vessel" has the meaning given the term in section 106 of title 46, United States Code.

(3) The term "Ready Reserve Force" has the meaning given the term in chapter 571 of title 46, United States Code.

(i) SUNSET.—The Maritime Administrator shall disband the working group upon the submission of the report required under subsection (f).

(j) [46 U.S.C. 7307 note] TEMPORARY REDUCTION OF LENGTHS OF CERTAIN PERIODS OF SERVICE. For the 3-year period beginning on the date of enactment of this Act—

(1) section 7307 of title 46, United States Code, shall be applied by substituting "18 months" for "3 years";

(2) section 7308 of such title shall be applied by

substituting "12 months" for "18 months"; and

(3) section 7309 of such title shall be applied by substituting "6 months" for "12 months".

(k) CENTERS OF EXCELLENCE FOR DOMESTIC MARITIME WORKFORCE TRAINING AND EDUCATION.—Section 51706 of title 46, United States Code, is amended—

(1) in subsection (a)—

(A) by striking "The Secretary" and inserting the following:

"(1) IN GENERAL.—The Secretary"

(B) by inserting ", after consultation with the Coast Guard," after "Transportation";

(C) by inserting ", for a 5-year period," after "designate"; and

(D) by adding at the end the following:

"(2) WITHDRAWAL OF DESIGNATION.—The Secretary of Transportation may withdraw a designation as a center of excellence for domestic maritime workforce training and education of a covered training entity upon discovery of adverse information, including discovery of information that the covered training entity has engaged in fraudulent or unlawful activities, or has been subjected to disciplinary or adverse administrative action by Federal, State, or other regulatory bodies."

(2) in subsection (b), by adding at the end the following:

"(5) ELIGIBLE USES OF GRANT FUNDS.—A center of excellence receiving a grant under this subsection shall—

"(A) carry out activities that are identified as priorities for the purpose of developing, offering, or improving educational or career training programs for the United States maritime industry workforce; and

"(B) provide training to upgrade the skills of the United States maritime industry workforce, including training to acquire covered requirements as well as technical skills training for jobs in the United States maritime industry."

; and

(3) in subsection (c)(1)—

(A) in subparagraph (B)(v), by striking "and" after the semicolon;

(B) in subparagraph (C), by striking the period at the end and inserting "; and"; and

(C) by adding at the end the following:

"(D) has—

"(i) not been subject to a disciplinary or adverse administrative action by Federal, State, or other regulatory bodies;

"(ii) no unresolved nonconformities from administrative audits by regulatory bodies; and

"(iii) not been subject to any adverse criminal action by a Federal, State, or local law enforcement authority."

SEC. 3535. [46 U.S.C. 57100 note] CONSIDERATION OF LIFE-CYCLE COST ESTIMATES FOR ACQUISITION AND PROCUREMENT OF VESSELS.

In carrying out the acquisition and procurement of vessels in the National Defense Reserve Fleet, the Secretary of Transportation, acting through the Administrator of the Maritime Administration, shall consider the life-cycle cost estimates of vessels during the design and evaluation processes to the maximum extent practicable.

SEC. 3536. LOANS FOR RETROFITTING TO QUALIFY AS A VESSEL OF THE UNITED STATES.

(a) IN GENERAL.—Section 53706(a) of title 46, United States Code, is amended by adding at the end the following:

"(8) Financing (including reimbursement of an obligor for expenditures previously made for) the reconstruction, reconditioning, retrofitting, repair, reconfiguration, or similar work in a shipyard located in the United States."

(b) PROHIBITION ON USE OF APPROPRIATED FUNDS.—Amounts appropriated to the Maritime Administration before the date of enactment of this Act shall not be available to be used for the cost of loan guarantees for projects receiving financing support or credit enhancements under section 53706(a)(8) of title 46, United States

Code, as added by this section.

SEC. 3537. [46 U.S.C. 50114 note] ACCOUNTABILITY FOR NATIONAL MARITIME STRATEGY.

(a) BIANNUAL BRIEFING.—

(1) REQUIREMENT.—Not less than twice annually, the Administrator of the Maritime Administration, in consultation with the National Security Council, the Secretary of State, the Secretary of Transportation, and the Secretary of Homeland Security, shall provide to the appropriate congressional committees briefings on the status of establishing the type of national maritime strategy required under section 50114 of title 46, United States Code. The Chief of Naval Operations, the Commandant of the Marine Corps, and the Commandant of the Coast Guard shall participate in each briefing required under this paragraph.

(2) USE.—The Administrator shall use the briefings required under paragraph (1) to augment and influence the national maritime strategy discussion with national security focused stakeholders across the administration, until an updated strategy is published and endorsed by the President of the United States.

(b) ELEMENTS.—As the national maritime strategy relates to national security, each briefing under subsection (a) shall include the following:

(1) Recommendations for a whole-of-Government approach to orchestrating national instruments of power to shape all elements of the maritime enterprise of the United States, domestic and international, on the high seas or domestic waterways.

(2) An assessment of great power competition in the maritime domain, to include opportunities for increased cooperation with allied and partner global maritime industry leaders to improve national shipbuilding and shipping, while promoting the international rules-based maritime order.

(3) An analysis of existing shipyards to build and capitalize on the virtuous cycle between commercial and military shipbuilding and repair, including areas of improvement.

(4) An analysis of opportunities for private or public

financing to increase the capacity, efficiency, and effectiveness of United States shipyards, including infrastructure, labor force, technology, and global competitiveness.

(5) An analysis of potential improvements to national or cooperative arrangements for sealift capacity and shipping, including for contested logistics.

(c) APPROPRIATE CONGRESSIONAL COMMITTEES.—In this section, the term "appropriate congressional committees" means—

(1) the congressional defense committees;

(2) and the Committee on Transportation and Infrastructure of the House of Representatives; and

(3) the Committee on Commerce, Science, and Transportation of the Senate.

* * * * * * *

DIVISION E—OTHER MATTERS

* * * * * * *

* * * * * * *

TITLE LVI—TRANSPORTATION AND INFRASTRUCTURE MATTERS

* * * * * * *

* * * * * * *

SEC. 5603. INTERNATIONAL PORT SECURITY ENFORCEMENT ACT.

Section 70108 of title 46, United States Code, is amended—

(1) in subsection (f)—

(A) in paragraph (1), by striking "provided that" and all that follows and inserting the following: "if—"

"(A) the Secretary certifies that the foreign government or international organization—

"(i) has conducted the assessment in

accordance with subsection (b); and

"(ii) has provided the Secretary with sufficient information pertaining to its assessment (including information regarding the outcome of the assessment); and

"(B) the foreign government that conducted the assessment is not a state sponsor of terrorism (as defined in section 3316(h))."

; and

(B) by amending paragraph (3) to read as follows:

"(3) LIMITATIONS.—Nothing in this section may be construed—

"(A) to require the Secretary to treat an assessment conducted by a foreign government or an international organization as an assessment that satisfies the requirement under subsection (a);

"(B) to limit the discretion or ability of the Secretary to conduct an assessment under this section;

"(C) to limit the authority of the Secretary to repatriate aliens to their respective countries of origin; or

"(D) to prevent the Secretary from requesting security and safety measures that the Secretary considers necessary to safeguard Coast Guard personnel during the repatriation of aliens to their respective countries of origin."

; and

(2) by adding at the end the following:

"(g) STATE SPONSORS OF TERRORISM AND INTERNATIONAL TERRORIST ORGANIZATIONS.—The Secretary—

"(1) may not enter into an agreement under subsection (f)(2) with—

"(A) a foreign government that is a state sponsor of terrorism (as defined in section 3316(h)); or

"(B) an entity designated by the Secretary of State

as a foreign terrorist organization pursuant to section 219 of the Immigration and Nationality Act (8 U.S.C. 1189); and

"(2) shall—

"(A) deem any port that is under the jurisdiction of a foreign government that is a state sponsor of terrorism as not having effective antiterrorism measures for purposes of this section and section 70109; and

"(B) immediately apply the sanctions described in section 70110(a) to such port."

Ocean Shipping Reform Act of 2022

Public Law 117-146

Ocean Shipping Reform Act of 2022

[(Public Law 117–146)]

[This law has not been amended]

AN ACT To amend title 46, United States Code, with respect to prohibited acts by ocean common carriers or marine terminal operators, and for other purposes.

Be it enacted by the Senate and House of Representatives of the United States of America in Congress assembled,

SECTION 1. [46 U.S.C. 101 note] SHORT TITLE.

This Act may be cited as the "Ocean Shipping Reform Act of 2022".

SEC. 2. PURPOSES.

Section 40101 of title 46, United States Code, is amended—

(1) by striking paragraph (2) and inserting the following:

"(2) ensure an efficient, competitive, and economical transportation system in the ocean commerce of the United States;"

(2) in paragraph (3), by inserting "and supporting commerce" after "needs"; and

(3) by striking paragraph (4) and inserting the following:

"(4) promote the growth and development of United States exports through a competitive and efficient system for the carriage of goods by water in the foreign commerce of the United States, and by placing a greater reliance on the marketplace."

SEC. 3. SERVICE CONTRACTS.

Section 40502(c) of title 46, United States Code, is amended—

(1) in paragraph (7), by striking "; and" and inserting a semicolon;

(2) in paragraph (8), by striking the period and inserting "; and"; and

(3) by adding at the end the following:

"(9) any other essential terms that the Federal Maritime Commission determines necessary or appropriate through a rulemaking process."

SEC. 4. SHIPPING EXCHANGE REGISTRY.

(a) IN GENERAL.—Chapter 405 of title 46, United States Code, is amended by adding at the end the following:

"SEC. 40504. [46 U.S.C. 40504] Shipping exchange registry

"(a) IN GENERAL.—No person may operate a shipping exchange involving ocean transportation in the foreign commerce of the United States unless the shipping exchange is registered as a national shipping exchange under the terms and conditions provided in this section and the regulations issued pursuant to this section.

"(b) REGISTRATION.—A person shall register a shipping exchange by filing with the Federal Maritime Commission an application for registration in such form as the Commission, by rule, may prescribe, containing the rules of the exchange and such other information and documents as the Commission, by rule, may prescribe as necessary or appropriate to complete a shipping exchange's registration.

"(c) EXEMPTION.—The Commission may exempt, conditionally or unconditionally, a shipping exchange from registration under this section if the Commission finds that the shipping exchange is subject to comparable, comprehensive supervision and regulation by the appropriate governmental authorities in a foreign country where the shipping exchange is headquartered.

"(d) REGULATIONS.—Not later than 3 years after the date of enactment of the Ocean Shipping Reform Act of 2022, the Commission shall issue regulations pursuant to subsection (a), which shall set standards necessary to carry out subtitle IV of this title for registered national shipping exchanges. For consideration of a service contract entered into by a shipping exchange, the Commission shall be limited to the minimum essential terms for service contracts established under section 40502 of this title.

"(e) DEFINITION OF SHIPPING EXCHANGE.—In this section, the term 'shipping exchange' means a platform (digital, over-the-counter, or otherwise) that connects shippers with common carriers for the purpose of entering into underlying agreements or contracts for the transport of cargo, by vessel or other modes of transportation."

(b) [46 U.S.C. 40504 note] APPLICABILITY.—The registration requirement under section 40504 of title 46, United States Code (as added by subsection (a)), shall take effect on the date on which the Federal Maritime Commission states the rule is effective in the regulations issued under such section.

(c) [46 U.S.C. 40501] CLERICAL AMENDMENT.—The analysis for chapter 405 of title 46, United States Code, is amended by adding at the end the following:

"40504. Shipping exchange registry."

SEC. 5. PROHIBITION ON RETALIATION.

Section 41102 of title 46, United States Code, is amended by adding at the end the following:

"(d) RETALIATION AND OTHER DISCRIMINATORY ACTIONS.—A common carrier, marine terminal operator, or ocean transportation intermediary, acting alone or in conjunction with any other person, directly or indirectly, may not—

"(1) retaliate against a shipper, an agent of a shipper, an ocean transportation intermediary, or a motor carrier by refusing, or threatening to refuse, an otherwise-available cargo space accommodation; or

"(2) resort to any other unfair or unjustly discriminatory action for—

"(A) the reason that a shipper, an agent of a shipper, an ocean transportation intermediary, or motor carrier has—

"(i) patronized another carrier; or

"(ii) filed a complaint against the common carrier, marine terminal operator, or ocean transportation intermediary; or

"(B) any other reason."

SEC. 6. PUBLIC DISCLOSURE.

Section 46106 of title 46, United States Code, is amended by adding at the end the following:

"(d) PUBLIC DISCLOSURES.—The Federal Maritime Commission shall publish, and annually update, on the website of the Commission—

"(1) all findings by the Commission of false detention and demurrage invoice information by common carriers under section 41104(a)(15) of this title; and

"(2) all penalties imposed or assessed against common carriers, as applicable, under sections 41107, 41108, and 41109, listed by each common carrier."

SEC. 7. COMMON CARRIERS.

(a) IN GENERAL.—Section 41104 of title 46, United States Code, is amended—

(1) in subsection (a)—

(A) in the matter preceding paragraph (1), by striking "may not" and inserting "shall not";

(B) by striking paragraph (3) and inserting the following:

"(3) unreasonably refuse cargo space accommodations when available, or resort to other unfair or unjustly discriminatory methods;"

(C) in paragraph (5), by striking " in the matter of rates or charges" and inserting "against any commodity group or type of shipment or in the matter of rates or charges";

(D) in paragraph (10), by adding ", including with respect to vessel space accommodations provided by an ocean common carrier" after "negotiate";

(E) in paragraph (12) by striking "; or" and inserting a semicolon;

(F) in paragraph (13) by striking the period and inserting a semicolon; and

(G) by adding at the end the following:

"(14) assess any party for a charge that is inconsistent or does not comply with all applicable provisions and regulations, including subsection (c) of section 41102 or part 545 of title 46, Code of Federal Regulations (or successor regulations);

"(15) invoice any party for demurrage or detention charges unless the invoice includes information as described in subsection (d) showing that such charges comply with—

"(A) all provisions of part 545 of title 46, Code of Federal Regulations (or successor regulations); and

"(B) applicable provisions and regulations, including the principles of the final rule published on May 18, 2020, entitled 'Interpretive Rule on Demurrage and Detention Under the Shipping Act' (or successor rule); or

"(16) for service pursuant to a service contract, give any undue or unreasonable preference or advantage or impose any undue or unreasonable prejudice or disadvantage against any commodity group or type of shipment."

; and

(2) by adding at the end the following:

"(d) DETENTION AND DEMURRAGE INVOICE INFORMATION.—

"(1) INACCURATE INVOICE.—If the Commission determines, after an investigation in response to a submission under section 41310, that an invoice under subsection (a)(15) was inaccurate or false, penalties or refunds under section 41107 shall be applied.

"(2) CONTENTS OF INVOICE.—An invoice under subsection (a)(15), unless otherwise determined by subsequent Commission rulemaking, shall include accurate information on each of the following, as well as minimum information as determined by the Commission:

"(A) Date that container is made available.

"(B) The port of discharge.

"(C) The container number or numbers.

"(D) For exported shipments, the earliest return date.

"(E) The allowed free time in days.

"(F) The start date of free time.

"(G) The end date of free time.

"(H) The applicable detention or demurrage rule on which the daily rate is based.

"(I) The applicable rate or rates per the applicable rule.

"(J) The total amount due.

"(K) The email, telephone number, or other appropriate contact information for questions or requests for mitigation of fees.

"(L) A statement that the charges are consistent with any of Federal Maritime Commission rules with respect to detention and demurrage.

"(M) A statement that the common carrier's performance did not cause or contribute to the underlying invoiced charges.

"(e) SAFE HARBOR.—If a non-vessel operating common carrier passes through to the relevant shipper an invoice made by the ocean common carrier, and the Commission finds that the non-vessel operating common carrier is not otherwise responsible for the charge, then the ocean common carrier shall be subject to refunds or penalties pursuant to subsection (d)(1).

"(f) ELIMINATION OF CHARGE OBLIGATION.—Failure to include the information required under subsection (d) on an invoice with any demurrage or detention charge shall eliminate any obligation of the charged party to pay the applicable charge."

(b) [46 U.S.C. 41102 note] RULEMAKING ON DEMURRAGE OR DETENTION.—

(1) IN GENERAL.—Not later than 45 days after the date of enactment of this Act, the Federal Maritime Commission shall initiate a rulemaking further defining prohibited practices by common carriers, marine terminal operators, shippers, and ocean transportation intermediaries under section 41102(c) of title 46, United States Code, regarding the assessment of demurrage or detention charges. The Federal Maritime Commission shall issue a final rule defining such practices not later than 1 year after the date of enactment of this Act.

(2) CONTENTS.—The rule under paragraph (1) shall only seek to further clarify reasonable rules and practices related to the assessment of detention and demurrage charges to address the issues identified in the final rule published on May 18, 2020, entitled "Interpretive Rule on Demurrage and Detention Under the Shipping Act" (or successor rule), including a determination of which parties may be appropriately billed for any demurrage, detention, or other similar per container charges.

(c) [46 U.S.C. 41104 note] RULEMAKING ON UNFAIR OR UNJUSTLY DISCRIMINATORY METHODS.—Not later than 60 days after the date of enactment of this Act, the Federal Maritime Commission shall initiate a rulemaking defining unfair or unjustly discriminatory methods under section 41104(a)(3) of title 46, United States Code, as amended by this section. The Federal Maritime Commission shall issue a final rule not later than 1 year after the date of enactment of this Act.

(d) RULEMAKING ON UNREASONABLE REFUSAL TO DEAL OR NEGOTIATE WITH RESPECT TO VESSEL SPACE ACCOMMODATIONS.—Not later than 30 days after the date of enactment of this Act, the Federal Maritime Commission, in consultation with the Commandant of the United States Coast Guard, shall initiate a rulemaking defining unreasonable refusal to deal or negotiate with respect to vessel space under section 41104(a)(10) of title 46, as amended by this section. The Federal Maritime Commission shall issue a final rule not later than 6 months after the date of enactment of this Act.

SEC. 8. ASSESSMENT OF PENALTIES OR REFUNDS.

(a) IN GENERAL.—Title 46, United States Code, is amended—

(1) in section 41107—

(A) in the section heading, by inserting "or refunds" after "penalties";

(B) in subsection (a), by inserting "or, in addition to or in lieu of a civil penalty, is liable for the refund of a charge" after "civil penalty"; and

(C) in subsection (b), by inserting "or, in addition to or in lieu of a civil penalty, the refund of a charge," after "civil penalty"; and

(2) section 41109 is amended—

(A) by striking subsections (a) and (b) and inserting the following:

"(a) GENERAL AUTHORITY.—Until a matter is referred to the Attorney General, the Federal Maritime Commission may—

"(1) after notice and opportunity for a hearing, in accordance with this part—

"(A) assess a civil penalty; or

"(B) in addition to, or in lieu of, assessing a civil penalty under subparagraph (A), order a refund of money (including additional amounts in accordance with section 41305(c)), subject to subsection (b)(2); and

"(2) compromise, modify, or remit, with or without conditions, a civil penalty or refund imposed under paragraph (1).

"(b) DETERMINATION OF AMOUNT.—

"(1) FACTORS FOR CONSIDERATION.—In determining the amount of a civil penalty assessed or refund of money ordered pursuant to subsection (a), the Federal Maritime Commission shall take into consideration—

"(A) the nature, circumstances, extent, and gravity of the violation committed;

"(B) with respect to the violator—

"(i) the degree of culpability;

"(ii) any history of prior offenses;

"(iii) the ability to pay; and

"(iv) such other matters as justice may require; and

"(C) the amount of any refund of money ordered pursuant to subsection (a)(1)(B).

"(2) COMMENSURATE REDUCTION IN CIVIL PENALTY.—

"(A) IN GENERAL.—In any case in which the Federal Maritime Commission orders a refund of money pursuant to subsection (a)(1)(B) in addition to assessing a civil penalty pursuant to subsection (a)(1)(A), the amount of the civil penalty assessed shall be decreased by any additional amounts included in the refund of money in excess of the actual injury (as defined in section 41305(a)).

"(B) TREATMENT OF REFUNDS.—A refund of money ordered pursuant to subsection (a)(1)(B) shall be—

"(i) considered to be compensation paid to the applicable claimant; and

"(ii) deducted from the total amount of damages awarded to that claimant in a civil action against the violator relating to the applicable violation."

(B) in subsection (c), by striking "may not be imposed" and inserting "or refund of money under subparagraph (A) or (B), respectively, of subsection (a)(1) may not be imposed";

(C) in subsection (e), by inserting "or order a refund of money" after "penalty";

(D) in subsection (f), by inserting ", or that is ordered to refund money," after "assessed"; and

(E) in subsection (g), in the first sentence, by inserting "or a refund required under this section" after "penalty".

SEC. 9. DATA COLLECTION.

(a) IN GENERAL.—Chapter 411 of title 46, United States Code, is amended by adding at the end the following:

"SEC. 41110. [46 U.S.C. 41110] Data collection

"The Federal Maritime Commission shall publish on its website a calendar quarterly report that describes the total import and export tonnage and the total loaded and empty 20-foot equivalent units per vessel (making port in the United States, including any territory or possession of the United States) operated by each ocean common carrier covered under this chapter. Ocean common carriers under this chapter shall provide to the Commission all necessary information, as determined by the Commission, for completion of this report."

(b) [46 U.S.C. 41110 note] RULE OF CONSTRUCTION.—Nothing in this section, and the amendment made by this section, shall be construed to compel the public disclosure of any confidential or proprietary data, in accordance with section 552(b)(4) of title 5, United States Code.

(c) [46 U.S.C. 41101] CLERICAL AMENDMENT.—The analysis for chapter 411 of title 46, United States Code, is amended by adding at the end the following:

"41110. Data collection."

SEC. 10. CHARGE COMPLAINTS.

(a) IN GENERAL.—Chapter 413 of title 46, United States Code, is amended by adding at the end the following:

"SEC. 41310. [46 U.S.C. 41310] Charge complaints

"(a) IN GENERAL.—A person may submit to the Federal Maritime Commission, and the Commission shall accept, information concerning complaints about charges assessed by a common carrier. The information submitted to the Commission shall include the bill of lading numbers and invoices, and may include any other relevant information.

"(b) INVESTIGATION.—Upon receipt of a submission under subsection (a), with respect to a charge assessed by a common carrier, the Commission shall promptly investigate the charge with regard to compliance with section 41104(a) and section 41102. The common carrier shall—

"(1) be provided an opportunity to submit additional information related to the charge in question; and

"(2) bear the burden of establishing the reasonableness of any demurrage or detention charges pursuant to section 545.5 of title 46, Code of Federal Regulations (or successor regulations).

"(c) REFUND.—Upon receipt of submissions under subsection (a), if the Commission determines that a charge does not comply with section 41104(a) or 41102, the Commission shall promptly order the refund of charges paid.

"(d) PENALTIES.—In the event of a finding that a charge does not comply with section 41104(a) or 41102 after submission under subsection (a), a civil penalty under section 41107 shall be applied to the common carrier making such charge.

"(e) CONSIDERATIONS.—If the common carrier assessing the charge is acting in the capacity of a non-vessel-operating common carrier, the Commission shall, while conducting an investigation under subsection (b), consider—

"(1) whether the non-vessel-operating common carrier is responsible for the noncompliant assessment of the charge, in whole or in part; and

"(2) whether another party is ultimately responsible in whole or in part and potentially subject to action under subsections (c) and (d)."

(b) [46 U.S.C. 41301] CLERICAL AMENDMENT.—The analysis for chapter 413 of title 46, United States Code, is amended by adding at the end the following:

"41310. Charge complaints."

SEC. 11. INVESTIGATIONS.

(a) AMENDMENTS.—Section 41302 of title 46, United States Code, is amended—

(1) in subsection (a), in the first sentence, by striking "or agreement" and inserting "agreement, fee, or charge"; and

(2) in subsection (b)—

(A) in the subsection heading, by striking "Agreement" and inserting "Agreement, fee, or charge"; and

(B) by inserting ", fee, or charge" after "agreement".

(b) REPORT.—The Federal Maritime Commission shall publish on a publicly available website of the Commission a report containing the results of the investigation entitled "Fact Finding No. 29, International Ocean Transportation Supply Chain Engagement".

SEC. 12. AWARD OF ADDITIONAL AMOUNTS.

Section 41305(c) of title 46, United States Codeis amended by striking "41102(b)" and inserting "subsection (b) or (c) of section 41102".

SEC. 13. ENFORCEMENT OF REPARATION ORDERS.

Section 41309 of title 46, United States Code, is amended—

(1) in subsection (a), by striking "reparation, the person to whom the award was made" and inserting "a refund of money or reparation, the person to which the refund or reparation was awarded"; and

(2) in subsection (b), in the first sentence—

(A) by striking "made an award of reparation" and inserting "ordered a refund of money or any other award of reparation"; and

(B) by inserting "(except for the Commission or any component of the Commission)" after "parties in the order".

SEC. 14. ANNUAL REPORT TO CONGRESS.

Section 46106(b) of title 46, United States Code, is amended—

(1) in paragraph (5), by striking "and" at the end;

(2) in paragraph (6), by striking the period and inserting "; and"; and

(3) by adding at the end the following:

"(7) an identification of any otherwise concerning practices by ocean common carriers, particularly such carriers that are controlled carriers, that are—

"(A) State-owned or State-controlled enterprises; or

"(B) owned or controlled by, a subsidiary of, or otherwise related legally or financially (other than a minority relationship or investment) to a corporation based in a country—

"(i) identified as a nonmarket economy country (as defined in section 771(18) of the Tariff Act of 1930 (19 U.S.C. 1677(18))) as of the date of enactment of this paragraph;

"(ii) identified by the United States Trade Representative in the most recent report required by section 182 of the Trade Act of 1974 (19 U.S.C. 2242) as a priority foreign country under subsection (a)(2) of that section; or

"(iii) subject to monitoring by the United States Trade Representative under section 306 of the Trade Act of 1974 (19 U.S.C. 2416)."

SEC. 15. TECHNICAL AMENDMENTS.

(a) Section 41108(a) of title 46, United States Code, is amended by striking "section 41104(1), (2), or (7)" and inserting "paragraph (1), (2), or (7) of section 41104(a)".

(b) Section 41109(c) of title 46, United States Code, as amended by section 8 of this Act, is further amended by striking "section 41102(a) or 41104(1) or (2) of this title" and inserting "subsection (a) or (d) of section 41102 or paragraph (1) or (2) of section 41104(a)".

(c) Section 41305 of title 46, United States Code, as amended by section 12 of this Act, is further amended—

(1) in subsection (c), by striking "41104(3) or (6), or 41105(1) or (3) of this title" and inserting "paragraph (3) or (6) of section 41104(a), or paragraph (1) or (3) of section 41105"; and

(2) in subsection (d), by striking "section 41104(4)(A) or (B) of this title" and inserting "subparagraph (A) or (B) of section 41104(a)(4)".

SEC. 16. DWELL TIME STATISTICS.

(a) DEFINITIONS.—In this section:

(1) DIRECTOR.—The term "Director" means the Director of the Bureau of Transportation Statistics.

(2) MARINE CONTAINER.—The term "marine container" means an intermodal container with a length of—

(A) not less than 20 feet; and

(B) not greater than 45 feet.

(3) OUT OF SERVICE PERCENTAGE.—The term "out of service percentage" means the proportion of the chassis fleet for any defined geographical area that is out of service at any one time.

(4) STREET DWELL TIME.—The term "street dwell time", with respect to a piece of equipment, means the quantity of time during which the piece of equipment is in use outside of the terminal.

(b) AUTHORITY TO COLLECT DATA.—

(1) IN GENERAL.—Each port, marine terminal operator, and chassis owner or provider with a fleet of over 50 chassis that supply chassis for a fee shall submit to the Director such data as the Director determines to be necessary for the

implementation of this section, subject to subchapter III of chapter 35 of title 44, United States Code.

(2) APPROVAL BY OMB.—Subject to the availability of appropriations, not later than 60 days after the date of enactment of this Act, the Director of the Office of Management and Budget shall approve an information collection for purposes of this section.

(c) PUBLICATION.—Subject to the availability of appropriations, not later than 240 days after the date of enactment of this Act, and not less frequently than monthly thereafter, the Director shall publish statistics relating to the dwell time of equipment used in intermodal transportation at the top 25 ports, including inland ports, by 20-foot equivalent unit, including—

(1) total street dwell time, from all causes, of marine containers and marine container chassis; and

(2) the average out of service percentage, which shall not be identifiable with any particular port, marine terminal operator, or chassis provider.

(d) FACTORS.—Subject to the availability of appropriations, to the maximum extent practicable, the Director shall publish the statistics described in subsection (c) on a local, regional, and national basis.

(e) SUNSET.—The authority under this section shall expire December 31, 2026.

SEC. 17. [46 U.S.C. 41301 note] FEDERAL MARITIME COMMISSION ACTIVITIES.

(a) PUBLIC SUBMISSIONS TO COMMISSION.—The Federal Maritime Commission shall—

(1) establish on the public website of the Commission a webpage that allows for the submission of comments, complaints, concerns, reports of noncompliance, requests for investigation, and requests for alternative dispute resolution; and

(2) direct each submission under the link established under paragraph (1) to the appropriate component office of the Commission.

(b) AUTHORIZATION OF OFFICE OF CONSUMER AFFAIRS AND DISPUTE RESOLUTION SERVICES.—The Commission shall maintain an Office of Consumer Affairs and Dispute Resolution Services to provide nonadjudicative ombuds assistance, mediation, facilitation, and arbitration to resolve challenges and disputes involving cargo shipments, household good shipments, and cruises subject to the jurisdiction of the Commission.

(c) ENHANCING CAPACITY FOR INVESTIGATIONS.—

(1) IN GENERAL.—Pursuant to section 41302 of title 46, United States Code, not later than 18 months after the date of enactment of this Act, the Chairperson of the Commission shall staff within the Bureau of Enforcement, the Bureau of Certification and Licensing, the Office of the Managing Director, the Office of Consumer Affairs and Dispute Resolution Services, and the Bureau of Trade Analysis not fewer than 7 total positions to assist in investigations and oversight, in addition to the positions within the Bureau of Enforcement, the Bureau of Certification and Licensing, the Office of the Managing Director, the Office of Consumer Affairs and Dispute Resolution Services, and the Bureau of Trade Analysis on that date of enactment.

(2) DUTIES.—The additional staff appointed under paragraph (1) shall provide support—

(A) to Area Representatives of the Bureau of Enforcement;

(B) to attorneys of the Bureau of Enforcement in enforcing the laws and regulations subject to the jurisdiction of the Commission;

(C) for the alternative dispute resolution services of the Commission; or

(D) for the review of agreements and activities subject to the authority of the Commission.

SEC. 18. TEMPORARY EMERGENCY AUTHORITY.

(a) DEFINITIONS.—In this section:

(1) COMMON CARRIER.—The term "common carrier" has the meaning given the term in section 40102 of title 46, United States Code.

(2) MOTOR CARRIER.—The term "motor carrier" has the meaning given the term in section 13102 of title 49, United States Code.

(3) RAIL CARRIER.—The term "rail carrier" has the meaning given the term in section 10102 of title 49, United States Code.

(4) SHIPPER.—The term "shipper" has the meaning given the term in section 40102 of title 46, United States Code.

(b) PUBLIC INPUT ON INFORMATION SHARING.—

(1) IN GENERAL.—Not later than 60 days after the date of enactment of this Act, the Federal Maritime Commission shall issue a request for information, seeking public comment regarding—

(A) whether congestion of the carriage of goods has created an emergency situation of a magnitude such that there exists a substantial, adverse effect on the competitiveness and reliability of the international ocean transportation supply system;

(B) whether an emergency order under this section would alleviate such an emergency situation; and

(C) the appropriate scope of such an emergency order, if applicable.

(2) CONSULTATION.—During the public comment period under paragraph (1), the Commission may consult, as the Commission determines to be appropriate, with—

(A) other Federal departments and agencies; and

(B) persons with expertise relating to maritime and freight operations.

(c) AUTHORITY TO REQUIRE INFORMATION SHARING.—On making a unanimous determination described in subsection (d), the Commission may issue an emergency order requiring any common carrier or marine terminal operator to share directly with relevant shippers, rail carriers, or motor carriers information relating to cargo throughput and availability, in order to ensure the efficient transportation, loading, and unloading of cargo to or from—

(1) any inland destination or point of origin;

(2) any vessel; or

(3) any point on a wharf or terminal.

(d) DESCRIPTION OF DETERMINATION.—

(1) IN GENERAL.—A determination referred to in subsection (c) is a unanimous determination by the commissioners on the

Commission that congestion of carriage of goods has created an emergency situation of a magnitude such that there exists a substantial, adverse effect on the competitiveness and reliability of the international ocean transportation supply system.

(2) FACTORS FOR CONSIDERATION.—In issuing an emergency order pursuant to subsection (c), the Commission shall tailor the emergency order with respect to temporal and geographic scope, taking into consideration the likely burdens on common carriers and marine terminal operators and the likely benefits on congestion relating to the purposes described in section 40101 of title 46, United States Code.

(e) PETITIONS FOR EXCEPTION.—

(1) IN GENERAL.—A common carrier or marine terminal operator subject to an emergency order issued pursuant to this section may submit to the Commission a petition for exception from 1 or more requirements of the emergency order, based on a showing of undue hardship or other condition rendering compliance with such a requirement impracticable.

(2) DETERMINATION.—The Commission shall make a determination regarding a petition for exception under paragraph (1) by—

(A) majority vote; and

(B) not later than 21 days after the date on which the petition is submitted.

(3) INAPPLICABILITY PENDING REVIEW.—The requirements of an emergency order that is the subject of a petition for exception under this subsection shall not apply to the petitioner during the period for which the petition is pending.

(f) LIMITATIONS.—

(1) TERM.—An emergency order issued pursuant to this section—

(A) shall remain in effect for a period of not longer than 60 days; but

(B) may be renewed by a unanimous determination of the Commission.

(2) SUNSET.—The authority provided by this section shall terminate on the date that is 18 months after the date of

enactment of this Act.

(3) INVESTIGATIVE AUTHORITY UNAFFECTED.—Nothing in this section shall affect the investigative authorities of the Commission as described in subpart R of part 502 of title 46, Code of Federal Regulations.

SEC. 19. BEST PRACTICES FOR CHASSIS POOLS.

(a) IN GENERAL.—Not later than April 1, 2023, the Federal Maritime Commission shall enter into an agreement with the Transportation Research Board of the National Academies of Sciences, Engineering, and Medicine under which the Transportation Research Board shall carry out a study and develop best practices for on-terminal or near-terminal chassis pools that provide service to marine terminal operators, motor carriers, railroads, and other stakeholders that use the chassis pools, with the goal of optimizing supply chain efficiency and effectiveness.

(b) REQUIREMENTS.—In developing best practices under subsection (a), the Transportation Research Board shall—

(1) take into consideration—

(A) practical obstacles to the implementation of chassis pools; and

(B) potential solutions to those obstacles; and

(2) address relevant communication practices, information sharing, and knowledge management.

(c) PUBLICATION.—The Commission shall publish the best practices developed under this section on a publicly available website by not later than April 1, 2024.

(d) FUNDING.—Subject to appropriations, the Commission may expend such sums as are necessary, but not to exceed $500,000, to carry out this section.

SEC. 20. [49 U.S.C. 31305 note] LICENSING TESTING.

(a) IN GENERAL.—Not later than 90 days after the date of enactment of this Act, the Administrator of the Federal Motor Carrier Safety Administration (referred to in this section as the "Administrator") shall conduct a review of the discretionary waiver authority described in the document issued by the Administrator entitled "Waiver for States Concerning Third Party CDL Skills Test Examiners In Response to the COVID-19 Emergency" and dated

August 31, 2021, for safety concerns.

(b) PERMANENT WAIVER.—If the Administrator finds no safety concerns after conducting a review under subsection (a), the Administrator shall—

(1) notwithstanding any other provision of law, make the waiver permanent; and

(2) not later than 90 days after completing the review under subsection (a), revise section 384.228 of title 49, Code of Federal Regulations, to provide that the discretionary waiver authority referred to in subsection (a) shall be permanent.

(c) REPORT.—If the Administrator declines to move forward with a rulemaking for revision under subsection (b), the Administrator shall explain the reasons for declining to move forward with the rulemaking in a report to the Committee on Commerce, Science, and Transportation of the Senate and the Committee on Transportation and Infrastructure of the House of Representatives.

SEC. 21. PLANNING.

(a) AMENDMENT.—Section 6702(g) of title 49, United States Code, is amended—

(1) by striking "Of the amounts" and inserting the following:

"(1) IN GENERAL.—Of the amounts"

; and

(2) by adding at the end the following:

"(2) NONAPPLICABILITY OF CERTAIN LIMITATIONS.—Subparagraphs (A) and (B) of subsection (c)(2) shall not apply with respect to amounts made available for planning, preparation, or design under paragraph (1)."

(b) EMERGENCY DESIGNATION.—Amounts for which outlays are affected under the amendments made by subsection (a) that were previously designated by the Congress as an emergency requirement pursuant to section 4112(a) of H. Con. Res. 71 (115th Congress), the concurrent resolution on the budget for fiscal year 2018, and to section 251(b) of the Balanced Budget and Emergency Deficit Control Act of 1985 are designated by the Congress as an emergency requirement pursuant to section 4001(a)(1) and section 4001(b) of S. Con. Res. 14 (117th Congress), the concurrent resolution on the budget for fiscal year 2022.

SEC. 22. REVIEW OF POTENTIAL DISCRIMINATION AGAINST TRANSPORTATION OF QUALIFIED HAZARDOUS MATERIALS.

(a) IN GENERAL.—Not later than 90 days after the date of enactment of this Act, the Comptroller General of the United States shall initiate a review of whether there have been any systemic decisions by ocean common carriers to discriminate against maritime transport of qualified hazardous materials by unreasonably denying vessel space accommodations, equipment, or other instrumentalities needed to transport such materials. The Comptroller General shall take into account any applicable safety and pollution regulations.

(b) CONSULTATION.—The Comptroller General of the United States may consult with the Commandant of the Coast Guard and the Chair of the Federal Maritime Commission in conducting the review under this section.

(c) DEFINITIONS.—In this section:

(1) HAZARDOUS MATERIALS.—The term "hazardous materials" includes dangerous goods, as defined by the International Maritime Dangerous Goods Code.

(2) OCEAN COMMON CARRIER.—The term "ocean common carrier" has the meaning given such term in section 40102 of title 46, United States Code.

(3) QUALIFIED HAZARDOUS MATERIALS.—The term "qualified hazardous materials" means hazardous materials for which the shipper has certified to the ocean common carrier that such materials have been or will be tendered in accordance with applicable safety laws, including regulations.

(4) SHIPPER.—The term "shipper" has the meaning given such term in section 40102 of title 46, United States Code.

SEC. 23. [46 U.S.C. 70105 note] TRANSPORTATION WORKER IDENTIFICATION CREDENTIALS.

(a) DEFINITION OF DIRECT ASSISTANCE TO A UNITED STATES PORT.—In this section:

(1) IN GENERAL.—The term "direct assistance to a United

States port" means the transportation of cargo directly to or from a United States port.

(2) EXCLUSIONS.—The term "direct assistance to a United States port" does not include—

(A) the transportation of a mixed load of cargo that includes—

(i) cargo that does not originate from a United States port; or

(ii) a container or cargo that is not bound for a United States port;

(B) any period during which a motor carrier or driver is operating in interstate commerce to transport cargo or provide services not in support of transportation to or from a United States port; or

(C) the period after a motor carrier dispatches the applicable driver or commercial motor vehicle of the motor carrier to another location to begin operation in interstate commerce in a manner that is not in support of transportation to or from a United States port.

(b) TRANSPORTATION WORKER IDENTIFICATION CREDENTIALS.—The Administrator of the Transportation Security Administration and the Commandant of the Coast Guard shall jointly prioritize and expedite the consideration of applications for a Transportation Worker Identification Credential with respect to applicants that reasonably demonstrate that the purpose of the Transportation Worker Identification Credential is for providing, within the interior of the United States, direct assistance to a United States port.

SEC. 24. USE OF UNITED STATES INLAND PORTS FOR STORAGE AND TRANSFER OF CARGO CONTAINERS.

(a) MEETING.—Not later than 90 days after the date of enactment of this Act, the Assistant Secretary for Transportation Policy, in consultation with the Administrator of the Maritime Administration and the Chairperson of the Federal Maritime Commission, shall convene a meeting of representatives of entities described in subsection (b) to discuss the feasibility of, and strategies for, identifying Federal and non-Federal land, including inland ports, for the purposes of storage and transfer of cargo containers due to port congestion.

(b) DESCRIPTION OF ENTITIES.—The entities referred to in subsection (a) are—

(1) representatives of United States major gateway ports, inland ports, and export terminals;

(2) ocean carriers;

(3) railroads;

(4) trucking companies;

(5) port workforce, including organized labor; and

(6) such other stakeholders as the Secretary of Transportation, in consultation with the Chairperson of the Federal Maritime Commission, determines to be appropriate.

(c) REPORT TO CONGRESS.—As soon as practicable after the date of the meeting convened under subsection (a), the Assistant Secretary for Transportation Policy, in consultation with the Administrator of the Maritime Administration and the Chairperson of the Federal Maritime Commission, shall submit to Congress a report describing—

(1) the results of the meeting;

(2) the feasibility of identifying land or property under the jurisdiction of United States, or ports in the United States, for storage and transfer of cargo containers; and

(3) recommendations relating to the meeting, if any.

(d) SAVINGS PROVISION.—No authorization contained in this section may be acted on in a manner that jeopardizes or negatively impacts the national security or defense readiness of the United States.

SEC. 25. REPORT ON ADOPTION OF TECHNOLOGY AT UNITED STATES PORTS.

Not later than 1 year after the date of enactment of this Act, the Comptroller General of the United States shall submit to Congress a report describing the adoption of technology at United States ports, as compared to that adoption at foreign ports, including—

(1) the technological capabilities of United States ports, as compared to foreign ports;

(2) an assessment of whether the adoption of technology at United States ports could lower the costs of cargo handling;

(3) an assessment of regulatory and other barriers to the adoption of technology at United States ports; and

(4) an assessment of technology and the workforce.

SEC. 26. AUTHORIZATION OF APPROPRIATIONS.

Section 46108 of title 46, United States Code, is amended by striking "$29,086,888 for fiscal year 2020 and $29,639,538 for fiscal year 2021" and inserting "$32,869,000 for fiscal year 2022, $38,260,000 for fiscal year 2023, $43,720,000 for fiscal year 2024, and $49,200,000 for fiscal year 2025".

ALASKA TOURISM RESTORATION ACT

PUBLIC LAW 117-14

Alaska Tourism Restoration Act

[(Public Law 117–14)]

[This law has not been amended]

AN ACT To restrict the imposition by the Secretary of Homeland Security of fines, penalties, duties, or tariffs applicable only to coastwise voyages, or prohibit otherwise qualified non-United States citizens from serving as crew, on specified vessels transporting passengers between the State of Washington and the State of Alaska, to address a Canadian cruise ship ban and the extraordinary impacts of the COVID-19 pandemic on Alaskan communities, and for other purposes.

Be it enacted by the Senate and House of Representatives of the United States of America in Congress assembled,

SECTION 1. [46 U.S.C. 101 note] SHORT TITLE.

This Act may be cited as the "Alaska Tourism Restoration Act".

SEC. 2. VOYAGE DEEMED TO BE FOREIGN.

(a) DEFINITION OF COVERED CRUISE SHIP.—

(1) IN GENERAL.—In this section, the term "covered cruise ship" means a vessel included on the list under paragraph (2) that—

(A) has been issued, operates in accordance with, and retains a COVID-19 Conditional Sailing Certificate of the Centers for Disease Control and Prevention; and

(B) operates in accordance with any restrictions or guidance of the Centers for Disease Control and Prevention associated with such Certificate, including any such restrictions or guidance issued after the date of enactment of this Act.

(2) LIST.—The vessels listed under this paragraph are the following:

(A) Carnival Freedom (IMO number 9333149).

(B) Carnival Miracle (IMO number 9237357).

(C) Crystal Serenity (IMO number 9243667).

(D) Discovery Princess (IMO number 9837468).

(E) Emerald Princess (IMO number 9333151).

(F) Eurodam (IMO number 9378448).

(G) Golden Horizon (IMO number 9793545).

(H) Grand Princess (IMO number 9104005).

(I) Hanseatic Inspiration (IMO number 9817145).

(J) Koningsdam (IMO number 9692557).

(K) NG Quest (IMO number 9798985).

(L) NG Sea Bird (IMO number 8966444).

(M) NG Sea Lion (IMO number 8966456).

(N) NG Venture (IMO number 9799044).

(O) Nieuw Amsterdam (IMO number 9378450).

(P) Noordam (IMO number 9230115).

(Q) Zuiderdam (IMO number 9221279).

(R) Majestic Princess (IMO number 9614141).

(S) Ovation of the Seas (IMO number 9697753).

(T) Radiance of the Seas (IMO number 9195195).

(U) Serenade of the Seas (IMO number 9228344).

(V) Eclipse (IMO number 9404314).

(W) Millennium (IMO number 9189419).

(X) Solstice (IMO number 9362530).

(Y) Norwegian Bliss (IMO number 9751509).

(Z) Norwegian Encore (IMO number 9751511).

(AA) Norwegian Jewel (IMO number 9304045).

(BB) Norwegian Spirit (IMO number 9141065).

(CC) Norwegian Sun (IMO number 9218131).

(DD) Ocean Victory (IMO number 9868869).

(EE) Pacific Princess (IMO number 9187887).

(FF) Pacific World (IMO number 9000259).

(GG) Quantum of the Seas (IMO number 9549463).

(HH) Queen Elizabeth (IMO number 9477438).

(II) Disney Wonder (IMO number 9126819).

(JJ) Regatta (IMO number 9156474).

(KK) Roald Amundsen (IMO number 9813072).

(LL) Ruby Princess (IMO number 9378462).

(MM) Sapphire Princess (IMO number 9228186).

(NN) Scenic Eclipse (IMO number 9797371).

(OO) Seabourn Odyssey (IMO number 9417086).

(PP) Seabourn Venture 2 (IMO 9862023).

(QQ) Seven Seas Mariner (IMO number 9210139).

(RR) Silver Shadow (IMO number 9192167).

(SS) Silver Wind (IMO number 8903935).

(TT) Star Breeze (IMO number 8807997).

(UU) Sylvia Earle (IMO number 9872327).

(VV) Westerdam (IMO number 9226891).

(WW) L'Austral (IMO number 9502518).

(XX) Silver Muse (IMO number 9784350).

(YY) Viking Orion (IMO number 9796250).

(b) CRITERIA.—A roundtrip voyage of a covered cruise ship transporting passengers between a port or place in the State of Alaska and a port or place in the State of Washington shall be deemed to have made a stop in a port or place of Canada, and deemed a foreign voyage, for purposes of the law of the United States, if—

(1) during the voyage, the covered cruise ship sends an email containing the information described in subsection (c) to—

(A) the Canada Border Services Agency;

(B) the Commissioner of Customs and Border Protection; and

(C) each alien crewman on such voyage who is in possession of a valid, unexpired nonimmigrant visa issued pursuant to subparagraph (C) or (D) of section 101(a)(15) of the Immigration and Nationality Act (8 U.S.C. 1101(a)(15)); and

(2) the voyage begins not later than February 28, 2022.

(c) EMAIL.—An email described in subsection (b)(1) shall contain the names of each alien crewman described in subparagraph (C) of such subsection.

(d) EMPLOYMENT OF ALIEN CREWMEN.—On the date on which a covered cruise ship sends an email to the Canada Border Services Agency in accordance with subsection (b)(1), each alien crewman described in subparagraph (C) of such subsection shall be deemed to have departed the United States, entered Canada, and been readmitted to the United States for purposes of complying with, during the applicable voyage described in subsection (b), the 29-day authorized stay pursuant to their nonimmigrant visas issued pursuant to subparagraph (C) or (D) of section 101(a)(15) of the Immigration and Nationality Act (8 U.S.C. 1101(a)).

(e) EXCEPTION.—Notwithstanding subsection (b), a voyage described in such subsection shall not be deemed a foreign voyage for purposes of section 446 of the Tariff Act of 1930 (19 U.S.C. 1446) or any other provision of law relating to levying duties or taxes on goods, including consumables, purchased for use onboard the covered cruise ship.

(f) APPLICABILITY.—This section shall not apply to a roundtrip voyage during any period for which the Director of the Centers for Disease Control and Prevention has issued an order under section 361 or 365 of the Public Health Service Act (42 U.S.C. 264 and 268) that requires covered cruise ships to suspend vessel operations.

(g) DURATION.—The authority provided under this section shall terminate on the earlier of—

(1) the date on which covered cruise ships are no longer prohibited by the Government of Canada, any political subdivision of Canada, or any port or province of Canada, from entering, berthing, or docking in Canadian waters of the Pacific Coast due to the COVID-19 pandemic; or

(2) March 31, 2022.

SEC. 3. MEDICAL AND SAFETY STANDARDS.

(a) IN GENERAL.—Chapter 35 of title 46, United States Code, is amended by adding at the end the following:

"SEC. 3510. [46 U.S.C. 3510] Additional medical and safety standards

"(a) AUTOMATED EXTERNAL DEFIBRILLATORS.—Not later than 1 year after the date of enactment of this section, the Secretary, in consultation with the Secretary of Health and Human Services and other appropriate Federal agencies, shall promulgate regulations to—

"(1) require that the owner of a vessel to which section 3507 applies install, and maintain in working order, automated external defibrillators on such vessel;

"(2) require that such defibrillators be placed throughout such vessel in clearly designated locations;

"(3) require that such defibrillators are available for passenger and crew access in the event of an emergency; and

"(4) require that automated external defibrillators, or adjacent equipment, allow passengers and crew to easily contact medical staff of the vessel.

"(b) DEFINITION OF OWNER.—In this section, the term 'owner' has the meaning given such term in section 3507."

(b) [46 U.S.C. 3501] CLERICAL AMENDMENT.—The analysis for chapter 35 of title 46, United States Code, is amended by adding at the end the following:

"Sec. 3510. Additional medical and safety standards."

www.ingramcontent.com/pod-product-compliance
Lightning Source LLC
Chambersburg PA
CBHW070046030426
42335CB00016B/1812

* 9 7 8 1 9 6 2 9 7 8 1 3 2 *